# Chu Hsi

Calligraphy of Chu Hsi: part of a letter to Liu Tzu-yü (Liu Yen-hsiu, 1097–1146). National Palace Museum, Taipei.

# Chu Hsi

## NEW STUDIES

WING-TSIT CHAN

UNIVERSITY OF HAWAII PRESS

HONOLULU

Publication of this book has been supported
by a grant from the National Endowment for
the Humanities, an independent federal agency.

Library of Congress Cataloging-in-Publication Data

Chan, Wing-tsit, 1901–

Chu Hsi : new studies / Wing-tsit Chan.

p.     cm.

Includes bibliographical references and index.

ISBN 0–8248–1201–8

1.   Chu, Hsi, 1130–1200.   I.   Title.

B128.C54C42   1989

181'.11—dc19      89–4799      CIP

University of Hawaii Press books are printed
on acid-free paper and meet the guidelines for
permanence and durability of the Council
on Library Resources.

# CONTENTS

v

# PREFACE

*Chu Hsi: New Studies* presents the results of research into the life and thought of Chu Hsi (1130–1200), indisputably the most influential thinker in Chinese history since Confucius and Mencius. Chu Hsi's ideas and works have profoundly affected Chinese, Korean, and Japanese institutions and thought. Originally, I composed several pieces in Chinese discussing topics on him that have been overlooked by Chinese, Korean, and Japanese writers, which were published in Taiwan and Hong Kong journals. Without my solicitation, these articles were reprinted in other journals in Taipei and the People's Republic of China. Encouraged by this favorable reception, I further investigated neglected topics on Chu Hsi, eventually writing more than a hundred essays. They form a book published in 1988 as the *Chu Tzu hsin-t'an-so* (New investigations on Master Chu) by the Student Book Company of Taipei. Since the material is new, I thought I should publish it in English also. However, the present work is not a translation. First of all, the 126 items have been reorganized into 33 chapters. Second, a considerable amount of material, especially that on Chu Hsi's calligraphic remains and his chronological biography, has been omitted. Third, much of the rest has been abridged. Finally, the presentation has often been altered to produce an approach suitable to English. With the exception of a few pages, I have excluded any excerpts from my previous publications in English, such as "Chu Hsi's Religious Life" and "Chu Hsi and the Academies," since these are easily available. My aim here is to present hitherto undisclosed material, as far as possible in Chu Hsi's own words, from the *Wen-chi,* the *Yü-lei,* and other sources. About a third of the book is on Chu Hsi's life, a third on his thought, and a third on his pupils and associates.

Since the material offered here is confined to neglected topics, the substance and length of the chapters are necessarily uneven. However, they are fully annotated. All quotations have been traced or accounted for, persons identified, titles translated, and terms explained. Asian names are given in the Asian manner, that is, family name first, except for contemporary people who have followed the Western practice. Honorific names have been used for Lu Hsiang-shan (Lu Chiu-yüan) and Wang Yang-ming (Wang Shou-jen) because practically all Asian writers use these honorifics. With a few exceptions where *pinyin* is used, transliterations are based on the Wade-Giles system. Dates for persons are given at the first occurrence in each chapter, except for pre-Ch'in (221–206 B.C.) Chinese philosophers with some exceptions, and Chu Hsi himself. Chinese calendar years are simply equated with Western years, except for people who happened to be born or die early in the following Western year (i.e., before the Chinese New Year). Chinese ages are counted according to the Oriental tradition, that is, by calendar year rather than by the twelve months following the actual birthday. Names of dynasties, provinces, and well-known cities are omitted from the Chinese glossary. Only four abbreviations have been used, as follows:

> *Wen-chi,* for the *Chu Tzu wen-chi* (Collection of literary works of Master Chu)
> *Yü-lei,* for the *Chu Tzu yü-lei* (Classified conversations of Master Chu)
> *SPPY,* for the *Ssu-pu pei-yao* (Essentials of the Four Libraries) edition
> *SPTK,* for the *Ssu-pu ts'ung-k'an* (Four Libraries series) edition

The abbreviation *cs* is also used after the year in which a civil service examination candidate received his *chin-shih* (presented scholar degree).

I wish to express my deep gratitude to my colleague Dr. Irene Bloom. She uncovered several of my mistakes, supplied additional material, and vastly improved my translation. Thanks also go to Professor Yü Ying-shih of Princeton University for suggesting several neglected subjects in the study of Chu Hsi. Most of these are now discussed herein. I want to thank Dr. Chu Ron-Guey most heartily for help on the bibliography, for tracing sources of quotations, for recommendations on matters of substance, and for contributing to the index.

WING-TSIT CHAN

# Chu Hsi

# – 1 –

# Biographical Account:
# The "Hsing-chuang"

THE "Chu Tzu hsing-chuang" is the primary source of information on the life of Chu Hsi (1130–1200). His biography in the *Sung shih* (History of the Sung dynasty) is based on it, and the successive chronological biographies *(nien-p'u)* of his life all have depended on it.

The philosophy, writings, and educational and political activities of Chu Hsi, the most influential Chinese thinker since Confucius and Mencius, have been studied in China, Korea, and Japan for many centuries, but certain aspects of his person and his life have been overlooked because they have been thought to be insignificant or purely private matters. The present work is devoted to these aspects rather than to a conventional biography, which I have written elsewhere.[1]

The "Hsing-chuang" was written by Chu Hsi's pupil and son-in-law, Huang Kan (1152–1221). The Master had perfect trust in him. When Chu Hsi built the Chu-lin Study in Chien-yang, Fukien, in 1194, he wrote Huang Kan and said, "When necessary, you, Chih-ch'ing, may be asked to take my place on the lecture platform."[2] The day before Chu Hsi died, he again wrote Huang Kan and said, "The trust of my Way lies with you. I have no more regrets."[3]

Chu Hsi died in 1200. At that time, the Court attacked his school bitterly, labeling it "false learning" *(wei-hsüeh)*. Obviously, this was not the time for a *hsing-chuang* to be written. The situation changed radically in 1208, however, when Chu Hsi was posthumously honored with the title Wen (Culture). His son Tsai (b. 1169) then asked Huang Kan to write the "Hsing-chuang." As Huang Kan said, "I waited for a year or two so that my learning career could be further advanced before I began to write,"[4] and "It took me another ten years or more to trace what I have heard and seen over the years to arrive at the final draft."[5] In the meantime, the draft was copied, passed around among friends, and discussed again and again. Huang himself said, "The biographical account of our

1

Master is merely a preliminary draft and is not yet in perfect order. I do not know who has passed it around."[6] Evidently, some fellow pupils had it printed and sent to others to solicit their opinions. One pupil, Ch'en Ch'un (1159–1223) wrote to Chu Tsai as follows:

> Subsequently, I received from Kuo Tzu-ts'ung[7] of Ch'ao-yang[8] the "Hsing-chuang" of our Master. The last paragraph of the printed copy does not have the writer's name, but I believe it was written by Chih-ch'ing. The general feeling of the account is proper and sound, but there are several places where the wording is not quite satisfactory. I do not know about the earlier paragraph, for I don't have a copy of it. For exam-ple, where it says, "The correct tradition has now arrived at the conclu-sion," I am afraid it should have been "The total substance now has its place." Again, the reference to "autumn frost" seems to lack warmth and tenderness. Also, where it says, "He has made contributions to the world and later generations," the point of his gathering and completing the teachings of various Neo-Confucians into a great concord is missing. Fur-thermore, subjects like astronomy, geography, musical scales, and military strategy are all matters of the Way, duties one owes to oneself, and con-crete and practical affairs. They are meant to manifest the substance and function of the clear character of the mind in its completeness, and are related to the idea of arriving at the highest good and pursuing the refined and the subtle to the limit. They should not be regarded as either refined or coarse. But the preceding passage is concluded with the greatness and brilliance of morality. Thus this section is divided into two segments, plac-ing these practical matters outside of morality as if they are not related to it.[9]

Ch'en Ch'un's criticisms were quite specific and to the point. There must have been similar reactions from other sources. Thinking and rethinking took Huang Kan another ten years or more: "I consulted the various accounts of our Master's life and funeral eulogies to make the final draft so as to check with like-minded friends and argue back and forth."[10] "I would accept an idea that was good and would correct any word that was wrong. Perhaps I have accommodated or yielded reluc-tantly, but I have never dared firmly to assert myself."[11] The result was a masterpiece of more than sixteen thousand words.[12] Aside from exten-sive quotations from Chu Hsi's famous memorials to the emperor, the "Hsing-chuang" reads, in part, as follows:

> After our Master returned home from T'ung-an,[13] he had a sinecure as a temple superintendent and lived at home for almost twenty years. His life was full of twists and turns and he was extremely poor, but he did not mind. His personal cultivation was full and rich, and his understanding of principles was clear and distinct. These qualities were even more plentiful in his actions. When he arrived at the prefecture,[14] he showed great com-

passion in his love for the people, as if their suffering was his own hidden sorrow. He lost no time in introducing beneficial measures and eliminating the harmful ones. . . .[15]

Our Master once drafted a memorial [in 1188] to urge ten measures, namely, discuss learning to rectify the mind, cultivate the person to regulate the family, avoid favorites so as to be close to the honest and the upright, reject personal kindness in order to uphold public justice, clarify moral principles in order to wipe out treachery, select teachers and tutors to assist the crown prince, be extremely careful in appointments so as to make clear the system, enforce discipline to promote social custom, economize on expenditures to strengthen the foundation of the state, and rectify political affairs in order to repel barbarians. These measures were intended to help the new regime. However, it happened that someone in the administration attacked the Learning of the Way (tao-hsüeh) as evil. Our Master firmly declined the new appointment.[16] He was then appointed a compiler in the Imperial Library and superintendent of a temple outside the capital. The appointment was never accepted. . . .[17]

Thereupon [in 1195] he drafted a memorial of more than ten thousand words to point out the danger of treacherous officials deceiving the emperor, thereby exposing the injustice done to the prime minister [Chao Ju-yü, 1140–1196].[18] The tone of the memorial was exceedingly bitter. The pupils took turns pleading with him to decide by means of divination. The result was the thirty-third hexagram, tun [retirement], changing to the thirteenth hexagram, t'ung-jen [companionship]. The Master withdrew in silence, burned the draft of his memorial, and called himself Tun-weng [Old man in retirement]. . . .[19]

In five decades, he served four emperors successively. He was an official outside the capital for only nine years and served in Court for only forty days. . . .[20]

His learning consisted of investigating principle to the utmost to extend one's knowledge and of returning to the self to practice in a concrete way. To abide in seriousness (ching, reverence) is to bring the beginning and the end to completion. He said that if one tries to extend knowledge without seriousness, one will be deluded and confused, and there will be no way to discern the ultimate objectives of moral principles; and if one tries to practice personally without seriousness, one will be lazy and dissipated, and there will be no way to bring about the reality of moral principles. . . . All things have their principles. Preserve the mind. . . . Investigate principle to the utmost. . . . Let there be no place for selfish human desires, but let there be ways to preserve the correctness of the Principle of Heaven. . . . The correct tradition of the Way lies in this. . . .[21]

According to his Way, as there is the T'ai-chi [Great Ultimate], yin and yang [passive and active cosmic forces] are distinguished. As there are yin and yang, the Five Agents [wu-hsing; Metal, Wood, Water, Fire, and Earth] are present to the fullest extent. When man and things are born with the endowment of the material forces (ch'i) of yin and yang and the Five Agents, the principle of the Great Ultimate is sufficiently present in each of them. One's destiny (ming) is what Heaven has endowed, one's nature is what one has received,[22] one's feelings react to external things, and one's mind unites nature and feelings.[23] Rooted in nature are the virtues of humanity, righteousness, propriety, and wisdom. As they are expressed in feelings, they are the beginnings of commiseration, shame and dislike, deference and compliance, and the sense of right and wrong[24] . . . .[25]

As to the visible actions in the cultivation of his person, his appearance was dignified and his words were firm. In walking, he was relaxed and respectful. In sitting, he was proper and straight. In his leisurely life, he would rise before dawn. He would wear a "deep" garment in which the jacket and skirt were attached, headgear of a wide cloth, and square-headed shoes. He would worship at the family shrine and then bow before the portrait of Confucius. He would then withdraw to his study. His stool and desk were in the correct position. All books and articles were always in good order. At meals, the arrangement of soup and food dishes had a definite place, and the use of spoons and chopsticks had a definite spot. When he was tired and rested, he would close his eyes and sit straight. When he had rested and stood up, he would walk slowly in regular steps. He would retire at midnight. Having awakened from sleep, he would cover himself with a quilt and sit down, sometimes until dawn. From youth to old age, whether in bitter cold or exceedingly hot weather, and whether in moments of haste or in seasons of danger, he would never depart for an instant from the principles of appearance and movement. In behaving at home, he was most filial in serving his parents and most loving in bringing up the children. In his married life, both husband and wife were dignified, and in their depth of gratitude toward each other they were contented. In religious sacrifices, no matter whether the occasion was major or minor, he was always sincere and serious. If he was amiss in ceremonies even in the least, he would be unhappy for the whole day. If, having sacrificed, no ritual had been violated, he would be overflowingly glad. At funerals his grief was complete. In food and mourning attire, he was always appropriate to the occasion. In treating guests, he never failed to extend a welcoming hand. To the best of his financial ability, he always enabled everyone to enjoy themselves to the utmost. He would extend his love to all relatives, whether near or far, and his respect to the community, including the most lowly. On auspicious or inauspicious occasions, such as celebrations or funerals, he never neglected the proper offerings. In his care for the poor and concern for survivors, his kindness was never deficient. For treating himself, he wanted no more in clothing than enough to cover the body, no more in food than enough to fill the stomach, and no more in shelter than enough to protect himself from wind and rain. What other people find unable to bear, he lived with at ease. . . .[26]

The works of Chou [Chou Tun-i, 1017–1073], the Ch'engs [Ch'eng Hao, 1032–1085, and Ch'eng I, 1033–1107], Chang [Chang Tsai, 1020–1077], and Shao [Shao Yung, 1011–1077][27] were to continue the tradition of the Way of Confucius and Mencius. Before long, however, their subtle words and great principles became stagnant and not prominent. Our Master gathered and developed them, and only then did they circulate abundantly in the world. . . . The doctrines of Taoism and Buddhism . . . and the selfishness of the school of utilitarianism prevailed together. . . . Our Master vigorously attacked them. . . . In his teaching, our Master considered the order of the *Great Learning,* the *Analects,* the *Book of Mencius,* and the *Doctrine of the Mean*[28] as the order to enter into the Way, with the classics to follow later. . . .[29]

I have heard that the correct tradition of the Way waited for the proper person before it was transmitted. . . . As our Master appeared, the Way transmitted from the Chou dynasty [1111–249 B.C.] on down suddenly became wide open like a bright sun in the middle of the sky, shining. . . .[30]

After he completed the "Hsing-chuang," Huang Kan wrote more than six hundred words to explain his selection of material. There were some who said that words should be reserved and not too explicit, that dates need not all be recorded, that the acceptance or declination of offices need not all be written down, that the advice to the emperor was too forthright, that criticisms of others were too blunt, that earlier scholars should not have been rejected too forcefully, and that the unorthodox schools should not have been attacked too vigorously. Huang Kan gave his explanation item by item. Actually, the "Hsing-chuang" does not contain any passages that are too explicit or too blunt. If we compare it with what Ch'en Ch'un suggested, we find that Huang Kan did accept a number of contrary opinions. "The correct tradition has now arrived at a conclusion" was changed to "The correct tradition now has its place," according to Ch'en Ch'un's suggestion. The reference to "autumn frost" was eliminated. The passage on gathering Neo-Confucian works and making them prominent must have been added in accordance with Ch'en's idea. Following Ch'en, too, a passage on astronomy, geography, and so on was included in the "Hsing-chuang."[31] Thus it appears that Huang Kan really "dared not fail to follow a single good word but in some places asserted his own opinion without completely following others."[32] When the "Hsing-chuang" was completed in 1217, he "left it inside a chest, thinking that before I die, I might still make some changes. Another four years passed. Now that my vital force and blood are getting much weaker and illness getting worse, I believe there cannot be any more additions or deletions." He therefore made a copy and sent his son to report it to the family temple.[33] There has never been a *hsing-chuang* that was written with such great care. To report to the family temple means "to lay before spiritual beings without question."[34] The "Hsing-chuang" is not Huang Kan's personal "final conclusion of a hundred years,"[35] but that of scores of his fellow pupils—and also that of the Chinese, Koreans, and Japanese who have studied this work over several centuries. When we read the "Hsing-chuang," we seem to be facing the man.

The "Hsing-chuang" has influenced all of East Asia. Hu Chü-jen (1434–1484), an outstanding Neo-Confucian of the Ming dynasty (1368–1644), often required his students to read it. He said,

> The "Chu Tzu hsing-chuang" is complete and thorough in learning, in principles, in the fundamental and the secondary, and in the refined and the coarse. I often told my beginning students to read it. The "Ming-tao hsing-chuang" [Biographical account of Ch'eng Hao][36] describes Ming-tao in a vast and refined way. However, because of his complete purity and total unity, unless one has cultivated oneself for a long time and reached a high level of development, one cannot understand it. I often wanted a student to read the "Chu Tzu hsing-chuang" first so that he would get a sense of pattern and style before he read the "Ming-tao hsing-chuang."[37]

Such was the importance that the Neo-Confucians attached to the "Hsing-chuang."

In Korea, the leading Neo-Confucian Yi Hwang (Yi T'oegye, 1501–1570) annotated it.[38] Although his annotations are brief, he supplemented the "Hsing-chuang" with material from various sources. The longest note appears under Chu Hsi's memorial of 1188, obviously to show that the twelve-thousand-word memorial did not overlook the matter of recovering the land from the Chin invaders. T'oegye quoted from Chu Hsi's pupil Yang Fu, who pointed out that the memorial says, "If the enemy is not destroyed, I beg to be executed," and that Chu Hsi merely wanted to put the government in order before recovering the land. Also, although the "Hsing-chuang" does not mention that Chu Hsi annotated the *Ch'u tz'u* (Songs of Ch'u) in 1195, T'oegye included the epilogue by Chu Hsi's pupil Yang Chi (1142–1213) to show Chu Hsi's concern over the sad state of the empire, which the *Ch'u tz'u* had expressed fourteen centuries earlier. Finally, Chu Hsi began to study with Li T'ung (1093–1163) in 1153. All previous accounts had emphasized that Li T'ung taught the young man to purify the mind by sitting quietly to discern its state before feelings of pleasure, anger, sorrow, and joy have been aroused. T'oegye was the first to bring out the fact that Li T'ung taught his student that "the principle is one but its manifestations are many" *(li-i fen-shu)*. This doctrine later became the backbone of Chu Hsi's philosophical system.

This last point is a good example of T'oegye's special insight, so it is no wonder his annotation has been highly regarded in Japan. As Kusumoto Sekisui (1832–1916) observed, "Earlier scholars said that only T'oegye could have written it. How true!" The Kimon School in Japan particularly praised the "Hsing-chuang." One of the three leaders of the school, Satō Naokata (1650–1719), wrote an epilogue to it in which he said, "If a student does not want to study Master Chu, that is the end of the matter. But if he does, he must scrutinize this work." The Kimon School included the "Hsing-chuang" in its curriculum for elementary schools. It also conducted discussion meetings on it and printed lectures on it. In his curriculum, Wakabayashi Kansai (1679–1732) proceeded from Chu Hsi's *Hsiao-hsüeh* (Elementary education) to the Four Books; to Chu Hsi and Lü Tsu-ch'ien's compilation, the *Chin-ssu lu* (Reflections on things at hand); to the Six Classics;[39] to the works of the Five Masters of the Northern Sung; and then to the "Chu Tzu hsing-chuang."[40] In so doing, he treated the latter almost like one of the Six Classics or one of the outstanding works of the Five Masters of the Northern Sung.

It was stated at the outset that the successive chronological biographies *(nien-p'u)* of Chu Hsi depend on the "Hsing-chuang," but it should be added that *hsing-chuang* and *nien-p'u* perform different functions. As has been said, "The *Chu Tzu nien-p'u* records the Master's search for teachers and friends, the details of his writing, his taking and leaving office, his advance and withdrawal, his conduct in government and his political measures in chronological order, whereas the 'Chu Tzu hsing-chuang' aims at bringing to light the refined principles and subtle ideas of his search and effort, and the profound objective of his accomplishing the Way and perfecting virtue. Here truly lies the continuation of Confucius and the transmission of the tradition of the Way."[41]

The first *Chu Tzu nien-p'u* was compiled by Chu Hsi's pupil Li Fang-tzu[42] in three chapters, and is often called the *Tzu-yang nien-p'u*, Tzu-yang referring to a mountain in Chu Hsi's ancestral place for which he named his study. Wei Liao-weng (1178–1237) wrote a preface for it.[43] The *Hsing-li ta-ch'üan* (Complete collection on nature and principle), compiled in 1415, quoted Li Fang-tzu at great length on Chu Hsi's words and activity, suggesting that this *nien-p'u* still existed at that time.

It is most likely that Li's *Nien-p'u* was published in more than one place with changes. When it was time for a revision, this was done by Yeh Kung-hui, in 1431, again in three chapters. Its preface, by Sun Yüan-chen, states that Yeh obtained an "old version" and corrected it, without specifying whether this was Li's original version. The epilogue, by Sun Shu-kung, says that the "old version" referred to the Fukien and Anhui editions. Presumably these were editions of Li's, probably altered and corrupted. At any rate, most scholars believe that Yeh's revision faithfully reflects Li's original compilation. Yeh's work was lost in China but fortunately preserved in Korea. From there it reached Japan, where it was printed in 1662. In 1972 it was reprinted in Taipei. Thus the earliest extant *Chu Tzu nien-p'u*, for centuries lost to China, is now back home.

Another revision was made by Tai Hsien (d. 1508) in 1506, in his *Chu*

*Tzu shih-chi* (True records of Master Chu). Chapters 2 to 4 are devoted
to the *nien-p'u*. In his own preface, Tai said that Li's *Nien-p'u* contained
corruptions and mistakes, and he improved it by adding materials from
the "Hsing-chuang," the *Chu Tzu wen-chi,* the *Chu Tzu yü-lei,* and so on.
Like Li's, Tai's *Nien-p'u* is in three chapters. I have compared the Yeh
revision with the Tai revision in thirty-six places.[44] Aside from the fact
that Tai added a few more events and provided a much fuller annotation, the two versions are surprisingly similar—indeed, almost identical. This shows that both were derived from the same source, that is,
Li's *Nien-p'u.* There are some differences, of course. Whereas Yeh said
that in 1130 Chu Hsi's father could not return home to Wu-yüan,
Anhui, because rebellion blocked the way, Tai added that Chu Hsi's
father was too poor to make the journey. For 1163, Yeh stated that Chu
Hsi studied Ch'an (Meditation) Buddhism; this is deleted in the Tai
version. Yeh recorded that in 1176 Chu Hsi went to Wu-yüan to visit
ancestral graves, but Tai added that he contemplated making his home
there. According to Yeh, when Chu Hsi submitted his 1188 memorial,
the emperor wasn't too annoyed until some ministers aggravated the
matter, but Tai said the emperor was very angry when he first read the
memorial. These minor discrepancies do not affect the essential character of Chu Hsi's biography in any significant way. Generally speaking,
the Tai version places more emphasis on Chu Hsi's writing.

The standard *nien-p'u* for the last two hundred years has been the *Chu
Tzu nien-p'u* by Wang Mao-hung (1668–1741), who devoted twenty
years to its preparation and went through four drafts. It was published
by his son in 1762, and is divided into four chapters, each in two parts.

Yeh's *Nien-p'u* was of course not available to Wang, and he was not
aware of Tai's. But he did consult Li Mo's *Chu Tzu nien-p'u* of 1552;
Hung Ch'ü-wu's *Chu Tzu nien-p'u* of 1700; the Fukien edition; and
Tsou Cho-ch'i's *Nien-p'u cheng-o* (Errors in the *Nien-p'u* corrected) of
circa 1738. Wang constantly referred to the Li and Hung versions,
especially the latter, and corrected them according to Huang Kan's
"Hsing-chuang," the *Wen-chi,* and the *Yü-lei.* He explained his choices
between the two versions at length, and his research was critical and
thorough. Discussions on these matters follow the main *nien-p'u* and are
entitled *Chu Tzu nien-p'u, k'ao-i* (Investigation into variants in the *Chu
Tzu nien-p'u*), in four chapters. Wang called the result of his research
simply *Nien-p'u.* The last part of his work consists of the "Chu Tzu lun-
hsüeh ch'ieh-yao-yü" (Master Chu's important sayings on learning), in
two chapters.

Li Mo's edition disappeared after the middle of the eighteenth century, for the *Ssu-k'u ch'üan-shu tsung-mu t'i-yao* (Essentials of the contents
of the *Complete Collection of the Four Libraries*), completed in 1781, does not
describe it. Instead, on the basis of indirect sources, it criticizes Li as

biased in omitting, for example, Chu Hsi's criticisms of Lu Hsiang-shan (Lu Chiu-yüan, 1139–1193) and Ch'en Liang (1143–1194).[45] Li Mo's account of Chu Hsi's famine relief measures, his association with Ch'en Liang, and his destruction of the temple dedicated to Ch'in Kuei (1091–1155), who made peace with the invading Chin, filled important gaps in Li Fang-tzu's *Nien-p'u.*[46]

Hung Ch'ü-wu's *Nien-p'u* is not included in the *Ssu-k'u ch'üan-shu tsung-mu t'i-yao* either, but a copy did emerge in Peking in 1936. It added considerable material to the traditional accounts of Chu Hsi's discussions on learning, his associations with Li T'ung, Chang Shih (1133–1180), and Lü Tsu-ch'ien (1137–1181), his debates with Lu Hsiang-shan and Ch'en Liang, and his criticisms of Buddhism and Taoism.[47]

None of these versions can compare with Wang Mao-hung's in reliability, however. By critically examining every piece of literary or historical evidence, by relying only on firsthand material, by judiciously evaluating the different accounts, and by carefully dating the essays, letters, and even sayings on learning, Wang practically transformed the *Nien-p'u* from a work of tradition to one of scholarship. Nevertheless, he was by no means free from defect. He could not escape the partisan spirit that had characterized the Chu Hsi School. For example, Chu Hsi had annotated the *Yin-fu ching* (Classic of secret accord) in 1175 and the *Ts'an-t'ung-ch'i* (The three ways unified and harmonized) in 1197. Wang does not even mention them, obviously because these are Taoist works. In 1196, Shen Chi-tsu memorialized the emperor to accuse Chu Hsi, falsely and recklessly, of ten crimes. The accusation finally led to the termination of Chu Hsi's rank and temple superintendency. Wang Mao-hung suggested that Shen's memorial was a fabrication by a follower of Wang Yang-ming (Wang Shou-jen, 1472–1529),[48] without realizing that the memorial is contained in a work of the early thirteenth century.[49] Notwithstanding these minor flaws, the remarkable thing about Wang's *Chu Tzu nien-p'u* is that it preserves the fundamental framework of Li Fang-tzu's *Chu Tzu nien-p'u* and supports Huang Kan's "Chu Tzu hsing-chuang" with ample evidence and a high level of scholarship.[50]

## Notes

1. See Herbert Franke, ed., *Sung Biographies* (Wiesbaden: Franz Steiner Verlag, 1976), pp. 282–290, and with correction, Wing-tsit Chan, ed., *Chu Hsi and Neo-Confucianism* (Honolulu: University of Hawaii Press, 1986), pp. 565–601.

2. *Sung shih* [History of the Sung dynasty] (Beijing: Chung-hua Book Co., 1977), ch. 430, biography of Huang Kan, p. 12778.

3. *Wen-chi,* 29:22b, letter to Chih-ch'ing (Huang Kan).

4. *Mien-chai chi* [Collected works of Huang Kan] (*Ssu-k'u ch'üan-shu chen-pen* [Precious works of the *Complete Collection of the Four Libraries*] ed.), 16:20b, letter in reply to Wang Yu-kuan; 36:48a, "Epilogue to the *Chu Tzu hsing-chuang.*"

5. *Ibid.*, 39:22b, "Report to the family temple upon completion of the 'Chu Tzu hsing-chuang.' "

6. *Ibid.*, 16:20b, letter in reply to Wang Yu-kuan.

7. Kuo Tzu-ts'ung's private name was Shu-yün, and he was a pupil of Chu Hsi. For an account of him, see my *Chu Tzu men-jen* [Master Chu's pupils] (Taipei: Student Book Co., 1982), p. 203.

8. A county in Kwangtung Province.

9. *Pei-hsi ta-ch'üan-chi* [Complete collected works of Ch'en Ch'un] (*Ssu-k'u ch'üan-shu chen-pen* ed.), 23:4a–b, letter to Chu Tsai.

10. *Mien-chai chi,* 36:49a, "Epilogue to the *Chu Tzu hsing-chuang.*"

11. See above, n. 5.

12. The "Hsing-chuang" constitutes ch. 36 of the *Mien-chai chi* and ch. 8 of *Huang Mien-chai chi,* an abridged edition. There is a fully annotated Japanese translation by Satō Hitoshi in his *Shushi gyōjō* [Biographical account of Master Chu] (Tokyo: Meitoku shuppansha, rev. 1984). There is also a Korean translation by Thomas Hosuck Kang, *Chuja haengjang* (Seoul: Munhwasa, 1975).

13. A county in southern Fukien. Chu Hsi was *chu-pu* (assistant magistrate) there from 1153 to 1156, when he was 24 to 27 years old. See chap. 2 below, n. 17.

14. This refers to Nan-k'ang, whose capital was in present Hsing-tzu County in Kiangsi. Chu Hsi was prefect there from 1179 to 1181.

15. *Mien-chai chi,* 36:7a.

16. In 1188, Chu Hsi was appointed junior expositor-in-waiting *(Ch'ung-cheng-tien shuo-shu).* This he declined.

17. *Mien-chai chi,* 36:25a–b.

18. In 1195, imperial relative Han T'o-chou (d. 1207), having consolidated all power in his own hand, expelled the prime minister, who later died in exile.

19. *Mien-chai chi,* 36:36b.

20. *Ibid.*, 36:38b. Actually, Chu Hsi served outside the capital for only seven years and a little over six months, and in Court for forty-six days.

21. *Ibid.*, 36:39b–40a.

22. This doctrine was derived from Ch'eng I. See the *I-shu* [Surviving works] 18:17a, in the *Erh-Ch'eng ch'üan-shu* [Complete works of the two Ch'engs] (*SPPY* ed.).

23. This is the doctrine of Chang Tsai in the *Chang Tzu yü-lu* [Recorded sayings of Master Chang] (*SPTK* ed.), pt. 3, p. 1a.

24. *Book of Mencius,* 2A:6.

25. *Mien-chai chi,* 36:40a–b.

26. *Ibid.*, 36:41b–42a.

27. These are often called the Five Masters of the Northern Sung (960–1126).

28. In 1190, Chu Hsi published the four works as the Four Books.

29. *Ibid.*, 36:43b–44b.

30. *Ibid.*, 36:48a–b.

31. *Ibid.*, 36:45b.

32. *Ibid.*, 36:49a.

33. See above, n. 5.

34. *Doctrine of the Mean,* ch. 29.

35. *Mien-chai chi,* 36:51a.

36. *I-ch'uan wen-chi* [Collection of literary works of Ch'eng I], ch. 7. "Ming-tao Hsien-sheng hsing-chuang" [Biographical account of Master Ch'eng Hao], 1a–7a, in the *Erh-Ch'eng ch'üan-shu.*

37. Hu Chü-jen, *Chü-yeh lu* [Records of occupying one's sphere of activity] (*Cheng-i-tang ch'üan-shu* [Complete library of the Hall of Rectifying the Way] ed.), 3:9b–10a, chapter on sages and worthies.

38. Yi T'oegye, *Chuja haengjang chie-chu* [Compiled annotation of the *Chu Tzu hsing-chuang*].

39. The Four Books are the *Great Learning,* the *Analects,* the *Book of Mencius,* and the *Doctrine of the Mean.* The Six Classics are the *Book of Odes,* the *Book of History,* the *Book of Rites,* the *Book of Changes,* the *Spring and Autumn Annals,* and the *Book of Music.* The *Book of Music* was lost before the third century B.C. and was replaced by the *Chou-li* [Rites of Chou] in the Sung dynasty (960–1279).

40. The material on the influence of the "Hsing-chuang" in Japan is drawn from Professor Yamazaki Michio's "Shushi gyōjō Taikei (T'oegye) shuchī no igi" [Significance of T'oegye's annotation of the *Chu Tzu hsing-chuang*) in the *T'oegye hakpo* [T'oegye journal], vol. 19 (August, 1978), pp. 131–141.

41. Wang Chung-lu's preface to the 1394 edition of the *Chu Tzu nien-p'u.*

42. Li Fang-tzu's courtesy name was Kung-hui and his literary name was Kuo-chai. He was a native of Shao-wu County, Fukien, and obtained the *chin-shih* (presented scholar) degree in 1214. He recorded more than 200 entries in the *Yü-lei* from 1188 on.

43. This preface is found in Tai Hsien's *Chu Tzu shih-chi* [True records of Master Chu] (*Chin-shih han-chi ts'ung-k'an* [Chinese works of the recent period] ed.), and in Wang Mao-hung's *Chu Tzu nien-p'u* [Chronological biography of Master Chu] (*Ts'ung-shu chi-ch'eng* [Collection of series] ed.).

44. See my *Chu Tzu hsin-t'an-so* [New investigations on Master Chu] (Taipei: Student Book Co., 1988), pp. 76–79.

45. *Ssu-k'u ch'üan-shu tsung-mu t'i-yao* [Essentials of the contents of the *Complete Collection of the Four Libraries*] (Shanghai: Commercial Press, 1933), pp. 1263, 1333.

46. This is pointed out by Hung Ching in his preface to Hung Ch'ü-wu's *Chu Tzu nien-p'u,* reproduced in Wang Mao-hung's *Chu Tzu nien-p'u,* ch. 1A, pp. 6–7.

47. This has been well brought out by Professor Jung Chao-tsu in his "Pa Hung Ch'ü-wu pen *Chu Tzu nien-p'u* [Epilogue on Hung Chü-wu's *Chu Tzu nien-p'u*] (*Yenching hsüeh-pao* [Yenching learned journal], no. 20, 1936), p. 210.

48. Wang Mao-hung, *Chu Tzu nien-p'u, k'ao-i* [Investigation into variants], ch. 4, p. 337, under the second year of Ch'ing-yüan (1196).

49. Yeh Shao-weng (c. 1175–1230), *Ssu-ch'ao wen-chien lu* [What was heard and seen in the four reigns] (*P'u-ch'eng i-shu* [Surviving works of P'u-ch'eng County] ed.), 4:10b–13b.

50. I have discussed these biographical accounts and Professor Jung Chao-tsu's studies in great detail in my *Chu Tzu hsin-t'an-so,* pp. 62–79.

# −2−

# Self-reflections

IN his conversations and letters, Chu Hsi often reflected on himself. The compilers of the *Yü-lei* placed those sayings in chapter 104, under "Master Chu discussing his own effort at learning," and in chapter 105, under "discussing his own commentaries on books." About half of the material in these two chapters makes up chapter 55 of the *Chu Tzu ch'üan-shu* (Complete works of Master Chu). Compiled in 1714 by Li Kuang-ti (1642–1718), the *Chu Tzu ch'üan-shu* also contains selections from Chu Hsi's letters, only a third of which are self-reflections. In addition, Professor Ch'ien Mu has compiled a section on Chu Hsi's self-accounts of his early years.[1] But all these accounts are incomplete, and in many cases sources are lacking. The following quotations have been gleaned from various sources and are divided into four sections— self-reflections that can be dated, reflections on life, reflections on his own works, and unfulfilled wishes. About half of this material does not appear in the works just mentioned, and all sources except a handful have been traced.

## Self-reflections That Can Be Dated

1. "When I was five or six, I was curious about what the sky was and what lay beyond it." (*Yü-lei,* ch. 45, sec. 30 [p. 1836].)

2. "When I was eight or nine and read the *Book of Mencius,* I was highly motivated when I came to the passage about Chess Ch'iu playing chess."[2] (*Ibid.,* ch. 121, sec. 10 [p. 4671].)

3. "As a child, I read the *Analects* and the *Book of Mencius.* Ever since then I have wanted to see books of the same high level but have not found any." (*Ibid.,* ch. 104, sec. 3 [p. 4151].)

4. "I read the Four Books[3] when I was young. I worked very hard." (*Ibid.*, sec. 1 [p. 4151].)

5. "When I was ten, a Taoist priest gave me a charm. When my elders saw it, they burned it." (*Ibid.*, ch. 3, sec. 80 [p. 87].)

6. "When I was eleven, my late father copied this prose-poem to give me. . . . Imperceptibly it has been fifty-nine years." (*Wen-chi,* supplementary collection, 8:10a–b, epilogue to his father's written copy of [Su Shih's (1037–1101)] *K'un-yang-fu* [Prose-poem on the war of K'un-yang in Honan].)

7. "When I was ten or more years old and read the saying 'The sage and I are the same in kind'[4] in the *Book of Mencius,* I was happy beyond words, and thought it was easy to become a sage. Only now do I realize that it is difficult." (*Yü-lei,* ch. 104, sec. 4 [p. 4151].)

8. "When I was twelve or thirteen, I heard that Venerable Fan [Fan Ju-kuei, 1102–1160] said that *hsieh-chü* [a measure to regulate oneself] means *chieh* [to knot]. He was very happy, believing that he had gone beyond earlier scholars." (*Ibid.,* ch. 16, sec. 251 [p. 589].)

9. "I received instruction on the *Analects* from my late father when I was thirteen or fourteen." (*Wen-chi,* 75:6b, preface to Chu Hsi's *Lun-yü yao-i* [Essential meanings of the *Analects*].)

10. "When I was young, Ping-weng [Sick old man; Liu Tzu-hui, 1101–1147] watched us closely. He did not allow us to read [works like the *Liao-chai chi* (Collection of literary writings of Ch'en Kuan [1057–1122])].[5] He wanted us to read discussions that were good. Reading under his supervision was really hard work." (*Yü-lei,* ch. 130, sec. 38 [p. 4976].)

11. "From the age of fourteen or fifteen on, I liked anything that I thought was good." (*Ibid.,* ch. 104, sec. 41 [p. 4167].)

12. "From the age of fourteen or fifteen, I had already set my mind on this [investigation of things, extension of knowledge, sincerity of the will, and the rectification of the mind]." (*Wen-chi,* 54:17b, first letter to reply to Ch'en Cheng-chi.)

13. "At the age of fifteen or sixteen, when I read the passage, 'If another man should succeed by one effort, you will use a hundred efforts. If another man should succeed by ten efforts, you will use a thousand efforts,'[6] I found Lü Yü-shu's [Lü Ta-lin, 1046–1092] explanation extremely satisfying. I was awed, inspired, and aroused by it." (*Yü-lei,* ch. 4, sec. 41 [p. 106].)

14. "The theory of the investigation of things has been fully discussed by Master Ch'eng [Ch'eng I, 1033–1107]. . . . From the age of fifteen or sixteen on, I read the book [the *Great Learning*] but did not understand the meaning of the investigation of things. For thirty years it was unsettled in my mind. In recent years I seek its meaning in practical tasks

and examine and compare it with other classics and commentaries, testing again and again its internal and external as well as its fundamental and secondary aspects. Only then do I know that the theory is correct." (*Wen-chi*, 44:37a, second letter in reply to Chiang Te-kung.)

15. "When I was fifteen or sixteen, I was interested in this [Ch'an (Meditation) Buddhism]. One day I met a monk in Ping-weng's place and talked with him. . . . Later, when I went to take the civil service examination, I used his ideas and talked nonsense. . . . I passed. [Original note:] (I was then nineteen)." (*Yü-lei*, ch. 104, sec. 38 [p. 4166].)

16. "From the time I was fifteen or sixteen, whenever I heard people talk about moral principles I knew they were good. However, only today do I understand." (*Ibid.*, ch. 33, sec. 84 [p. 1363].)

17. "In my study as a young man, I already loved Neo-Confucianism at age sixteen. At seventeen, I was as well informed as scholars today. Later I acquired Hsieh Hsien-tao's [Hsieh Liang-tso, 1050–1120] [commentary on] the *Analects* and was very happy. I studied it thoroughly."[7] (*Ibid.*, ch. 115, sec. 41 [p. 4435].)

18. "As a youth, I foolishly made up my mind to study. My interest was aroused by the theories of the Master."[8] (*Wen-chi*, 80:4b–5a, account of the temple for Hsieh Liang-tso.)

19. "In his *Shih-pien* [Examination of the *Book of Odes*], Cheng Yü-chung [Cheng Ch'iao, 1102–1160] contended that the poem 'Chiang Chung Tzu' [Begging Chung Tzu][9] was simply a love poem and not an admonition to Chung Tzu. I knew from my youth that his theory was correct." (*Yü-lei*, ch. 23, sec. 27 [p. 8711].)

20. "In my youth I always looked down upon it [the *T'ang-chien* (Mirror of the T'ang dynasty)],[10] considering it unduly simple and traditional. As I see it now, the *T'ang-chien* is truly so." (*Ibid.*, ch. 108, sec. 20 [p. 4266].)

21. "From the age of fifteen or sixteen to twenty, I did not want to read books on history." (*Ibid.*, ch. 104, sec. 23 [p. 4159].)

22. "From the time I was sixteen or seventeen, I worked hard at reading books. At that time I felt no limit in any direction. I merely exerted my energy." (*Ibid.*, sec. 8 [p. 4153].)

23. "Before my capping ceremony, I read the literary writings of Master Nan-feng [Tseng Kung, 1019–1083]. I loved their serious expressions and correct principles. I often read them at home." (*Wen-chi*, 83:12b, epilogue to Tseng Nan-feng's calligraphic folio.)

24. "I was orphaned at fourteen. At sixteen the mourning was over. At that time, in religious sacrifices we merely followed old ceremonies in the family. Although the rites were not complete, they were in very good order. My late mother was very serious about religious observ-

ances. When I reached seventeen or eighteen, I investigated the rites of various schools and the rites became quite complete." (*Yü-lei,* ch. 90, sec. 109 [p. 3676].)

25. "When I was seventeen or eighteen, I read the *Doctrine of the Mean* and the *Great Learning.* Each morning, as I got up, I recited them ten times. Even now I can recite from memory the *Great Learning.*" (*Ibid.,* ch. 16, sec. 22 [p. 509].)

26. "I read [the *Book of Mencius*] from age seventeen or eighteen to twenty. I tried to understand it sentence by sentence but did not apprehend it thoroughly. After I was twenty I realized that was not the way to read it." (*Ibid.,* ch. 105, sec. 36 [p. 4180].)

27. "I remember when I went to take the civil service examination as a young man, I looked down on the examining official and said, 'How could he understand what is in my mind?' Nowadays people try to accommodate the thoughts of the examining official, thus making the matter even worse." (*Ibid.,* ch. 121, sec. 21 [p. 4677].)

28. "As a young man, I loved antiquity. The family was too poor to have books on bronze and stone inscriptions. I always took delight in reading the prefaces, epilogues, and passages on critical research in what Master Ou-yang [Ou-yang Hsiu, 1007–1072] collected [in his *Chi-ku lu* (Records of a collection of antiquity)]." (*Wen-chi,* 75:2a, essay on family collection of stone carvings.)

29. "When I was young, I was able to write only fifteen or sixteen essays. Later, that enabled me to pass the civil service examination. A person should be able to write essays. But when he gets the degree, that is all there is to it." (*Yü-lei,* ch. 107, sec. 32 [p. 4247].)

30. "When I was eighteen or nineteen, I had the opportunity to pay homage to Master Hsü [Hsü Ts'un][11] in Ch'ing-hu [Clear Lake]. I was told about the doctrines of self-mastery and returning to humanity[12] and the doctrine of knowing words and nourishing the strong moving power."[13] (*Wen-chi,* 81:21b, epilogue to Hsü Ch'eng-sou's poem.)

31. "After I received the civil service examination degree, I insisted on reading books. People hindered me from left and right, but I paid no attention. I just went on and read by myself." (*Yü-lei,* ch. 104, sec. 24 [p. 4159].)

32. "Before I was twenty, I acquired the *Shang-ts'ai yü-lu* [Recorded sayings of Hsieh Liang-tso] to read. At first I used red ink to mark the correct passages, but they appeared different on second glance. Then I marked them with white ink three times and then with black ink. After several times, they became quite different from the first time." (*Ibid.,* sec. 12 [p. 4157].)

33. "When I was about twenty, I already understood the general idea of the *Book of History* to be like this [i.e., to have moral principles implicit

in its comments]. Now my understanding is more refined. Time flies. Without realizing it, five decades have gone by." (*Ibid.,* sec. 9 [p. 4154].)

34. "From the time I was twenty, I wanted to get at the innermost of moral principles. Once I was reading Shang-ts'ai's *Lun-yü* [*shuo*] [Explanation of the *Analects*]. At first I marked passages with red ink, then green ink, and then yellow ink. After several times, I finally used black ink. That was to get at the essence." (*Ibid.,* ch. 120, sec. 18 [p. 4612].)

35. "When I was twenty and came to this passage [Ch'eng I's comment on the third hexagram, *t'un* (accumulate to the point of bursting)],[14] I suspected that it was not satisfactory, but I had no other theory on which to base [my suspicion]. I had to accede to the explanation but was never satisfied. Only later did I see that I was wrong." [*Ibid.,* ch. 70, sec. 12 [p. 2778].)

36. "From twenty on, I felt that the individual prefaces in the *Book of Odes*[15] were without meaning. If one ignores the individual prefaces and only ponders the poems, one will feel that its principles are penetrating." (*Ibid.,* ch. 80, sec. 43 [p. 3302].)

37. "I shall now urge you gentlemen to reject external affairs and concentrate your effort on investigating principles. From the age of twenty, I have been doing this." (*Ibid.,* ch. 104, sec. 45 [p. 4167].)

38. "When I was young, I passed through P'u-t'ien[16] and heard Lin Ch'ien-chih [Lin Kuang-ch'ao, 1114–1178] and Fang Tz'u-jung speaking about a certain doctrine in a very spirited manner. I was much aroused and elated. When I went home to think about it, for several hours I forgot both sleep and food." (*Ibid.,* ch. 132, sec. 55 [p. 5096].)

39. "Formerly, when I was *chu-pu* [assistant magistrate] in T'ung-an,[17] I kept close account of the taxes and custom duties. Every day I checked the items and signed my name to avoid any corruption by officials." (*Ibid.,* ch. 106, sec. 1 [p. 4193].)

40. "When I was *chu-pu* in T'ung-an, whenever I went after overdue taxes, I always told people beforehand." (*Ibid.,* sec. 2 [p. 4193].)

41. "When I was *chu-pu* in T'ung-an and requested a seal of approval, an army commander used a Taoist seal, for assistant officials wanted money before giving the approval. I jokingly said that it is impossible to be both a military man and a Taoist priest." (*Ibid.,* sec. 4 [p. 4194].)

42. "Now in T'ung-an I see that official families, rich households, officials, and merchants sell their land and property and refuse to work, and by holding onto their remaining power try to sit through their difficulties. . . . Whenever there was a case in the county that came before me for settlement, I always finished it in one day. Unless this is done, village folk will be in danger of having to look for shelter and food and of losing work. Merchants and rich people could hold on for a long period,

putting the village folk in a difficult position, so they would complain." (*Wen-chi,* 43:4a, ninth letter in reply to Ch'en Ming-chung [Ch'en Tan].)

43. "I remember when I was young in T'ung-an, I heard the sound of bells and drums at night. Before their sound ended, my mind was already drifting. Consequently, I became alarmed and realized that in learning one must concentrate one's mind and dedicate one's will to it." (*Yü-lei,* ch. 104, sec. 33 [p. 4163].)

44. "Later, when I became *chu-pu* in T'ung-an, as I could not go to sleep, I suddenly realized that [sprinkling and sweeping the ground][18] and [investigating the principles of things with care and refinement until one enters into the spirit][19] are distinguished as being fundamental and secondary and being great and small." (*Ibid.,* ch. 49, sec. 42 [p. 1914].)

45. "When I was in T'ung-an, one day I happened to go into the mountains for an inspection. At night a thought suddenly came to me. . . . If it is not sprinkling and sweeping the ground, it must be investigating the principles of things with care and refinement until one enters into the spirit. One need not do anything else." (*Ibid.,* sec. 43 [p. 1915].)

46. "I used to waste a great deal of thought. . . . Why was it that you gentlemen said that secondary things are fundamental? Later, when I went from T'ung-an to another county on official business, I kept thinking along the way. Only then could I think the matter through." (*Ibid.,* sec. 44 [p. 1916].)

47. "Formerly, when I was *chu-pu* in T'ung-an, I went to the country and stayed in a Buddhist monastery. The bedding was thin and I could not sleep. Just as I was thinking about the chapter on Tzu-hsia's pupils,[20] I heard a cuckoo's call that was very touching. Whenever I hear a cuckoo now, I recall that time." (*Ibid.,* sec. 55 [p. 1920].)

48. "Formerly, when I was *chu-pu* in T'ung-an, a scholar in the county school interpreted the *Book of History* in this way [that studying and teaching others are both study]. I thought his interpretation was new and clever, and I was happy." (*Ibid.,* ch. 79, sec. 58 [p. 3237].)

49. "Formerly, I was in T'ung-an. . . . When my term was up, I was in the capital waiting for official approval to leave. My luggage had been sent out, and I had no books to read. I borrowed a copy of the *Book of Mencius* from the keeper of the inn where I was staying. I read it thoroughly and only then did I understand the implications of the chapter on nourishing the moving strong power."[21] (*Ibid.,* ch. 104, sec. 14 [p. 4157].)

50. "I was formerly a *chu-pu* in T'ung-an. When my term was up, I went to Ch'üan-chou City to wait for official permission to leave. I borrowed books at the inn and obtained a copy of the *Book of Mencius.* I read

it carefully and only then did I find its original meaning." (*Ibid.*, sec. 13 [p. 4157].)

51. "In the autumn of the sixteenth year of *Shao-hsing* [1156], I had served as an official in T'ung-an for three years. My successor appointed by the Ministry of Personnel had not arrived. The official residence was deteriorating daily and could no longer be used for shelter. I had made a request to the county for repairs. It then happened that I was ordered to visit the neighboring prefectures. I took the opportunity personally to take my family, old and young, and send them home to the east. When I returned in the following spring to T'ung-an, the doors and chambers had collapsed and I could no longer enter. I therefore stayed at the house of Mr. Ch'en of the county." (*Wen-chi*, 77:5a–b, account of Wei-lei Cottage.)

52. "At first I studied under P'ing-shan [Liu Tzu-hui] and Chi-hsi [Hu Hsien, 1086–1162]. Chi-hsi studied under Wen-ting [Hu An-kuo, 1074–1138] and loved Buddhism and Taoism. Wen-ting's learning is all right for government, but he has not arrived at the Way. At any rate, Chi-hsi really had no insight into Buddhism and Taoism. P'ing-shan passed the civil service examination as a young man. When he was an official in P'u-t'ien County, he had as a guest a Buddhist priest. He could meditate and achieved an insight after several days. When he got old, he returned home to study Confucian works. He thought Confucianism agreed with Buddhism. He therefore wrote the 'Sheng-ch'uan lun' [Essay on the sacred transmission]. Later P'ing-shan passed away but Chi-hsi survived. Because I thought I had learned nothing about the Way, I went to see Yen-p'ing [Li T'ung, 1093–1163]." (*Yü-lei*, ch. 104, sec. 37 [p. 4164].)

53. "Later, I went to the post in T'ung-an. I was then twenty or twenty-five. When I first saw Master Li [Li T'ung], I talked with him. Master Li merely said [Ch'an Buddhism] was wrong. I suspected that he had not understood it and quizzed him again and again. Master Li was a simple and solemn person but was not skillful at conversation. He merely told me to read the words of the Sage [Confucius] and the Worthy [Mencius]. Thereupon I temporarily left Ch'an alone. In my mind I thought that Ch'an was all right but that I should read the books of Confucius anyway. I read them again and again, day after day, and gradually found the words of the Sage and the Worthy interesting. As I looked back on Buddhism, I gradually discovered its defects, full of cracks." (*Ibid.*, sec. 38 [p. 4166].)

54. "When I first saw Master Li, I expressed a great number of ideas. Master Li said, 'How is it that you can understand so many lofty ideas but do not understand things right in front of you? The Way is not mysterious. When you try to grasp it through the concrete effort devoted to daily affairs, you will naturally see it.' Only later did I understand what he meant." (*Ibid.*, ch. 101, sec. 76 [p. 4082].)

55. "When I was young, I was ignorant and studied Ch'an. Master Li, however, said strongly that it was wrong. Later, when I examined the matter, I found this side more interesting. As this side advanced an inch, the other side retreated an inch, and has now completely melted away. In the final analysis, there is no advantage in studying Buddhism." (*Ibid.*, sec. 39 [p. 4167].)

56. "At that time, when I studied, although I achieved some understanding, whenever I failed to understand, I let it go. After I saw Master Li, I learned how to direct my effort." (*Ibid.*, ch. 98, sec. 35 [p. 3992].)

57. "I have now come to Yen-p'ing to see Venerable Li Yüan-chung [Li T'ung] and ask him about the doctrine that there is one thread running through [Confucius' teaching], namely, conscientiousness *(chung)* and altruism *(shu)*.[22] He said, '*Chung* and *shu* were precisely Tseng Tzu's insight. When disciples asked him, he explained to them what he understood. [The one thread and *chung-shu*] are not two different things.' " (*Wen-chi*, 37:3a–b, first letter to Compiler Fan.)

58. "In the past, when I tried to understand principles, I also had this defect [of looking for intangibles]. Later, Master Li told me to look for principles in the classics. Afterward, I paid close attention to the classics and deduced some concrete principles. Then I realized that previous thinkers had been wrong." (*Yü-lei*, ch. 104, sec. 27 [p. 4160].)

59. "Someone asked: 'Sir, does your theory of *chung-shu* in your letters [*Wen-chi*, 37:3a–6a] to Compiler Fan [Fan Ju-kuei] agree with your [*Lun-yü*] *chi-chu* [Collected commentaries on the *Analects*]?' The Master said: 'The letters were written before I was thirty; the theory is generally correct. But the way I expressed the idea was not quite right. My views now are somewhat different.' " (*Ibid.*, ch. 27, sec. 100 [p. 1121].)[23]

60. "My commentaries on the *Analects* and the *Book of Mencius* and my explanation of terms are given as notes following the text. I want people to digest every word, whether refined or coarse and whether fundamental or secondary. I have worked on them since I was thirty and have not yet finished revising. I have not been careless or hasty. Readers must be very careful." (*Ibid.*, ch. 116, sec. 37 [p. 4462].)

61. "I made progress before thirty. After thirty, there has not been much progress." (*Ibid.*, ch. 104, sec. 44 [p. 4167].)

62. "Before I was forty, like others I devoted myself to literary composition. Since then, I have had no time for that. However, the compositions I did since then are no different from what I wrote when I was about twenty." (*Ibid.*, ch. 139, sec. 17 [p. 5303].)

63. "I wanted to set up a shrine in Yün-ku [Cloud Valley][24] for the Ancient Sage [Confucius], accompanied by the Four Worthies[25] and with the two Ch'engs[26] and other masters on the right. But I did not get around to doing it." (*Ibid.*, ch. 90, sec. 28 [p. 3640].)

64. "I remember when I was in Nan-k'ang,[27] I wanted to fix up the altar of the Sage in the school, but I was not able to do it. Then I told my successor that there should not be an image for the Sage. It was proper to set up a tablet at the spring and autumn sacrifices. Since that is impossible now, the only thing to do is to have an image sitting on the floor. Only in this way does it conform to the rites." (*Ibid.*, sec. 20 [p. 3638].)

65. "He [Lu Hsiang-shan] came to Nan-k'ang. I invited him to lecture. He spoke about the distinction between righteousness and advantage."[28] (*Ibid.*, ch. 119, sec. 17 [p. 4590].)

66. "When I was in Nan-k'ang, as soon as there was a drought, [I ordered] money and goods to be collected." (*Ibid.*, ch. 106, sec. 5 [p. 4194].)

67. "When I was in Nan-k'ang . . . I generally used dispatches [between prefectures instead of the petitions used at the time by smaller prefectures to larger ones]. At first officials were scared, but I told them that this was according to law. There is no harm in proceeding like this." (*Ibid.*, sec. 8 [p. 4196].)

68. "Formerly, when I was in Nan-k'ang, it was wrong for government teachers to give subjects for essays [out of context]. I could not help petitioning to order the prefectural school not to do this. In recent departmental examinations [in the national capital], subjects remain as they were before." (*Ibid.*, ch. 118, sec. 56 [p. 4557].)

69. "When my term in Nan-k'ang was about to end, someone let a horse gallop in the city and it trampled a child almost to death. I was then in the school and ordered that the man be brought to the judicial court. The next day I assigned the case to a clerk. In the evening I passed by the official building. The clerk said, 'As ordered in the morning, the man has been flogged according to law.' I could not help being suspicious, for when I returned to the judicial court, the man's hat and shoes were in neat condition, with no sign of his having been flogged. Thereupon I interrogated the official and the offender [and sentenced the offender to imprisonment]. The next day, the official was whipped and dismissed. A friend happened to be present and said, 'He [the offender] is a member of a [well-known] family. Why humiliate him?' I said, 'When life and death are at stake, why be lenient? If a member of a [well-known] family can be allowed to gallop a horse and trample a person, in the future he will do something worse.' " (*Ibid.*, ch. 106, sec. 7 [pp. 4195–4196].)

70. "I took great pains in the past. Thinking over principles is like crossing a dangerous wooden bridge. The slightest slip makes a great deal of difference. As soon as one loses one's footing, one falls. I took great pains. After fifty, I felt my energy was weakening. I realized that whether or not one understands principles depends on a very subtle dif-

ference, but my energy was not up to it. That is why all my commentaries on the *Great Learning,* the *Doctrine of the Mean,* the *Analects,* and the *Book of Mencius* were done before [I was] fifty. Since then, I haven't progressed much." (*Ibid.,* ch. 104, sec. 46 [p. 4168].)

71. "On the occasion of a discussion on accepting gifts by investigating officials on their inspection trips, the Master said, 'According to recent regulations, one is allowed [to do so] once in a term.' Chih-ch'ing [Huang Kan, 1152–1221] said, 'As I see it, one should accept only a certain amount.' The Master said, 'When I was in Chekiang East,[29] I never accepted anything.' " (*Ibid.,* ch. 106, sec. 20 [p. 4201].)

72. "When I was commissioner in Chekiang East, there was a woman in Shao-hsing County who had an affair with the son of her late husband's sister. The man promptly became her second husband [literally, 'man following in the footsteps of the husband']. He controlled the family's property and squandered the money without restraint. The [woman's] son felt this was unfair and came to sue. At first I refused to hear the case because of their family relationship. After he followed me for several tens of *li,*[30] his sincerity was touching and I accepted the case. . . . When a person's crime has reached this point and the official does not punish him, how can the father not harbor a sense of great injustice in his grave? . . . When the second husband was pursued at great speed, he jumped into a well. His crime could not be concealed." (*Ibid.,* sec. 21 [p. 4202].)

73. "I feel that only this year [1190] am I free from doubt." (*Ibid.,* ch. 104, sec. 47 [p. 4169].)[31]

74. "I had reached sixty-one years old before I began to see in my readings how principles are." (*Ibid.,* ch. 115, sec. 33 [p. 4428].)

75. "In the past I spoke arbitrarily. That did not help matters. Only now can I see clearly that in every word the Sage tells me is the truth. Only now, when I am sixty-one years old, do I realize this." (*Ibid.,* ch. 104, sec. 46 [p. 4169].)

76. "One day when I had completed trial court in Chang-chou,[32] a scholar was waiting in the hall to ask me whether he could study with me. He lived in [neighboring] Ch'üan-chou. His parents wanted him to pursue the civil service examination and disliked his studying [Neo-Confucianism]. Because he hadn't come with his parents' approval, I told him to go home, get their permission, and come again. Only then would it be all right. But he had an insight, and that was something special." (*Ibid.,* ch. 120, sec. 56 [p. 4635].)

77. "The Master suddenly lamented, . . . saying, '. . . I feel I have not made much progress. On the higher level [of principles] there still seems to be an obstruction.' He also said, 'On the higher level, I feel I have penetrated only half of it.' " (*Ibid.,* ch. 104, sec. 49 [p. 4170].)[33]

78. "In T'an-chou[34] it was customary not to receive guests on the

first and fifteenth day of the month. That was the case at all offices. But I broke the rule and ordered that guests be received on all days." (*Ibid.*, ch. 106, sec. 45 [p. 4222].)

79. "Now in Court[35] I debated with several gentlemen about which temple in which to enshrine Hsi-tsu,[36] almost to the point of shouting with anger. Because of that, I eventually left the capital. Otherwise, I would surely have been chased out." (*Ibid.*, ch. 90, sec. 52 [p. 3658].)

80. "I heard that on a certain day there was going to be a discussion meeting on [enshrining Hsi-tsu in the temple for distant ancestors]. I declined to attend. If I had gone, I would surely have quarreled with the several gentlemen." (*Ibid.*, ch. 107, sec. 8 [p. 4231].)

81. "Even if I understand [principles], I am old and will soon die. How many years can I enjoy them? But I failed to understand more than ten years ago. It is regrettable to die now. [Original note:] Winter, *ping-ch'en* [1196]." (*Ibid.*, ch. 104, sec. 48 [p. 4169]. Chu Hsi was then sixty-seven years old.)

82. "Beginning last year, I have found it difficult to kneel down to kowtow. It was especially difficult in the winter. In the spring of this year,[37] I could barely stand. I therefore asked a substitute to perform the kowtow, but now I can't even stand. Not only the ancients but also many today are not feeble at seventy or eighty. I don't understand why I have declined like this." (*Ibid.*, ch. 90, sec. 109 [p. 3677].)[38]

83. "The Chekiang area is a hotbed of trickery and utilitarianism. Its influence will be like wildfire in twenty or thirty years, and will do a great deal of harm. I am now sixty or seventy years old, with not many years in this world, and may die any day. I now share this idea with you gentlemen. It will prove to be true in the future." (*Ibid.*, ch. 94, sec. 205 [p. 3825].)

84. "I am now sick to the point of death. In the past several years, in view of such doctrines [utilitarianism] in the Chekiang area in general, I have exerted my energy with the hope of checking their spread, but working hard has proved to be futile. I don't know what the situation will be after I close my eyes. It is awful; it is lamentable." (*Ibid.*, ch. 73, sec. 32 [p. 2941].)

85. "It was not my request that I go to the palace to lecture [before the emperor] morning and evening;[39] it was a traditional practice. At that time, however, I thought it would do no good to retain the lecture-ship for too long. Although I lectured twice every day, making the text clear and explaining point by point, it was merely a routine. As I look at the matter now, it was merely like a piece of stationery." (*Ibid.*, ch. 132, sec. 86 [p. 5106].)

86. "[In 1196, Yang Fang][40] was about to leave and asked for instruction. The Master said, 'What I talk about every day is nothing but the Way. You should exert effort on it.' . . . Thereupon he said, 'I have drifted for twenty years and I merely talked [about the Way] and passed

on. Only now do I realize that one should cultivate it.' " (*Ibid.*, ch. 119, sec. 5 [p. 4577].)

87. "People are afraid of imprisonment for party politics. If one looks at the matter calmly, one does not understand why. Take the case of Yang Tzu-chih [Yang Fang]. The other day when he saw me about to present a memorial, he came to urge me to stop. He even knit his eyebrows and made all kinds of expressions. I told him, 'Why do you have to do this? I am saying what I have been saying all along. If all people kept silent, no good men would go forward [to help the emperor].' " (*Ibid.*, ch. 107, sec. 21 [p. 4244].)

88. "The prefectures and counties were intensely searching for [Ts'ai Yüan-ting, 1135–1198] to arrest him. I don't understand what offense he has committed."[41] (*Ibid.*, ch. 107, sec. 22 [p. 4245].)

89. "Someone urged the Master to dismiss his pupils, close his door, and reduce his activity to avoid trouble. The Master said, 'Whether one encounters blessing or calamity is up to fate.' " (*Ibid.*, sec. 27 [p. 4246].)

90. "At the time, the persecution of 'false learning' was very vigorous. . . . The Master said, 'My head now feels like it is only glued to my neck.' He also said, 'From time immemorial, no sage has ever been murdered.' " (*Ibid.*, sec. 33 [p. 4248].)

## Reflections on Life

91. "Take my study. When did I have teachers and friends to confine me to anything? And when were there many books? I merely exerted myself." (*Ibid.*, ch. 121, sec. 53 [p. 4690].)

92. "I dare not consider myself unable to understand, but I achieved [what I have learned] by accumulating it bit by bit." (*Ibid.*, ch. 104, sec. 41 [p. 4167].)

93. "In the old days, when I learned to play the flute, I played without heed, claiming that I would follow the rules after I had learned to play. But that was not the case and I never learned. I realize that in learning one must take care at the beginning." (*Ibid.*, ch. 55, sec. 41 [p. 2089].)

94. "Throughout life I have not been lazy. Even when I am seriously ill, I single-heartedly go forward to do things. By nature I [simply] cannot be lazy." (*Ibid.*, ch. 120, sec. 29 [p. 4617].)

95. "Throughout life, I have not been able to write by simply patching [things] together. Simply putting [them] together does not help." (*Ibid.*, ch. 139, sec. 129 [p. 5336].)

96. "Throughout life, I have hated writing essays the most. I did it only when I could not resist people's requests." (*Ibid.*, ch. 104, sec. 57 [p. 4172].)

97. "When I was traveling, many people requested poems and epi-

logues. To me, [the answer to] why man endures along with Heaven, Earth, the sun and the moon really cannot be found in these things [poems and epilogues]." (*Ibid.*, ch. 107, sec. 63 [p. 4255].)

98. "I don't set up a body of writing. Ordinarily, I only engage in discussion." (*Ibid.*, ch. 118, sec. 88 [p. 4571].)

99. "Asked whether he accepted birthday gifts in office, the Master said, 'No. But sometimes that is not practicable. As a prefect, one does not have to accept, for [a prefect] is free to do whatever he likes. But perhaps when an inspecting commissioner is present, the only thing to do is to follow the custom and accept, since on his birthday one has to make a gift to him. I did this in T'an-chou [1194]. In Nan-k'ang [1179–1181] and Chang-chou [1190–1191] I neither accepted nor presented any.' " (*Ibid.*, ch. 87, sec. 157 [p. 3583].)

100. "People often do not want to receive guests. I don't know why. If I had no guests for a month, or [even] for a day, it would be like being seriously ill for a month. Today I talked with a guest and feel relaxed in my mind. I don't know how those who close their doors and do not see people pass their time." (*Ibid.*, ch. 107, sec. 44 [p. 4250].)

101. "In my life, I have written many pieces to decline official appointments." (*Ibid.*, sec. 70 [p. 4257].)

102. "Question: 'What do you wear on death anniversaries, Sir?' Answer: 'I simply wear a loose jacket of white silk and a light bluish cap. I cannot be too elaborate.' " (*Ibid.*, ch. 87, sec. 157 [p. 3582].)

103. "On the fifteenth day of the seventh month, people eat vegetarian meals and employ Buddhist priests. I do not follow that." (*Ibid.*, ch. 190, sec. 132 [p. 3684].)

104. "Question: 'While observing seasonal religious sacrifices [such as spring sacrifice], how about popular festivals [such as New Year's]?' Answer: 'Both have been retained in my family.' " (*Ibid.*, sec. 133 [p. 3684].)

105. "I myself have a mourning dress, silk jacket, and a silk cap. I wear them on death anniversaries." (*Ibid.*, sec. 141 [p. 3686].)

106. "Throughout my life, I have often dreamed of old friends and relatives. If on the following day I did not receive a letter from them or see them, inevitably other people would talk about them. As I see it, these are correct dreams. The rest are all incorrect." (*Ibid.*, ch. 86, sec. 70 [p. 3530].)

## Reflections on His Own Works

107. "In reading books, one must be willing to make an effort. In the past it was difficult for me to succeed. I therefore dare not lightly tell people what to do. When I could not resist annotating or writing commentaries, what I have done is to select from a wide area the refined and

subtle passages of the several masters and seniors so people may read them. They are simple and essential." (*Ibid.*, ch. 121, sec. 79 [p. 4702].)

108. "In explaining the classics, every word I use has been weighed carefully before I dare write it down." (*Ibid.*, ch. 105, sec. 2 [p. 4174].)

109. "My explanation of books is like textual annotation. In many cases only one or two words are used, and in others no explanation is necessary. However, that is only the way to explain books. It is also necessary to teach people not to be careless in reading books." (*Ibid.*, sec. 3 [p. 4174].)

110. "When I alter the words of a classic, there must be a purpose; it is not done lightly. One should understand the purpose of the alteration." (*Ibid.*, sec. 4 [p. 4175].)

111. "It is often the case that in explaining the works of the several masters [Ch'eng I, etc.], I dare not quote some of their very good passages because their ideas are not found in the original text." (*Ibid.*, sec. 5 [p. 4175].)

112. "I worked hardest on the *Great Learning*. When Wen Kung [Ssu-ma Kuang, 1019–1086] wrote the [*Tzu-chih*] *t'ung-chien* [Comprehensive mirror for the aid of government], he said that he devoted all the energy in his life to the work. I did the same thing with the *Ta-hsüeh chang-chü* [Commentary on the *Great Learning*]. The *Lun-Meng* [*chi-chu*] [Collected commentaries on the *Analects* and the *Book of Mencius*] and the *Chung-yung* [*chang-chü*] [Commentaries on the *Doctrine of the Mean*] did not take a lot of exertion." (*Ibid.*, ch. 14, sec. 51 [p. 412].)

113. "I have repeatedly revised the *Ta-hsüeh Chung-yung* [*chang-chü*] (Commentaries on the *Great Learning* and the *Doctrine of the Mean*] but have never reached the point beyond revision. Only recently does the *Ta-hsüeh* [*chang-chü*] seem to contain very few defects. Ideas are most thoroughly expressed in discussions. As soon as they are written down, they don't measure up to even ten or twenty percent of the discussion." (*Wen-chi*, 54:10b, first letter in reply to Ying Jen-chung.)

114. " 'For more than forty years I have thought over the *Lun-Meng* [*chi-chu*]. I have weighed every word in them and would not allow myself to be offtrack. Students should pay close attention to my explanations.' Further remark: 'In explaining the words of the Sage and the Worthy, one principle must follow another, as one part of water follows another. Then the current will not be impeded.' Still further remark: 'Each time I look at the *Chung-yung chieh* [Explanation of the *Doctrine of the Mean*], I do not have much doubt. In the case of the *Ta-hsüeh* [*chang-chü*], however, while I am reading, doubts arise. I have never been completely satisfied and therefore I have never stopped revising it.' " (*Ibid.*, ch. 19, sec. 61 [p. 704].)

115. " 'In my *Yü-Meng chi-chu* [Collected commentaries on the *Analects* and the *Book of Mencius*], not a single word may be added and not a

single word may be deleted. You gentlemen should read them carefully.'
He said again: 'Not a single word more and not a single word less.' "
(*Ibid.*, sec. 59 [p. 703].)

116. "When I read books in the past, I put in a lot of work. I had a
whole trunk of commentaries on the *Analects* and the *Book of Mencius* by
various scholars. When I read a paragraph, I would always look up
many of them. I would investigate and look for ideas and systems on the
basis of their theories. After I was satisfied with what I had found, I
decided which was right and which was wrong. I would write out several words of what was right. I also copied down what was good.
Although they cannot compare with the [*Lun-Meng*] *chi-chu,* which are
succinct but thorough, the outline was already definite. The present
*Chi-chu* are an abridgment of those notes. But people do not pay attention; they hold on to their preconceptions and read these works carelessly. If one consults one or two paragraphs of the [*Lun-Meng*] *ching-i*
[Essential meanings of the *Analects* and the *Book of Mencius*] to see why
certain passages [of the various masters selected for the *Ching-i*] have
been chosen or rejected [for the *Chi-chu*], one will understand." (*Ibid.*,
ch. 120, sec. 17 [p. 4610].)

117. "In my writing of the *Huo-wen* [Questions and answers on the
Four Books], I have all along wanted the student to understand their
correct intentions. Those who read these works should see which theories cited in them should be examined and which should not. They
should overlook those that need not be examined so as to allow the correct intentions to become clearer." (*Ibid.*, ch. 121, sec. 33 [p. 4682].)

118. "The Master said that one does not have to read the *Lun-yü huo-
wen* [Questions and answers on the *Analects*]. When asked for an explanation, he said, 'It is fragmentary.' " (*Ibid.*, ch. 105, sec. 35 [p. 4181].)

119. "Formerly, I compiled this work [the *Meng Tzu yao-chih* (Essential meanings of the *Book of Mencius*)]. As I see it now, it is unnecessary.
The *Book of Mencius* teaches people directly, in a clear manner. It is good
enough." (*Ibid.*, sec. 37 [p. 4182].)

120. "Formerly, when I wrote the *Shih-chieh* [Explanation of the *Book
of Odes*], I used the individual prefaces [to each poem]. Where a preface
did not make sense, I explained it away. But I always felt uncomfortable. When I explained [a poem] the second time, although I retained
the individual preface and sometimes argued for it, in the end I failed to
see the original intention of the poet. Later I woke up to the fact that if
all the individual prefaces are overlooked, the odes naturally make
sense. I therefore eliminated all former theories. Only then did the
intention of the poems become lively." (*Ibid.*, ch. 80, sec. 71 [p. 3313].)

121. "In most cases I have not followed the individual prefaces in my
explanation of the *Book of Odes*. Even if my explanations are no good, at
most I have offended the writers of the prefaces. If I had only relied on

the prefaces and had not investigated the intention of each poem as expressed in both its earlier and later parts, I would have offended the sages and worthies." (*Ibid.*, sec. 96 [p. 3324].)

122. "In the past I read several scores of theories on the *Book of Odes,* and I remember every one of them in its entirety. . . . I read them thoroughly. Only after a long time have I dared decide which theory is correct and which is not." (*Ibid.*, sec. 97 [p. 3325].)

123. "As soon as I arrived in Ch'angsha [1194], I wanted you gentlemen to come to work on the *Li-pien* [Compilation of the text on rites]. But I found there was too much work to do, and I did not intend to stay long. Therefore I gave up the idea. [Several months] later, when I got to the capital, things were more settled. I drew up a plan and issued a call throughout the country for specialists on ritual texts to come for the compilation. People like Yü Cheng-fu were asked to come. Today everything was stopped." (*Ibid.*, ch. 84, sec. 37 [p. 3479].)[42]

124. "My explanations of the 'Hsi-ming' [Western inscription] and the 'T'ai-chi-[t'u shuo]' [Explanation of the diagram of the Great Ultimate] are accumulations of several scores of years of work. Not a single word is the result of my personal ideas." (*Wen-chi,* 38:30a, letter in reply to Huang Shu-chang.)

125. "The fundamentals of self-cultivation are completely covered in the *Hsiao-hsüeh* [Elementary education], while refined and subtle principles are fully treated in the *Chin-ssu lu* [Reflections on things at hand]." (*Yü-lei,* ch. 105, sec. 22 [p. 4179].)

126. "The *Chin-ssu lu* is worth reading. The Four Books are the ladders to the Six Classics.[43] The *Chin-ssu lu* is the ladder to the Four Books." (*Ibid.*, sec. 23 [p. 4179].)

127. "Everything in the *Chin-ssu lu* is intimately connected with man's life and can save him from defects." (*Ibid.*, sec. 26 [p. 4179].)

128. "The *Hsiao-hsüeh* has much to say on respect and reverence and little on prevention and prohibition." (*Ibid.*, sec. 21 [p. 4178].)

129. "Only the first part of 'Jen-shuo' [Treatise on humanity][44] is good." (*Ibid.*, sec. 42 [p. 4184].)

## Unfulfilled Wishes

130. "I wanted to build a family temple with five rooms. It was beyond my financial ability to do so." (*Ibid.*, ch. 90, sec. 49–50 [p. 3657].)

131. "I often think that, in about ten years, the children's marriages will have been carried out. Then I can put aside all domestic chores and seclude myself in this place [Yün-ku in Mount Lu]." (*Wen-chi,* 78:4b, "Yün-ku chi" [Account of Cloud Valley].)

132. "Asked about the *Lun-yü huo-wen* [Questions and answers on the

*Analects*], the Master said: 'This was written fifteen years ago. The ideas there are not like mine today. At the time I wanted to revise it. As time went on, my energy became weak. That task is a huge one. Eventually I abandoned it." (*Yü-lei,* ch. 105, sec. 34 [p. 4184].)

133. "Wang's [Wang An-shih, 1021–1086] new commentaries on the classics do have their good points. He devoted his whole life to them. How can they be without insight? . . . Once I wanted to go through them and summarize their fine points, but have had no time to do so." (*Ibid.,* ch. 130, sec. 13 [p. 4968].)

134. "The *Book of History* is difficult to punctuate. Take the 'Ta-kao' [Great announcement] in the *Chou-shu* [Books of Chou] section. Some sentences are very long. Present readers have broken them up and therefore have failed to understand them. I wanted to write a *Shu-shuo* [Explanation on the *Book of History*]. In the end it was never done." (*Ibid.,* ch. 78, sec. 15 [p. 3148].)

135. "[The ritual texts] are scattered in different places. I have not been able to collect them. How terrible! Every day there are too many things to deal with, and I cannot concentrate. If I had the leisure of several months and the assistance of one or two friends, the task would be accomplished. While I was at Court, I wanted to petition the Court to set up a specific bureau, summoning several friends from all quarters who are specialists on ritual works to do the compilation. When the book was finished and was about to be presented to the Court, I would then petition the Court to appoint them as officials to reward them. That would also assist the Court's intention to gather and utilize idle talents. However, before I started the project, I left the capital." (*Ibid.,* ch. 84, sec. 37 [p. 3479].)

136. "Once I had the desire to write a section on Hsiao Ho's [d. 193 B.C.] and Han Hsin's [d. 197 B.C.] first meeting with Emperor Kao-tsu [r. 106–195 B.C.], a section on Teng Yü's [2–58] first meeting with Emperor Kuang-wu [r. 25–57], and a section on the time [in 207 when] Wu-hou [Chu-ko Liang, 181–234] first met with the Hsien-chu [earlier ruler, i.e., Liu Pei, 162–223], and have these several sections, together with Wang P'o's *P'ing-pien ts'e* [Plan to pacify the borders], constitute a book." (*Ibid.,* ch. 135, sec. 15 [p. 5170].)

137. "I once wrote the *T'ung-chien kang-mu* [Outline of the *Tzu-chih t'ung-chien*] and theorized that [certain dynasties like the Three Kingdoms, 220–280, dividing China] had no orthodoxy *(cheng-t'ung).* This book has not been brought up to date. Gentlemen of later times will see something worthwhile in it." (*Ibid.,* ch. 105, sec. 55 [p. 4189].)

138. "When I read the *Nü-chieh* [Admonitions for women], I found it incomplete and in some places superficial. Po-kung [Lü Tsu-ch'ien, 1137–1181] also considered it defective. When I was at leisure, I wanted to select ancient sayings in another anthology like the *Hsiao-hsüeh,* in

several parts, with items like 'Correctness and Tranquillity,' 'Humility and Weakness,' 'Filial Piety and Love,' 'Peace and Cordiality,' 'Diligence and Carefulness,' 'Thrift and Simplicity,' 'Generosity and Charity,' and 'Discussion and Learning.' Whatever of Pan Chao's [52?–125] book [the *Nü-chieh*] is worth including will be selected. . . . Being ill and tired, I cannot gather and inspect the material. Kindly review these items thoroughly to see if anything is missing, and if so, please supply it. If such a book can be compiled, it will be something." (*Wen-chi*, 35:27b, fifteenth letter to Liu Tzu-ch'eng [Liu Ch'ing-chih].)

139. "The poems of Tu [Tu Fu, 712–770] contain many misprints. The *Cheng-i* [Corrections of variants] by Ts'ai Hsing-tsung is, of course, good but not exhaustive. Once I wanted to enlarge it and write a *Tu shih k'ao-i* [Investigation into the variants in Tu Fu's poems], but in the end I didn't have the time." (*Yü-lei*, ch. 140, sec. 21 [p. 5343].)

140. "I have always wanted to compose a poem to describe why the water of the Ku-lien [Cave][45] is good, but it is very difficult to express. Generally, whenever the water touches the mouth, it is as if there is nothing, and it is [also] very smooth. But I have not been able to describe these two qualities." (*Ibid.*, sec. 59 [p. 5351].)

141. "Once I wanted to use Ssu-ma's [Ssu-ma Kuang, 1019–1086] book, consult the theories of various thinkers, make adjustments with deletions and additions, draw up an outline, show the items, and append it to the end [of Chang Shih's (1133–1180) *San-chia li-fan* (Models of rituals by three authors)]. . . . However, because of illness I was not able to do so." (*Wen-chi*, 83:14b, epilogue on the *San-chia li-fan*.)

## Notes

1. Ch'ien Mu, *Chu Tzu hsin-hsüeh-an* [New anthology and critical accounts of Master Chu] (Taipei: San-min Book Co., 1971), vol. 3, pp. 37–47.

2. *Book of Mencius*, 6A:2. Chess Ch'iu was teaching two people. One was concentrating while the other was thinking about shooting a swan.

3. The Four Books are the *Great Learning*, the *Analects*, the *Book of Mencius*, and the *Doctrine of the Mean*.

4. *Book of Mencius*, 6A:7.

5. Ch'en Kuan was too Buddhistic for Liu Tzu-hui. The *Liao-chai chi* is lost. Selections are found in the *Sung-Yüan hsüeh-an* [Anthology and critical accounts of Sung and Yüan Neo-Confucians] (*SPPY* ed.), 35:4a–5a, chapter on Ch'en Kuan, etc. For Ch'en's Buddhist interest, see *ibid.*, 5a–6b.

6. *Doctrine of the Mean*, ch. 20.

7. Hsieh's commentary is no longer extant.

8. Referring to Hsieh Liang-tso.

9. *Book of Odes*, ode no. 76.

10. The *T'ang-chien* [Mirror of the T'ang dynasty] was written by Fan Tsu-yü (1041–1099).

11. Hsü Ts'un's courtesy name was Ch'eng-sou.

12. *Analects,* 12:1.

13. *Book of Mencius,* 2A:2.

14. *I chuan* [Commentary on the *Book of Changes*], 1:14b–15a, in the *Erh-Ch'eng ch'üan-shu* [Complete works of the two Ch'engs] (*SPPY* ed.).

15. In the *Book of Odes,* there is an individual preface to each poem interpreting it as a moral admonition.

16. A county in Fukien.

17. A county in Fukien. Chu Hsi was *chu-pu* (assistant magistrate) there from 1153 to 1156. The *chu-pu,* literally a clerk, actually performed the functions of a magistrate.

18. *Analects,* 19:12.

19. *Book of Changes,* "Appended Remarks," pt. 2, ch. 5.

20. *Analects,* 19:12. Ch'eng I's comment: "From sprinkling and sweeping the ground to investigating things with care and refinement until one enters into the spirit, there is one principle penetrating through all." (*I-shu* [Surviving works], 15:8a, in the *Erh-Ch'eng ch'üan-shu.*)

21. *Book of Mencius,* 2A:2.

22. *Analects,* 4:14.

23. Chu Hsi's letters to Fan Ju-kuei are found in the *Wen-chi,* 37:3a, 6a.

24. Chu Hsi built a cottage in Yün-ku in Mount Lu, Fukien, in 1175.

25. The Four Worthies were Yen Tzu, Tzu-ssu, Tseng Tzu, and Mencius.

26. The two Ch'engs were Ch'eng Hao (1032–1085) and Ch'eng I (1033–1107).

27. Chu Hsi was prefect in Nan-k'ang from 1170–1181.

28. *Analects,* 4:16.

29. Chu Hsi was commissioner of affairs of ever-normal granaries, tea, and salt in Chekiang East in 1181.

30. A *li* is one-third of a mile.

31. This was recorded by T'ung Po-yü in 1190, when Chu Hsi was sixty-one.

32. Chu Hsi was prefect in Chang-chou, Fukien, in 1190.

33. This was recorded by Yeh Ho-sun in 1191, when Chu Hsi was sixty-two.

34. Chu Hsi was prefect in T'an-chou, present Changsha in Hunan Province, in 1193.

35. Chu Hsi was lecturer-in-waiting in 1194.

36. Hsi-tsu was the historical founder of the Sung dynasty. The debate was about whether this founder should be enshrined in a special temple, as Chu Hsi contended, or in the temple for other ancestors, as others argued.

37. The year referred to is 1198 or 1199.

38. This was recorded by Shen Hsien from 1198 on.

39. See above, n. 35.

40. Yang Fang's courtesy name was Tzu-chih. He obtained the *chin-shih* (presented scholar) degree in 1163. For him, see my *Chu Tzu men-jen* [Master Chu's pupils] (Taipei: Student Book Co., 1982), pp. 267–268.

41. Because the government attacked Chu Hsi and his school as "false learning," Chu Hsi was dismissed from the government as well as from his temple

guardianship. Ts'ai Yüan-ting, a close associate, was banished to Tao-chou (present Tao County, Honan) in 1197, where he died a year later. For him, see the *Sung-Yüan hsüeh-an,* ch. 62, chapter on Ts'ai Yüan-ting, and my *Chu Tzu men-jen,* pp. 331–332.

42. Chu Hsi was then seriously ill and passed away several days later.

43. The Six Classics are the *Book of Odes,* the *Book of History,* the *Book of Rites,* the *Book of Changes,* the *Autumn and Spring Annals,* and the *Book of Music.* The *Book of Music* was lost before the third century B.C. and was replaced by the *Chou-li* [Rites of Chou] in the Sung dynasty (960–1279).

44. The "Jen-shuo" [Treatise on humanity] is found in the *Wen-chi,* 67:20a–21b. See ch. 11 below.

45. The Ku-lien Cave is in Mount Wu-i in Fukien.

# Names and Family

## Names

CHU Hsi was born at noon on the fifteenth day of the ninth month in the year *keng-hsü* (1130) of the Chien-yen period (1127–1130) at the home of Cheng An-tao in Yu-hsi County, Nan-chien Prefecture, Fukien Province. His father gave him the childhood name Shen-lang (Young man of Shen) to commemorate the place of his birth, Yu-hsi, whose name had originally been Shen-hsi (Shen river) but had been changed because of a taboo for a prince in Fukien.[1] He was also given the childhood name Chi-yen—Chi because he was the youngest son, and Yen in reference to Yen-p'ing, an old name for Nan-chien.

His regular name was Hsi (bright), and he ranked fifty-second in the order of his generation. There are two significant points about the name Hsi. First, it is a single name. This practice, common among some families, began in the Chu family with the fifteenth generation, four generations before Chu Hsi's time, and lasted until the middle of the eighteenth century. Even today, a number of Chu Hsi's descendants have single names. According to a table of twenty generations,[2] there has been only one exception since the tradition began, and that was Chu Hsi's grandson, En-lao. Chu Hsi was still living when En-lao was born, and presumably it was he who named the child. The double name appears in the *Wen-chi*,[3] so either Chu Hsi made an exception, which I doubt very much, or En was later respectfully called En-lao (Venerable En) and his name collated as such in the *Wen-chi*.

The second characteristic of the name Hsi is that, like the other single names in the Chu family of that generation, it contains a part that means one of the Five Agents (*wu-hsing*, Metal, Wood, Water, Fire, and Earth)—in this case, the fire radical. Professor Miura Kunio has suggested that this tradition began with Chu Hsi's father.[4] To fulfill this requirement, in some cases obscure characters were used and in others the characters did not truly contain one of the five elements. Each generation used the same element for its names; for example, Chu Hsi's three sons all had the earth radical in their names, all seven grandsons had the metal radical, and all six great-grandsons the water radical. This applied only to male members of the family. By the eleventh generation after Chu Hsi, exceptions began to appear. The system probably broke down soon afterward, but exactly when needs further research. Miura Kunio, following Morohashi Tetsuji (1883–1982), believes that the order originated with Tung Chung-shu's (176–104 B.C.) doctrine of the Five Agents producing one another in a cycle.[5] I rather think that Chu Hsi's father was thinking of Tung's matching the Five Agents with the Five Constant Virtues (humanity, righteousness, propriety, wisdom, and faithfulness), for the idea of cycles did not fit in with the idea of continuous generations.[6]

When Chu Hsi was sixteen or seventeen, his teacher, Liu Tzu-hui (1101–1147) gave him the courtesy name *(tzu)* Yüan-hui (Origination that is hidden) and composed a poem to celebrate the occasion.[7] Later, Chu Hsi felt that *yüan* was the first quality of Change,[8] which he did not deserve, and chose to use the name Chung-hui (Hui the junior). Chu Hsi always used this name, never Yüan-hui, although people always addressed him as Yüan-hui, not Chung-hui.[9]

Throughout his life, Chu Hsi used a number of literary names *(hao)*. In 1175, when he built a thatched hut in Yün-ku (Cloud Valley) on top of Mount Lu, 70 *li*[10] from the seat of Chien-yang County in Fukien, he called it Hui-an (Secluded Cottage) and used the terms in his own name. Beginning in 1174 he often called himself Hui-weng (Old man Hui), and in his later years called himself Yün-ku lao-jen (Old man of Cloud Valley). After he reconstructed the White Deer Hollow Academy in 1179, he styled himself Pai-lu-tung-chu (Head of White Deer Hollow). He used the title Jen-chih-t'ang-chu (Master of the Hall of Righteousness and Wisdom) after 1183, when he built the Wu-i Ching-she (Study on Mount Wu-i), which incorporated the Jen-chih-t'ang. In 1185 Chu Hsi was given a sinecure as superintendent of the Yün-t'ai Temple.[11] Thereafter he used the titles "Yün-t'ai yin-li (Official of Yün-t'ai in retirement), Yün-t'ai chen-i (True retiree of Yün-t'ai), Yün-t'ai wai-shih (official of Yün-t'ai outside the national capital), and Yün-t'ai tzu (Master of Yün-t'ai). Likewise, he adopted the title Sung-kao yin-li (Official in retirement at the high peak of Sung) when he was appointed superintendent of the Ch'ung-fu Temple at Mount Sung[12] in 1188, and Hung-ch'ing wai-shih upon appointment to the Hung-ch'ing Temple in the southern capital in Honan in 1191. In 1195 he built the Chu-lin Ching-she (Bamboo Grove Study) in Chien-yang. Because the study was surrounded by water, he called himself Ch'ang-chou ping-sou (Sick man at Ch'ang-chou). By that time his health was deteriorating, and he also used the name Hui-an ping-sou. In 1195 he adopted his last literary name, Tun-weng (Old man in retirement).[13]

When he annotated the *Ts'an-t'ung-ch'i* (Three ways unified and harmonized) in 1197, Chu Hsi used the pseudonym K'ung-t'ung tao-shih Tsou Su (Tsou Su the K'ung-t'ung Taoist), Tsou being the Chu state in ancient times, *su* being the original pronunciation of *hsi,* and *k'ung-t'ung* meaning youthful ignorance. Apparently he wanted to apologize for annotating a Taoist work.

Some names applied to him are actually mistakes or misprints, such as Hui-an t'ung-sou, Ch'ang-chou tiao-sou, Ch'ang-tzu ping-sou, and Yün-ku hao-jen. There is no evidence that Chu Hsi ever used any of these. As for the name Cho-chai, it derives from a misreading of the text, for Chu Hsi merely wrote an essay on someone's Cho-chai Study.[14] He was posthumously honored as Wen Kung (Venerable gentleman of culture) in 1208 and as Hui Kuo-kung (State duke of Hui-chou) in 1228, Hui-chou referring to his ancestral place in Anhui (now in Kiangsi). Because he once named his study the Tzu-yang Study after Tzu-yang Mountain in Hui-chou, and because he settled down in his later years in K'ao-t'ing in Chien-yang, a place his father loved and thought of living in, scholars have honored him as Master of Tzu-yang and Master of K'ao-t'ing.

When Chu Hsi signed his name, he often named a place to show where he came from. His sense of ancestry was exceedingly strong. In his writings, more than fifty times he called himself "Chu Hsi of Hsin-an." Sometimes he used Tan-yang or Wu-chün (Prefecture of Wu) instead. Hsin-an belonged to Tan-yang Prefecture in Han times (206 B.C.–A.D. 220), but was separated from it and became a new prefecture in the Wu state. It was renamed Hsin-an in 265 and Hui-chou in 1121. Because P'ing-ling Mountain is in the northern part of Hui-chou, Chu Hsi also signed his name "Chu Hsi of P'ing-ling."

## Parents

Chu Hsi's father came from Hui-chou. Both Tzu-yang and K'ao-t'ing are place names that recall his father, and there is no doubt that his father loomed large in his mind. His father's name was Sung, and his courtesy name was Ch'iao-nien. He was born on the twenty-third day of the intercalary second month, 1097, in Sung-yen Village, Wan-nien Township,[15] Wu-yüan County, Hui-chou Prefecture. In 1118 he obtained the *chin-shih* (presented scholar) degree and was appointed county sheriff *(wei)* in Cheng-ho County, Chien-chou Prefecture, in Fukien. He took his family, including his own father, to Fukien. When his father died, Chu Sung could not return to Hui-chou because of poverty.[16] He therefore buried his father on the side of Hu-kuo Temple, 20 *li* west of the city of Cheng-ho. At the time he associated with Lo Ts'ung-yen (1073–1135) and Li T'ung (1093–1163), through whom he learned of the doctrines transmitted by the Ch'eng brothers (Ch'eng Hao, 1032–1085, and Ch'eng I, 1033–1107). Chu Sung called his study Wei-chai (Soft Leather Study), following the example of the ancients who wore soft leather to slow down their quick tempers.[17] When the mourning period was over in 1128, he was appointed sheriff in Yu-hsi. He arrived in the seventh month and his term was up in the fifth month of the following year. He was then appointed superintendent of customs at Shih-ching Trading Center, Hsiu-jen Village, K'ai-chien Township, Ch'üan-chou Prefecture. In the following year, because of war, he left his position and took his family to Cheng-ho and then to Yu-hsi. Thus the family shuttled between Chien-chou and Nan-chien prefectures. In 1130, he and his wife were staying at the I-chai Study of Cheng An-tao (1073 *cs*) in Yu-hsi County, where Chu Hsi was born.

In 1134 Chu Sung was called to the capital in Lin-an (present Hangchow) for an audience. As a result he was appointed correcting editor *(cheng-tzu)* of the Imperial Library *(pi-shu-sheng)*. After observing mourning for his wife, he was called again for an audience. In 1138 he was appointed collator *(chiao-shu-lang)* of the Imperial Library. He was then shifted to assistant editor *(chu-tso tso-lang)* and collator in the bureau of history *(shih-kuan)*. At that time Ch'in Kuei (1091–1155) was talking peace with the invading Chin, which Chu Sung and others protested. Chu was sent away to be prefect of Jao-chou,[18] but he declined the post and requested a sinecure as superintendent of the Ch'ung-tao Temple in T'ai-chou. Thus he terminated his political career in 1140 and went to live in Chien-yang County, later moving to the capital of Chien-chou Prefecture. He died in the southern section of the city in 1143, at the age of forty-seven. One account says he died in Huan-hsi Ching-she (Study Surrounded by Water) in the southern part of the city.[19] But since all other accounts say he died in a private home, the residence was probably made into an academy later, as an honor to him. On his deathbed, Chu Sung wrote to Hu Hsien (1086–1161), Liu Mien-chih (1091–1149), and Liu Tzu-hui in Wu-fu Village, Ch'ung-an County, and told Chu Hsi to study with them. Thus in 1143, when Chu Hsi was fourteen, he moved to Wu-fu Village with his mother. The next year he buried his father by the side of the Ling-fan Temple of Hsi-t'a Mountain in the vicinity of Wu-fu Village. In 1170 he moved the grave to the foot of the O-tzu-feng in Pai-shui, in the same area, and because the place was wet, moved it once more to the north of the Buddhist temple on the middle level of Chi-li Mountain, Shang-mei Village, Wu-i Township, Ch'ung-an County.[20]

*Mother*

We know very little about Chu Hsi's mother. Huang Kan's (1152–1221) "Chu Tzu hsing-chuang" (Biographical account of Master Chu) only gives her family name. The biography of Chu Hsi in the *Sung shih* (History of the Sung dynasty) does not even mention her. Fortunately, we have Chu Hsi's own writing about his mother. According to him, she was from the Chu family (different from Chu Sung's) of Hui-chou, which owned almost half the business in the prefectural capital. Her father was Chu Ch'üeh, a learned scholar and philanthropist who died at the age of eighty-three. By that time the family fortune had declined. His wife was Miss Yü from the same prefecture. They had three sons and a daughter.[21] Chu Hsi added that his mother was born in the seventh month of 1100. She was married at eighteen. She received the title *ju-jen* (Related person)[22] because of her husband's position as Imperial Library collator. A virtuous woman, kind and gentle, she served her parents-in-law well and endured poverty without complaint. She lived until the age of seventy. She and Chu Sung had three sons, two of whom died in infancy; Chu Hsi was the youngest. They also had five daughters, the youngest of whom was married to Liu Tzu-hsiang, who was *chu-pu* (assistant magistrate) of Ch'ang-ting County, Fukien;[23] her father affectionately called her *hsiao-wu-niang* (little fifth young lady).[24] In a letter to a friend, Chu Hsi described his mother as "pure and devoted in moral character. She served her mother-in-law in the most filial and respectful manner. My grandmother was very strict but my mother was obedient. In managing the family she was lenient but enforced discipline. She always personally took part in the preparation of seasonal religious sacrifices. Her treatment of her bride's maid and servants was kind, without the slightest trace of jealousy."[25]

After his mother died in 1169, Chu Hsi buried her the following year in the Han-ch'üan (Cold Spring) area on the south side of T'ien-hu Mountain near Ch'ung-t'ai Village, Chien-yang County, a hundred *li* from his father's grave.[26] He built the Han-ch'üan Ching-she (Cold Spring Study) there. According to Yeh Kung-hui's *Chu Tzu nien-p'u* (Chronological biography of Master Chu) and the *nien-p'u* in Tai Hsien's *Chu Tzu shih-chi* (True records of Master Chu), he lived by the side of the grave but went home to Wu-fu Village on the first and fifteenth days of the month to perform religious rites. The three later chronological accounts that Wang Mao-hung consulted also tell of Chu Hsi maintaining this tradition. Wang contended, however, that the Ching-she was a place for study and discussion, not for mourning, and therefore rejected the notion of Chu Hsi's monthly journeys. It is true that the distance between the Han-ch'üan area and Wu-fu Village, where the religious rites were performed, was too great for frequent travel. The chronological accounts probably recorded Chu Hsi's standard practice, which was not necessarily followed every month. There is no reason the Ching-she could not have been used for both study and mourning. We know that Chu Hsi took religious rites about his mother very seriously and always wore black on her anniversary dates. When a pupil asked why, he replied, "Have you not heard that 'The mourning of a superior man lasts through life'?"[27]

Yet if we know very little about the life of Chu Hsi's mother, we know even less about that of his wife. In the Chinese tradition, family affairs are considered absolutely private and not for public record, which is undoubtedly why biographies of Chu Hsi almost never mention his wife. Huang Kan's "Hsing-chuang" merely says, "He married a Liu who was posthumously given the title *shih-jen* [Person of great virtue].[28] She was the daughter of Master Ts'ao-t'ang [Liu Mien-chih] of Pai-shui. Ts'ao-t'ang was one of those with whom Wei-chai [Chu Sung] told Master Chu to study. She died in the *ting-yu* year of the Ch'ien-tao reign and was buried in a grave reserved for her and her husband."[29] Yeh Kung-hui's *Chu Tzu nien-p'u*, under the year 1176, says, "Lady Liu died in the eleventh month." In the second month of the following year, she was buried in Ta-lin Valley in T'ang-shih Village[30] in Chien-yang County. A cottage there was called Shun-ning (To follow and to be at peace).[31] Its pavilion was called Tsai-ju (Outstanding).[32] Chu Hsi was to be buried by her side. The names of the pavilion and cottage and the plan for burial together indicate that their married life must have been quite happy. We do not know when Chu Hsi's wife was born or married, but we do know that her father died in 1149. It is known that she gave birth to their first son in 1153 and died in 1176. If we suppose that she was born in 1133 (three years Chu Hsi's junior), married in 1149, and gave birth to the youngest daughter in 1175, then their marriage lasted for twenty-eight years.

## Children

Chu Hsi's marriage produced three sons and five daughters, seven grandsons, nine granddaughters, six great-grandsons, and seven great-granddaughters.[33] The eldest son was Shu, courtesy name Shou-chih, born in 1153. A bright boy, he received training at home but tended to be lazy. At the age of twenty-one, he was sent to Chin-hua in Chekiang to study with Lü Tsu-ch'ien (1137–1181). When he left home, Chu Hsi wrote down strict instructions for him, including no drinking or making loud noises and exactly what to say on certain occasions.[34] In his correspondence with Lü he often expressed great concern about his son's behavior and academic progress, and Lü always reassured him that all was well. Lü Tsu-ch'ien's brother, Lü Tsu-chien (d. 1200), liked Shu very much.[35] Shu boarded with Lü Tsu-ch'ien's pupil, P'an Ching-hsien (1137–1192). Shu had been engaged to the second daughter of

Hsiang An-shih (d. 1208), who was his own age, but the girl died before marriage.[36] P'an liked Shu enough to offer him his own daughter in marriage. At the time the girl was only thirteen, much younger than Chu Hsi had thought. But since Shu was over twenty, the marriage was performed in the following year (1174).[37] We know that Shu failed to copy a couple of essays requested by his father.[38] Altogether, he lived in Chin-hua for six years, going home once for his mother's funeral and twice to take the civil service examination. Finally he took his wife and child home to try the examination once more, but failed for the third time. Now evidently matured, he became more interested in learning and did some copying for his father,[39] but never served as an official. He died in Chin-hua in 1191 at the age of thirty-nine, leaving his wife, two sons, and four daughters.

As soon as he heard about the death of his son, Chu Hsi resigned as prefect of Chang-chou and requested a superintendency of a temple in order to return home and arrange for the funeral. The *Yü-lei* contains four passages describing how seriously and meticulously Chu Hsi attended to Shu's funeral and anniversaries. This shows his deep feeling for his son. In his correspondence with pupils and friends, he repeatedly expressed extreme grief over the loss. He did not teach his son to compose poems, and had thought that Shu was not versed in the art. After Shu's death, however, a pupil, Hsü Chin-chih, showed Chu Hsi the poems Shu had written on social occasions. Chu Hsi could not refrain from shedding tears.[40]

His second son was Yeh, courtesy name Wen-chih, born in 1154, a year after Shu. Chu Hsi had wanted a scholar from Chien-yang to teach the boys,[41] and there is evidence that they were sent to study with Ts'ai Yüan-ting.[42] Chu Hsi was anxious that Yeh marry early.[43] In 1180 Yeh and Shu took the civil service examination together, but both failed.[44] As a result of Chu Hsi's official status, Yeh was appointed supervisor of wine storage in the new commercial center in Te-ch'ing County, Hu-chou, in present Chekiang. At that time Chu Hsi was prefect of Nan-k'ang in Kiangsi. Because the famine situation was grave, Chu Hsi worked very hard and his heart trouble became serious. Yeh was immediately called to take care of him,[45] and also assisted Chu Hsi in his printing business.[46] When Chu Hsi became critically ill, Yeh hurriedly went from his home in Wu-fu Village to Chien-yang. Two days later, Chu Hsi passed away. Thus Yeh was the only son by his deathbed. Yeh himself died nine years later, in 1209, leaving his wife and four sons. He was buried in the Lung-yin Temple in San-ch'ü Village in Chien-yang.[47]

Chu Hsi's third son was Tsai, courtesy name Ching-chih, born in 1169. Chu Hsi was disturbed at not being able to secure a teacher for him.[48] Hsü Shun-chih was expected to come from Yu-hsi, since it was too far to send the boy there, but Hsü got married, and as a result Tsai never had a tutor.[49] It is not known whether he took the civil service examination. Once, when asked whether he had been taught anything special at home, Tsai said, "Ordinarily I just listened to the discussion between my father and his friends. Sometimes, privately, he merely pointed out my defects. One day he taught me the *Great Learning* and said, 'I devoted my whole life to this book. One must understand it before reading other books.' "[50]

When Chu Hsi became prefect of Nan-k'ang in 1179, Tsai, then eleven years old, was the only family member to accompany him.[51] Tsai himself had a long political career. Tai Hsien's *Chu Tzu shih-chi* gives the long list of his successive positions.[52] He followed in his father's footsteps in some cases, such as serving as *chu-pu*, prefect of Nan-k'ang, superintendent of ever-normal granaries, tea, and salt, and so on. Like his father, he declined a number of posts and preferred the sinecure of superintending a temple. The day before Chu Hsi died, he wrote Tsai to tell him to return home early to collect his writings, and lamented, "For years father and son have had no chance to see each other."[53] He died in 1239 at seventy-nine. We know that he had four sons, that he was buried behind the Yung-an Temple in the capital of Chien-ning Prefecture, and that he posthumously received the title Duke of Chien-an Prefecture.

Chu Hsi's eldest daughter was Sun, who was married to Liu Hsüeh-ku, the son of Liu Tzu-hui's adopted son Liu P'ing (1138–1185). We know nothing else about her, but do find that Hsüeh-ku, his father Liu P'ing, Chu Shu, Chu Tsai, and others accompanied Chu Hsi on a visit to Mi-an on Mount Lu, Kiangsi, in 1181,[54] and that Chu Hsi wrote a poem about an orchid Hsüeh-ku gave him.[55]

The second daughter, Tui, was married to one of Chu Hsi's most outstanding pupils, Huang Kan, who became a renowned scholar but was very poor. Once Chu Hsi wrote him and said,

> It is most fortunate that this girl found a home in a virtuous family to serve a worthy man. But she lost her mother at an early age and thus missed instructions on proper behavior. Furthermore, because the family is poor, it has not been able to provide a generous dowry. For this I am very much ashamed and deeply regretful. I suppose your mother, being a kind lady, can surely overlook things. . . . Because of his features and spirit, grandson Lo should grow up to be an accomplished person. . . . Grandson Fu also seems to be gradually developing. It is worth watching.[56]

Another letter inquired about the well-being of the two boys.[57] The Lo boy liked a picture of a lion at Chu Hsi's home very much. It was a painting by the famous painter Lu T'an-wei (fifth century A.D.). Chu

Hsi sent to Huang Kan and told him to lift Lo up to look at it but not let him scratch it, and wrote that he hoped Lo would grow up to be like a lion whose "roar will crack the skulls of a hundred animals."[58] Chu Hsi also sent two of his other grandsons to study with Huang Kan.[59]

The third daughter, Ssu, was born in the *kuei-ssu* year (1173). We are told that she lost her mother at age four, was betrothed to a member of the Chao family at fifteen, was a young woman of fine character, was her father's pet, and expressed the desire to be buried with her mother.[60] From Chu Hsi's letters to friends, we learn that she was sick for over a hundred days and then passed away.[61] Chu Hsi composed a rhymed inscription on her death. During her lifetime, Chu Hsi was teaching and writing at home and must have developed special affection for her. The inscription is in three-character form, as if to make it easier for the girl to understand, since she did not have the learning her brothers had.

Chu Hsi was not the innovator of the three-character form. Precedents can be found in the *Great Learning*[62] and the *Hou-Han shu* (History of the Later Han dynasty).[63] Chu Hsi himself, however, wrote two additional inscriptions in the three-character style.[64] Can we say that his three-character pieces inspired his pupil, Ch'en Ch'un (1159–1223), who wrote the *Ch'i-meng ch'u-sung* (Elementary verses for the beginner) in the three-character style?[65] We may also wonder whether the *San-tzu ching* (Three-character classic), which has been the first primer for schoolchildren since the thirteenth century, owes its origin to Chu Hsi or to Ch'en Ch'un.[66]

Nothing is known of Chu Hsi's fourth daughter except that she was married to Fan Yüan-yü, son of Chu Hsi's pupil Fan Nien-te. Neither is anything known about the fifth daughter except that she died several years after Ssu. Once Chu Hsi wrote Ch'en Wen-wei (1154–1239) that he had lost a small grandchild.[67] And the day before he himself died, Chu Hsi wrote Fan Nien-te asking him to continue his work on ritual texts and to arrange for the marriage of a grandchild.[68] But in neither case did Chu Hsi name the grandchild to whom he was referring.

## Notes

1. Wang Mao-hung, *Chu Tzu nien-p'u* [Chronological biography of Master Chu] (*Ts'ung-shu chi-ch'eng* [Collection of series] ed.), ch. 1, p. 1; *k'ao-i* [Investigation into variants], ch. 1, p. 243, under the sixth year of Ch'ing-yüan (1120). Liang Chang-chu (1775–1849) asserted in his *Ying-lien ts'ung-hua, hsü-hua* [Talks on couplets, further talks] (*Kuo-hsüeh chi-pen ts'ung-shu* [Basic sinological series] ed.), p. 191, that Chu Hsi was named Yu-lang after the Yu River in Yu-hsi County, but gave no evidence.

2. Tai Hsien, *Chu Tzu shih-chi* [True records of Master Chu] (*Chin-shih han-chi ts'ung-k'an* [Chinese works of the recent period series] ed.), pp. 43–73, genealogy.

3. *Wen-chi,* 94:27a, Chu Hsi's account of his son's burial.

4. Miura Kunio, *Shushi* (Tokyo: Kōdansha, 1979), p. 201.

5. *Ibid.,* 201.

6. For a detailed discussion of the generation names in the Chu family, see my *Chu Tzu hsin-t'an-so* [New investigations on Master Chu] (Taipei: Student Book Co., 1988), sec. 6, on generation names of the Chu family.

7. This poem is found in Wang Mao-hung's *Nien-pu,* pp. 4–5. I have annotated it in my *Chu Tzu hsin-t'an-so,* sec. 5, on Liu Tzu-hui's poem.

8. In the first hexagram in the *Book of Changes,* the Four Qualities of Change are: *yüan heng li chen* (origination, flourishing, advantage, and firmness).

9. Chu Ron-Guey has brought to my attention that in the *Nan-p'ing hsien-chih* [Accounts of the Nan-p'ing County] (1928 ed.), 17:27a, Chu Hsi is mentioned as Chung-hui. This exception is unique.

10. A *li* is one-third of a mile.

11. The Yün-t'ai Temple was at Mount Hua in Shensi. It had been occupied by the invading Chin; Chu Hsi's superintendency was merely nominal and required neither official duty nor residence there.

12. In Honan Province.

13. For the reason for the name Tun-weng (Old man in retirement) see ch. 1 above, p. 3.

14. For reference to the *Wen-chi* on these names, mistaken names, titles, official titles when Chu Hsi was prefect, etc., see my *Chu Tzu hsin-t'an-so,* sec. 3, on what Chu called himself. This essay also goes into the place names noted below.

15. This is according to Yeh Kung-hui, *Chu Tzu nien-p'u* [Chronological biography of Master Chu] (*Chin-shih han-chi ts'ung-k'an* ed.), p. 55, and Tai Hsien's *Chu Tzu shih-chi,* p. 75, both under the fourth year of Chien-yen (1130). According to Wang Mao-hung's *Nien-p'u,* p. 1, under the same year, it was Yung-p'ing Township. I have followed Yeh and Tai because their sources are earlier.

16. Some accounts said Chu Sung could not return to Hui-chou because the road was blocked by Fang La's rebellion. But Wang Mao-hung pointed out on p. 202 of his *Nien-p'u* that the rebellion took place in 1120–1121, whereas Chu Sung's father died in 1125. Wang cited the authority of Chu Hsi himself. See the *Wen-chi,* 94:22b, account of moving his father's grave.

17. *Wen-chi,* 97:18a, "Biographical account of Honorable Chu [Chu Hsi's father]."

18. Present Shang-jao County, Kiangsi.

19. Chu Yü (*fl.* 1722), *Chu Tzu wen-chi ta-ch'üan lei-pien* [Classified compilation of the complete collection of literary works of Master Chu] (1722 ed.), Bk. I, chronological biography, p. 3b.

20. For the biography of Chu Sung, see the *Wen-chi,* 97:17a–26b, Chu Hsi's biographical account of his father; 94:22b–23b, Chu Hsi's account of the moving of his father's grave; and supplementary collection, 8:8b–9b, Chu Hsi's epilogue to Chu Sung's letter to his father-in-law; and Gao Ling-yin, "Chu Hsi

hsing-tsung k'ao" [Investigation into Chu Hsi's travel] (*Chung-kuo che-hsüeh shih lun-ts'ung* [Anthology on the history of Chinese philosophy], no. 1, 1984), pp. 413–416.

21. *Wen-chi*, 98:24b–26a, Chu Hsi's account of his grandfather-in-law.

22. *Ju-jen* (Related person) was the lowest of seven ranks for the wife of an official.

23. *Wen-chi*, 94:23b–24a, Chu Hsi's account of the burial of his mother; 97:25b–26a, Chu Hsi's account of his father.

24. *Ibid.*, supplementary collection, 8:8b, Chu Hsi's epilogue to Chu Sung's letter to his father-in-law.

25. *Ibid.*, 38:46b, Chu Hsi's fourth letter to Ch'en Chün-chü (Ch'en Fu-liang).

26. *Ibid.*, 94:23b–24a, Chu Hsi's account of his mother's burial.

27. *Yü-lei*, ch. 90, sec. 143 (p. 3686). The quotation comes from the *Book of Rites*, "Chi-i" [Meaning of sacrifice], sec. 5.

28. *Shih-jen* [Person of great virtue] was the second lowest of seven ranks for the wife of an official.

29. *Mien-chai chi* [Collected works of Huang Kan] (*Ssu-k'u ch'üan-shu chen-pen* [Precious works of the *Complete Collection of the Four Libraries*] ed.), 36:47a–b, biographical account of Master Chu. There was no *ting-yu* year in the Ch'ien-tao reign.

30. Yeh Kung-hui, *Chu Tzu nien-p'u*, p. 104, under the third year of Ch'un-hsi (1176). This has been repeated in subsequent chronological accounts, including Wang Mao-hung's *Nien-p'u*, p. 65. T'ang-shih was later called Chia-ho Village.

31. In Chang Tsai's (1020–1077) "Hsi-ming" [Western inscription], the concluding remark says, "In life I follow and serve Heaven and Earth. In death I shall be at peace."

32. The term comes from the *Lieh Tzu*, ch. 1 (*SPTK* ed., called *Ch'ung-hsü chih-te chen-ching* [True classic of the perfect virtue of simplicity and vacuity]), 1:5a.

33. *Mien-chai chi*, 36:47b–48a. Tai Hsien, *Chu Tzu shih-chi*, pp. 44–48, added grandsons En-lao and Ch'in.

34. *Wen-chi*, supplementary collection, 8:6a–8b, "To my eldest son Shu."

35. *Ibid.*, 1:7b, twenty-sixth letter to Huang Chih-ch'ing (Huang Kan).

36. *Ibid.*, separate collection, 3:13b, second letter to Liu Tzu-ch'eng (Liu Ch'ing-chih).

37. *Ibid.*, regular collection, 33:26a, thirty-eighth letter to Lü Po-kung (Lü Tsu-ch'ien).

38. *Ibid.*, 34:34b–35a, ninety-third letter to Lü Po-kung.

39. *Ibid.*, supplementary collection, 1:21b, eighty-sixth letter to Huang Chih-ch'ing (Huang Kan); separate collection, 3:5b, first letter to Ch'eng Yün-fu (Ch'eng Hsün).

40. *Ibid.*, regular collection, 83:22b–23a, "An inscription on my son's poetic folio."

41. *Ibid.*, 39:5a, letter in reply to K'o Kuo-ts'ai (K'o Han).

42. *Ibid.*, 44:3a, fourth letter, and 4a, fifth letter, in reply to Ts'ai Chi-t'ung (Ts'ai Yüan-ting).

43. *Ibid.*, 33:26a, thirty-eighth letter in reply to Lü Po-kung.

44. *Ibid.*, 34:29b, eighty-fifth letter in reply to Lü Po-kung.

45. *Ibid.*, p. 28b.

46. *Ibid.*, 60:1b, first letter in reply to Chou Ch'ün-jen (Chou P'u).

47. Tai Hsien, *Chu Tzu shih-chi*, p. 45, genealogy.

48. *Wen-chi*, 39:19a, eightieth letter in reply to Hsü Shun-chih (Hsü Sheng).

49. *Ibid.*, 35:17a, seventh letter in reply to Liu Tzu-ch'eng.

50. *Yü-lei*, ch. 14, sec. 50 (p. 412).

51. *Wen-chi*, 26:23b, a short note to the assistant councilor.

52. Tai Hsien, *Chu Tzu shih-chi*, pp. 46–48.

53. Ts'ai Ch'en, "Chu Wen Kung meng-tien chi" [Account of Chu Hsi's death], in the *Ts'ai-shih chiu-ju shu* [Nine Confucians in the Ts'ai family] (1868 ed.), 6:59b, quoted in Wang Mao-hung, *Chu Tzu nien-p'u*, ch. 4B, p. 228, under the sixth year of Ch'ing-yüan (1120).

54. *Wen-chi*, 84:30a, account of a visit to Mi-an.

55. *Ibid.*, 2:4a.

56. *Ibid.*, supplementary collection, 1:10a, thirty-fourth letter in reply to Huang Chih-ch'ing.

57. *Ibid.*, 16a, fifty-ninth letter.

58. *Ibid.*, 12a, fortieth letter.

59. *Ibid.*, 14b, 17b, and 19b, the fifty-first, sixty-fifth, and seventy-third letters. The name of one of the two grandchildren, Chun, does not appear in Huang Kan's "Chu Tzu hsing-chuang," 36:47b, or Tai Hsien's *Chu Tzu shih-chi*, pp. 48–56, genealogy. There must be a mistake somewhere.

60. *Ibid.*, 93:1a, "Nü Ssu mai-ming" [Inscription for the burial of daughter Ssu].

61. *Ibid.*, regular collection, 27:22b, letter to Huang Chin-shu; separate collection, 4:13a, letter to Lin Ching-po (Lin Ch'eng-chi).

62. The *Great Learning*, ch. 2.

63. *Hou-Han shu* [History of the Later Han dynasty] (*SPTK* ed.), 13:23a–b, "Record of the Five Agents."

64. *Wen-chi*, 85:4b, 5a, inscriptions on the window and the wine cup.

65. *Pei-hsi ta-ch'üan chi* [Complete collected works of Ch'en Ch'un] (*Ssu-k'u ch'üan-shu chen-pen* [Precious works of the *Complete Collection of the Four Libraries*] ed.), 16:6b–7a.

66. For a discussion on this question, see my *Chu Tzu hsin-t'an-so*, pp. 672–674.

67. *Wen-chi*, 59:32a, letter in reply to Ch'en Ts'ai-ch'ing (Ch'en Wen-wei).

68. See above, n. 53.

# – 4 –

# Ways of Living:
# Residences, Dress,
# and Travel

O N Chu Hsi's private life, most writers have hardly gone beyond what Huang Kan (1152–1221) wrote in his "Hsing-chuang" (Biographical account).[1] We are told very little about the way he dressed or traveled. Whether he ever made Mount Wu-i his regular residence is still controversial. We propose to discuss these matters as far as available materials allow.

## Residences

As mentioned in chapter 3 above, Chu Hsi was born in someone's home in Yu-hsi County in northern Fukien. At fourteen, following his father's dying wishes, he took his mother farther north to Wu-fu Village in order to study with Hu Hsien (1086–1162), Liu Mien-chih (1091–1149), and Liu Tzu-hui (1101–1147).[2] Tzu-hui's elder brother, Liu Tzu-yü (1097–1146), built a house beside his own for Chu Hsi and his mother. Chu Hsi called the place Tzu-yang Tower, recalling the Tzu-yang Mountain in his ancestral place in Wu-yüan.[3] Many mountain peaks could be seen from the window, and numerous bamboos surrounded the house,[4] which was Chu Hsi's residence for some fifty years.

Wu-fu Village is in Ch'ung-an County in northern Fukien, about 150 *li*[5] southeast of the county seat. Of the three teachers, Chu Hsi studied most with Liu Tzu-hui. There is a Master Chu Lane in the village, which is, according to tradition, the route he walked to school. Across from the T'an-hsi stream in the village is Sha-mao (Silk Hat) Mountain, which looks like a screen *(p'ing)*. Hence Tzu-hui called himself P'ing-shan (Screen Mountain), and scholars have honored him as Master of P'ing-shan. About 150 *li* to the northwest is Mount Wu-i. Among the numerous scenic spots is the Shui-lien-tung (Water Curtain

44

Cave), which can accommodate several hundred people. Inside the cave is a stone inscription which says that Liu P'ing-shan and other scholars lectured there. Based on this inscription there is a strong tradition that Liu P'ing-shan taught there and that Chu Hsi attended his teachings. It is quite plausible that P'ing-shan occasionally lectured in the cave and that Chu Hsi accompanied him. But their residences were in Wu-fu Village.

There is much evidence that Wu-fu Village was Chu Hsi's long-term residence. In a letter to Ts'ai Yüan-ting (1135–1198) he said, "Yesterday I finished in Wu-fu the writing you wanted. Since I returned home, I have been busy all the time. Also because I have not conducted a divination for the burial, my mind has not been settled."[6] Chu Hsi was referring to moving his father's grave to a new site in 1170.[7] From this we know that in 1170, when he was forty-one years old, he was still living in Wu-fu Village. When Lü Tsu-ch'ien (1137–1181) visited him in 1175 to compile the *Chin-ssu lu* (Reflections on things at hand), Lü went to Wu-fu Village on the first day of the fourth month, according to his own account, and stayed in Chu Hsi's study.[8] In the *Yü-lei*, we have a conversation recorded by Wan Jen-chieh that says, "The Master asked me about my endeavors since I had taken leave from him. I answered, 'I have carefully adhered to your instruction and dared not be amiss. Formerly, I could not help being skeptical about your theories. But since I last arrived in Wu-fu Village, I have realized that your principles are decidedly unchangeable.' "[9] Wan was originally a follower of Lu Hsiang-shan (1139–1193). He came to Nan-k'ang[10] in Kiangsi when Chu Hsi was prefect there (from 1179 to 1181) and became his pupil. Wan recorded more than four hundred conversations with Chu Hsi, including the one just cited.[11] He saw the Master again in 1188.[12] This conversation must have taken place during his second visit. In other words, before Chu Hsi left for the national capital to report to the emperor in the third month of 1189, he lived and taught in Wu-fu Village.

The most telling evidence, however, is offered by Chu Hsi himself. In 1191 his term expired as prefect at Chang-chou in southern Fukien. He left the prefecture in the fourth month and went to Chien-yang County in northern Fukien in the fifth month. He wrote Ch'en Liang (1143–1194) and said, "My home in Wu-fu Village is not pleasant to look at. I do not choose to return there and have decided to settle here. However, there are only several hundred cash in my purse. Hardly ten or twenty percent of the work [on the home] had been done and the purse is exhausted. I shall have to go into debt before finishing the work. I regret very much that I was too hasty in making plans, but the scenery here is attractive."[13] He also wrote his pupil Wu Pi-ta, saying, "I am now temporarily living here near the city. The task of handling affairs and receiving guests is more than double that at the mountain. It is now not feasible to return to Wu-fu Village and I plan to settle right here. I have already bought an old house to which I can move next year. At present I have built a small tower. It will be finished in another ten days. The mountains and rivers here are elegant, clear, and secluded. They are most enjoyable."[14]

The mountain referred to in his letter to Wu Pi-ta is Wu-i. For forty years Chu Hsi frequented this mountain and in 1183 built the Wu-i Ching-she (Wu-i Study) there.[15] He gathered many followers and attracted many visitors, so that Wu-i became an intellectual center. As he wrote in a poem, "With lute and books, I have almost become a guest of the mountain for forty years."[16] In the decade after establishing the Ching-she, Chu Hsi probably stayed at Wu-i more often than not, but his regular residence remained in Wu-fu Village. As he wrote Ch'en Liang in 1185, "Early last month I went to the city and then returned home. After handling a number of affairs, I went to Wu-i until I came home yesterday."[17]

The following year, Ch'en wanted to tour Wu-i. In response Chu Hsi wrote,

> Because it is cold in the winter and hot in the summer, this mountain is not inhabitable. Only in the spring when it is warm and in the fall when it is cool, and when flowers display their colors and dew is light and trees are clear, is it time for an enjoyable visit in the two seasons. This spring I came only once and did not have time to stay overnight. Because of illness I have not been able to come since the fall. Affairs [at the Ching-she] have been much neglected. If you can come next spring, we can visit there for several days.[18]

From these letters we know that Chu Hsi's sojourns at Wu-i could be either long or short. Generally speaking, before he built the Ching-she, his stays were comparatively short, and afterward they were comparatively long. He probably did consider moving to Wu-i at one time, because in a poem he referred to Wu-fu Village as his "old residence" and talked about "moving east" (to Wu-i),[19] but this appears to have been a passing thought.

Before the Wu-i Ching-she, Chu Hsi had the Han-ch'üan Ching-she (Cold Spring Study), which he built in 1170 beside his mother's grave.[20] Since all the chronological biographies say that he stayed in the Ching-she every day and went home (presumably to Wu-fu Village) every first and fifteenth day of the month, they give the impression that Chu Hsi made his home there. Whether he actually made the monthly trips will be discussed later. The chronological biographies also say that in 1197,

when the government was persecuting Chu Hsi's *tao-hsüeh* (Learning of
the Way) as "false learning," and when the prefectural and county
offices were pursuing Ts'ai Yüan-ting for arrest, Chu Hsi and Ts'ai
stayed together overnight at the Cold Spring Study. However, Wang
Mao-hung (1668–1741) proved beyond any doubt that this story is a
fabrication.[21]

Since the Cold Spring Study was on the south side of T'ien-hu
Mountain, it was easily accessible. Consequently, whenever Chu Hsi
went there, guests filled the hall.[22] Sometimes he and friends stayed
there for more than ten days,[23] and he also took his two sons there.[24]
Such frequent visits[25] show that Chu Hsi deeply loved the Cold Spring
Study. But he also said "I hurriedly went to the Cold Spring Study"[26]
and "I hurriedly went to the Cold Spring Study today but returned in
the evening,"[27] indicating that he did not always stay for long. When
Lü Tsu-ch'ien came to visit him in 1175, he went first to Wu-fu Village,
and they then spent about ten days at the Cold Spring Study. Afterward
they toured Mount Wu-i with friends before going on to the Goose Lake
Temple in Kiangsi to meet Lu Hsiang-shan, his brother, and others.
Several days after Chu Hsi returned home, he ascended the peak of
Mount Lu. He praised the mountain as "elegant and open, unlike the
human world, but the air is too light for a lengthy stay."[28]

What lured Chu Hsi to this mountain was Yün-ku (Cloud Valley). In
a poem, he said that for thirty years he had lived by the side of P'ing-
shan (Screen Mountain) in a village and near markets, which did not
agree with his desire for quiet. He had heard that west of Hsi-shan
(Western Mountain) there was a valley deep but open, and he vowed to
sell his small property to build a place there.[29] Screen Mountain refers
to Wu-fu Village, and Western Mountain was where Ts'ai Yüan-ting
lived. Chu Hsi did not carry out his wishes completely, but in his "Yün-
ku chi" (Account of Cloud Valley) he wrote,

> Cloud Valley is on top of Mount Lu, 70 *li* northwest of Chien-yang
> County. . . . I acquired it in 1170. I built a thatched hall there and called
> it Hui-an [Secluded Cottage]. A stream runs southwest for 7 *li*. . . . Rock
> cliffs rise for more than a hundred feet, from which a waterfall plunges
> down. . . . In the bamboo grove is the Hui-an with three rooms. . . .
> There are several tens of *mu*[30] of rice-field that can be cultivated. There is
> a cottage inhabited by Buddhists and Taoists. . . . It is more than 80 *li*
> from my home in the southwest, so it is utterly impossible for people to
> visit, and I have come only once or twice a year. However, my friend
> Ts'ai Chi-t'ung [Ts'ai Yüan-ting] lives 20 *li* or more north of the moun-
> tain. He has found it possible to visit a number of times. From the plan-
> ning in the beginning to the completion of the compound, all has been due
> to him.[31]

This account was written in the seventh month of 1175, a month after Chu Hsi returned from the meeting at Goose Lake Temple. The whole structure was a very simple affair. In a poem, he said that the cottage could not stand either the rain or the wind, and that straw had to be hurriedly added to the roof.[32]

Because Cloud Valley was far from Wu-fu Village and was on a mountaintop, it took a whole day by carriage to make the trip. Chu Hsi recalled in a poem his hunger, thirst, and fatigue during the journey.[33] Ordinarily it took two days to make the trip. As Chu Hsi wrote in a poem, he and his friends started from Screen Mountain and arrived at Cloud Valley the next evening.[34] Still, he liked the place enough to stay for more than ten days at a time.[35] We no longer know where Cloud Valley was, but it must be quite near the Cold Spring Study. In a letter to Ts'ai Yüan-ting, Chu Hsi said that after sacrifices to his mother's grave at the Cold Spring, he immediately ascended Mount Lu. I believe both the Cold Spring Study and the Secluded Cottage were his country villas. His earlier desire to return to Cloud Valley was never fulfilled.

In 1191, he finally moved from Wu-fu Village to K'ao-t'ing in Chien-yang County. The scenery at K'ao-t'ing was exceedingly beautiful. Chu Hsi's father had once passed through it and loved it, declaring that it was worth settling there, and fulfilling his father's wish was the main reason that Chu Hsi made the move. There were of course other reasons as well, which can be seen in Chu Hsi's letter to his teacher Hu Hsien. When Fan Ju-kuei (1102–1160) died, his family wanted to settle in T'ai-ning County in Fukien. Chu Hsi wrote his teacher and recommended Chien-yang. He offered three advantages, namely, that Chien-yang was better for visiting graves, for discussions and teaching, and for making a living. Since Hu Hsien died in 1162, when Chu Hsi was only thirty-three, the attraction of Chien-yang must have made a deep impression on Chu Hsi early on. For one thing, Chien-yang was not far from his mother's grave, and after Chu Hsi settled there he moved his father's grave to Chi-li Mountain, Shang-mei Village, Wu-i Township, Ch'ung-an County. The new site was not only closer to Chien-yang but dear to his father, who had once expressed the desire to enjoy the flowers and wine at Chi-li Mountain.[36] Because of poverty, Chu Hsi ran a printing business there to supplement his income.[37]

We have mentioned that Chu Hsi bought an old house in Chien-yang, but he finally built a new one. In a letter to Chu Lu-shu he said, "When I returned last year, I was careless in financial planning. I foolishly built a small house, and moved in only recently. But expenditures numbered in the hundreds [of cash]. I have borrowed everywhere. Still my family has not completely come together. I regret that I did not think matters over carefully."[38]

Chu Hsi arrived in Chien-yang on the twenty-fourth day of the fifth month in 1191, temporarily living in the Huang-mei Temple in the T'ung-yao Bridge area (this was probably the old house he bought). When the new house was finished in the sixth month of 1192, he reported to his ancestors in a religious ceremony at the family shrine.[39] We know very little about the new residence except that K'ao-t'ing was at the foot of Yü-chen Mountain in San-kuei Village, west of the county seat of Chien-yang. Chu Hsi called the place Tzu-yang Shu-t'ang (study), Tzu-yang again referring to the Tzu-yang Mountain in Hui-chou, where his father came from. In the study there was a chamber called Ch'ing-jui-ko (Clear and Secluded Chamber).[40] The house was in ruin in Yüan times (1217–1368) and was repaired during the Ming (1368–1644), but ceased to exist long ago. Today K'ao-t'ing has thirty-six villages. Twenty-five of these have families named Chu, all descendants of Chu Hsi. Chu Hsi lived in K'ao-t'ing for not quite eight years before he died, and one of those years he was mostly away from home. What makes Chien-yang immortal is the Chu-lin Ching-she (Bamboo Grove Study) he founded in 1194, which was an intellectual magnet in Chu Hsi's last years and remained a famous academy for centuries.

## Dress

Chu Hsi's dress seems to be a trivial matter, yet Huang Kan took special care in his "Hsing-chuang" to note that the Master dressed in a "deep" garment, a headgear of wide cloth, and square-toed shoes. Moreover, the chronological biographies (nien-p'u) emphatically state that as soon as his official status was terminated, Chu Hsi received guests in the simple dress (yeh-fu) of a commoner. Obviously, Chu Hsi took his dress very seriously. Yet these two bits of information are all we know about the matter. Writers who mention his dress generally repeat the scant information in the biographical account and the chronological biographies. A study of Chu Hsi's dress would be welcome. Not being a specialist on the subject, I do not propose to make such a study, but I have gathered from various sources pertinent passages on how he dressed, and hope that this information will stimulate further research. In the meantime, it should help to answer a number of questions, such as whether or not Chu Hsi was a conservative in the matter of dress.

1. The "Hsing-chuang" says, "In his leisurely life, he would rise before dawn. He would wear a 'deep' garment,[41] a headgear of wide cloth, and square-toed shoes. . . . For treating himself, he wanted no more in clothing than enough to cover the body, no more in food than enough to fill the stomach, and no more in shelter than enough to protect himself from wind and rain."[42]

2. "The Master would early in the morning present incense [to vari-

ous shrines]. In the spring and summer, he wears a 'deep' garment. In the winter he wears a hat of black silk. His upper garment is made of cloth with wide sleeves and a black hem, and the lower garment [skirt] is made of thin white silk, like the garment of Lien-hsi [Chou Tun-i, 1017–1073]. When he receives an official who is on duty or other officials, he appears in a tight garment."[43]

3. "Asked about [his] system of dress, the Master said, 'There is no system. Since most painted portraits are like this, I imitate them.' Asked about the measurement, he said, 'There is no basis to go by. Although ritual works talk briefly about the matter, the explanation is not clear.' "[44]

4. "The Master saw that the dress worn by Cheng-fu [Yü Cheng-fu] was made of white cotton with a round neckline that was black. The Master asked him what style it was, and Cheng-fu replied, 'It is T'ang dynasty [618–907] style.' The Master said no more. Thereafter, he changed his clothing style [to be that of T'ang]."[45]

5. Chu Hsi wrote a treatise on the "deep" garment that he wore, describing the measurement and material, and mentioning the large belt, black silk cap, headgear of wide cloth, and black shoes, but he did not go into the history of the garment or its use. The two conversations recorded in the Yü-lei also deal exclusively with material and color.[46]

6. "Asked what kind of dress he wears on death anniversaries [of his ancestors], the Master said, 'I merely wear a light robe of white raw silk and thin dark bluish headgear. I cannot have too many kinds of dress.' Asked what the bluish headgear is made of, he answered, 'Either light thin silk or raw silk will do. I use thin silk.' Asked whether on his birthday he accepts an offering of wine from juniors, he said, 'No.' Asked if he changes his clothing, he also said 'No.' . . . Asked about the method of fashioning the dark bluish headgear, he said, 'It is like a lined turban, with four tassels. It resembles a scarf-cap.' "[47]

7. "Asked about his system of dress, the Master said, 'I have mourning dresses, raw silk robes, and raw silk headgear. I wear them on death anniversaries.' "[48]

8. "The Master said, 'On death anniversary days, one should wear a black robe and a black hat.' "[49]

9. "On the death anniversaries of his father and mother, after performing religious sacrifices, he wore thin raw silk, dark bluish headgear for the whole day. One day when he arrived at the chamber in the evening, he still wore white headgear and had not taken it off. Upon being asked, he answered, 'I heard that is the plan of my younger brother-in-law Ch'eng Yün-fu [Ch'eng Hsün, 1135–1196].' "[50]

10. "When I was chu-pu [assistant magistrate] at T'ung-an [from 1153 to 1156], the Court gave an order for all officials to wear a hat. I found it an obstacle when I rode in a sedan chair. Later I added a circle of bamboo on top of the sedan."[51]

11. "Whenever the Master was ill and pupils came to visit, he always adjusted his hat to the right position, sat down, and bowed. He displayed his sentiment to the fullest in every way, without feeling tired of the reception in the least. . . . [When he lectured in the evening and there was a guest in the audience,] as the guest withdrew, he would always stand to see that his carriage started. Only when the guest no longer turned his head did he withdraw to disrobe."[52]

12. "On the occasion of discussing how those in popular society were not wearing caps or belts, he said, 'In running the empire, there are things that cannot be delayed for a day and there are things that can be corrected gradually. Those that cannot be delayed for a day refer to starting things. Those that can be corrected gradually refer to maintaining things.' "[53]

13. When Chu Hsi's official status was terminated in 1199, he began to receive guests in the simple dress of a commoner. In his *Nien-p'u,* Wang Mao-hung quotes Chu Hsi's public notice on receiving guests, which says briefly, "Venerable Lü Ying-yang [Lü Hsi-che, c. 1036–c. 1114] once said, 'It was proper etiquette for people in the capital and Lo-yang whose official status had ended to dress in everyday simple dress when they dealt with people, but regrettably that was not so in outlying districts.' His idea was very profound. Compared to the light robe of white raw silk *(liang-shen),* the attire of the jacket above and the skirt below with a large belt and square-toed shoes is not rustic. Its convenience is that when the belt is tightened, it is proper etiquette, and when it is loosened, one is at leisure. Furthermore, if people in remote areas can see the old custom of the capital when imperial ancestral glory was high and realize how beautiful the attire is, it may be a help in promoting morals."[54]

Wang was quoting from the *Nien-p'u* of Li Mo (1552) and Hung Ch'ü-wu (1700), but earlier chronological biographies by Yeh Kung-hui (1401) and Tai Hsien (d. 1508; published 1513), which were not available for Wang to consult, already contained the passage. This means that it may be traced to the earliest chronological biography, which was written by Chu Hsi's pupil Li Fang-tzu. A short treatise entitled "On Receiving Guests after Retirement from Office" is included in the *Wen-chi* and explains that the main reason for Chu Hsi's simple dress was his inability to move around because of his poor health.[55]

14. According to the "Hsing-chuang," "When the Master was seriously ill and near death, . . . he put himself in the correct position, adjusted his dress and cap, and passed away resting on the pillow."[56]

15. In his "Chu Wen Kung meng-tien chi" (Account of Chu Hsi's death), Ts'ai Ch'en (1167–1230) said, "On the ninth day [April 23, 1200], at the fifth watch [about 4:00 A.M.], . . . the Master held the pen as usual, but he could no longer swing it. In a moment he laid down the

pen and rested on the pillow. By mistake his hand touched his headgear. He looked at me for me to adjust it."[57]

16. The *Sung shih* (History of the Sung dynasty) says, "When Chu Hsi was about to die, he gave Kan [Huang Kan] his 'deep' garment and some works he had written."[58] But Wang Mao-hung showed this story to be a farfetched borrowing from the idea of dharma transmission by Buddhist patriarchs.[59]

## Travel

Biographers of Chu Hsi, whether in China, Japan, or Korea, have relied mainly on Huang Kan's "Hsing-chuang," supplemented with the biography in the *Sung shih* and perhaps with some details from the chronological biographies. These are adequate as far as Chu Hsi's movements of historical significance are concerned. But Chu Hsi loved to tour scenic spots, visited friends in many places, lectured in even more, and, during the years he suffered political persecution (1196–1200), lived quietly in a number of localities. Where did he go? How long did he stay? By what means did he travel? Aside from his trips to Wu-yüan to visit ancestral graves in 1150 and 1176, his tour of Mount Heng with Chang Shih (1133–1180) and others in 1167, his meeting at the Goose Lake Temple with Lu Hsiang-shan, and his tour of Mount Lu in 1181, the chronicles hardly mention his other travels, and those that are included are only briefly noted. There is nothing like the detailed and statistical survey Kusumoto Bun'yū made of Wang Yang-ming's (1472–1529) visits to Buddhist temples, for example.[60]

What we need is a comprehensive survey and detailed account of Chu Hsi's travels, which is possible not only by carefully scrutinizing both his writings and contemporary accounts, but also by examining the county and prefectural records of all the places he visited. Obviously, this requires a cooperative effort of many people over many years. Gotō Toshimizu devoted a whole section in his book on Chu Hsi to his tour of Mount Heng,[61] thus introducing a new topic in Chu Hsi studies. Recently, Professor Gao Ling-yin published an article on Chu Hsi's travel that is the most detailed of its kind.[62] The following is directed toward three traditions about Chu Hsi's travels that have thus far been accepted, although many questions about them remain to be answered.

*"He went on foot for several hundred* li." According to Huang Kan's "Hsing-chuang," "Master Li Yen-p'ing [Li T'ung, 1093–1163] studied with Master Lo Yü-chang [Lo Ts'ung-yen, 1072–1135], and Master Lo studied with Master Yang Kuei-shan [Yang Shih, 1053–1135]. Yen-p'ing was a schoolmate of Wei-chai [Chu Sung, 1097–1143, Chu Hsi's

father]. When the Master [Chu Hsi] returned home from T'ung-an [in 1158] he did not regard several hundred *li* as too far and walked on foot to become a pupil."[63] This has been repeated in the *Sung shih*'s biography of Chu Hsi,[64] but none of the chronological biographies tells this story.[65] My question is not whether Chu Hsi went on foot but whether he walked for several hundred *li*. What Huang Kan wanted to convey was how eager Chu Hsi was to learn from Li T'ung, since Li T'ung inherited the doctrines of the Ch'eng brothers (Ch'eng Hao, 1032–1085, and Ch'eng I, 1033–1107) in a direct line of transmission, and this was Chu Hsi's second visit to Li. I suppose most readers understand Huang Kan's intention. Strictly speaking, as scholars in Chien-yang told me in 1983, Chu Hsi must have used a boat, carriage, and horse along the way. Li T'ung was then living in Yen-p'ing,[66] which is 250 kilometers from T'ung-an as the bird flies. The route winds over mountains and rivers; it takes at least five days to walk. Although it was by no means impossible for Chu Hsi to walk the entire distance, it is not likely that he did so. This raises the question of how he traveled. Did he use a sedan chair? Did he ride in a carriage or on horseback? Did he go by boat? Did he walk? These questions are worth investigating.

According to Chu Hsi himself, "When the capital was at the height of its glory, officials only rode on horseback. Even attendants also rode on horseback. Only a greatly honored elder or a high official who was sick was permitted to ride in a sedan chair. Even he would humbly decline and would not take it right away. Nowadays, all officials, great or small, ride in sedan chairs. Even people like eunuchs and messengers use the sedan chair."[67] When he was *chu-pu* in T'ung-an, Chu Hsi did ride in a sedan chair, as we have already seen. But when he went to Yen-p'ing,[68] there was no longer an official sedan chair; moreover, he had waited in T'ung-an for months after the termination of his office. He was appointed late in 1158 to be superintendent of a Taoist temple, a sinecure that involved no duty and very little salary, so he could not afford to hire a sedan chair for a journey of several days. In addition, from Chu Hsi's youth, his father had taught him the doctrines of the Ch'eng brothers, and from his youth Ch'eng I had refused to ride in a sedan chair. After Ch'eng I was banished to Szechuan, he visited some cliffs with two imperial emissaries. They insisted on riding in sedan chairs, but Ch'eng I declined to do so. When asked why, he answered, "I cannot bear to ride. Clearly human beings are used to take the place of animals. It is all right when one is sick or the road is muddy."[69]

It is likely that Chu Hsi was influenced by Ch'eng I. He said that "When Nan-hsüan [Chang Shih] was home, whenever he needed to go out to attend affairs, he always went with his younger brother in sedan chairs."[70] Chu Hsi merely stated the fact and did not criticize Chang Shih and his brother. In answering a pupil's question on abiding in seriousness and investigation of principle to the utmost, he said, "It is like going out. When it is necessary to ride in a sedan chair, ride in it. When it is necessary to ride on horseback, do so. And when it is necessary to walk, then walk."[71] This conversation was recorded in 1199, the year before he died. It gives the impression that Chu Hsi approved of riding in a sedan chair. However, this record was given as a note. In the text itself his words were, "If a person wants to make a trip, if there is a horse, he should ride on a horse, or if there is a carriage, he should ride in a carriage. If there is no carriage, then he should walk." There is no mention of sedan chairs. My belief is that, after he left T'ung-an, Chu Hsi would not ride in a sedan chair but did not criticize those who did. At any rate, there is no evidence of his riding in a sedan chair after he was assistant magistrate in T'ung-an.

Since Cloud Valley is on top of Mount Lu, Chu Hsi often had to climb there on foot. From a poem we know that once when he was climbing it rained hard and he got wet.[72] Another poem tells us that he climbed along but forgot his fatigue because of the scenery.[73] There are many poems in the *Wen-chi* describing his walking to many places. He told Ts'ai Yüan-ting in a letter that he went up to Mount Lung-hu (Dragon Lake) and the road was very slippery.[74] The mountain was 50 *li* west of Shao-wu in Fukien. At its summit was Dragon Lake, which vehicles could not reach. Unless one rode on horseback, one had to go on foot. Chu Hsi must also have walked a good deal on Mount Wu-i. When I visited the mountain in 1983, there were many places where I had to go on foot. When Chu Hsi went to Yen-p'ing, he probably went on foot for some, if not most, of the distance.

Sometimes he used a horse. He and friends toured Mount Heng in 1167 almost entirely on horseback. Many poems written on that trip have titles such as "Composed on Horseback," "In Snow and on Horseback," and the like.[75] Halfway between Wu-fu Village and Mount Wu-i, there is still the "Horse Rest Station." Although few people use it for that purpose today, its name indicates that during Chu Hsi's time people traveled on horseback. The area around Mount Wu-i consists of many hills and streams. The Wu-i River curves nine times. When I traveled the river, like many others I went on a bamboo raft, although small boats were available. The Wu-i Ching-she could not be reached except by boat and then on foot. In the *Wen-chi,* more poems were composed on board a boat than on horseback. After all, the chief means of transportation in China, in Chu Hsi's time as today, was by boat, and Fukien was no exception. Furthermore, boats provide meals and sleeping accommodations. On board one can discuss learning with friends, read, and write. Some of Chu Hsi's epilogues were written on boats.[76]

*"He took to the road with only one vehicle."* In his travels, Chu Hsi also used carriages. Once he was about to get into a carriage but became sick.[77] On another occasion he wanted to drive his own carriage to a nearby county, but because he could not afford to supply the necessary food he had to cancel the trip.[78] On still another occasion, when he heard someone reading in a farmhouse, he immediately descended from his vehicle.[79] There were many instances of this sort. In addition, he sometimes used the combination of horseback and carriage. In a poem about going up Cloud Valley, he said that in the morning he caressed the horse and in the evening he greased the vehicle.[80] On his ten-day tour of Mount Lu in Kiangsi in 1181, he and his party used carriages almost exclusively.[81] In a poem about his visit to Mount Lu in Kiangsi, Chu Hsi began by saying that he started in a vehicle from the edge of a Fukien mountain and ended up in the front of a mountain in Nan-k'ang.[82] This indicates that he made the trip from Fukien to Nan-k'ang to become prefect there in 1179 by riding in a carriage.

Chu Hsi's most famous journey by carriage took place in 1181, when he was appointed superintendent-designate in charge of affairs of ever-normal granaries, tea, and salt in the present Anhui and Chekiang area, where people were starving. As the "Hsing-chuang" tells us, "Because people were starving at the time, he took to the road in a single vehicle on the very day" he received the appointment.[83] The *Sung shih* and the various chronological biographies all repeated this. No one has ever questioned Chu Hsi's sense of duty or awareness of urgency. But what was his route? How long did it take? Questions like these have not be asked or answered. When Chu Hsi was appointed prefect of Nan-k'ang in 1178, he declined the post four times. He finally started for Nan-k'ang in the first month of 1179 and arrived in the third month. In a note to the government he said, "I have reluctantly assumed office following the recent imperial order. I dared not bring my family for a lengthy stay. I only brought a small boy who is a little over ten years old."[84] This boy was his third son, Tsai, who was then eleven years old. In a letter to another official he said that he "came alone as a visitor. I have brought a son and a nephew here, but there are no women to take care of the household."[85] We do not know who this nephew was, but he was probably someone who joined them to help with Tsai. Before the journey Chu Hsi also wrote Lü Tsu-ch'ien and said, "I have here only three or five loads of baggage and a son and a nephew. It is not much trouble to go to live there."[86] All these comments deal with his going to the post at Nan-k'ang. He did not plan to stay long and therefore he traveled lightly. Neither the "Hsing-chuang" nor the chronological biographies say that he went in a single vehicle.

On his journey to the famine-struck area, however, the records definitely state that he went in a single vehicle. Did he do the driving him-

self? Was there an attendant with him? We have no information on
these matters. We do know that he did not bring books with him. In a
letter to a friend he said, "Because I came in a single vehicle, there were
no books for me to consult."[87] According to the "Hsing-chuang,"
"During his administration, while in office, whenever he went out, he
always rode in a single vehicle. He shunned attendants. Although he
covered a large area, people did not know about it."[88] In its biography
of Chu Hsi, the *Sung shih* echoed this.[89] In his chronological biography
of 1431, however, Yeh Kung-hui added that Chu Hsi brought with him
all the provisions he needed and did not involve the prefectures or counties in the least.[90] Tai Hsien's *Nien-p'u,* in his *Chu Tzu shih-chi* (True
records of Master Chu), agreed.[91] Since the records are unanimous in
stating that Chu Hsi shunned attendants, he must have driven alone all
the way from Fukien to Chekiang in 1181. However, when he was at
Nan-k'ang in 1179 he was suffering from a foot ailment,[92] so it is
unlikely that he drove alone over such a long distance at that time. The
main reason for his immediate departure for Chekiang in a single vehicle was probably that people were already starving. An additional reason may have been to avoid social engagements that would delay his
arrival. However, these are mere speculations. Only specialists can
determine the facts.

*"He always went home on the first and fifteenth day of the month."* As already
noted, Chu Hsi's mother died in 1169. He buried her on the south side
of T'ien-hu Mountain in Chien-yang County, built the Cold Spring
Study beside her grave, and went home to Wu-fu Village the first and
fifteenth day of each month to perform religious sacrifices.[93] But in his
"Hsing-chuang" Huang Kan did not say anything to this effect. The
earliest account is found in Yeh Kung-hui's *Chu Tzu nien-p'u* (1431)
under the sixth year of the Ch'ien-tao period (1170). In a note Yeh says,
"Everyday he lived by the side of the grave. On the first and fifteenth
days of the month, he would go home to perform religious sacrifices."
This is repeated in Tai Hsien's *Chu Tzu shih-chi* of 1513, again under the
year 1170. In both cases the character for the first day of the month
*(shuo)* is misprinted as the character for dawn *(tan),* but as Wang Mao-
hung pointed out, this has been corrected in the Fukien edition of the
*Chu Tzu nien-p'u.*[94] Since the tradition was repeated in all the chronological biographies, it may have originated in the earliest *nien-p'u* on Chu
Hsi, written by his pupil Li Fang-tzu (1214 *cs*), which is no longer
extant. Our question is whether the statement is literally true. By
"home" the chronological biographies must mean Wu-fu Village,
because that was where Chu Hsi and his family lived. But the village is
some 80 or 90 *li* from the grave. It took two days to make a one-way
trip, or three or four days for a round-trip. It is incredible that Chu Hsi

would have spent seven or eight days on the road every month. We have already shown that he did not stay at the Cold Spring Study for long periods of time. Thus the statement in the records must mean that whenever he was at the Cold Spring Study, Chu Hsi would go home to Wu-fu Village so he could perform religious sacrifices. In a letter to Ts'ai Yüan-ting, Chu Hsi told him that on the eighth or ninth day of the month he would go to the Cold Spring Study, and that he hoped Yüan-ting would come on the eleventh or twelfth.[95] We can assume that Chu Hsi was home in Wu-fu Village on the first of the month and would return home on the fifteenth, after spending a couple of days at the Cold Spring Study with his friend Yüan-ting.

## Notes

1. On Huang Kan's "Hsing-chuang," see ch. 1 above, pp. 1–11.

2. For the three teachers, see ch. 2 above, pp. 13–14, and ch. 5 below, p. 62.

3. Wu-yüan County, originally in Hui-chou prefecture in Anhui, is now in Kiangsi.

4. *Wen-chi,* 9:9a.

5. A *li* is one-third of a mile.

6. *Wen-chi,* supplementary collection, 2:25a, one hundred twentieth letter in reply to Ts'ai Chi-t'ung (Ts'ai Yüan-ting).

7. On Chu Hsi's moving his father's grave, see ch. 3 above, p. 35.

8. *Tung-lai Lü T'ai-shih wen-chi* [Collection of literary works of Lü Tsu-ch'ien, member of the Han-lin Academy] (*Hsü Chin-hua ts'ung-shu* [Supplement to the Chin-hua series] ed.), ch. 15, "Records of arrival in Fukien."

9. *Yü-lei,* ch. 115, sec. 3 (p. 4412).

10. Present Hsing-tzu County.

11. For Wan Jen-chieh, see my *Chu Tzu men-jen* [Master Chu's pupils] (Taipei: Student Book Co., 1982), pp. 248–249.

12. This is according to Tanaka Kenji, "Shumon deshi shiji nenkō" [Chu Hsi's pupils' years in attendance], *Tōhō gakuhō* [Oriental journal], no. 48 (1975), p. 302.

13. *Wen-chi,* supplementary collection, 7:8a, letter to Ch'en T'ung-fu (Ch'en Liang).

14. *Ibid.,* regular collection, 52:10b, eighth letter in reply to Wu Po-feng (Wu Pi-ta).

15. For more on the Wu-i Ching-she, see ch. 21 below.

16. *Wen-chi,* 9:3b.

17. *Ibid.,* 36:28a, ninth letter in reply to Ch'en T'ung-fu.

18. *Ibid.,* p. 30a, eleventh letter.

19. *Wen-chi,* 9:9a.

20. See ch. 3 above, p. 36.

21. Wang Mao-hung, *Chu Tzu nien-p'u* [Chronological biography of Master Chu] (*Ts'ung-shu chi-ch'eng* [Collection of series] ed.), *k'ao-i* [Investigation into variants], ch. 4, p. 339, under the third year of Ch'ing-yüan (1197).

22. *Wen-chi,* supplementary collection, 2:2b, sixth letter in reply to Ts'ai Chi-t'ung; repeated in 2:21a, ninety-third letter.

23. *Ibid.,* regular collection, 44:21b, seventh letter in reply to Fang Po-mu (Fang Shih-yao); also 33:26a, thirty-ninth letter in reply to Lü Po-kung (Lü Tsu-ch'ien).

24. *Ibid.,* 39:44b, ninth letter in reply to Fan Po-ch'ung (Fan Nien-te).

25. *Ibid.,* 44:4a, fifth letter in reply to Ts'ai Chi-t'ung; 44:11a, eighth letter.

26. *Ibid.,* separate collection, 1:9a, second letter to Lin Ching-po (Lin Ch'eng-kuei).

27. *Ibid.,* supplementary collection, 2:3b, thirteenth letter in reply to Ts'ai Chi-t'ung.

28. *Ibid.,* regular collection, 33:27b, fortieth letter in reply to Lü Po-kung. For the meeting at the Goose Lake Temple, see ch. 26 below.

29. *Ibid.,* 4:9a.

30. A *mu* is one-sixth of an acre.

31. *Ibid.,* 78:2a–4b, "Account of Cloud Valley."

32. *Ibid.,* 6:18a.

33. *Ibid.,* 6:14b. T'an-hsi in the poem refers to Wu-fu Village, because the T'an-hsi stream was there.

34. *Ibid.,* 6:22a.

35. *Ibid.,* 6:14a, and 44:33a, tenth letter to Fang Po-mu.

36. *Ibid.,* 97:26a, Chu Hsi's biographical account of his father.

37. For Chu Hsi's printing enterprise, see ch. 5 below, pp. 77–81.

38. *Wen-chi,* separate collection, 5:13b, letter to Chu Lu-shu.

39. *Ibid.,* regular collection, 86:15a, report to the family shrine on moving the residence.

40. *Ibid.,* 83:24b–25b, epilogue to the biographical account of Li Ts'an-chung (Li Tseng).

41. *Shen-i,* literally "deep garment," the chief characteristic of which is that the jacket and the skirt are attached.

42. *Mien-chai chi* [Collected works of Huang Kan] (*Ssu-k'u ch'üan-shu chen-pen* [Precious works of the *Complete Collection of the Four Libraries*] ed.), 36:41b, biographical account.

43. *Yü-lei,* ch. 107, sec. 54 (p. 4252). This was recorded by Wang Kuo after 1194.

44. *Ibid.,* sec. 55 (p. 4253). This was recorded by Huang I-kang after 1193. "Ritual works" refer to the "Yü-tsao" [Jade pendants], "Shen-i" ["Deep" gown], etc. of the *Book of Rites.*

45. *Ibid.,* ch. 138, sec. 141 (p. 5292). This was recorded by Wang Kuo after 1194.

46. *Wen-chi,* 68:5a–7a, "The System of the 'Deep' Garment"; *Yü-lei,* ch. 87, sec. 180–181 (p. 3594).

47. *Yü-lei,* ch. 87, sec. 157 (pp. 3582–3583). This was recorded by Shen Hsien after 1198.

48. *Ibid.,* ch. 90, sec. 141 (p. 3786). The conversation was recorded by Fu Kuang after 1194.

49. *Ibid.,* sec. 142 (p. 3686).

50. *Ibid.,* sec. 145 (p. 3687). This conversation was also recorded by Wang Kuo after 1194.

51. *Ibid.,* ch. 91, sec. 9 (p. 3692), a conversation recorded by Huang I-kang after 1194. How the bamboo circle overcame the obstacle is not clear.

52. *Ibid.,* ch. 107, sec. 57 (p. 4253). This was recorded by Yeh Ho-sun after 1191.

53. *Ibid.,* ch. 108, sec. 7 (p. 4259).

54. Wang Mao-hung, *Chu Tzu nien-p'u,* ch. 4B, p. 225, under the fifth year of Ch'ing-yüan (1199).

55. *Wen-chi,* 74:29b–30a.

56. *Mien-chai chi,* 36:46a, biographical account.

57. Ts'ai Ch'en, "Chu Wen Kung meng-tien chi" [Account of Chu Hsi's death], in the *Ts'ai-shih chiu-ju shu* [Works of nine Confucians in the Ts'ai family] (1868 ed.), 6:60a.

58. *Sung shih* [History of the Sung dynasty] (Beijing: Chung-hua Book Co., 1977), ch. 439, biography of Huang Kan, p. 12778.

59. See Wang Mao-hung, *Chu Tzu nien-p'u, k'ao-i,* ch. 4, p. 344.

60. Kusumoto Bun'yū, *Ō Yōmei no zenteki shisō kenkyū* (Nagoya: Nisshindō shoten, 1958), pp. 113–133.

61. Gotō Toshimizu, *Shushi* (Tokyo: Hyōronsha, 1943), pp. 117–123.

62. Gao Ling-yin, "Chu Hsi hsing-tsung k'ao" [Investigation of Chu Hsi's travel], in *Chung-kuo che-hsüeh-shih lun-ts'ung* [History of Chinese philosophy series], no. 1 (1984), pp. 413–434.

63. *Mien-chai chi,* 36:39a, biographical account.

64. *Sung shih,* ch. 429, biography of Chu Hsi, p. 12769.

65. See, for example, Wang Mao-hung, *Chu Tzu nien-p'u,* p. 13.

66. Present Nan-p'ing County in central Fukien.

67. *Yü-lei,* ch. 127, sec. 57 (p. 4900).

68. On Yen-p'ing and Li Yen-p'ing (Li T'ung), see ch. 2 above, p. 19, and ch. 3, p. 35.

69. *Wai-shu* [Additional works], 10:3a, in the *Erh-Ch'eng ch'üan-shu* [Complete works of the two Ch'engs] (*SPPY* ed.).

70. *Yü-lei,* ch. 103, sec. 52 (p. 4149).

71. *Ibid.,* ch. 121, sec. 58 (p. 4692).

72. *Ibid.,* ch. 5, sec. 20 (p. 137).

73. *Wen-chi,* 6:13a, "On traveling to the peak of Mount Lu [in Fukien]."

74. *Ibid.,* supplementary collection, 2:20a, eighty-ninth letter in reply to Ts'ai Chi-t'ung (Ts'ai Yüan-ting).

75. See *ibid.,* regular collection, ch. 5.

76. *Ibid.,* 82:1a; 84:27b.

77. *Ibid.,* 34:6a, sixtieth letter in reply to Lü Po-kung.

78. *Ibid.,* 33:10b, fourteenth letter in reply to Lü Po-kung.

79. *Ibid.,* 76:13b, "Preface to the *Collection of Literary Works of Temple Superintendent Hsieh.*"

80. *Ibid.,* 6:22a.

81. See *ibid.,* 7:16a, account of the visit to the northern part of Mount Lu.

82. *Ibid.,* 7:1b.

83. *Mien-chai chi,* 36:10b, biographical account.

84. *Wen-chi,* 26:23b, note to an official.

85. *Ibid.,* p. 2b, letter to Assistant Bureau Director Yüan.

86. *Ibid.,* 34:25a, eighty-third letter in reply to Lü Po-kung.

87. *Ibid.*, 37:26b, first letter to Kuo Ch'ung-hui.

88. *Mien-chai chi,* 36:13b, biographical account.

89. *Sung shih,* ch. 429, biography of Chu Hsi, p. 12756.

90. Yeh Kung-hui, *Chu Tzu nien-p'u* (*Chin-shih han-chi ts'ung-k'an* [Chinese works of the recent period series] ed.), under the year 1180 (p. 135).

91. Tai Hsien, *Chu Tzu shih-chi* [True records of Master Chu] (*Chin-shih han-chi ts'ung-k'an* ed.), p. 132.

92. See *Wen-chi,* 22:15b, note to request a temple superintendency; 26:24a, note to State Councilor Chou (Chou Pi-ta).

93. See ch. 3 above, p. 36.

94. Wang Mao-hung, *Chu Tzu nien-p'u, k'ao-i,* ch. 1, p. 262, under the sixth year of Ch'ien-tao (1170).

95. *Wen-chi,* supplementary collection, 2:2a, second letter in reply to Ts'ai Chi-t'ung.

# – 5 –

# Chu Hsi's Poverty

THERE are two important reasons for writing on the subject of Chu Hsi's poverty. One is that, in a great many of some two thousand letters preserved in the *Wen-chi,* Chu Hsi stated (but did not complain about) how poor he was. There are very few words by other writers on this subject, so it is time to substantiate the painful fact. The second reason is that Confucianism, especially Neo-Confucianism, has been considered the bastion of the landed class. It has often been asserted that Chinese scholars came from wealthy families. If so, Chu Hsi, the most influential Confucian thinker in the last two thousand years, should have been a rich man. Facts must be brought out to determine whether or not he was. Evidence is not easy to gather, but pieces of information, however minute, must be collected to show once and for all that Chu Hsi was among the poorest scholars in Chinese history. This can be seen in his family heritage, temple emoluments, official salary, dire financial state, printing business, acceptance of gifts, and endurance of poverty.

## Family Heritage

Chu Hsi came from a once-wealthy family that had possessed much land. For three generations, including that of his grandfather, family members did not have to serve in the government but relied on income from their land. By the time of Chu Hsi's father, however, the family wealth had declined. When his father, Chu Sung (1097–1143), was appointed county sheriff of Cheng-ho County[1] in Fukien Province, he had to mortgage a hundred *mu*[2] before he could move his family from Wu-yüan County in Hui-chou (Anhui)[3] to Fukien. When Chu Sung's father died, he did not have enough money to bury him in Hui-chou and therefore had to bury him in Cheng-ho County. According to Li

Fang-tzu's chronological biography *(nien-p'u)* of Chu Hsi, the journey to Hui-chou was prevented by the rebellion of Fang La, which blocked the road. But as Wang Mao-hung (1668–1741) pointed out, the rebellion took place in 1120–1121, whereas Chu Sung's father died in 1125. Wang therefore concluded that Li Fang-tzu was wrong.[4] Besides, Chu Hsi himself said that the journey was prevented by poverty: "Because of poverty he [Chu Sung] could not return [to Hui-chou] and therefore buried [his father] in Fukien."[5] As to the land Chu Sung had mortgaged, according to the *Chu Tzu nien-p'u* compiled by Li Mo (d. 1556), Yü Chi (1272–1348), in his "Account of Returning the Land," briefly said, "The Venerable Chang Tun-i, who was of the same community and who was a professor in Chien-chou,[6] redeemed the land. In his calculation, in ten years the rentals from the land would pay for it and he would then return the land to the Chu family. When the Official of the Personnel Department [Chu Hsi's father] died in the *kuei-hai* year [1143], he wrote a letter of condolence to Wen Kung [Chu Hsi] during the funeral and returned the land. In the *kung-wu* year [1150] Wen Kung visited ancestral graves in Wu-yüan. He designated the rentals from the land for the upkeep of the graves."[7] That Chang Tun-i should have redeemed the land for the Chu family proves that the Chu family was not financially able to do so.

Chu Hsi's father had once been a high official. His family was not destitute. However, during his last years he had no official position and probably no income. When, on his deathbed, Chu Sung wrote his friends in Wu-fu Village in Ch'ung-an County to take care of his wife and son, maintenance must have been a key factor in addition to a good education for the youngster. When Chu Hsi and his mother moved to Wu-fu Village, Liu Tzu-yü (1097–1146) built a house beside his own for them. As Chu Hsi later recalled, "The Honorable Vice Minister [Liu Tzu-yü] considered it his duty to care for the orphaned and poor."[8] This refers to the fact that, at fourteen years of age, Chu Hsi had lost his father and had no assets. This is what the *Sung shih* (History of the Sung dynasty) means when it says, "His family being poor, he went in his youth to be under the protection of his father's friend Liu Tzu-yü."[9]

Following his father's wishes, Chu Hsi studied under Hu Hsien (1086–1162), Liu Tzu-hui (1101–1147), and Liu Mien-chih (1091–1149). The latter liked him enough to give his daughter to him in marriage. Liu Mien-chih's family was traditionally wealthy.[10] But in 1196, at the height of government persecution of Chu Hsi's learning as "false," when Shen Chi-tsu wrote a memorial to the emperor attacking Chu Hsi and stating that he had "married the daughter of Liu Kung [1122–1178], and after Liu died put under his control tremendous wealth of tens of thousands [of cash],"[11] Shen did not get the name straight.

## Temple Emoluments

Chu Hsi loved nothing better than to live quietly, write, and teach. To support himself, he would petition for a temple emolument. Altogether he petitioned twenty times, received appointment eleven times for six different temples, and served for twenty-two years and seven months. In the Sung dynasty (960–1279), probably no one served more often or for a longer total period than he.

The system of temple emolument can be traced to the T'ang dynasty (618–907), but it developed during the Sung and ceased afterward. The concept was similar to modern fellowships awarded by governments or foundations to scholars for writing or research. According to the "Record of Government Offices" of the *Sung shih* (History of the Sung dynasty),

> In the Sung system, the institution of temple emolument was launched to treat the elderly and the worthy favorably. At first the number was small but it increased in the Hsi-ning period [1068–1077]. . . . At that time the Court was restructuring the government. Fearing the tired and the elderly might not be able to carry on their duties, it was designed to remove them and appoint them to temple superintendencies so they could continue to receive a salary. Wang An-shih [1021–1086] also took the opportunity to remove those who opposed him. Consequently, he decreed that the number of superintendents be unlimited. . . . From the Shao-hsing period [1131–1162] on, many scholar-officials were in dire straits and there were not enough positions for them. Therefore . . . the principle was to depend on them for potential responsibility. The purpose was commendable. However, while in the beginning it was for the purpose of pacifying the maladjusted, as the system developed, it tended more and more to heedless applications and reckless awards.[12]

As Chu Hsi himself observed,

> At first the system of temple emoluments did not exist in the dynasty. . . . After Wang Chieh-fu [Wang An-shih] instituted his New Laws, he was worried that scholar-officials of the world might dispute him, but he was afraid of criticism should he suppress or dismiss them. He therefore started the system of temple emolument to deal with those who opposed him. However, the appointment was not easy to get. Only those of the rank of censor or prefect, or those specially favored, could get it. Those below the [rank of] prefect were all appointed from among the departments. Later the grants were relaxed, and now it is relaxed even more, to the point that anyone can get it.[13]

Another source informs us that "the system of temple emolument outside the national capital was started in the Hsi-ning period. The purpose of Wang Ching Kung [Wang An-shih] was to handle those who opposed him."[14] Chu Hsi was referring to this system of emolument for temples outside the national capital.

The emolument system developed not only from the Sung rulers' desire to favor the elderly and the worthy and to pacify their own critics, but also from the fact that they themselves were devout followers of the Taoist religion, promoting it and worshiping their ancestors in some of the temples in question. During the Southern Sung (1127–1279) there were only seven temples in the capital and forty-one outside. Successful applicants over sixty years old were appointed to large temples. The terms were two to three years; salaries varied. There was no duty to speak of, and the appointee did not need to reside at the temple.[15] It was under these conditions that Chu Hsi repeatedly petitioned and many times received appointments. They were as follows:

1. *Superintendent* (chien) *of the Nan-yüeh (Southern peak) Temple in T'an-chou*[16] *from the twelfth month of 1158 to the fifth month of 1162.* Chu Hsi obtained the *chin-shih* (presented scholar) degree in 1148, at the age of nineteen, and in 1151 was appointed *chu-pu* (assistant magistrate) of T'ung-an County in Ch'üan-chou in southern Fukien, which was about 600 *li*[17] from his home in Ch'ung-an, with the rank of left *ti-kung-lang* (dignitary for meritorious achievement), the lowest of thirty-seven grades for a civil official. He arrived in T'ung-an in the seventh month of 1153; in the seventh month of 1156, his term was up. As Huang Kan (1152–1221) tells us in his "Chu Tzu hsing-chuang" (Biographical account of Master Chu), "After four years he was anxious to return home to serve his mother and to teach. In the twenty-eighth year [1158] he petitioned for a temple emolument. He was appointed superintendent of the Nan-yüeh Temple in T'an-chou."[18] Chu Hsi petitioned in the eleventh month and received the appointment a month later. He then returned to Ch'ung-an to teach. The superintendency was the lowest of four ranks for a temple emolument. During the Northern Sung (960–1126), temple emoluments were set up for all the Five Peaks,[19] but during the Southern Sung (1127–1279), only the Nan-yüeh Temple in Hunan was not occupied by the invading Chin. The temple was located at Heng Mountain in southwest Heng-shan County. At the time of Chu Hsi's appointment, the incumbent was an investigating censor. For a young man of twenty-nine to receive the honor of such an emolument testifies to Chu Hsi's reputation and his accomplishments at T'ung-an.

2. *Reappointment to the Nan-yüeh Temple from the sixth month of 1162 to the twelfth month of 1163.* In 1162, Chu Hsi was thirty-three years old. His term as temple superintendent was up in the fifth month. He petitioned for a temple emolument, and on the nineteenth day of the sixth month he was reappointed to the Nan-yüeh Temple. As the "Hsing-chuang" tells us, "His term was up in the thirty-second year [of Shao-hsing,

1162]. He petitioned again. As Emperor Hsiao Tsung [r. 1163–1189] ascended the throne, he was reappointed."[20] On the twelfth day of the eleventh month in the following year, he was appointed a professor of the military academy (wu-hsüeh po-shih). While he waited in Ch'ung-an to take office, his superintendency was automatically terminated due to his new appointment.

3. *Reappointment to the Nan-yüeh Temple from the fifth month of 1165 to the twelfth month of 1167.* In the spring of 1165 Chu Hsi was urged to assume his office at the military academy. He left home in the fourth month. As he approached the temporary capital of Hangchow, he found that the government was suing for peace with the invading Chin. He objected and requested a temple emolument, which was granted in the fifth month. Having accepted the appointment, he returned home to Ch'ung-an. Two years later, in the twelfth month of 1167, he was appointed a compiler (p'ien-hsiu) in the Shu-mi-yüan (privy council in charge of military affairs). While waiting at home to assume office, his term as superintendent was terminated. According to Wang Mao-hung, Chu Hsi was to succeed Shih Yüan-chih as compiler. He had to wait at home because Shih's tenure was not yet up.[21] In 1169, the government urged him three times to take office, but in the ninth month his mother passed away. As Chu Hsi himself said,

> After four [calendar] years as chu-pu at T'ung-an in Ch'üan-chou, I returned home. Because my mother was getting old and the family was poor, I could not wait [while unemployed] and petitioned for a temple emolument. I served two terms but before the second term was up I was summoned for an audience in Court and was appointed a professor at the military academy. I was anxious to have some emolument to support my mother and requested an emolument once more. Again, before the end of my tenure, I was appointed to be a compiler at the privy council. But because I was mourning the death of my mother, I would not assume office.[22]

The third tenure at the Nan-yüeh Temple was comparatively longer, but like the previous one it was terminated before it was up.

4. *Director (chu-kuan) of the Ch'ung-tao Temple in T'ai-chou from the sixth month of 1174 to the sixth month of 1176.* In 1173, when Chu Hsi was forty-five years old, on the twenty-eighth day of the fifth month, an imperial edict conferred on him the rank of left hsüan-chiao-lang (dignitary for propagation of teachings) in charge of the Ch'ung-tao Temple in T'ai-chou, with residence anywhere to suit his convenience. The new rank was twenty-sixth among the thirty-seven for a civilian official. The temple was 20 *li* northwest of T'ien-t'ai County in Chekiang, and director was a grade higher than superintendent. According to Huang Kan's

"Hsing-chuang," "The Master considered that [the purpose of] granting a temple emolument along with a promotion in rank was to reward an accomplishment, promote the worthy, and care for the elderly generously. Now that he suddenly got the award for nothing, it meant that in asking for less he had received more instead. He declined because this was contrary to principle. The next year [1174] he again declined but [finally] accepted the appointment because the emperor insisted on it."[23] In his statement of thanks for the appointment, Chu Hsi said, "In view of your great kindness, I dare not stubbornly decline. I have, looking in the direction of your palace, accepted your kindness on the twenty-third day of the sixth month."[24] Two years later, in the sixth month of 1176, he was designated librarian (pi-shu-lang) of the Imperial Library (pi-shu-sheng). With this appointment, his tenure at the temple came to an end.

5. Director of the Ch'ung-yu Temple on Mount Wu-i from the eighth month of 1176 to the eighth month of 1178. Chu Hsi was not successful in declining the librarianship. When he declined it again in the eighth month and requested a temple emolument, he was granted the directorship of the Ch'ung-yu Temple. The temple was about 30 li northwest of Ch'ung-an. His tenure lasted until the eighth month of 1178, when he was appointed prefect of Nan-k'ang Commandery.[25] He declined the office twice and requested a temple emolument three times. It was not until the third month of 1179 that he assumed office as prefect. But in the fifth and sixth months and the first, third, and fourth months of the following year, he petitioned again and again for a temple emolument. One of these requests was rejected; the rest were simply ignored. As Chu Hsi said in his official document declining the post as prefect of Nan-k'ang, "It has been more than twenty years since I retired from a term as an official. . . . I served several times as a temple official but that involved no official duty."[26] The term "temple official" refers to Chu Hsi's positions at the Nan-yüeh, Ch'ung-tao, and Ch'ung-yu temples. The "Hsing-chuang" also says, "After the Master returned from T'ung-an, he received a temple emolument and lived at home for almost twenty years. He was in abject poverty but that did not bother him."[27] Here Huang Kan's "almost twenty years" and Chu Hsi's own "more than twenty years" are synonymous: both mean merely a long time, and do not suggest that the three temple tenures amounted to twenty years. Between these tenures, Chu Hsi served in the government, waited at home to assume office, or mourned his mother. These activities were not concurrent with his temple tenures, so his emolument was interrupted. Actually, over the course of twenty years or so, Chu Hsi served as a temple official five times, for a total of twelve and a half years. During this period his emolument was meagre, and he received no salary for the other eight years. The "Hsing-chuang" also

says, "The Master requested a temple emolument five times."[28] These requests took place after his term as prefect of Nan-k'ang.

6. *Director of the Ch'ung-tao Temple in T'ai-chou from the second month of 1183 to the second month of 1185.* Chu Hsi took office at Nan-k'ang in the third month of 1179. When his term expired in the third month of 1181, he was appointed superintendent-designate in charge of ever-normal granaries, tea, and salt *(ch'ang-p'ing ch'a-yen kung-shih)* in Chiang-nan West.[29] While waiting to take office, he returned home on the twenty-seventh day of the third intercalary month. In the seventh month he was named to serve in the imperial archive *(chih-pi-ko),* an appointment that he declined three times. However, in the eighth month he was transferred to the position of superintendent-designate in charge of ever-normal granaries, tea, and salt in Chekiang East.[30] He accepted this appointment and left in a single vehicle on the very day he received the order because there was a great famine in the Chekiang area. He served in this capacity for a little over a year; on the twelfth day of the ninth month in the following year, he left because he was promoted. He declined the promotion but requested a temple emolument in the eleventh month, and was given the post at the Ch'ung-tao Temple. His term there lasted for two years.[31]

7. *Director of the Yün-t'ai Temple in Hua-chou from the fourth month of 1185 to the fourth month of 1187.* At the conclusion of his term at the Ch'ung-tao Temple, Chu Hsi requested a temple emolument again. In the fourth month of 1185 he was appointed to a two-year term as director of the Yün-t'ai Temple. This temple was originally in Shensi. According to Chu Hsi it contained an image of Emperor Shen-tsung (r. 1068–1085).[32] After the temple fell to the Chin, the post existed in name only. In the third month of 1187 Chu Hsi was put in charge of the Hung-ch'ing Temple of the southern capital, and his term at Yün-t'ai expired.

8. *Director of the Hung-ch'ing Temple of the southern capital from the fourth to the seventh month in 1187.* In 1014 Ying-t'ien[33] Prefecture was made the southern capital and imperial ancestors were offered sacrifice in the Hung-ch'ing Temple, with the images of T'ai-tsu (r. 960–975) and T'ai-tsung (r. 976–997) standing at their sides.[34] Although Chu Hsi was transferred to this temple in the third month, he waited until his two-year term at the Yun-t'ai Temple was up in the fourth month before he assumed his new title. In a letter to Liu Ch'ing-chih (1139–1195) he said, "Yesterday I received the imperial appointment to the Hung-ch'ing Temple. I wrote a poem, which says, 'The original temple in the old capital had been covered with smoke and dust for a long time / The sadness of the white-haired temple official is expressed anew / I faced a thousand doors but announced myself in vain / I don't know when I shall be able to pay homage to the true image.' As my years are declining and I am easily moved, unconsciously my tears and snivel gather

across my face."[35] Chu Hsi sighed because there was an image of Emperor Shen-tsung in the temple. He was then fifty-eight, and probably had white hair himself.

Several months later, the emperor thought Chu Hsi should be appointed to office because he had been in retirement for some time. Consequently, Chu Hsi was appointed judicial intendant of Chiang-nan West *(Chiang-nan hsi-lu t'i-t'ien hsing-yüeh)*. While he was waiting to take office, he could retain his temple post. He declined the new appointment twice but finally accepted, terminating his temple tenure. He left to take office on the eighteenth day of the third month of 1188. As the "Hsing-chuang" says, "The Master was prefect at Nan-k'ang and served in Chekiang East. For the first time he could put his learning into practice. The result of his measures was remarkable but he was not employed further. He withdrew and served as an official of the Ch'ung-tao, Yün-t'ai, and Hung-ch'ing temples for five years."[36] Here Huang Kan meant five calendar years, from the second month of 1183 to the seventh month of 1187. On his way to the post in Chiang-nan West, Chu Hsi declined the position of judicial intendant twice and requested a temple emolument twice. On the seventh day of the sixth month, he was summoned to the Yen-ho Palace for an audience with the emperor. The next day he was appointed a director in the army ministry *(ping-pu lang-kuan)*, but he declined with the excuse of a foot ailment, requesting a temple emolument instead. On the tenth day he was told to assume the post of judicial intendant. In the following month he declined once more, again with the excuse of a foot ailment, and petitioned for a temple emolument.

9. *Director of the Ch'ung-fu Temple on Mount Sung in the western capital from the seventh month of 1188 to the eighth month of 1189.* As a result of review in the seventh month of 1188, Chu Hsi was promoted to the rank of *ch'ao-feng-lang* (dignitary for court service) to serve in the Pao-wen-ko (an archive where the imperial calligraphy was preserved) and be in charge of the Ch'ung-fu Temple. After he failed in the eighth month to decline both the new rank and the archive appointment, he agreed to serve. The Ch'ung-fu Temple was originally at the foot of Mount Sung in Teng-feng County in Honan. After the Sung government moved south, only the emoluments of temples outside the temporary capital were retained. The rank of *ch'ao-feng-lang* was the twenty-second among the thirty-seven for civil officials. Thus Chu Hsi was promoted four ranks above his previous rank of *hsüan-chiao-lang*. In the tenth month he was summoned to the palace for an interview, and the following month he presented a sealed memorial. A note to the memorial says, "All along I enjoyed temple emoluments for nine terms, which I did not deserve."[37]

On the twenty-first day of the twelfth month, Chu Hsi was appointed junior expositor-in-waiting *(Ch'ung-cheng-yüan shuo-shu)* and concurrently put in charge of the West T'ai-i Temple. This temple was inside Lin-an (Hangchow), the temporary capital. Its prestige was very high, and to be appointed to a concurrent position meant especially favorable treatment. But Chu Hsi declined the expositor position and requested a temple emolument outside the capital. He was appointed a compiler of the Imperial Library on the eleventh day of the first month of 1189, while retaining charge over the Ch'ung-fu Temple. He declined the job of compiler but kept the temple position. Thus his term for the Ch'ung-fu Temple was never interrupted and the offer of the T'ai-i Temple position never accepted. His Ch'ung-fu Temple tenure was not terminated until the eighth month, when he was appointed assistant regional finance commissioner *(chuan-yün fu-shih)* of Chiang-nan East (in Kiangsu and Anhui). The Ch'ung-fu Temple tenure was comparatively longer, lasting for two years and nine months. After he declined the offer to be regional commissioner, he was sent in the eleventh month to be prefect at Chang-chou in southern Fukien.

10. *Director of the Hung-ch'ing Temple of the southern capital from the ninth day of the third month of 1191 to the twelfth month of 1193.* Chu Hsi was sixty-one years old in 1190. From the twenty-fourth day of the fourth month of 1190 to the twenty-ninth day of the fourth month of the following year, he was prefect at Chang-chou. In the tenth month of 1190 he requested a temple emolument but was denied. When his eldest son died in the beginning of 1191, he strongly requested a temple emolument to go home to attend to the burial. He was appointed a compiler in the Imperial Library in the third month of 1191 and was also put in charge of the Hung-ch'ing Temple. The temple tenure lasted until he was appointed pacification commissioner *(an-fu-shih)* of Ching-hu South based at T'an-chou (Ch'ang-sha).

11. *Supervisor* (t'i-chü) *of the Hung-ch'ing Temple of the southern capital from the twelfth month of 1194 to the twelfth month of 1196.* Chu Hsi arrived at T'an-chou on the fifth day of the fifth month in 1194. Emperor Kuang-tsung (*r.* 1190–1194) died in the seventh month and was succeeded by Ning-tsung (*r.* 1195–1224), who summoned Chu Hsi to the capital. Chu Hsi left T'an-chou in the eighth month and entered the capital on the second day of the tenth month. On the tenth day he began to lecture on the *Great Learning* before the new emperor. But because he offended the Court officials in his memorials, because these officials attacked Chu Hsi and his School, because he opposed the decision on imperial burial sites, and possibly because his lectures bored the emperor, he was released nine days later from his lecturership. In the twelfth month of 1194 he was appointed *t'i-chü* of the Hung-ch'ing Temple. *T'i-chü* was the highest of four ranks for temple officials. Nevertheless, the attack on him gained momentum. A year later, Chu Hsi was dismissed from the government and his temple tenure was terminated. Thus his more than

twenty years of temple emolument came to an end along with his political career.

## Official Salary

We have no information on Chu Hsi's income. Surely his pupils brought gifts as tuition, but we do not know how often or how much. Shen Chi-tsu's accusation that he selected pupils only from wealthy families is utterly baseless.[38] There were gifts from admirers and officials but, as we shall see, Chu Hsi declined many of them. He wrote many biographies, tomb inscriptions, prefaces, epilogues, and accounts for which he must have been paid an honorarium. Once, however, he received a set of books instead of cash.[39] In the period when he was a temple official, his only regular income was the meager temple emolument. According to the *Sung shih,* a temple superintendent in the Northern Sung received 15 *kuan* a month. With minor adjustments, this scale was followed during the Southern Sung. In this period the salary for *ch'ao-feng ta-fu* was 35 *kuan;* for *ch'ao-feng-lang,* 30 *kuan;* for *hsüan-chiao-lang,* 15 *kuan;* and for *ti-kung-lang,* 12 *kuan.* Besides the salary, there were subsidies in the form of silk, rice, and the like. In addition, several *kuan* were given as supplementary payment. Altogether, a temple superintendent received about 50 *kuan* besides commodities. Each *kuan* consisted of a thousand cash. In the Southern Sung, because of depreciation, a *kuan* was worth six hundred cash in the capital and four hundred outside.[40]

Commodity prices and the cost of living at that time are difficult to determine. According to Chu Hsi's report on one area under his jurisdiction, the cost of rice was from 17 to 40 cash per one tenth of a peck.[41] Kinugawa also estimated that during the Southern Sung the price of one tenth of a peck of rice ranged from 30 to 50 cash.[42] In other words, each *kuan* could buy only about four pecks of rice, and each person required about three pecks a month.[43] Thus a temple emolument alone was barely enough to pay for the food of a family. It is no wonder that throughout his life Chu Hsi told friends that he was poverty-stricken. After he returned from T'ung-an he petitioned for a temple emolument because his mother was old and the family was poor. When he was waiting to assume office as professor of the military academy, he wrote his friend K'o Han (c. 1106–1177), "Since there are still three years of waiting, I cannot [afford to] do so. The pressure of poverty is extremely strong. Any moment I will have to request a temple emolument."[44] In 1167, when he was appointed compiler in the privy council, he sent a communication to the Minister of State Affairs that said, "The family is really poor and the parent old. . . . I hope you will help me in appointing me to the temple position."[45] In 1173 he again pleaded that "The family being poor, I beg to be appointed superintendent of a temple once more."[46] In a letter to his friend Liu Tzu-ch'eng he said, "My tenure for temple emolument will be up in three or four days. Some days ago, incidentally, I asked Yu Yen-chih [Yu Mao, 1127–1194] to request for me again. I simply have to get it. I am very sorry to do this again because of poverty."[47] In another letter he said, "As to myself, my debts have not been all paid, and rice for food is insufficient. I am afraid I shall be a temple official permanently."[48]

This shows that Chu Hsi was not happy being a temple official but had to depend on emoluments for sustenance. In still another letter to Liu he said, "You, my friend, have safely returned home. Furthermore, you have a temple emolument to supplement your official salary and should have no more worries about clothing and food."[49] Whereas Liu had two sources of income, Chu Hsi often depended on a temple emolument alone, so his financial stringency can readily be seen. In the years when he received no temple emolument, obviously the situation was worse. In a letter to Prime Minister Chou Pi-ta (1126–1204) he said, "It has been a year since I lost my temple emolument in the eighth month of last year [1189]. My situation of poverty and illness can be known without saying."[50]

Chu Hsi served as a government official several times when the salaries were higher. The salary for *chu-pu* during the Shao-hsing period was only 7 *kuan* per month.[51] This, plus 12 *kuan* for the rank of *ti-kung-lang*, add up to less than twenty. Compensation for other offices was higher. That for a professorship at the military academy was 20 *kuan;* for prefect, from 7 to 60 *kuan,* depending on the population; for superintendent in charge of ever-normal granaries, tea, and salt, 30 *kuan;* for judicial intendant, 20 *kuan;* and for lecturer-in-waiting, 15 to 25 *kuan.*[52] All these figures are necessarily estimates. Besides these basic salaries, there were subsidies, both in *kuan* and in commodities. When the pay for the rank was added, even with depreciation, the total monthly amount was several hundred *kuan.*

When there was a surplus, Chu Hsi readily contributed it to a public cause. While he was prefect at Nan-k'ang, he wrote his good friend Lü Tsu-ch'ien (1137–1181), "West of the three cliffs of Mount Lu is a waterfall plunging into a rock niche. Although not tall, the approach of the waterfall is very strong. Formerly it was called 'The Sleeping Dragon.' There used to be a small temple but that has disappeared. I recently came to that spot and could not help contributing part of my official salary to erect a simple building in which I hope K'ung-ming's[53] portrait will be painted on the wall."[54] He contributed his salary to building a pavilion there, also.[55] In a subsequent letter he said, "Following precedent, two images have been set up in the two temples of the academy. . . . I dared not squander government money. As to the

Sleeping Dragon Temple I talked about in my last letter, I also used my salary and dared not squander government money."[56] According to the account of the White Deer Hollow Academy, he also contributed 487 *mu* of rice field to the academy.[57]

## Dire Financial State

Chu Hsi's dire financial state can be seen with regard to his building projects as well. In the course of his life, he built several cottages and studies. In 1170, after he buried his mother in Han-ch'üan-wu (Cold Spring Plateau) in Chien-yang County, he built a study, the Han-ch'üan Ching-she, nearby. In 1175, he also built a hut, called Hui-an (Secluded Cottage), in Yün-ku (Cloud Valley) on top of Mount Lu, 70 *li* northwest of Chien-yang. He had acquired the land in 1170 and now built a thatched hall with three rooms, behind which he built a thatched cottage. It took several years to finish the pavilions and to acquire the land north of the mountain from the Shih family. When the project was completed in 1175, Chu Hsi wrote the "Yün-ku chi" (Account of Cloud Valley) to describe it in detail.[58]

Eight years later, in the fourth month of 1183, he built the Wu-i Ching-she at the foot of Ta-yin-p'ing (Great Hidden Screen) by the fifth turn of the Wu-i River of Mount Wu-i, 30 *li* northwest of Ch'ung-an. Work began in the first month and was finished in the fourth. The Ching-she compound covered an area of several *mu*. The main building had three rooms. On the left foot of the Screen, at Shih-men-wu (Stone Gate Cove), a house was built to accommodate scholars, and southwest of the Stone Gate, a house to accommodate Taoists and Buddhists. There were pavilions and groves of trees to please the eye and the mind. Chu Hsi wrote an account and poems with an introduction to commemorate the structure.[59]

In 1194 Chu Hsi built the Chu-lin Ching-she (Bamboo Grove Study), later called the Ts'ang-chou Ching-she, beside his residence in K'ao-t'ing in Chien-yang County. When the study was finished, on the thirteenth day of the twelfth month, he led his pupils to report to Confucius in a religious ceremony.[60]

It may be asked how such a poor man was able to build such elaborate structures. Hui-an in Cloud Valley was made possible mostly through the financial help of Chu Hsi's pupil Ts'ai Yüan-ting (1135–1198). Even so, a number of projected pavilions did not materialize. The land was probably inexpensive because the place was not easily accessible and only a small part of it could be cultivated. Moreover, the thatched Hui-an could not withstand wind or rain. In a poem Chu Hsi said of it, "After six years, more straw had to be added in a hurry."[61] The "Account of Cloud Valley" says, "I wanted to build a small pavilion . . . but I had no time to do so. . . . There are several tens of *mu* of rice-field that can be cultivated. . . . It is more than 80 *li* from my home in the southwest, so it is utterly impossible for people to visit, and I have come only once or twice a year. However, my friend Ts'ai Chi-t'ung [Ts'ai Yüan-ting] lives 20 *li* or more north of the mountain. He has found it possible to visit a number of times."[62]

The Wu-i Ching-she was also a simple affair. It consisted of thatched buildings and wooden gates, taking advantage of local materials and natural scenery. The Chu-lin Ching-she was necessitated by the increasing number of Chu Hsi's pupils; it was not for pleasure. As Tai Hsien (1496 *cs*) has noted in his *nien-p'u* under 1194, "After Master Chu returned home, the number of pupils greatly increased. At this point, the Ching-she was built."[63] Since it took only one month to build, it could not have been lavish.[64]

The simplicity of the buildings was necessitated by Chu Hsi's inability to afford luxury, but it was also due to his disapproval of elaborate structures. In 1194, after his lecture before the emperor, he stayed in the palace and personally memorialized the emperor on four subjects. One was that Emperor Kuang-tsung not repair the several hundred buildings in the Eastern Palace. Chu Hsi told the emperor that while the citizens were starving, it was unconscionable for him to spend the money on his own comfort.[65] In a letter to Liu Ch'ing-chih he said, "I hear that the plan for the Lien-hsi Study is very elaborate. In my humble opinion, it is not necessary. If later on no one could live there, it will be wasted. It is better to simplify the whole scheme, use and strengthen its support, and buy some land to provide for the guard so the study will be lasting. Only then will it be good."[66] Once he criticized P'eng Kuei-nien (1142–1206) for building a mansion, saying, "I hear that P'eng Tzu-shou [P'eng Kuei-nien] built a very large residence. Why is that necessary?"[67] He also criticized Liu Kung for building a lavish mansion.[68]

In 1179, as prefect of Nan-k'ang, Chu Hsi restored the White Deer Hollow Academy. In his official communication to report on the reconstruction, he said, "There is already a commandery school in the commandery for the purpose of training students. The academy restored at the White Deer Hollow consists of no more than three or five small rooms to mark the old relic so that it will not be neglected. I dare not foolishly squander government money and waste people's energy."[69] In all these cases, his policy of thrift is unmistakable.

As to his own buildings, in most cases Chu Hsi was simply unable to afford what he wanted. In a letter to his friend Ho Hao (1128–1175) he said, "Previously, I miscalculated and foolishly remodeled and expanded my poor house for purposes of receiving guests and performing religious sacrifice. Once the work began, both money and energy were exhausted. But the situation is such that work cannot be stopped in mid-course. In the last several days I have been extremely bothered, almost to the point of having no time to eat or to breathe."[70] Later in the letter he mentioned that the following spring he was going east to visit ancestral graves. This refers to his second visit to Wu-yüan in 1176. Thus it must have been the house in Wu-fu Village in Ch'ung-an that became too small for social and religious functions, not the cottage in the Cloud Valley, which, being far away, he used only occasionally.

In 1184 Chu Hsi wrote Ch'en Liang (1143–1194), "In recent years, my financial stringency is particularly severe. Poems are completed but my house is not. And I cannot afford messengers to go between friends."[71] At the time, Chu Hsi was superintendent of the Ch'ung-tao Temple of T'ai-chou; his poverty was to be expected. In 1191 he wrote his pupil Wu Pi-ta, "It is not feasible to return to Wu-fu Village now. I have decided to settle down here and have bought an old house from someone. I shall move in next year. Now I am constructing a small tower. The work will be done in about ten days."[72] In a letter to a friend, he said, "Arranging for [my son's] funeral and building a house will take place next year. Right now I am building a small study hall (shu-yüan) as a place for entertainment, handling affairs, and rest. Later it can also be used to store books and for relaxation. However, a great deal of energy and money have been spent, and I don't know what the situation will be next year."[73] By the small shu-yüan, he must have meant the small tower. At that time, Chu Hsi had just finished his term as prefect at Chang-chou and decided to move from Ch'ung-an to Chien-yang. Even with the salary of a prefect, he could only afford to buy an old house. In another letter to Ch'en Liang, he said that he was not returning to Wu-fu Village but had decided to settle in Chien-yang, adding that "there are only several hundred cash in my purse. Hardly ten or twenty percent of the work has been done and the purse is exhausted. I shall have to go into debt before finishing the work. I regret very much that I was too hasty in making plans."[74] In a letter to Chu Lu-shu, he also said that he had been careless in planning for a small house, which had incurred a good deal of debt for him.[75]

Chu Hsi also wanted to establish a family temple of five rooms, with the rear room as a long hall that would be partitioned into four rooms for ancestral tablets.[76] But his family altar was actually in a corner of the living room. When a pupil asked him about his plans for a temple, he replied he could not build one "simply because I am financially unable to do so."[77] Chu Hsi was exceedingly serious about observing rituals, yet he was denied a temple in his home. The extent to which he was financially restrained cannot be exaggerated.

His poverty was apparent not only in his building projects but in other respects as well. He gave his daughter in marriage to Huang Kan, who became an outstanding pupil. In a letter to his son-in-law he said, "It is most fortunate that this girl found a home in a virtuous family to serve a worthy man. But she lost her mother at an early age and thus missed instructions on proper behavior. Furthermore, because the family is poor, it has not been able to provide a generous dowry. For this I am very much ashamed and deeply regretful."[78] Being very careful about political appointments, Chu Hsi would not try to gain any favor for his son-in-law. In reply to his pupil Wu Nan, who had asked for a favor, he said, "From your letter I know you were going to the capital. I believe you must have arrived. However, I am now out of office and am far away. How can I seek by some means an office or a favor in examinations for anybody? If I were able to do so, relatives like Huang Chih-ch'ing [Huang Kan] should figure first in my schemes."[79]

Huang Kan was extremely poor. Chu Hsi finally urged him to take the civil service examinations and enter the government, which he did. But his poverty was well known. In his "To My Children with a Sigh," Huang Kan said that "I deprived you of powder and salt, and your faces, in front of me, appear green and yellow. When you are cold in the winter, you have no soft furs to wear, and when you are hungry in the morning, there is no soft rice for you to eat."[80] In a letter to Huang Kan, Chu Hsi said, "I am planning to build a study in the back of the house. The scale is very large. When you come home later, you may be asked to hang up your signboard [to teach] and be in charge. After this building, it will not be difficult to plan for a small house for you."[81] But in a later letter he said, "I have found the foundation for a house here but money is not available yet."[82] There is no mention in either the *Wen-chi* or the *Yü-lei* of whether or not the house was finally erected. In all probability, because of Chu Hsi's poverty, his wish was never fulfilled.

Chu Hsi sent his eldest son, Shu, to study with Lü Tsu-ch'ien. In a letter to Lü he said, "I should send my oldest son to you to study with you right away. However, the move would involve much expenditure. Next spring I shall bring him myself."[83] This shows that Chu Hsi could not afford to send a companion with his son at the time he wrote. In 1180 he wrote Lü again to have Shu come home for a visit as soon as possible, saying, "I have heard from Shu-tu [P'an Ching-hsien (1137–1193), with whom the son was boarding]. It seems that Shu-tu will not permit my son to come. This time I have broken a rule to send someone by borrowing not a little from various sources. If my son does not make the trip, the money will be wasted. In the future, I am afraid I shall not be able to send anyone, and that will be troublesome. Kindly say a good word [to Shu-tu] so my son can return home early."[84]

It has been pointed out that Chu Hsi borrowed more than once. When he said he broke a rule, he merely meant that as a general rule he did not want to be in debt. If his son did not make the trip this time, he would have to send someone again for him and that would require borrowing once more. When the *Sung shih* says, "Frequently he borrowed from others to meet expenses," it is not exaggerating.[85]

When Chu Hsi became sick in 1186, Ch'en Liang sent a messenger to inquire of his illness, but Chu Hsi was unable to return the courtesy in the same way. In his reply he said, "Being poor and simple in my private life, I am unable to send a messenger to inquire of your activities, but you have taken the trouble of sending a messenger to inquire about my health."[86] Ch'en Liang lived in Chekiang, far away from Chu Hsi's residence in Fukien, and sending a messenger was costly. When Ch'en Liang returned home in 1193 after receiving the highest degree in the civil service examination, Chu Hsi wanted to send someone to congratulate him but was not able to do so, and could only send a letter.[87]

When Ch'eng Shen-fu passed away, Chu Hsi wrote his pupil Lin Yung-chung and said,

> At the present time my financial stringency is indescribable. I have tried to cut down all expenses and still there is not enough for daily upkeep. I wished I could send a small condolatory gift but cannot afford to do so. I have already spoken to his younger brother about it. There is still "writings money" in your place. Please use one thousand cash. My office in the government has already sent an official document and some fragrant tea to his younger brother's place. Please express my humble feeling by offering incense and tea before his tablet.[88]

Another example is that Chu Hsi's pupil Wu Po-feng once presented him with books and medicine. In reply he said, "I have nothing now to return your courtesy."[89] When Wu died, he wrote Huang Hsün (1147–1212), "I wanted to send a messenger to bring a letter of condolence and to mourn in his home, but that was beyond my ability."[90] When Lü Tsu-ch'ien's wife passed away, Chu Hsi wished to send an offering of condolence but was prevented from doing so because of poverty.[91] Perhaps he had too many social obligations and had to retrench, but his lack of financial resources was real and he was not making an excuse. The "writings money" probably consisted of honoraria for writing biographies and the like that Lin Yung-chung had collected to meet unexpected expenses.

Chu Hsi's pupils often helped him make copies of his writings. But in his late years, when he was working on ritual texts, government persecution of Chu Hsi's "false learning" was severe and some pupils tried to avoid getting involved. As he told a pupil, "Only in the last several months have I begun to attend to the ritual texts, and I have tidied up more than ten chapters. But I am bothered because no one is available for copying. Wherever I could depend on people, they all fear complicity in 'false learning' and decline to help. Those who could help are far away and cannot meet immediate needs. The only resort is to hire someone to copy, but the cost is high and I cannot afford it."[92] Chien-yang was a center of publication, and so must have had an ample supply of copyists whose wages were reasonable, yet Chu Hsi could not afford to hire anyone.

Wei Ch'eng-chih was a wealthy person. Chu Hsi said, "This autumn his struggle with a debtor caused the debtor's death. He was free only after all his holdings were taken away, and in addition he had to borrow. Now his family of four or five is desperate. It is quite pitiable, but I have no means of saving them." He also said he wanted to invite people for a visit but "a poor family cannot finance it."[93] Thus his poverty restricted him in a number of ways.

In many of his letters Chu Hsi told his friends how poor he was. We read such expressions as "poverty driving me to take the civil service examinations," "living in poverty to serve my parent," "poor family and heavy burden," "serving my parent under financial hardship," "poor and ill," "living in poverty," "daily encroachment of poverty and illness," "increasingly poor every day," "heavy pressure of poverty and illness," "complication of poverty and illness," "indescribable poverty and illness," "activities beyond the ability of a poor family," and many more.[94] In his funeral address for Chang Shih (1133–1180), Chu Hsi described himself as "a poor student of grass."[95] He told his pupil Huang Hao that he "had no other hope than to have enough to eat in declining years."[96] Indeed, few thinkers in Chinese history have been as poverty stricken as Chu Hsi. As the "Hsing-chuang" put it, he led a very thrifty life, needing only enough clothing to cover his body and food to fill his stomach, and took situations in stride that others would have found unbearable.[97] The *Sung shih* also says, "The basket and gourd were frequently empty, but he was at ease. He shared his simple and coarse food with those pupils who came from a distance."[98] When Hu Hung (1163 *cs*) visited Chu Hsi, he too received simple fare. But Hu Hung was offended, and when he became a high official, he wrote a memorial attacking Chu Hsi. Hu's revenge finally led to Chu Hsi's dismissal from government. One may say, therefore, that Chu Hsi was definitely a victim of his own poverty.

## Printing Business

Because his income was negligible, Chu Hsi had to supplement it, which he did by printing books. Since this was a very minor part of his life, neither the "Hsing-chuang" nor the *Sung shih* mentions it, nor is there a word about it in the chronological biographies or in any account

of his life. Perhaps because there is very little material on the subject—
or because it is felt that the business was beneath the dignity of Chu Hsi
—no writer has even referred to it. Yet in a letter to Lü Tsu-ch'ien concerning a pirated edition of his *Lun-yü ching-i* (Essential meanings of the
*Analects*) and his *Meng Tzu ching-i* (Essential meanings of the *Book of Mencius*) in I-wu County, Chu Hsi wrote,

> The cost of the publication was fairly high. Many people contributed to it
> and the circulation has been pretty good. Now suddenly there is this trou-
> ble, which is not merely an inconvenience to me. Please inquire about the
> matter as soon as you can, and say something to stop it. I am sure the
> pirate will listen to you. Otherwise, here is an official communication
> which I shall trouble you to seal and present to Venerable Shen as soon as
> possible. If he [the pirate] can be stopped before he has invested much
> money, neither of the two sides will be hurt. . . . This step is rather ridicu-
> lous, but because of poverty, I have to find food and cannot help going to
> this extent. I hope you will understand.[99]

Clearly friends had contributed to the publication of his books to enable
him to supplement his income, only to suffer from a dishonest busi-
nessman.

Chu Hsi must have printed many of his own works. His pupil Chan
I-chih (1151 *cs*) thought there were both pros and cons to such publication because of the government prohibition on Chu Hsi's "false learning." In reply Chu Hsi said,

> I deeply appreciate your kind thoughts about the benefit and harm of
> printing books. In my humble opinion, what I have written is not yet in
> good order. Whenever I read it again, there is surely going to be some
> revision. . . . Government money should not be used to publish private
> books. . . . I am now presenting to you the printed copy with correc-
> tions. . . . The printing of the collection of literary works of Ch'in-fu
> [Chang Shih] has taken a long time but is not yet finished. It is difficult to
> talk with vulgar people who only love profit. However, I have personally
> urged him. As soon as I receive a copy, I shall send it on to you.[100]

From this we can see that Chu Hsi did not publish his books with government money or without careful revision. This being the case, unless
Chan could publish for him, he would have to do it himself.

In another letter to Chan he said,

> I have proofread *The Explanation of the Book of History.* Just before I was
> going to send it to you, I casually went over it and found the pupils' proof-
> reading to be uneven and had to go over it myself. There are also many
> places that should be revised. However, [the commentary on the] *Analects*

has already been corrected in many places. I don't know if any further revision is necessary. I am afraid it needs to be reprinted. It is better to follow the old edition with notes in between the text for more appropriate style. . . . If it is necessary to revise [it], please delegate people who are well-informed and careful, and supervise them personally. Calculate the number of words carefully. If the number is insufficient, it does no harm to leave empty spaces. If the number is too great, you will have to double the line, as in notes. Do not give this copy directly to the carver, for fear he might want to save labor, lift off the pasted sheet, leave uncorrected what should be corrected, and thus do harm in the long run.[101]

Undoubtedly, Chan I-chih supervised the printing. Undoubtedly, too, Chu Hsi was meticulous in the preparation and proofreading of the publication.

There is also a letter to Liu Hsüeh-ku in which Chu Hsi said,

I have a small favor to ask you. Here are ten thousand sheets of paper with which I wish to print the classics, philosophers, the *Chin-ssu lu* [Reflections on things at hand], the *Hsiao-hsüeh* [Elementary education], and two ritual texts. But judging by the edition samples, the paper will not be sufficient for printing the classics and philosophers, although more than enough for the Four Books.[102] My idea is to use the greater half of the paper to print the classics and philosophers, and the rest to print the other works. This seems to be feasible. However, four thousand sheets have yet to come. I am now dispatching to you six thousand sheets. Please go ahead and begin printing. Also check the number of sheets to be sure none is missing; I shall send you the rest in three to five days. I have some money toward the cost of carving and ink, and I have borrowed the rest. I have asked Venerable Kao to give it to you. You may make the payment.[103]

Liu Hsüeh-ku was married to Chu Hsi's oldest daughter. Since in an earlier letter to him Chu Hsi mentioned Ts'ai Yüan-ting's banishment of 1197, the printing business must have been located in Chien-yang. The more significant point to note is that Chu Hsi attended even to small details of the business.

In all probability, the printing business was delegated to Chu Hsi's second son, Yeh. Perhaps Chu Hsi himself had to attend to it during Yeh's absence. In a letter to a pupil he said,

Because my son has gone to take the civil service examinations and has not returned home, I have asked an acquaintance to get the books you want to buy and give them to the messenger. The accounts are on a separate sheet which you can examine. The money certificates you sent are not enough to pay the bill. I have cashed several certificates to make the purchase. But not all the purchases have been made. Also, about completing the reprinting of the *Han shu* [History of the Han dynasty], I do not know what kind of paper you want and what size. The printer dares not go ahead. When convenient, please let me know in detail and printing will be resumed.[104]

This case involved both buying and printing books, indicating the extent of the operation.

In the *Yü-lei* we have a record of P'eng Shih-ch'ang, who headed the Hsiang-shan Academy, visiting Chu Hsi in 1196. When Chu Hsi asked him why he had come to Chien-yang, P'eng answered that the academy lacked books in its library and that he had come to procure them.[105] P'eng must have been referring to the classics and to Neo-Confucian works such as the *Lun-yü ching-i, Meng Tzu ching-i, Chin-ssu lu,* and *Hsiao-hsüeh.* Such books were probably not available on the general Chien-yang market which was devoted to popular literature and to essays for aiding candidates in preparing for civil service examinations. It is possible that P'eng came to Chien-yang especially to buy the books Chu Hsi printed.

In addition to his son Yeh, Chu Hsi's pupil Lin Yung-chung handled money for him, as evidenced by Chu Hsi's letter inquiring, "How much 'writings money' is still with you after what you sent me recently? . . . I have folded my hands to wait for this money before printing can be continued. Otherwise, there will be an interruption and a waste of energy."[106]

Chu Hsi's friend Chang Shih was not pleased with his printing enterprise. As he wrote,

I have heard from someone who has come here that you have printed a small number of books to help your finances. I believe what has been reported, and know that you are under the pressure of huge expenditure. When I first heard about it, I thought there was no harm in it. But as I think it over, I am afraid it is to some extent unsatisfactory. When I asked the person who came here, he dared not conceal the fact. At present our Way is isolated, with few adherents. If you print this type of literature to help yourself with the profit derived from it, I am very much afraid that when people hear about it, they will think of all kinds of things and our Way will lose its efficacy even more. Although you may feel that you are at ease with yourself and do not care what people say, still in the end it is not in harmony with affairs and principles. Because of poverty there is no harm in engaging in some other kind of business. I am not absolutely sure about this matter. I don't know what you think. I have heard Tzu-fei [Sung Hsiang, 1159 *cs*] say that your social expenses are very high. It will be fine if you can reduce them. I don't know if I am correct in this either.[107]

Since Chang Shih died in 1180, before Chu Hsi moved to Chien-yang, Chu Hsi's printing business must have been started long before, in Ch'ung-an.

In reaction to Chang Shih's letter, Chu Hsi wrote Lin Yung-chung, "Ch'in-fu [Chang Shih] does not approve my printing books but said that it would do no harm to do something else for a livelihood. I do not understand him at all. I am afraid that to do something else would be even more degrading."[108] Chang Shih was a very close friend. He and Chu Hsi admonished each other with absolute sincerity. But he did not know in detail the real situation of Chu Hsi's printing business, nor did he offer any concrete suggestions as to what other business might be helpful to Chu Hsi's livelihood. We do not know what Chang Shih meant when he referred to the "small number of books" that Chu Hsi was printing. Had he known they were the *Chin-ssu lu, Hsiao-hsüeh,* and so on, he probably would have realized that Chu Hsi printed books partly to promote Neo-Confucianism and to help bring the Confucian Way out of isolation. Chu Hsi definitely entered the printing business because of poverty, but he was also attempting to prevent pirating of his own and others' works. Most important of all, he was promoting Neo-Confucian studies.

## Acceptance of Gifts

The "Hsing-chuang" tells us that "in dealing with guests, he always entertained to the best of the family's ability and enjoyed to the highest degree."[109] Undoubtedly, there were a good many social occasions over the years. We have already noted a number of cases when Chu Hsi's poverty prevented him from giving gifts, but there are also many cases in the *Wen-chi* where gifts were given. When Lü Tsu-ch'ien's wife died, although at first Chu Hsi was unable to mourn her, later he did send someone to bring condolence money.[110] When Chang Shih died, he sent a messenger to offer libations,[111] and when Lu Chiu-ling (1132–1180) passed away, he also sent a person to make libations.[112] When his pupil Fang Lei was suffering from great pain, Chu Hsi wrote him, "I wanted to find some money to help with your medical expenses but have [previously] been unable to do so. However, by hook or by crook, I have [now] found fifty thousand cash to send you. You, my friend, should take special measures to rest and not worry." He also gave him three taels of *jinsen*.[113] On another occasion he presented Ch'en Liang with "a piece of white woolen to make a winter garment."[114]

In the other direction, Chu Hsi's pupil Fang Shih-yao (1148–1199) sent him some freshly picked tea,[115] and the Buddhist priest Chih-nan Shang-jen sent him fine, yellow dried bamboo shoots, dried laver, and so on. In the latter case, Chu Hsi returned the favor with twenty cans of *an-lo* (happy) tea powder, miscellaneous rubbings, and three stitched volumes of T'ang dynasty (618–907) poetry.[116] He also made many gifts of books and pamphlets, too numerous to recount here.

All these gifts were matters of social courtesy. In serious cases of accepting or rejecting a gift, Chu Hsi was guided only by what was right. As the *Sung shih* says, "If it was contrary to moral principles, he would not accept even a penny."[117] When Chu Hsi's eldest son, Shu, died, Ch'en Liang sent a person to offer libations. Chu Hsi responded, "Your messenger was robbed in Chiang-shan County [in Chekiang] and lost heavily. He also brought two rolls of silk and said they were given to him by someone as a replacement. I dare not keep the silk. It is now packed for the government to be returned to its original owner."[118] This shows that he would not accept a gift not intended for him. Another time, a certain young man by the name of Wu sent a messenger bearing gifts. In reply, Chu Hsi wrote him,

> I have not become acquainted with you. When I asked the messenger, I found that you are young and have a father at home who should be honored. But your letter, poems, and essays are rude and undisciplined, and you behave like a well-experienced person. You have gone as far as to present a gift to a person to whom you should not be giving anything, and have done so without invoking the name of your father or elder brother. This does not seem to indicate any innate knowledge or innate ability to love your parents or to respect elders. . . . There is no justification for accepting your gifts of stationery, ink-slabs, and ink-bars. I have not opened the package but have given it back to the messenger.[119]

This shows that he would not accept an inappropriate gift.

When Vice Minister Chao Ju-yü (1140–1196) offered to build a house for him, Chu Hsi wrote him to say, "This is a private dwelling and should not burden the government. . . . In the spring a few friends here wanted to build one for me and I declined."[120] Chao also pitied Chu Hsi for his poverty and sent part of his own salary to him. In a letter to Chao, he replied, "It is the normal lot of a poor, old bookish person to have simple and coarse food. I had not realized that some young people who consider that to be novel readily spread the word and caused you, a compassionate person, to worry deeply about me to the extent of quickly rendering me help. . . . I dare not accept your great kindness and have asked the messenger to return the gift to you. If in the future it should happen that my poverty becomes worse than it is today, I shall report it to you so that your generosity may finally be accepted."[121] In his administration Chao had evidently alienated his people, as Chu Hsi pointed out to him: "Even small children all harbor a feeling of injustice. I am afraid you are not aware of this. Although you have gone far astray, there is still an opportunity for correction." With this admonition, Chu Hsi accepted Chao's gifts of *jinsen,* and the like, as a sign of respect.[122]

A note to a letter to Lin Yung-chung says, "From the first month I have declined the gifts of the prefecture."[123] We do not know the date of this letter, but in it Chu Hsi asks whether Lin has resigned from his professorship of around 1173. Thus we know that it was written when Chu Hsi was living at home with the support of a temple emolument. Why he should decline a gift from a prefecture is not explained, but it is safe to assume that it was a matter of principle. Throughout his life, Chu Hsi declined official posts many times, by and large because of his moral principles. In a letter to Lin he said, "I dare not accept official salary because I have no high position or high degree. It would be against the law. I do not mean to hold myself aloof."[124]

When friends made gifts that were appropriate, however, Chu Hsi gladly accepted them. Ch'en Liang once sent fragrant tea, Szechuan silk, and Soochow stationery, which Chu Hsi received without hesitation, although in the case of excessive presents, he begged Ch'en to withdraw them.[125] Moreover, the presents Ch'en Liang offered did not affect Chu Hsi in the least in his debate with Ch'en on the issue of righteousness versus profit, or on that of the sagely king and the despot. In the *Yü-lei* we read,

> Upon talking about poverty, the Master said, "If friends give money, it is correct to accept it if no principle is violated. [Mencius] clearly said, 'If one's treatment is according to the Way and one's dealings conform to ceremony,'[126] Confucius would have accepted. If friends do not entrust you with legitimate matters but benefit you with money, that decidedly will not do."[127]

When he was prefect at Nan-k'ang (1179–1181) and Chang-chou (1190–1191), Chu Hsi would neither accept nor give birthday gifts. In T'an-chou (1194), however, he accepted birthday gifts because it was the practice and, in the case of officials of parallel political divisions, gave gifts to them on their birthdays.[128]

Chu Hsi once remarked to his students,

> It breaks my heart to see officials squander public money. . . . There were no definite rules for making gifts. Whether the gift was big or small depended on their whim. People in the government have told me that gifts made to officials passing through could be one thousand or five thousand cash. Later this was continued or no gift was made at all. Therefore I said, "This won't do. There is a public treasury here. Officials passing through should be given an amount appropriate to their rank. Only this is just. Why should the gift be looked upon as personal favor?" I therefore introduced definite regulations.[129]

To Chu Hsi, there was no difference between a personal and an official gift, since both must conform to moral principles.

## Endurance of Poverty

These accounts of Chu Hsi's poverty and his insistence on moral principles are reminiscent of stories about Yen Hui (521–490 B.C.?), Confucius' most virtuous pupil, who would not allow his joy to be affected by
the fact that he had only a single bamboo dish of rice to eat, a single
gourd dish to drink from, and a mean, narrow lane to live in.[130] Chu
Hsi "had been used to hunger and cold for a long time,"[131] "felt that it
is one's normal lot to withdraw and retire in poverty and illness,"[132] and
believed that "when we come to this situation, we should only direct our
effort to the endurance of poverty."[133] As he told his son-in-law Huang
Kan, "The pressure of livelihood is extraordinary. But principle and
fate are like this. The only thing to do is firmly to endure it."[134] In a letter to Lü Hsien (possibly his pupil) he said, "Poverty is the norm of a
scholar. If it does not affect his conduct, that is excellent."[135] In a letter
to a friend, Lü Shao-hsien, he said, "Your letter tells me of your abject
poverty. This is normal for us. You should strongly hold onto your life
so you will not fail the instructions of your forebears."[136] This was the
conviction with which Chu Hsi conducted his own life from youth to
old age.

In his *Mu-chai chi* (Account of the Shepherd's Studio) Chu Hsi said,
"In spite of the worry of danger and hunger, I have never neglected my
mindfulness for a single day. . . . Confucius said, 'Poor but cheer-
ful.'[137] . . . Should one allow poverty to disturb his will? . . . I am
devoting this effort to arriving at sagehood."[138] This is why he endured
poverty throughout life and adhered to the Way. As he himself put it,
"In my pursuit of learning in life, I merely learn to endure poverty and
adhere to the Way. It is precisely for this that friends have come from
afar for consultation."[139] In other words, the fact that Chu Hsi has been
a central figure in the intellectual life of China since Sung times is due
not merely to his completion of Neo-Confucian thought but also to his
great moral power in enduring poverty and adhering to the Way. In
1173, in appointing him to be in charge of Ch'ung-tao Temple, the
imperial edict said, "Chu Hsi was at peace with poverty and adhered to
the Way (*an-p'ing shou-tao*). His integrity and humility were commend-
able."[140] We may say that *an-p'ing shou-tao* was a way of life chosen by
Chu Hsi himself, admired by friends, and recognized by the Court.

## Notes

1. The capital of Ch'eng-ho County was in present Chien-chou County.
2. A *mu* is one-sixth of an acre.
3. Now in Kiangsi.
4. Wang Mao-hung, *Chu Tzu nien-p'u* [Chronological biography of Master

Chu] (*Ts'ung-shu chi-ch'eng* [Collection of series] ed.), *k'ao-i* [Investigation into variants], ch. 1, p. 242.

5. *Wen-chi,* 94:22a, account of moving his father's grave.

6. Present Nan-p'ing Special District in Fukien.

7. Quoted by Wang Mao-hung, *Chu Tzu nien-p'u,* p. 7. Yü Chi's account is found in full in Tai Hsien, *Chu Tzu shih-chi* [True records of Master Chu], (*Chin-shih han-chi ts'ung-k'an* [Chinese works of the recent period series] ed.), ch. 11.

8. *Wen-chi,* 90:1b, tomb inscription for Liu P'ing-shan (Liu Tzu-hui).

9. *Sung shih* [History of the Sung dynasty] (Beijing: Chung-hua Book Co., 1977), ch. 429, biography of Chu Hsi, p. 12767.

10. *Wen-chi,* 90:21a, tomb inscription for Liu Mien-chih.

11. Yeh Shao-weng, *Ssu-ch'ao wen-chien lu* [Records of what was heard and seen during the four reigns] (*P'u-ch'eng i-shu* [Surviving works of P'u-ch'eng County] ed.), 4:3b, "Faction during the Ch'ing-yüan period (1195–1200)."

12. *Sung shih,* ch. 170, "Account of Government Offices," pp. 4080–4082.

13. *Yü-lei,* ch. 128, sec. 28 (p. 4929).

14. Wang Ming-ch'ing, *Hui-ch'en ch'ien-lu* [Sweeping the dust: Earlier records], ch. 2, sec. 26.

15. See Liang T'ien-hsi, *Sung-tai tz'u-lu chih-tu k'ao-shih* [Investigation on temple emolument in the Sung period] (Hong Kong: Privately published, 1978), pp. 52, 245, 246.

16. Present Changsha in Hunan Province.

17. A *li* is one-third of a mile.

18. *Mien-chai chi* [Collected works of Huang Kan] (*Ssu-k'u ch'üan-shu chen-pen* [Precious works of the *Complete Collection of the Four Libraries*] ed.), 36:2a, biographical account.

19. The Five Peaks are Mount T'ai or the Eastern Peak in Shantung Province; Mount Hua or the Western Peak in Shensi; Mount Heng or the Southern Peak in Hunan; Mount Heng or the Northern Peak in Hopei; and Mount Sung or the Central Peak in Honan.

20. *Mien-chai chi,* 36:2b, biographical account.

21. Wang Mao-hung, *Chu Tzu nien-p'u, k'ao-i,* ch. 1, p. 260, under the third year of Ch'ien-tao (1167).

22. *Wen-chi,* 22:7a, "Official document of the Chien-ning Prefecture."

23. *Mien-chai chi,* 36:5b, biographical account. See also *Wen-chi,* 22:4b–5b, "Official document of appeal to decline a temple emolument."

24. *Wen-chi,* 22:9a.

25. Its capital was in present Hsing-tzu County in Kiangsi.

26. *Wen-chi,* 22:12a.

27. *Mien-chai chi,* 36:6a, biographical account.

28. *Ibid.,* 36:10a, biographical account.

29. Eleven prefectures in Anhui and Chekiang.

30. Six prefectures in Chekiang.

31. The term ended in the first month according to Liang T'ien-hsi, *Sung-tai tz'u-lu chih-tu k'ao-shih,* p. 499, but in the second month according to Wang Mao-hung, *Chu Tzu nien-p'u,* ch. 3A, p. 124, under the twelfth year of Ch'un-hsi (1185).

32. *Yü-lei*, ch. 128, sec. 29 (p. 4929).

33. The capital of Ying-t'ien Prefecture was in present Shang-ch'iu County, Honan Province.

34. Liang T'ien-hsi, *Sung-tai tz'u-lu chih-tu k'ao-shih*, pp. 59–60.

35. *Wen-chi*, separate collection, 3:14b, letter to Liu Tzu-ch'eng (Liu Ch'ing-chih). The poem is also found in the regular collection, 9:6b.

36. *Mien-chai chi*, 36:16a, biographical account.

37. *Wen-chi*, 11:37b, sealed memorial of *wu-shen* (1188).

38. Yeh Shao-weng, *Ssu-ch'ao wen-chien-lu*, 4:13a, "Faction during the Ch'ing-yüan Period (1195–1200)." See ch. 31 below, p. 552.

39. Chu Hsi wrote a biography for Liu Tzu-ho (Liu Ching-chih). Liu's son gave him the *Han shu* [History of the Han dynasty], which Chu Hsi turned over to the White Deer Hollow Academy. See *Wen-chi*, 81:24a, "Epilogue on the *Han shu* Preserved in the White Deer Hollow Academy."

40. *Sung shih*, ch. 172, "Record of Government Offices," pp. 4116, 4129, 4134–4135; Liang T'ien-hsi, *Sung-tai tz'u-lu chih-tu k'ao-shih*, pp. 289, 291, 295; Kinugawa Tsuyoshi, *Sung-tai wen-kuan feng-chi chih-tu* [System of compensation for civilian officials in the Sung period], trans. by Cheng Liang-sheng (Taipei: Commercial Press, 1977), p. 36.

41. *Wen-chi*, 21:9a, "Official Document Exposing the Delinquency of Magistrate Wang Chih-chung of Chiang-shan County."

42. Kinugawa, *Sung-tai wen-kuan feng-chi chih-tu*, p. 90.

43. *Wen-chi*, 16:15b, "Official Document Reporting the Termination of the Tenure at Nan-k'ang"; Kinugawa, *Sung-tai wen-kuan feng-chi chih-tu*, p. 91.

44. *Wen-chi*, 39:4a, letter in reply to K'o Kuo-ts'ai (K'o Han).

45. *Ibid.*, 22:2b, "Second Official Document in Reply to the Directive to Hurry to Assume Office."

46. *Ibid.*, 22:4b, fifth official document declining an appointment.

47. *Ibid.*, 35:23a, eleventh letter to Liu Tzu-ch'eng.

48. *Ibid.*, 35:20b, ninth letter.

49. *Ibid.*, 35:27b, fifteenth letter.

50. *Ibid.*, 27:25b, letter to Prime Minister Chou (Chou Pi-ta).

51. *Sung shih*, ch. 271, "Record of Government Offices," p. 4108; Kinugawa, *Sung-tai wen-kuan feng-chi chih-tu*, p. 37.

52. *Sung shih*, ch. 171, "Record of Government Offices," pp. 4130, 4113, 4114; ch. 172, 4131–4133; Liang T'ien-hsi, *Sung-tai tz'u-lu chih-tu k'ao-shih*, p. 298; Kinugawa, *Sung-tai wen-kuan feng-chi chih-tu*, p. 47.

53. K'ung-ming refers to Chu-ko Liang (181–234), a celebrated hero who attempted to restore the Han dynasty (206–220 A.D.). He was compared to the Sleeping Dragon.

54. *Wen-chi*, 34:10b–11a, sixty-eighth letter in reply to Lü Po-kung (Lü Tsu-ch'ien).

55. This is recorded both in Yeh Kung-hui's *Chu Tzu nien-p'u* [Chronological biography of Master Chu] (*Chin-shih han-chi ts'ung-k'an* [Chinese works of the recent period series] ed.), and in Tai Hsien's *Chu Tzu shih-chi* under the year 1180.

56. *Wen-chi*, 34:12b–13a, sixty-ninth letter in reply to Lü Po-kung.

57. *Pai-lu shu-yuan chih* [Account of the White Deer Hollow Academy], (1622 ed.), 16:1a, chapter on land proceeds.

58. *Wen-chi,* 78:2a–5a, "Yün-ku chi" (Account of Cloud Valley).

59. *Ibid.,* 9:2b–4a.

60. *Ibid.,* 86:12a–b, "Report to the Ancient Sage upon the Completion of the Ch'ang-chou Ching-she."

61. *Ibid.,* 6:18a.

62. *Ibid.,* 78:4b, "Account of Cloud Valley."

63. Tai Hsien, *Chu Tzu shih-chi,* pp. 193–194, under the fifth year of Ch'un-hsi (1194).

64. Wang Mao-hung, *Chu Tzu nien-p'u,* p. 214.

65. *Wen-chi,* 14:19b, "Note on Personally Memorializing on Four Things after Lecturing before the Emperor."

66. *Ibid.,* 35:20a, ninth letter in reply to Liu Tzu-ch'eng (Liu Ch'ing-chih).

67. *Yü-lei,* ch. 120, sec. 121 (p. 4661).

68. *Ibid.,* ch. 132, sec. 68 (p. 5101).

69. *Wen-chi,* 20:9b, "Official Communication to Report on the Restoration of the White Deer Hollow Academy."

70. *Ibid.,* 40:9b–20a, fourth letter in reply to Ho Shu-ching (Ho Hao).

71. *Ibid.,* 36:21b–22a, sixth letter in reply to Ch'en T'ung-fu (Ch'en Liang).

72. *Ibid.,* 52:10b, letter to Wu Po-feng (Wu Pi-ta).

73. *Ibid.,* 51:25a, seventh letter in reply to Huang Tzu-keng (Huang Hsün).

74. *Ibid.,* supplementary collection, 7:8a, letter to Ch'en T'ung-fu (Ch'en Liang).

75. *Ibid.,* separate collection, 5:13b, letter to Chu Lu-shu.

76. *Yü-lei,* ch. 90, sec. 51 (p. 3657).

77. *Ibid.,* sec. 49 (p. 3657).

78. *Wen-chi,* supplementary collection, 1:10a thirty-fourth letter in reply to Huang Chih-ch'ing (Huang Kan).

79. *Ibid.,* regular collection, 54:32a, fourth letter in reply to Wu I-chih (Wu Nan).

80. *Mien-chai chi,* 40:17a–b, poems.

81. *Wen-chi,* supplementary collection, 1:19b–20a, seventy-sixth letter in reply to Huang Chih-ch'ing.

82. *Ibid.,* 1:20a–b, eightieth letter.

83. *Ibid.,* regular collection, 33:25a, thirty-seventh letter in reply to Lü Po-kung (Lü Tsu-ch'ien).

84. *Ibid.,* 34:30b, eighty-seventh letter in reply to Lü Po-kung.

85. *Sung shih,* ch. 429, biography of Chu Hsi, pp. 12767–12768.

86. *Wen-chi,* 36:30a, eleventh letter in reply to Ch'en T'ung-fu (Ch'en Liang).

87. *Ibid.,* 36:31b, thirteenth letter.

88. *Ibid.,* separate collection, 6:5b, seventh letter to Lin Tse-chih (Lin Yung-chung).

89. *Ibid.,* regular collection, 52:11a, eighth letter in reply to Wu Po-feng.

90. *Ibid.,* 51:27b, letter in reply to Huang Tzu-keng (Huang Hsün).

91. *Ibid.,* 33:10z, fourteenth letter in reply to Lü Po-kung.

92. *Ibid.,* 53:13a, twenty-second letter in reply to Liu Chi-chang (Liu Fu).

93. *Ibid.,* separate collection, 4:5a, fifth letter to Liu Kung-fu (Liu Kung).

94. *Ibid.,* 22:37a; 43:1a; 22:26a, 37:5a; 25:12b, 39:25b; 40:4b, 40:27b; separate collection, 6:6a; 4:9b; regular collection, 52:38b; 23:8a.

95. *Ibid.*, 87:9b, funeral address for Chang Ching-fu (Chang Shih).

96. *Ibid.*, 46;8b, second letter in reply to Huang Shang-po (Huang Hao).

97. *Mien-chai chi*, 36:42a, biographical account.

98. *Sung shih*, ch. 429, biography of Chu Hsi, p. 12767.

99. *Wen-chi*, 33:19a, twenty-eighth letter in reply to Lü Po-kung.

100. *Ibid.*, 27:16a–17a, third letter in reply to Chan I-chih (Chan T'i-jen).

101. *Ibid.*, 27:19a–b, fourth letter to Chan I-chih.

102. The Four Books are the *Great Learning,* the *Analects,* the *Book of Mencius,* and the *Doctrine of the Mean.*

103. *Wen-chi,* separate collection, 5:4a, second letter to Hsüeh-ku (Liu Hsüeh-ku).

104. *Ibid.,* regular collection, 60:1b, letter in reply to Chou Ch'un jen (Chou P'u).

105. *Yü-lei,* ch. 124, sec. 68 (p. 4783).

106. *Wen-chi,* separate collection, 6:6a, seventh letter to Lin Tse-chih (Lin Yung-chung).

107. *Nan-hsüan Hsien-sheng wen-chi* [Collection of literary works of Chang Shih] (*Chin-shih han-chi ts'ung-k'an* ed.), 21:11a–b (pp. 685–686), twenty-ninth letter in reply to Chu Yüan-hui (Chu Hsi).

108. *Wen-chi,* extra collection, 6:6a, seventh letter to Lin Tse-chih.

109. *Mien-chai chi,* 36:42a, biographical account.

110. *Wen-chi,* 34:17a, seventy-sixth letter in reply to Lü Po-kung (Lü Tsu-ch'ien).

111. *Ibid.,* 34:24a, eighty-second letter.

112. *Ibid.,* 34:31b, eighty-ninth letter.

113. *Ibid.,* separate collection, 5:2a–b, third letter to Fang Keng-tao (Fang Lei).

114. *Ibid.,* supplementary collection, 7:8b, letter to Ch'en T'ung-fu (Ch'en Liang).

115. *Ibid.,* regular collection, 44:26b, sixteenth letter to Fang Po-mu (Fang Shih-yao).

116. *Ibid.,* extra collection, 5:11a, letter to Priest Chin-nan Shang-jen.

117. *Sung shih,* ch. 429, biography of Chu Hsi, p. 12768.

118. *Wen-chi,* supplementary collection, 7:8b, letter to Ch'en T'ung-fu.

119. *Ibid.,* regular collection, 55:27a, letter in reply to young man Wu.

120. *Ibid.,* 27:2b, second letter to Chief Chao (Chao Ju-yü).

121. *Ibid.,* 27:8a, fifth letter.

122. *Ibid.,* .

123. *Ibid.,* separate collection, 6:5a, seventh letter to Lin Tse-chih (Lin Yung-chung).

124. *Ibid.,* separate collection, 6:10b, sixteenth letter.

125. *Ibid.,* regular collection, 36:20a, 29a, 31b, sixth, eleventh, and thirteenth letters in reply to Ch'en T'ung-fu (Ch'en Liang).

126. *Book of Mencius,* 5B:4.

127. *Yü-lei,* ch. 13, sec. 129 (p. 385).

128. *Ibid.,* ch. 87, sec. 147 (p. 3583).

129. *Ibid.,* ch. 126, sec. 11 (p. 4198).

130. *Analects,* 6:9.

131. *Wen-chi,* 25:18b, letter to Councilor of State Kung (Kung Mao-liang).

132. *Ibid.,* 22:6b, fourth official communication to resign from appointment to a temple post.

133. *Ibid.,* 54:33a, letter in reply to Chao Ch'ang-fu (Chao Fan).

134. *Ibid.,* supplementary collection, 1:21b, eighty-eighth letter to Huang Chih-ch'ing (Huang Kan).

135. *Ibid.,* regular collection, 39:2b, letter in reply to Lü Hsien.

136. *Ibid.,* 64:23b, second letter in reply to Lü Shao-hsien.

137. *Analects,* 1:15.

138. *Wen-chi,* 77:7a–b, "Account of the Shepherd's Studio."

139. *Ibid.,* 54:32a, fourth letter in reply to Wu I-chih (Wu Nan).

140. *Ibid.,* 22:4b, first official communication to decline the appointment of a temple post.

# −6−

# Wine and Song;
# Smiles and Anger;
# Sternness and Humor

Most people have the impression that Chu Hsi was a very serious man. Some even believe he was severe in carrying out justice (I shall discuss this problem later, in chapter 31). But although Chu Hsi took everything seriously, he also had his lighter moments. It may come as a surprise that he smiled often and had quite a sense of humor. We shall begin with his love of wine and song.

## Wine and Song

In a poem called "Home Brewed Wine," Chu Hsi wrote that his ailing body was restricted by rules but that he loved to entertain guests. In a footnote he explained that of late he had been obliged to abstain from drinking alcohol.[1] From an earlier sentence, which says that his hair was turning white, we know that his self-imposed discipline took place in his later years. In a letter to Chang Shih (1133–1180) he said, "In recent days I have the tendency of chasing after external things. My mind loves to do so and cannot stop itself. In all such cases I have followed the precedent of abstaining from alcohol. I have stopped the tendency completely and it seems an easy matter."[2] This shows that even before Chang Shih passed away, Chu Hsi abstained from drinking. He once urged his friend Chao Fan (1143–1229) "by all means to abstain from writing poems and to stop drinking."[3] Chao Fan enjoyed writing poems. He often used poems in place of letters. Chu Hsi once praised his poems as "fairly compassionate."[4] But in discussing Chao Fan's poetry with his pupil Lin Yung-chung, Chu Hsi said,

> Today people do not devote their efforts to discussing moral principles but to writing poems and literary compositions. In so doing, they have degenerated into secondary matters. What is worse, they do not model

90

themselves after good writers but after bad ones. In writing poems they do not learn from the Six Dynasties [222–589] or Li [Li Po, 699–762] and Tu [Tu Fu, 712–770], but only from rough ones. Even if they learn perfectly well, what is the use? And what if they do not learn well?[5]

What Chu Hsi meant was not that one should not write poems at all, but that one should not write bad poems. Similarly, he did not mean to say that one should have nothing to do with wine, but that one should not drink beyond one's capacity.

Throughout his life, Chu Hsi himself drank wine and wrote poetry. When he wrote Chang Shih about stopping the mind altogether, he did not mean ceasing to think completely, but only stopping wayward thought. As was said of Confucius, "There was no limit for himself, but he had never gone to the point of being disorderly."[6] Therefore, by "stop" Chu Hsi meant to stop short of disorderliness. When he sent his eldest son, Shu (Shou-chih), to study with Lü Tsu-ch'ien (1137–1181), he laid down strict rules for him to follow. Among them was "not to drink."[7] Here the prohibition was complete, for although Shu was twenty-one years old, he was not yet married and had not proved that he could manage himself.

From his poems, one gets the impression that Chu Hsi drank very often and under many circumstances. He drank alone,[8] in company,[9] with companions,[10] with neighbors,[11] with fellow travelers,[12] and with Taoists.[13] He drank in the morning[14] and in the evening.[15] He drank under the moon,[16] in the snow,[17] and amidst flowers.[18] Whether it was in a boat,[19] by a pond,[20] on the roadside,[21] on top of a mountain,[22] in a straw hut[23] or in a lavish inn,[24] he would enjoy a cup of wine. His capacity must have been great, for he could drink from a cup,[25] a large container,[26] or a bottle.[27] Sometimes he drank one cup,[28] sometimes three cups,[29] and sometimes he did not realize that there was a bottom to the cup.[30] He even treated wine as tea and "did not care if he got drunk in a rustic person's house."[31] In the Wen-chi, drinking appears in the title of many a poem.[32]

By being drunk,[33] of course, Chu Hsi meant slightly intoxicated.[34] Sometimes he was comfortably drunk and fell asleep;[35] other times he was drunk to a very high degree.[36] In extreme cases he had to be assisted in walking[37] or had to lean on a cane.[38] In most cases he would fall asleep. Liu Kung (1122–1178) once asked him to write a preface for a collection of the literary works of Venerable Wang. He wrote Liu to say,

Not long ago you asked me to write a preface for the collection of literary works of Venerable Wang. Much to your disappointment I replied that I was afraid I was not able to do so. Recently, I happened to be drinking with Hsiang P'ing-fu [Hsiang An-shih, d. 1208], got drunk, and went to sleep. In the middle of the night I woke up and could not go back to sleep. As my thoughts wandered, ideas seemed to rush in. In no time I had tens and hundreds of words. I suddenly got up, as if in fear, and sat down. I lit a lamp and wrote the preface down. In my humble opinion, it is good enough to be the preface of the collection of Venerable Wang. I don't know what you will think about it.[39]

This is the "Wang Mei-hsi wen-chi hsü" (Preface to the collection of literary works of Wang Mei-hsi [Wang Shih-p'eng, 1112–1171]), a work of some twelve hundred words.[40] There is no doubt that on this occasion wine contributed to Chu Hsi's inspiration.

Another time, Chu Hsi was in a boat under a new moon with his pupils Lin Tse-chih (Lin Yung-chung) and Fan Po-ch'ung (Fan Nien-te). The two pupils had had some drinks and gone to sleep, but the Master was awake. He then composed a poem in which he wrote, "Let us ask the visitors with drunken eyes: Do you know if the journey is difficult?"[41] In 1167, accompanied by these two pupils, Chu Hsi had visited Chang Shih in Changsha to discuss the problem of equilibrium and harmony. In the eleventh month, they had ascended Mount Heng. During seven days of touring the mountain, they had braved wind and snow. Hence the poem refers to the difficulty of this journey. In this case, wine had warmed the feelings between Master and pupils. On another occasion when Chu Hsi had drunk several cups of wine, his pupil Wu Shou-ch'ang asked him for some calligraphy, which he cheerfully provided in both large and small characters.[42]

Despite Chu Hsi's enjoyment of wine, he would not allow it to influence his heartfelt feelings. For example, he once went to Wu-yüan, in present Kiangsi, to visit his ancestral graves, and was urged by the local community to pay homage at the Wu-t'ung Temple. Local people there believed the temple deity to possess spiritual power. Before they made a trip they always prayed and made offerings at the temple, and any scholar passing through would worship there by writing his name on a piece of paper and thus declaring himself a disciple of the deity. Chu Hsi, however, refused to do so. That evening, Chu Hsi drank some wine at the community banquet and his internal organs were disturbed all night. The local people attributed the illness to his failure to pay homage to the temple deity, but Chu Hsi said, "It is my fortune to have come here. My ancestral graves are nearby. If the deity can bring fortune or misfortune to bear upon me, may he bury me immediately by the side of my ancestral graves. It would be quite convenient."[43]

In 1196, having offended Han T'o-chou (d. 1207), who controlled the government, Chu Hsi was dismissed from his lecturership-in-waiting as well as his superintendency of a Taoist temple. In the following year his friend Ts'ai Yüan-ting (1135–1198) was banished to Tao-chou[44] as a means of persecuting Chu Hsi. Officials in various prefectures and counties were searching for Ts'ai to arrest him. According to the *Yü-lei,*

> The Master went to the Chang-an Temple to wait for Ts'ai, who was passing through by boat on his way to banishment. The Master met him outside the temple gate. They sat in the room of the head priest. Aside from ordinary greetings, not a word was said about Ts'ai's sad and difficult journey. He asked Ts'ai about the doubtful points in the *Ts'an-t'ung-ch'i* [Three ways unified and harmonized], which he had been reading for days. Ts'ai answered freely and easily. A little later, pupils brought in wine. They all drank and became drunk. The Master sat between rows of pupils on the bridge in front of the temple and drank. He drank some more when he went back to the temple. Feeling drunk, he went to sleep. When he drank on the bridge, Chan Yüan-shan [Chan T'i-jen, 1143–1206] withdrew. The Master said, "This man has an air of wealth and nobility."[45]

According to Ts'ai's biography in the *Sung shih* (History of the Sung dynasty), "Hsi and several hundred of his pupils had a farewell banquet in a desolate temple. Many participants sighed and some even wept. Hsi glanced at Yüan-ting as usual. Thereupon he sighed heavily and said, 'The feeling of mutual love among friends and the unyielding will of Chi-t'ung [Tsai Yüan-ting] may both be said to be evident.' "[46] Even in times of a crisis, drinking had no effect on Chu Hsi.

Chu Hsi was not known as a skillful player of the lute, but he could sing, especially after some wine. In a poem, he said that he could hold the lute but could not play, but as he approached a wine vessel, he would utter a long sigh.[47] When he sang in exhilaration from drinking, his power became strong and his diction clear and beautiful.[48] As he said in another poem, after three cups of wine his undaunted spirit was aroused and his sonorous chanting seemed to flow from the mountain peak.[49] Back in the spring of 1150, he had gone to Wu-yüan to visit his ancestral graves. At that time, Tung I stood by his side at the community banquet. Since everyone was intoxicated with wine, they took turns singing. Chu Hsi sang a verse of the "Li-sao" (Encountering sorrow) by Ch'ü Yüan (343–277 B.C.?). Everyone was surprised that he sang with gusto and a sonorous voice.[50] Chang Shih did not approve of Chu Hsi's singing aloud, however, nor did he hesitate to admonish him in a letter: "Many messengers have told me that at banquets you were elated after some wine. Your power became vigorous and you sang a song of lament in a heroic manner. Things like this must have been due to the habits of blood and vital power in your ordinary life that you have not eliminated. This should not be considered a small defect."[51] Chang

Shih must have gotten the impression that Chu Hsi went beyond the normal bounds, undoubtedly due to the exaggeration of the messengers. Had Chang Shih lived longer or seen Chu Hsi more often, he would have realized that his worry was unfounded.

To sing, chant, or recite was almost routine with Chu Hsi, as with most Chinese literati. He often engaged in these activities when he strolled or traveled with his students, sometimes for the enjoyment of the moment and sometimes to dispel sadness and sorrow. As one pupil recorded, on numerous occasions he would wander about with students, walking to and fro and looking here and there, all the time chanting softly.[52] Chu Hsi's pupil Wu Shou-ch'ang loved to discuss poetry with the Master. As he recalled,

> The Master would look at a river, a rock, a blade of grass, or a tree, not blinking his eyes for a whole day whenever he came to something interesting. After serving some rounds of wine, he would move to another location. When he was quite drunk he would sit cross-legged. After reciting from the classics, the histories, the philosophers, and the collections, he would even recite memoirs or miscellaneous literature in finished style. When he was slightly drunk, he would chant classical literature. His power and rhythm were clear and strong. According to what I have heard, the Master loved to recite Ch'ü Yüan's "Li-sao," K'ung-ming's [Chu-ko Liang, 181–234] "Ch'u-shih piao" [Manifesto on the military expedition], Yüan-ming's [T'ao Ch'ien, 365–427] "Kuei-ch'ü-lai-tz'u" [Homeward bound], and some poems of Tu Tzu-mei [Tu Fu]. That is all.[53]

Once, when Chu Hsi was resting downstairs with a foot ailment, he chanted Tu Fu's poem on the old cedar several times.[54] In this poem Tu Fu praised Chu-ko Liang's loyalty, comparing him to an old cedar. According to Yeh Wei-tao, when Chu Hsi chanted Tu Fu's poem, he had in mind high officials' sueing for peace with the Chin invaders in 1137.[55] Thus even wine and song served a high purpose for him.

## Smiles and Anger

Ming-tao (Ch'eng Hao, 1032–1085) was warm, while I-ch'uan (Ch'eng I, 1033–1107) was stern. This is well known to students of Chinese thought. As told in the *Wai-shu* (Additional works) of the Ch'eng brothers, "Chu Kung-yen [Chu Kuang-t'ing, 1037–1094] went to see Ming-tao in Ju-chou.[56] After he returned, he told people, 'Kuang-t'ing sat in the spring wind for a month.' When Yu [Yu Tso, 1053–1123] and Yang [Yang Shih, 1053–1135] first went to see I-ch'uan, I-ch'uan sat with his eyes closed. The two pupils stood by his side. When he woke up, he looked at them and said, 'Are you young gentlemen still here? The day is late. You may rest.' As they went out, the snow had accumulated for one foot."[57] Neither their *I-shu* (Surviving works) nor their *Wai-shu* contains a record of the two Ch'engs' smiles or anger, in sharp contrast to the *Yü-lei,* which contains more than one such account. This is because the *I-shu* and the *Wai-shu* contain recorded sayings, whereas the *Yü-lei* contains conversations. And as we shall see, the personality of Chu Hsi combined those of the Ch'eng brothers.

In a way, among Chu Hsi's several hundred pupils, Ch'en Ch'un (1159–1223) understood him best. As Ch'en Ch'un described Chu Hsi, "He was dignified and awesome as you looked at him, but warm and intimate when you approached him. In dealing with people, he was happy and pleasant all day, warm like a spring wind that is peaceful and worthy of embracing. When a thing should not be done, however, his judgment was like the severity of thunder, which is stern and cannot be violated."[58] In other words, Chu Hsi could smile and he could also be angry. The *Yü-lei* notes his smile or anger on more than ten occasions. The circumstances varied and cannot be generalized. When he smiled in answering a pupil's question about personality and humanity *(jen),*[59] responded to a question on the well-field system,[60] discussed the policy of Emperor Kao-tsu of the Han dynasty (206 B.C.–A.D. 220),[61] or commented on Mencius' doctrine of the Four Beginnings,[62] Chu Hsi was dealing with no one situation. His smile can only be taken as an expression of his warm personality. Incidentally, the last two cases just mentioned occurred during the same conversation, which is the only time Chu Hsi is said to have smiled twice.

When he talked about ancient rites, sometimes he smiled faintly, sometimes he waited for a long time before smiling, and sometimes he smiled when he reached a certain point. For example, the ancient custom of having someone impersonate the object of worship and offer wine to the participants until they became intoxicated was surely ludicrous, and only when Chu Hsi got to this point in the story did he smile.[63] Another example occurred when his pupil Fu Hsü first became an official. Fu Hsü wanted to call on the Master wearing his official cap and belt, but Pao Yang stopped him, saying that if Fu Hsü had worn the cap and belt, he would have violated ritual. But Chu Hsi replied that after all, those were governmental orders. After a long while, Chu Hsi also smiled and said, "Hsien-tao's [Pao Yang's] system is a transcendental one," meaning he was Buddhistic.[64] On yet another occasion, when a pupil remarked that ancient rites were difficult to practice, he simply smiled. This time the smile seemed to mean disapproval, for in Chu Hsi's teaching the standard for rites is not whether they are difficult or easy to practice, but whether one practices them with seriousness *(ching,* reverence).[65] When asked about the Confucian saying that one cannot conceal one's character,[66] Chu Hsi smiled and said that Mencius looked at a person's pupils to see if they were bright or dull,[67] a method that must have appeared interesting to him.[68] When a pupil first saw him and asked if there was one word that could be a guide for life,[69] Chu Hsi's smile seemed to suggest a criticism, implying that one must learn in every way and should not adhere to just one word.[70]

Ts'ai Yüan-ting had associated with Chu Hsi for a long time. He was once advised not to make a trip to Ch'üan-chou in southern Fukien, so he went to Chu Hsi for a decision. Chu Hsi smiled and did not answer. Only after a long time did he say, "Do it if you find ease in your mind though trouble in your body, and do it if there is more righteousness than profit."[71] Ts'ai was a specialist in the *Book of Changes* and could have found his own answer. Nevertheless, to be at ease in one's mind and to seek righteousness is a serious matter. Thus Chu Hsi's smile was a serious indication, not a lighthearted expression.

A lighthearted smile was evident in the case of Wu Shou-ch'ang. He first studied Ch'an (Meditation) Buddhism and later came to study with Chu Hsi, bringing his son along with him. On one or two occasions, Chu Hsi almost joked with him, as we shall see when we come to the topic of humor. One day, Shou-ch'ang asked the Master why there was *jen* (humanity, the universal virtue) in the flying of the hawk and the leaping of the fish, as told in the *Doctrine of the Mean*.[72] Chu Hsi waited for quite a while, then smiled and said, "You love Ch'an. This is somewhat like Ch'an. Why don't you tell me something about Ch'an?" Shou-ch'ang replied, "I dare not." Chu Hsi said, "Isn't it the cloud in the blue sky and the water in the vase?" Shou-ch'ang dared not reply. The Master said, "You may as well try." Shou-ch'ang said, "At present he is precisely I, but I am not he." Chu Hsi said, "Why don't you say, 'At present I am precisely he'?" Then he went on to say, "You must understand other parts of the *Doctrine of the Mean* and do that carefully. When you get to that point, you have only to refer to it lightly and you will naturally understand. You will have no more doubt, and you won't have to ask people."[73] Ordinarily, Chu Hsi was very stern toward pupils with an interest in Ch'an, but he felt quite comfortable with Shou-ch'ang. Perhaps his smile had a magical effect in turning Shou-ch'ang away from Ch'an.

Although Chu Hsi did not smile often, his smile was quite meaningful, as the above cases have indicated. More cases will be cited when we come to Chu Hsi's sense of humor; in the meantime, we turn to his anger. As far as we know from the *Yü-lei,* Chu Hsi was angry on only three occasions. Once, his pupil Kan Chieh asked him how can it be proved that man's nature contains the Five Constant Virtues of humanity, righteousness, propriety, wisdom, and faithfulness. This angered Chu Hsi, who replied, "You look like a child. You always talk freely about nature and destiny." He then turned to the group and said, "Let him come and touch nature. The more you try to catch nature, the farther it goes away. Fundamentally, principle has a true order. The substance of the Five Constant Virtues cannot be measured. It functions in the Five Teachings,[74] in filial piety toward parents, and in loyalty to the ruler." He continued, "There must be a foundation, such as commiseration, which we know issues from humanity. . . . Nature is everywhere before us. Let us direct our efforts to what is clear and evident." He went on to say, "Substance cannot be seen. Let us devote our efforts to function, and substance is included in it." The following evening he said, "Last night Chieh-fu [Kan Chieh] wanted to see the Five Constant Virtues in nature. There is no reason why he did not understand how things such as commiseration are issued. As there are humanity, righteousness, propriety, and wisdom, there are things like commiseration."[75] Kan Chieh's oral and written questions, as well as the conversations he recorded, all deal with nature and principle, yet he failed to understand that there are the Five Constant Virtues i  nature. Furthermore, he was looking for substance and overlooked function. Chu Hsi must have been greatly disappointed. No wonder he was displeased.

On a second occasion, Chu Hsi's anger was even greater. According to the *Yü-lei,* "The Master fell sick with asthma. For days pupils had not asked any questions. One evening he sent an attendant to call the pupils into his chamber. The pupils did not ask any questions then, either. The Master angrily said, 'You gentlemen just sit idle. What do you do? Why not go home? What is the use in coming here from so far away?' "[76] In his teaching, he encouraged pupils to ask questions, and even when he was ill he continued to discuss various topics with them. Obviously, his students did not want to aggravate his discomfort, but they failed to realize that he was relentless in his effort. The day before he died, when pupils came to visit and inquired about his condition, he sat up and told them, "I appreciate your bothering to come from afar. But principle is like this. We all have to work hard and stand firm before there can be any progress."[77] We can readily see that the stronger the effort he wanted his pupils to make, the stronger his feeling became.

The third instance of Chu Hsi's anger was recalled by Wang Kuo after 1194: "One day when the Master happened to talk about someone who accepted a bribe, his anger was shown in his appearance. He said, 'As I see it, such people are like actors who wear masks.' Then he said further, 'They say public officials should not covet money, but magistrates demand it.' He went on to cite case after case and sighed heavily."[78]

## Sternness and Humor

From the foregoing, one gathers that Chu Hsi was a very stern person. His attitude was always careful and dignified, and he was particularly

serious about rituals. The following items from the *Yü-lei* show how
stern he was:

1. "One year some time ago [1179] I went to Kiangsi. When I was
talking with Tzu-shou [Lu Chiu-ling, 1132–1180], Liu Ch'un-sou [Liu
Yao-fu, 1175 *cs*][79] went to sit alone in a corner in the back and paid no
attention to anything, imitating a Taoist in meditation. I scolded him
and said, 'Even if what Venerable Lu and I say is not worth listening to,
still we are a few years older [than you]. Why misbehave like this?' "[80]
Yao-fu went to study with Lu Hsiang-shan at seventeen, entered the
National University *(t'ai-hsüeh)* at twenty-four, became a monk at
twenty-nine, and died at forty-four. He was indeed a queer person.

2. "Someone was in attendance but fell asleep. The Master reprimanded him."[81]

3. "There was a pupil who, whenever he finished bowing, would
retract his left hand into his sleeve. The Master said, 'Sir, why do you
always pull in one of your hands? It does not seem to be proper
behavior.' "[82]

4. "Every evening when pupils gathered, one who was older than the
rest engaged in gossip as soon as he sat down. The Master reprimanded
him, saying, 'Sir, you are already forty years old. You still do not
understand what you read. As soon as you sit down, you talk about
other people's affairs. On recent evenings, you gentlemen have engaged
in idle talk until the second watch [10 p.m.]. In a gathering like this,
why don't you reflect on yourselves and do your own work instead of
talking about the nonessential?' He then sighed for a long while."[83]

5. "A pupil asked about the difficulty of appearing dignified. The
Master said, 'If one's mind is serious, one's appearance will be dignified. Dignity is not something one can create externally.' Ch'en Ts'ai-
ch'ing [Ch'en Wen-wei, 1154–1239] also talked about the nine appear-
ances.[84] The next morning Ts'ai-ch'ing used his right hand to pull the
left sleeve of his light robe of white raw silk to one side. The Master
said, 'Last night you said that "the expression of the hand should be
respectful,"[85] and now you act like this.' Ts'ai-ch'ing was abashed,
quickly crossed his hands, bowed, and said, 'I had forgotten.' The Master said, 'Should one forget learning for oneself? Formerly, Hsü Chieh-
hsiao [Hsü Chi, 1028–1103] went to see Hu An-ting [Hu Yüan, 993–
1059]. As he withdrew, his head turned slightly to the side. An-ting
suddenly shouted, "The appearance of the head should be straight."
Chieh-hsiao thought to himself that not only should the head be
straight; the mind should also be straight. From then on he had no more
perverse thoughts. A seeker of learning must be like this before it can be
all right.' "[86]

6. "Ho-sun [Yeh Wei-tao] begged to ask a question. At the end he
lowered his voice and the Master could not hear. Thereupon he said,

'Sir, you are from an elegant community. Why is your voice like this? You have begun well, but lately you have seemed gradually to become lazy. Confucius said, "His speech is firm and decided."[87] If you keep on like this, in the end it will do you no good. You will not see principles clearly, and will gradually enter into darkness. You will be befuddled and uncertain, and unable to reach the realm of brightness and correctness. In speech one must be clear in every word and every sentence. One must see what is right and what is wrong.' "[88]

7. "A small boy added some charcoal and stirred up the fire, which scattered in disorder. The Master said, 'You may put the fire out. I do not want it this way. This is just building a fire without seriousness. This is why the Sage taught children to be very careful in everything like sprinkling and sweeping the ground, and in answering and replying.[89] Young people in my father-in-law's family, regardless of whether or not they are virtuous, are always tidy when they appear in public. This is because they were taught by elders from the very start. When one lives away from elders, one's disposition becomes quite different.' "[90]

Huang Kan's (1152–1221) "Hsing-chuang" (Biographical account) tells us that Chu Hsi's "appearance was dignified and his words were firm. In walking, he was relaxed and respectful. In sitting, he was proper and straight."[91] One cannot avoid the impression that he was a stern man, and the above accounts deepen that impression. But he also had a sense of humor, although no writer has ever portrayed that side of his personality. There are accounts in the *Yü-lei* and the *Wen-chi* that show that he could be humorous at times, as the following selections testify:

1. As mentioned above, when Wu Shou-ch'ang came to study with Chu Hsi, he brought his son Hao along with him. A conversation recorded by Shou-ch'ang in the *Yü-lei* runs this way: "The Master asked me what books Hao had been taught in recent days. I replied that in the forenoon Fang Po-mu [Fang Shih-yao] teaches him to study the *Analects* and to listen to the explanation of some of its moral principles. In the afternoon he recites some essays by the Su family [Su Hsün, 1009–1066; Su Shih, 1037–1101; and Su Ch'e, 1039–1112] and the like, so that he can learn to write contemporary [literary] compositions. The Master smiled and said, 'In the morning you give him medicated soap [to strengthen his health] and in the afternoon you give him powdered medicine [to relieve the "heat"].' Then he grew serious and said, 'It is good enough to teach him only the *Book of Odes* and the *Book of History*.' "[92]

2. Another conversation recorded by Shou-ch'ang: "The Master asked me, 'What did you learn when you went to see [the Ch'an priest] Shu-shan?'[93] I replied, 'Let us take that and return it to the wall.' He

said, 'Do you know how to take it back to the wall or don't you?' I wanted to reply, 'It is all in there,' but I dared not. It happened the Master wrote on the fan in my hand, 'I have always been thinking of the third month in Chiang-nan [south of the Yangtze River]. All the flowers are fragrant wherever the partridge sings.' He held up the pen, looked at me, and asked, 'Do you know? Or don't you know?' I replied, 'It is all in here.' "[94]

3. "The Master divided the backyard of the archery hall in the pre-fectural capital[95] into nine squares like the character *ching* [well]. In the central square a pile of rocks made a high platform. In the square above it he built a straw hut with three windows. The railings of the left window are patterned after the *t'ai* [peace] hexagram, those of the right window after the *p'i* [obstructed] hexagram, those of the rear window after the *fu* [to return] hexagram, and the leaves of the front door are patterned after the *po* [to heal] hexagram.[96] The front of the hut is con-nected to a small house. In the front square is a small straw pavilion. In the three squares on each side are peach and prune trees interspersed with plums. Around the nine squares is bamboo. Today he wandered in the garden, smiled, and told his pupils, 'These are the form of the Nine Categories[97] and the Eight Trigrams[98] above, and the system of the Nine Fields[99] and the Eight Strategic Positions[100] below.' "[101]

4. Chu Hsi told his pupils: "Wang Kung-ch'en [1012–1085] built a high tower and Wen Kung [Ssu-ma Kuang, 1019–1086] built a room underground. People at the time said, 'One man penetrated Heaven and the other entered the Eart' K'ang-chieh [Shao Yung, 1011–1077] told Venerable Fu [Fu Pi, 1004–1083], 'What a strange thing: One man lives in a tree and the other in a cave.' "[102]

5. He also told his pupils: "Mo Ti [468–376 B.C.?][103] and Kung-shu Ch'iao[104] argued as they did. In the final analysis, one argument over-comes the other ad infinitum. One of them said, 'I know how to resist you, but wouldn't tell you.' The other said, 'I know how to attack you, but wouldn't tell you.' "[105]

6. A poem that Chu Hsi sent to Chiang Wen-ch'ing (Chiang Ssu) and Liu Shu-t'ung (Liu Huai) says:

> From time immemorial poets have been poor,
> Two more persons have now been added to the crowd
> I should laugh at friends of Hunan,
> In two years they have been blown into the dust of a city.

A note to it says, "This is to make fun of Tzu-meng [Yu K'ai], who is afraid of the discomfort of being driven to poverty."[106] All three men were Chu Hsi's pupils.

7. In answering a pupil's question on the *Book of Changes*, Chu Hsi

said, "The mind of King Wen [*r.* 1171–1122 B.C., to whom the sixty-four hexagrams have been attributed] was already unlike the broadness and openness of that of Fu-hsi [the legendary emperor to whom the Eight Trigrams were attributed]. He was in a hurry and had to speak out. The mind of Confucius [to whom the "ten wings" of the *Book of Changes* are attributed] was unlike the broadness and greatness of that of King Wen. He was in a hurry and had to speak out on principles. That is why the original purpose [of divination] was lost. Both of them paid no attention to the purpose of the sage's drawings of the trigrams, but each talked about his own set of principles. And what I-ch'uan [Ch'eng I] later spoke about seems to have been somewhat like the Changes of Confucius, but went further. . . . This is my theory, as I see the matter. I don't know what later people will think." He then added, "When Tung-p'o [Su Shih] finished his commentary on the *Book of Changes,* he told people, 'Since the *Book of Changes,* no one has written a book like mine.' "[107]

8. "When Wang Kuo returned from Wen-ling,[108] he reported to the Master what he had heard about Duke Yüeh's [Yüeh Fei, 1103–1141] answer to the emperor's [Kao-tsung] inquiry on peace in the empire, in which he had said, 'There will be peace in the empire when civil officials refuse to accept money and military officials do not care about their lives.' The Master merely smiled and said, 'Since then, even military officials also accept money.' "[109]

9. Chu Hsi's "Poem in Praise of Regulated Breathing" says, "I maintain the singleness of mind and dwell in peace of spirit. I shall live to a thousand and two hundred years."[110] This piece of humor is unique because, unlike the rest, it uses exaggeration.

10. In a letter to his son-in-law Huang Kan, Chu Hsi said, "I do not know if grandson Lo will remember me. He liked the painting of a lion on the wall. Here is the painting for him."[111] Of course, Lo did not forget his grandfather; Chu Hsi said so just for a smile.[112]

## Notes

1. *Wen-chi,* 3:15b.

2. *Ibid.,* 31:14b, twenty-seventh letter in reply to Chang Ching-fu (Chang Shih).

3. *Ibid.,* supplementary collection, 6:1b letter to Chao Ch'ang-fu (Chao Fan).

4. *Yü-lei,* ch. 140, sec. 57 (p. 5351).

5. *Ibid.,* sec. 73 (p. 5354).

6. *Analects,* 10:8.

7. *Wen-chi,* supplementary collection, 8:6b, instructions to Chu Hsi's eldest son, Shu (Shou-chih).

8. *Ibid.,* regular collection, 1:19a, 22a.

9. *Ibid.*, 3:13a.

10. *Ibid.*

11. *Ibid.*, 2:19a.

12. *Ibid.*, 8:9a.

13. *Ibid.*, 9:4b.

14. *Ibid.*, 2:8a.

15. *Ibid.*, 5:16b.

16. *Ibid.*, 2:2a.

17. *Ibid.*, 5:14a.

18. *Ibid.*, 1:7a.

19. *Ibid.*, 5:15b.

20. *Ibid.*, 6:19b.

21. *Ibid.*, 5:6a.

22. *Ibid.*, 5:7b.

23. *Ibid.*, 1:22a.

24. *Ibid.*, 3:13a.

25. *Ibid.*, 3:13b, 4:3a.

26. *Ibid.*, 3:3b.

27. *Ibid.*, 5:16b.

28. *Ibid.*, 5:21a.

29. *Ibid.*, 6:5a, 7:6b.

30. *Ibid.*, 4:1b.

31. *Ibid.*, 5:17b.

32. For example, *ibid.*, 1:19a, 1:22a, 4:1b, 6:7b, 6:8b, 9:14b, 10:2a.

33. *Ibid.*, 2:23a, 6:5a.

34. *Ibid.*, 6:7b.

35. *Ibid.*, 8:6a.

36. *Ibid.*, 2:2a.

37. *Ibid.*, 2:23a.

38. *Ibid.*, 5:20b.

39. *Ibid.*, separate collection, 4:4b, fifth letter to Liu Kung-fu (Liu Kung).

40. The "Wang Mei-hsi wen-chi hsü" [Preface to the collected literary works of Wang Mei Hsi] is found in *ibid.*, 75:28a–30b.

41. *Ibid.*, 5:15b.

42. *Yü-lei,* ch. 127, sec. 67 (p. 4256).

43. *Ibid.*, ch. 3, sec. 79 (p. 85).

44. Present Tao County in Hunan Province.

45. *Yü-lei,* ch. 107, sec. 24 (pp. 4245–4246).

46. *Sung shih* [History of the Sung dynasty] (Beijing: Chung-hua Book Co., 1977), ch. 444, biography of Ts'ai Yüan-ting, p. 12875.

47. *Wen-chi,* 1:19a.

48. *Ibid.*, 2:19a.

49. *Ibid.*, 5:8a.

50. Yeh Kung-hui, *Chu Tzu nien-p'u* [Chronological biography of Master Chu] (*Chin-shih han-chi ts'ung-k'an* [Chinese works of the recent period series] ed.), p. 64, under the twentieth year of Shao-hsing (1150). This episode is repeated in subsequent chronological biographies.

51. *Nan-hsüan Hsien-sheng wen-chi* [Collection of literary works of Master

Chang Shih] (*Chin-shih han-chi ts'ung-k'an* ed.), 20:11a (p. 659), eleventh letter in reply to Chu Yüan-hui (Chu Hsi).

52. *Yü-lei,* ch. 107, sec. 57 (p. 4253).

53. *Ibid.,* sec. 52 (p. 4252).

54. *Ibid.,* ch. 127, sec. 44 (p. 4892).

55. *Ibid.*

56. Present Lin-ju County in Honan Province. Ch'eng Hao was superindendent of wine in Ju-chou in 1083.

57. *Wai-shu* [Additional works], 12:7b–8a, in the *Erh-Ch'eng ch'üan-shu* [Complete works of the two Ch'engs] (*SPPY* ed.).

58. *Pei-hsi ta-ch'üan chi* [Complete collected works of Ch'en Ch'un] (*Ssu-k'u ch'uan-shu chen-pen* [Precious works of the *Complete Collection of the Four Libraries*] ed.), 17:4a, "An Account of Master Chu, Lecturer-in-waiting."

59. *Yü-lei,* ch. 26, sec. 36 (p. 1042).

60. *Ibid.,* ch. 90, sec. 42 (p. 3648).

61. *Ibid.,* (p. 3654).

62. *Book of Mencius,* 2A:6, where Mencius taught that "the feeling of commiseration is the beginning of humanity, the feeling of shame and dislike is the beginning of righteousness, the feeling of deference and compliance is the beginning of propriety, and the feeling of right and wrong is the beginning of wisdom."

63. *Yü-lei,* ch. 90, sec. 70 (p. 3667).

64. *Ibid.,* ch. 91, sec. 9 (p. 3693). Pao Yang was a follower of both Chu Hsi and Lu Hsiang-shan, but inclined more toward Lu. For Pao Yang, see my *Chu Tzu men-jen* [Master Chu's pupils] (Taipei: Student Book Co., 1982), pp. 69–70.

65. *Ibid.,* ch. 89, sec. 16 (p. 3608).

66. *Analects,* 2:10.

67. *Book of Mencius,* 44:16.

68. *Yü-lei,* ch. 24, sec. 28 (p. 924).

69. *Analects,* 15:23.

70. *Yü-lei,* ch. 118, sec. 88 (p. 4567).

71. *Ibid.,* ch. 120, sec. 126 (p. 4662).

72. *Doctrine of the Mean,* ch. 12, quoting the *Book of Odes,* ode no. 239.

73. *Yü-lei,* ch. 118, sec. 80 (p. 4565).

74. The Five Teachings are righteousness on the part of the father, affection on the part of the mother, friendliness on the part of the elder brother, respect on the part of the younger brother, and filial piety on the part of the son.

75. *Yü-lei,* ch. 115, sec. 43 (p. 4436).

76. *Ibid.,* ch. 121, sec. 106 (p. 4716).

77. Ts'ai Ch'en (1167–1230), "Chu Wen Kung meng-tien chi" [Account of Chu Hsi's death], in the *Tsai-shih chiu-ju shu* [Works of nine Confucians in the Ts'ai family] (1868 ed.), 6:59a. This account is quoted in Wang Mao-hung (1668–1741), *Chu Tzu nien-p'u* [Chronological biography of Master Chu] (*Ts'ung-shu chi-ch'eng* [Collection of series] ed.), pp. 227–229.

78. *Yü-lei,* ch. 107, sec. 50 (p. 4251).

79. For Liu Ch'un-sou, see my *Chu Tzu men-jen,* pp. 312–313.

80. *Yü-lei,* ch. 121, sec. 102 (p. 4714).

81. *Ibid.*

82. *Ibid.*, sec. 103 (p. 4715,

83. *Ibid.*, sec. 101 (pp. 4713–4714).

84. *Book of Rites,* "Jade Pendants," sec. 29, talks about how dignified the hand, the foot, the mouth, the eye, etc., should be.

85. *Ibid.*

86. *Yü-lei,* ch. 114, sec. 7 (p. 4387).

87. *Analects,* 19:9, referring to the superior man.

88. *Yü-lei,* ch. 114, sec. 23 (p. 4397).

89. *Analects,* 19:12.

90. *Yü-lei,* ch. 7, sec. 17 (p. 203).

91. *Mien-chai chi* [Collected works of Huang Kan] (*Ssu-k'u ch'üan-shu chen-pen* [Precious works of the *Complete Collection of the Four Libraries*] ed.), 36:41b, biographical account.

92. *Yü-lei,* ch. 118, sec. 85 (p. 4566).

93. We do not know who Shu-shan was.

94. *Yü-lei,* ch. 118, sec. 87 (p. 4566).

95. The prefectural capital referred to here is Chang-chou, in southern Fukien. Chu Hsi was prefect there in 1190.

96. These are the eleventh, twelfth, twenty-fourth, and twenty-third hexagrams, respectively, in the *Book of Changes.* Each consists of six continuous or broken lines in various combinations.

97. The Nine Categories are given in the "Great Norm" chapter of the *Book of History.* The first category is the Five Agents (Five Elements), namely, Water, Fire, Wood, Metal, and Earth; and the second category is the Five Activities, namely, appearance, speech, seeing, hearing, and thinking; etc.

98. The Eight Trigrams have been ascribed to the mythical emperor Fu-hsi, who designed eight figures of three continuous or broken lines to represent the various elements of the cosmos.

99. This refers to the Nine Fields of antiquity. Little is known about them. According to one theory, there were books on these fields, now lost.

100. The Eight Strategic Positions are supposed to have been arranged by the mythical Yellow Emperor. Chu-ko Liang (181–234) applied them and made them famous.

101. *Yü-lei,* ch. 106, sec. 35 (p. 4217).

102. *Ibid.*, ch. 138, sec. 55 (p. 5275).

103. Mo Ti, or Mo Tzu, was the founder of the Mo School. For his debate with Kung-shu, see the *Mo Tzu,* ch. 50.

104. Kung-shu Ch'iao refers to Kung-shu Pan, a contemporary of Confucius, native of Lu, and famous mechanist worshiped by Chinese carpenters as their patron deity. Here Chu Hsi or the pupil who recorded the conversation used the character *kung* (skill) for another character *kung* (duke) in Kung-shu's name, and called his private name *ch'iao* (skill), probably thinking of Mencius' praise of Kung-shu's skill in the *Book of Mencius,* 4A:1.

105. *Yü-lei,* ch. 138, sec. 144 (pp. 5292–5293).

106. *Wen-chi,* 9:14a. For the three pupils, see my *Chu Tzu men-jen,* pp. 80, 241, 310.

107. *Yü-lei,* ch. 66, sec. 20 (pp. 2592–2593).

108. Ch'üan-chou Prefecture, in southern Fukien, was called Wen-ling because its climate was warm *(wen)*.

109. *Yü-lei,* ch. 112, sec. 58 (p. 4358).

110. *Wen-chi,* 86:6a.

111. *Ibid.,* supplementary collection, 1:12a, fortieth letter in reply to Huang Chih-ch'ing (Huang Kan).

112. See ch. 3 above, pp. 39–40, for more details about this painting.

# – 7 –

# Memory, Dreams, Divination, and Popular Beliefs

THE preceding chapter dealt with Chu Hsi's emotions; this one will be devoted to his intellect. Put differently, the last chapter focused on how Chu Hsi felt, whereas this chapter examines how his mind worked. Neither is systematic or comprehensive, for we are not engaged in an encyclopedic or textbook presentation but in an investigation of areas hitherto unexplored. Chu Hsi talked so much about divination that one might think he practiced it all the time, yet there are surprisingly few instances of this on record. On the contrary, he seems to have used myriad historical facts and written records to guide his thinking and actions, and his memory for these was truly phenomenal.

## Memory

The *Yü-lei* consists of 140 chapters, in which about four thousand conversations between Chu Hsi and his pupils are recorded. Except for a few cases when students presented written questions and the Teacher gave written replies, the questions and responses occurred at random. In his answers, Chu Hsi quoted or referred to the classics or to historical events more than ten thousand times, always from memory. It is true that in the old educational system, students were required to memorize the Four Books[1] and the Five Classics.[2] But Chu Hsi cited many more classics, histories, books of philosophy and collections—including dates, measurements, and a thousand or so poetic lines—all in response to any question on any subject. It is amazing that he could draw on these resources from memory. Most of the conversations were impromptu affairs in the evening, when one or more pupils happened to visit him together. Obviously, there was no opportunity to check his sources, even assuming he had them on hand. The *Yü-lei* records only one instance of Chu Hsi consulting an original text. During one of several conversations concerning Yin T'un's (Yin Ho-ching, 1071–1142) commentary on the *Analects,* Chu Hsi asked Ching-chih (Huang Hsien-tzu) to bring him the *Ho-ching yü-lu* (Recorded sayings of Yin T'un) to consult.[3] As far as I know, all Chu Hsi's other references to or citations of various works were made off the cuff.

Chu Hsi wrote a great deal. His writings were often copied for circulation, to send to friends for comments or in answer to questions. Sometimes his son Shu[4] or others[5] copied for him. Ordinarily he hired a professional copyist, but because of poverty he could not always do so.[6] Occasionally he had to do the proofreading himself,[7] and he often complained that he could not get anyone to copy his work[8] or that he himself had no time to do so.[9] These cases usually concerned his correspondence rather than casual conversations. Yet if he often had difficulty getting someone to copy his writings for him, it is logical to conclude that he would also have had difficulty finding people to check sources for him, whether for his writings or his conversations with pupils and friends.

Because he had no chance to check his sources, Chu Hsi did make mistakes. "The Principle of Heaven is the product of my personal realization" is a well-known saying by Ch'eng Hao (1032–1085). Chu Hsi surely knew it well, but on one occasion he attributed it to Ch'eng I (1033–1107),[10] possibly by mistake, or perhaps because he assumed the idea was shared by both brothers, as was true in most cases. Another time, he quoted Tung Chung-shu's (176–104 B.C.) saying as "Human nature is simple substance. It cannot be perfected *(ch'eng)* without education," and went on to criticize Tung for the word *ch'eng,* which he called "utterly injurious to principle."[11] If Chu Hsi had checked Tung's *Ch'un-ch'iu fan-lu* (Luxuriant gems of the *Spring and Autumn Annals),* he would have found that *ch'eng* does not appear in the sentence in question, which says, "Nature is the simple material of heavenly substance, while goodness is the transformation of kingly instruction."[12] Although Chu Hsi had not altered Tung's meaning, he would not have concentrated on the word *ch'eng* if he had checked the text. Perhaps we should not take such a mistake too seriously, for Chu Hsi was thinking of Tung's doctrine, not his literal expression.

In his *Chu Tzu ssu-shu chi-chu tien-chü k'ao* (Investigation into the textual evidence of Master Chu's *Collected Commentaries on the Four Books),* Ōtsuki Nobuyoshi has pointed out 175 places where Chu Hsi gave new interpretations in his commentaries. His general conclusion is that Chu Hsi was very original. But he also mentions that Chu Hsi mistook the *K'ung Tzu chia-yü* (School sayings of Confucius) for the *Shuo-yüan* (Collection of discourses); the chapter on funeral ceremonies of the *I-li* (Book of ceremonial) for its chapter on "Having done the evening [wailing]"; the sayings of Fan Tsu-yü (1041–1098) for those of Hsieh Liang-tso (1050–c. 1120); and the agriculturists in the *Shih chi* (Historical records) for the agriculturists in the *Han shu* (History of the Han dynasty).[13] There are also cases where mistakes were made by those who recorded Chu Hsi's conversations. For instance, in one place it is noted that "the Master mentioned his name, but it is now forgotten."[14] In another, Chu Hsi is said to have remarked that the Chin people "hunted along the Yalu River and in the summer went to a mountain," but the recorder adds that "the name has been forgotten."[15] Clearly it was the recorder, not Chu Hsi, who did not remember the name of the mountain. When Ch'eng I is quoted as saying, "The sage has no beginning, and therefore his mind cannot be seen," the note says, "This is meaningless. There must be a mistake."[16] Undoubtedly the mistake was made by the recorder rather than Chu Hsi.

In some cases there seems to be a mistake but in reality there is none. For example, Chu Hsi attributed the saying, "Talk about nature and not about material force is incomplete, and talk about material force but not about nature is unintelligible,"[17] to Ch'eng Hao and also to Ch'eng I.[18] This was not a lapse in memory, because the brothers did share the same ideas. When Chu Hsi simply referred to "Master Ch'eng," without specifying which brother he meant, he was not being indefinite or vague but was conscious of this fact.[19] The same is true of his understanding of the explanation of righteousness and profit on the part of Su the father and Su the son. On the one hand he regarded the theory that profit is the harmonization of what is right as the doctrine of Su Shih (1037–1101),[20] but on the other hand he ascribed it to Shih's father, Hsün (1009–1066).[21] There is no contradiction here because the doctrine was common to both father and son. Chu Hsi was thoroughly aware of this, for he said, "The senior Su held that righteousness is too strong to be peaceful; only with profit in it can it be peaceful. That is nonsense. . . . Later, Tung-p'o [Su Shih] also applied this doctrine in his commentary on the *Book of Changes*. The nonsense is even worse."[22]

In cases where Chu Hsi committed no error but merely failed to recall a detail, he used expressions like "such-and-such a prince,"[23] "such-and-such a king,"[24] "such-and-such a scripture,"[25] or "Kuei-shan [Yang Shih, 1053–1135] wrote the "Yang-hao-t'ang chi" [Account of the Hall of Nourishing the Strong Moving Power] for so-and-so."[26] In such cases, Chu Hsi may either have forgotten the name or considered it not important enough to specify. Once he said, "So-and-so recorded that whenever Liu Yüan-ch'eng [Liu An-shih, 1048–1125] met people, he engaged in very little conversation during the visit." At first glance, it seems that Chu Hsi could not remember the name of the recorder. However, Chu Hsi added that in fact "Yüan-ch'eng was unrestrained in conversation and had no scruples about anything at all."[27] He may have purposely omitted the name of the recorder in order not to embarrass him with this contradiction. He was frank to admit it when he actually forgot something. In discussing Lü Tsu-ch'ien's (1137–1181) five rules for selecting essays for his *Wen-chien* (Mirror of literature), Chu Hsi mentioned four rules and then said honestly, "I have forgotten one of the rules."[28] And in the *Wen-chi*, in a letter to Liu Ch'ing-chih (1139–1195), he said, "I have forgotten Mr. Chu Ts'en's courtesy name. Please let me know."[29]

Mistakes or lapses of memory such as those just mentioned are very few. Given the more than ten thousand conversations recorded in the *Yü-lei* and *Wen-chi*, this small number tends to indicate that they are the exception rather than the rule. Moreover, there are many cases that show Chu Hsi's remarkable memory for details. He could state specifically that there were 175 soldiers for every 15 military vehicles in the state of Ch'u,[30] and that Prince Shen-sheng's military expedition took place in the twelfth month of the second year of Duke Min's rule (660 B.C.).[31] He remembered very clearly, too, that in the state of Chin the ancestral tablet for a noble of low rank was 1.2 inches high and 4.5 inches wide.[32] Nor was Chu Hsi guessing when he said that the diameter of an ancient carriage was 6 feet.[33] When Yü Ta-ya visited him, he immediately said, "It has been three years since we have seen each other. How have you been?"[34] This was not the only time he remembered how long it had been since he had seen a pupil or a friend. In discussing Buddhist scriptures, the recorder of the conversation added a note that says, "The Master cited their chapter numbers in great detail, too numerous to be recorded here."[35] When Chu Hsi explained a certain poem in the *Book of Odes,* he summarized the central ideas in each verse.[36] When he answered questions on his *Lun-yü chi-chu* (Collected commentaries on the *Analects*), he cited from five to nine interpretations for each chapter, in each case giving the name of whoever advocated the theory.[37]

The most amazing case is his quotation of Su Hsün's essay. In instructing his pupil Ch'eng Tuan-meng (1143–1191), Chu Hsi said,

I have seen that the senior Su said that, "When I read the *Book of Mencius,* the *Analects,* the *Han Fei Tzu,* and the works of other sages, I sat straight rigidly and read all day for eighteen years. In the beginning, when I entered into the matter, I was apprehensive. As I looked extensively to the outside, I was startled and afraid. After I had read for a long time, I became more and more refined and the understanding in my mind became wide and far-reaching. I felt that people's words should be like these, but I still dared not utter them myself. Eventually, [the words] I wanted to say increased every day. As I could not control myself, I gave it a try and wrote them down. After having read them two or three times, they seemed to have arrived easily well blended in one piece."[38]

The whole passage must have come from memory, for it is most unlikely that Su Hsün's *Chia-yu chi* (Collected works of the Chia-yu period; 1056–1063) was readily available for Chu Hsi to consult. If one compares the passages he recited to the original in the *Chia-yu chi*,[39] one finds that Chu Hsi was faithful almost to the letter. The only difference is that in the original, the *Analects* precedes the *Book of Mencius* and there is the word *erh* (and) before "rigidly." Also, the original has "seven or eight years" instead of "eighteen years," so the latter is obviously a misprint. There is no doubt, therefore, that Chu Hsi recited the passage, as recorded, from memory, for if an editor had later checked it against the original, he would have added *erh* and put the *Analects* and the *Book of Mencius* in proper order. It was not unusual for a scholar to quote the classics extensively from memory, but to quote Su Hsün at such length shows that Chu Hsi had a memory of which few people can boast.

## Dreams

Material on Chu Hsi in relation to dreams is extremely rare. Fortunately, there is enough to show that even in this matter his philosophy of principle is predominant. According to the *Yü-lei,*

> Tou [Tou Ts'ung-chou][40] said of himself that dreams had him confused. The Master said, "*Hun* [the heavenly component of the soul] and *p'o* [the earthly component] interact to constitute sleep. The mind is still there and can think as usual. That is how dreams come about." Thereupon Chu Hsi said of himself that in the several days when he was sick, he only dreamed about explaining the *Book of History,* and formerly, in an official place, he only dreamed of deciding on legal cases. Tou said, "These are still daily affairs." The Master said, "Though these are daily affairs, still they should not appear in dreams."[41]

This conversation was recorded by Liao Te-ming after 1173. We do not know the exact year, but since Tou and his younger brother went to Chien-yang to study with Chu Hsi in 1186, this conversation must have taken place in Chu Hsi's later years.

Lo Ta-ching of the Southern Sung (1127–1279) wrote in his *Ho-lin yü-lu* (Jade-like dew from the forest of cranes) an anecdote concerning Chu Hsi as follows:

> Liao Te-ming was an outstanding pupil of Chu Wen Kung [Chu Hsi]. When he was young, he dreamed of going to an audience with the emperor. The receptionist came out and asked for his calling card. When he took one out of his sleeve, he found it was inscribed *hsüan-chiao-lang* [dignitary for propagation of teachings].[42] Later, when he passed the civil service examination and was awarded a title, he was appointed an official

in Fukien with the rank of *hsüan-chiao-lang*. Recalling his earlier dream, he was afraid that his official career would end in this rank and was unwilling to accept the appointment. He went to Wen Kung for advice. Wen Kung said, "A man is different from articles. Take a pen. It can only be a pen and cannot be an ink-slab. A sword can only be a sword and cannot be a lute. Each has an unalterable course from the time of its formation to its destruction. Man is different. His mind is unobstructed and intelligent and embodies all principles. Blessing and catastrophe, fortune and misfortune vary according to it, and it is difficult to predict a definite course. When you go to take office, you should only enrich and expand your moral nature and vigorously pursue good work. Your earlier dream is not worth bothering about." Te-ming accepted the instruction with a bow. From then on, he rose in his career and achieved a correct [higher] rank.[43]

Te-ming's courtesy name was Tzu-hui. He was a native of Shun-ch'ang County in Fukien and obtained a *chin-shih* (presented scholar) degree in 1169.[44] There are thirty sections in chapter 123 of the *Yü-lei* about the Master's instructions to him, but no reference to the dream, although such a dream is most likely. In any case, Chu Hsi's reliance on moral principles and not dreams is obvious.

Another section of the *Yü-lei* says,

Upon talking about dreams, the Master said, "The Sage [Confucius] practiced seriousness (*ching*, reverence) at all times. He practiced seriousness even in small, unimportant things. Only later Confucians began to talk big and got nowhere. In the *Chou-li* [Rites of Chou] there is an official in charge of dreams.[45] What importance does a dream have? Nevertheless, the Sage regarded it as an affair. Throughout my life, I have often dreamed of old friends and relatives. If on the following day I did not receive a letter from them or see them, inevitably other people would talk about them. As I see it, these are correct dreams. The rest are all incorrect.[46]

Chu Hsi did not continue to explain what makes dreams correct or incorrect, but moral principles would no doubt have been his criteria.

## Divination

If Chu Hsi did not rely on dreams to guide his thoughts and actions, did he rely on divination? He wrote the *Chou-i pen-i* (Original meanings of the *Book of Changes*) and the *I-hsüeh ch'i-meng* (Study of the *Book of Changes*). In addition, more of Chu Hsi's recorded conversations concern this classic than any other except the *Analects*. In addition, of the 622 sections in the *Chin-ssu lu* (Reflections on things at hand), compiled by Chu Hsi and Lü Tsu-ch'ien, 106 come from Ch'eng I's *I chuan*

(Commentary of the *Book of Changes*). Finally, to Chu Hsi the *Book of Changes* was primarily for divination. Thus the importance of divination to him is perfectly clear. This being the case, he ought to have practiced it frequently throughout his life, as was the custom of intellectuals and peasants alike. Yet only two occasions connecting him to divination have been recorded. Can we assume that divination was so common, like eating and sleeping, that no mention of it needed to be made? First of all, we must examine the two cases.

As Huang Kan (1152–1221) wrote in his "Chu Tzu hsing-chuang" (Biographical account of Master Chu),

> The Master greatly worried that Han T'o-chou [d. 1207] wielded all power in his own hands. He had repeatedly spoken to the emperor [about this]. In addition, he personally wrote several letters and sent his pupils secretly to make it clear to the prime minister [Chao Ju-yü, 1140–1196] to reward Han substantially but not allow him to participate in the government. . . . After the prime minister was expelled, governmental power rested entirely with T'o-chou. The Master thought to himself that although he had retired from government, he still held a title and should not remain silent. Thereupon [in 1195] he drafted a memorial of more than ten thousand words to point out the danger of treacherous officials deceiving the emperor, thereby exposing the injustice done to the prime minister. The tone of the memorial was exceedingly bitter. The pupils took turns appealing to him to have the matter decided by means of divination. The result was the thirty-third hexagram, *tun* [retirement], changing to the thirteenth hexagram, *t'ung-jen* [companionship]. The Master withdrew in silence, burned the draft of his memorial, and called himself Tun-weng [Old man in retirement].[47]

This was in 1195.

The account in the various chronological biographies *(nien-p'u)* is slightly different. According to Yeh Kung-hui's chronological biography of 1431, the earliest *nien-p'u* in existence, Chu Hsi's draft memorial consisted of several tens of thousands of words, and it was Ts'ai Yüan-ting (1135–1198) who suggested the divination.[48] This account was repeated both in Tai Hsien's (d. 1508) *Nien-p'u*[49] and in Wang Mao-hung's (1668–1741),[50] but they state that the result was the *tun* hexagram changing to the thirty-seventh hexagram, *chia-jen* (family), instead of *t'ung-jen*. Whether the draft memorial was "more than ten thousand words" or "tens of thousands of words" is irrelevant, and whether one or more pupils urged divination is immaterial, for they did not affect Chu Hsi's decision. However, whether the hexagram changed to "family" or "companionship" is important, because it was this that led to Chu Hsi's decision to burn the draft of his memorial. The matter therefore requires some scrutiny.

To this day, scholars are almost evenly divided as to whether the variation was *chia-jen* or *t'ung-jen*. In his annotation of Huang Kan's "Hsing-chuang," the leading Korean Neo-Confucian, Yi Hwang (Yi T'oegye, 1501–1570), accepted *t'ung-jen*.[51] The *Sung shih chi-shih pen-mo* (Full account of the factual records of the *History of the Sung Dynasty*) also used *t'ung-jen*.[52] So have a number of Chinese and Japanese scholars, including Ch'ien Mu[53] and Yasuoka Masahiro.[54] On the other side, in addition to Tai Hsien and Wang Mao-hung, Chou Yü-t'ung,[55] Gotō Toshimizu (1892–1961),[56] Satō Hitoshi,[57] and Chang Li-wen[58] have all followed Wang Mao-hung and used *chia-jen*. I believe Wang is correct. Wang wrote,

> The *Nien-p'u* says that the result was the *tun* hexagram changing to *t'ung-jen*. The "Hsing-chuang" says the same. But in the separate collection [of the *Wen-chi,* Chu Hsi's] letter in reply to Liu Te-hsiu says, 'The result was *tun* changing to *chia-jen,* being the divination of the bottom, divided line of *tun* and the "good to retire" of the fourth, undivided line from the bottom.'[59] If the variation was *t'ung-jen,* the divination would only affect the bottom line of *tun.* Both the *Nien-p'u* and the "Hsing-chuang" probably made the mistake on the basis of hearsay. I have now corrected them.[60]

In the *Wen-chi* there is also a letter from Chu Hsi to Vice Minister Chang that says, "Several days ago, I divined according to the *Book of Changes* and happened to find the bottom line of the hexagram *tun.* Since this has been revealed in divination, what can they do to me? What is the use of escaping from it?"[61] Wang did not quote this letter, nor have other writers referred to it. When the bottom line of the *tun* hexagram, which is divided, changes into an undivided line, the hexagram becomes that of *t'ung-jen.* The *t'ung-jen* in Yeh Kung-hui's chronological biography may be based on this letter.

Wang Mao-hung said, however, that if the variation had been *t'ung-jen,* the divination would have affected only the bottom line of *tun.* The explanation of the bottom line of *tun* says, "This divided line shows a retiring tail. The situation is dangerous. No movement in any direction should be made." Its abstract meaning is that "if no movement be made, what disaster can there be?" Wang's contention that the variation was actually *chia-jen* can be understood only in connection with the phrase "good to retire." "Good to retire" refers to the fourth line from the bottom, for which the explanation is, "Good to retire means that in a superior man, this will lead to good fortune, and in the inferior man, this will lead to misfortune." When the bottom line of *tun* changes from a divided to an undivided line and the fourth line changes from an undivided line to a divided line, the hexagram becomes *chia-jen.* Thus Wang Mao-hung was right in his contention that if the relationship is that of *chia-jen,* or family, harmony must be preserved. Hence Chu Hsi's retirement.

Nevertheless, Wang's statement that the mistake in the chronological biography he consulted and in Huang Kan's biographical account is a product of hearsay is not entirely convincing. Tai Hsien's *Nien-p'u* was not available to Wang. Had he consulted Tai's work, he would not have considered the mistake in the *Nien-p'u* to be due to hearsay. As for the theory that Huang Kan heard the wrong story, I have my doubts. After all, the divination dealt with a crisis, and there were several pupils on the scene. When the story was transmitted from mouth to mouth, it must have been conveyed with great seriousness, and I doubt very much that *chia-jen* was twisted into *t'ung-jen.* It is more likely that the mistake was made when Huang Kan's "Hsing-chuang" was copied, and was then perpetuated in the *Nien-p'u.* There are certainly mistakes in the "Hsing-chuang." For example, it says that Chu Hsi's wife died in the *ting-yu* year of the Ch'ien-tao period (1165–1173).[62] But there was no *ting-yu* year in that period, and in fact Chu Hsi's wife died in 1176.

Regardless of whether the divination revealed the hexagram for "family" or that for "companionship," would Chu Hsi's subsequent actions have been any different? According to the various chronological biographies, pupils pleaded with Chu Hsi not to present his memorial, saying that it would lead to catastrophe, but he refused to listen. At that point Ts'ai Yüan-ting asked that the matter be decided by divination. What is significant about the episode is that Chu Hsi did not take the initiative to divine. In the final analysis, whether the divination actually affected his decision to burn his draft memorial must remain unknown to everyone but himself.

The second divination took place two years later, in 1197. In the *Yü-lei,* we are told that

> Chi-t'ung [Ts'ai Yüan-ting] was about to be banished, and Court officials said the Master would also be punished. After the Master finished his meal, he came downstairs, walked to the west several times, and then sat down cross-legged. Ho-sun [Yeh Wei-tao, 1220 *cs*] withdrew and returned to the *ching-she* [Bamboo Grove Study] to tell his fellow pupils. Han-ch'ing [Fu Kuang] divined and got the [sixty-second] hexagram, *hsiao-kuo* [slight excess]. [The explanation of its fifth line from the bottom says,] "The prince shoots his arrow and takes the bird in a cave." He said, "There will be no danger to our Master, but Ts'ai will be hurt." He forthwith went downstairs with his younger brother Wan. The Master was seated and sleeping soundly but awoke at the noise made by his pupils and immediately bowed to them. When they asked about the matter concerning Venerable Ts'ai, he said, "The counties and prefectures are searching for him urgently [with the intention to] arrest him. I do not know what crime he has committed." Thereupon he explained in detail to Cheng-ch'un [Wan

Jen-chieh] the points about the *Book of Mencius* that Wan had asked him
about that morning but had failed to understand.[63]

The upshot was that Ts'ai was banished to Tao-chou[64] in an attempt to
intimidate Chu Hsi, and died in Heng-chou on his way to Tao-chou.

As in the first divination, it was not Chu Hsi who took the initiative
in this case; indeed, he was not even present. But this time the purpose
of the divination was not merely to offer a course of action but to foretell
fortune or misfortune. We do not know whether or not Chu Hsi held
this belief. The fact that he immediately began to discuss the *Book of
Mencius* may indicate that he was nonchalant about it. We do know that
he was definitely opposed to divination as a way of foretelling future
events. When asked whether it was true that divination could foretell
events several generations in the future, as reported in the *Tso chuan*
(Tso's commentary), he answered, "This is impossible. Only when
descendants wanted to usurp and steal offices did they manufacture this
[idea] to cheat their superiors and deceive their inferiors."[65] He also
said, "The *ch'i* [material force] of the *ch'ien* [Heaven, male] hexagram is
strongest in the fourth month, and that of the *k'un* [Earth, female] hexagram in the tenth month. One should not say that people born in these
months are all good."[66]

So far as we know, Chu Hsi also swore only once. According to the
*Yü-lei,* Chu Hsi said, "If a single word of my commentary on this paragraph has violated Mencius' ideas, may Heaven reject me."[67] The
paragraph in question is the *Book of Mencius* 2A:2, on the "strong, moving power" *(hao-jan chih ch'i).* This is what Chu Hsi's commentary says:

> *Hao-jan* means strong and great operation, and *ch'i* [material or vital force]
> is that which pervades and animates the body. Originally, it is strong and
> moving; it becomes weak through lack of nourishment. Mencius alone
> knew how to nourish it skillfully to restore it to its original state. For only
> when one knows words can one understand moral principles and be free
> from doubt about affairs in the world, and only when one nourishes the
> *ch'i* can one accompany it by moral principles and be free from fear about
> things in the world. This is how one can take up great responsibility and
> yet maintain an undisturbed mind. . . . Exceedingly great, it is limitless,
> and exceedingly strong, it cannot be twisted. It is the correct *ch'i* of
> Heaven and Earth which man receives for his life. It is so in whole or in
> part.[68]

## Popular Beliefs

Chu Hsi's attitude was basically rationalistic, but he was not immune to
popular practices and beliefs. His attitude toward strange phenomena
follows the tradition of Ch'eng I, who explained all phenomena in terms

of principle. Ch'eng I even dismissed Po-yu, a ghost who allegedly would spread the word that he was going to kill people,[69] as "a special principle."[70] For example, Chu Hsi refused to believe that eclipses were omens of disaster. To him, an eclipse of the sun or moon was due to a decline of the yang or yin *ch'i* (active or passive cosmic material force), and any such deviation could be calculated. As he saw it, ancient people viewed eclipses as premonitions due to their ignorance about the calendar.[71] Similarly, he thought thunder was merely *ch'i,* like firecrackers. "When the force is contracted to the extreme, it has to explode."[72] But he also said, "Although thunder is merely *ch'i,* because there is *ch'i* there must be physical shape. Take a rainbow. It is a group of small raindrops with the sun shining upon them, thus forming their image. Because a rainbow has physical shape, it can suck in water or wine. When a family has it, it can be monstrous or auspicious."[73] It can be argued that what is monstrous or auspicious is so to the family, but to say that a rainbow can absorb water or wine borders on belief in monstrosity. Nevertheless, in his explanation of thunder, Chu Hsi followed the rationalistic line. In commenting on the noise of thunder in the tenth month, he said, "I am afraid it is a case of the material force of yang being aroused, and therefore the heavy snow is a good omen for rich harvest. The snow is not the cause of the rich harvest, but it congeals the yang force on the ground. In the coming year it develops and produces all things."[74] An omen is, after all, a matter of principle.

Ch'eng I thought that hail was produced by lizards spitting water.[75] To Chu Hsi, "At first, there is probably no such principle, but on closer examination there is, except that it is incorrect to say that hailstones are completely the product of lizards."[76] Clearly he believed that lizards could produce hail, but he added that "we don't know what the principle is. If the Creator used this creature to produce hail, the Creator would be insignificant."[77] In Chu Hsi's view, since the character *pao* (hail) consists of the character *yü* (rain) and the character *pao* (to wrap), "What makes hail is that the material force wraps around [rain]."[78] Moreover, according to Chu Hsi, the lizard resembles the dragon in shape and belongs to yin. When this material force is affected and responds, the result is hail.[79] Popular folklore held that the dragon produces rain. On this, Chu Hsi said, "The dragon is a water animal. When it emerges and interacts with the active cosmic material force to produce humidity, there is rain. Ordinarily, however, rain comes from the dampness of the interaction of yin and yang; it is not necessarily produced by the dragon."[80] Thus Chu Hsi explained both hail and rain in terms of yin and yang. Yet he still believed in dragons, saying that their eyes shone like bronze plates.[81] He also believed in unicorns. He expressed doubt that the unicorn had influenced Confucius' writing of the *Spring and Autumn Annals,* or that the completion of the *Annals* had

influenced the appearance of the unicorn. But he did say that the unicorn appeared at the wrong time, was killed, and that this was an evil
omen.[82] While his skeptical spirit is impressive, he nevertheless believed
not only in the unicorn but also in its appearance as an omen.

Although Chu Hsi was not completely free from traditional popular
beliefs in strange phenomena, he did tend to be more rational than
Ch'eng I, in that he interpreted most abnormal occurrences in terms of
yin and yang. A will-o'-the-wisp, for example, was to him merely material force that had not yet dispersed.[83] So was the Buddha-lamp. As we
read in the *Yü-lei,*

> What common people call a Buddha-lamp is light emitted because the
> material force is very strong. It may be precious material force or it may
> be the light of flying insects or rotten leaves. . . . Formerly, someone put
> some light in a box. When he looked inside the next day, there were only
> rotten leaves. . . . Formerly, someone followed Wang Sheng-hsi [Wang
> Ying-ch'en, 1118–1176] to O-mei Mountain. When he looked around at
> the beginning of the fifth watch [about 4:00 a.m.], he saw a spread of
> white air. Gradually it became round with a reflection like a mirror. In it
> was the image of the Buddha. As the man folded his head-scarf with his
> hand, the Buddha in the reflection also folded his head-scarf. He then real-
> ized that it was the reflection of himself.[84]

Among Buddhist beliefs, Chu Hsi objected most vigorously to the
doctrine of transmigration. To him, "The doctrines of 'stealing a
fetus'[85] and 'grabbing the blessing'[86] are all lies."[87] According to his
reasoning, "The Buddhists say that after a man dies he becomes a
ghost, and the ghost in turn becomes a man. If this were the case, the
world would always have so many people coming and going. There
would be no creation, and neither production nor reproduction. This is
absolutely unreasonable."[88] Since he did not believe in transmigration,
neither did he believe in the Taoist idea of everlasting life. According
to him,

> People say that immortals do not die. It is not true that they do not die,
> but they gradually dissolve without being conscious of it. They can refine
> through alchemy their vital force *(ch'i)* and physical shape in such a way
> that the rudiments all disappear and only the clear and unobstructed *ch'i*
> remains. Consequently, they can rise high up and transform themselves.
> . . . But in time the *ch'i* will have to dissipate. For example, the immortals
> the people talked about in the Ch'in [221–206 B.C.] and Han [206 B.C.–
> A.D. 220] periods no longer appear.[89]

When a pupil asked if there were immortals, Chu Hsi answered, "Who
can say there aren't? There is truly this principle, but the effort

involved is generally difficult."[90] Again Chu Hsi's explanation is based on the theory of *ch'i*, which, in its purity, can rise up and transform itself. As for Buddhist followers who prayed to ascend to Heaven, to Chu Hsi they were merely witches who tried to fool people.[91] Tradition regarded Lord Wu-i as an immortal, but to Chu Hsi he was "a recluse admired by people, and regarded as an immortal after his death."[92] In short, "One should not say that there are no immortals, but even if there are, what is the mystery about them? They have nothing to do with us. Why should we bother about them?"[93] As Confucius taught, "Devote yourself earnestly to the duties due to men, and respect spiritual beings but keep them at a distance."[94]

Chu Hsi also explained what folklore called a wronged soul or possession by a ghost in terms of *ch'i*. He said,

> Eighty percent of what common folk say is nonsense, but twenty percent is true. In most of these cases, a person's life span was not up when he was drowned or killed, or died of a sudden illness. Since his *ch'i* is not yet exhausted, he can therefore possess people. There are also cases where a person dies suddenly and his *ch'i* has not yet completely dissipated. That is due to the richness of his original endowment, but eventually the *ch'i* will disperse, for essence and *ch'i* are combined to produce man and things. Since "The wandering away of spirit becomes change,"[95] there will be no more *ch'i*. For instance, people talk about immortals. But they only talk about immortals of the recent period, and immortals of antiquity are no longer to be seen. The *Tso chuan* [Tso's commentary] tells us the story of Po-yu doing violence, but we no longer see his ghost today."[96]

According to the account in the *Tso chuan,* Tzu-ch'an (d. 496 B.C.) later adopted someone as his heir, thus pacifying the wronged soul Po-yu, so that the *ch'i* of injustice evaporated. Chu Hsi gave two instances that may be good illustrations of this explanation. When he was prefect in Chang-chou, a woman and her lover murdered her husband. The murdered man's *ch'i* of injustice did not disperse and his ghost haunted people. After the woman and her lover were tried and executed, the haunting stopped.[97] In another case, a ghost was doing violence in a certain locality. After people used explosives to destroy the tree on which the ghost depended, the violence ceased. As Chu Hsi understood it, the force of an unjust death had not dispersed until the explosive shocked it into dispersion.[98] Like thunder, hail, and rainbows, he believed that the ghosts of human beings would eventually dissipate.[99]

Material force, of course, affects ghosts, but it affects human beings even more. According to Chu Hsi, people who have pig's hair on their chests or who make noises like a pig in their sleep are endowed with the *ch'i* of a pig.[100] It was also claimed that when ignorant people prayed as a group, a deity would show his spiritual efficacy. As Chu Hsi explained it, "When the minds of many people are concentrated on one spot, there is naturally warmth, and consequently there is the principle of the spirit. This is why in religious sacrifices flesh and blood are often used. The purpose is to utilize their *ch'i* of life."[101]

The basic principle underlying all this is the Confucian doctrine of one *ch'i* operating in the entire universe, and thus affecting the influence and response among all things. Although Chu Hsi's own philosophy was based on principle, he was careful to add that principle can never be detached from *ch'i*. But the extent to which this influence and response among things actually operates is unclear in his thinking, especially in regard to human action. Once he remarked, "Yüan-shan [Chan T'i-jen, 1143–1206] loved to calculate *ch'i* and talk about prophecy. This is unreliable. Everything depends on the Mandate of Heaven, but it also depends on human effort. As soon as there is a thing, man should try to understand it, that is all."[102] By this he meant that one should cultivate one's moral life and leave everything to Heaven. There is no need to talk about fate or to engage in fortune-telling. When one's energy is exerted, there will be a result. Thus it depends on man's effort.[103]

Despite this rationalism, Chu Hsi also seems to have believed in superstitions. In a letter to Ts'ai Yüan-ting he said, "I happened to go to your house and learned that there was a newborn son there that day. I was very happy. My declining and crude steps usually bring bad luck. Ever since the age of thirty or so, whenever I have reached someone's home, the newborn baby has turned out to be a girl. This happened in several places. Only this year, happily, has it been a boy."[104] This seems to indicate that Chu Hsi accepted superstitions, although we find no other evidence for this belief. Ts'ai and the Master were intimate friends, so Chu Hsi's comment may have been intended merely as an interesting aside.

However, regarding Chu Hsi's eldest son Shu's (1163–1191) burial, Chang Shih (1133–1180) wrote him to say, "Has your daughter-in-law finished the burial? . . . Social custom in recent years puts great stock in the prophecy of yin-yang specialists [geomancers], but of course a superior man does not do that. What I heard may be wrong, and the harmful effect that can develop from such a prophecy may be exaggerated. Please think the matter over."[105] Chang Shih's reaction must have been based on the report that Chu Hsi was waiting for a geomancer to make the decision. In fact, in a letter to Ch'en Liang (1143–1194), Chu Hsi virtually said so: "In the matter of the burial of my late son, a cemetery has been found. But a yin-yang specialist said the burial should not take place until the summer of next year. The coffin is now in the funeral home by the grave."[106] Could it be that the decision was made by his daughter-in-law, and that Chu Hsi gave his approval in deference to her? There seems to be evidence to support such a contention, as the next case will show.

Chu Hsi's pupil Hu Yung wrote to ask him whether to divine for an auspicious day and a place of good fortune for the burial of his father. In reply, Chu Hsi said, "Master I-ch'uan [Ch'eng I] vigorously demolished popular beliefs, but at the same time said that a place should be selected [for burial] where the wind is favorable and the land rich. This being the case, the site should have a good contour, with the terrain embracing the grave as if with folded hands, and there should be no empty spot. But one should not follow the advice of a geomancer."[107] Moreover, there is a conversation in the *Yü-lei* that proves that Chu Hsi did not believe in fortune or misfortune in the selection of a site but in its natural qualities instead. When pupils maintained that a certain temple had spiritual efficacy, he responded, "Yang-shan Temple is extremely magnificent. This is because through divination an excellent spot among mountains and rivers was found. The shrine at the back of the temple is both secluded and quiet. The foundation of the temple is at the edge of the mountain. Though the mountain is small, its range begins at a great distance. When the range reaches the edge of this stream, all the surrounding mountains seem to pay homage to it. The foundation of the shrine is also good."[108] Here the result of the divination is interpreted in purely naturalistic, almost aesthetic terms, with no reference to good or bad fortune.

The most famous case of Chu Hsi's argument for choosing a burial site based on its natural characteristics was his debate with Court officials about where to bury Emperor Hsiao-tsung (r. 1163–1189). Despite the officials' insistence that the grave should face north, Chu Hsi argued for a place where the soil was rich, not endangered by rocks or water, and free from the risks of warfare or excavation. He was arguing not only for positive natural qualities for the site but also for permanence and peace. In the end his opposition led to his dismissal from government, but he stood his ground without regret.[109]

We are not saying that Chu Hsi was strictly rationalistic and never bowed to popular beliefs. There are two passages in the *Yü-lei* to show that he did. One says, "Our Master did not purposely differ from popular customs. Someone whose new house was not ready when the year-end was fast approaching, because the outer door had not been built, asked the Master, 'If I move in and there is a superstition, what should be done? What about using the side door?' The Master said, 'To go out the front door accords with principle. Using the side door would be contrary to custom.' "[110] Here not contradicting custom is synonymous with following popular custom. Another passage says, "The Master asked Chih-ch'ing [Huang Kan] the reason for not moving into the house. Answer: 'The outer door has not been built.' The Master said, 'There are still two more days left before the New Year. You can start work. Furthermore, if after you move into the new house there is some superstition, what will happen? The third day of the month is a "red mouth"[111] day.' "[112] These passages clearly show that Chu Hsi accepted at least some superstitions.

Although Chu Hsi was not entirely free from popular beliefs, he was advanced compared to most of his contemporaries, and even some intellectuals today. The *Book of Odes* says, "King Wen [r. 1171–1122 B.C.?] ascends and descends / On the left and the right of the Lord."[113] In explaining this poem Chu Hsi said, "If you say that King Wen was really on the left and right of the Lord-on-High, and that there is really a Lord-on-High like the sculptured image in the world, it will not do. But since the sages say so, there must be such a principle."[114] By principle Chu Hsi meant religious, not scientific principle. Religious sacrifice requires absolute sincerity on the one hand, and belief in *ch'i,* through which the sacrifice communicates, on the other. That is why Chu Hsi said, "If you say there is nothing that comes to enjoy your sacrifice, why sacrifice? What is it that is solemn above and causes people to worship in reverence and awe? But if you say that there is a deity riding on a cloud-chariot who comes, that is absurd."[115] Again he said,

Things like being killed by a deity are merely the flourishing and decline of the *ch'i* of the Five Agents.[116] If one wants to reason, there is such a principle. But people of later generations reason too minutely and too rigidly. If one understands the matter and sees through it, as Shang-ts'ai [Hsieh Liang-tso, 1050–c. 1120] said, "If I want it, there it will be. If I do not want it, there it will not be."[117] That will be all right.[118]

Another passage in the *Yü-lei* will serve as the concluding remark of this chapter. Chu Hsi said, "The principle of life and death, and spiritual beings, is certainly not what the Buddhists say or what common folk perceive. And yet there is something clearly evident, which cannot be inferred by reasoning. One must understand this type of thing."[119]

## Notes

1. The Four Books are the *Great Learning,* the *Analects,* the *Book of Mencius,* and the *Doctrine of the Mean.*

2. The Five Classics are the *Book of Odes,* the *Book of History,* the *Book of Rites,* the *Book of Changes,* and the *Spring and Autumn Annals.*

3. *Yü-lei,* 36, sec. 33 (p. 1525).

4. *Wen-chi,* separate collection, 3:5b, first letter in reply to Ch'eng Yün-fu (Ch'eng Hsün).

5. *Ibid.*, regular collection, 49:25a, fourteenth letter in reply to T'eng Te-chang (T'eng Kung).

6. *Ibid.*, 53:13a, twenty-second letter in reply to Liu Chi-chang (Liu Fu).

7. *Ibid.*, supplementary collection, 20:20b, ninety-first letter in reply to Ts'ai Chi-t'ung (Ts'ai Yüan-ting).

8. *Ibid.*, 2:21a, ninety-second letter in reply to Ts'ai Chi-t'ung; regular collection, 39:5a, first letter in reply to K'o Kuo-ts'ai (K'o Han); 63:22a, fifth letter in reply to Sun Ching-fu (Sun Tzu-hsiu); 40:31b, ninth letter in reply to Ho Shu-ching (Ho Hao); 38:30b, letter in reply to Keng Chih-chih (Keng Ping); 61:35a, fifth letter in reply to Tseng Ching-chien (Tseng Chi).

9. *Ibid.*, 62:1a, first letter in reply to Chang Yüan-te (Chang Hsia).

10. *Yü-lei,* ch. 98, sec. 64 (p. 4001).

11. *Ibid.*, ch. 125, sec. 51 (p. 4806).

12. Tung Chung-shu, *Ch'un-ch'iu fan-lu* [Luxuriant gems of the *Spring and Autumn Annals*] (*SPTK* ed.), 10:8b, treatise no. 36, "Concrete Nature."

13. Ōtsuki Nobuyoshi, *Chu Tzu ssu-shu chi-chu tien-chü k'ao* [Investigation into the textual evidence of Master Chu's *Collected Commentaries on the Four Books*] (Taipei: Student Book Co., 1976) pp. 82, 118, 164, 401.

14. *Yü-lei,* ch. 132, sec. 15 (p. 5081).

15. *Ibid.*, ch. 133, sec. 20 (p. 5123).

16. *Ibid.*, ch. 53, sec. 88 (p. 2062).

17. *I-shu* [Surviving works] 6:2a, in the *Erh-Ch'eng ch'üan-shu* [Complete works of the two Ch'engs] (*SPPY* ed).

18. Chu Hsi attributed this saying to Ch'eng I in *Yü-lei,* ch. 4, sec. 48 (p. 108) and ch. 59, sec. 42 (p. 2195), and to Ch'eng Hao in ch. 4, sec. 64 (p. 113), ch. 62, sec. 62 (p. 2370), and *Wen-chi,* 44:19a, letter in reply to Fang Po-mu (Fang Shih-yao).

19. See ch. 19 below, section on "Ch'eng Tzu."

20. *Yü-lei,* ch. 22, sec. 59 (pp. 836–837).

21. *Ibid.*, sec. 66 (p. 840); ch. 68, sec. 123 (p. 2716).

22. *Ibid.*, ch. 36, sec. 4 (p. 1517).

23. *Ibid.*, ch. 139, sec. 71 (p. 5321).

24. *Ibid.*, ch. 126, sec. 58 (p. 4841).

25. *Ibid.*, sec. 71 (p. 4848).

26. *Ibid.*, ch. 52, sec. 79 (p. 1978).

27. *Ibid.*, ch. 68, sec. 97 (pp. 2709–2710).

28. *Ibid.*, ch. 122, sec. 24 (p. 4727).

29. *Wen-chi,* separate collection, 3:13b, second letter to Liu Tzu-ch'eng (Liu Ch'ing-chih).

30. *Yü-lei,* ch. 83, sec. 96 (p. 3436).

31. *Ibid.*, sec. 105 (p. 3440).

32. *Ibid.*, ch. 90, sec. 81 (p. 3670).

33. *Ibid.*, ch. 38, sec. 53 (p. 1605).

34. *Ibid.*, ch. 113, sec. 33 (p. 4380).

35. *Ibid.*, ch. 126, sec. 6 (p. 4823).

36. *Ibid.*, ch. 81, sec. 104 (p. 3362).

37. *Ibid.*, ch. 30–33. See ch. 23 below, p. 378 and n. 36, p. 392.

38. *Ibid.*, ch. 121, sec. 6 (p. 4664).

39. Su Hsün, *Chia-yu chi* [Collected works of the Chia-yu period] (*SPPY* ed.), 11:3a–b, first letter to Ou-yang Hsiu.

40. For Tou Ts'ung-chou, see my *Chu Tzu men-jen* [Master Chu's pupils] (Taipei: Student Book Co., 1982), pp. 360–361.

41. *Yü-lei*, ch. 114, sec. 45 (pp. 4410).

42. *Hsüan-chiao-lang* was the title of the twenty-sixth out of thirty-seven ranks for civilian officials.

43. Lo Ta-ching, *Ho-lin yü-lu* [Jade-like dew from the forest of cranes] (*Ts'ung-shu chi-ch'eng* [Collection of series] ed.), ch. 13, pp. 144–145.

44. For Liao Te-ming, see my *Chu Tzu men-jen*, p. 287.

45. *Chou-li*, Office of Spring, under the office of divination.

46. *Yü-lei*, ch. 86, sec. 70 (p. 3530).

47. *Mien-chai chi* [Collected works of Huang Kan] (*Ssu-k'u ch'üan-shu chen-pen* [Precious works of the *Complete Collection of the Four Libraries*] ed.), 36:36a–b, biographical account.

48. Yeh Kung-hui, *Chu Tzu nien-p'u* [Chronological biography of Master Chu] (*Chin-shih han-chi ts'ung-k'an* [Chinese works of the recent period series] ed.), p. 228, under the first year of Ch'ing-yüan (1195).

49. Tai Hsien, *Chu Tzu shih-chi* [True records of Master Chu] (*Chin-shih han-chi ts'ung-k'an* ed.), p. 196, also under 1195.

50. Wang Mao-hung, *Chu Tzu nien-p'u* (*Ts'ung-shu chi-ch'eng* [Collection of series] ed.), ch. 4B, p. 216, also under 1195.

51. Yi T'oegye, *Chuja haengjang chipshu* [Compiled annotation of the "Chu Tzu hsing-chuang"] (Kyoto: Asakura Gisuke ed.), p. 48b.

52. *Sung shih chi-shih pen-mo* [Full account of the factual records of the *History of the Sung Dynasty*] (Peking: Chunghua Book Co., 1955) p. 684.

53. Ch'ien Mu, *Sung-Ming li-hsüeh kai-lun* [General account of Sung and Ming New-Confucianism] (Taipei: Chinese Cultural Publication Enterprise Committee, 1953), p. 115.

54. Yasuoka Masahiro, *Shushigaku nyumon* [Introduction to the Study of Chu Hsi] (Tokyo: Meitoku shuppansha, 1974), p. 61.

55. Chou Yü-t'ung, *Chu Hsi* (Shanghai: Commercial Press, 1931), p. 16.

56. Gōtō Toshimizu, *Shushi* (Tokyo: Hyōronsha, 1943), p. 187.

57. Satō Hitoshi, *Shushi* (Tokyo: Shūeisha, 1985), p. 247.

58. Chang Li-wen, *Chu Hsi ssu-hsiang yen-chiu* [Study of Chu Hsi's thought] (Beijing: Chinese Social Science Press, 1981), p. 78.

59. *Wen-chi*, separate collection, 1:13b, sixth letter in reply to Liu Te-hsiu (Liu Kuang-tsu).

60. Wang Mao-hung, *Chu Tzu nien-p'u, k'ao-i* [Investigation into variants], ch. 4, p. 335, under the first year of Ch'ing-yüan (1195).

61. *Wen-chi*, supplementary collection, 5:6a, letter to Vice Minister Chang Mao-hsien (Chang Yung).

62. *Mien-chai chi*, 36:47a.

63. *Yü-lei*, ch. 107, sec. 22 (pp. 4244–4245).

64. Present Tao County in Hunan Province.

65. *Yü-lei*, ch. 83, sec. 25 (p. 3408).

66. *Ibid.*, ch. 68, sec. 4 (p. 2677). Ch'ien (Heaven, male) and *k'un* (Earth, female) are the first and second hexagrams in the *Book of Changes*.

67. *Ibid.*, ch. 52, sec. 88 (p. 1983).

68. *Meng Tzu chi-chu* [Collected commentaries on the *Book of Mencius*], comment on 2A:2.

69. *Tso chuan* [Tso's commentary], Duke Chao, seventh year (537 B.C.).

70. *I-shu* [Surviving works], 3:6a, in the *Erh-Ch'eng ch'üan-shu* [Complete works of the two Ch'engs] (*SPPY* ed.).

71. *Yü-lei,* ch. 2, sec. 33 (p. 34); sec. 38 (p. 35).

72. *Ibid.*, sec. 52 (p. 38).

73. *Ibid.*, sec. 54 (p. 38).

74. *Ibid.*, sec. 53 (p. 38).

75. *I-shu,* 10:2b.

76. *Yü-lei,* ch. 2, sec. 56 (p. 38).

77. *Ibid.*, ch. 3, sec. 14 (p. 55).

78. *Ibid.*, ch. 2, sec. 56 (p. 39).

79. *Ibid.*

80. *Ibid.*, sec. 50 (p. 37).

81. *Ibid.*, ch. 138, sec. 104 (p. 5285).

82. *Ibid.*, ch. 83, sec. 117 (p. 3444). See also ch. 190, sec. 34 (p. 3644).

83. *Ibid.*, ch. 63, sec. 112 (p. 2455).

84. *Ibid.*, ch. 126, sec. 108 (p. 4862).

85. "Stealing a fetus" refers to stealing someone's soul and implanting it in a fetus through transmigration.

86. "Grabbing the blessing" refers to taking the inheritance due to the natural heir.

87. *Yü-lei,* ch. 126, sec. 103 (p. 4860).

88. *Ibid.*, ch. 3, sec. 19 (pp. 57–58).

89. *Ibid.*, ch. 125, sec. 59 (pp. 4809–4810). See also ch. 63, sec. 112 (pp. 2454–2455).

90. *Ibid.*, ch. 4, sec. 97 (p. 129).

91. *Ibid.*, ch. 106, sec. 25 (p. 4204).

92. *Wen-chi,* 76:26b, account of the map of Mount Wu-i. Chu Hsi loved this mountain intensely and built a study there. As he said in his account, the deity had been worshiped since the Han dynasty and regarded as the residing deity of Mount Wu-i, but we do not know much about him.

93. *Yü-lei,* ch. 114, sec. 40 (p. 4409).

94. *Analects,* 6:20.

95. *Book of Changes,* "Appended Remarks," pt. 1, ch. 4.

96. *Yü-lei,* ch. 63, sec. 132 (pp. 2464–2465); See also ch. 3, sec. 20 (p. 61, and above, n.1.

97. *Ibid.*, ch. 3, sec. 43 (p. 69).

98. *Ibid.*, sec. 19 (p. 60).

99. *Ibid.*, sec. 15 (p. 56).

100. *Ibid.*, sec. 50 (p. 72).

101. *Ibid.*, ch. 87, sec. 169 (p. 3590). See also ch. 3, sec. 80 (p. 86).

102. *Ibid.*, ch. 138, sec. 67 (p. 5277).

103. *Ibid.*, sec. 101–102 (p. 5284).

104. *Wen-chi,* 44:10b, eighth letter in reply to Ts'ai Chi-t'ung (Ts'ai Yüan-ting).

105. *Nan-hsüan Hsien-sheng wen-chi* [Collected works of Master Chang Shih] (*Chin-shih han-chi ts'ung-k'an* ed.), 23:12a (p. 735), fifty-third letter in reply to Chu Yüan-hui (Chu Hsi).

106. *Wen-chi,* supplementary collection, 7:8a, letter to Ch'en T'ung-fu (Ch'en Liang).

107. *Ibid.,* regular collection, 63:1b, first letter to in reply to Hu Po-liang (Hu Yung).

108. *Yü-lei,* ch. 3, sec. 80 (p. 86–87).

109. See the *Wen-chi,* 15:32a–36b, memorial on the imperial grave site. See also Wang Mao-hung, *Chu Tzu nien-p'u,* pp. 201–202.

110. *Yü-lei,* ch. 107, sec. 74 (p. 4257).

111. The term *ch'ih-k'ou,* literally "red mouth," may refer to the day on which families posted strong words on the door to ward off evil.

112. *Yü-lei,* ch. 107, sec. 75 (p. 4257).

113. *Book of Odes,* ode no. 235.

114. *Yü-lei,* ch. 3, sec. 57 (p. 76). See also ch. 81, sec. 134 (p. 3371).

115. *Ibid.,* ch. 3, sec. 68 (p. 81).

116. The Five Agents (or Five Elements) are Metal, Wood, Water, Fire, and Earth.

117. *Shang-ts'ai yü-lu* [Recorded sayings of Hsieh Liang-tso] (*Chin-shih han-chi ts'ung-k'an* ed.), pt. 1, p. 16a (p. 31).

118. *Yü-lei,* ch. 138, sec. 100 (p. 5282).

119. *Ibid.,* ch. 3, sec. 12 (pp. 53–54).

# – 8 –

# Traditions and Legends about Chu Hsi

STANDARD biographies of Chu Hsi tell us nothing about him of a mythical nature. He is portrayed as a man of unusual wisdom, tremendous scholarship, and remarkable accomplishment. Inevitably, however, a number of folktales have grown up around him. We shall recount these chronologically, beginning with his childhood.

Chu Hsi himself wrote that when he was five or six, he wondered what the sky was and what lay outside it.[1] According to Huang Kan (1152–1221), the question arose during a conversation between Chu Hsi and his father. Amazed, Chu Sung gave his son the *Classic of Filial Piety* to read. Having finished it, the boy wrote, "If I do not live up to this, I am not human." Another time he was playing with a group of boys in a sandpit. Sitting up straight, he was drawing something with his finger. It turned out to be the Eight Trigrams.[2] These stories are repeated in various chronological biographies *(nien-p'u)* of Chu Hsi, although they assign the events to different years, from age four to age eight.[3] Chu Yü *(fl.* 1722), the sixteenth-generation descendant of Chu Hsi, claimed that the site of his drawing the Eight Trigrams still existed.[4]

These stories point to nothing mysterious about Chu Hsi, but merely show his talents, and certainly he was a talented person. The tradition about his father's choice of a location, however, is related to a belief in geomancy. When his father wanted to select a place, perhaps for a house or for his grave, the geomancer said, "Wealth will be only like this, and high position will only be like this. But when a child is born, he will be like Confucius." And sure enough, Chu Hsi became a great Confucian.[5]

Another tradition concerns the seven dark spots on Chu Hsi's cheek. Many of his portraits, whether drawn on paper or carved in stone, show

126

seven spots on his right check in the pattern of the Big Dipper. The obvious suggestion is that his life was mandated by Heaven. Wang Mao-hung (1668–1741), in his *Chu Tzu nien-p'u* (Chronological biography of Master Chu), noted that "the Fukien edition [of the *nien-p'u*] said, 'There are seven black spots on the right cheek of Wen Kung [Chu Hsi]. People of the time considered that extraordinary.' Neither Li's edition [Li Mo's *Chu Tzu nien-p'u* of 1552] nor Hung's edition [Hung Ch'ü-wu's *Chu Tzu nien-p'u* of 1700]) recorded it."[6] The significant point is that Wang did not mention this in the regular chronological biography section but in the section devoted to his research notes, thus indicating that he did not quite believe in the legend. Neither Yeh Kung-hui's *Chu Tzu nien-p'u* of 1431 nor the *nien-p'u* in Tai Hsien's (d. 1508) *Chu Tzu shih-chi* (True records of Master Chu) mentions the matter. The "Chu Tzu hsing-chuang" (Biographical account of Master Chu) written by Huang Kan and the biography in the *Sung shih* (History of the Sung dynasty)[7] are silent on it as well. Nor is there any evidence in Chu Hsi's self-admonition on his self-portrait,[8] in Ch'en Liang's (1143–1194) eulogy on Chu Hsi's portrait,[9] in that of the Buddhist monk Yüan-wu K'eng-an,[10] or in any of the Chu Hsi shrines or portraits recorded in Tai Hsien's *Chu Tzu shih-chi*.[11] Ku Ch'i-yüan (1599 *cs*), in his *Shuo-lüeh* (Brief accounts), recorded all the strange physiological cases, such as double eyelids or a purple birthmark on the back, since ancient times, but did not mention Chu Hsi's birthmarks. This shows that at the end of the sixteenth century, there was not yet such a tradition about Chu Hsi.

The earliest account of these dark spots is the Fukien edition of the *Chu Tzu nien-p'u,* written at the beginning of the Ch'ing Dynasty (1644–1911). There were several editions, one of which is Chu Yü's *Nien-p'u.* According to him, "There were seven dark spots on the right cheek of Wen Kung in the form of a constellation [the Great Dipper]. People of the time considered that extraordinary." This may be the edition referred to by Wang Mao-hung. The account continues, "Governor Li Ch'ou-yüan [Li Kuan] of the Ming dynasty [1368–1644] was a native of Feng-ch'eng County.[12] He was once the magistrate of Wu-yüan.[13] He received an account passed on by local elders that said, 'When Lady Ch'eng, the fourth-generation ancestor of Wen Kung, was buried on the official burial ground, there were seven rocks on the ground. That is why Wen Kung was born with seven birthmarks.' " Chu Yü further noted,

When I visited the grave of Wen Kung's grandfather in Cheng-ho County [Fukien], the landscape was magnificent. The grave seemed to embrace everything with nothing missing. The sandy river, which reaches the capital of Cheng-ho, is called Seven-Star River, with a parade of seven rocks

along the river. The river originates in Hsi-chin, converges with Sung-hsi
River, and runs from east to west for more than 300 *li*[14] to the capital. The
grave, being on the state burial ground, provided the spiritual protection
of an ancestor, resulting in the birth of Wen Kung with seven birthmarks.[15]

To Chu Yü, Heaven and Earth had worked together to produce these
extraordinary birthmarks.

By the middle of the Ming dynasty, the tradition of the Dipper-like
birthmarks must have been quite prevalent, because the biographical
account of Ch'en Hsien-chang (1428–1500) states that he, too, had
seven black spots in the shape of the Great Dipper on his right cheek,[16]
and this is repeated in his biography in the *Ming shih* (History of the
Ming dynasty).[17] Ch'en's pupil Lin Kuang, however, questioned it,
saying, "This was Master Chu's facial feature. If Pai-sha [Ch'en
Hsien-chang] also had it, why have we not seen it?"[18]

Several stories have been told about Chu Hsi's birth, undoubtedly
due to the impulse to give him a divine character. Chu Yü tells us that
"the residence where Chu Hsi was born is now the Nan-hsi Academy. It
faces some mountains that resemble the Chinese character *wen,* and the
mountain where the house was situated resembles the Chinese character *kung.* Hence, the degree Wen Kung [Lord of Culture] was conferred
to him posthumously. The mountain is now called the Wen Kung
Mountain."[19] And according to Liang Chang-chü (1775–1849), both
Mount Wen and Mount Kung are in Yu-hsi County, where Chu Hsi
was born. On his birthday, the two mountains shed strong light, forming the two characters *wen-kung.*[20] Similarly, the *Yen-p'ing fu-chih*
(Records of Yen-p'ing prefecture) says that Mount Wen is on the edge
of Ch'ing-yin River and Mount Kung is across the river. Both were
covered with trees, but when Chu Hsi was born, a wildfire destroyed
their forests and revealed their true shapes, which resemble the characters *wen* and *kung.*[21]

According to Tai Hsien's *Nien-p'u,* when Chu Hsi was born, the well
in the ancestral house in Wu-chou emitted auspicious air.[22] This was
elaborated on by Chu Yü. From various other sources, Chu Yü related
that the house was on South Street in Wu-yüan. In 1097, white air
issued from the well and looked like a rainbow, and on that day Chu
Hsi's father was born. According to the account, Chu Hsi once said that
when his father was born, the white air from the well lingered for a
whole day like a rainbow, so the well was named Rainbow Well. In
1130, the account concludes, the auspicious air from the well lingered
like clouds, and on the third day Chu Hsi was born.[23] Commenting on
this account, Wang Mao-hung remembered, "In 1130, war was ram-
pant. Wu-chou was far away from Yu-hsi. Even if there was auspicious

air from the well, how could it be known [in Yu-hsi]? The account even said that the air prevailed for three days and then Wen Kung was born. Undoubtedly, this is farfetched."[24] It should be added that in his biographical account of his father, Chu Hsi never mentioned auspicious air.[25]

There is also the story of a retired gentleman of the Sung dynasty (960–1279) who lived on Men-yüeh (Full moon) Mountain. He raised a female horse that gave birth to a colt with a dragon's head. Elders in the community told him that when Confucius edited and corrected the Six Classics,[26] the unicorn appeared. Now that Chu Hui-an (Chu Hsi) honors the Four Books,[27] they said, a dragon-horse is born, which is the portent for a sage. When Chu Hsi heard about this, he said he didn't deserve the compliment. Later, when a search was made to find the horse, it had disappeared.[28]

Other efforts have been made to turn Chu Hsi into a diviner. Chu Hsi had written a couplet for a farmer wishing him a good harvest. During the disorder in the Chia-ching period (1522–1566), many counties were in ruin but that farmer's county was spared;[29] this was then said to indicate that Chu Hsi could foresee such events. The story about the age of a grave is even more specific. According to Hsü Po of the Ming dynasty, in I-wu County of Chekiang was the grave of Liu Hao, a prefect in the Sung dynasty. In the *wu-ch'en* year of the Lung-ch'ing period (1568), his descendant Shang-kung was repairing the grave tablet. When he had dug down several feet, he found a brick about a foot square on which was carved Chu Hsi's calculation of the years of the grave, which said, "In the *wu-ch'en* year of the T'ien-sheng period (1028), a burial took place on this mound. Through spiritual protection, dukes and marquises were produced in the eighteen generations. Descendants will continue in an unbroken line and follow the examples of their forebears without cessation. After 541 years, a descendant of seventeen or eighteen will repair the grave. There will be a new tablet from *wu-ch'en* to *wu-ch'en*, and there will be repair after repair for a thousand years." The poem bore the signature of Chu Hsi. The account marvels at its exactness, because from the *wu-ch'en* year of T'ien-sheng to the *wu-ch'en* year of Lung-ch'ing was indeed 541 years, and Shang-kung was seventeen years old. The account adds that Liu Hao's great-grandsons Hui and Hsi were Chu Hsi's pupils, which was why Chu Hsi wrote the poem carved on the stone.[30] One trouble with this story is that none of Chu Hsi's pupils was named Liu Hui or Liu Hsi.

Hsü Po also wrote that

once Chu and Lü Tung-lai [Lü Tsu-ch'ien, 1137–1181] were reading together in the Yün-ku [Cold Valley] Study. As Chu Hsi devoted his whole energy to writing, his spirits were high and he did not feel tired at all. Tung-lai, however, always felt tired late in the evening and had to rest before he worked again. He was ashamed that his energy did not measure up to that of Chu Hsi. He asked Wen Kung about his vigor. [Chu Hsi told him that] as he sat at night, there seemed to be something under the desk that touched his feet. After stepping on it for a long time, he said, his energy greatly increased. Several years later, Wen Kung suddenly saw a spiritual being one evening whose many eyes ejected more than a hundred lights. The spiritual being declared, "The star of many eyes has appeared." From then on, the thing under the desk never came again. When night came, Wen Kung got under a quilt and went to sleep.[31]

This narration seems unclear. Perhaps some sentences are missing. Lü visited Chu Hsi's Cold Spring Study in the fourth month of 1175 and left the next month. The Cloud Valley Lodge was not built until the seventh month, by which time Lü had returned to his home in Chin-hua, Chekiang. But regardless of the confusion of the Cold Spring Study with the Cloud Valley Lodge, the purpose of the tale is clear—namely, to show that a spiritual being was serving Chu Hsi.

A more interesting and clearer story concerns Chu Hsi in the Wu-i area of Fukien. Mount Wu-i is exceedingly scenic, with a famous river that winds in nine turns. According to the tale, a young and beautiful woman came to Chu Hsi and told him that her family lived across from the fifth turn of the river. Her family was Hu and her private name was Li-niang (Beautiful maiden), she said. She wanted to become a pupil, so Chu Hsi taught her the classics. She came every day and served him tea and food. She also fanned him when it was hot and started the fire when it was cold. Gradually the two began living together as husband and wife. One day Chu Hsi took a walk to the P'ing-lin ferry station. Suddenly a man and a woman, both very dark and with protruding eyes, called Chu Hsi and told him that he looked sick. They told him that the young lady who was serving him was really a fox *(hu)* spirit who had come to steal his jade bowl, the fount of his wisdom, but Chu Hsi refused to believe them. They then whispered something into Chu Hsi's ear and suddenly vanished. Chu Hsi was bothered by what he had heard and could not go to sleep. For three nights he stayed awake. All this time Li-niang was with him but eventually became tired and fell asleep. As she slept, a pair of jade chopsticks protruded from her nose. When the chopsticks finally fell to the ground and broke, they reflected the shape of a fox. Li-niang then awoke and confessed that she was a fox spirit who had been cultivating herself as a fairy in Mount Wu-i for a thousand years. The couple, she added, were really turtle spirits she had been training to be fairies. Because they plotted to get Chu Hsi's jade bowl and her jade chopsticks, she had condemned them to be ferry paddlers. Now that her chopsticks were broken she would have to leave, and would lie forever in the cave of Nan-ming-ching. At that point, thunder struck. Pointing to two black shadows, Li-niang cried and said, "They are the ones who have broken us up." In his distress Chu Hsi picked up his brush, which flew out the window like an arrow, hitting the couple. They immediately resumed their true forms and became the stone turtles by the Wu-i River. When Chu Hsi turned his head, Li-niang had already disappeared. Later, when Chu Hsi took a walk and approached the flower beds of Nan-ming-ching, he found a dead fox. With tears he buried it and set up a tablet on which were carved the words "Madame Hu (Fox)."[32]

Tourists enjoying the delightful scenery of the Wu-i River ride on bamboo rafts, as I did in 1983. When they come to the eighth turn of the river, they see two dark gray rocks in the shape of turtles, and the woman who poles the raft tells them about the legend of the turtles. This is not mere entertainment, for it indicates how deeply the lore about Chu Hsi has entered the fabric of folk society. People in the Wu-i area believe that Chu Hsi was such a good and wise person that spirits really did come to serve him.

A similar story prevailed in the area of Mount Lu in Kiangsi, where in 1179 Chu Hsi reconstructed the White Deer Hollow Academy, which became the model for academies in all of China for centuries thereafter. As the Mount Lu version has it, a fox spirit disguised as a young woman came to live with Chu Hsi. She brought a pearl that she persuaded Chu Hsi to swallow and that became the source of his wisdom. Later, a green toad spirit, also disguised as a young woman, came to live with him. Eventually the two women quarreled and exposed their secrets. The next day they were gone. When Chu Hsi found the dead fox and toad under a bridge near the academy, he buried them in the academy grove with all the proper ceremonies and set up a stone tablet in their memory.[33]

According to the Mount Lu story, Chu Hsi lived at the academy for life and was buried there, whereas in fact he was in the area for only two years and his official residence while there was several miles from the academy itself. It is also interesting that the number of fairies has doubled compared to the story told in the vicinity of Mount Wu-i. This suggests that the tradition originated in Fukien, a hotbed of mysteries, and later spread to Kiangsi.

Chu Hsi served as prefect of Chang-chou in southern Fukien in 1190, for exactly one year. Surprisingly, the traditions about him in this area are all perfectly mundane and involve not a single fairy. These stories, conveniently collected in a scholarly historical study, may be briefly summarized as follows:

1. *The White Cloud Cave Study.* Chu Hsi found White Cloud Cave an ideal place to read and wanted to build a study there, but the bricks and

tiles he needed were at the foot of the mountain. He told the people that the tiles would fly up the mountain. Being curious, many people gathered at the foot of the mountain. Chu Hsi told each of them to carry several bricks and tiles up the hill. When people realized it was all a joke, they knew they had been taken for a ride.

2. *Shrimps and snails.* Monks at the cave were of course vegetarians. One day someone presented Chu Hsi with a dish of fried shrimps and snails. He threw the leftovers into a stream. Somehow they revived and have continued to flourish to this day.

3. *Tzu-yang (Chu Hsi) tea.* Behind the Chu Hsi Shrine is a pond where the water is always dark. It is believed to be the pond where Chu Hsi washed his ink-slab. In the pavilion behind it, a tablet reads, "The site where Wen Kung lectured on the classics." The tea produced in the area of White Cloud Cave is especially fragrant and is called Tzu-yang tea.

4. *Front-door screens.* Every house in Chang-chou has a bamboo screen at the front door so people cannot look in from the outside but can see from the inside out. According to local tradition, this was one of the reforms Chu Hsi instituted in Chang-chou, primarily for the privacy of women.

5. *Bound feet.* Another custom begun by Chu Hsi, according to Chang-chou folk, was bound feet. At the bottom of the shoes, a piece of wood about an inch thick was held together with a single nail, supposedly to prevent women from running away from home. There were also the Wen Kung dress, the Wen Kung cane, Wen Kung shoes for men, and a unit of measure called the Wen Kung peck.[34]

6. *Ch'en Ch'un.* Ch'en Ch'un (1159–1223), a native of Chang-Chou, was one of Chu Hsi's most outstanding pupils. He came to study with the Master when Chu Hsi became prefect of Chang-chou in 1190. According to the legend, when Chu Hsi heard that Ch'en Ch'un was an excellent painter, he personally came to request a picture of the moon. Ch'en said he was not yet ready to paint. After a servant came several times for the painting, Ch'en picked up the stem of a sugarcane, looked at the full moon, swiftly drew a line, and gave the picture to the servant. The servant thought the picture was too poor for Chu Hsi's taste and bought one in the market instead. Upon examining it, Chu Hsi knew it could not have come from Ch'en Ch'un's brush, and was exhilarated when the servant produced the drawing by Ch'en Ch'un.

7. *Ch'en Ch'un's daughter's dowry.* Ch'en was a poor schoolteacher and could not afford the usual dowry for his daughter. Instead, he gave her several barrels of his own paintings. Her new mother-in-law was not pleased and used them as cooking fuel. By the time Ch'en Ch'un's daughter discovered what she was doing, only one painting, that of a red sun, was left. She told her mother-in-law that the paintings were her

father's choice pieces. Luckily, she added, the red sun picture had been saved, because it could warm the wheat when hung up in the winter. Her mother-in-law did not believe her, but it proved to be true. At that point, however, the painting turned into smoke and disappeared.[35]

8. *Getting rid of the frogs.* Chu Hsi wanted a quiet evening for study but was annoyed by the sound of frogs. Following the example of Han Yü (768–824), who sacrificed to the crocodiles in Ch'ao-chou, Kwangtung, and told them to go away, Chu Hsi wrote a sacrificial address and advised the frogs to keep quiet. When that did not stop their noise, he made many paper cangues to throw into the pond and warned the frogs of their fate unless they left immediately. The next morning each frog wore a cangue. Chu Hsi pardoned them and told them to go away. Thereafter, the pond was quiet. It was later named Tuan-wa-ch'ih (Pond clear of frogs). People of Chang-chou believed that the thriving green frogs were descendants of the repentant frogs. One account points to Chu Hsi's poem on the frogs[36] as proof of the event, while another says the event had nothing to do with Chu Hsi but was the act of a certain Minister P'an.[37]

9. *The evil monk.* A monk in the K'ai-yüan Temple in the capital of Chang-chou was really a rat spirit. He had a trap door on the floor. When he saw a beautiful worshiper, he would trap her in the basement for his pleasure. Officials feared his power and paid homage to him upon arrival, but Chu Hsi refused to do so. The rat spirit was angry and released water from a well to flood the city, hoping to drown Chu Hsi. Chu Hsi took the plaque from the door of the official building and threw it and his own clothing into the water, which soon flowed away. When people in the city shouted that the water level had reached the roofs of their houses, the rat spirit was happy and stopped the water from the well, not realizing that the official building was on high ground. When Chu Hsi sent people to search for the plaque and they found it on top of the well, he had a piece of stone placed on the opening of the well. From then on, the water level never rose above the stone. In revenge, the rat spirit bit a beam in the roof of the main hall of the official building, hoping that the beam would fall and kill Chu Hsi. However, when Chu Hsi noticed that one end of the beam was about to fall, he pointed his brush at the beam and it stayed put. The hall has since been taken down to make room for a boulevard.[38]

10. *The pagoda over a well.* According to legend, women in Chang-chou were licentious. This puzzled Chu Hsi when he arrived. Upon examining the city plan, he concluded that the pattern of the bridges and streets was responsible. The North Bridge, he thought, looked like a pillow. Kung-fu (Public office) Street and Shih-jen-ch'iao (Bridge of great humaneness) Street looked like a person's two arms. North Bridge Boulevard looked like a person's body. At the well there was a fork,

which resembled two legs. He decided that the well was the female organ. Women were licentious because they drank the water from the well. Therefore he built a pagoda on top of the well. The pagoda was called the Hsien-t'ung (All through) Pagoda, and the well Mei-jen (Beautiful women) Well.[39]

Chu Hsi lived in Chien-yang in northern Fukien for many more years than in Chang-chou, yet only one story has prevailed about him there. The story was told to me when I visited the place in 1983. According to the tradition, when Chu Hsi was near death, he asked an old woman to come to see his broken ink-slab, which was to be buried with him. Later, when the old woman's son tried to rob the grave, he encountered rocks and could not dig any further. The old woman told him, "Master Chu was extremely poor. Only a broken ink-slab was buried with him. I saw that myself." Upon hearing this, the son gave up the idea of robbing the grave.

When Chu Hsi became sick on the second day of the third month of 1200, several of his pupils were with him. Ts'ai Ch'en (1167–1230) wrote a very detailed day-to-day account of his illness and death. On the ninth day of the month (April 23), Chu Hsi was discussing the funeral rituals with his students but then was no longer able to speak. He wanted to pick up a brush but was so weak that it dropped beside his pillow. Gradually his breath stopped. It was exactly noon. "On that day," Ts'ai wrote, "a big storm destroyed houses. Large trees were uprooted. In no time, a flood caused hills to crumble."[40] In the minds of his pupils, Chu Hsi was a man approaching the status of Confucius, so his death, according to tradition, was accompanied by falling trees and landslides. Obviously, they believed that Heaven and Earth responded to their Master's death. Chu Hsi did not believe in survival in the personal sense. The day before he died he told his pupils, "The principle is like this. You must work hard and stand firm on the ground. Only then can there be progress."[41]

Strangely enough, we have only one story about Chu Hsi's afterlife. In the *Hsü-shih pi-ching* (Hsü Po's literary notes), it is recorded that in the Hsien-ch'en period (1265–1274), P'eng Tan-hsüan from Szechuan visited Mount Wu-i. Wandering into a thatched hut, he saw two scholars in high hats and wide sashes facing each other and eating dinner. They invited P'eng to join them. On the table were a pig's head, a goat's lung, and a chicken. Their conversation concerned the primodial diagram and commentaries on the *Book of Changes*—all over his head, P'eng said. When he inquired about their names, the one on the right said that his family name was Wei but that he had no courtesy name because he was a rustic person in the mountains, and the one on the left would not answer. P'eng then begged to leave, since evening was drawing near. The next day, he brought a servant and some gifts with him but could not find the way. When he entered a rich man's house and told his story, the rich man said "How strange! Yesterday we sacrificed in Wen Kung's shrine with exactly the food you saw on the table." Only then did P'eng realize that the man on the left had been Chu Hsi and the one on the right Wei Liao-weng (1178–1237).[42]

From the above, we may conclude that among Chinese philosophers Chu Hsi has probably been mythologized more than anyone except Confucius. All the legends point to his wisdom rather than to supernatural power. There is no account that he performed any miracle. Most of the stories are clearly fabrications but some might be true. Some are for scholars, while others are for ordinary folk. All show how deeply Chu Hsi has influenced the Chinese people and how highly they have regarded him.

# Notes

1. *Yü-lei*, ch. 45, sec. 30 (p. 1836).

2. *Mien-chai chi* [Collected works of Huang Kan] (*Ssu-k'u ch'üan-shu chen-pen* [Precious works of the *Complete Collection of the Four Libraries*] ed.), 36:1b–2a, biographical account. The Eight Trigrams consist of continuous or broken lines representing the various elements of the universe.

3. See Yeh Kung-hui, *Chu Tzu nien-p'u* [Chronological biography of Master Chu] (*Chin-shih han-chi ts'ung-k'an* [Chinese works of the recent period series] ed.), p. 57; Tai Hsien (d. 1508), *Chu Tzu shih-chi* [True records of Master Chu] (*Chin-shih han-chi ts'ung-k'an* ed.), pp. 76–77; Wang Mao-hung, *Chu Tzu nien-p'u* (*Ts'ung-shu chi-ch'eng* [Collection of series] ed.), ch. 1, p. 2.

4. Chu Yü, *Chu Tzu wen-chi ta-ch'üan lei-pien* [Classified compilation of the complete collection of literary works of Master Chu] (1722 ed.), Bk. I, 1:3a.

5. Ch'u Jen-huo, *Chien-hu chi* [Collection of a hard gourd] (*Ch'ing-tai pi-chi ts'ung-k'an* [Ch'ing dynasty notes series] ed.), fourth collection, 2:7a.

6. Wang Mao-hung, *Chu Tzu nien-p'u, k'ao-i* [Investigation into variants], ch. 1, p. 243, under the fourth year of Shao-hsing (1130).

7. *Sung shih* [History of the Sung dynasty] (Beijing: Ching-hua Book Co., 1977), ch. 429, biography of Chu Hsi.

8. *Wen-chi*, 85:5a, 11a.

9. *Ch'en Liang chi* [Collected works of Ch'en Liang] (Peking: Chung-hua Book Co., 1974), p. 110.

10. *Ch'ung-an hsien-chih* [Accounts of Ch'ung-an County] (Yung-cheng [1723–1736] of the Ch'ing dynasty ed.), ch. 8; *Ch'ung-an hsien hsin-chih* [New accounts of Ch'ung-an County] (1941 ed.), 20:5b (p. 520).

11. Tai Hsien, *Chu Tzu shih-chi*, chs. 11–12.

12. A county in Kiangsi.

13. Now Wu County in Kiangsi.

14. A *li* is one-third of a mile.

15. Chu Yü, *Chu Tzu wen-chi ta-ch'üan lei-pien*, Bk. I, chronological biography, p. 2a.

16. According to Jen Yu-wen, *Pai-sha Tzu yen-chiu* [Study of Master Ch'en Hsien-chang] (Hong Kong: Chien-shih Meng-chin Study, 1970), p. 29.

17. *Ming shih* [History of the Ming dynasty] (*SPPY* ed.), 283:1b, biography of Ch'en Hsien-chang.

18. Lin Kuang, *Nan-ch'uan ping-nieh chi* [The hard life of Lin Kuang], p. 27, quoted by Jen Yu-wen, *op. cit.*, p. 29.

19. Chu Yü, *Chu Tzu wen-chi ta-ch'üan lei-pien,* Bk. I, chronological biography, p. 1b.

20. Liang Chang-chü, *Ying-lien ts'ung-hua* [A series of talks on couplets] *Kuo-hsüeh chi-pen ts'ung-shu* [Basic Sinological series] ed.), p. 191.

21. *Yen-p'ing fu-chih* [Records of Yen-p'ing prefecture] (1873 ed.), 5:1b–2a.

22. Tai Hsien, *Chu Tzu shih-chi,* p. 75.

23. Chu Yü, *Chu Tzu wen-chi ta-ch'üan lei-pien,* Bk. I, chronological biography, pp. 1b, 2a.

24. Wang Mao-hung, *Chu Tzu nien-p'u, k'ao-i,* ch. 1, pp. 242–243, under the fourth year of Chien-yen (1130).

25. *Wen-chi,* 97:17b–26a, biographical account of Chu Sung.

26. The Six Classics are the *Book of Odes,* the *Book of History,* the *Book of Rites,* the *Book of Changes,* the *Spring and Autumn Annals,* and the *Book of Music.* The last classic was lost before the third century B.C. and was replaced by the *Chou-li* [Rites of Chou] during the Sung dynasty (960–1279).

27. The Four Books are the *Great Learning,* the *Analects,* the *Book of Mencius,* and the *Doctrine of the Mean.*

28. Chu Kuo-chen, *Yung-t'ung hsiao-p'in* [Sketches of the Welling-up Pavilion] (Peking: Chung-hua Book Co., 1959), p. 502.

29. Ting Ch'uan-ching, *Sung-jen i-shih lei-pien* [Classified compilation of anecdotes of the people of the Sung dynasty] (Taipei: Commercial Press, 1966), p. 862, quoting Hsieh Chao-chih, *Ch'ang-hsi so-yü* [Trivial talks of Fu-ning Prefecture].

30. Hsü Po, *Hsü-shih pi-ching* [Hsü Po's literary notes] (Taipei: Student Book Co., 1971), 8:29a–b (pp. 781–782).

31. Quoted in the *Chu Hsi chi-ch'ih hsüeh-p'ai Fu-chien ti-fang-shih tzu-liao* [Data of the local history about Chu Hsi and his school in Fukien], compiled by the Institute of Chinese Philosophy of Hsia-men University (1981), p. 68. However, I have not been able to find this material in Hsü Po's *Hsü-shih pi-ching.*

32. *Wu-i-shan min-chien ch'uan-shuo* [Folk traditions of Mount Wu-i] (Foochow: Fu-chien People's Press, 1981), pp. 20–28.

33. Carl F. Kupfer, "The White Deer Grotto University," *Sacred Places in China* (Cincinatti: Western Methodist Book Co., 1911), p. 75. I am grateful to Professor John W. Chaffee of New York State University at Binghamton for supplying me with this material.

34. Weng Kuo-liang, *Chang-chou shih-chi* [Historical traces of Chang-chou] (Peking: Peking University, 1935), pp. 8–10.

35. *Ibid.,* pp. 34–35.

36. *Wen-chi,* 9:10:9b.

37. Weng Kuo-liang, *Chang-chou shih-chi,* pp. 37–39.

38. *Ibid.,* pp. 59–60.

39. *Ibid.,* p. 92.

40. Ts'ai Ch'en, "Chu Wen Kung meng-tien chi" [Account of Chu Hsi's death], in the *Ts'ai-shih chiu-ju shu* [Works of nine Confucians in the Ts'ai family] (1868 ed.), 6:60a.

41. *Ibid.*, p. 59a.

42. Hsü Po, *Hsü-shih pi-ching*, 8:34b–35a (pp. 792–793).

# *Li* and Philosophical
# Categories

NEO-CONFUCIANISM is often called *Li-hsüeh* (School of Principle) in Chinese, so there is no question that *li* (principle) is the central concept in the entire Neo-Confucian movement. This chapter, however, is not concerned with a systematic or comprehensive story of the concept. More than twenty years ago I did just that in a long article in the *Tsing Hua Journal of Chinese Studies,* which was reproduced in *Neo-Confucianism, Etc., Essays by Wing-tsit Chan*[1] and also translated in a Chinese journal and a Chinese anthology.[2] Although the two English publications are rather obscure, the essay is not reprinted here because the present work deals only with material not previously available in any language. What is new about *li* is Chu Hsi's saying, "*Li* produces *ch'i* [material force]."

At the International Conference on Chu Hsi in Honolulu in 1982, Professor Yamanoi Yū presented a paper entitled "The Great Ultimate and Heaven in Chu Hsi's Philosophy," in which he quoted Chu Hsi's saying, "*T'ai-chi* [the Great Ultimate] created yin-yang [passive and active cosmic forces] means that *li* creates *ch'i.*" He mentioned in a note that the saying is quoted in the *Chou Tzu ch'üan-shu* (Complete works of Master Chou)[3] and the *Hsing-li ching-i* (Essential ideas of nature and principle),[4] but that "I have not been able to identify its original source. I shall be profoundly grateful if I am informed of it."[5] Professor Yamanoi had also cited Chu Hsi's saying, "Although *ch'i* is produced by *li,* once *ch'i* is produced, *li* no longer controls it."[6] But that was not what he was asking about. When I returned home from the conference, I made a thorough search without success. In the following year I happened to participate in a colloquium at the Chinese Academy of Social Sciences in Beijing, where someone gave me a copy of the *Zhongguo zhexueshi yanjiu* (Research in the history of Chinese philosophy) that contained an article by Chen Lai. In it Chen Lai said that Chu Hsi's saying, "*Li* creates *ch'i*," is found in Lü Nan's (1479–1542) *Sung ssu-tzu ch'ao-shih* (Selections from the four masters of the Sung period), and called the reader's attention to Lü's note that says, "It is correct to say that there is principle in material force but wrong to say that principle produces material force."[7] By the four masters, Lü actually meant five—namely, Chou Tun-i (1017–1073), Ch'eng Hao (1032–1085), Ch'eng I (1033–1107), Chang Tsai (1020–1077), and Chu Hsi; he evidently considered the Ch'eng brothers as one because their opinions were largely identical. In the preface to the section on Chu Hsi, as Chen Lai pointed out, Lü had this to say: "I have selected from the *Yü-lüeh* [Brief selection of sayings] compiled by Master Chu's pupil, Yang Yü-li [1193 *cs*], leaving out duplicate [sayings] and including those that are relevant to life." On the strength of this, Chen Lai concluded that the saying came from Yang Yü-li's *Chu Tzu yü-lüeh*. He added that the anthology was noted in the bibliographical section of both the *Sung shih* (History of the Sung dynasty) and the *Ming shih* (History of the Ming dynasty), but not in the *Ssu-k'u ch'üan-shu* (Complete collection of the Four Libraries). The supplement of the latter does mention that there was an 1834 edition, but since the work is not in the catalogue of any library, it is probably lost.[8]

As to why the saying is not found in the *Yü-lei*, I have a different interpretation from that of Chen Lai. In his opinion, the *Chu Tzu yü-lüeh* prevailed in the southeast around 1220–1221, so that the compiler of the *Yü-lei*, Li Ching-te (*fl.* 1263), must have seen it. According to Chen Lai, the *Yü-lei* focused on Chu Hsi's thought system in its entirety, while the *Yü-lüeh* is made up of Chu Hsi's refined sayings that can be used for self-admonition and teaching others. Consequently, "Li Ching-te did not take such selected sayings seriously [or] . . . give them careful examination."[9] My interpretation is rather different. After all, Li Ching-te was a very careful person. In the compilation, he "took in what was left out [of the collections that made up the *Yü-lei*] and corrected what was mistaken. By comparing the recorded sayings, more than 1,150 duplicates were eliminated. It took several years to compile."[10] I believe Li Ching-te eliminated the saying in question because it duplicated others. The *Yü-lei* already contains the saying, "Because there is this principle, there is produced afterward this material force."[11] It also incudes the saying, already quoted, that "although *ch'i* is produced by *li*, once *ch'i* is produced, *li* no longer controls it."[12] These render an additional saying unnecessary.

More important, the question of whether principle exists before material force or vice versa has generated a great deal of controversy. Chu Hsi said, "Fundamentally, principle and material force cannot be spoken of as prior or posterior. But if we must trace their origin we are obliged to say that principle is prior. However, principle is not a separate entity. It exists right in material force. Without material force, principle would have nothing to adhere to."[13] Someone asked about the theory that there is principle first and then material force. Chu Hsi answered,

> You don't have to say it this way. How do we know if there is principle first and then material force, or material force first and then principle? Neither of these can be speculated on. But I imagine that material force operates according to principle. As material force gathers, principle is also there. Material force can integrate and create, but principle has no intention and does not deliberate or create."[14]

This is what is meant by principle not controlling material force. The statement in the *Yü-lüeh* that principle produces material force makes principle an active agent and does not convey the idea that principle operates in the natural way. In commenting on the classical saying, "What Heaven imparts to man is called human nature,"[15] Chu Hsi said, "Nature is principle. By means of yin, yang, and the Five Agents,[16] Heaven creates and transforms the myriad things. Material force thereby perfects physical shape, and principle is also endowed."[17] In the final analysis, both principle and material force are created by Heaven, which means that material force is not produced by principle.

Moreover, since principle is the key category in Neo-Confucianism, it is not out of place to point out Chu Hsi's contributions to Chinese philosophical categories. There is no question that Chu Hsi discussed such categories more than any other Chinese writer, since he lived for a long time and left us with an enormous amount of material. The *Wen-chi* alone contains almost two thousand letters by him, while the recorded conversations in the *Yü-lei* constitute 140 chapters. And these do not include his almost one hundred other works. Strangely enough, none of the categories he discussed can be claimed as his own, for he created none. Terms like *hsiao* (filial piety), *ti* (brotherly respect), *chung* (loyalty), *hsin* (faithfulness), *jen* (humanity), *i* (righteousness), *li* (propriety), *chih* (wisdom), *ke* (investigation), *chih* (extension), *ch'eng* (sincerity), *cheng* (correctness), *chung* (central), *yung* (ordinary), *i-fa* (after manifestation), *wei-fa* (before manifestation), and so on originated in the Four Books;[18] *yu* (being), *wu* (nonbeing), *ts'ai* (capability), *hsing* (nature), and others came from the metaphysics of Wei (220–265) and Chin (265–420) times; and *T'ai-chi, li, ch'i,* and the like were derived from the Neo-Confucians of the Northern Sung (960–1126). Strictly speaking, all originated in pre-Ch'in (221–206 B.C.) thought.

Hence it is impossible to pinpoint a philosophical category that Chu Hsi employed for the first time. This is almost incredible for a thinker who has influenced Chinese, Korean, and Japanese thought more than any other person in the last seven hundred years, but it results from the fact that Chu Hsi always used traditional categories even though he usually gave them new meanings. Two examples will suffice. First, he defined *jen* as "the character of the mind and the principle of love."[19] Ch'eng I (1033–1107) had equated *jen* with seeds of grain,[20] on the theory that "the mind of Heaven and Earth is to produce things."[21] Chu Hsi went a step further and declared that "the mind of Heaven and Earth is to produce things. In the production of men and things, they received the mind of Heaven and Earth as their mind."[22] Ch'eng I had said, "*Jen* is the correct principle of the world."[23] But Chu Hsi thought that was too vague and did not cover the substance of *jen*.[24] Therefore, he proceeded to explain *jen* as the character of the mind, for to him "*Jen* is the complete character of the original mind, and there is thus the Principle of Heaven."[25] Traditionally, *jen* had been understood as love, an idea that reached its height in Han Yü (768–824), who regarded *jen* as universal love.[26] In criticizing him, Ch'eng I said that love is feeling while *jen* is nature, and that although the man of *jen* loves universally, it is wrong to regard love as *jen*.[27] Chu Hsi gave *jen* a more philosophical meaning by saying that it is the principle of love, and no explanation since has gone beyond Chu Hsi's interpretation.

The second example is that of *wu-chi* (the ultimate of nonbeing). The term comes from the *Lao Tzu*,[28] and both Liu Tsung-yüan (773–819)[29] and Shao Yung (1011–1077)[30] had used it, but the meaning had always remained hidden. Chou Tun-i had adopted a Taoist priest's diagram of the Great Ultimate, in which the first circle represents that *wu-chi*, followed by the circle of *T'ai-chi*, which embraces yin and yang. In his "T'ai-chi-t'u shuo" (Explanation of the diagram of the Great Ultimate), Chou began by saying "*Wu-chi* and *T'ai-chi*," but he never explained what he meant.[31] Chu Hsi gave a specific explanation for the first time, saying, "The operation of Heaven has neither sound nor smell.[32] It is really the pivot of all transformations and the basis of all varieties and categories of things. It is not that outside the Great Ultimate there is another Ultimate of Nonbeing."[33] On the Taoistic category of *wu-chi*, Chu Hsi carried on an extensive discussion with his pupils[34] and engaged in a bitter debate through correspondence with Lu Hsiang-shan (1139–1193) in 1188–1189. To Lu, adding *wu-chi* on top of *T'ai-chi* was adding a bed above a bed,[35] but to Chu Hsi, *wu-chi* simply meant being without spatial restriction or physical shape and was not a thing distinct from the Great Ultimate.[36] In spite of Lu's objection, *wu-chi* remains an important category in Chinese philosophy.

Chu Hsi also contributed to the order of categories without deliberately doing so. In compiling the *Chin-ssu lu* (Reflections on things at hand) in collaboration with Lü Tsu-ch'ien (1137–1181), he arranged the anthology in fourteen chapters without titles, except for a general description of the main purpose of each chapter. A second-generation pupil, Yeh Ts'ai (*fl.* 1248), was the first to use titles, putting Chu Hsi's descriptions in simple terms: (1) The substance of Tao (the Way), (2) Learning, (3) Extension of knowledge, (4) Preserving one's mind and nourishing one's nature, (5) Self-discipline, (6) The way of the family, (7) Serving or not serving in the government, (8) The substance of government, (9) Methods of government, (10) Governmental affairs, (11) Teaching, (12) Caution, (13) Heterodox schools, and (14) Sages and worthies.[37] Ever since, this has been the standard order of philosophical categories. Works like the *Yü-lei* of 1170, the *Hsing-li ta-ch'üan* (Great collection of Neo-Confucianism) of 1415, the *Chu Tzu ch'üan-shu* (Complete works of Master Chu) of 1714, and the *Hsing-li ching-i* (Essential ideas of nature and principle) of 1715 all followed the chapter arrangement of the *Chin-ssu lu,* and these works have dominated Chinese thought for centuries. In a sense, the order follows that in the *Great Learning,* which starts with the investigation of things and proceeds through the extension of knowledge, the sincerity of the will, the rectification of the mind, the cultivation of the self, the regulation of the family, ordering the state, and, finally, world peace. However, the order of the *Chin-ssu lu* is more refined and starts with the substance of Tao. Thus the most important philosophical category heads the list.

## Notes

1. "The Evolution of the Neo-Confucian Concept of *Li* as 'Principle,' " *Tsing Hua Journal of Chinese Studies,* Taipei, N.S. Vol. 4, no. 2 (February, 1964), pp. 123–149. Reprinted in my *Neo-Confucianism, Etc., Essays by Wing-tsit Chan* (Hong Kong: Oriental Society, 1969), pp. 45–87.

2. Chinese translation by Wan Hsien-fa, in *The Young Sun,* Hong Kong, vol. 31, no. 6 (serial no. 366), (October, 1966), pp. 18–25; vol. 31, no. 7 (serial no. 367), (November, 1966), pp. 11–20. Reprinted in Hsiang Wei-hsin and Liu Fu-tseng, eds., *Chung-kuo che-hsueh ssu-hsiang lun-chi: Sung-Ming p'ien* [Essays on Chinese philosophy and thought: The Sung and Ming periods] (Taipei: Cowboy Publishing Co., 1976), pp. 57–91.

3. *Chou Tzu ch'üan-shu* [Complete works of Master Chou Tun-i] (*Kuo-hsüeh chi-pen ts'ung-shu* [Basic Sinological series] ed.), ch. 1, p. 6.

4. Li Kuang-ti, *Hsing-li ching-i* [Essential ideas of nature and principle] (*SPPY* ed.), 1:4a.

5. Wing-tsit Chan, ed., *Chu Hsi and Neo-Confucianism* (Honolulu: University of Hawaii Press, 1986), pp. 86–91.

6. *Yü-lei,* ch. 4, sec. 65 (p. 114).

7. Lü Nan, *Sung ssu-tzu ch'ao-shih* [Selections from the four masters of the Sung period] (Taipei: World Book Co., 1962), p. 361.

8. Chen Lai, in *Zhongguo zhexueshi yanjiu* [Research in the history of Chinese philosophy], Beijing, 1983, no. 2, p. 85.

9. *Ibid.,* p. 86.

10. *Yü-lei,* Li Ching-te's epilogue dated 1263.

11. *Ibid.,* ch. 1, sec. 5 (p. 2).

12. See above, n. 6.

13. *Yü-lei,* ch. 1, sec. 11 (p. 4).

14. *Ibid.,* sec. 13 (pp. 4–5).

15. *Doctrine of the Mean,* ch. 1.

16. The Five Agents (or Five Elements) are Metal, Wood, Water, Fire, and Earth.

17. Chu Hsi, *Chung-yung chang-chü* [Collected commentaries on the *Doctrine of the Mean*], comment on ch. 1.

18. The Four Books are the *Great Learning,* the *Analects,* the *Book of Mencius,* and the *Doctrine of the Mean.*

19. Chu Hsi, *Lun-yü chi-chu* [Collected commentaries on the *Analects*], comment on 1:2; and *Meng Tzu chi-chu* [Collected commentaries on the *Book of Mencius*], comment on 1A:1, etc.

20. *I-shu* [Surviving works], 18:2a, in the *Erh-Ch'eng ch'üan-shu* [Complete works of the two Ch'engs] (*SPPY* ed.).

21. *Wai-shu* [Additional works], 3:1a, in the *Erh-Ch'eng ch'üan-shu.*

22. *Wen-chi,* 67:20a, "Jen-shuo" [Treatise on humanity].

23. *I-ch'uan ching-shuo* [Ch'eng I's explanation of the classics], 6:2b, in the *Erh-Ch'eng ch'üan-shu.*

24. *Yü-lei,* ch. 25, sec. 20 (p. 976).

25. *Ibid.,* sec. 21 (p. 976).

26. *Han Ch'ang-li ch'üan-chi* [Complete works of Han Yü] (*SPPY* ed.), 15:1a, "Inquiry on the Way."

27. *I-shu,* 18:1a.

28. *Lao Tzu,* ch. 28.

29. *Liu Ho-tung ch'üan-chi* [Complete works of Liu Tsung-yüan] (*SPPY* ed.), 14:9a, "Answers about Heaven."

30. Shao Yung, *Huang-chi ching-shih shu* [Supreme principles governing the world] (*SPPY* ed.) 7A:25b, "Outer Chapter on Viewing Things," pt. 1.

31. *Chou Tzu ch'üan-shu,* ch. 1, p. 4, "Explanation of the Diagram of the Great Ultimate."

32. *Doctrine of the Mean,* ch. 33, quoting the *Book of Odes,* ode no. 235.

33. Chu Hsi's commentary on the "Explanation of the Diagram of the Great Ultimate" in the *Chou Tzu ch'üan-shu,* ch. 1.

34. See the *Yü-lei,* ch. 94.

35. *Hsiang-shan ch'üan-chi* [Complete works of Lu Hsiang-shan] (*SPPY* ed.), 2:4b–7b, first letter to Chu Yüan-hui (Chu Hsi).

36. *Wen-chi,* 36:7b–10b, fifth letter in reply to Lu Tzu-ching (Lu Hsiang-shan).

37. Yeh Ts'ai, *Chin-ssu lu chi-chieh* [Collected explanations of *Reflections on Things at Hand*]. For a description of this work, see my translation of the *Chin-ssu lu* entitled *Reflections on Things at Hand* (New York: Columbia University Press, 1967), pp. 338–339.

# – 10 –
# *T'ai-chi*

THE philosophical category of *T'ai-chi* (the Great Ultimate) is treated neither systematically nor comprehensively here, for material on the subject abounds in Chinese, Korean, Japanese, and even English publications.[1] Instead, the present discussion is concerned only with problems that are new and on which there is nothing yet written in English—in this case, the use of the term *hun-lun* to describe *T'ai-chi*, and whether *T'ai-chi* is important in Chu Hsi's system.

Discussing Ch'en Ch'un (1159–1223), one of Chu Hsi's foremost pupils, in his *Chung-kuo che-hsüeh ssu-hsiang shih* (History of Chinese philosophical thought), Professor Stanislaus Lokuang said, "Chu Hsi regarded the Great Ultimate as principle. Ch'en Ch'un carefully adhered to his teacher's doctrines, but in explaining the original substance of the Great Ultimate he added the term *hun-lun* [undifferentiated] and thus differed from Chu Hsi's thought."[2] This is an original observation. Kusumoto Masatsugu's (1889–1963) *Sō-Min jidai jugaku shisō no kenkyū* (Study of Confucian thought in the Sung and Ming periods) is the most extensive study of Ch'en Ch'un in modern times. In it he particularly emphasized that Ch'en Ch'un employed the principle of the undifferentiated *(hun-tun)* to explain *T'ai-chi*. Kusumoto was not exaggerating when he characterized Ch'en Ch'un's thought as refined.[3] Ch'en Ch'un loved to use the term *hun-lun*. In his *Pei-hsi tzu-i* (Neo-Confucian terms explained), Ch'en used it five times under the category of "one thread running through all," twelve times under that of *T'ai-chi*, three times under "centrality and harmony," twice in his essay on "The Source of Teachers and Friends," and ten times in the sections on *T'ai-chi* in "Recovered Passages."[4] No one else had used the term so often. Yet *hun-lun* basically means "undifferentiation" and is essentially identical with Chu Hsi's explanation of *wu-chi* (ultimate of nonbeing) in the sense of being soundless and odorless. Chu Hsi himself also used *hun-lun* to explain *wu-chi* and said, "In the state of *hun-lun,* before any differentiation appeared, the two cosmic forces of yin and yang were merged in a subtle and hidden way."[5] In teaching pupils, he also employed the term. For example, "When a student first reads some writing, he merely sees something *hun-lun.* In time he will see two or three pieces until he sees ten pieces or more. Only then can he achieve progress."[6] Again, he said, "Seriousness (*ching,* reverence) cannot be explained in terms of *hun-lun.* One must inspect every event. The great essential is not to let go."[7]

But in actually describing (rather than explaining) *wu-chi,* Chu Hsi was not prone to use the term *hun-lun,* probably because it carried with it too much of Taoist mysticism. In his words, "*T'ai-chi* means precisely the ultimate of principle. . . . Now that you have explained it in terms of the great centrality, and have also discussed it as the state of undifferentiation of *ch'ien* [Heaven] and *k'un* [Earth] [i.e., yang and yin] and as the time of undifferentiation in the process of the great evolution, I am afraid that is unsatisfactory."[8] He also said,

> From your letter, you are saying precisely that there is something outside everyday affairs shimmering brilliantly and circulating to and fro. This is the same as what you quoted in your letter as "the reality of *wu-chi*"[9] and "the spirit of the valley that never dies."[10] What is called "a pure man who transcends and is no longer attached to any class of Buddhas or sentient beings"[11] is a Buddhist phrase. It is the leader of the spirit of the valley. . . . The language of the *Analects* and the *Book of Mencius* is plain and clear, and is devoid of this kind of mysterious utterance.[12]

Instead, Chu Hsi loved to quote the saying, "The operations of Heaven have neither sound nor smell"[13] to characterize *wu-chi.* He said, "*Wu-chi* is so called precisely because it has neither spatial restriction nor physical shape. It seems to exist prior to things, but it is not absent after the existence of things. It seems to lie outside yin and yang, but it has never ceased operating in the midst of them. It seems to penetrate the whole substance and is present everywhere, but it cannot be spoken of as basically having sound or smell."[14] He also said, "What is called 'Wu-chi erh T'ai-chi' does not mean that on top of the Great Ultimate there is separately an Ultimate of Nonbeing. It merely says that the Great Ultimate is not a thing, as in the saying, 'The operations of Heaven have neither sound nor smell.' "[15] Again, he said, "What is called *wu-chi* is to bring out the wonder of its being soundless and odorless."[16]

All this is not at variance with Ch'en Ch'un's description. As Ch'en Ch'un said,

*Wu-chi* means infinity; it merely describes principle as having no shape or appearance, spatial restriction or physical form, very much like the description of the operations of Heaven as having neither sound nor smell. *T'ai* means to the highest degree, and *T'ai-chi* is the greatest extent to the highest degree. Since it cannot be described, it is called *t'ai*. This simply means that although principle has no shape or appearance, spatial restriction or physical form, it is the basis and the axis of all transformations. It is called *T'ai-chi* because it is completely merged as one and undifferentiated *(hun-lun)* to the highest degree.[17]

Ch'en Ch'un was certainly remarkable in describing *T'ai-chi* as *hun-lun*, but he did not depart from his teacher.

As to whether or not *T'ai-chi* is an important concept in Chu Hsi's philosophical system, that depends on what one perceives Chu Hsi's system to be. Certainly the concept of *T'ai-chi* is cardinal in his metaphysics. In an earlier article I have shown in detail how Chu Hsi had to utilize Chou Tun-i's (1017–1073) "T'ai-chi-t'u shuo" (Explanation of the diagram of the Great Ultimate) despite the Taoist origin of the term *wu-chi*, for without it the relation between principle and material force cannot be explained.[18] In spite of this central importance, Professor Yamanoi Yū, in his 1982 paper entitled "The Great Ultimate and Heaven in Chu Hsi's Philosophy," declared that "the word *t'ai-chi* was neither woven closely into Chu Hsi's philosophical system nor given its proper place within it. For Chu Hsi's theoretical system, the word *t'ai-chi* is not an indispensable one."[19] This conclusion is utterly different from the general opinion among Chu Hsi specialists. Professor Yamanoi is a world-renowned authority on Neo-Confucianism and president of Japan's Society for Chinese Philsophy. He was not purposely making a shocking statement but drew his conclusion from solid scholarship.

According to Professor Yamanoi, the term *T'ai-chi* is used in the *Wen-chi* about 260 times, and in the *Yü-lei* about 350 times. Moreover, "almost all the cases in which this term is used belong to the contexts where Chu Hsi interpreted the word *t'ai-chi* described in the 'T'ai-chi-t'u shuo' or in the 'Appended Remarks' of the *Book of Changes*, or to the contexts where he discussed some philosophical issues relevant to these works. There are very few instances where Chu Hsi used this term when he developed his own theory or expressed his own opinions without regard to the 'T'ai-chi-t'u shuo' or the *Book of Changes*."[20] He cited four passages that may express Chu Hsi's philosophical views without any direct relationship to the two works he had mentioned, but added that "the very fact that there are only four examples among hundreds bespeaks my point that the word *t'ai-chi* did not become one of the words that could sustain Chu Hsi's philosophical system."[21] Yamanoi was the first to point out that these four passages have no direct relationship with the "T'ai-chi-t'u shuo" or the *Book of Changes,* a unique and sharp observation indeed.

In the *Wen-chi,* Chu Hsi criticized the interpretation of *T'ai-chi* as *chung* (centrality).[22] His discussion centered on the meaning of the word *chi* (ultimate or extreme), which has no direct relation with the *Book of Changes* or the "T'ai-chi-t'u shuo." It may be argued that the controversy about *chung* sprang from Chu Hsi's debate with Lu Hsiang-shan (1139–1193) on the "T'ai-chi-t'u shuo"[23] in 1188–1189, but if there was any connection, it was indirect. Furthermore, the discussion with Chang Shih (1133–1180) took place before the debate with Lu. The *Wen-chi* includes Chu Hsi's "T'ai-chi shuo" (Treatise on the Great Ultimate).[24] Half of this treatise is devoted to topics based on quotations from the *Book of Changes,* such as *yüan heng li chen* (origination, flourishing, advantage, and firmness),[25] "the state of absolute quiet," and "when acted on immediately penetrates all things,"[26] and on Ch'eng I's (1033–1107) famous saying, "Activity and tranquillity have no beginning, and yin and yang have no starting point."[27] But the other half quotes the opening of the *Doctrine of the Means* as saying, "What Heaven imparts to man is called human nature," and is devoted to a discussion of nature, destiny, feelings, centrality, and harmony.

Moreover, the *Yü-lei* contains the saying, "The Great Ultimate is nothing other than principle."[28] This is the core of Chu Hsi's thought system and is not an explanation of either the *Book of Changes* or the "T'ai-chi-t'u shuo." It has the same meaning as another saying, "The Great Ultimate is merely the principle of Heaven, Earth, and the myriad things."[29] If one argues that the latter saying is followed by the famous quotation from Ch'eng I and is therefore related to the *Book of Changes,* it can also be argued that the quotation from Ch'eng I describes the Great Ultimate in general rather than the *Book of Changes.* Besides, there is another saying in the *Yü-lei* about the Great Ultimate that clearly has nothing to do with either the *Book of Changes* or the "T'ai-chi-t'u shuo." A pupil asked about Ts'ai Chi-t'ung's (Ts'ai Yüan-ting, 1135–1198) saying that "there is the operation of principle and there is an order. First there is the operation and then there is the order." The Teacher said, "It is difficult to say which is the first. Chi-t'ung mentioned the Great Ultimate to show that all principles are the same. Hold onto his theory if you like."[30] There are also discussions in the *Yü-lei* on Shao Yung's (1011–1077) doctrine that "Tao is the Great Ultimate"[31] and "The mind is the Great Ultimate,"[32] which is clearly unrelated to either of the two works.[33] Nevertheless, Professor Yamanoi's keen observation that most of the discussions in the *Yü-lei* and the *Wen-chi* on the Great Ultimate are related to the *Book of Changes* or the "T'ai-chi-t'u shuo" is an admirable discovery.

Professor Yamanoi also said,

More decisive on this issue is that the word *t'ai-chi* was used nowhere in the *Ssu-shu chi-chu* (Collected commentaries on the Four Books).[34] Even in the *Ssu-shu huo-wen* (Questions and answers on the Four Books), the word *t'ai-chi* is not used except in the brief remark that "When Master Chou [Chou Tun-i] appeared, he advocated the doctrines of *t'ai-chi,* yin-yang, and the Five Agents."[35] Moreover, even this one example belongs to the context where Chu Hsi pointed out the greatness of what Chou Tun-i's "T'ai-chi-t'u shuo" had achieved. Never did he aim at elucidating Mencius' doctrine of nature by the notion of *T'ai-chi* there. Nowhere did Chu Hsi use the word *t'ai-chi* to annotate or elucidate the Four Books.[36]

This is another keen observation that no one else has made. To Professor Yamanoi, the *Ssu-shu chi-shu* and the *Ssu-shu huo-wen* are Chu Hsi's most important works, and almost all Chu Hsi specialists share this view. Not only do the Four Books form the core of Chu Hsi's system, but many of his key ideas come from his commentaries on them. For example, his famous formulation, "The clear character is what man received from Heaven. It is vacuous [devoid of obstruction], intelligent, and not beclouded. All principles are contained therein and all events proceed from it," is from his comment on the opening passage of the *Great Learning.*[37] Both his definition of *jen* (humanity) as "the principle of love and the character of the mind" and his definition of *li* (propriety) as "the measures and patterns of the Principle of Heaven and the regulation of human affairs" are from his comments on the *Analects.*[38] He said, "In my *Yü-Meng chi-chu* [Collected commentaries on the *Analects* and the *Book of Mencius*], not a single word may be added and not a single word deleted."[39] He also said, "For more than forty years I have thought over the *Lun-Meng* [*chi-chu*] [Collected commentaries on the *Analects* and the *Book of Mencius*]. I have weighed every word in them and would not allow myself to be offtrack."[40]

Indeed, just three days before Chu Hsi died, he revised his commentary on the chapter on sincerity of the will in the *Great Learning.*[41] Thus it is not an exaggeration to say that the *Ssu-shu chi-chu* is the key to Chu Hsi's philosophical system. When Professor Yamanoi said that the concept of the Great Ultimate was not woven into the thoughts of Chu Hsi, he probably had this in mind. However, the Great Ultimate is a concept in cosmology and ontology, whereas the doctrines in the Four Books are relevant to daily affairs. These doctrines are based on principle, and principle in turn is based on the Great Ultimate. Perhaps Professor Yamanoi considers metaphysics to be of secondary importance in Chu Hsi's system. If so, his conviction may serve to steer other scholars away from an overemphasis on metaphysics in Chu Hsi.

Incidentally, the fact that Chu Hsi was still working on his commentary on the *Great Learning* at the very end of his life is a celebrated story well known to scholars. But it is never mentioned that, as Professor Yü

Ying-shih has called to my attention, the same account of Chu Hsi's death tells us that, after the revision of the *Great Learning,* he continued to revise a paragraph of his annotation of the *Ch'u-tz'u* (Elegies of Ch'u). The significance of this remains a matter of speculation. Scholars agree that Chu Hsi annotated the *Ch'u-tz'u* in 1195 to show his concern about the political persecution of Neo-Confucianism, just as Ch'ü Yüan (343–277 B.C.) originally wrote the *Ch'u-tz'u* to express his sadness over the political situation of his time. The account of Chu Hsi's death goes on to note his eagerness concerning the compilation of ritual texts. Thus his last intellectual concern was with rituals, to which he devoted practically his whole life.

## Notes

1. For a source in English, see Wing-tsit Chan, ed., *Chu Hsi and Neo-Confucianism* (Honolulu: University of Hawaii Press, 1986), chaps. 6–9, 11, 18, and pp. 8–10.

2. Stanislaus Lokuang, *Chung-kuo che-hsüeh ssu-hsiang shih* [History of Chinese philosophical thought]: *The Sung Period* (Taipei: Student Book Co., 1978), p. 67.

3. Kusumoto Masatsugu, *Sō-Min jidai jugaku shisō no kenkyū* [Study of Confucian thought in the Sung and Ming Periods] (Tokyo: Hiroike Gakuen Press, 1962), pp. 291–293.

4. See my translation of Ch'en Ch'un's *Pei-hsi tzu-i* entitled *Neo-Confucian Terms Explained* (New York: Columbia University Press, 1986), pp. 94–96, 115–120, 122–125, 178–182, and 188–192.

5. *Yü-lei,* ch. 94, sec. 16 (p. 3758).

6. *Ibid.,* ch. 10, sec. 15 (p. 257).

7. *Ibid.,* ch. 8, sec. 27 (p. 214).

8. *Wen-chi,* 37:31b–32a, third letter in reply to Ch'eng K'o-chiu (Ch'eng Ch'iung).

9. Chou Tun-i, "Explanation of the Diagram of the Great Ultimate," in the *Chou Tzu ch'üan-shu* [Complete works of Master Chou] (*Kuo-hsüeh chi-pen ts'ung-shu* [Basic sinological series] ed.) ch. 1, p. 14.

10. *Lao Tzu,* ch. 6.

11. *Lin-chi Hui-chao Ch'an-shih yü-lu* [Recorded sayings of Ch'an Master Hui-chao of Lin-chi] in the *Taishō daizōkyō* [Taishō edition of the Buddhist canon], vol. 47, p. 496.

12. *Wen-chi,* 45:42b–43a, eighteenth letter in reply to Liao Tzu-hui (Liao Te-ming).

13. *Doctrine of the Mean,* ch. 33, quoting the *Book of Odes,* ode no. 235.

14. *Wen-chi,* 36:9b, fifth letter in reply to Lu Tzu-ching (Lu Hsiang-shan).

15. *Ibid.,* 49:10a–b, thirteenth letter in reply to Wang Tzu-ho (Wang Yü).

16. *Ibid.,* 45:11b, first letter in reply to Yang Tzu-chih (Yang Fang).

17. *Neo-Confucian Terms Explained,* pp. 116–117.

18. See my "Chu Hsi's Completion of Neo-Confucianism," in Françoise

Aubin, ed. *Étude Song—Sung Studies in memorium Étienne Balazs,* Paris: Ser. II, no. 1 (1973), pp. 59–90. Reprinted in my *Chu Hsi: Life and Thought* (Hong Kong: Chinese University Press, 1987), pp. 103–138. Chinese translation by Wan Hsien-fa in *Chinese Cultural Renaissance Monthly,* no. 12 (December, 1974), pp. 1–14; *Sinological Monthly,* no. 37 (January, 1975), pp. 20–43; and my *Chu-hsüeh lun-chi* [Essays on Chu Hsi Studies] (Taipei: Student Book Co., 1982), pp. 1–35.

19. *Chu Hsi and Neo-Confucianism,* p. 82.

20. *Ibid.*

21. *Ibid.,* pp. 82–83.

22. *Wen-chi,* 31:17a, twenty-ninth letter in reply to Chang Ching-fu (Chang Shih); 54:10a, letter in reply to Yü Shou-weng (Yü T'ing-ch'un).

23. *Ibid.,* 36:8a–9a, 12a, fifth and sixth letters in reply to Lu Tzu-ching (Lu Hsiang-shan).

24. *Ibid.,* 67:16a–b, "T'ai-chi shuo" (Treatise on the Great Ultimate).

25. These are the Four Qualities of the first hexagram, *ch'ien* (Heaven, male), in the *Book of Changes.*

26. This is from the commentary on the second hexagram, *k'un* (Earth, female), in the *Book of Changes.*

27. *I-ch'uan ching-shuo* [Ch'eng I's explanations of the classics], in the *Erh-Ch'eng ch'üan-shu* [Complete works of the two Ch'engs] (*SPPY* ed.), 1:1b–2a, "Explanation of the *Book of Changes.*"

28. *Yü-lei,* ch. 1, sec. 4 (p. 2).

29. *Ibid.,* sec. 1 (p. 1).

30. *Ibid.,* ch. 6, sec. 13 (p. 161).

31. Shao Yung, *Huang-chi ching-shih shu* [Supreme principles governing the world] (*SPPY* ed.), 7A:23a, "Outer Chapter of Viewing Things."

32. *Ibid.,* 8A:25a, "Outer Chapter of Viewing Things."

33. *Yü-lei,* ch. 100, sec. 31 (p. 4050).

34. The Four Books are the *Great Learning,* the *Analects,* the *Book of Mencius,* and the *Doctrine of the Mean.*

35. Chu Hsi, *Meng Tzu huo-wen* [Questions and answers on the *Book of Mencius*] (Pao-ku-t'ang [Hall of Precious Bestowment] ed. of the *Chu Tzu-i-shu* [Surviving works of Master Chu]), 11:4a, comment on 6A:6. The Five Agents (or Five Elements) are Metal, Wood, Water, Fire, and Earth.

36. *Chu Hsi and Neo-Confucianism,* p. 83.

37. Chu Hsi, *Ta-hsüeh chang-chü* [Collected commentaries on the *Great Learning*], comment on the opening sentence.

38. Chu Hsi, *Lun-yü chi-chu* [Collected commentaries on the *Analects*], comments on 1:2 and 1:12.

39. *Yü-lei,* ch. 19, sec. 59 (p. 703).

40. *Ibid.,* sec. 61 (p. 704).

41. Ts'ai Ch'en, "Chu Wen Kung meng-tien chi" [Account of Chu Hsi's death], in the *Ts'ai-shih chiu-ju shu* [Works of nine Confucians in the Ts'ai family] (1868 ed.), 6:59a.

# 11

# Chu Hsi's "Jen-shuo"
# (Treatise on Humanity)

C HU Hsi's philosophical thought centered on the basic concepts of the Great Ultimate *(T'ai-chi)*, principle *(li)*, material force *(ch'i)*, humanity *(jen)*, righteousness *(i)*, equilibrium *(chung)*, and harmony *(ho)*. In these he perpetuated the doctrines of the Ch'eng brothers (Ch'eng Hao, 1032–1085, and Ch'eng I, 1033–1107) and added his own innovative views to compete with the prevailing philosophical schools of Hunan, Kiangsi, and Chekiang. To this end he carried on debates with Lu Hsiang-shan (1139–1193) of Kiangsi on the problem of the Great Ultimate,[1] with Chang Shih (1133–1180) of Hunan on the issue of equilibrium and harmony,[2] and with Ch'en Liang (1143–1194) of Chekiang on the questions of righteousness versus profit and the way of the sagely king versus the way of the powerful despot.[3] But there was no debate on the central concept of *jen* (humanity), as if Chu Hsi were not much concerned with it. In reality, however, after he compiled the *Lun-yü yao-i* (Essential meanings of the *Analects*) in 1163 at the age of thirty-four, Chu Hsi hardly passed a day without thinking and talking about *jen*. His ideas on it are found in his commentaries, letters, and conversations. The number of people with whom he discussed *jen*, both in person and in his correspondence, far exceeded the number with whom he discussed other topics. His correspondence on *jen*, now preserved in the *Wen-chi*, includes letters to Chang Ching-fu (Chang Shih), Lü Po-kung (Lü Tsu-ch'ien), Ho Shu-ching (Ho Hao), Hu Kuang-chung (Hu Shih), Wu Hui-shu (Wu I), Shih Tzu-chung (Shih Tun), Lin Hsi-chih (Lin Ta-ch'un), Lin Tse-chih (Lin Yung-chung), Hu Po-feng (Hu Ta-yüan), Lü Tzu-yüeh (Lü Tsu-chien), "Venerable Sir," Yü Chan-chih (Yü Yü), Chou Shun-pi (Chou Mu), Chou Shu-chin (Chou Chieh), Fang Pin-wang (Fang I), Li Yao-ch'ing (Li T'ang-tzu), Ch'en An-ching (Ch'en Ch'un), Yang Chung-ssu (Yang Tao-fu), Ch'en Ch'i-chih (Ch'en Chih), and Hsü Chü-fu (Hsü Yü). The degree of fervent discussion can readily be seen.[4]

Besides his correspondence, Chu Hsi wrote the "Jen-shuo," a 824-character treatise now preserved in chapter 67 of the *Wen-chi*. It is divided into two sections, the first on *jen* as "the character of the mind" *(hsin chih te)*, and the second on *jen* as "the principle of love" *(ai chih li)*. He also criticized the theories of *jen* forming one body with all things and *jen* as consciousness of pain. In addition, he drew the "Jen-shuo-t'u" (Diagram of the "Treatise on Humanity") which appears at the end of chapter 105 of the *Yü-lei*—and in chapter 18 below (p. 281). The diagram was drawn after many years of discussion on *jen* and numerous revisions of the treatise. To Chu Hsi, the concept of *jen* was clearly far more important than those of the Great Ultimate and other philosophical categories. Why was this? As Chu Hsi himself confided, he simply could not help it.

## The Motive

In a letter to Lü Tsu-ch'ien (1137–1181), Chu Hsi wrote,

> Of course this treatise is superficial and lacks reserve. But in my humble opinion, in the teaching of the ancients there was already a clear explanation of terms like this beginning with elementary education, unlike the superficial, abstract, and artificial interpretations of later generations. In their learning, they understood the term clearly, but a principle like this must be put into actual practice. Therefore, in the School of the Sage [Confucius] the important task has been to search for humanity. The reason is that having understood the term to some extent, one has to strive to arrive at that state. People today have completely failed to understand. This being the case, what they are seeking eagerly is something of which they are ignorant throughout life. How can they be expected to love to discuss it and to know where to devote their effort? Therefore, although my words today are simple and plain compared to those of the ancients, I cannot help uttering them.[5]

Two points should be noted in this letter, namely, Chu Hsi's explanation of the term *jen* and his emphasis on the necessity of putting it into concrete practice. But one must first comprehend the principle of *jen* before one can practice it. In a letter to Lü Tsu-ch'ien's brother, Lü Tsu-chien (d. 1196), Chu Hsi said,

> *Jen*, of course, cannot be interpreted purely from the point of view of function, but one must understand the principle that *jen* has the ability to function. Only then will it do. Otherwise, the term will be meaningless and

cannot be explained. Take the sentence, "Origination is the leading quality of goodness."[6] It means the original substance which is the starting point of the origination of all things and which can function. One should not regard the original substance of *jen* as one thing and its function as another. . . . Generally speaking, the meaning of *jen* must be found in one idea and one principle. Only then can we talk on a high level about a principle that penetrates everything. Otherwise, it will be the so-called vague Thusness and stupid Buddha-nature,[7] and the word *jen* will be left dangling. I have written my humble treatise precisely for this reason.[8]

The idea in this passage is similar to that in the letter to Lü Tsu-ch'ien —namely, that the concept of *jen* must be understood before its substance and function can be distinguished.

In his letter to Wu I, Chu Hsi said,

Generally speaking, in recent years scholars do not like to talk about *jen* in terms of love. Therefore, when they see that the Master Gentleman [Ch'eng I] talked about the mind of Heaven and Earth in terms of one yang [positive cosmic force] element producing things,[9] they are certain to be sadly dissatisfied, and furthermore, to ascribe ideas over and above what is originally intended and make abstract inferences without realizing that the way Heaven and Earth exercise their mind is none other than this. If we talk about *jen* beyond this sense, we will degenerate into emptiness and fall into quiescence, and substance and function, and the fundamental and the secondary, will have no relation to each other.[10]

This letter puts special emphasis on the interpretation of *jen* as love, which is rooted in the mind of Heaven and Earth to produce things. The purpose is still to clarify the concept of *jen*.

From the above, we can see that Chu Hsi had three reasons for writing the "Jen-shuo." First, scholars of his time wrote on the subject of *jen* in great confusion. Chang Shih, Lin Ta-ch'un, Chou Chieh, Yang Tao-fu, and "Venerable Sir" each wrote a treatise on *jen*. Strange doctrines sprang up, with no agreement among them. Especially mistaken were the theories that *jen* meant forming one body with all things and of *jen* as consciousness. Thus Chu Hsi wrote his treatise to clarify the meaning of the term. Second, he wanted to show that the concept *jen* as love is based on the notion that the mind of Heaven and Earth is to produce things, and thereby prevent scholars from falling into the errors of emptiness and quiescence. The "Jen-shuo" says, "I fear scholars talk about *jen* without reference to love. I have therefore propounded this particular doctrine of *jen* to make the idea clear." Third, Chu Hsi wanted to correct the erroneous theory that substance and function are two different things.

## Main Ideas of the "Jen-shuo"

Although the "Jen-shuo" is short, its ideas are well thought out. It starts with the sentences, "The mind of Heaven and Earth is to produce things. In the production of man and things, they receive the mind of Heaven and Earth as their mind." The first sentence is a quotation from Ch'eng I;[11] the second was added by Chu Hsi himself. Chu Hsi continues, "The moral qualities of the mind of Heaven and Earth are four: origination, flourishing, advantage and firmness,[12] and origination unites and controls all their operations." In the human mind, "There are also Four Virtues, namely: humanity, righteousness, propriety, and wisdom,[13] and humanity embraces all their functions." "Therefore, with reference to the character of the mind . . . we can only say that it is *jen.*" "For *jen* as constituting the Way consists of the fact that the mind of Heaven and Earth to produce things is present in everything. Before the feelings are aroused, this substance is already existent in its entirety. After feelings are aroused, its function is infinite. Thus if we can truly realize *jen* and preserve it, we have in it the spring of all virtues and the root of all good deeds. This is why the Confucian School always urged students to exert anxious and unceasing effort in the pursuit of *jen.*" Self-mastery, respect and reverence, conscientiousness and altruism, filial piety and brotherly respect—all are ways to preserve this mind and put it into practice. Before the feelings are aroused, it is nature, which is identical with *jen.* As feelings are aroused, it becomes love. That is why Chu Hsi defined *jen* as "the principle of love." Though nature and feelings seem to belong to different spheres, their interpenetration make them one system, like arteries and veins. But among followers of the Ch'eng brothers,

> Some [notably Yang Shih, 1053–1135] say that love is not *jen* and regard the unity of all things and the self as *jen,* while others [notably Hsieh Liang-tso, 1050–c. 1120] maintain that love is not *jen* but explain *jen* in terms of the possession of consciousness by the mind.[14] . . . From what they call the unity of all things and the self, it can be seen that *jen* involves love for all, but unity is not the reality that makes *jen* a substance. From the way they regard the mind as the possession of consciousness, it can be seen that *jen* includes wisdom, but that is not the real reason why *jen* is so called. . . . To talk about *jen* in general terms of the unity of things and the self will lead people to be vague, confused, neglectful, and make no effort to be alert. The bad effect—and there has been one—may be to consider other things as oneself. To talk about *jen* in specific terms of consciousness will lead people to be nervous, irascible, and devoid of any quality of depth. The bad effect—and there has been one—may be to consider [selfish] desire as principle. In one case, [the mind] forgets [its objec-

tive]. In the other, [there is artificial effort to] help [it grow].[15] Both are wrong.

This is the gist of the "Jen-shuo."

## When Was the Treatise Written?

We do not know exactly when the "Jen-shuo" was written. Liao Te-ming (1169 cs) asked, "Sir, in the 'Jen-shuo' that you wrote some time ago, you generally consider the mind to embrace the principle of love, and that is why it is called jen. But now in your [Meng Tzu] chi-chu [Collected commentaries on the Book of Mencius], commenting on the sentence 'Jen is the human mind,'[16] you take it to mean 'the master of dealing with all changes.' How about it?"[17] This was recorded by Liao after 1173, suggesting that the "Jen-shuo" was written before the compilation of the [Meng Tzu] chi-chu in 1177. However, Chu Hsi said, "For more than forty years I have thought over the Lun-Meng [chi-chu] [Commentaries on the Analects and the Book of Mencius],"[18] and several days before he died he was still revising his commentary on the Great Learning. Thus what is found in the Lun-Meng chi-chu may very well have been written after the "Jen-shuo."

In any case, the writing of the treatise must have taken a long time, although it also must not have been completed too late. In his letter to Lü Tsu-ch'ien on jen, Chu Hsi said that Ch'in-fu (Chang Shih) had written that he had no more doubts about the "Jen-shuo." He added that he "wanted to write the [I-Lo] yüan-yüan lu [Records of the origin of the school of the Ch'engs] to include all the deeds and writings of the various gentlemen, from Chou [Chou Tun-i, 1017–1073] and the Ch'engs on. I am troubled not to have the material or the complete accounts of various scholars of the Yung-chia School. I have, therefore, written Shih-lung [Hsüeh Chi-hsüan, 1134–1173] to ask him to search and send them to me."[19] The fact that Chang Shih had no more doubts about the "Jen-shuo" indicates that the treatise had assumed its final form. Only then did Chu Hsi conceive the idea of compiling the I-Lo yüan-yüan lu and find that the material needed to do so was not yet available. The Yüan-yüan lu was completed in the sixth month of 1173. Assuming it took a year or two to write, the idea of compiling it must have occurred around 1171, by which time the final draft of the "Jen-shuo" must also have been written. Professor Tomoeda Ryūtarō believes that the treatise was completed about 1173, when Chu Hsi was forty-four.[20] My opinion is that it was finished before, not after, that year.

We do not know how many years Chu Hsi debated with Chang Shih on the "Jen-shuo." There are four letters to Chang Shih in the *Wen-chi* devoted to discussions on the treatise.[21] In his funeral address for Chang Shih, Ch Hsi said that for almost ten years they had debated back and forth, finally coming to an agreement.[22] Although this is a general statement, it must include their discussions on the "Jen-shuo," and indeed, the four letters are clear evidence of this fact. When Chu Hsi visited Chang Shih at Changsha in 1167, one of the topics for discussion was *jen*.[23] Although Chang Shih said he had no more doubts, that did not necessarily mean the two men were in complete agreement. As Chu Hsi said, in their former discussion he and Chang Shih "still had one or two points of disagreement."[24] Thus the final draft of the treatise must have been preceded by years of discussion with Chang Shih. We may say that the "Jen-shuo" was largely finished by 1171, but it must have been started many years earlier.

Because one of the letters in which Chu Hsi discussed the "Jen-shuo" with Chang Shih contains the sentence, "In your letter you consider what I say in the 'K'e-chai [chi]' [Account of the studio of self-mastery] to be better,"[25] and the "K'e-chai chi" was written in 1172, Professor Mou Tsung-san has determined that the first draft of the "Jen-shuo" was written before that date.[26] His theory is correct. However, he also maintains that Chu Hsi wrote the "Jen-shuo" two or three years after he had established the new doctrine of equilibrium and harmony in 1169; that his debates with scholars on the subject generally took place after he was forty-three years old (1172); and that the final draft was also written after this date. I am afraid he puts the matter too late, for we know that in 1172 Chang Shih had no more doubts. It may be argued that Chu Hsi said in his letter, "I wanted to make some revisions but have had no time to do so," indicating that when the "K'e-chai chi" was written, the "Jen-shuo" was not yet completed. However, I am convinced this is not the case, because the letter also says, "Formerly, I presented the 'Jen-shuo' to you." "Formerly" may refer either to the first draft of a numbers of years before, to the final draft of only a year or two earlier, or even to some intermediate version. We do not know what it was that Chu Hsi had wanted to revise. He went on to say that Chang Shih "did not understand this completely." The entire emphasis in the "K'e-chai chi" is on self-mastery, which is not a key idea in the "Jen-shuo." Perhaps Chu Hsi did not make the revision, whatever it was, but even after he finished the treatise, he continued to discuss it with scholars. As late as 1185 he discussed it in a letter to Lü Tsu-chien,[27] in which he also referred to his debate with Ch'en Liang during the same year.[28] If Chu Hsi had wanted to make revisions even at this late date, there ought to have been no problem in doing so, just as after the *Lun-Meng chi-chu* was finished, he continued to make changes in it.

Based on the dates mentioned above, we may conclude that Chu Hsi's discussions on the "Jen-shuo" took place for many years after 1165 or 1166, when Chu Hsi was thirty-six or thirty-seven, and culminated in about 1171, when he was forty-two. In any case, the completion of the "Jen-shuo" preceded not only that of the *Yüan-yüan lu* but also that of the *Chin-ssu lu* (Reflections on things at hand) in 1175; the *Ssu-shu chi-chu* (Collected commentaries on the Four Books)[29] and the *Ssu-shu huo-wen* (Questions and answers on the Four Books) in 1177; his publication of the Four Books in 1190; and the "Yü-shan chiang-i" (Yü-shan lecture) in 1194.[30] Although the Four Books are the foundation of Chu Hsi's doctrines and the Yü-shan lecture their outline, Chu Hsi's thoughts had come to maturation in the "Jen-shuo" twenty years earlier.

## Important Phrases

The "Jen-shuo" contains two key phrases, "the character of the mind" and "the principle of love." These two refrains occur in more than ten places in the *Lun-yü chi-chu* (Collected commentaries on the *Analects*) and the *Meng Tzu chi-chu* (Collected commentaries on the *Book of Mencius*). In the former, it is said in the comments on *Analects* 1:2 that "*Jen* is the principle of love and the character of the mind," and on 18:1 that "*Jen* does not violate the principle of love and has a way of preserving the character of the mind." In the latter, in a comment on 1A:1, it is said that "*Jen* is the character of the mind and the principle of love." In the *Lun-yü huo-wen* (Questions and answers on the *Analects*), it is also said that "The principle of love is the reason for the character of the mind."[31] In other places, the phrases "the character of the mind" and "the complete character of the mind" often occur, as do "the mind of *jen* is the mind to love people," "the foundation of *jen* is love," and "to love people is the application of *jen*."[32] Thus the use of "the character of the mind" and "the principle of love" is not incidental but the result of decades of careful deliberation. As Chu Hsi said, "In my *Yü-Meng chi-chu* [Collected commentaries on the *Analects* and the *Book of Mencius*], not a single word may be added and not a single word deleted."[33] He also said, "For more than forty years I have thought over the *Lun Meng* [*chi-chu*]. I have weighed every word in them and would not allow myself to be offtrack."[34]

### Origin of the Phrases

In his *Kairoku* (Records of the sea), Yamazaki Bisei (1797–1863) noted that in the *Ryūgan tekagami* (Paragon of the dragon niche) *jen* is explained thus: "Pronounced *jen*. It is the character of the mind and the principle of love." Since the *Ryūgan tekagami* was written in 997 and the *Lun-Meng chi-chu* was completed 180 years later, in 1177, he concluded that the two phrases were originally Buddhist and were borrowed by Chu Hsi.[35] But as Yamaguchi Satsujō (1882–1948) pointed out, the preface of the *Ryūgan tekagami* says the book consists of some 26,430 words, whereas the edition that Yamazaki used contains 39,428 words. In the notes to this longer edition are notations such as "present addition," and in the case of *jen* the enlarged edition has added, "It means affectionate love." Yamaguchi therefore decided that the phrases "the character of the mind" and "the principle of love" were obviously later additions.[36] Accordingly, Fujitsuka Chikashi (1879–1948) said, "These phrases are found in the Korean enlarged edition of the *Ryūgan tekagami*. Both the *Kairoku* of Yamazaki Bisei and the *Kobun kyūshō kō* (Investigation of ancient texts) of Shimada Kan (1879–1915) are based on this reprint for their conclusions. How can they be relied on?"[37]

Yamaguchi did not believe that Chu Hsi borrowed his key phrases from Buddhism, but he did assert that he borrowed from Chang Shih. According to Yamaguchi, Chang Shih's comment on *Analects* 12:22 says, "As we investigate human nature, its principle of love is *jen* and its principle of knowledge is wisdom." Chang's *Lun-yü chieh* (Explanation of the *Analects*) was written in 1173, while Chu Hsi's *Chi chu* was completed after his *Lun-Meng ching-i* (Essential meaning of the *Analects* and the *Book of Mencius*) and *Lun-Meng huo-wen*. The *Ching-i* was compiled in 1172, a year earlier than Chang's *Lun-yü chieh,* but the *Huo-wen* was completed in 1177, four years after the *Lun-yü chieh*. For the sake of argument, Yamaguchi concluded that had the phrases "the character of the mind" and "the principle of love" not been used in the *Ching-i,* Chang Shih might have been the first to use them in his *Lun-yü chieh*.[38] We do not know in what month of 1173 the *Lun-yü chieh* was completed, but Chu Hsi's *Yüan-yüan lu* was finished in the sixth month of that year, at which time the "Jen-shuo" had assumed its final form. Even if Chang Shih finished the *Lun-yü chieh* in the first month of 1173, did Chu Hsi see it, immediately borrow the phrase "the principle of love," and insert it in his "Jen-shuo"? Would this have been typical of Chu Hsi, who did not add or delete a word without a long period of thinking? Did his many discussions with Chang Shih on the "Jen-shuo" take place only during these several months of 1173? And even supposing that "the principle of love" did come from Chang Shih, where would "the character of the mind" have come from? In his reply to Chu Hsi, Chang Shih said, "I have read your letter several times and have been greatly benefited. What you called the principle of love has certainly opened me up."[39] Thus we can see that it was Chu Hsi who inspired Chang Shih, not vice versa. It is therefore more convincing to say that Chang Shih borrowed from Chu Hsi, rather than the other way around. Ōtsuki Nobuyoshi regarded "the principle of love" and "the character of the mind" as new meanings contributed by Chu Hsi.[40]

This is not his own opinion but the consensus of scholars over the centuries.

### The Character of the Mind

The central concepts of the "Jen-shuo" are "the character of the mind" and "the principle of love." What do these mean? "The character of mind" is sometimes rendered as "the Way of the mind"[41] and "the character of nature."[42] Hu Hung (1106–1161) had said in his *Hu Tzu chih-yen* (Master Hu's understanding of words) that "*Jen* is the way of the mind,"[43] which could have inspired Chu Hsi. The words *tao* (way) and *te* (character) are interchangeable. Nevertheless, *tao* refers to function, whereas *te* refers to substance. There was a special reason for Chu Hsi to use the term "character." He said, "It is like saying that being moist is the character of water and being dry and hot is the character of fire."[44] The chief character of *jen* is *sheng,* to produce or to give life. In commenting on the *Book of Mencius* 5A:11, he said, "*Jen* is the character of the mind. As Master Ch'eng [Ch'eng I] has said, 'The mind is comparable to seeds of grain. The nature of growth is *jen.*' "[45] Chu Hsi's idea was derived from Ch'eng I's doctrine of *sheng-sheng* (production and reproduction, perpetual renewal of life). Ch'eng I's novel interpretation of *jen* as seeds was a breakthrough in the philosophy of *jen*. And just as *jen* is comparable to seeds, Ch'eng I said, so "the mind is the principle of production."[46] He also said, "The mind of Heaven and Earth is to produce things."[47] Chu Hsi agreed with this. The first sentences of the "Jen-shuo" are "The mind of Heaven and Earth is to produce things. In the production of man and things, they receive the mind of Heaven and Earth as their mind." This is the basic point of the "Jen-shuo," a point that provoked a great deal of discussion among scholars. We shall deal with it in more detail below.

Because *jen* has the connotation of growth, it can include the Four Virtues of humanity, righteousness, propriety, and wisdom. Ch'eng I said, "Spoken of separately, it is one of the several, but spoken of collectively, it embraces all four."[48] Chu Hsi also agreed with this. His pupil Ch'en Ch'un (1159–1223) once asked, "*Jen* is the character of the mind. Are righteousness, propriety, and wisdom also characters of the mind?" Chu Hsi answered, "They are all characters of the mind, but *jen* alone embraces all of them."[49] And in answering a similar question from Huang Kan (1152–1221), he said, "They all are, but *jen* is the greatest."[50] What he meant by "embraces all of them" and "is the greatest" is that "spoken of together, all four are characters of the mind, but *jen* is the master."[51] In other words, "*Jen* being the character of the mind, it possesses all the other three. . . . What is called the character of the mind here is similar to what Master Ch'eng meant by 'collectively, it embraces all four.' "[52]

Although Chu Hsi agreed with Ch'eng I, his "Jen-shuo" is original in many respects. Ch'eng I had said, "*Jen* is the correct principle of the world."[53] Chu Hsi did not adopt this definition but coined his own—namely, "the character of the mind." Many of his pupils were skeptical about this and questioned him repeatedly, either in person or by letter. Chu Hsi thought Ch'eng I's definition too broad or too vague,[54] for righteousness, propriety, and wisdom can also be correct principles of the world.[55] To Chu Hsi, Ch'eng I was speaking only in general terms, not about the substance of *jen*.[56] If correct principle is applied to *jen*, it would be the character of the mind.[57] That is to say, *jen* is not a general principle of the world but the correct principle of the mind; it "is merely the correct principle of my mind."[58] Hence, in answering his pupil Ch'eng Hsün's letter, in which Ch'eng had equated *jen* with the Principle of Heaven, Chu Hsi said, "This statement should be fully explained and not dismissed like this."[59] Elsewhere he noted, "It is necessary to say that *jen* is the complete character of the original mind, and there is thus the Principle of Heaven,"[60] and because "*jen* is the complete character of the original mind, if the innate mind of the Principle of Heaven as it naturally is has been preserved and not lost, whatever one does will be orderly and harmonious."[61]

Thus the character of the mind is of course the substance of *jen*,[62] and is of course internal, not external.[63] As Chu Hsi said, "One must see what the feeling is if one loses or preserves the character of the mind, and then one can see what *jen* really is."[64] The "Jen-shuo" says,

> "Be respectful in private life, be serious *(ching)* in handling affairs, and be loyal in dealing with others."[65] This is the way to preserve the mind. "Be filial in serving parents, be respectful in serving the elder brother,[66] and be altruistic in dealing with others."[67] These are the ways to practice this mind. [The *Analects* also say,] "One obtains *jen* if one seeks it."[68] The fact that [Po-i and Shu-ch'i] yielded the throne to each other, fled, and later appealed [to King Wu (r. 1121–1104 B.C.)] not to send a military expedition [against the Shang dynasty (c. 1751–1112 B.C.)], choosing to starve to death [after the Shang fell],[69] was because of their ability not to lose the mind.

Preserving, practicing, and not losing all refer to the character of the mind. There are only two questions on the "Jen-shuo" in the *Yü-lei*. One was asked by Shen Hsien, who inquired about the mind of Heaven and Earth to produce things, a point discussed below. The other was asked by Kan Chieh, who inquired about preserving and not losing the character of the mind. Kan Chieh asked, "Sir, in your "Jen-shuo" you say this is to preserve [*jen*] and this is not to lose [*jen*], but at the same time you say that when one practices this, *jen* is in it, but practicing is not *jen*." Chu Hsi answered, "Of course it is not all right to call it *jen*, but to say that it is not *jen* is simple to deny it is *jen* in so many words.

Mencius went on to explain *jen,* but Confucius did not do this."[70] What Kan Chieh meant was that practice belongs to worldly affairs, whereas *jen* is character. At bottom, *jen* is man's mind, while righteousness is man's path.[71] Chu Hsi himself also said, "*Jen* is the character of the mind. As soon as one preserves this mind, there will be nothing but *jen.* Take the saying, 'To master oneself and return to propriety [is *jen*].'[72] What the saying calls for is that after selfish desires have been eliminated, the mind is forever preserved. It does not cover practice."[73]

There is clearly a difference between principle and worldly affairs. However, since Chu Hsi interpreted *jen* as the character of the mind, and since this character means the spirit of life, ideas must be expressed in practice. Here Chu Hsi seems to contradict himself. As Ch'en Ch'un explained, "*Jen* is the complete character of the mind. It includes and controls all the other four virtues. Righteousness, propriety, and wisdom are impossible without *jen.* This is so because *jen* is the principle of production in the mind, always operating in the process of production and reproduction without cease, and remaining from the beginning to the end without interruption."[74] This means that *jen* is the principle of production and reproduction, operating everywhere in actual practice.

### The Principle of Love

As Chu Hsi explained it, "*Jen* is the principle of love. Principle is the root, while love is the sprout. The love of *jen* is comparable to the sweetness of sugar and the sourness of vinegar. Love is the taste."[75] The principle of love is also "comparable to the root of a plant and the spring of water."[76] Love is active while principle is tranquil.[77] Here the word "principle" should be emphasized. Lü Tsu-ch'ien interpreted "the principle of love" as "the beginning of activity and the way of growth," but Chu Hsi considered that the word "beginning" was too weak.[78]

By love, Chu Hsi meant the principle of *jen* in the mind. This mind is expressed in filial piety and brotherly respect. Before these feelings are aroused, what is preserved in the mind is only the principle of love.[79] Chang Shih had explained the passage "Filial piety and brotherly respect are the root of *jen*"[80] by saying that "beginning with filial piety and brotherly respect, the way of *jen* will grow indefinitely." Commenting on this, Chu Hsi said, "Here the word *jen* refers precisely to the principle of love."[81] Because it is this principle, it has the spirit of life of *jen,* which has to be expressed. Liao Te-ming asked about *jen* as the principle of love, saying, "Sir, in the 'Jen-shuo' that you wrote some time ago, you generally consider the mind to embrace the principle of love, and that is why it is called *jen.* But now in your [*Meng Tzu*] *chi-chu* [Collected commentaries on the *Book of Mencius*], commenting on the sentence '*Jen* is the human mind,'[82] you take it to mean 'the master of dealing with all changes.' How about it?" Chu Hsi answered:

You don't have to look at it this way. Nowadays, when people talk about *jen* they mostly look upon it as something abstract. That won't do. At the time [of the presence of mind], the sprouts of humanity, righteousness, propriety, and wisdom are already there, but have not yet been activated. . . . Propriety is basically the principle of culture. As it is activated, it becomes deference and humility. Wisdom is basically the principle of discrimination. As it is activated, there are the right and wrong.[83]

If the mind is merely considered the master of dealing with the tens of thousands of transformations, *jen* as the spirit of growth will be lost.

The principle of love is the same as the original substance of *jen*. In a letter in reply to Hu Shih, Chu Hsi said,

Of course it is wrong simply to equate *jen* with love, but the principle of love is the substance of *jen*. Since Heaven, Earth, and the ten thousand things form one body with the self, of course love should cover everything, but that is not the reason that *jen* is the principle of love. We must realize that humanity, righteousness, propriety, and wisdom are all characters of nature, the principle that originally exists by itself without any artificial manipulation. But *jen* is the principle of love and the way of growth. Because of this, it can include the Four Virtues and is the essential of learning.[84]

To say that *jen* is the principle of love means that "*jen* is nature while love is feeling." In other words, "Love is the feeling of *jen* and *jen* is the nature of love,"[85] but the two cannot be separated.[86] Questioned about *jen* as the principle of love, Chu Hsi said,

The term will become clear if you look at the mind, nature, and feeling separately. Undifferentiated within one's person is the master, which is the mind. There are humanity, righteousness, propriety, and wisdom, which are one's nature. When these are expressed, they become commiseration, shame and dislike, deference and humility, and the sense of right and wrong. These are feelings. Commiseration is love, the beginning of *jen*. *Jen* is substance, while love is function.[87]

Someone asked, "Why is *jen* the principle of love?" Chu Hsi answered,

Man is endowed with the best of the Five Agents[88] at birth. Therefore, his mind is constituted so that before it is activated it possesses the nature of humanity, righteousness, propriety, wisdom, and faithfulness as its substance, and after it is activated it has the nature of commiseration, shame and dislike, respect and reverence, the sense of right and wrong, and truthfulness as its function. For the spirit of Wood is *jen*,[89] which is the principle of love. . . . All this is the Principle of Heaven as it surely is, and why the human mind is wonderful. From this we can infer that *jen* is the principle of love.[90]

He also said,

> *Jen* is the principle of love, while love is the function of *jen*. It is simply
> called *jen* before it is activated, when it has neither shape nor shade. It is
> called love only after it is activated, when it has shape and shadow. Before
> it is activated and called *jen*, it can include righteousness, propriety, and
> wisdom. After it is activated and called commiseration, it can include
> respect and reverence, deference and humility, and the sense of right and
> wrong. We call these the Four Beginnings,[91] "beginning" being com-
> parable to sprouts or buds. Commiseration is the beginning that issues
> from *jen*.[92]

In his explanation of the principle of love, Ch'en Ch'un said,

> *Jen* is the totality of the mind's principle of production. It is always produc-
> ing and reproducing without cease. Its clue becomes active in the mind.
> When it sets forth, naturally there is the feeling of commiseration. As the
> feeling of commiseration grows in abundance to reach a thing, it becomes
> love. Therefore, *jen* is the root of love, commiseration the sprout from the
> root, and love the sprout reaching its maturity and completion. Looking
> at it this way, we can easily see the vital connection between *jen* as the prin-
> ciple of love and love as the function of *jen*.[93]

Ch'en Ch'un understood his teacher's ideas quite well.

From this we know that Chu Hsi regarded love as active and as the
force of production. Before it is activated, love is nature, is the substance of *jen*, and includes the Four Virtues. When it is aroused and
expressed as feeling because of its activity and growth, it includes the
Four Beginnings. However, nature and feeling are not to be separated,
for substance and function are not bifurcated. The principle of love is
original with one's nature, and does not become so because of impartiality. Since one's nature is pure, one can penetrate Heaven, Earth,
and the ten thousand things, yet one does not become *jen* after such penetration.

### The Character of the Mind and the Principle of Love

Thus far the character of the mind and the principle of love have been
treated separately, but this does not mean that they are two different
things. In his elucidation of *jen*, Chu Hsi combined the two, a point that
should not be overlooked. However, *jen* is neither love nor the mind,
nor love and mind combined. Chu Hsi said, "Love is not *jen*; the principle of love is *jen*. The mind is not *jen*; the character of the mind is *jen*."[94]
Therefore *jen* combines the character of the mind and the principle of
love. Moreover, Chu Hsi explained *jen* not only in terms of the mind
but also in terms of principle. He said, "*Jen* is the principle of love. That

is why it is the character of the mind. Because it is principle, it is therefore character. The relation between the two is a necessary one and neither can be lacking."[95] In other words, principle is the cause and character is the effect. In the final analysis, Chu Hsi's explanation of *jen* is in
terms of principle. Therefore Ch'en Ch'un said, "*Jen* may be spoken of
in terms of principle or in terms of mind. . . . When Wen Kung [Chu
Hsi] said that *jen* is the character of the mind and the principle of love,
he was speaking in terms of principle."[96]

According to Chu Hsi, in the *Analects* and the *Book of Mencius* there are
cases where *jen* is spoken of purely from the point of view of the character of the mind, such as "Master oneself and return to propriety,"[97] "Be
respectful in private life,"[98] and "Humanity is man's mind."[99] There
are also cases where *jen* is spoken of purely from the point of view of the
principle of love, such as "Filial piety and brotherly respect are the root
of *jen*,"[100] "The man of *jen* loves others,[101] "The mind of commiseration
[is *jen*],"[102] and so forth.[103] But this does not mean that the two aspects
are two different things. The difference between them is only that
between substance and function, and between being spoken of collectively or separately. When Chu Hsi said that *jen* is the principle of love,
he meant what Ch'eng I intended in saying that "spoken of separately,
it is one of the four"[104]—that is, humanity, righteousness, propriety,
and wisdom spoken of separately; when he said that *jen* is the character
of the mind, he meant what Ch'eng I intended in saying that "spoken
of collectively, it embraces all four"[105]—that is, the Four Virtues spoken
of together.[106] Chu Hsi said, "The character of the mind is spoken of
from the combination of the Four Beginnings, while the principle of
love is spoken of merely from the whole and part of *jen* itself, the issuing
forth of which is love, while its principle is *jen*. *Jen* includes the Four
Beginnings because of the operation of its spirit of life."[107] He also said,
"Righteousness, propriety, and wisdom are all present in the mind, but
humanity is merged as one. Separately speaking, *jen* is the master of
love. Collectively speaking, it includes the other three virtues."[108] In
other words,

> The principle of love is spoken of separately as one thing, while the char-
> acter of the mind is spoken of collectively as including the four. Therefore,
> when spoken of together, all the four are characters of the mind and *jen* is
> the master. Spoken of separately, *jen* is the principle of love; righteousness,
> the principle of appropriateness; propriety, the principle of respect and
> reverence, deference and humility; and wisdom, the principle of discrimi-
> nating what is right and wrong.[109]

The character of the mind and the principle of love can also be
spoken of as substance and function. Chu Hsi said, "To speak of the

character of the mind collectively, before it is activated it is substance, and after it is activated it is function. To speak of the principle of love separately, *jen* is substance and commiseration is function."[110] Ch'en Ch'un said, "The character of the mind refers, collectively, to substance, while the principle of love refers, separately, to function."[111] But regardless of whether one is speaking collectively or separately, of substance or of function, *jen* cannot be divided in two. It is not the case that aside from the character of the mind there is a separate principle of love.[112] That is why Chu Hsi said, "The character of the mind is the same as the principle of love. They are not two different things."[113] The character of the mind as the substance of *jen* is the mind of Heaven and Earth to produce things, and the principle of love as the function of *jen* is "the warm and rich air of spring in which the mind of Heaven and Earth is revealed. By summer the force of life grows, by autumn the force of life is collected, and by winter the force of life is stored."[114] The central point here is that the character of the mind and the principle of love are both forces of life. A pupil asked, "To be completely merged without any selfishness is the principle of love. Is the practice of *jen* with realization in the self the character of the mind?" Chu Hsi answered, "It is all right to explain the terms this way, but I am afraid it is not thorough enough as far as the fundamental is concerned."[115] By "the fundamental," Chu Hsi meant Ch'eng I's doctrine of *jen* as comparable to seeds.[116]

There is a long passage by Chu Hsi that summarizes the ideas brought forth above:

> The [*Lun-meng*] *chi-chu* explains *jen* as the principle of love and the character of the mind. Love is commiseration, which is feeling. Its principle is called *jen*. With reference to the character of the mind, character is merely love. When it is called the character of the mind, it means the controlling power of love. In the way man is made up, his principle is the principle of Heaven and Earth and his material force is the material force of Heaven and Earth. Principle has no trace and cannot be seen; it can be seen in material force. One must realize that the idea of *jen* means a warm and harmonious force without differentiation. Its material force is the material force of the positive cosmic element (yang) and spring of Heaven and Earth, and its principle is the mind of Heaven and Earth to produce things. . . . Disciples in the Confucian School generally only asked about the task of practicing *jen*. As to the whole and part of *jen,* each of them had understood the idea. . . . There is only one *jen*. Although spoken of separately, numerous principles are embraced in it, and although spoken of collectively, numerous principles are embraced in it.[117]

We have here the cardinal ideas of the "Jen-shuo."

Scholars understood the principle of love and the character of the mind differently. Perhaps the most sophisticated among them were Chu Hsi's pupils Li T'ang-tzu and Hsü Yü. Li T'ang-tzu said,

> "Comforting the old, being faithful to friends, and cherishing the young"[118] are of course *jen,* but they are also love. . . . The reason for comforting, being faithful, and cherishing is principle, not love. . . . Therefore love belongs to feeling and is one of the items of *jen.* Principle belongs to nature and the totality of the way of *jen.* Hence love is not *jen* but the principle of love is *jen.* . . . The mind is the master of nature and feeling. Since it is the master of nature, all principles of why a thing is so are present in the mind, and since it is the master of feeling, all principles of why a thing should be so issue forth from the mind. In this process principle is fully realized and love operates, because the mind is the master. This being the case, isn't *jen* the character of the mind?

Commenting on this, Chu Hsi said, "Your explanation of the principle of love is close to the truth, but with regard to the character of the mind you should think of Master Ch'eng's analogy of seeds."[119] Li's interpretation in terms of what is and what should be, and of the mind as the master of nature and feeling, is truly refined, but he overlooked the mind of Heaven and Earth to produce things and *jen* as seeds, and thus overlooked the opening passage of the "Jen-shuo."

Hsü Yü said,

> The character of the mind is the way to produce. This is so because the mind of Heaven and Earth is to produce things, and man receives it as his mind, which is called *jen.* Its substance is identical with Heaven and Earth and penetrates all things. Its principle unites all goodness and includes the Four Beginnings. . . . Spoken of collectively, it is the character of the mind. Spoken of separately, it is the principle of love. The foundation of what is spoken of collectively issues forth to become the function of what is spoken of separately, and the function of what is spoken of separately is combined to become the foundation of what is spoken of collectively. They should not be bifurcated as two different things that are big and small, fundamental and secondary. Because the principle of *jen* has not been clearly understood, people have been misled by material endowment and beclouded with selfish desires, causing the way of growth to stop and the Principle of Heaven to cease operation. . . . If man can personally realize *jen,* he will make sure that not the slightest selfishness can be injected into the substance of production and reproduction, so that it will operate and penetrate, reaching everywhere and covering everything. Only then can the character of the mind and the principle of love be fully realized.

Commenting on this, Chu Hsi said, "The general idea of this passage is correct, but the principle of love should not be understood [purely] as function. You should ponder this. In time, things will become smooth and harmonious, and what is right and what is wrong will naturally be seen.[120]

Hsü's interpretation is superior to Li's because Hsü emphasized the way of production. But his idea of identification with Heaven and Earth was a notion that Chu Hsi did not easily accept. In his reply to Chou Mu (1141–1202), the Master said,

> What is called the character of the mind is the same as what Master Ch'eng called seeds of grain, and what is called the principle of love is precisely *jen* as love before it is activated and love as *jen* that has been activated. You should only think along these lines and need not introduce extraneous conceptions that will only confuse the issue. If one understands *jen* at this point, it is all right to be identified with Heaven and Earth and the ten thousand things. If one does not understand this and forthwith considers forming one body with Heaven and Earth and the ten thousand things as *jen,* there will be no solution.[121]

As to the task of practicing *jen,* Chu Hsi repeatedly said that if one personally realizes and thinks about the character of the mind and the principle of love, one will understand *jen.*[122] Personal realization means effort. A pupil said, "When one compares the love that has been activated, one knows that it is the character of the mind. And when one points to *jen* that has not been activated, one knows that it is the principle of love." Chu Hsi commented,

> One must clearly see the principle in places where one applies oneself to the concrete task. Then the particular meaning will emerge. Take "Mastering oneself and returning to the propriety."[123] How should these be done to become *jen?* "Be respectful in private life and be serious in handling affairs,"[124] and "When you go abroad, behave to everyone as if you were receiving a great guest."[125] Mastering oneself and returning to propriety is basically not *jen,* but one must find out from mastering oneself and returning to propriety wherein *jen* lies, personally realize it in the way relevant to oneself, and not seek it outside.[126]

Professor Mou Tsung-san vigorously opposes Chu Hsi's doctrine of the principle of love and the character of the mind. He regards Chu Hsi as following Ch'eng I's theory of *jen* as nature and love as feeling; dividing the substance of *jen* into the three portions of mind, nature, and feeling; splitting principle and material force into two categories; and explaining *jen* according to the formula of "the character of the mind and the principle of love." In this way, he says, Chu Hsi made *jen* static and dead. The *jen* Chu Hsi talked about is "merely the existing principle of existentialism, quietly lying there," according to Professor Mou. Therefore it is not concrete, vital, or alive. The character of the mind is

merely the character of the operation of the material force, for the Four
Virtues are rooted in origination, flourishing, advantage, and firmness,[127] which are but the four stages of the transformation of the two
material forces of yin and yang (passive and active cosmic forces).[128]

Professor Mou agrees with Ch'eng Hao and Lu Hsiang-shan's theory
that mind is principle. To him, the mind is the original mind, not the
mind that commands and unites nature and feeling; likewise, nature is
the original nature, not the nature different from feeling that involves
material force. Hence Professor Mou thinks that Chu Hsi rigidly
adhered to Ch'eng I's line of thought and that his theoretical construction was based on the idea that *jen* is the character of the mind and the
principle of love—a formula decidedly different from the linear, direct
system of Confucius and Mencius as understood by other Sung dynasty
(960–1279) Confucians.[129] Since Mou's standpoint is that "mind is
principle," whereas Chu Hsi's was that "nature is principle," naturally
they cannot be expected to agree. To Ch'eng I and Chu Hsi, *jen* was a
force of growth and the mind was the principle of growth. To say that
their idea of *jen* was a static one is hardly fair. According to Professor
Ch'ien Mu, Chu Hsi's "doctrine that *jen* is the character of the mind
and the principle of love is a synthesis of the ideas of Ch'eng I and Lu
Hsiang-shan. Later scholars who arbitrarily put Chu Hsi on the side of
Ch'eng I and declare him different from Lu really have failed to examine the matter clearly."[130]

### *Jen* as Forming One Body with Things and *Jen* as Consciousness

The "Jen-shuo" puts forth the theory that *jen* is the character of the
mind and the principle of love. On this basis Chu Hsi criticized two
doctrines. One is that *jen* means forming one body with things. Its chief
representative was Yang Shih. Chu Hsi held that forming one body with
things does not really make *jen* a substance. The other is the doctrine
that *jen* is consciousness, as advocated by Hsieh Liang-tso. To Chu Hsi,
this theory does not explain what *jen* itself is. But in neither case did
Chu Hsi go into detail. Having made these main points in the "Jen-
shuo," he proceeded to say that, generally speaking, those who advocate the theory of forming one body will cause people to be vague, confused, and perhaps to treat things as the self, while those who advocate
the theory of *jen* as consciousness will cause people to get excited and
perhaps confuse selfish desires with principle. He did not explain further.

There has been a great deal of discussion on these two theories, but it
is not necessary to go into them here except to quote Professor T'ang
Chün-i. According to him, Chu Hsi regarded impartiality as what pre-

cedes *jen* and forming one body as what follows *jen,* and therefore regarded neither as being its substance. As to consciousness, T'ang holds that it refers to *jen* as including wisdom, for the mind can be conscious of principle and does possess the character of wisdom. Thus consciousness is the last expression of *jen* but is not *jen* itself. This explanation by T'ang is simple and perfectly clear. He goes on to say that Chu Hsi was different from previous thinkers, who only discussed *jen* in one respect:

> Chu Hsi views *jen* from what precedes it, namely impartiality; from what follows it, namely, forming one body with things; from the inside, namely, the nature of consciousness of the mind; and from the outside, namely, the feeling resulting from the consciousness of things. Above, it penetrates Heaven. Below, it permeates man. As the root, it exists in the one principle in the self. As branches, it scatters to become the ten thousand things —from love, respect, appropriateness, and the discrimination of right and wrong, to loving people and benefiting things. All these are delineated. In this discussion of *jen* from what is before and what is after, from the inside and the outside, from above and below, and from the root and branches, there is, of course, a refined and careful idea.[131]

This amounts to a eulogy for the "Jen-shuo."

Professor Mou looks at the matter differently. To him, forming one body with things is the manifestation of the true mind, which is precisely substance in the true sense. He also says that the consciousness of people's pain is precisely that which explains what *jen* itself is. In his view, Chu Hsi's assertion that the doctrine of *jen* as forming one body is inadequate and the doctrine of *jen* as consciousness goes too far is absolutely absurd.[132] Mou's analysis of the "Jen-shuo" is extremely sophisticated.[133] His refutation is also in sharp contrast to T'ang's standpoint. Chu Hsi rejected the two doctrines because *jen* as forming one body with things deals with only one aspect of *jen,* and *jen* as consciousness does not distinguish between substance and function. In other words, the former fails to understand substance and the latter attends exclusively to function. For Chu Hsi, *jen* is a complete virtue with both substance and function, which come from the same source and are not two different things.

## Discussions on the "Jen-shuo"

Both before and after the "Jen-shuo" was finalized, it must have circulated extensively among pupils and friends, for the response to it was great. The "Jen-shuo" was the focus of many of the discussions about the mind of Heaven and Earth to produce things, the character of the mind, the principle of love, forming one body with things, and the theory of *jen* as consciousness. Chu Hsi's replies to Wu I on the mind of Heaven and Earth to produce things, the character of nature, the principle of love, and consciousness[134] do not explicitly refer to the "Jen-shuo," but the fact that the order of topics is the same as that in the "Jen-shuo" makes it plausible that the questions pertained to the treatise. His discussions with Chang Shih on the "Jen-shuo" consist of four letters in the *Wen-chi* and two in Chang's literary collections on the "Jen-shuo."[135]

The first letter to Chang Shih explains every sentence of the "Jen-shuo."[136] Chu Hsi's treatise begins with the statement that "the mind of Heaven and Earth is to produce things." Chang Shih found fault with this, but Chu Hsi insisted that the aim of Heaven and Earth is to give life and that the sentence is not wrong. In reply, Chang Shih said, "The sentence that 'the mind of Heaven and Earth is to produce things' is all right as ordinarily understood, but I am afraid it makes better sense merely to say that there is the mind of Heaven and Earth to produce things and that man receives this mind as his mind."[137]

What Chang Shih was saying is that Heaven and Earth do not consciously produce things, but that man receives from them the mind to produce things. This suggestion was not accepted. Chang Shih also questioned whether "the mind that cannot bear to see the suffering of others can embrace [or encompass] the Four Beginnings [of the feelings of commiseration, shame and dislike, deference and compliance, and right and wrong]." To Chu Hsi, however, "That the mind that cannot bear to see the suffering of others can embrace the Four Beginnings is comparable to the fact that humanity can embrace the Four Virtues of humanity, righteousness, propriety and wisdom." Later, Chang Shih wrote to say that although the mind that cannot bear to see the suffering of others can embrace the Four Beginnings, it is better to generalize and call it humanity.[138] To Chang Shih, the substance of the man of *jen* is always good, but Chu Hsi felt that Chang Shih did not understand that *jen* is the source of all virtues. Chang Shih thought that "when spoken of along with righteousness, propriety, and wisdom, the manifestation of humanity becomes the mind that cannot bear the suffering of others." Chu Hsi felt this was unsatisfactory, because humanity, righteousness, propriety, and wisdom "are all rooted in the mind. They are principles before manifestation." Chang Shih held that "the way of the man of *jen* embraces everything," but Chu Hsi wanted to know why it embodies everything.

Chang Shih also considered that "what Master Ch'eng [Ch'eng I] criticized was defining *jen* as love." This is a criticism of Chu Hsi's statement in the "Jen-shuo" that "what Master Ch'eng criticized was defining the expression of love as *jen*." Chu Hsi countered, "Master Ch'eng said, 'Humanity is nature while love is feeling. How can one regard love as humanity?' This saying explicitly disapproves of treating feeling as nature, but does not say that the nature of humanity is not expressed in the feeling of love, or that humanity in love is not based on the nature of humanity."

Moreover, Chang Shih took the meaning of *yüan* (origination) as going beyond producing things. Chu Hsi thought it was a great defect to say this, for he believed that *yüan* is the source not only of things but of all virtues.[139] Chang Shih replied, "When I said the other day that the meaning of *yüan* goes beyond the production of things, it leads to the suspicion that I was only talking about producing things and thus did not fully bring out the idea of *yüan* as production and reproduction [in all spheres of life]. Now you have fully explained the concept of production."[140]

Finally, Chang Shih believed that the man of *jen* loves everything but that there is a distinction in the application of *jen*, whereas Chu Hsi regarded making the distinction as the task of righteousness. "Although humanity and righteousness are not separated, in their function they each have their own sphere and should not be confused."

Chu Hsi's second letter on the "Jen-shuo"[141] is his reply to Chang Shih's response to his first letter.[142] Chang Shih had contended that the substance of *jen* is impartiality *(kung)*. When one is impartial, he said, there will not be the selfishness that divides the self and others, and thus love will prevail everywhere. To Chu Hsi, however, "*Jen* is the character of nature and the foundation of love. . . . If impartiality, which is extended to the whole world and which eliminates the selfishness that divides the self and others, is considered the substance of *jen*, I am afraid that that impartiality is totally devoid of feeling, like the emptiness of wood and stone."

Chu Hsi's third letter is concerned with the theory of *jen* as consciousness.[143] Chang Shih had written Chu Hsi on the theory, but his letter is no longer extant. In his reply Chu Hsi said, "The man of *jen* has consciousness, it is true, but consciousness itself is not *jen*. Who is going to make the mind know, or make it conscious? . . . However, consciousness is merely the functioning of wisdom. Only the man of *jen* can have both *jen* and wisdom. Therefore it is all right to say that a man of *jen* certainly has consciousness, but is not all right to say that the mind's consciousness is *jen*."

Chu Hsi's fourth letter stresses the point that neither impartiality nor forming one body with things is the substance of *jen*. Chang Shih had written that "one forms one body with Heaven and Earth because man and things share the secret of production and reproduction inherent in the mind of Heaven and Earth, and this is the principle of love."[144] In response, Chu Hsi said that when one is impartial one looks upon Heaven and Earth and things as one body and loves all, but added that "the principle of love is an original principle that exists by itself and is not the result of forming one body with Heaven and Earth and all things."[145]

In this debate, Chu Hsi won most of the arguments, although sometimes he went too far in criticizing his friend. For example, Chang Shih merely said that the man of *jen* is always good, but Chu Hsi criticized him for not knowing that *jen* is the highest good; also, Chang Shih only said that love is prevalent everywhere, but Chu Hsi censured him for not recognizing the substance of *jen*. Moreover, Chu Hsi's understanding of consciousness left something to be desired. As Professor Mou Tsung-san has pointed out, "Chu Hsi mistakenly considers the consciousness of *jen* as the consciousness of wisdom. Because of this misunderstanding, he has confined consciousness to wisdom."[146] Mou's analysis of Chu Hsi's four letters is extremely refined.[147] He does not completely agree with Chang Shih, but in every case considers Chu Hsi to be wrong.

In the *Wen-chi* there are also two letters to Ho Hao (1128–1175) on the "Jen-shuo."[148] A survey of the *Yü-lei* and the *Wen-chi* shows that the opening sentence of the "Jen-shuo," about the mind of Heaven and Earth, generated the most controversy. To Ho Hao, the mind of Heaven and Earth is *jen* because when the yang element grows, the spirit of unceasing production and reproduction is revealed; however, Chu Hsi thought that to wait for the yang element to grow would divide the process into two sections, because that theory leaves the yang element before its return unaccounted for.[149] Chu Hsi's student Shen Hsien did not understand the idea that the mind of Heaven and Earth is to produce things. The Teacher explained it to him, saying, "The mind of Heaven and Earth is simply to produce. Everything has to be produced before there can be a thing. . . . This is a general discussion on the substance of *jen*. Within it are items and specifications."[150] We do not know whether this clarified matters for Shen, but Chu Hsi's discussions with Chang Shih, reported above, in all likelihood satisfied him. As Chu Hsi told Hu Shih, "I recently received two letters from Ch'in-fu [Chang Shih] on the 'Jen-shuo' in which he raised many critical questions. I have answered them all. Lately he has written to say that he no longer has any doubts."[151]

Due to these discussions, the "Jen-shuo" was modified in some respects. As Chu Hsi wrote Lü Tsu-ch'ien, "The 'Jen-shuo' has recently been revised further, becoming clearer and more refined than before."[152] Comparing the treatise with Chang Shih's questions and objections, we can see that the passage about the Four Beginnings being encompassed by the mind that cannot bear to see others' suffering is no longer found in the treatise. Nor does the final treatise refer to Mencius' idea that the man of *jen* loves all, an omission obviously due to Chang

Shih's argument. But Chu Hsi held firmly to the doctrine that the mind of Heaven and Earth is to produce things. In his letter to Ho Hao, he said,

> I have maintained that *jen* is the mind of Heaven and Earth, and that man and things receive this mind as their mind. Although this idea is the product of my personal opinion of the moment, I humbly believe that it opens up precisely the point that there is no separation between Heaven and man. In this respect, the treatise seems to be refined and thorough. If one follows this matter through, one will see that in the undifferentiated unity between *jen* and the mind is naturally a distinction.[153]

For Chu Hsi to say that he had opened up the point that there is no separation between Heaven and man seems a bold statement, but it does not mean that he was completely satisfied with the "Jen-shuo." On the contrary, he himself said that only the earlier section of the treatise is satisfactory.[154] Probably he meant that the latter section dealing with the theories of *jen* as consciousness and as forming one body with all things does not clearly explain why they are not *jen*. Be that as it may, in Chu Hsi's "Jen-shuo," the doctrine of *jen* reaches its highest point of development in the history of Chinese thought. As Ch'en Ch'un put it, scholars from the Han dynasty (206 B.C.–A.D. 220) on "have lost the fundamental idea of the law of the mind traditionally transmitted in the Confucian School. Wen Kung [Chu Hsi] was the first to describe *jen* as the character of the mind and the principle of love. For the first time the explanation of *jen* is to the point."[155]

## The Diagram of the "Jen-shuo"

The "Jen-shuo-t'u" (Diagram of the "Treatise on Humanity") is reproduced below in chapter 18 (p. 281). The important points are given in the comment following the diagram and need not be repeated here. Suffice it to say that the diagram's general emphasis on practice and its inclusion of impartiality twice both suggest Chang Shih's influence on Chu Hsi.

## Chang Shih's "Jen-shuo"

Chang Shih also wrote a "Jen-shuo," which has sometimes been confused with Chu Hsi's treatise. Under the title of Chu Hsi's treatise there is a note which says, "The Chekiang edition erroneously considers Master Nan-hsüan's [Chang Shih's] 'Jen-shuo' as the Master's 'Jen-shuo' and considers the Master's 'Jen-shuo' as its preface."[156] Even Chu Hsi's pupil Ch'en Ch'un thought that Chu Hsi had written both of the "Jen-shuo," one of which had gotten into Chang Shih's literary collection by mistake.[157] Another pupil, Hsiung Chieh (1199 *cs*), took Chang's treatise to be Chu Hsi's.[158] In reality, each man wrote his own treatise, and there is no basis for believing that one is the preface to the other. Chang Shih's "Jen-shuo" is preserved in chapter 18 of the *Nan-hsüan Hsien-sheng wen-chi* (Collection of literary works of Master Chang Shih). The whole treatise consists of 477 characters, plus notes totaling 33 characters, so it is not quite half the length of Chu Hsi's "Jen-shuo." It says, in brief,

> In man's nature the Four Virtues of humanity, righteousness, propriety, and wisdom are present. Humanity is the principle of love, righteousness the principle of appropriateness, propriety the principle of deference, and wisdom the principle of knowledge. . . . In man's nature there are only these four, and they control the ten thousand goodnesses. What is called the principle of love is the mind of Heaven and Earth to produce things, from which *jen* is born. Thus *jen* is the leader of the Four Virtues and can embrace all of them. Because in man's nature there are these Four Virtues, when they are expressed in feelings the feeling of commiseration penetrates all of them. That is why nature and feeling are respectively substance and function, and the way of the mind is the master of nature and feeling. Because man is beclouded by selfish desires, he loses the principle of nature and becomes devoid of *jen*. . . . The essential point in the practice of *jen* lies in self-mastery. . . . Nothing can becloud the principle of love, which penetrates Heaven and Earth and all things like arteries and veins, and which functions everywhere. Therefore, to designate love as *jen* is to be blind to its substance, for *jen* is the principle of love, and to designate impartiality as *jen* is to lose its reality, for impartiality is what enables man to be *jen*. . . . Only the man of *jen* can extend it and be appropriate; that is what is preserved by righteousness. . . . This being the case, the student must consider searching for *jen* as essential, and in the practice of *jen* consider self-mastery as the way.[159]

Readers may well be amazed at the similarity between this treatise and that of Chu Hsi. Practically all its major ideas are found in both treatises, except that Chang's treatise puts more emphasis on the ideas of self-mastery, eliminating becloudedness, and knowing what to preserve. Chang's treatise also stresses how the man of *jen* can preserve righteousness, propriety, and wisdom. Chu Hsi rejected Yang Shih's doctrine that forming one body with things is *jen*, while Chang Shih rejected impartiality, which means practically the same thing. Chu Hsi criticized Hsieh Liang-tso's theory that consciousness is *jen*, while Chang Shih merely said that the man of *jen* can be conscious and cannot be darkened. Their major difference is that Chu Hsi talked about the two aspects of the character of the mind and the principle of love, whereas Chang Shih spoke only about the principle of love.

It may be argued that Chang's treatise came first and that that is why Chu Hsi's is fuller. However, in his letter to Lü Tsu-ch'ien, Chu Hsi mentioned that Chang Shih had written him to say that Chang's own "Jen-shuo" had been revised, and in the same letter, Chu Hsi also mentioned Lü's promise to write a preface for the *I-Lo yüan-yüan lu* [Records of the origin of the school of the Ch'engs].[160] Since the *Yüan-yüan lu* was completed in 1173, two years after Chu Hsi's "Jen-shuo," Chang Shih's "Jen-shuo" must have been written later. As to why Chang Shih chose to write a "Jen-shuo" after Chu Hsi had written one, there is a possible explanation: he accepted the concept of *jen* as produced by the mind of Heaven and Earth, but did not accept the idea that the mind of Heaven and Earth is to produce things. Hence Chang Shih refrained from talking about the character of the mind. Chu Hsi's "Jen-shuo" tends to be theoretical. Although it says that the student should eagerly search for *jen,* it does not prescribe any method for doing so. In contrast, Chang Shih elaborated on the ability of the man of *jen* to extend to the point of preserving righteousness, propriety, and wisdom. Most importantly, he emphasizes the point that to practice *jen,* one must master oneself.

Chu Hsi's "Jen-shuo" quotes the *Analects* on self-mastery once, but only in passing. We know that Chang Shih considered Chu Hsi's "K'e-chai chi" [Account of the studio of self-mastery] to be superior to Chu Hsi's "Jen-shuo," thus implying that the latter was deficient on self-mastery. Chang Shih may have written his "Jen-shuo" to make up for Chu Hsi's deficiency, since for Chang Shih, self-mastery was a key virtue. This can be seen in Huang Tsung-hsi's *Sung-Yüan hsüeh-an* (Anthology and critical accounts of the Neo-Confucians of the Sung and Yüan dynasties), whose only quote from Chang Shih's "Jen-shuo" is the shortest sentence on self-mastery in it.[161] Yet it is not true that Chu Hsi neglected self-mastery. In a letter to Lü Tsu-ch'ien he maintained that learning and self-mastery must be pursued equally, and added that in a letter to Chang Shih he had written one or two paragraphs on the defect of ignoring self-mastery.[162] (The letter referred to is lost, so Chu Hsi must have written more than four letters to Chang Shih on the "Jen-shuo.")

Chu Hsi also wrote a letter to Chang Shih specifically on the latter's "Jen-shuo," taking exception to a number of points in Chang's draft.[163] He said that his friend "only talks about nature but not feeling, and furthermore, does not say that the mind penetrates both nature and feeling, thus seeming to oppose nature to mind." In the final text of Chang Shih's "Jen-shuo," there are sentences expressing the ideas that nature and feeling are mutually penetrated as substance and function, and that the mind is the master of nature and feeling—undoubtedly additions due to Chu Hsi's criticism. Chu Hsi had also objected to Chang Shih's statement that "when one is broad and extremely impartial and inter-penetrates, like arteries and veins, with Heaven and Earth and things, the principle of love will be obtained internally and the function of love will be expressed externally." To Chu Hsi, "The principle of love is native to one's nature. It prevails because of broadness and extreme impartiality, but it is not the product of broadness and extreme impartiality." The final draft of Chang's "Jen-shuo" says, "If one is broad and extremely impartial, the principle of love originally present in nature will not be beclouded . . . and, like arteries and veins, will pene-trate Heaven and Earth and all things and function everywhere." This shows that Chang Shih adopted Chu Hsi's theory that the principle of love exists before forming one body with things. Moreover, Chang's statement that "to designate impartiality as *jen* is to lose its reality," together with its note, which quotes Ch'eng I's saying that "one should not forthwith point to impartiality as *jen*,"[164] is obviously a revision made because of Chu Hsi's criticism.

However, Chang Shih strongly adhered to the idea of impartiality. Therefore, in the final text there is the sentence, "Impartiality is why a person can be *jen*." In the original draft, Chang Shih had said "Every-thing in the world is part of my humanity," to which Chu Hsi objected, "Things are things and *jen* is my mind. Why do you take things to be my mind?" The original sentence does not appear in the final draft, another indication of Chang's respect for Chu Hsi's opinion. Actually, as Professor Mou Tsung-san has pointed out, Chang Shih did not equate things with the mind but merely meant that everything is pene-trated by the operation of the substance of *jen*.[165] Comparing the earlier draft to the final draft, we must conclude that Chang Shih modified his "Jen-shuo" in accordance with Chu Hsi's opinions. This is further evi-dence that Chang Shih's "Jen-shuo" is later than Chu Hsi's.

## Did Chu Hsi Write Chang Shih's "Jen-shuo"?

At the International Conference on Chu Hsi held in Honolulu, Hawaii in 1982, Professor Satō Hitoshi presented a paper on Chu Hsi's "Jen-shuo"[166] in which he stated that both Ch'en Ch'un and Hsiung Chieh failed to realize that Chu Hsi had nothing to do with Chang Shih's "Jen-shuo." In 1981, I had published an essay in Chinese on Chu Hsi's "Jen-shuo," of which the material here is a translation. It was reprinted in my *Chu-hsüeh lun-chi* (Studies on Chu Hsi),[167] but appeared too late for the conference. After the conference, Dr. Liu Shu-hsien published his reflections, which read in part:

> The *Nan-hsüan wen-chi* [Collection of literary works of Master Chang Shih] was completely compiled by Chu Hsi. He deleted all letters and essays

that did not conform to his own line of thought and regarded them as Chang Shih's immature work of early years. Is it possible that Nan-hsüan never revised his early draft into the final form after it had met with Chu Hsi's criticism? After Nan-hsüan's death, Chu Hsi wrote another "Jen-shuo" based on his agreement with Nan-hsüan, included it in the *Nan-hsüan wen-chi* as Nan-hsüan's own work, and published it as such. That is why some pupils such as Ch'en Ch'un and Hsiung Chieh regarded this "Jen-shuo" as the work of Chu Hsi. In my understanding, unless this was the situation, it is fundamentally impossible to imagine that Chu Hsi's personal pupils got confused in such a manner. Of course, probably because of his limited ability to express himself in English, Professor Satō basically did not give any answer to the question I raised. Mr. [Wing-tsit] Chan answered for him and said that Ch'en Ch'un was not with Chu Hsi at the time and that Hsiung Chieh's understanding was greatly deficient, and that that was why such a confusion resulted. But I consider such an answer to be unsatisfactory. Ch'en Ch'un was Chu Hsi's favorite pupil in his late years and "defended the Teacher with great energy" [quote from Ch'üan Tsu-wang, 1705–1755].[168] Since he decidedly said that Chu Hsi wrote two versions of the "Jen-shuo," he must have had some basis [for this]. Probably Chu Hsi wrote another "Jen-shuo," accepted Nan-hsüan's criticism, put in an essay the concept of self-mastery, and adopted Nan-hsüan's sayings such as "Heaven, Earth, and the ten thousand things penetrate one another like blood and arteries." To commemorate his deceased friend, he took this essay as Nan-hsüan's final conclusion and included it in the *Nan-hsüan wen-chi*. Such a scenerio is certainly not beyond the imagination.[169]

Professor Liu's theory is both original and bold, but I hold to my opinion and agree with Professor Satō that Chu Hsi and Chang Shih each wrote a "Jen-shuo." As the *Ssu-k'u ch'üan-shu tsung-mu t'i-yao* (Essentials of the contents of the *Complete Collection of the Four Libraries*) states, Hsiung Chieh "was extremely superficial and there is nothing to recommend him."[170] But Ch'en Ch'un did not become a pupil of Chu Hsi until 1190. By that time, Chu Hsi's "Jen-shuo" had been finished for twenty years. Since several writers had written a "Jen-shuo" and each one had been copied and passed around, it was natural for Ch'en Ch'un, living in an isolated village, to believe that his Teacher had written two treatises on *jen*. The "Jen-shuo" issue was no longer alive, and Ch'en was not familiar with Chu Hsi's "Jen-shuo." As he told a pupil, "Wen Kung has two treatises on *jen*. Have you seen them? One treatise got into the *Nan-hsüan wen-chi* by mistake, and the other recently reached me from Wen-ling."[171] Thus Ch'en was simply not well informed. As to putting Chang Shih's name on a treatise of his own, this would have been entirely out of character for Chu Hsi. He was never known to employ such devious means, and he could easily have commemorated his friend in a straightforward way.

# Notes

1. *Wen-chi,* 36:7a–16b, fourth, fifth, and sixth letters in reply to Lu Tzu-ching (Lu Hsiang-shan).

2. *Ibid.,* 30:19a–20b; 32:4a–6a, 24a–26b; 64:28b–29b, third, thirty-third, thirty-fourth, and forty-eighth letters in reply to Chang Ch'in-fu (Chang Shih), and letter to the gentlemen of Hunan.

3. *Ibid.,* 36:19a–28b, fourth through ninth letters in reply to Ch'en T'ung-fu (Ch'en Liang).

4. *Ibid.,* 31:4b–8a, 32:16b–24b, 35:6b (Chang Ching-fu); 33:15a–16a (Lü Po-kung); 40:29a–30e (Ho Shu-ching); 42:8a (Hu Kuang-chung); 42:17b–19b (Wu Hui-shu); 42:35a–36a (Shih Tzu-chung); 5:13a (Lin Hsi-chih); 43:28a (Lin Tse-chih); 46:26a–29a (Hu Po-feng); 47:7b–8a, 26b–28a (Lü Tzu-yüeh); 47:7b (Venerable Sir); 50:25a (Yü Chan-chih); 50:34a (Chou Shun-pi); 54:14b (Chou Shu-chin); 56:12b–13b (Fang Pin-wang); 57:2b–3a (Li Yao-ch'ing); 57:10a–11a (Ch'en An-ch'ing); 58:2b–3b (Yang Chung-ssu); 58:21a (Ch'en Ch'i-chih); and 58:28b–29b (Hsü Chu-fu).

5. *Ibid.,* 33:15b, twenty-fourth letter in reply to Lü Po-kung (Lü Tsu-ch'ien).

6. This is from the commentary on the first hexagram, *ch'ien* (Heaven, male), in the *Book of Changes.*

7. *Yün-men Wen-yen Ch'an-shih yü-lu* [Recorded sayings of the Ch'an Patriarch Wen-yen of Yün-men Mountain], in the *Hsü-tsang-ching* [Supplementary Buddhist canon], first collection, B, *Ku-tsun-su yü-lu* [Recorded sayings of ancient elders], 17:189a.

8. *Wen-chi,* 47:26b–27a, twenty-fifth letter in reply to Lü Tzu-yüeh (Lü Tsu-chien).

9. *I chuan* [Commentary on the *Book of Changes*], 2:33a, in the *Erh-Ch'eng ch'üan-shu* [Complete works of the two Ch'engs] (*SPPY* ed.).

10. *Wen-chi,* 42:18a, tenth letter in reply to Wu Hui-shu (Wu I).

11. *Wai-shu* [Additional works], 3:1a, in the *Erh-ch'eng ch'üan-shu.* The *Wai-shu* does not specify whether this saying was uttered by Ch'eng I or Ch'eng Hao, but it is generally accepted as Ch'eng I's saying. In his *Ming-tao ch'üan-shu* [Complete works of Ch'eng Hao], Shen Kuei of the Ming dynasty (1368–1644) ascribed it to Ch'eng Hao.

12. These are the Four Qualities of the *ch'ien* hexagram in the *Book of Changes.*

13. *Book of Mencius,* 2A:6.

14. Yang Shih's doctrine may be found in the *Kuei-shan wen-chi* [Collection of literary writings of Yang Shih] (1590 ed.), 11:1b; 26:3a; and the *Kuei-shan yü-lu* [Recorded sayings of Yang Shih] (*SPTK* ed.), 2:10b. Hsieh Liang-tso's doctrine may be found in the *Shang-ts'ai yü-lu* [Recorded sayings of Hsieh Liang-tso] (*Chin-shih han-chi ts'ung-k'an* [Chinese works of the recent period] ed.), pt. 1, p. 2b, 13a–b; pt. 2, p. 1a.

15. *Book of Mencius,* 2A:2.

16. *Ibid.,* 6A:11.

17. *Yü-lei,* ch. 59, sec. 155 (p. 2239).

18. *Ibid.,* ch. 19, sec. 61 (p. 704).

19. *Wen-chi,* 33:12a–b. The "scholars of the Yung-chia school" refers to the

historians and utilitarians active in the area of Yung-chia County in southeastern Chekiang Province.

20. Tomoeda Ryūtarō, *Shushi no shisō keisei* [Formation of Master Chu's thought] (Tokyo: Shunjūsha, 1979), p. 114.

21. *Wen-chi*, 32:16b–26b, forty-second through forty-seventh letters in reply to Chang Ch'in-fu (Chang Shih).

22. *Ibid.*, 87:9b, funeral address for Chang Shih.

23. *Yü-lei*, ch. 103, sec. 41 (p. 4142).

24. *Ibid.*

25. *Wen-chi*, 32:21a, "Further Discussion on the 'Jen-shuo.' " The "K'e-chai chi" [Account of the studio of self-mastery] is found in the *Wen-chi*, 77:15a–16b.

26. Mou Tsung-san, *Hsin-t'i yü hsing-t'i* [Substance of the mind and substance of nature] (Taipei: Cheng-chung Book Co., 1969), vol. 3, p. 229.

27. *Wen-chi*, 47:27a, twenty-fifth letter in reply to Lü Tzu-yüeh (Lü Tsu-chien).

28. *Ibid.*, 36:27a, ninth letter in reply to Ch'en T'ung-fu (Ch'en Liang).

29. The Four Books are the *Great Learning*, the *Analects*, the *Book of Mencius*, and the *Doctrine of the Mean*.

30. The "Yü-shan chiang-i" [Yü-shan lecture] is found in the *Wen-chi*, 74:17b–22a. Yü-shan is a county in Kiangsi. See also ch. 23 below.

31. Chu Hsi, *Lun-yu huo-wen* [Questions and answers on the *Analects*] (*Chin-shih han-chi ts'ung-k'an* ed.), 1:12a (p. 27), comment on 1:3.

32. Chu Hsi used the phrase "the character of the mind" in comments on the *Analects* 1:3, 6:5, 7:29, 15:8; and on the *Book of Mencius* 6A:11. He used "the complete character of the mind" in comments on the *Analects* 7:6, 33; 8:7; 12:1 and 2. "The mind of *jen* is the mind to love people" occurs in a comment on the *Book of Mencius* 4A:1; and "the foundation of *jen* is love" on 4A:27. "To love people is the application of *jen*" is used in reference to the *Analects* 12:22. "The principle of love" appears in the *Lun-yü huo-wen* 1:7b (p. 18); "the character of the mind" is found in *ibid.*, 6:5b (p. 260), 12:1a–b (pp. 423–424), and 18:2a (p. 625).

33. *Yü-lei*, ch. 19, sec. 57 (p. 703).

34. *Ibid.*, sec. 61 (p. 704).

35. Yamazaki Bisei, *Kairoku* [Records of the sea], ch. 20.

36. Yamaguchi Satsujō, *Jin no kenkyū* [Study of *jen*] (Tokyo: Iwanami Book Co., 1936), pp. 370–371.

37. Quoted in Ōtsuki Nobuyoshi, *Chu Tzu ssu-shu chi-chu tien-chü k'ao* [Investigation into the textual evidence of Master Chu's *Collected Commentaries on the Four Books*] (Taipei: Student Book Co., 1976), p. 5.

38. Yamaguchi, *Jin no Kenkyū*, pp. 376–377.

39. *Nan-hsüan Hsien-sheng wen-chi* [Collection of literary works of Master Chang Shih] (*Chin-shih han-chi ts'ung-shu* ed.), 20:12a (p. 661), thirteenth letter in reply to Chu Yüan-hui (Chu Hsi).

40. Ōtsuki, *Chu Tzu ssu-shu chi-chu tien-chü k'ao*, p. 5.

41. *Wen-chi*, 30:28b, ninth letter in reply to Chang Ch'in-fu; 32:25b, forty-seventh letter.

42. *Ibid.*, 42:19a, tenth letter in reply to Wu Hsi-shu.

43. *Hu Tzu chih-yen* [Master Hu's understanding of words] (*Yüeh-ya-t'ang ts'ung-shu* [Hall of Kwangtung elegance series] ed.), 1:1a.

44. *Wen-chi*, 60:18a, second letter in reply to Tseng Tse-chih.

45. *I-shu* [Surviving works], 18:2a, in the *Erh-Ch'eng ch'üan-shu.*

46. *Ibid.,* 21B:2a.

47. *Wai-shu*, 3:1a.

48. *I chuan*, 1:2b.

49. *Yü-lei*, ch. 20, sec. 95 (p. 751).

50. *Ibid.,* ch. 25, sec. 27 (p. 979).

51. *Ibid.,* ch. 20, sec. 103 (p. 752).

52. *Ibid.,* sec. 102 (p. 752).

53. *I-ch'uan ching-shuo* [Ch'eng I's explanations of the classics], 6:2b, in the *Erh-Ch'eng ch'üan-shu.*

54. *Yü-lei*, ch. 25, sec. 21, 22 (pp. 976–977).

55. *Ibid.,* sec. 23 (p. 977).

56. *Ibid.,* sec. 20 (p. 976).

57. *Ibid.,* sec. 24 (p. 978).

58. *Ibid.,* ch. 45, sec. 19 (p. 1830).

59. *Wen-chi*, 41:12b, fourth letter in reply to Ch'eng Yün-fu (Ch'eng Hsün).

60. *Yü-lei*, ch. 25, sec. 21 (p. 976).

61. *Ibid.,* sec. 22, (pp. 976–977).

62. *Ibid.,* ch. 95, sec. 12 (p. 3839).

63. Chu Hsi, *Lun-yü chi-chu* [Collected commentaries on the *Analects*], comment on 7:29.

64. *Wen-chi,* supplementary collection, 9:1a, letter in reply to Liu Tao-chung (Liu Ping).

65. *Analects,* 13:19.

66. *Classic of Filial Piety,* ch. 14.

67. *I-shu*, 11:5b.

68. *Analects,* 7:14.

69. According to tradition, the lord of Ku-chu had wanted to transmit the throne to Shu-ch'i, his younger son. When he died, Shu-ch'i yielded to his elder brother Po-i, but Po-i declined and they both fled rather than take the throne. Later, when King Wu launched a military expedition against the Shang dynasty, out of loyalty the brothers tried to prevent it, but failed. Thereupon they retired to live on berries on a mountain and eventually starved to death.

70. *Yü-lei*, ch. 105, sec. 45 (p. 4186).

71. *Book of Mencius,* 6A:11.

72. *Analects,* 12:1.

73. *Wen-chi*, 59:8a, letter in reply to Li Yüan-han.

74. *Pei-hsi tzu-i* [Ch'en Ch'un's explanation of terms], sec. 59 (*Hsi-yin-hsüan ts'ung-shu* [Studio where time is highly valued series] ed., 1:26a–b). See my translation entitled *Neo-Confucian Terms Explained* (New York: Columbia University Press, 1986), pp. 75–76.

75. *Yü-lei*, ch. 20, sec. 87 (p. 748).

76. *Wen-chi*, 60:18a, second letter in reply to Tseng Tse-chih.

77. *Yü-lei*, ch. 20, sec. 98 (p. 751).

78. *Wen-chi*, 33:12a–b, eighteenth letter in reply to Lü Po-kung (Lü Tsu-ch'ien).

79. *Yü-lei,* ch. 20, sec. 127 (p. 767).

80. *Analects,* 1:2.

81. *Wen-chi,* 31:21b, thirtieth letter in reply to Chang Ching-fu (Chang Shih). The same idea is expressed in the *Yü-lei,* ch. 20, sec. 94 (p. 750).

82. *Book of Mencius,* 6A:11.

83. *Yü-lei,* ch. 59, sec. 155 (p. 2239).

84. *Wen-chi,* 42:8b, fifth letter in reply to Hu Kuang-chung (Hu Shih).

85. *Yü-lei,* ch. 6, sec. 117 (p. 191).

86. *Ibid.,* ch. 20, sec. 90 (pp. 748–749).

87. *Ibid.*

88. The Five Agents (or Five Elements) are Metal, Wood, Water, Fire, and Earth.

89. In Cheng Hsüan's (127–200) commentary on the first chapter of the *Doctrine of the Mean,* the Five Agents are equated with the Five Constant Virtues of humanity, righteousness, propriety, wisdom, and faithfulness.

90. *Lun-yü huo-wen* 1:7b (p. 18), comment on 1:2.

91. In the *Book of Mencius,* 2A:6, the Four Beginnings are the starting points of the Four Virtues of humanity, righteousness, propriety, and wisdom.

92. *Yü-lei,* ch. 20, sec. 93 (p. 750).

93. *Pei-hsi tzu-i,* sec. 50 (pt. 1, p. 24b); *Neo-Confucian Terms Explained,* p. 71.

94. *Yü-lei,* ch. 20, sec. 124 (p. 765).

95. *Ibid.,* sec. 97 (p. 751).

96. *Pei-hsi tzu-i,* sec. 73 (pt. 1, p. 32a); *Neo-Confucian Terms Explained,* p. 84.

97. *Analects,* 12:1.

98. *Ibid.,* 13:19.

99. *Book of Mencius,* 7B:16.

100. *Analects,* 1:2.

101. *Ibid.,* 4:2.

102. *Book of Mencius,* 2A:6.

103. *Yü-lei,* ch. 20, sec. 113 (p. 760). See also sec. 106 (p. 753).

104. *I chuan,* 1:2b.

105. *Ibid.*

106. *Ibid.,* sec. 101 (pp. 751–752).

107. *Ibid.*

108. *Ibid.,* sec. 109 (p. 755).

109. *Ibid.,* sec. 103 (p. 752).

110. *Ibid.,* sec. 104 (p. 750).

111. *Pei-hsi tzu-i,* sec. 73 (pt. 1, p. 32a); *Neo-Confucian Terms Explained,* p. 84.

112. *Yü-lei,* ch. 20, sec. 101 (p. 753).

113. *Wen-chi,* 51:38b, letter in reply to Wan Cheng-ch'ou (Wan Jen-chieh).

114. *Yü-lei,* ch. 20, sec. 103 (p. 754).

115. *Ibid.,* sec. 111 (p. 757).

116. *Ibid.,* sec. 111 (p. 758).

117. *Ibid.,* ch. 6, sec. 78 (pp. 179–180).

118. *Analects,* 5:25.

119. *Wen-chi,* 57:2b–3a, letter in reply to Li Yao-ch'ing (Li T'ang-tzu).

120. *Ibid.,* 58:29a–b, first letter in reply to Hsü Chu-fu (Hsü Yü).

121. *Ibid.,* 50:34b, fifth letter in reply to Chou Shun-pi (Chou Mu). Also in the *Yü-lei,* ch. 20, sec. 111 (pp. 758–759).

122. *Yü-lei*, ch. 6, sec. 87 (p. 185).

123. *Analects*, 12:1.

124. *Ibid.*, 13:19.

125. *Ibid.*, 12:2.

126. *Yü-lei*, ch. 20, sec. 112 (pp. 759–760).

127. These are the Four Qualities of the first hexagram, *ch'ien* (Heaven, male), in the *Book of Changes*.

128. Mou Tsung-san, *Hsin-t'i yü hsing-t'i*, vol. 3, pp. 232, 242, 245–246.

129. *Ibid.*, p. 243.

130. Ch'ien Mu, *Chu Tzu hsin-hsüeh-an* [New anthology and critical accounts of Master Chu] (Taipei: San-min Book Co., 1971), vol. 2, pp. 54–55.

131. T'ang Chün-i, *Chung-kuo che-hsüeh yüan-lun: Yüan-hsing-pien* [Origin and development of Chinese philosophical ideas: Volume on nature] (Hong Kong: New Asia Research Institute, 1968), pp. 390–399.

132. Mou Tsung-san, *Hsin-ti yü hsing-t'i*, vol. 3, pp. 249–252.

133. *Ibid.*, pp. 234–252.

134. *Wen-chi*, 42:17b–19a, tenth letter in reply to Wu Hui-shu (Wu I).

135. *Ibid.*, 32:16b–21b; *Nan-hsüan Hsien-sheng wen-chi*, 20:7b (p. 652), ninth letter in reply to Chu Yüan-hui (Chu Hsi); 21:5b (p. 674), twenty-first letter.

136. *Ibid.*, 32:16a–18b, letter in reply to Chang Ching-fu (Chang Shih) on the "Jen-shuo."

137. *Nan-hsüan Hsien-sheng wen-chi*, 21:5b (p. 674), twenty-first letter in reply to Chu Yüan-hui.

138. *Ibid.*, 20:7b (p. 652), ninth letter.

139. *Wen-chi*, 32:17b–18a. *Yüan* is the first of the Four Qualities of origination, flourishing, advantage, and firmness in the process of change, according to the commentary on the first hexagram, *ch'ien*, in the *Book of Changes*.

140. *Nan-hsüan Hsien-sheng wen-chi*, 20:7b (p. 652), ninth letter in reply to Chu Yüan-hui.

141. *Wen-chi*, 32:19a–b, "Further discussion on the 'Jen-shuo.' "

142. *Nan-hsüan Hsien-sheng wen-chi*, 21:5b–6a (pp. 674–675), twenty-first letter to Chu Yüan-hui.

143. *Wen-chi*, 32:20a–b, "Further discussion on the 'Jen-shuo.' "

144. *Nan-hsüan Hsien-sheng wen-chi*, 20:7a (p. 651), ninth letter to Chu Yüan-hui.

145. *Wen-chi*, 32:20a–b, "Further discussion on the 'Jen-shuo.' "

146. Mou Tsung-san, *Hsin-t'i yü hsing-t'i*, vol. 3, p. 280.

147. *Ibid.*, pp. 259–281.

148. *Wen-chi*, 40:29a–30a, sixteenth and seventeenth letters in reply to Ho Shu-ching (Ho Hao).

149. *Ibid.*, p. 29a.

150. *Yü-lei*, ch. 105, sec. 44 (p. 4186).

151. *Wen-chi*, 42:8a, fifth letter in reply to Hu Kuang-chung (Hu Shih).

152. *Ibid.*, 33:15a, twenty-fourth letter in reply to Lü Po-kung (Lü Tsu-ch'ien).

153. *Ibid.*, 40:29b, seventeenth letter in reply to Ho Shu-ching.

154. *Yü-lei*, ch. 105, sec. 42 (p. 4184).

155. *Pei-hsi tzu-i*, sec. 71 (pt. 1, 31a–32a). See my translation, *Neo-Confucian*

*Terms Explained,* pp. 81–83. Also *Sung-Yüan hsüeh-an* [Anthology and critical accounts of the Neo-Confucians of the Sung and Yüan dynasties] (*SPPY* ed.), 68:2a–b.

156. *Wen-chi,* 67:20a, "Treatise on *Jen.*"

157. *Pei-hsi ta-ch'üan-chi* [Complete collected works of Ch'en Ch'un] (*Ssu-k'u ch'üan-shu chen-pen* [Precious works of the *Complete Collection of the Four Libraries*] ed.) 26:5b, fifth letter in reply to Ch'en Po-tsao (Ch'en I).

158. Hsiung Chieh, *Hsing-li ch'ün-shu chü-chieh* [Punctuation and explanation of books on nature and principle] (*Chin-shih han-chi ts'ung-k'an* ed.), 8:8a–10b (p. 367–372).

159. *Nan-hsüan Hsien-sheng wen-chi,* 18:1a–b.

160. *Wen-chi,* 33:18a–b, twenty-seventh letter in reply to Lü Po-kung (Lü Tsu-ch'ien). See also above, p. 155.

161. *Sung-Yüan hsüeh-an [Anthology and critical accounts of the Neo-Confucians of the Sung and Yüan dynasties] (SPPY* ed.), 50:11a, chapter on Chang Shih.

162. *Wen-chi,* 33:20a–b, thirtieth letter in reply to Lü Po-kung.

163. *Ibid.,* 32:23a–24b, forty-seventh letter in reply to Ch'in-fu on his "Jen-shuo."

164. *I-shu,* 3:3a.

165. Mou Tsung-san, *Hsien-t'i yü hsing-t'i,* vol. 3, p. 295.

166. Professor Satō's paper is published in Wing-tsit Chan, ed., *Chu Hsi and Neo-Confucianism* (Honolulu: University of Hawaii Press, 1986), pp. 212–227.

167. Wing-tsit Chan, *Chu-hsüeh lun-chi* [Studies on Chu Hsi] (Taipei: Student Book Co., 1982), pp. 37–68.

168. In the *Sung-Yüan hsüeh-an,* introduction to ch. 68 on Ch'en Ch'un.

169. Liu Shu-hsien, "Further examination of Chu Hsi's 'Treatise on *Jen,*' the concept of the Great Ultimate, and orthodox tradition of the Way—Reflections on participating at the International Conference on Chu Hsi [in Chinese]," in *Shih-hsüeh p'ing-lun* [Historical tribune], no. 5 (January, 1983), p. 173–188.

170. *Ssu-k'u ch'üan-shu tsung-mu t'i-yao* [Essentials of the contents of the *Complete Collection of the Four Libraries*] (Shanghai: Commercial Press, 1933), p. 1919.

171. *Pei-hsi ta-ch'üan chi,* 26:5b, fifth letter in reply to Ch'en Po-tsao. Wen-ling is an elegant name for Ch'üan-chou Prefecture in southern Fukien.

# 12

# Chu Hsi on *T'ien*

T*'ien* means three different things in Chu Hsi's system of thought. When a pupil asked about the meaning of *t'ien* in the classics, Chu Hsi answered, "This must be understood by oneself. Some say that *t'ien* refers to the blue sky and others say that it means the master *(chu-tsai)*. And there are times when it simply means principle *(li)*".[1] Asked about the theory that *t'ien* is identical with principle, he said, "*T'ien* is of course principle, but the blue sky is also *t'ien*. What is above and has a master is also *t'ien*."[2] This idea was derived from Ch'eng I (1033–1107), who said, "Spoken of collectively, *t'ien* is the Way *(tao)*. . . . Spoken of separately, it is called *t'ien* in the sense of physical shape, the Lord *(ti)* in the sense of a master, passive and positive cosmic forces *(kuei-shen)* in the sense of function, spirit *(shen)* in the sense of its wonderful operation, and *ch'ien* in the sense of nature and feeling."[3]

## *T'ien* as the Blue Sky

Here Chu Hsi largely followed tradition but added a new meaning. As recorded in the *Yü-lei*, he said,

> In the beginning of the universe there was only material force consisting of yin [passive cosmic force] and yang [active cosmic force]. This force moved and circulated, turning this way and that. As it gained speed, a mass of sediment was compressed [pushed together], and since there was no outlet for this, it consolidated to form the Earth in the center of the universe. The clear part of material force formed the sky, the sun, the moon, and the stars and zodiacal spaces. It is only on the outside that the encircling movement perpetually goes on. The Earth exists motionless in the center of the system, not at the bottom.[4]

The two forces of yin and yang are water and fire.[5] "The circulation of the sky is ceaseless, rotating day and night."[6] Shao Yung (1011–1077) had said, "The woodcutter asked the fisherman, 'What does the sky depend on?' Answer: 'It depends on the Earth.' 'What does the Earth rely on?' Answer: 'It relies on Heaven.' 'In that case, what do Heaven and Earth depend on?' Answer: 'They mutually depend on each other. What Heaven depends on is the physical shape and what the Earth depends on is the material force.' "[7] Chu Hsi clarified this by saying, "By virtue of its material force, Heaven depends on the physical shape of the Earth, and by virtue of its physical shape, the Earth depends on the material force of Heaven."[8] When asked by a pupil whether Heaven and Earth can be destroyed, he replied, "No, they cannot be destroyed, only gradually humankind will become inhuman to the extreme, everyone will be fighting, creating a general chaos, and men and things will all perish. The world will then begin anew."[9] This idea of a new world is a novel concept. Of course it could have come out of the traditional idea of cycles, but the Buddhist doctrine of the long period between the creation and recreation of the universe *(kalpa)* must also have exerted some influence. This can be seen in Chu Hsi's answer to the pupil's further question about the birth of the first man, in which he referred to the Buddhist theory of sudden emergence or unconditional creation.[10]

Of special significance is Chu Hsi's discovery of the nature of fossils. In discussing how the universe changes, he said, "There are shells of conchs implanted in rocks. The rocks were formerly mud, and conchs lived in water. What is low has changed to high, and what is soft has changed to hard. When one thinks deeply about this matter, one can find evidence for it."[11] He also said, "Now on the high mountains there are implants of oyster shells. This means that low ground has become high ground. Furthermore, oysters had to live in sand and mud, but now they are found in rocks. This means that what was soft has become what is hard."[12] When Hu Shih (1891–1962) said that Chu Hsi realized what are fossils three hundred years before Leonardo da Vinci, he was stating a simple fact.[13] Of course Chu Hsi's insight came from his philosophy of change rather than from purely scientific observation, but he nevertheless uncovered a concrete scientific fact.

## *T'ien* as Principle

To interpret *t'ien* in the sense of principle is of course to be expected of Chu Hsi. The quotation by Ch'eng I cited above shows that this idea is derived from him, but Chu Hsi refined it and gave it a new meaning. In his commentary on the *Analects* 3:13, Chu Hsi said, "*T'ien* is identical with principle."[14] In his commentary on the *Book of Mencius* 4A:7, he also said, "*T'ien* is what the tendency of principle should be."[15] Elsewhere he said, "*T'ien* is nothing but principle. That a large state should serve a small state and that a small state should serve a large state are what should be according to principle. When one is naturally in accordance with Heaven *(T'ien)*, it is said that one delights in Heaven. When one does not dare violate principle, it is said that one stands in awe of Heaven."[16]

Traditionally, to sin against, obey, violate, delight in, or stand in awe of Heaven had been understood in terms of Heaven being an anthropomorphic deity. To interpret Heaven in the sense of principle was a new proposition, and a daring one at that. On the passage, "We cannot hear his [Confucius'] views on human nature and the Way of Heaven," Chu Hsi commented, "Nature is the principle of Heaven that man has received, and the Way of Heaven is the original substance of the Principle of Heaven. In reality, they are just one principle."[17] Although Ch'eng I had said that, collectively speaking, *t'ien* is the Way, in his comment on a pupil's inability to hear Confucius' view on the Way of Heaven, he merely said that Confucius' view was perfect.[18] But Chu Hsi explicitly identified *t'ien* with principle, thus carrying the interpretation a step further.

Chu Hsi said, "*T'ien* is where principle comes from."[19] This seems to say that *t'ien* comes before principle. He also said, "There is only one principle in the universe. Heaven receives it to become Heaven, Earth receives it to become Earth, and all those born in the universe receive it to become their nature."[20] This seems to say that Heaven comes after principle, so some scholars think that Chu Hsi contradicted himself here. But in reality, principle is above time and cannot be described as before or after. When Chu Hsi went on to say that "the operation of principle is omnipresent," he merely meant that everything in the world has to follow principle before it can fulfill its nature to become a thing, not that everything in the world is born of principle. Moreover, when a pupil inquired whether it is not true that Heaven is spoken of from the point of view of what is natural; *ming* (mandate, destiny) from the point of view of its operation and its endowment in things; nature from the point of view of its totality, from which everything receives its own share to be born; and principle from the point of view of everything having a specific principle *(tse)* of its being, "Chu Hsi gave an affirmative answer."[21] He also said, "Principle is the substance of Heaven, *ming* is the function of principle, and nature is what man receives."[22] But Heaven and *ming* are not two different things, "for spoken of from the point of view of principle, it is Heaven, and spoken of from the point of view of man, it is *ming*. In reality, they are only one."[23] Again, he said, "Heaven is spoken of in terms of principle, and *ming* is spoken of in terms of appointment. They are not two different things."[24] In the final analysis, Heaven is identical with _ming,_ and _ming_ is the function of principle.

## The Master and _Ti_

Heaven is none other than a blue physical form, but since it is also principle, it must have a master.[25] Chu Hsi said, "Now it won't do to say that there is someone in Heaven to pass judgment on sins, but it also won't do to say that there is no master whatsoever. In a matter like this, one must see for oneself."[26] When asked who the master is, he replied, "Naturally there is a master, for Heaven is the strongest and most positive thing. It naturally rotates like this without cease. There must be a master for it to do so. In this respect one must see for oneself; it is not something that can be fully explained in words." Thereupon he cited Chuang Tzu's words, "Who manipulates this? Who masterminds this?"[27] and finally added, "Chuang Tzu also understood this principle."[28] Chuang Tzu had continued, "Who, resting inactive himself, pushes them [the sky, etc.] into circulation? I wonder, is there a mechanism that cannot stop? I wonder, do they revolve and cannot stop themselves?" The answer of the Taoists is naturalism, mechanism, or skepticism. For the Confucians, however, the tradition of the Lord on High is too strong to ignore. Therefore Chu Hsi insisted that there must be a master. As the Ch'eng brothers had said, "In the _Book of Odes_ and the _Book of History,_ whenever there is the idea of a master, the word _ti_ [lord] is used, and whenever there is the idea of all-embracing and all-covering, the word _t'ien_ is used."[29]

The _ti_ in the _Book of Odes_ and the _Book of History_ is undoubtedly an anthropomorphic deity. In the Taoist religion it is called the Jade Emperor, the Great Lord of Three Purities, and the like. Chu Hsi replaced these names with "principle." He said, "In the cases of affection between father and son, and righteousness between ruler and minister,[30] although according to principle this should be so, still there must be a principle above to direct them. But it is not as in Taoism, where there is really a Great Lord of Three Purities dressed up and sitting there."[31] Put simply, "The fundamental factor of _ti_ is principle."[32] On the basis of this, Chu Hsi interpreted the passage in the _Book of Odes_ where it says, "[King Wen, _r._ 1161–1122 B.C.] was on the left and right of _ti,_"[33] as follows: "[King Wen] examined the Principle of Heaven and did this or that. This is the meaning in ancient commentaries."[34] As a matter of fact, K'ung Ying-ta's (574–648) sub-commentary on the _Book of Odes_ still retained the notion of an anthropomorphic deity: "[King Wen] always watched the ideas of the Heavenly Lord, followed what the Lord considered to be proper, obeyed it and carried it out in action."[35]

In contrast, Chu Hsi interpreted *ti* strictly as principle. Nevertheless, the idea of a master is basically mysterious, belonging to the sphere of personal belief, and cannot be rationally determined. Therefore Chu Hsi repeatedly urged pupils to find out for themselves. He said, "This is what it is according to principle. It won't do if you say that there was really a King Wen moving up and down, nor will it do if you say that the poet talked nonsense."[36] It is recorded in the *Book of History* that the Heavenly Lord bestowed on the ruler Kao-tsung an able minister.[37] On the basis of this account, a pupil asked whether there really was a Heavenly Lord who conversed with the ruler. To this, Chu Hsi responded, "Nowadays people only explain *ti* in terms of a master, considering *ti* to have neither physical shape nor form. I am afraid this will not do. But if one likens it to what the world calls the Jade Emperor, I am afraid that will not do either. In the end, what this principle is, no scholar can say."[38] What Chu Hsi meant is that we do not know whether there is a Heavenly Lord, but if there is, he must follow principle.

## "The mind of Heaven and Earth is to produce things"

Where is the generating force of the master? According to Chu Hsi, it is in the mind of Heaven and Earth. A pupil asked, "With reference to the mind of Heaven and Earth and the principle of Heaven and Earth, principle is moral principle. Is mind the will of a master?" Answer: "The mind is the will of a master, it is true, but what is called master is precisely principle itself. It is not true that outside the mind there is principle, or that outside principle there is a mind." Further question: "Are the word *hsin* [mind] and the word *ti* similar?" Answer: "The word *jen* [man] resembles the word *t'ien,* and the word *hsin* resembles the word *ti*."[39] Again, Chu Hsi said, "The mind of Heaven and Earth— principle is in it,"[40] and "This mind cannot be said to be unintelligent, but it does not deliberate as in the case of man."[41]

What does the mind of Heaven and Earth want to do? It wants to produce things. The concept of production (*sheng,* to generate, to give life) can be traced back to ancient times. The *Book of Changes* says, "Change means production and reproduction (*sheng-sheng*)."[42] It also says, "The great characteristic of Heaven and Earth is to produce."[43] Ch'eng I said, "The mind of Heaven and Earth is to produce things."[44] This became the central idea in Chu Hsi's discussion of *t'ien.* His discussion on the mind of Heaven and Earth to produce things is several times longer than his discussions on *t'ien, ti,* and *chu-tsai.* Chu Hsi and Chang Shih (1133–1180) debated on Ch'eng I's saying for some years, but Chu Hsi held firmly to Ch'eng I's idea.[45] It is not an exaggeration to say that this concept is as important in Chu Hsi's system of thought as those of *T'ai-chi* (the Great Ultimate) and *jen* (humanity).

As Chu Hsi saw it, "Heaven and Earth have no other business except to have the mind to produce things. The material force of one origin [the Great Ultimate, including principle and material force] revolves and circulates without a moment of rest, doing nothing except creating the myriad things."[46] This mind has never ceased. From time immemorial, the process of production and reproduction has been going on. As in the case of growth in the spring and preservation in the winter, the principle has never been interrupted.[47] As to why this has been the case, Chu Hsi offered no definite explanation. However, several reasons can be discerned from his conversations. First, for a thing to be, it has to be produced: "The mind of Heaven and Earth is simply to produce. All things must be produced before they can be things. As in the case of the sprouts of plants and the flourishing of their branches, all must be produced before they become so. The reason man and things are in the process of infinite production and reproduction lies in their principle of production."[48] Second, there is the mutual propelling forward of yin and yang. Chu Hsi said, "In its expansion, it becomes yang, and in its dark moments, it becomes yin. When is it not the mind of Heaven and Earth?"[49] Third, there is the air of spring: "The air of spring is warm and rich, from which we can see that the mind of Heaven and Earth to produce things. Summer is the growth of the creative air, autumn is its contraction, and winter is its preservation. If there were no intention to produce things in the spring, there would be none of the remaining seasons."[50] Fourth, there is the pressing of the generative force. According to Chu Hsi, "The mind of Heaven and Earth is to produce things. Take for example the cooking of rice in a pot. The force rises from the bottom to the top and then turns downward. It simply turns around inside until the rice is cooked. Heaven and Earth simply embrace a great many forces inside, without any outlet. As the forces turn around once, they produce one kind of thing. They have no aim but simply to produce things."[51] These four explanations of the ceaseless production of Heaven and Earth express the same idea. There is some duplication, but the fourth explanation is the most interesting, because it shows that the power of Heaven and Earth to produce things is so strong that it cannot be stopped.

## The Mind of Heaven and Earth
## in the Hexagram *Fu* (to return)

The easiest way to see that the mind of Heaven and Earth is to produce things is to look at the yang line at the bottom of the *fu* hexagram in the *Book of Changes*. A hexagram consists of six lines which may be continuous (yang) or broken (yin), with the movement from the bottom of the hexagram to the top. In the *fu* hexagram, the bottom line is a yang line, which means incipient growth. The explanation of its component lines says, "In the operation of Heaven, seven days make up a cycle. . . . In the *fu* hexagram, the mind of Heaven and Earth can be seen."[52] Concerning this point, Chu Hsi deliberated a great deal. In his conversations with students and correspondence with friends, he often discussed this question. His main idea was that

> *fu* is not the mind of Heaven and Earth, but in *fu* we can see the mind of Heaven and Earth. . . . The bottom line of this hexagram shows why the mind of Heaven and Earth is to produce things. The hexagram is so called because of the emergence of the yang element at the starting point. . . . Because of its return, the shooting forth of yang can be seen at the bottom, and because of the return we can see the mind of Heaven and Earth.[53]

Chu Hsi noted that "the Sage [Confucius] said that in the *fu* hexagram the mind of Heaven and Earth can be seen. The point when activity vaguely begins is the best time to observe that the force of growth never stops."[54] He also said, "The yang element is exhausted beyond the top line but returns at the bottom line. In this the Sage could see the mind of Heaven and Earth. What returns is the material force. There is a reason it returns. If there were no mind of Heaven and Earth to produce and reproduce without cease, the force of yang, once exhausted, would be finished and could not continue."[55]

In his commentary on the passage "In the hexagram of *fu* the mind of Heaven and Earth can be seen," Ch'eng I remarked, "The yang element returns at the bottom, which shows the mind of Heaven and Earth to produce things. Former Confucians all considered that the mind of Heaven and Earth can be seen in tranquillity, without knowing that it is seen in the beginning of activity."[56] Ch'eng I had in mind Wang Pi (226–249), who, in his commentary on the *Book of Changes,* had this to say: "Silent and complete nonbeing is the foundation. Therefore when activity ceases in the world, the mind of Heaven and Earth can be seen."[57] In commenting on Ch'eng I's words, Chu Hsi said,

> This paragraph of I-ch'uan's [Ch'eng I] means that the character of Heaven and Earth is to produce and reproduce. The process of origination, flourishing, advantage, and firmness[58] constitutes the mind to produce things. However, in its tranquillity and return, it is the substance [of Change] that has not been aroused, while in its activity that penetrates everything, it is the function that has been aroused. When the yang element returns, its initial emergence is extremely subtle. Of course it seems to be tranquil, but actually it is the incipient moving force of activity. Its tendency gets stronger every day, and all things depend on it to begin. Such is the beginning of the operations of the Mandate of Heaven, and the commencement of creation and development in which the mind of

Heaven and Earth to produce and reproduce unceasingly can be seen. When it is tranquil and before it is aroused, it is the substance of this mind. Although it is everywhere, it is not yet revealed. This is why Master Ch'eng considered the beginning of activity as the mind of Heaven and Earth, thus putting forward function to include substance.[59]

These words contain a subtle criticism of Ch'eng I's theory, for both tranquillity and activity are only half the story of the mind of Heaven and Earth. Besides, although the beginning of activity is subtle, it is already the start of creation. In Chu Hsi's mind, "Creation cannot be seen in the return itself, but in it one can see the mind to create."[60] Chang Shih once wrote Chu Hsi, contending that activity implies tranquillity and suggesting that the mind of Heaven and Earth can still be seen in tranquillity. For Chu Hsi, however, there could be neither activity without tranquillity nor tranquillity without activity; the movement of yin and yang alternate and become the root of each other.[61] "One must view the matter from both activity and tranquillity, yin and yang, and good and evil," he said.[62] This is why he rejected Lao Tzu's idea of maintaining steadfast tranquillity at the return of things.[63]

Chu Hsi not only disagreed that only in tranquillity or activity can the mind of Heaven and Earth can be seen, he also disagreed that only in *fu* can the mind of Heaven and Earth be seen. In his words,

When the Sage amplified the *Book of Changes,* he said, "In *fu* the mind of Heaven and Earth can be seen." It is wrong for people to say today that only in *fu* can the mind of Heaven and Earth be seen. All sixty-four hexagrams show the mind of Heaven and Earth. He merely saw in the *fu* hexagram the sudden return of the yang element, and amplified it in this way. In our discussion we should know that there are the active mind and the tranquil mind, as there are the good mind and the evil mind. One must see the matter according to the situation.[64]

He also said, "We must realize that the mind of Heaven and Earth is none other than origination, flourishing, advantage, and firmness."[65] In other words, the mind of Heaven and Earth to produce things includes the whole creative process and is not limited to the return of the yang element. Consequently, Chu Hsi asked, "Why only in *fu* can the mind of Heaven and Earth be seen?"[66] Practically speaking, there is no conflict between seeing the mind of Heaven and Earth in the *fu* hexagram and seeing it in all sixty-four hexagrams. The fact that, when the yin element on top of the *fu* hexagram is exhausted, it returns to yang at the bottom is a clear indication that yin and yang alternate and become the root of each other. It is only wrong to claim that in *fu* alone can the mind of Heaven and Earth be seen.

## *T'ien-hsin* (The mind of Heaven)

In all these discussions, the phrase "the mind of Heaven and Earth" is used. As far as we know, there is only one case each in the *Wen-chi* and *Yü-lei* where Chu Hsi used "the mind of Heaven" *(t'ien-chih-hsin)* to replace "the mind of Heaven and Earth."[67] Moreover, his employment of *t'ien-hsin* to mean the mind of Heaven and Earth occurs only twice in the *Wen-chi.*[68] In addition, he quoted Chang Tsai's (1020–1077) use of the term three times.[69] Everywhere else, Chu Hsi used the term *t'ien-hsin* to mean "the sovereign's mind," which has nothing to do with the mind of Heaven and Earth.[70]

## Having a Mind *(yu-hsin)* and Having no Mind *(wu-hsin)*

The question arises whether or not the mind of Heaven and Earth to produce things is a conscious mind. Chu Hsi concluded that since there is the mind to produce things, it must be a conscious one. Otherwise, he thought, an ox would produce a horse and a peach tree would produce plums.[71] But this mind is free from deliberation or manipulation, and therefore it is called "the mind without a mind *(wu-hsin)*."[72] Questioned about Ch'eng I's saying, "Heaven and Earth have no mind except to complete things and transform things. The sage has mind but takes no artificial action,"[73] Chu Hsi replied, "This is to say in what respect Heaven and Earth have no mind."[74] He also said, "When the myriad things are born and grow, that is the time when Heaven and Earth have no [deliberative] mind. When dried and withered things desire life, that is the time when Heaven and Earth have [a nondeliberative] mind."[75] These words are intriguing, for the birth and growth of the myriad things occur according to principle. Because the Principle of Heaven is perfectly impartial, there is no need for a master to deliberate and manipulate, and principle is said to have no mind. In the case of dried and withered things desiring life, the Principle of Heaven is an indication of the will to live. When yin is exhausted and returns to yang, the mind of Heaven and Earth can be seen.

## "Man and things receive this mind as their mind"

Chang Tsai said, "Heaven has no mind. Its mind is in man's mind. One man's private opinion cannot represent fully the mind of Heaven, but when the minds of all people agree, that will be a moral principle, and that is Heaven. Therefore what we call Heaven or the Lord is completely the feeling of the people."[76] This idea is derived from the *Book of History,* quoted in the *Book of Mencius,* that "Heaven sees as my people see; Heaven hears as my people hear."[77] To this Chu Hsi gave a philosophical interpretation. In the opening passage of his "Jen-shuo" he said, "The mind of Heaven and Earth is to produce things. In the production of man and things, they receive the mind of Heaven and Earth as their mind." The first sentence is a quotation from Ch'eng I,[78] while the second is Chu Hsi's own.[79] As he explained, "Heaven and Earth apply this mind universally to all things. Man receives it and it thus becomes man's mind, and things receive it and it thus becomes the mind of things. As grass and plants, birds and animals come into contact with it, it becomes their mind. There is only one mind of Heaven and Earth."[80]

The mind of Heaven and Earth means the macrocosm, while a man or a thing means the microcosm. "In the production of the myriad things by Heaven and Earth, there is the mind of Heaven and Earth in everything."[81] This conforms to Chu Hsi's philosophy that there is a Great Ultimate in each and every thing. Ch'eng I said, "The mind is the principle of production. As there is the mind, a body must be provided for it so it can produce. The feeling of commiseration is the principle of production in man."[82] As Chu Hsi explained it, " 'The mind is the principle of production' means the mind is the way of production. 'The feeling of commiseration is the principle of production in man' means that man receives the mind of Heaven and Earth at birth. The mind of Heaven and Earth is simply to produce things."[83] He also said, "If there were no mind of Heaven and Earth to produce things, there would not be the body. As soon as there is a body of blood and breath, the mind of Heaven and Earth to produce things is present in it."[84]

Man is not only endowed with the mind of Heaven and Earth. In the tradition of Heaven seeing as the people see and hearing as the people hear, his mind is the expression of the mind of Heaven and Earth. Commenting on the Confucian saying, "It is man that can make the Way great,"[85] Chu Hsi said, "Man is the mind of Heaven and Earth. If there were no man, no one would attend to Heaven and Earth."[86] This does not mean that man is superior to Heaven but indicates the unity of man and Heaven. As he said, "I have maintained that *jen* [humanity] is the mind of Heaven and Earth, and that man and things receive this mind as their mind. Although this idea is the product of my personal opinion of the moment, I humbly believe that it opens up precisely the point that there is no separation between Heaven and man."[87]

For Heaven and Earth, the mind is to produce things; in man, the mind is to practice *jen*. At birth, man receives the material force of Heaven and Earth. "That is why the mind is *jen*, and because it is *jen*, it will produce."[88] *Jen* is the leader of all good deeds. Because of *jen* all virtues, like righteousness, propriety, and wisdom, are naturally produced.[89] *Jen* possesses the spirit of life. The mind is also like Heaven and Earth giving birth to things, producing and reproducing without end.[90]

That is why Ch'eng I said, "The mind is comparable to seeds of grain. The nature of growth is *jen*."[91] Chang Tsai said, "Make up your mind for the sake of Heaven and Earth."[92] In his commentary on this saying, Chang Po-hsing (1652–1725) remarked, "The mind of Heaven and Earth is to produce and reproduce and transform the myriad things, and their nature and destiny are thereby correct. Confucians also make this their mind, assisting and participating in the process of nourishing things, bringing order throughout Heaven and Earth, and making sure that man really fulfills his nature to the best of his ability."[93] Full realization of nature leads to *jen*, and *jen* leads to sagehood. In sagehood, Heaven and man are united as one.

## Notes

1. *Yü-lei*, ch. 1, sec. 22 (p. 8).
2. *Ibid.*, ch. 79, sec. 67 (p. 3240).
3. *I chuan* [Commentary on the *Book of Changes*], 1:1a, in the *Erh-Ch'eng ch'üan-shu* [Complete works of the two Ch'engs] (*SPPY* ed.). *Ch'ien* (Heaven, male) is the first hexagram in the *Book of Changes*. Its Four Qualities are origination, flourishing, advantage, and firmness.
4. *Yü-lei*, ch. 1, sec. 23 (p. 8).
5. *Ibid.*, sec. 33 (p. 10).
6. *Ibid.*, sec. 25 (p. 9).
7. *Shao Tzu ch'üan-shu* [Complete works of Master Shao Yung] (1606 ed.), ch. 7, "Additional Works," "Conversation between the Fisherman and the Woodcutter," p. 4a.
8. *Yü-lei*, ch. 1, sec. 26 (p. 9).
9. *Ibid.*, ch. 1, sec. 39 (p. 11).
10. *Ibid.*
11. *Ibid.*, ch. 94, sec. 16 (p. 3759).
12. *Ibid.*, ch. 94, sec. 17 (p. 3761).
13. Hu Shih, *The Chinese Renaissance* (Chicago: University of Chicago Press, 1934), p. 59.
14. Chu Hsi, *Lun-yü chi-chu* [Collected commentaries on the *Analects*], comment on 3:13.
15. Chu Hsi, *Meng Tzu chi-chu* [Collected commentaries on the *Book of Mencius*]; comment on 4A:7.
16. *Ibid.*, 1B:3.
17. *Lun-yü chi-chu*, comment on 5:12.
18. For the quotation by Ch'eng I, see above, n. 3. For his comment on the Way of Heaven, see his *Ching-shuo* [Explanations of the classics], 6:5a, in the *Erh-Ch'eng ch'üan-shu*.
19. *Meng Tzu chi-chu*, comment on 7A:1.
20. *Wen-chi*, 70:5a, "On reading [Hu Hung's *Huang-wang*] *ta-chi* [Great principle of the universe]."
21. *Yü-lei*, ch. 5, sec. 1 (p. 133).
22. *Ibid.*, sec. 2 (p. 133).
23. *Meng Tzu chi-chu*, comment on 5B:6.

24. *Wen-chi,* 40:30a, eighteenth letter to Ho Shu-ching (Ho Hao).

25. *Yü-lei,* ch. 68, sec. 10 (p. 2679).

26. *Ibid.,* ch. 1, sec. 22 (p. 8).

27. *Chuang Tzu,* ch. 14, "Revolution of Heaven" (*SPTK* ed., *Nan-hua chen-ching* [True classic of Chuang Tzu], 5:35b).

28. *Yü-lei,* ch. 68, sec. 11 (p. 2679).

29. *I-shu* [Surviving works], 2A:13b, in the *Erh-Ch'eng ch'üan-shu.* It is not specified which of the Ch'eng brothers uttered this. In all probability the two shared the same idea. On this topic, see ch. 19 below, section on "Ch'eng Tzu."

30. *Book of Mencius,* 3A:4.

31. *Yü-lei,* ch. 25, sec. 83 (p. 1001).

32. *Ibid.,* ch. 1, sec. 21 (p. 8).

33. *Book of Odes,* ode no. 235.

34. *Yü-lei,* ch. 81, sec. 135 (p. 3372).

35. K'ung Ying-ta, *Mao-shih cheng-i* [Correct meanings of Mao's edition of the *Book of Odes*] (*Shih-san ching chu-shu* [Commentaries and sub-commentaries of the Thirteen Classics], World Book Co. ed.), ch. 16, p. 236 (p. 504).

36. *Yü-lei,* ch. 81, sec. 134 (pp. 3371–3372).

37. *Book of History,* "Yüeh-ming" [Charge to Yüeh], pt. 1, sec. 2.

38. *Yü-lei,* ch. 79, sec. 46 (p. 3233).

39. *Ibid.,* ch. 1, sec. 17 (pp. 5–6).

40. *Wen-chi,* 58:5a, second letter in reply to Huang Tao-fu (Huang Ch'iao-chung).

41. *Yü-lei,* ch. 1, sec. 16 (p. 5).

42. *Book of Changes,* "Appended Remarks," pt. 1, ch. 5.

43. *Ibid.,* pt. 2, ch. 1.

44. *Wai-shu* [Additional works], 3:1a, in the *Erh-Ch'eng ch'üan-shu.*

45. On this debate, see ch. 11 above, pp. 170–171.

46. *Yü-lei,* ch. 1, sec. 18 (p. 6). See also ch. 69, sec. 86 (p. 2754).

47. *Ibid.,* ch. 63, sec. 12 (p. 2031); ch. 27, sec. 107 (p. 1125).

48. *Ibid.,* ch. 105, sec. 44 (p. 4186).

49. *Wen-chi,* 25:11b, letter to Prefect Fu of Chien-ning Prefecture.

50. *Yü-lei,* ch. 20, sec. 117 (p. 754).

51. *Ibid.,* ch. 53, sec. 14 (p. 2033).

52. *Book of Changes,* twenty-fourth hexagram, *fu* (to return), "Yao-tz'u" (Explanation of component lines).

53. *Wen-chi,* 42:18a, tenth letter in reply to Wu Hui-shu (Wu I).

54. *Yü-lei,* ch. 71, sec. 42 (p. 2849).

55. *Wen-chi,* 32:4b, thirty-third letter in reply to Chang Ch'in-fu (Chang Shih).

56. *I chuan,* 2:33a.

57. *Chou-i chu* [Commentary on the *Book of Changes*], in *Wang Pi chi chiao-shih* [Collected works of Wang Pi collated and annotated] (Beijing: Chung-hua Book Co., 1980), p. 336.

58. These are the Four Qualities of Change. See the *Book of Changes,* the first hexagram, *ch'ien* (Heaven, male).

59. *Yü-lei,* ch. 71, sec. 50 (p. 2852).

60. *Ibid.,* sec. 53 (p. 2854).

61. *Wen-chi*, 32:26a, forty-seventh letter in reply to Chang Ch'in-fu (Chang Shih). Chang's letter to Chu Hsi is no longer extant.

62. *Ibid.*, 49:2a, second letter in reply to Wang Tzu-ho (Wang Yü).

63. *Yü-lei*, ch. 71, sec. 53 (p. 2858). For Lao Tzu's doctrine of return, see the *Lao Tzu*, ch. 16.

64. *Ibid.*, sec. 60 (p. 2858).

65. *Wen-chi*, 40:29a, sixteenth letter in reply to Ho Shu-ching (Ho Hao). See also 67:1a, "Treatise on Origination, Flourishing, Advantage, and Firmness."

66. *Ibid.*, 47:22b, twentieth letter in reply to Lü Tzu-yüeh (Lü Tsu-chien).

67. *Wen-chi*, 57:36b, written questions from Ch'en An-ch'ing (Ch'en Ch'un). *Yü-lei*, ch. 95, sec. 96 (p. 3874).

68. *Wen-chi*, 11:8b, memorial of 1162; 76:7b, postscript to Prime Minister Li's (Li Kang) memorial.

69. *Cheng-meng* [Correcting youthful ignorance], ch. 7, "Broadening the Mind," sec. 1, in the *Chang Tzu ch'üan-shu* [Complete works of Master Chang Tsai] (*SPPY* ed.), 2:21a. Chu Hsi quoted the phrase *t'ien-hsin* in the *Yü-lei*, ch. 98, secs. 61 and 68 (p. 4001); ch. 95, sec. 127 (p. 3887).

70. See, for example, *Wen-chi*, 13:6b, memorial of 1181.

71. *Yü-lei*, ch. 1, sec. 18 (p. 6).

72. *Ibid.*, ch. 4, sec. 24 (p. 96).

73. Ch'eng I, *I-ch'uan ching-shuo* [Ch'eng I's explanation of the classics], 1:2a, in the *Erh-Ch'eng ch'üan-shu*, "Explanation of the *Book of Changes.*"

74. *Yü-lei*, ch. 1, sec. 18 (p. 6).

75. *Ibid.* sec. 19 (p. 7).

76. *Chang Tzu ch'üan-shu*, 4:7b, "Chou-li" [Rites of Chou].

77. *Book of History*, "The Great Oath," pt. 2, sec. 7, quoted in the *Book of Mencius*, 5A:5.

78. *Wai-shu*, 3:1a.

79. *Wen-chi*, 67:20a, "Jen-shuo" [Treatise on humanity].

80. *Yü-lei*, ch. 1, sec. 18 (p. 7).

81. *Ibid.*, ch. 27, sec. 63 (p. 1107).

82. *I-shu*, 21B:2a.

83. *Yü-lei*, ch. 95, sec. 96 (p. 3874). See also ch. 53, sec. 90 (p. 2062).

84. *Ibid.*, ch. 53, sec. 10 (p. 2031).

85. *Analects*, 15:28.

86. *Yü-lei*, ch. 45, sec. 66 (p. 1850).

87. *Wen-chi*, 40:29b, seventeenth letter in reply to Ho Shu-ching (Ho Hao).

88. *Yü-lei*, ch. 5, sec. 30 (p. 138).

89. *Wen-chi*, 32:17b, reply to Chang Ch'in-fu (Chang Shih) on the "Jen-shuo."

90. *Yü-lei*, ch. 5, sec. 31 (p. 138).

91. *I-shu*, 18:2a.

92. *Chang Tzu yü-lu* [Recorded sayings of Master Chang Tsai] (*SPTK* ed.), pt. 2, p. 6b.

93. Chang Po-hsing, *Chin-ssu lu chi-chieh* [Collected explanations of *Reflections on Things at Hand*] (*Cheng-i-t'ang ch'üan-shu* [Complete library of the Hall of Rectifying the Way] ed.), 2:50b.

# -13-

# The Principle of Heaven
# vs. Human Desires

T HE terms "Principle of Heaven" *(t'ien-li)* and "human desires" *(jen-yü)* are derived from the "Records of Music" chapter of the *Book of Rites*. There it says, "When like and dislike cannot be regulated inside and desires tempt from the outside, if one is unable to return to the self [the original mind], the Principle of Heaven will be destroyed. . . . When man degenerates to the level of things, the Principle of Heaven is destroyed and human desires are indulged in to the extreme."[1] From the very start, the Principle of Heaven and human desires stand at opposite poles, incompatible with each other. Chang Tsai (1020–1077) contrasted them sharply, saying, "Those who understand higher things return to the Principle of Heaven, while those who understand lower things succumb to human desires."[2] He also said, "To understand the Principle of Heaven is to face light when none of the phenomena is hidden, while to indulge in human desires to the extreme is merely to look at the shadow and only trifle in a thing."[3]

It seems that to Chang Tsai, principle and desires were irreconcilable. But he also said,

> The relation between the mouth and the stomach on the one hand and food and taste on the other, and between the nose and tongue on the one hand and smell and taste on the other, are all cases of [physical] nature's attacking and seizing. He who understands virtue will have a sufficient amount, that is all. He will not allow sensual desires to be a burden to his mind, the small to injure the great, or the secondary to destroy the fundamental.[4]

In his commentary, Wang Fu-chih (1619–1692) explained, "What is possessed by one's nature cannot be cut off. He who understands virtue realizes that what he has received from Heaven is not confined to this, but satisfies his material force according to his capacity so as to stop his attacking and seizing."[5] Here "according to his capacity" means to go neither too far nor not far enough, which is the traditional doctrine in the Confucian School.

This tradition was continued by the Ch'eng brothers (Ch'eng Hao, 1032–1085, and Ch'eng I, 1033–1107), who clarified the meaning of the Principle of Heaven. They said, "All things are nothing but the Principle of Heaven. What has one to do with it? . . . Everything is what it should be according to the Principle of Heaven. When has man anything to do with it? To have anything to do with it [to meddle with it] must be pure selfishness."[6] They also said, "What is meant by the Principle of Heaven is that this moral principle knows no limit. 'It does not exist because of [sage-emperor] Yao; nor does it cease to exist because of [wicked king] Chieh.' . . . Originally, it lacks nothing. All principles are sufficient in themselves."[7] Again, they said, " 'If one cannot return to the self, the Principle of Heaven will be destoryed.' What is meant by the Principle of Heaven is that all principles are self-sufficient in themselves and that originally it lacks nothing. Therefore if one returns to the self and is sincere, there is nothing more to be said."[8] And finally, "If people are blind to the Principle of Heaven, it is only because they are disturbed by excessive desires."[9] These are all sayings by both the brothers, who often shared the same ideas.

Ch'eng I himself said, "Rules of propriety (li) are same as principle (li). If it is not the Principle of Heaven, it is a selfish desire. Although one may have the intention to do good, it is still against the rules of propriety. When there are no more human desires, there is the Principle of Heaven."[10] He also said, "Seriousness (ching) is nothing but concentrating on one thing. When one concentrates on one thing, one does not go to the east or to the west. In that case, one only remains in the center, not going here or going there. In that case, there is nothing but the internal. When that is preserved, the Principle of Heaven naturally becomes clear."[11] Again, he said, "What exists before Heaven and what exists after Heaven conforms to the Principle of Heaven. Human desires are false";[12] "The human mind corresponds with human desires, while the mind of the Way corresponds with the Principle of Heaven";[13] and "The human mind is precarious; it corresponds with human desires. The mind of the Way is subtle; it corresponds with the Principle of Heaven."[14] From these sayings it can be seen that Ch'eng I emphasized the distinction between principle and desires. To him, "desires" meant selfish, manipulative desires, which was why he saw them as precarious and false.

Ch'eng Hao said, "Good and evil in the world are both the Principle of Heaven. What is called evil is not originally evil. It becomes evil only because of deviation from the Mean."[15] He also said, "Good and evil among things are both the Principle of Heaven. In the Principle of Heaven, some things must be good and others bad, for 'it is the nature of things to be unequal.' We should examine the matter and should not enter into evil ourselves and be dragged down by any particular thing."[16] Again, he said, "The student need not seek afar but can search right here in himself. All he has to do is understand the Principle of Heaven and be serious."[17] But most important is what Ch'eng Hao said of himself: "Although I have learned some of my doctrines from others, the concept of the Principle of Heaven I realized by myself."[18] This celebrated saying has been cited frequently.

Principle *(li)* and the Principle of Heaven *(t'ien-li)* are often inter-changeable. If *t'ien* is interpreted as nature, of course, the Principle of Heaven originally lacks nothing and all principles are sufficient in themselves. But the Principle of Heaven realized by Ch'eng Hao is not limited to nature. It is at once the fundamental principle of the universe and the highest good for man—what Liu Shih-p'ei (1884–1919) called "the universal principle common to the minds of all men, and what the *Book of Odes* describes as specific principle *(tse)* in the saying, 'Heaven produces the teeming multitude. As there are things there are their specific principles.' "[19]

In his sub-commentary on the "Record of Music," K'ung Ying-ta (574–648) interpreted principle as nature *(hsing),*[20] as in the *Doctrine of the Mean,* namely, "What Heaven imparts to man."[21] This being the case, the Principle of Heaven is not only philosophical and ethical but also religious, for its final goal is the unity of Heaven and man. That is why the two Ch'engs strongly emphasized sincerity and seriousness, for the Principle of Heaven is the final objective of self-cultivation. According to Professor Mou Tsung-san, the primary meaning of the Principle of Heaven for Ch'eng Hao is principle in terms of its substance, which is completely good, everlasting, and self-existing; the secondary meaning is principle in terms of what is real, including its various natural tendencies. Thus Professor Mou holds that Ch'eng Hao's basic idea of the Principle of Heaven is its primary meaning, with its secondary meaning referred to only incidentally.[22] Actually, the two Ch'engs talked about preserving the Principle of Heaven through sincerity and seriousness more often than they spoke of the real substance of the Principle of Heaven. In their minds, the Principle of Heaven is the supreme command to do good.

Generally speaking, Chu Hsi's ideas on the Principle of Heaven and human desires were derived from the two Ch'engs, but he expanded them and refined them, thus giving them a special flavor. These ideas fall under nine headings, discussed below.

## The Principle of Heaven

In his letter in reply to Ho Shu-ching (Ho Hao, 1128–1175), Chu Hsi said,

> The Principle of Heaven is undifferentiated, it is true. However, since it is called principle, it has the meaning of an order (t'iao-li). Therefore, each of the Four Virtues of humanity, righteousness, propriety, and wisdom in it immediately becomes a moral principle without mixture or confusion. It is described as undifferentiated because before the virtues have issued forth no one can see their beginning, and they cannot be identified as any particular principle. But it is not true that humanity, righteousness, propriety, and wisdom are not distinguished and only later are produced as something with physical shape and appearance. We must know that the Principle of Heaven is the general name for humanity, righteousness, propriety, and wisdom, and that they are the specific aspects of the Principle of Heaven.[23]

There are two important points in this passage: that the Principle of Heaven is identical with the Four Virtues, and that the Principle of Heaven has an order. Both are Chu Hsi's developments beyond the thoughts of the two Ch'engs. As Chu Hsi said, "Every thing and every affair is the operation of the Principle of Heaven. . . . What goes on in our daily life is nothing but the Principle of Heaven."[24] In other words, every thing and every affair is an occasion for the realization of the Four Virtues.

Chu Hsi defined rules of propriety (li) as the measure and pattern (chieh-wen) of the Principle of Heaven,[25] meaning that rites or rules of propriety are the regulated arrangements of the Principle of Heaven. That is why he said, "Rules of propriety are the Principle of Heaven."[26] He also quoted Ch'eng I's aphorism that "rules of propriety are identical with principle," and went on to say, "What he was saying is that rules of propriety belong to the Principle of Heaven in opposition to the self, which belongs to human desires. He did not define rules of propriety as principle or say that they are really interchangeable."[27] A pupil asked, "When the term 'rules of propriety' is used instead of 'principle,' is it because rules of propriety are concrete, have a finite measure, and are related to an actual situation?" Chu Hsi answered, "If you only talk about principle, you will be abstract. Rules of propriety are the measure and pattern of the Principle of Heaven. They teach people to have some standard."[28]

## Human Desires

According to Chu Hsi, "To eat and to drink is the Principle of Heaven, but to demand delicious taste is a human desire."[29] He also said,

"Among external things that tempt people, nothing is stronger than the desires for food and sex. But if we investigate into the foundation, they are, of course, indispensable to man, for he cannot be without them. However, in them there is a distinction between the Principle of Heaven and human desires on which one should not err even to the smallest degree."[30] This matter of degree is concerned not with whether the taste is delicious but with one's demand. If one insists that food be delicious, one is selfish. To Chu Hsi, "Human desires do not necessarily refer to the enjoyment of sound or color, material benefits, or the extravagance of shelter or travel. Whatever one harbors in one's mind that is slightly off the Way, that is human desire."[31] He also said, "Originally, there are human desires in the Principle of Heaven. Only when it operates in a wrong way is a human desire produced."[32] By "Originally, there are human desires," Chu Hsi meant that human nature is originally good, not evil. Only when nature loses its correctness does it degenerate into evil. Hence "desires" here mean incorrect or selfish desires.

Sometimes another character, *yü* with the heart radical at the bottom, *YÜ*, is used to designate desire that is selfish, incorrect, or reckless. However, *yü* is usually used for *YÜ*. Therefore, in Chinese literature human desires *(jen-yü)* and selfish desires *(ssu-yü)* always mean bad desires *(YÜ)*. Scholars who attack Chu Hsi either take "human desires" to mean all human desires, or purposely twist its meaning that way. They claim that Chu Hsi advocated suppressing the desires for food and sex, without realizing that he merely advocated the suppression of incorrect, selfish desires. Chu Hsi clearly said, "In human desires, there is naturally the Principle of Heaven."[33] He also said, "As there is the Principle of Heaven, there are human desires, for the Principle of Heaven must have a place to settle. If the settling is out of place, human desires will be produced."[34] Any fair-minded reader will understand that, in this last quotation, the first use of "human desires" is neutral in meaning, whereas the second is evil. In other words, if desires for food and sex are correct, that is the Principle of Heaven and not selfish human desires: "When man and woman live together, it is a human affair that is close at hand, but the Way operates in it."[35] In short, everything must follow the Way.

Ch'eng I once said, "The human mind is selfish desire, while the mind of the Way is the Principle of Heaven."[36] To Chu Hsi,

The words "selfish desire" are too heavy. . . . There is only one mind. When the Principle of Heaven is completely present and can be revealed anywhere, it is called the mind of the Way. When there is any deliberation or scheming, it is called the human mind. Deliberation and scheming are not always evil. The mind is called selfish desire because if even an iota of it does not naturally issue from the Principle of Heaven, it will be a selfish desire.[37]

Thus, "The statement 'the human mind is selfish desire' does not mean what common folk call selfish desire. When there is the slightest intention to manipulate, although it may be said originally to issue from the mind of the Way, still it has never left the sphere of human desires."[38]

A pupil once asked, "Many former scholars said that the mind of the Way is the mind of nature bestowed by Heaven, and that the human mind is the mind of human desires. Now that you have correlated them, is it correct?" Chu Hsi answered,

> If the human mind is so very bad, it must be completely eliminated before the mind of the Way becomes clear. . . . The human mind is our body with consciousness and desires, as in the case of "I desire humanity"[39] and "I follow what my heart desires."[40] When the desire of our nature is affected by external things and becomes activated, how can we avoid that desire? Only when external temptation causes us to fall will it be harmful. . . . Take the case of food. When one is hungry or thirsty and desires to eat one's fill, that is the human mind. However, there must be moral principle in it. Some should be eaten and some not. . . . This is the correctness of the mind of the Way.[41]

This is what Chu Hsi meant by there being only an iota of difference between morality and selfishness, the Principle of Heaven and human desires.

## The Opposition between Principle and Desires

Chu Hsi said, "There are only two paths for man, namely, the Principle of Heaven and human desires. If something is not the Principle of Heaven, it is a human desire. This means that there is nothing belonging neither to the Principle of Heaven nor to human desires."[42] He also noted that "although the Principle of Heaven and human desires do not coexist, since they are earlier or later, impartial or selfish, depraved or correct, they cannot but be opposed to each other."[43] Therefore, "The Principle of Heaven and human desires are always opposed," somewhat like an ink-slab, the upper side being the Principle of Heaven and the underside being human desires.[44] Put differently, "There are two extremes to every thing. What is right is the impartiality of the Principle of Heaven. What is wrong is the selfishness of human desires."[45]

In his memorial of 1181, Chu Hsi said, "Where the mind is directed —there lies the difference between the Principle of Heaven and human desires. Because the two are distinguished, whether they are impartial or selfish and whether they are depraved or correct can be determined. The Principle of Heaven is the mind as it originally is. If it is not followed, the mind will become selfish and also depraved."[46] This distinction between impartiality and selfishness, correctness and depravity can also be seen in righteousness versus profit: "Righteousness is what is proper according to the Principle of Heaven, whereas profit is the desire of human feelings."[47] In sum, "What is good is the Principle of Heaven and what is evil is human desires,"[48] and "Good and evil are the concrete substance of the Principle of Heaven and human desires."[49]

## No Definite Demarcation between Principle and Desires

Although the Principle of Heaven and human desires are opposed, "There is no hard and fast demarcation between them."[50] Yet neither can they take the place of each other: "There is only one mind. It only depends on how the Principle of Heaven and human desires rise and fall in it."[51] Again, "There is only one mind in man. As the Principle of Heaven prevails, human desires will disappear, and as human desires win out, the Principle of Heaven will be destroyed. There has never been a case where the Principle of Heaven and human desires have been mixed."[52] Similarly, "When one wins, the other withdraws, and when the other wins, the first withdraws. There has never been a case where both have stood in the middle, neither advancing nor withdrawing."[53] Hence the difference between them is extremely small and subtle.[54]

## The Choice between Principle and Desires

Since the difference between principle and desires is so subtle, "One must investigate and make a decision between the Principle of Heaven and human desires."[55] Chu Hsi said, "The difference between the Principle of Heaven and human desires is very little. That is why Master Chou [Chou Tun-i, 1017–1073] merely talked about *chi* [incipient activating force]. But one must distinguish them early. That is why Hung-ch'ü [Chang Tsai, 1020–1077] often talked about *yü* [preparation]."[56] Chu Hsi was referring to Chou Tun-i's theory of *chi*, "the subtle, incipient, activating force giving rise to good and evil,"[57] which holds that whenever the mind is activated in the slightest degree, good and evil are determined. Chang Tsai said, "When preparation is made within myself, it is seeking an advantage outside,"[58] implying that one must make an effort beforehand.

As Chu Hsi put it, "It is easy for human desires to advance quickly, but the Principle of Heaven is difficult to recover."[59] Therefore, it is necessary "to think carefully about affairs in one's daily life and to realize which is the Principle of Heaven and which are human desires,"[60] for "to differentiate the Principle of Heaven and human desires and to determine whether a proper degree or measure has been attained depends especially on whether or not the mind can master the situation."[61] Indeed, "In the midst of gathering things and holding on to self-cultivation, the student should examine at the point of the beginning of thoughts which is the Principle of Heaven and which are human desires, and take the one but reject the other."[62] To Chu Hsi, "The task of the investigation of things is none other than to understand that there are the Principle of Heaven and human desires in things and to examine them in each case."[63]

## Having Few Desires (kua-yü) and Having No Desire (wu-yü)

Mencius said, "To nourish the mind, nothing is better than to have few desires."[64] Chu Hsi considered having few desires to be good and not evil, for one should not be able to count one's evil desires in any number.[65] If one wants this and also wants that, that is equivalent to having many desires.[66] In commenting on Mencius, Chu Hsi said, "Although desires like those of the mouth, nose, ears, and eyes are indispensable to man, if one has many and does not restrain oneself, one will inevitably lose one's original mind. This is something against which the student must guard himself."[67] Ch'eng I had said, "The extension of knowledge lies in nourishing it, and in nourishing knowledge nothing is better than to have few desires."[68] Commenting on this statement, Chu Hsi noted, "If the Way is followed, both [knowledge and desires] will be nourished, but if the Way is not followed, one will harm the other."[69] Moreover, if the Way is followed, "The few desires will not be disturbing and knowledge will become clearer."[70] Thus it will not do merely to depend on having few desires; one must still investigate things.[71]

Chu Hsi's point here is that what matters is not whether one has many or few desires but whether the desires one does have are correct. It is dangerous to have many desires without restraint. In the case of selfish desires, of course there should be fewer and fewer until there are none. That is why he said, "Now it is necessary to have few and then get to the point of having none."[72] Chou Tun-i had said, "I declare that, in nourishing, the mind does not stop at having few desires and preserving the mind. If one has few desires and then gets to the point of having none, sincerity will be established and understanding will be penetrating."[73] Commenting on this passage, Chu Hsi said,

> Talking about reaching the ultimate point, of course that is true, but to reach the point of having no desires one must necessarily go through having few desires. If one talks about reaching the point [of having none] and does not follow an order, there is no way for one to advance. If one talks about the ultimate point and does not follow an order, I am afraid one may be satisfied with a small accomplishment. Therefore Master Chou's doctrine serves to stimulate in this regard.[74]

The term "having no desire" *(wu-yü)* comes from the *Lao Tzu*.[75] In Chou Tun-i's "Explanation of the Diagram of the Great Ultimate," following the sentence, "The sage settles these affairs by the principles of the Mean, correctness, humanity, and righteousness, regarding tranquillity as fundamental," there is a note that says, "Having no desire, there will be tranquillity."[76] In his *T'ung-shu* (Penetrating the *Book of Changes*), Chou also said, "The essential way is to [concentrate on] one thing. [Concentrating on] one thing means having no desire. Having no desire, one is vacuous [absolutely pure and peaceful] while tranquil, and straight."[77] As just mentioned, Chou held that having no desire, "One's sincerity will be established and understanding will be penetrating."[78]

Those who attack Neo-Confucianism have ignored Chou's emphasis on tranquillity and concentrated on criticizing his idea of having no desires and condemning him for cutting off feelings, not realizing that to the Neo-Confucians, human desires meant selfish desires. Selfish desires have a way of arousing people, rendering tranquillity impossible. As Chu Hsi said, "Because desires are aroused and feelings overcome [reason], one cannot be tranquil."[79] He also said, "The doctrine of Master Chou is simply that 'having no desires, there will be tranquillity.' Generally speaking, his idea is to regard tranquillity as fundamental."[80] Explaining the term "having no desires," Li Kuang-ti (1642–1718) said, "Having no desires comes from the preservation of sincerity and being careful about the subtle, incipient activating force. When sincerity is preserved and the subtle, incipient activating force is cared for, one will have no desires and will be sincere. Concentrating on one thing means having no desires and being sincere."[81]

## Similarity in Substance but Difference in Function

Hu Hung (1106–1161) wrote the *Chih-yen* (Understanding of words) and postulated that "the Principle of Heaven and human desires are the same in substance but different in function. They are the same in operation but different in feelings. A gentleman who is keen in his cultivation should clearly distinguish them."[82] In his *Hu Tzu chih-yen i-i* (Doubts on *Master Hu's Understanding of Words*), Chu Hsi strongly criticized this proposition:

The idea of this chapter is likewise that human nature is neither good nor evil. . . . We don't know the origin of the Principle of Heaven, but it is in man at his birth. Human desires come about when one is restricted by one's physical shape, mixed in one's material force, a slave to habits, and confused in one's feelings. . . . I am afraid it is wrong to merge the Principle of Heaven and human desires in one spot. . . . The original substance is in reality only the Principle of Heaven, without any human desire in it.[83]

In the *Yü-lei,* Chu Hsi also said,

The defect of Master Hu lies in his theory that human nature is neither good nor evil. In substance there is only the Principle of Heaven, not [self-ish] human desires. It is wrong to say that they are the same in substance. Perhaps there are occasions when they are the same in operation but different in feelings. For example, taste to the mouth, colors to the eye, sound to the ear, smell to the nose, and comfort to the four limbs are the same in the sage and in an ordinary person. This means they are the same in operation. But the sage does not indulge his feeling for these, and that is why he is different from the ordinary person.[84]

Chu Hsi added, "With the sage and the worthy, everything is the Principle of Heaven, whereas with the inferior man, everything is selfish desire."[85] This is where the two are the same in operation but different in feelings. In this respect Chu Hsi agreed with Hu Hung, but he also noted, "The difference between the Principle of Heaven and human desires is very little. Where the operations are the same but the feeling different, one must sharply examine and clearly discriminate."[86]

## The Sage-King and the Powerful Feudal Lord

Ch'en Liang (1143–1194), who advocated utilitarianism, theorized that "righteousness and profit advance together, and the kingly way and the way of the powerful feudal lord operate at the same time."[87] He declared that "since the way of the sage-king and the way of the power-ful feudal lord can be used in a mixture, the Principle of Heaven and human desires can operate together."[88] To Ch'en Liang, "The Three Dynasties had followed [the Way] to the fullest extent, whereas the Han [206 B.C.–A.D. 220] and the T'ang [618–907] did not go to the fullest extent."[89] That is to say, the difference between the Three Dynasties and the Han and T'ang dynasties is a matter of degree, not substance.

Chu Hsi, however, strongly argued the opposite. He said,

You have only said that they have not followed to the fullest extent, but have not talked about why they have not followed to the fullest extent. You are comparing the accomplishments of the sage-rulers in the arena of profit and desires. When you see something vaguely similar, you immedi-ately assert that the behavior of the sage-rulers is no more than this. What is called "An infinitesimal mistake in the beginning will lead to an infinite mistake at the end"[90] lies here.[91]

In an earlier letter to Ch'en Liang, Chu Hsi had conceded that "although perhaps the rulers of Han and T'ang sometimes unintentionally conformed to the Way, totally speaking, their minds were on profit and desires. This is why the sage-emperors Yao and Shun and the sage-kings of the Three Dynasties were utterly different from Emperor Kao-tsu [r. 206–195 B.C.] of Han and Emperor T'ai-tsung [r. 627–649] of T'ang, and they cannot be grouped together in the end."[92] Chu Hsi's denunciation of the Han and T'ang rulers was undoubtedly too severe, but in terms of the Principle of Heaven versus selfish human desires, his conclusions were inevitable.

## Tai Chen's Attack on Neo-Confucianism

Chu Hsi's standpoint and those of Hu Hung and Ch'en Liang were quite different. Both Hu and Ch'en simply defended their positions. Tai Chen (1724–1777), in contrast, attacked his opponents in vigorous and bitter terms. He accused the Neo-Confucians of the Sung period (960–1279) of regarding principle "as if it were a thing,"[93] of "killing people with principle,"[94] and of "cutting off desires."[95] However, no Neo-Confucian had ever said that principle is like a thing. Manchu emperors made use of Neo-Confucianism to imprison and even execute political dissidents, it is true, but Neo-Confucians never killed anyone with principle or even proposed to do such a thing. Nor does the idea of cutting off desires appear in the writings of the Ch'eng brothers or Chu Hsi. Chu Hsi did say, "The student must entirely eliminate human desires and fully recover the Principle of Heaven."[96] But this means "manifesting the Principle of Heaven and destroying human desires"[97] —that is, wiping out all selfish desires so that the Principle of Heaven can be manifest, not destroying all desire for food and sex. As Ch'eng I said, "The three hundred rules of ceremonies and the three thousand rules of conduct are not intended to cut off people's desires and impose on them something they cannot do. They are meant to prevent their [selfish] desires and discipline them against excess so that they will enter the Way."[98]

Tai Chen, however, claimed that the Neo-Confucians "looked upon people's crying of starvation, the grief and sorrow of men and women, and even their groping for life at the point of death, all as human desires. They consider cutting off all desires to be the Principle of Heaven as it originally is."[99] He also said, "All the hunger and cold, grief and sorrow, food and sex, and all the feelings of normal emotions and hidden sentiments are called human desires. They realized throughout their life that desires were difficult to control. What they called the preservation of principle is but an empty name. In reality, they wanted only to destroy feelings and desires altogether."[100] None of these statements resembles what the Ch'engs or Chu Hsi actually said. Perhaps Tai Chen had other reasons for his vehement feelings. In explaining Chou Tun-i's "having no desire, there will be tranquillity," Tai Chen did not refer to Chou's ideas of sincerity and tranquillity but simply equated his notion with the "taking no action" of Lao Tzu and Chuang Tzu.[101] Ch'eng I had explained seriousness as "concentrating on one thing and not getting away from it,"[102] which Tai Chen said is the same as Lao Tzu's doctrine of "embracing the one" and "having no desire."[103] But Ch'eng I had interpreted seriousness in terms of concentrating on one thing, saying, "Concentrating on one thing is none other than being tidy and serious."[104] This is nothing like "having no desire" or "taking no action."

All this is well known to students of Neo-Confucianism, but Tai Chen twisted its meaning. His opposition to Chu Hsi's doctrine of physical nature and his criticism of the Neo-Confucian distinction of the Principle of Heaven and human desires as too severe do have philosophical justification. However, his reckless attack on the Sung Neo-Confucians represents not Tai Chen the celebrated authority of evidential research but Tai Chen the frustrated scholar. Ironically, when Tai Chen said that "to restrain oneself and not to err is the way to follow the Principle of Heaven,"[105] that "principle is feelings that do not err,"[106] and that "when one's feeling does not go too far or not far enough, that is principle,"[107] he was in complete agreement with Chu Hsi. Although Tai Chen attacked Chu Hsi vigorously, in the final analysis he did not leave the confines of Chu Hsi's Neo-Confucianism.

## Notes

1. *Book of Rites,* "Record of Music," sec. 1.
2. *Cheng-meng* [Correcting youthful ignorance], ch. 6, "Sincerity and Enlightenment," sec. 34, in the *Chang Tzu ch'üan-shu* [Complete works of Master Chang Tsai] (*SPPY* ed.), 2:18a.
3. *Ibid.,* ch. 7, "Broadening the Mind," sec. 13 (*Chang Tzu ch'üan-shu,* 2:22b).
4. *Ibid.,* ch. 6, "Sincerity and Enlightenment," sec. 36 (*Chang Tzu ch'üan-shu,* 2:18b).
5. Wang Fu-chih, *Chang Tzu Cheng-meng chu* [Commentary on Master Chang's *Cheng-meng*] (Beijing: Ku-chi Press, 1956), p. 88.
6. *I-shu* [Surviving works], 2A:13a, in the *Erh-Ch'eng ch'üan-shu* [Complete works of the two Ch'engs] (*SPPY* ed.).
7. *Ibid.,* 2A:13b. The quotation comes from the *Hsün Tzu,* essay no. 17 on Heaven.
8. *Ibid.,* 2A:14b.
9. *Ibid.,* 2A:22a.
10. *Ibid.,* 15:1b.

11. *Ibid.,* 15:5a.

12. *Ibid.,* 24:1a.

13. *Wai-shu* [Additional works], 2:4a, in the *Erh-Ch'eng ch'üan-shu.*

14. *Ibid.,* 3:2a. The concepts of the human mind and the mind of the Way are derived from the *Book of History,* "Counsel of Great Yü," sec. 15.

15. *I-shu,* 2A:1b.

16. *Ibid.,* 2A:5b. The quotation comes from the *Book of Mencius,* 3A:4.

17. *Ibid.,* 2A:5b.

18. *Wai-shu,* 12:4a.

19. *Li-hsüeh tzu-i t'ung-shih* [General explanation of terms in the School of Principle], p. 2a, in the *Liu Shen-shu Hsien-sheng i-shu* [Surviving works of Liu Shih-p'ei], quoting the *Book of Odes,* ode no. 260, which is repeated in the *Book of Mencius,* 6A:6.

20. K'ung Ying-ta, *Li-chi cheng-i* [Correct meanings of the *Book of Rites*] (World Book Co. *Shih-san-ching chu-shu* [Commentaries and sub-commentaries of the Thirteen Classics] ed.) ch. 37, p. 301 (p. 1529).

21. *Doctrine of the Mean,* ch. 1.

22. Mou Tsung-san, *Hsin-t'i yü hsing-t'i* [Substance of mind and substance of nature] (Taipei: Cheng-chung Book Co., 1968), vol. 2, pp. 79–81.

23. *Wen-chi,* 40:36a, twenty-seventh letter in reply to Ho Shu-ching (Ho Hao). For the Four Virtues, see the *Book of Mencius,* 6A:6.

24. *Yü-lei,* ch. 40, sec. 10 (p. 1634).

25. Chu Hsi, *Lun-yü chi-chu* [Collected commentaries on the *Analects*], comment on 1:12.

26. Chu Hsi, *Lun-yü huo-wen* [Questions and answers on the *Analects*] (*Chin-shih han-chi ts'ung-k'an* [Chinese works of the recent period series] ed.), 12:2b (p. 426), comment on 12:1.

27. *Ibid.,* p. 3b (p. 426), comment on 12:1.

28. *Yü-lei,* ch. 41, sec. 22 (p. 1671).

29. *Ibid.,* ch. 13, sec. 22 (p. 356).

30. Chu Hsi, *Ta-hsüeh huo-wen* [Questions and answers on the *Great Learning*] (*Chin-shih han-chi ts'ung-k'an* ed.), p. 21b (p. 42), comment on ch. 5.

31. *Wen-chi,* 31:14b–15a, second letter to Liu Kung-fu (Liu Kung).

32. *Ibid.,* 40:39b, twenty-ninth letter in reply to Ho Shu-ching (Ho Hao).

33. *Yü-lei,* ch. 13, sec. 16 (p. 355).

34. *Ibid.,* sec. 15 (p. 355).

35. *Wen-chi,* 46:25b, second letter in reply to Hu Po-feng (Hu Ta-yüan).

36. *Wai-shu,* 2:4a. See also 3:2a; *I-shu,* 24:1b.

37. *Wen-chi,* 32:7a, thirty-seventh letter to Chang Ching-fu (Chang Shih). See also 40:29a, fifteenth letter in reply to Ho Shu-ching.

38. *Ibid.,* 42:20a, eleventh letter in reply to Wu Hui-shu (Wu I).

39. *Analects,* 7:29.

40. *Ibid.,* 2:4.

41. *Yü-lei,* ch. 62, sec. 41 (pp. 2362–2363).

42. *Ibid.,* ch. 41, sec. 22 (p. 1670).

43. *Wen-chi,* 42:7b, fifth letter in reply to Hu Kuang-chung (Hu Shih).

44. *Yü-lei,* ch. 13, sec. 21 (p. 356).

45. *Ibid.,* sec. 30 (p. 358).

46. *Wen-chi,* 13:7b, second memorial of 1181.

47. *Lun-yü chi-chu,* comment on 4:16.

48. *Wen-chi,* 62:20b, letter in reply to Fu Ch'eng-tzu.

49. *Ibid.,* 53:31b, fifty-first letter in reply to Hu Chi-sui (Hu Ta-shih).

50. *Yü-lei,* ch. 13, sec. 25 (p. 356).

51. *Ibid.,* sec. 27 (p. 357).

52. *Ibid.,* sec. 17 (p. 356).

53. *Ibid.,* sec. 26 (p. 357).

54. *Wen-chi,* 37:19b, letter in reply to Cheng Ching-wang (Cheng Po-hsiung). See also 64:37b, tenth letter in reply to Liu Kung-tu (Liu Meng-jung); *Yü-lei,* ch. 13, sec. 20 (p. 356).

55. *Wen-chi,* 55:25a, letter in reply to Yen Tzu-chien.

56. *Yü-lei,* ch. 13, sec. 19 (p. 356).

57. Chou Tun-i, *T'ung-shu* [Penetrating the *Book of Changes*], ch. 3. For an English translation, see my *A Source Book in Chinese Philosophy* (Princeton, N.J.: Princeton University Press, 1963), p. 466.

58. *Chen-meng,* ch. 4, "Spiritual Transformation," sec. 15, in the *Chang Tzu ch'üan-shu,* 2:14b.

59. *Wen-chi,* 43:1a, letter in reply to Ch'eng Ming-chung (Ch'en Tan).

60. *Yü-lei,* ch. 41, sec. 14 (p. 1663). See also ch. 42, sec. 30 (p. 1722).

61. *Wen-chi,* 32:6b, thirty-sixth letter to Chang Ch'in-fu (Chang Shih).

62. *Ibid.,* 51:1a, letter in reply to Tung Shu-chung (Tung Chu).

63. *Yü-lei,* ch. 15, sec. 26 (p. 459).

64. *Book of Mencius,* 7B:35. In the *Lao Tzu,* ch. 19, it is also said, "Reduce selfishness, have few desires."

65. *Yü-lei,* ch. 61, sec. 68 (p. 2340).

66. *Ibid.,* sec. 67 (p. 2340).

67. Chu Hsi, *Meng Tzu chi-chu* [Collected commentaries on the *Book of Mencius*], commenting on 7B:35.

68. *Wai-shu,* 2:4a.

69. *Yü-lei,* ch. 18, sec. 60 (p. 650).

70. *Ibid.,* sec. 62 (pp. 650–651).

71. *Ibid.,* sec. 59 (p. 650).

72. *Ibid.,* ch. 61, sec. 71 (p. 2340).

73. *Chou Tzu ch'üan-shu* [Complete works of Master Chou Tun-i] (*Kuo-hsüeh chi-pen ts'ung-shu* [Basic sinological series] ed.), ch. 17, p. 334, "Account of the Nourishing the Mind Pavilion."

74. Chu Hsi, *Meng Tzu huo-wen* [Questions and answers on the *Book of Mencius*] (*Chin-shih han-chi ts'ung-k'an* [Chinese works of the recent period series] ed.), 14:10a (p. 207), comment on 6B:35.

75. *Lao Tzu,* chs. 3, 34, 37, 57.

76. *Chou Tzu ch'üan-shu,* ch. 2, p. 23, "Explanation of the Diagram of the Great Ultimate."

77. *T'ung-shu,* ch. 20. For an English translation, see *A Source Book in Chinese Philosophy,* p. 473.

78. See above, n. 73.

79. *Yü-lei,* ch. 94, sec. 99 (p. 3787).

80. *Ibid.,* sec. 103 (p. 3788).

81. Chou Tun-i, *T'ung-shu* [Penetrating the *Book of Changes*] (*SPPY* ed.), supplement, "Jung-tsun t'ung-shu p'ien" (Li Kuang-ti's treatise on the *T'ung-shu*), p. 2b.

82. This passage does not appear in the *Hu Tzu chih-yen* [Master Hu's understanding of words] (*Yüeh-ya-t'ang ts'ung shu* [Hall of Kwantung elegance series] ed.) in six chapters, but is quoted in Chu Hsi's *Hu Tzu chih-yen i-i* [Doubts on *Master Hu's Understanding of Words*].

83. *Wen-chi*, 73:41b–42a, "Hu Tzu chih-yen i-i." The *I-i* is also appended to the *Hu Tzu chih-yen*. See also *Yü-lei*, ch. 43, sec. 57 (p. 1767).

84. *Yü-lei*, ch. 101, sec. 182 (p. 4119). See also sec. 183–186 (pp. 4119–4121).

85. *Ibid.*, ch. 117, sec. 7 (p. 4476). See also ch. 40, sec. 33 (p. 1643).

86. *Wen-chi*, 37:15b, second letter to Liu Kung-fu.

87. *Ch'en Liang chi* [Collected works of Ch'en Liang] (Beijing: Chung-hua Book Co., 1974), ch. 20, p. 281, letter of 1184 to Chu Yüan-hui (Chu Hsi).

88. *Ibid.*, p. 295, letter of 1186 to Chu Yüan-hui.

89. *Ibid.*, p. 289, letter of 1185. The Three Dynasties were the Hsia (2183–1752 B.C.?), Shang (1751–111 B.C.?), and Chou (1111–249 B.C.).

90. *I-wei t'ung-kua-jen* [Apocryphal treatise on the *Book of Changes:* On the understanding of verification of divination], pt. 1, p. 5a.

91. *Wen-chi*, 36:27a, ninth letter in reply to Ch'en T'ung-fu (Ch'en Liang).

92. *Ibid.*, p. 25a–b, eighth letter.

93. Tai Chen, *Meng Tzu tzu-i shu-cheng* [Commentary on the meanings of terms in the *Book of Mencius*], sec. 5, 10, 27, 33, 40, 41, 43. For an English translation of some sections, see *A Source Book in Chinese Philosophy*, pp. 711–722.

94. *Ibid.*, sec. 10, 40, 43.

95. *Ibid.*, sec. 40, 43.

96. *Yü-lei*, ch. 13, sec. 28 (p. 357).

97. *Ibid.*, ch. 12, sec. 71 (p. 329).

98. *I-shu*, 25:6b.

99. *Meng Tzu tzu-i shu-cheng*, sec. 40.

100. *Ibid.*, sec. 43.

101. *Ibid.*, sec. 10, 43.

102. *I-shu*, 15:1a.

103. *Meng Tzu tzu-i shu-cheng*, sec. 43; *Lao Tzu*, ch. 10, 22. For Lao Tzu's use of the phrase "having no desire," see above, n. 75.

104. *I-shu*, 15:6b.

105. *Meng Tzu tzu-i shu-cheng*, sec. 11.

106. *Ibid.*, sec. 2, 10.

107. *Ibid.*, sec. 3.

# -14-

# *Ming*
# (mandate, destiny,
# order, fate)

I N the preface of the 1508 edition of Ch'en Ch'un's (1159–1223) *Pei-hsi tzu-i* (Ch'en Ch'un's explanation of terms), published by the Shou-fan shu-t'ang (Long-lasting vassal state study) of the Ming (1368–1644) royal house, it is said,

> In the case of *ming* in the *Doctrine of the Mean,* Wen Kung [Chu Hsi] merely interpreted *ming* as "to command." The Master [Ch'en Ch'un], however, defined it as "an order from a superior or an official order," etc. He also said that "the word *ming* has two meanings—it can be spoken of in terms of principle *(li),* and it can be spoken of in terms of material force *(ch'i).* In actuality, principle does not lie outside of material force."

The first quotation definitely indicates that Ch'en Ch'un said something new, and the second may also give the impression that Ch'en Ch'un surpassed Chu Hsi in his definition. Yet neither is true, as Ch'en Ch'un would have been the first to point out.

Ch'en Ch'un wrote the *Pei-hsi tzu-i* in twenty-six categories, with *ming* as the first. The category of *ming* has nine sections, which can be summarized under four headings:

1. "*Ming* is like an order, an order from a superior or an official order."[1]

2. "The word *ming* has two meanings—it can be spoken of in terms of principle and it can be spoken of in terms of material force. In actuality, principle does not lie outside of material force. . . . Take the sayings, 'What Heaven imparts *(ming)* to man is called human nature';[2] 'At fifty I knew the Mandate *(ming)* of Heaven';[3] and 'Investigate principle to the utmost and fully develop one's nature until one's destiny *(ming)* is fulfilled.'[4] In all these cases, the term *ming* is spoken of purely in terms

of principle. . . . When *ming* is spoken of in terms of material force, there are two kinds. One is with respect to wealth or poverty, honor or humble station, longevity or brevity of life, and calamity or blessing. As in the cases of 'Life and death are the decree *(ming)* of Heaven'[5] and 'Everything is destiny *(ming),*'[6] *ming* is considered from the inequality of the degree of one's endowment of material force. It is the *ming* [destiny, fate] of one's given lot *(ming-fen).* The other kind is the *ming* in Mencius' saying, 'The virtue of humanity in the relationship between father and son, the virtue of righteousness in the relationship between ruler and minister—these are [endowed in people in various degrees] according to fate *(ming).*'[7] This is considered in terms of the inequality of the degree of purity or impurity in the endowment of material force. They refer to whether a person is wise or stupid, virtuous or not."[8]

3. "The Mandate of Heaven is the operation of the Way of Heaven whereby things are endowed. Spoken of in terms of the principles of origination, flourishing, advantage, and firmness,[9] it is called the Way of Heaven."[10] "These four can be discussed in relation to material force or principle."[11] " 'Does Heaven give an order *(ming)* in many words?'[12] According to principle, it should be that way, that is all."[13]

4. " 'That which is done without man's doing is from Heaven. That which happens without man's causing it to happen is from the Mandate of Heaven.'[14] . . . While the mandate is the Mandate of Heaven, it is revealed only when man gives it a concrete form. Therefore fortune or misfortune, calamity or blessing comes from Heaven and becomes a mandate when it reaches man."[15]

All four points are from Chu Hsi and are important in his discussion of *ming.* Scholars have correctly said that Ch'en Ch'un carefully adhered to Chu Hsi's teachings and elaborated on his fundamental ideas. There is no separate chapter or section in the *Yü-lei* on *ming;* conversations concerning it are included in chapter 4, which is on physical nature. Very little is said about it in the *Wen-chi.* However, there are many conversations in the *Yü-lei* concerning the concept of *ming* in the *Analects,* the *Book of Mencius,* the *Book of Changes,* and the thought of the Ch'eng brothers (Ch'eng Hao, 1032–1085, and Ch'eng I, 1033–1107). Generally speaking, Chu Hsi's discussion of *ming* can be considered in five respects, as described below.

## What Is *Ming?*

As Chu Hsi explained it, "It is like the order of the sovereign. It is like an official order, prescribing the functions of an office."[16] Also, "The word *ming* is like a ruler ordering a person to assume a certain office and delegating him to do certain things,"[17] and "What is called *ming* is like the Son of Heaven ordering me to become a such-and-such official."[18]

In thus interpreting *ming*, Chu Hsi introduced a new meaning. What is new is not that *ming* means to order but that it means to order someone to do something. This is a departure from Ch'eng I's explanation of *ming* as "an order designating the rank."[19] Commenting on this definition, Chu Hsi remarked, "I am afraid it is unsatisfactory to say that *ming* is an order designating the rank."[20] In bestowing a rank, there need not be any duty to perform, but Chu Hsi's emphasis is on carrying out one's duty.

## *Ming* as Principle or Material Force

Chu Hsi said,

> *Ming* is what is given by Heaven, as in the common saying that *ming* is the order of Heaven. But there are two kinds of *ming*. It can be spoken of in terms of material force, because in the endowment of man there is inequality in a greater or lesser amount and in purity or impurity, as in the sayings, "If my Way is to fall, it is *ming*"[21] and "It is *ming* whether to obtain an office or not."[22] It can be spoken of in terms of principle. In the operation of the Way of Heaven, what is endowed in man becomes the nature of humanity, righteousness, propriety, and wisdom,[23] as in the sayings, "At fifty I knew the Mandate of Heaven"[24] and "What Heaven imparts to man is called human nature."[25] Both [principle and material force] are endowed by Heaven and it is therefore called *ming*.[26]

He also said, "In giving *ming* to man, Heaven's order comes in different degrees such as a greater or lesser endowment and a longer or shorter span of life, and also comes in degrees of purity or impurity and imbalance or balance. In all cases, it is *ming*."[27] This is the same as the record in the *Yü-lei:* "The Master said there are two kinds of *ming*. One has reference to one's poverty or wealth, honor or humble station, death or life, longevity or brevity of life. The other has reference to one's purity or impurity, correctness or partiality, wisdom or stupidity, worthiness or unworthiness. One belongs to material force and the other to principle."[28] He also said, "There is only one *ming*. It can be spoken of in terms of principle and it can be spoken of in terms of material force. What Heaven has endowed in man is principle, while the reason for man's longevity or brevity, and success or failure, is due to material force. Principle is refined and subtle and is difficult to describe, but man should not rely entirely on the course of material force to the point of giving up human effort."[29] Again, he said, "There is only one *ming*, but in the words of the Sage and the Worthy [Confucius and Mencius], sometimes it is spoken of in terms of principle and sometimes it is spoken of in terms of material force. This chapter ['At fifty I knew the Mandate of Heaven'] is spoken of in terms of principle, whereas those who say that prominence or obscurity depend on *ming* [fate] are speaking in terms of material force."[30]

This interpretation is also new. Ch'eng I had said, "Honor or humble station, and longevity or brevity of life are due to *ming* [fate]. Humanity, righteousness, propriety, and wisdom are also due to *ming* [mandate]."[31] It could be said that Ch'eng I divided *ming* into two kinds, but he did not explain it in terms of principle and material force, whereas Chu Hsi did speak of it in these terms. However, principle and material force are not to be separated; as Chu Hsi said, "They cannot be separated, for without material force Heaven has no way to order *(ming)* people, and without material force man has no way to receive the order *(ming)* of Heaven."[32] Although Chu Hsi tied *ming* to both principle and material force, to him principle was fundamental. As he said, "When Heaven gives an order, it is something like 'The Lord on High is greatly infuriated.'[33] It is simply that according to principle it should be so. Nothing in the world is honored more highly than principle, and therefore we call it the Lord."[34] Ch'en Ch'un heard Chu Hsi make this remark personally.[35] Elsewhere Chu Hsi said, "The Mandate of Heaven is the correct principle given by Heaven."[36] Such was his emphasis on principle.

Although principle and material force cannot be separated, there is a distinction between them. For this reason, Chu Hsi criticized Hou Chung-liang (*fl.* 1100)[37] and said,

> All things receive the *ming* [mandate] from Heaven to be born and obtain the substance of their principle. Therefore the virtues of humanity, righteousness, propriety, and wisdom are rooted in the mind and constitute one's nature. Having been born, one follows the evolution of one's material force, and therefore the changes of rising and falling, and greater or lesser degrees of things, are open to one's fate, from which there is no escape. What is called *ming* in this chapter ['If my Way is to prevail, it is *ming* (decree). If it is to fall, it is *ming*'][38] refers to the evolution of material force. But Master Hou explained it in terms of the Principle of Heaven. He has not examined the difference between principle and material force.[39]

Ch'eng I did not make a clear distinction between principle and material force. No wonder his pupil was not free from the same defect.

## *Ming* and Nature *(hsing)*

Both *ming* and nature are principle. Chu Hsi said, "Principle in the world is simply good and is never evil. The name 'nature' is given when things are produced. There is only principle. It is called *ming* [order] with respect to Heaven and nature with respect to man."[40] He also said,

"*Ming* is like a royal edict, while nature is like official duty,"[41] and "*Ming* is something like an order, while nature is the duty that should be performed, like a registrar rounding up the record and the county sheriff making an inspection."[42] Again, he noted, "I once made an analogy. *Ming* is like an appointment from the Court and nature is like the profession of an official."[43] Elsewhere, he explained further:

> *Ming* [mandate] is what Heaven bestows on things that Heaven cannot refrain from doing, and nature is what I have received from this *ming* in its totality to be born. Therefore speaking from the point of view of *ming* [mandate], *ming* may be called origination, flourishing, advantage, and firmness[44]—and the four seasons and the Five Agents,[45] as well as the multitude of things and the thousands of transformations, all come out of them. Speaking from the point of view of nature, it may be called humanity, righteousness, propriety, and wisdom—and the Four Beginnings[46] and the Five Constant Virtues,[47] as well as the principle of the ten thousand things and affairs, are all united in them. Although there is the distinction of nature and *ming* in man and Heaven, their principle is the same, and although there is a variety of material endowments in man and things, their principle is not different.[48]

This explanation is derived from Ch'eng I, but is fuller. Ch'eng I had said, "What is given by Heaven is called *ming* [mandate], and what is endowed in me is called nature,"[49] and "What Heaven has endowed is *ming,* and what things have received is nature."[50] Chu Hsi did not go beyond these words. However, Ch'eng I had said, "It is nature that the five [mouth, eye, ear, nose, and the four limbs] have desires, but that is our lot. If not all desires are fulfilled, that is *ming* [fate]. We should not say that since we have them in our nature we want to be sure to fulfill them." To this, Chu Hsi added, "I humbly note that the fact that not all desires are fulfilled is not limited to poverty and humble station. Even when one's honor and wealth reach the highest degree, there are still measures and limits. That is also *ming* [fate]."[51]

Ch'en Ch'un was rather brief on *ming* in relation to principle and material force, but dealt at length on the inequality of *ming*. Sections 3, 6, and 9 of his *Pei-hsi tzu-i* concentrate on this question, and are comparatively longer than the other sections on the category of *ming*.[52] It is interesting to note that Chu Hsi did not pair *ming* with nature but with Heaven. Since what Heaven imparts to man is nature, for all practical purposes, Heaven is no different from nature.

## Human Effort and *Ming*

In the Confucian tradition, "to be content with fate *(an-ming),*" "obeying fate *(shun-ming),*" "waiting for destiny *(ssu-ming)* [while cultivating one's person]," "establishing destiny *(li-ming),*" and "correct destiny *(cheng-ming)*" are all concerned with human effort. Chu Hsi said, "*Ming* that is correct comes from principle, whereas *ming* that is altered comes from physical endowment. Essentially, both are the bestowment of Heaven. . . . One should fulfill this Way oneself, and then whatever *ming* one may encounter will be the correct *ming.*"[53] He also quoted Chang Tsai (1020–1077) as saying, "In nourishing life, one leaves one's *ming* to Heaven, but in practicing the Way, one demands fulfillment in the self,"[54] and said that Chang Tsai's "words are simple but cover everything."[55] About the tradition that Confucius seldom talked about *ming,*[56] Chu Hsi said, "The reason Confucius seldom talked about *ming* is that fortune and misfortune, blessing and calamity are all *ming*. If he had talked about *ming* a great deal, I am afraid people would leave everything to fate and human effort would be abandoned. That is why he seldom talked about fate."[57]

Chu Hsi also said,

What is called *ming* is like the emperor ordering me to become a certain official. As to the duties of that office—whether they are easy or difficult, what can be done and what cannot be done—all that is fate at that moment. All one can do is proceed. . . . Therefore the superior man is apprehensive and cautious, as if on the brink of a deep gulf or treading on thin ice.[58] This is because he wants to obey the *ming* [order] that is correct and not the *ming* that is incorrect.[59]

Again, he said,

Not only should one not allow any double-mindedness regardless of longevity or brevity of life, one should also cultivate one's person and wait for fate *(ming)* [to take its own course]. Only then can one establish one's destiny *(ming).*[60] If one has a life span of a hundred years, in these hundred years one must do everything right. If one has a life span of one day, within that one day one must also do everything right. Only that will do.[61]

Not to allow any double-mindedness, to cultivate one's person while waiting, and to establish one's destiny all come from the *Book of Mencius*. In his commentary on the passage, Chu Hsi said, "Not to have any double-mindedness is to know Heaven to the highest degree. To cultivate one's person and wait until death means to serve Heaven throughout life, and to establish destiny means to preserve completely what Heaven has bestowed and not harm it with human artificiality."[62] This interpretation is new, for no previous commentator had ever said such a thing. Ch'en Ch'un fully understood Chu Hsi's interpretation, which is why he said, "When human effort has been exhausted, everything is laid bare and no human attempt can alter it. That is an act of

Heaven."[63] On the surface, Ch'en Ch'un seems to encourage human effort but discourage human "attempts." However, here effort implies doing one's duty, whereas an attempt involves manipulation. Ch'en Ch'un was echoing Chu Hsi's idea of not harming *ming* with human artificiality.

## Investigation of Principle to the Utmost, Full Development of Nature, and Fulfillment of Destiny

The Ch'eng brothers regarded these three to be simultaneous. Ch'eng Hao said, "The investigation of principle to the utmost, the full development of nature, and the fulfillment of destiny[64]—these three things are to be accomplished simultaneously. There is basically no time sequence among them. The investigation of principle to the utmost should not be regarded merely as a matter of knowledge. If one really investigates principle to the utmost, even one's nature and destiny can be fulfilled."[65] He also said, "The investigation of principle to the utmost, the full development of one's nature, and the fulfillment of destiny are one thing."[66] Ch'eng I said, "The investigation of principle to the utmost, the full development of nature, and the fulfillment of destiny are only one thing. As principle is investigated to the utmost, one's nature is fully developed, and as one's nature is fully developed, destiny is fulfilled."[67]

Chang Tsai considered this view of the two Ch'engs to be "erroneous in being too hasty. There should be an order in this matter. One must investigate principle to the utmost before one can fully develop one's nature. By extension in kind, one can then develop the nature of others. Having fully developed the nature of others, one must then develop the nature of all things together. Only then can one reach the Way of Heaven."[68] Chu Hsi chose to follow Chang Tsai rather than the Ch'eng brothers. He said, "Both Masters Ch'eng were speaking in terms of understanding, and what they said is not as useful as Master Chang's theory. The investigation of principle to the utmost pertains to understanding, whereas fully developing nature pertains to action. I feel Masters Ch'eng were too hasty in what they said."[69]

Concerning this point, Ch'en Ch'un did not utter a single word. Perhaps investigation of principle in order to develop human nature has no direct relationship with the meaning of terms. Ch'en Ch'un emphasized the Mandate of Heaven, with the stress on establishing destiny. Not only did Ch'en Ch'un set up a special category for *ming,* he also headed his work with it. He was convinced that in the operation of the Mandate of Heaven, man has to fulfill the duty of practicing humanity and establishing righteousness. Chu Hsi repeatedly taught him to seek the Source, which is none other than the Principle of Heaven; and directed to man, it is the Mandate of Heaven. No wonder Ch'en Ch'un placed *ming* ahead of all other categories.

Gotō Toshimizu (1893–1961) compiled the *Shushi shisho shūchū sakuin* (Index to Master Chu's *Collected Commentaries on the Four Books*) and the *Shushi shisho wakumon sakuin* (Index to Master Chu's *Questions and Answers on the Four Books*.[70] In both cases he included a special section on *ming,* which immediately follows the leading section on Heaven. It is not known whether Ch'en Ch'un's *Pei-hsi tzu-i* influenced Professor Gotō. Ch'en's work has been very popular among Japanese Neo-Confucians, perhaps more so than among Chinese Neo-Confucians. It would be natural if it directly or indirectly affected Professor Gotō's work. Unfortunately, it is too late to ask him personally.

# Notes

1. *Pei-hsi tzu-i* [Ch'en Ch'un's explanation of terms], sec. 1 (*Hsi-yin-hsüan ts'ung-shu* [Studio where time is highly valued series] ed.), pt. 1, p. 1a. For an English rendering, see my translation entitled *Neo-Confucian Terms Explained* (New York: Columbia University Press, 1986), p. 37.

2. *Doctrine of the Mean,* ch. 1.

3. *Analects,* 2:4.

4. *Book of Changes,* "Remarks on the Trigrams," ch. 1.

5. *Analects,* 12:5.

6. *Book of Mencius,* 7A:2.

7. *Ibid.,* 7B:24.

8. *Pei-hsi tzu-i,* sec. 2 (pt. 1, pp. 1a–2a); *Neo-Confucian Terms Explained,* p. 38.

9. These are the Four Qualities of the first hexagram, *ch'ien* (Heaven, male), in the *Book of Changes.*

10. *Pei-hsi tzu-i,* sec. 2 (pt. 1, p. 1b); *Neo-Confucian Terms Explained,* p. 38.

11. *Ibid.,* sec. 5 (pt. 1, p. 4a); *Neo-Confucian Terms Explained,* p. 42.

12. *Book of Mencius,* 5A:6.

13. *Pei-hsi tzu-i,* sec. 6 (pt. 1, 4b); *Neo-Confucian Terms Explained,* p. 43.

14. *Book of Mencius,* 5A:6.

15. *Pei-hsi tzu-i,* sec. 7 (pt. 1, pp. 5b–6a); *Neo-Confucian Terms Explained,* p. 44.

16. *Yü-lei,* ch. 58, sec. 14 (p. 2158); ch. 4, sec. 38 (p. 101); ch. 5, sec. 45 (p. 143).

17. *Ibid.,* ch. 44, sec. 108 (p. 1814).

18. *Ibid.,* ch. 42, sec. 46 (p. 1727).

19. *I-shu* [Surviving works], 9:3b, in the *Erh-Ch'eng ch'üan-shu* [Complete works of the two Ch'engs] (*SPPY* ed.).

20. Chu Hsi, *Lun-yü huo-wen* [Questions and answers on the *Analects*] (*Chin-shih han-chi ts'ung-k'an* [Chinese works of the recent period series] ed.), 11:6b (p. 412), comment on 11:18.

21. *Analects,* 14:38.

22. *Book of Mencius,* 5A:18.

23. *Ibid.,* 2A:6.

24. *Analects*, 2:4.

25. *Doctrine of the Mean*, ch. 1.

26. *Yü-lei*, ch. 4, sec. 29 (pp. 2321–2322).

27. *Ibid.*, ch. 58, sec. 14 (p. 2158).

28. *Ibid.*, ch. 4, sec. 87 (p. 123).

29. *Ibid.*, ch. 36, sec. 6 (p. 1518).

30. *Lun-yü huo-wen*, 2:7a (p. 85), comment on 2:4.

31. *I-shu*, 24:3b.

32. *Yü-lei*, ch. 4, sec. 87 (p. 123).

33. *Book of History*, "Hung-fan" [Grand plan], sec. 3.

34. *Yü-lei*, ch. 4, sec. 37 (pp. 100–101).

35. *Pei-hsi tzu-i*, sec. 8 (pt. 1, p. 6a); *Neo-Confucian Terms Explained*, p. 45.

36. Chu Hsi, *Lun-yü chi-chu* [Collected commentaries on the *Analects*], comment on 16:8.

37. Hou Chung-liang's courtesy name was Shih-sheng. He was a pupil and distant relative of the Ch'eng brothers. For him, see the *Sung-Yüan hsüeh-an* [Anthology and critical accounts of Neo-Confucians of the Sung and Yüan dynasties] (*SPPY* ed.), 30:2b, biography of Hou Chung-liang.

38. *Analects*, 14:38.

39. *Lun-yü huo-wen*, 14:19b (p. 514), comment on 14:38.

40. *Yü-lei*, ch. 5, sec. 15 (p. 134).

41. *Ibid.*, sec. 3 (p. 134).

42. *Ibid.*, ch. 4, sec. 40 (p. 103).

43. *Wen-chi*, 58:28a, first letter in reply to Ch'en Wei-tao.

44. See above, n. 9.

45. The Five Agents (or Elements) are Metal, Wood, Water, Fire, and Earth.

46. The Four Beginnings are the feeling of commiseration as the beginning of humanity; the feeling of shame and dislike as the beginning of righteousness; the feeling of deference and compliance as the beginning of propriety; and the feeling of right and wrong as the beginning of wisdom. See the *Book of Mencius*, 2A:6.

47. The Five Constant Virtues are humanity, righteousness, propriety, wisdom, and faithfulness.

48. Chu Hsi, *Chung-yung huo-wen* [Questions and answers on the *Doctrine of the Mean*] (*Chin-shih han-chi ts'ung-k'an* ed.), p. 3a (p. 5), comment on ch. 1.

49. *I-shu*, 6:8a.

50. *I chuan* [Commentary on the *Book of Changes*], 1:2a, in the *Erh-Ch'eng ch'üan-shu*.

51. Chu Hsi, *Meng Tzu chi-chu* [Collected commentaries on the *Book of Mencius*], comment on 7B:24.

52. *Pei-hsi tzu-i*, sec. 3, 6, 9 (pt. 1, p. 2a); *Neo-Confucian Terms Explained*, pp. 37–38, 42–44, 45–46.

53. *Yü-lei*, ch. 4, sec. 93 (p. 126).

54. I cannot locate this saying in the *Chang Tzu ch'üan-shu* [Complete works of Master Chang Tsai].

55. *Meng Tzu chi-chu*, comment on 7B:24.

56. *Analects*, 9:1.

57. *Yü-lei,* ch. 36, sec. 1 (p. 1515).

58. Paraphrase of the *Book of Odes,* ode no. 195.

59. *Yü-lei,* ch. 42, sec. 46 (p. 1727).

60. Paraphrase of the *Book of Mencius,* 7A:1.

61. *Yü-lei,* ch. 60, sec. 43 (p. 2268).

62. *Meng Tzu chi-chu,* comment on 7A:1.

63. *Pei-hsi tzu-i,* sec. 6 (pt. 1, p. 5b); *Neo-Confucian Terms Explained,* pp. 43–44.

64. *Book of Changes,* "Remarks on the Trigrams," ch. 1.

65. *I-shu,* 2A:2b.

66. *Ibid.,* 11:3b.

67. *Ibid.,* 18:9a.

68. Quoted in *ibid.,* 10:5a.

69. *Yü-lei,* ch. 77, sec. 26 (p. 3127).

70. These two books were published by Hiroshima University in 1954 and 1955, respectively.

# – 15 –

# Substance and Function

THE tradition of substance *(t'i)* and function *(yung)* is a long one.[1] Generally speaking, Chu Hsi's doctrine of substance and function was derived from Ch'eng I's (1033–1107) famous sayings, "Substance and function come from the same source, and there is no gap between the manifest and the subtle,"[2] "The mind sometimes refers to its substance and sometimes refers to its function,"[3] and "Substance exists in the Way *(tao)*."[4] But Chu Hsi's scope was far more extensive and his analysis far more refined than those of Ch'eng I, and remained unmatched by later Neo-Confucians. What Chu Hsi called *t'i* is not the *t'i* in *t'i-tuan*, for *t'i-tuan* refers to form in its whole and parts, whereas here *t'i* means substance or reality. After all, *t'i-tuan* denotes no more than the character *(te)* of a thing.[5] Substance explains why a thing is so, whereas function explains how a thing is so. As Chu Hsi said, "Pleasure, anger, joy, and sorrow are functions, whereas the reason for pleasure, anger, joy, and sorrow is substance."[6] He also said, "Substance is the reason for being, whereas function is its utility. Take, for example, the hearing of the ear or the seeing of the eye. It is naturally so and is substance, whereas to direct the eye to see things or to turn one's ear to listen is function."[7]

Nevertheless, substance is not the Way, for the Way involves both substance and function. Ch'eng I had said, "Water flows without stop and things grow infinitely. In all these, substance exists in the Way."[8] In his own explanation, Chu Hsi said, " 'Substance exists in the Way' means that substance can be seen through the Way. The Way cannot be seen; it is revealed in the flowing from the start. Unless there are things and affairs, how can the Way be seen? This is how the substance of many things and affairs exists in the Way."[9] He compared the substance of the Way to the skeleton of the Way,[10] but he never explained what this

222

skeleton is. Chu Hsi never wrote a comprehensive or systematic treatise on the subject, although he discussed many topics in terms of substance and function. From these discussions, six principles can be discerned, as described below.

## Substance and Function Are Different

Chu Hsi said, "As to what is before and after physical shape, there is a distinction. One must clearly differentiate that one is substance and the other is function before one can say that they come from the same source. One must differentiate that one is form and the other is principle before one can say that there is no gap. If there is only one thing, there is no need to say that they come from the same source or that there is no gap between them."[11] He also said, "The student must distinguish between what has not been aroused and what has already been aroused before he can say that they come from the same source. While the source is the same, that they are different as substance and function remains unchanged."[12]

Chu Hsi had a great deal to say on the difference between substance and function and offered many examples. In the case of Change, Change is substance, and *ch'ien* (strength) and *k'un* (obedience) are function.[13] Likewise, yin (passive cosmic force) and yang (active cosmic force), tranquillity and activity, and the state of absolute quiet and inactivity and the state immediately penetrating all things when acted on are separately substance and function.[14] Of the Four Qualities of Change, advantage and firmness are substance while origination and flourishing are function.[15] Principle and form, the subtle and the manifest,[16] the present and the future,[17] and Heaven and Earth on the one hand and *kuei-shen* (negative and positive spiritual forces) on the other[18] are all substance and function, respectively, and not to be confused.

In the case of the Way, the Way is substance, while moral principles are function.[19] The hidden *(yin)* aspect of the Way is the subtlety of substance, while the reaching far and wide *(fei)* aspect is the pervasiveness of function.[20] The Way of Heaven is substance; the way of man is function.[21] The great foundation is substance; the universal path is function.[22] The mind and nature, nature and feeling,[23] the state before feelings are aroused and the state after they are aroused,[24] equilibrium *(chung)* and harmony *(ho)*,[25] humanity *(jen)* and love,[26] conscientiousness *(chung)* and altruism *(shu)*,[27] and humanity, righteousness, propriety, and wisdom on the one hand and commiseration, shame and dislike, respect and reverence, and the sense of right and wrong on the other[28] are all respectively substance and function. Other cases, such as the ear being substance and hearing function,[29] virtue being substance and capability function,[30] and holding fast to seriousness in order to preserve its substance while investigating principle to the utmost in order to extend its function,[31] are discussed below.

## Substance and Function Are Not Separated

Substance and function are of course different, but they are not separated. Chu Hsi said,

> What has not been aroused is substance, while what has been aroused is function. With reference to the state before the feelings are aroused, humanity, righteousness, propriety, and wisdom are all merged in it. They cannot be imagined and the application of their functions cannot be observed. With reference to the state where the feelings have been aroused, everything in one's daily life is important and relevant to the self, and the principle that has not been aroused always operates in it. Essentially, substance and function have never been separated.[32]

He also said,

> When [the mind] is tranquil, things and affairs have not reached it, and thoughts and deliberations have not started to emerge. Nature is merged and undifferentiated, and moral principles are completely present in it. What is called equilibrium is why the mind becomes substance and why it is absolutely quiet and inactive. When it is active, things and affairs reach it one after another, and thoughts and deliberations begin to emerge. The seven feelings [pleasure, anger, sorrow, joy, love, dislike, and desire] successively function, each with its own master. What is called harmony is why the mind becomes function, and why it immediately penetrates all things when acted upon. However, the nature that is tranquil cannot help but be active, and the feeling that is active necessarily has a degree and measure. Thus whether the mind remains absolutely quiet or penetrates everything, it operates everywhere and penetrates thoroughly, in which case substance and function are never separated.[33]

This being the case, although equilibrium and harmony are distinguished as substance and function, in reality they are not apart from each other. Accordingly, Chu Hsi set up an imaginary conversation that goes like this: Question: "Are equilibrium and harmony really two things?" Answer: "Since one is called substance and the other function, how can they not be two things? However, when we examine the reality of substance and function, one is the substance of the other, and the other is the function of it. As in the case of the ear and the eye that can hear and see, and seeing and hearing coming from the eye and ear, they are from the very beginning not two different things."[34] Elsewhere, he said, "Substance and function are not separated. For example, the body is substance, and to rise up and walk is function."[35]

Since substance and function are not separated, there is certainly no substance without function. In Chu Hsi's view, the Buddhists hold onto emptiness and silence, and therefore they have substance without function.[36] Once a pupil asked Ch'eng I if, in the state of equilibrium before the feelings of pleasure, anger, sorrow, and joy are aroused, the ear hears nothing and the eye sees nothing. Ch'eng I answered, "Although the ear hears nothing and the eye sees nothing, nevertheless the principle of hearing and seeing must already be there before hearing and seeing are possible."[37] Commenting on this passage, Chu Hsi said, "This is impossible according to principle."[38] To him, the ear hearing nothing and the eye seeing nothing were no different from the Buddhists having substance without function.

Chu Hsi also felt that Lu Hsiang-shan (1139–1193) had failed to understand that substance and function are not separated, in that Lu "talks about the substance that is empty and regards encountering everything as function." That is to say, "Whenever he sees a section, he immediately says that it is function and not substance. For example, in talking about a ruler, when there are no dots to mark the length, it is substance, and whenever there are dots, it is not substance but function. Or in talking about a balance, when there are no dots to mark the weight, that is substance, and whenever there are dots, that is not substance but function."[39] As Chu Hsi saw it, Lu's error consisted in having function without substance and substance without function. Therefore he criticized Lu's teaching as being equivalent to Ch'an (Meditation) Buddhism.

To explain how substance and function are not separated, there is nothing better than Chu Hsi's theory of the mind. This theory can be traced to Chang Tsai's (1020–1077) doctrine that the mind unites and commands nature and feeling,[40] a doctrine that was further developed by Ch'eng I, who said that the mind sometimes refers to its substance and sometimes to its function. Chu Hsi constructed his theory that substance and function prevail together on the basis of this idea. To him, nature is substance while feeling is function, and the mind commands them both.[41] As he put it, "Humanity, righteousness, propriety, and wisdom are nature and substance, whereas commiseration, shame and dislike, deference and humility, and the sense of right and wrong are feelings and function. It is the mind that commands nature and feelings and includes substance and function."[42] In other words, "The mind is the master of the body. That which constitutes its substance is nature, while that which constitutes its function is feeling."[43] In his diagram of the "Jen-shuo" (Treatise on humanity), Chu Hsi considered the mind to command everything and to nourish everything completely, without any differentiation. He also regarded the mind as including both the state before feelings are aroused and humanity as its substance, and both the state after feelings are aroused and commiseration as its function.[44] Because the nature of the mind is humanity, "there is nothing that humanity does not command, and therefore there is nothing that commiseration does not penetrate. This is precisely the wonder of the fact that substance and function are not separated."[45] Hence "Nature and mind are merely substance and function. According to principle, can substance and function be separated from each other?"[46]

That substance and function are not separated can also be seen in their continuity. Before function comes substance, and before substance comes function, one succeeding the other without break.[47] This is not a theory of cycles. Shao Yung (1011–1077) loved to talk about cycles, but to Chu Hsi, "K'ang-chien [Shao Yung] always insisted on talking about the period in between. . . . He always insisted on talking about the period between yin and yang or between activity and tranquillity. . . . Consequently, there is a gap. Therefore it is not as good as Master Ch'eng's saying that substance and function come from the same source and that there is no gap between the manifest and the subtle."[48] Chu Hsi once said, "With reference to substance and function, there must be substance before there can be function."[49] This seems to say that substance is prior to function, and that therefore there is a gap. But since function is merely the operation of substance, it is necessary to have the great foundation established first of all. "Therefore, although substance and function are distinguished as tranquil and active, substance must be firmly established before function can operate. In reality, they are not two different things."[50] That is why he said, "In an instant of thought both substance and function are present. As what is aroused in the mind goes away, what is not yet aroused in the mind comes in. There is no gap between them and nothing is obstructed."[51]

## Substance and Function Come from the Same Source

This is a celebrated saying by Ch'eng I that has become a basic concept of Neo-Confucianism. But Ch'eng I never explained how they come from the same source. It is easy for scholars to interpret the saying to mean that the origin of substance and function is the same. This is, of course, its primitive meaning. But it was only after Chu Hsi expanded the concept and refined it that it became a key element in Neo-Confucian thought—and Chu Hsi's most celebrated utterance as well. "The same source" does not mean the same origin; it means that there is function in substance and substance in function. In other words, substance and function involve each other. Some may argue that this is the Buddhist theory of the one and the many embracing each other. This theory may have influenced Chu Hsi, but the fact remains that his statement is the logical development of the idea that substance and function are not separated. Thus he had no need to depend on Buddhism. Besides, in Buddhism substance and function have never been given equal weight.

Chu Hsi said,

> The Great Ultimate naturally embraces the principle of activity and tranquillity, but activity and tranquillity should not be taken to distinguish substance and function as two different things, for tranquillity is the substance of the Great Ultimate and activity is the function of the same Great Ultimate. Take, for example, a fan. There is only one fan. When it is waved, that is function, and when it is laid down, that is substance. When it is laid down, there is only one principle, and when it is waved, there is also only one principle.[52]

What Chu Hsi meant by "the same source" is none other than the "only one principle" of the fan. The important point is that in substance there is function and in function there is substance:

> "Substance and function come from the same source." Although substance shows no trace, there is already function in it. "There is no gap between the manifest and the subtle" means that in the manifest there is already the subtle. Before the existence of Heaven and Earth, the ten thousand things are already present. This means that in substance there is function. After the establishment of Heaven and Earth, the principle remains. This means that in the manifest there is the subtle.[53]

Thus substance and function not only are not separated but also embrace or encompass each other. This idea was the foundation for the doctrine of the Ming (1368–1644) Neo-Confucians that substance and function are the same. Chu Hsi said, "Speaking from the point of view of principle, function is in substance. That is what is called the same source. Speaking from the point of view of forms, the manifest cannot exclude the subtle. That is what is called having no gap."[54] He also said, "Substance and function coming from the same source means that from the point of view of principle, principle is substance and form is function, but in principle there is form. Hence the source is the same. The manifest and the subtle having no gap means that from the point of view of form, form is manifest and principle is subtle, but in form there is principle. Hence there is no gap."[55]

Chu Hsi and his very good friend, Chang Shih (1133–1180), debated for more than ten years on various questions. Although they agreed on the fundamentals, they argued over many points. Chang Shih declared that "the substance of wisdom is active but tranquillity is in it, and the substance of humanity is tranquil but activity is in it." Chu Hsi praised him and said, "This principle is excellent."[56] In both the *Wen-chi* and the *Yü-lei*, the subject of substance and function coming from the same source is discussed many times, for it is the central concept in Chu Hsi's doctrine of substance and function.

## Everything Has Its Own Substance and Function

It has already been said that there is substance in function and function in substance. This does not mean that substance and function are interchangeable, for substance remains substance and function remains function. Hence Chu Hsi went on to say, "In reality, the difference between substance and function, and between the manifest and the subtle, cannot be said not to exist." This means that substance cannot be taken as function and function cannot be taken as substance. However, everything has its own substance and its own function. Thus in Chu Hsi's system of substance and function, every fact or principle has both substance and function. The mind can be spoken of in terms of substance and also in terms of function. The same is true of humanity, righteousness, wisdom, the Way, and virtue. Humanity has its own substance and function, and righteousness also has its own substance and function.[57]

In his commentary on the sentence in the *Analects* that "the man of wisdom delights in water," Chu Hsi said, "The man of wisdom delights in water that flows everywhere without stagnation." Here he was speaking in terms of function. In his comment on the sentence in the same chapter that "the man of wisdom is active," he said, "Activity and tranquillity refer to substance." Here he was speaking in terms of substance.[58] There is no contradiction in this commentary; Chu Hsi was simply saying that wisdom has both substance and function. When a pupil said that the Way embraces both substance and function and that virtue also embraces substance and function, he gave his approval.[59] Everything, therefore, can be viewed as substance or function. As he himself noted, "From the perspective of yin and yang, righteousness is substance and humanity is function. From the perspective of preserving the mind and regulating affairs, humanity is substance and righteousness is function."[60] He also said, "Speaking from the point of view of what is above physical shape, what is empty and tranquil is of course substance, while what is revealed in things and affairs is function. Speaking from the point of view of what has physical shape, however, things and affairs are substance and the principle that is revealed is function."[61] Again, "Speaking in terms of yang, yang is substance and yin is function. Speaking in terms of yin, yin is substance and yang is function."[62] Substance and function are relative here, but since they come from the same source, each preserves its nature as both substance and function.

## Substance and Function Have No Fixed Position

Since a thing can be substance and/or function, neither substance nor function can be fixed in time or place. When humanity and righteousness are spoken of together, humanity is substance and righteousness is function, but when humanity is spoken of alone, it includes both substance and function,[63] since righteousness, propriety, and wisdom are contained in it.[64] Also, "With reference to the Four Beginnings,[65] in terms of substance and function, substance is primary and function is secondary. But in terms of the starting point, the beginning of the starting point is primary and the end of the starting point is secondary. The two theories do not hinder each other."[66] Take the case of humanity. Mencius interpreted it as man's mind,[67] but Ch'eng I understood it as nature.[68] As Chu Hsi saw it, the two are not contradictory, for Ch'eng I distinguished substance and function in what he said, while Mencius combined them.[69] Chu Hsi said, "For the meaning of humanity, Mencius spoke of it in the sense of the mind that penetrates both substance and function and commands both nature and feelings. In contrast, Master Ch'eng spoke of it in the sense of nature, analyzing its seeming similarity [with feeling], and distinguisheed it as substance [and feeling] and as function."[70]

In the case of equilibrium (chung), "The chung in chung-ho [equilibrium and harmony] refers specifically to what has not been aroused [substance], while the chung in chung-yung [central and universal, the Mean] includes both substance and function."[71] Thus chung has two meanings: equilibrium in the state before the feelings are aroused, and the Mean according to the circumstance (shih-chung). As Chu Hsi said, "The chung in chung-yung is that which is going neither too far nor not far enough. Its fundamental idea is the Mean according to the circumstance. Traced to its foundation, the chung [equilibrium] in the state before the feelings of pleasure, anger, sorrow, and joy are aroused becomes the chung in shih-chung. The chung [equilibrium] before the feelings are aroused is substance, while the chung [the Mean] in shih-chung is function. Thus the term chung involves both equilibrium and harmony."[72] He explained further that "chung-ho [equilibrium and harmony] is spoken of in terms of nature and feeling, while chung-yung [central and universal, the Mean] is spoken of in terms of moral principles. In reality they are the same. When chung is paired with ho, chung is substance and ho is function, referring to the states before and after the feelings are aroused. When chung is paired with yung, we have to turn around and say that yung is substance while chung is function. . . . When chung-ho is paired with chung-yung, chung-ho is substance and chung-yung is function."[73]

It can readily be seen that Chu Hsi's system of substance and function is highly complicated, with substance and function crisscrossing in all directions in a variety of ways never encountered before or since Chu Hsi's time. When a pupil asked about the saying in the *Analects,* "Among the functions of rites, the most valuable is that it establishes harmony,"[74] Chu Hsi's answer was long, thorough, and did not mince words. The pupil asked: "Shang-ts'ai [Hsieh Liang-tso, 1050–c. 1120] said, 'Rites and music are different in function but the same in substance.'[75] Thus the mind is substance, and reverence [from rites] and harmony [from music] are function. In your [*Lun-yü*] *chi-chu,* however, you said that 'Reverence is substance and harmony is function.' Why is there this discrepancy?" Chu Hsi answered,

> Speaking from the point of view of the mind, the mind is substance and reverence and harmony are function. When reverence and harmony are spoken of as a pair, then reverence is substance and harmony is function. Generally speaking, substance and function have no fixed position. They can shift. For example, when one faces north, then here is south and there is north. When one moves to the north, then in the north there are its north and south. Substance and function are not fixed. The substance and function in this place appertain here, while the substance and function in that place appertain there. This principle knows no limit and is applicable in any direction, penetrating hundreds of items and thousands of details.

Then he pointed with his finger and added, "Clearly there is one layer after another. It is the same no matter how you look at it. When it is turned over and over, it is the same. For example, when talking about the Two Modes [yin and yang], the Great Ultimate is the Great Ultimate [substance] and the Two Modes are function. When talking about the Four Forms [major and minor yin and yang], the Two Modes are the Great Ultimate and the Four Forms are function. In terms of the Eight Trigrams, the Four Forms are the Great Ultimate and the Eight Trigrams are function."[76]

## The Same in Substance but Different in Function

The theory that rites and music differ in function but are the same in substance was entirely agreeable to Chu Hsi. As he explained it, "Rites aim primarily at reverence, and music aims primarily at harmony. Hence they are different in function. But they are both based on the mind and hence are the same in substance. However, reverence and harmony are only one thing. When reverence obtains, there will be harmony, and when harmony obtains, there will naturally be reverence."[77] This means that not only reverence and harmony but all virtues issue from the mind, for the one foundation diversifies into many manifestations. This is Ch'eng I's theory of principle being one while manifestations are many.[78] In explaining that conscientiousness *(chung)* and altruism *(shu)* are the way of the one thread that runs through everything,[79] Chu Hsi said, "To devote oneself to the fullest extent is conscientiousness, which is the substance of the Way. To extend oneself to others is altruism, which is the function of the Way. Conscientiousness is the substance of altruism. That is how manifestations are many but their principle is one. Altruism is the function of conscientiousness. That is how principle is one but its manifestations are many."[80] He also said, "Perfect sincerity that is unceasing is the substance of the Way, and that is how the many manifestations come from the one foundation. That all things enjoy their being is the function of the Way, and that is how the one foundation is revealed in many manifestations. Looked at this way, the reality of the one thread running through all things can be seen."[81] The earlier passage deals with ethics while the latter deals with metaphysics, but the principle is the same.

Although Chu Hsi accepted Hsieh Liang-tso's theory of sameness in substance but difference in function, he was extremely critical of Hu Hung's (1106–1161) theory that "the Principle of Heaven and [selfish] human desires have the same substance but different functions and have the same operation but different feelings."[82] In Chu Hsi's words, "Perhaps there are cases when they have the same operation but different feelings," but "In substance there is only the Principle of Heaven and no [selfish] human desires."[83] On this point Chu Hsi not only declared it to be "incorrect" in his *Hu Tzu chih-yen i-i* (Doubts on *Master Hu's Understanding of Words*),[84] he also discussed Hu's mistakes with Hu's pupil and Chu Hsi's own good friend, Chang Shih.[85] What he criticized, however, was the theory that the Principle of Heaven and human desires have the same substance, not the theory that things can have the same substance but different functions. Whatever has substance must have function, and therefore the substance can be known from the function: "When we have found the function, we can know the substance, for function springs from substance."[86] For example, from the fact that water runs without stop can be seen the natural state of the substance of the Way.[87] In short, because there is substance there must be function, and because there is function there must be substance. They are two sides of the same coin, and they come from the same source. The concept of substance and function is a cornerstone in Chu Hsi's organic conception of the universe.

## Notes

1. See my article on *T'i-yung* in Wei Cheng-t'ung, ed., *Chung-kuo che-shüeh tz'u-tien ta-ch'üan* [Complete dictionary of Chinese Philosophy] (Taipei: Buffalo Press, 1983), pp. 853–856.

2. Ch'eng I, *I chuan* [Commentary on the *Book of Changes*], preface.

3. *I-ch'uan wen-chi* [Collection of literary works of Ch'eng I], 5:12a, letter to Lü Ta-lin on equilibrium, in the *Erh-Ch'eng ch'üan-shu* [Complete works of the two Ch'engs] (*SPPY* ed.).

4. Quoted by Chu Hsi in his *Lun-yü chi-chu* [Collected commentaries on the *Analects*], comment on 9:16. See the *I-shu* [Surviving works], 19:3b, in the *Erh-Ch'eng ch'üan-shu*.

5. *Yü-lei*, ch. 32, sec. 91 (p. 1324).

6. *Ibid.*, ch. 17, sec. 50 (p. 619). The four feelings refer to the *Doctrine of the Mean*, ch. 1.

7. *Ibid.*, ch. 6, sec. 22 (p. 162).

8. See above, n. 4.

9. *Yü-lei*, ch. 36, sec. 116 (pp. 1557–1558).

10. *Ibid.*, sec. 114 (p. 1557). See also ch. 6, sec. 20 (p. 162).

11. *Wen-chi*, 48:17b, forty-first letter in reply to Lü Tzu-yüeh (Lü Tsu-chien).

12. *Ibid.*, 35:2a, letter in reply to Lü Po-kung (Lü Tsu-ch'ien). See also below, n. 16.

13. *Yü-lei*, ch. 75, sec. 103 (p. 3076). *Ch'ien* (Heaven, male) and *k'un* (Earth, female) are the first and second hexagrams, respectively, in the *Book of Changes;* their chief qualities are strength and obedience.

14. *Ibid.*, ch. 1, sec. 1 (p. 1). The two states refer to the *Book of Changes*, "Appended Remarks,'', pt. 1, ch. 10.

15. *Ibid.*, ch. 69, sec. 86 (p. 2754). The Four Qualities are those of the first hexagram, *ch'ien*, in the *Book of Changes*.

16. *Wen-chi*, 40:38b, twenty-ninth letter in reply to Ho Shu-ching (Ho Hao).

17. *Yü-lei*, ch. 6, sec. 21 (p. 162).

18. *Ibid.*, ch. 68, sec. 17 (p. 2681).

19. *Ibid.*, ch. 52, sec. 107 (p. 1991).

20. *Ibid.*, ch. 63, sec. 53 (p. 2432). For *fei* and *yin*, see the *Doctrine of the Mean*, ch. 12. Also Chu Hsi, *Chung-yung chang-chü* [Commentary on the *Doctrine of the Mean*], comment on ch. 12.

21. *Ibid.*, ch. 27, sec. 34 (p. 1080).

22. *Chung-yung chang-chü*, comment on ch. 1.

23. *Yü-lei*, ch. 5, sec. 65 (p. 148); ch. 27, sec. 47 (p. 1092); *Wen-chi*, 40:36b, twenty-eighth letter in reply to Ho Shu-ching (Ho Hao).

24. *Yü-lei*, ch. 5, sec. 62 (p. 146).

25. Chu Hsi, *Chung-yung huo-wen* [Questions and answers on the *Doctrine of the Mean*] (*Chin-shih han-chi ts'ung-k'an* [Chinese works in the recent period series] ed.), p. 10b (p. 20), comment on ch. 1.

26. *Yü-lei*, ch. 20, sec. 100 (p. 751).

27. *Ibid.*, ch. 27, sec. 9 (p. 1074); sec. 3–4 (p. 1080); sec. 44 (p. 1089).

28. *Ibid.*, ch. 6, sec. 40 (p. 166); *Wen-chi*, 50:37a, fifth letter in reply to Cheng Tzu-shang (Cheng K'o-hsüeh); Chu Hsi, *Meng Tzu chi-chu*, [Collected commentaries on the *Book of Mencius*], comment on 2A:6.

29. *Yü-lei*, ch. 1, sec. 12 (p. 4).

30. *Ibid.*, ch. 24, sec. 50 (p. 933).

31. *Wen-chi*, 59:20b, letter in reply to Wu Tou-nan (Wu Jen-chieh).

32. Chu Hsi, *Meng Tzu huo-wen* [Questions and answers on the *Book of Mencius*] (*Chin-shih han-chi ts'ung-k'an* ed.), 13:8b (p. 176), comment on 7A:15.

33. *Wen-chi,* 32:24b–25a, forty-seventh letter in reply to Chang Ch'in-fu (Chang Shih).

34. *Chung-yung huo-wen,* p. 11b (pp. 21–22), comment on ch. 1.

35. *Yü-lei,* ch. 17, sec. 50 (p. 619).

36. *Ibid.,* ch. 59, sec. 160 (p. 2243). Also ch. 126, sec. 80 (p. 4853).

37. *I-shu,* 18:15a.

38. *Yü-lei,* ch. 126, sec. 7 (p. 4823).

39. *Ibid.,* ch. 6, sec. 22–23 (p. 163).

40. *Chang Tzu yü-lu* [Recorded sayings of Master Chang Tsai] (*SPTK* ed.), pt. 3, p. 1a.

41. *Yü-lei,* ch. 5, sec. 65 (p. 148).

42. *Wen-chi,* 56:14b, fourth letter in reply to Fang Pin-wang (Fang I).

43. *Ibid.,* 40:36b, fortieth letter in reply to Ho Shu-ching (Ho Hao); *Yü-lei,* ch. 5, sec. 66–76 (pp. 148–153).

44. *Yü-lei,* ch. 105, sec. 43 (p. 4185). For the "Jen-shuo," see ch. 11 above. For the diagram of it, see p. 281 below.

45. *Wen-chi,* 40:29b, seventeenth letter in reply to Ho Shu-ching.

46. *Ibid.,* p. 25b, eleventh letter.

47. *Yü-lei,* ch. 1, sec. 1 (p. 1).

48. *Ibid.,* ch. 71, sec. 58 (p. 2857).

49. *Ibid.,* ch. 53, sec. 42 (2041).

50. *Chung-yung chang-chü,* comment on ch. 1.

51. *Wen-chi,* 30:20a, fourth letter to Chang Ch'in-fu (Chang Shih).

52. *Yü-lei,* ch. 94, sec. 29 (pp. 3766–3767).

53. *Ibid.,* ch. 67, sec. 37 (p. 2631).

54. *Wen-chi,* 30:12b, seventh letter in reply to Minister Wang (Wang Ying-ch'en).

55. *Ibid.,* 40:38b, twenty-ninth letter in reply to Ho Shu-ching (Ho Hao).

56. *Ibid.,* 31:26b, letter to Chang Ch'in-fu on his *Explanation of the Analects.*

57. *Yü-lei,* ch. 6, sec. 130 (p. 194). See also ch. 94, sec. 87 (p. 3783).

58. Chu Hsi, *Lun-yü chi-chu* [Collected commentaries on the *Analects*], comment on 6:21. See also *Yü-lei,* ch. 32, sec. 86 (p. 1322).

59. *Yü-lei,* ch. 95, sec. 24 (p. 3843).

60. *Meng Tzu huo-wen,* 1:2a (p. 3), comment on 1A:1.

61. *Wen-chi,* 48:16b, fortieth letter in reply to Lü Tzu-yüeh (Lü Tsu-chien).

62. *Yü-lei,* ch. 6, sec. 21 (p. 162).

63. *Ibid.,* sec. 68 (p. 186).

64. *Ibid.,* ch. 62, sec. 9 (p. 2349).

65. The Four Beginnings refer to the *Book of Mencius,* 2A:6, where it is said that the feeling of commiseration is the beginning of humanity; the feeling of shame and dislike is the beginning of righteousness; the feeling of deference and compliance is the beginning of propriety; and the feeling of right and wrong is the beginning of wisdom.

66. *Wen-chi,* 59:11b, letter in reply to Ho Chü-yüan.

67. *Book of Mencius,* 6A:11.

68. *I-shu,* 18:1a.

69. *Yü-lei,* ch. 20, sec. 128 (p. 768).

70. *Wen-chi,* 35:4a, ninety-sixth letter in reply to Lü Po-kung (Lü Tsu-ch'ien).

71. *Ibid.*

72. *Yü-lei,* ch. 62, sec. 9 (p. 2349).

73. *Ibid.,* ch. 63, sec. 8 (p. 2417).

74. *Analects,* 1:12.

75. Hsieh Liang-tso, *Lun-yü shuo* [Explanation of the *Analects*], comment on 1:12.

76. *Yü-lei,* ch. 22, sec. 65 (pp. 838–839). For the Great Ultimate, the Two Modes, etc., see *Book of Changes,* "Appended Remarks," pt. 1, ch. 11.

77. *Ibid.,* sec. 63 (p. 837).

78. *I-ch'uan wen-chi,* 5:12b.

79. Reference to the *Analects,* 4:15.

80. Chu Hsi, *Lun-yü huo-wen* [Questions and answers on the *Analects*] (*Chin-shih han-chi ts'ung-k'an* ed.), 4:17b (p. 188), comment on 4:15.

81. *Lun-yü chi-chu,* comment on 4:14.

82. *Wen-chi,* 73:41b, "Hu Tzu chih-yen i-i" [Doubts on *Master Hu's Understanding of Words*].

83. *Yü-lei,* ch. 101, sec. 182 (p. 4119).

84. *Wen-chi,* 73:42a, "Hu Tzu chih-yen i-i."

85. As related in *Wen-chi,* 58:28a, first letter in reply to Hsü Chü-fu (Hsü Yü).

86. *Yü-lei,* ch. 42. sec. 103 (p. 1745).

87. *Ibid.,* ch. 36, sec. 118 (p. 1558).

# – 16 –

# The Two-Wheel Pattern

As Wang Mao-hung (1668–1741) observed,

From the sixth year of Ch'ien-tao [1170], in his letters to Lü Tung-lai [Lü Tsu-ch'ien, 1137–1181][1] and Liu Tzu-ch'eng [Liu Ch'ing-chih, 1139–1195],[2] he [Chu Hsi] singled out the two sayings of Master Ch'eng [Ch'eng I, 1033–1107]. The fundamental principle of his learning throughout life was firmly patterned on them. They are the same as "Honoring the moral nature (tsun-te-hsing) and following the path of inquiry and study (tao-wen-hsüeh)" in the Doctrine of the Mean[3] and "Seriousness (ching, reverence) means to straighten the internal life and righteousness means to square the external life" in the Greater Commentary of the Book of Changes.[4] From the time of antiquity, the transmissions of the sages and worthies all match like the pieces of a tally. In the fifth year of Shao-hsi [1194], he wrote Sun Ching-fu [Sun Tzu-hsiu] and said, "Master Ch'eng's two sayings, 'Self-cultivation requires seriousness,' [and] 'The pursuit of learning depends on the extension of knowledge,'[5] are like the two wheels of a vehicle or two wings of a bird. There has never been a case when a vehicle or a bird has been able to proceed with only one of them."[6] This is especially clear and clean-cut. Twenty-five years had passed and his words did not change even an iota.[7]

We have already brought out the truth of this last statement in our discussion of Chu Hsi's doctrine of substance and function.[8] The same pattern can be seen in his doctrine on meditation and reading.[9] It can also be discerned in his doctrines of the wu-chi (ultimate of nonbeing) and T'ai-chi (Great Ultimate), li (principle) and ch'i (material force), hsing (nature) and ch'ing (feelings), and almost everything else he talked about. What follow are three areas in which the two-wheel pattern is especially firm and clear.

235

## Honoring the Moral Nature and Following the Path of Inquiry and Study

Writers are fond of considering Chu Hsi as representing the School of Principle *(Li-hsüeh)* and Lu Hsiang-shan (1139–1193) as representing the School of Mind *(Hsin-hsüeh)*. They regard Lu as advocating honoring the moral nature and Chu as advocating following the path of inquiry and study. Furthermore, they see the meeting of Chu, Lu, and others at the Goose Lake Temple in 1175 as having been for the purpose of resolving their philosophical differences–the chief difference being precisely that of honoring the moral nature versus following the path of inquiry and study. According to this view, the conflict between the School of Principle and the School of Mind over the next few centuries was a confrontation between honoring the moral nature and following the path of inquiry and study.

I once shared this view to some extent.[10] Upon further investigation, however, I found that the topics of discussion at the 1175 meeting were confined to the question of what was easy and simple versus fragmentation and isolated details, and to the order of the nine hexagrams. I also found that in their informal conversations, those present touched upon Lü Tsu-ch'ien's commentary on the *Book of History,* Lu Tzu-shou's (Lu Chiu-ling, 1132–1180) new composition, and the Lus' pupil Ts'ao Li-chih (Ts'ao Chien, 1147–1183). On the way to the meeting, Lu Hsiang-shan composed a poem to match one written by his elder brother Tzu-shou. Part of Hsiang-shan's poem reads, "Work that is easy and simple will in the end be lasting and great / Understanding that is devoted to isolated details will end up in aimless drifting." Thus the participants' argument "in tens of rounds" probably concerned the matter of easiness and simplicity, which are the qualities of the first and second hexagrams, respectively, of the *Book of Changes.*[11] These were the only topics of discussion and conversation at the meeting that we are aware of.[12] The subject of honoring the moral nature versus following the path of inquiry and study was not even mentioned. That the meeting ended with displeasure on both sides cannot be denied. Later, Chu Hsi repeatedly wrote friends to say that Lu Hsiang-shan was too self-confident and narrow. But not once did he mention that honoring the moral nature and following the path of inquiry and study was a point in dispute.

Throughout the history of Neo-Confucianism, due to the partisan spirit of the followers of the two schools, honoring the moral nature and following the path of inquiry and study have been taken as irreconcilable opposites. The one who started this trend was probably Lu Hsiang-shan himself. In his letter to Hsiang An-shih (d. 1208), Chu Hsi said,

> Generally speaking, from Tzu-ssu on, the method of teaching was to regard honoring the moral nature and following the path of inquiry and study as the essentials for one's effort. But now Tzu-ching [Lu Hsiang-shan] only advocates honoring the moral nature, while I myself ordinarily have tended more toward following the path of inquiry and study. Consequently, his followers are mostly admirable in their conduct. But he is completely careless in the understanding of moral principles and, furthermore, talks about a kind of artificial principle to cover up and will not yield. On my part, although I dare not talk recklessly about moral principles, nevertheless, in the important task of helping others and helping oneself, I have not exerted sufficient effort. From now on I must return to the self and exert myself, doing away with shortcomings and collecting the strong points so that I won't fall on one side.[13]

This is a fair judgment of Chu Hsi himself and of Lu, inculcating as it does the noble spirit of eliminating weak points and adding strong points to arrive at the Mean. When Lu heard about this, he said, "Chu Yüan-hui [Chu Hsi] wishes to do away with two shortcomings and collect two strong points, but I thought that is impossible. If one does not know how to honor the moral nature, how can there be any following the way of inquiry and study?"[14] Thus Lu did not allow the dual emphasis on honoring the moral nature and following the path of inquiry and study as taught by Tzu-ssu in the *Doctrine of the Mean*. To him, Chu Hsi did not know how to honor the moral nature because he tended to the side of following the path of inquiry and study. Did Chu Hsi really fail to honor the moral nature, or did he begin to honor the moral nature only after Lu Hsiang-shan criticized him? We must consider the matter thoroughly.

In the *Doctrine of the Mean* it is said, "Therefore the superior man honors the moral nature and follows the path of inquiry and study. He achieves breadth and greatness and pursues the refined and subtle to the limit. He seeks to reach the greatest height and brilliancy and follows the path of the Mean. He goes over the old so as to find out what is new.[15] He is earnest and deep and highly respects all propriety."[16] In his commentary on the passage, Chu Hsi said, "Honoring the moral nature is the way to preserve the mind and reach the highest degree of what is great in the substance of the Way. Following the path of inquiry and study is the way to extend knowledge and reach the highest degree of what is small in the substance of the Way. The two are the great fundamentals of moral cultivation and the consolidation of the Way."[17] There are three important points in this commentary: (1) the equation of honoring the moral nature and following the path of inquiry and study with preserving the mind and the extension of knowledge; (2) the idea that the two reach the highest degree of what is great and what is small in the substance of the Way; and (3) the assertion that the two are important fundamentals of one's learning. The discussions on the two concepts in the *Wen-chi* and the *Yü-lei* do not go beyond these three points, except to detail and refine them.

Strangely enough, there are only twenty or thirty places where honoring the moral nature and following the path of inquiry and study are discussed in the *Wen-chi* and the *Yü-lei;* in the latter they appear mostly in chapter 64, where the passage from the *Doctrine of the Mean* is discussed. Does this mean that the two concepts are unimportant in Chu Hsi's system of thought? Let us first see how he understood them.

According to Chu Hsi's *Chung-yung chang-chü* (Commentary on the *Doctrine of the Mean*), "To honor means to revere and to comply. Moral nature means the correct principle that we receive from Heaven. To follow means to proceed along."[18] In answer to a pupil, Chu Hsi said, "Moral nature means the nature of moral principles."[19] He also said, "To honor is simply to lift up a thing and venerate it, and to follow simply means to proceed, like going to act on it."[20] He explained,

> Things like "Being respectful in private life and being serious in handling affairs,"[21] and "Let one's words be sincere and truthful, and one's deeds be earnest and reverential,"[22] and so on, are all moral nature. As to inquiry and study, it is very broad and many items are involved. Every thing and every affair is inquiry and study. It is endless. . . . To look upon a thing as important and not to neglect it is to honor it. . . . Take the case of this fan. You do not know how to make it yourself and go to ask people to show you how to make it. After you have heard people teach you how to make it, you must go ahead and make it. Only then is it following the path of inquiry and study. But if you only ask and then leave it alone and do not make it, that is not following the path of inquiry and study.[23]

In the *Doctrine of the Mean,* from honoring the moral nature to highly respecting all propriety, there are altogether ten items. Chu Hsi considered the ten "as having no space between,"[24] for "they are one thing in general, but there must be degrees before they can be complete."[25] At the same time, he separated honoring the moral nature, achieving breadth and greatness, seeking to reach the greatest height and brilliancy, going over the old, and being earnest and deep into one group, and following the path of inquiry and study, pursuing the refined and subtle to the limit, following the path of the Mean, finding out what is new, and highly respecting all propriety into another.[26] The former group describes action, while the latter describes knowledge.[27] The former set includes the five items that deal with what is great, while the latter set includes the five items that deal with what is small.[28] As Chu Hsi put it, "From honoring the moral nature to being earnest and deep is the upper section, where they are undifferentiated and all merged, while from following the path of inquiry and study to highly respecting all propriety is the lower section, where they are detailed and close together."[29] He also said, "The five items from honoring the moral nature to being earnest and deep are efforts directed toward one's moral nature, while from following the path of inquiry and study to highly respecting all propriety are efforts toward one's inquiry and study."[30]

In other words, "Honoring the moral nature, achieving breadth and greatness, seeking to reach the greatest height and brilliancy, going over the old, and being earnest and deep are simply honoring the moral nature, while pursuing the refined and subtle to the limit, following the path of the Mean, finding out what is new, and highly respecting all propriety are simply following the path of inquiry and study."[31] Consequently, honoring the moral nature and following the path of inquiry and study embrace all eight items that follow them:[32]

> Honoring the moral nature and following the path of inquiry and study are fundamental principles, while the rest are efforts in detail. Because one can honor the moral nature, one can achieve breadth and greatness, seek to reach the greatest height and brilliancy, go over the old, and be earnest and deep. . . . Because one can follow the path of inquiry and study, one can pursue the refined and the subtle to the limit, follow the path of the Mean, find out what is new, and highly respect all propriety.[33]

The ten different items are now combined into two and even one thing. As Chu Hsi said, "Originally, these are two different items, and they are further divided into ten. In reality, there are only two things, and the two things are simply one thing, which is honoring the moral nature. One applies honoring the moral nature to follow the path of inquiry and study. Hence it is said to honor the moral nature and follow the path of inquiry and study."[34]

Honoring the moral nature and following the path of inquiry and study are basically one thing, but there is no harm in separating them into two. The details of the task of inquiry and study are numerous, while the effort of honoring the moral nature is simple.[35] Honoring the moral nature is fundamental, while following the path of inquiry and study is secondary. As Chu Hsi wrote his friend, "The fundamental of this learning is to honor the moral nature."[36] To Chu Hsi, honoring the moral nature is a firm base, "only [equipped] with which can the task of learning be handled":[37] "If one does not honor the moral nature, one will be lazy and negligent. How can one advance in learning?"[38] "If one can honor the moral nature, one can therefore follow the path of inquiry and study, for once the fundamental has been attained, the secondary will naturally follow."[39]

When Chu Hsi delivered a lecture at Yü-shan[40] in his later years, he said,

> In their teaching for us, the Sage [Confucius] and worthies followed the
> proper order of beginning and end, root and branches. Nothing, whether
> refined or coarse, big or small, was left out. Therefore, as soon as honor-
> ing the moral nature is mentioned, there is the task of following the path of
> inquiry and study. Although an effort should be devoted to each in itself,
> they are not distinctly two separate things. . . . Therefore, in the learning
> of the superior man, when he has been able to honor the moral nature to
> preserve what is great in himself, he should follow the path of inquiry and
> study to pursue to the limit what is small in himself. . . . Here the student
> should, of course, hold honoring the moral nature as fundamental, but he
> should also make the greatest effort in following the path of inquiry and
> study. What is important is to enrich and develop the one along with the
> other. Then there will be complete embracement and total penetration,
> and nothing will be missing from the totality and substance of the Way.[41]

Since in his later years Chu Hsi considered honoring the moral nature
to be fundamental and to function along with following the path of
inquiry and study, this excerpt may be taken as his final conclusion on
the subject. He repeatedly expressed the view that honoring the moral
nature and following the path of inquiry and study should proceed
together. On the one hand, he said, "In our discussion, we tend to the
one side of honoring the moral nature. In that case, the advantage will
be only on that side. If there is no effort at following the path of inquiry
and study, there will be only that advantage, any action will be handi-
capped, and nothing can be done."[42] On the other hand, because pupils
devoted effort to investigating principle and gradually ignored things
relevant to the self, Chu Hsi taught them to honor the moral nature.[43]
He said, "Unless you do this, what you have learned and what you
have held onto will be one-sided and incomplete."[44] What he called
"two feet,"[45] "effort on both sides,"[46] and "functioning for each
other"[47] all mean the mutual development of honoring the moral nature
and following the path of inquiry and study.

It could be argued that the letters and conversations referred to above
may have taken place after 1183, when Lu Hsiang-shan remarked that
Chu Hsi did not know how to honor the moral nature, and that it was
only when stimulated by Lu that Chu Hsi turned away from a one-
sided emphasis on following the path of inquiry and study to stress both
sides. But the fact is that Chu Hsi's letters to Lü Tsu-ch'ien and Liu
Ch'ing-chih in 1170, to which Wang Mao-hung referred,[48] antedate Lu
Hsiang-shan's remark by more than ten years. Even in his letter to
Hsiang P'ing-fu (Hsiang An-shih), to which Lu's remark was directed,
Chu Hsi merely said that he tended more toward following the path of
inquiry and study—not that he completely emphasized one side.
Because of this tendency, he wanted to make up with the merit of one for
the demerit of the other. Even after 1188, Chu Hsi recognized that hith-

erto he had not talked sufficiently on the side of honoring the moral nature, which he now wanted to rectify.[49]

Thus, although Chu Hsi did not meet the standard he set for himself, his standard was nevertheless unmistakable. In his writing and teaching throughout his life, he always aimed at balancing equally on "two feet." Knowledge and action proceeding together; abiding in seriousness and investigating principle to the utmost; enlightenment and sincerity advancing together; seriousness and righteousness supporting each other; extensive study of literature and restraining oneself with rules of propriety; holding onto seriousness and extending knowledge—all these are like the two wheels of a vehicle or two wings of a bird. They have the same meaning as honoring the moral nature and following the path of inquiry and study. This is summed up in Ch'eng I's saying, "Self-cultivation requires seriousness. The pursuit of learning depends on the extension of knowledge," which Chu Hsi loved to quote.

The outstanding Neo-Confucian of the Yüan dynasty (1277–1368), Wu Ch'eng (1249–1333), wrote the "Account of the Studio of Honoring the Moral Nature and Following the Path of Inquiry and Study," in which he said, "Four generations after Ch'eng I came Chu Hsi. In the refinement of literary meanings and in the discussion of sentences and words, there has been no one to surpass him since the time of Mencius. His followers have often stagnated in this and allowed their minds to degenerate."[50] What Wu meant was that Chu Hsi was one-sided in favor of following the path of inquiry and study. This is why Wang Yang-ming (1472–1529), in his essay "Master Chu's Final Conclusions Arrived at Late in Life," after selecting excerpts from thirty-four of Chu Hsi's letters to friends, quotes Wu's account almost in full to show that in his late years, Chu Hsi turned more and more to moral cultivation and gradually came to the position held by Wang himself.[51] Although, in an epilogue to Wu's account, Li Tsu-t'ao tried to explain that Wu was not criticizing Chu Hsi but merely wanted to correct the intellectual atmosphere of his own time, Wu had already exerted a strong influence and affirmed the impression that Chu Hsi had ignored honoring the moral nature. As a result, even Huang Tsung-hsi (1610–1695) asserted that Chu Hsi regarded following the path of inquiry and study as fundamental,[52] and his son, Huang Po-chia (fl. 1695) followed him.[53] From the foregoing discussion, it is clear that nothing could be further from the truth.

## Enlightenment and Sincerity

In his prose-poem for the White Deer Hollow Academy, Chu Hsi wrote, "Let enlightenment and sincerity advance together, and let seriousness and righteousness stand side by side."[54] The first half of the passage was derived from the *Doctrine of the Mean,* which says, "Given sincerity, there will be enlightenment, and given enlightenment, there will be sincerity";[55] the second half was derived from "Master Ch'eng," who said, "With seriousness and righteousness supporting each other, go straight ahead. They are the starting points from which one can reach the level of the virtue of Heaven."[56] According to Chu Hsi, this was Ch'eng Hao's (1032–1085) rather than Ch'eng I's (1033–1107) utterance.[57] The concept of seriousness and righteousness as a pair originated in the *Book of Changes,* where it is said, "Seriousness means to straighten the internal life and righteousness means to square the external life."[58] Since Chu Hsi's time, the aphorisms "Enlightenment and sincerity advance together" and "Seriousness and righteousness support each other" have been famous slogans in Neo-Confucianism. Huang Kan (1152–1221) quoted them in a letter.[59] They also appear three times in Lo Ch'in-shun's (1465–1547) *K'un-chih chi* (Knowledge painfully acquired),[60] and they are repeated in Huang Tsung-hsi's *Ming-ju hsüeh-an* (Anthology and critical accounts of the Neo-Confucians of the Ming dynasty).[61]

What is intriguing is that while Huang Kan used "enlightenment and sincerity," and Lo Ch'in-shun used "sincerity and enlightenment," Huang Tsung-hsi used both. That led me to suspect that the shift from the School of Principle in the Sung (960–1279) to the School of Mind in the Ming (1368–1644) was accompanied by a change from "enlightenment and sincerity" to "sincerity and enlightenment." In his rearrangement of the chapter order in the *Great Learning,* Chu Hsi put the chapter on the investigation of things ahead of the one on the sincerity of the will. Perhaps placing enlightenment ahead of sincerity in his prose-poem was a conscious reflection of the sequence in the *Great Learning.* Wang Yang-ming, however, strongly opposed Chu Hsi's arrangement and insisted on returning to the ancient version, in which sincerity precedes the investigation of things. That being the case, Wang should have used "sincerity and enlightenment," not "enlightenment and sincerity." But in Wang's *Ch'uan-hsi lu* (Instructions for practical living), after quoting "Given sincerity, there will be enlightenment, and given enlightenment, there will be sincerity" from the *Doctrine of the Mean,* he said that "enlightenment and sincerity mutually produce each other," not "sincerity and enlightenment produce each other."[62]

Since the two produce each other, it really does not matter which comes first. From the fact that Huang Tsung-hsi used both phrases, it is clear that the issue does not lie in the two but in nature and education. The *Doctrine of the Mean* says, "It is due to our nature that enlightenment results from sincerity. It is due to education that sincerity results from enlightenment."[63] In his commentary on this passage, Chu Hsi said, "The virtue of the sage is always substantial and his brilliance is always shining. These are within his nature. It is the way of Heaven. In the learning of the worthy, first he must understand what is good and then he can make the good substantial. He arrives through education. It is the way of man."[64]

This theory about the sage and the worthy came from Ch'eng I. In his "Treatise on What Yen Tzu Loved to Learn," Ch'eng I said, "In the learning of the superior man, the first thing is to be clear in one's mind and to know where to go, and then act vigorously in order that one may arrive at sagehood. This is what is meant by sincerity resulting from enlightenment. Therefore the student must exert his own mind to the utmost. If he does so, he will know his own nature, and if he knows his own nature, examines his own self, and makes it sincere, he becomes a sage."[65] However, Chu Hsi did not completely agree with Ch'eng I's interpretation of enlightenment and sincerity. To Ch'eng I, "Enlightenment means that one learns from the outside and gets the meaning inside, while sincerity is what one gets from the inside but also covers the outside. At bottom they are the same."[66] Ch'eng I also said, "The way of Confucius, when demonstrated in action as described in chapter 10 of the *Analects,* is enlightenment resulting from sincerity. When one learns to become Confucius by living according to this chapter, it is sincerity resulting from enlightenment. But their goals are the same."[67] Commenting on these statements, Chu Hsi said,

> Master Ch'eng's various theories were recorded by his pupils. To explain sincerity and enlightenment in terms of the inside and outside, and the way and action, does not seem to be to the point. Only the passage where it is said that the first thing is to be clear in one's mind—that is, to explain enlightenment in terms of knowledge and to explain sincerity in terms of action—is really his teaching. It is in the "Treatise on What Yen Tzu Loved to Learn" written by the Master himself.[68]

Chu Hsi strictly adhered to the teaching of the *Doctrine of the Mean,* which distinguishes nature and education. The sage becomes so by nature, whereas the task of the worthy is to learn. Both the sage and the worthy involve the inside and outside as well as the way and action, and therefore these cannot be perceived as the distinction between enlightenment and sincerity.

Chang Tsai (1020–1077) clearly distinguished nature and education. He said,

> We must know that there is a difference between going from sincerity to enlightenment and going from enlightenment to sincerity. In going from sincerity to enlightenment, one must first fulfill one's nature until principle is investigated. This means that one must first understand one's nature and then investigate principle. In going from enlightenment to sin-

cerity, one must first investigate principle to the utmost until nature is fulfilled. That means one must first understand through learning, and by
extension reach the nature bestowed by Heaven.[69]

Ch'eng I did not agree with this. When someone remarked to him, "I
am afraid it is going too far to say that one goes from enlightenment to
sincerity and from sincerity to enlightenment," Ch'eng I replied, "It is
correct to say that one could go from enlightenment to sincerity, but it is
wrong to say that one could go from sincerity to enlightenment, for sincerity is the same as enlightenment."[70] Commenting on this remark,
Chu Hsi said,

> When Master Chang separated nature and education as two different
> ways, he was talking about the process of learning and not about the dif-
> ferent levels of the sage and the worthy, and that was why he said one
> could proceed from sincerity to enlightenment. Although Master Ch'eng's
> criticism is all right, he did not go into the purpose of Master Chang's
> remark and was therefore mistaken. I am afraid that when he said that
> "Sincerity is the same as enlightenment," he was not free from error.[71]

Pupils of Ch'eng I differed in their interpretations of nature and education. To Lü Ta-lin (1046–1092),

> From sincerity to enlightenment means that one acts according to one's
> nature, while from enlightenment to sincerity means that one makes an
> effort to return to one's nature.[72] Acting according to one's nature refers
> to the completion of virtue. That is the nature of the sage. To return to
> nature refers to the intention to learn. That is the education of the worthy.
> The completion of virtue means to arrive at the point that is concrete and
> unchanging, from which all moral principles arise. All principles of the
> world, whatever the eye sees or the ear hears, will be known without delib-
> eration and understood without words. This is called "Given sincerity,
> there will be enlightenment." To intend to learn means to extend one's
> knowledge to investigate principles in the world to the utmost. Then all
> principles of the world will be understood and one will ultimately arrive at
> the point of being concrete and unchanging. One will then be extremely
> simple and easy and act as though there is nothing. This is what is meant
> by "Given enlightenment, there will be sincerity."[73]

To Yu Tso (1053–1123), "From sincerity to enlightenment means to
come from the self, and that is why it is called nature. From enlightenment to sincerity means to come from the outside, and therefore it may
be called education. Sincerity is based on nature, and therefore there is
always enlightenment, while the enlightened person cultivates a particular goodness, and therefore can attain sincerity." And to Yang Shih
(1053–1135), "From sincerity to enlightenment is the Way of Heaven,

and that is why it is called nature, while from enlightenment to sincerity is the way of man, and that is why it is called education. The ways of Heaven and man are the same, but where the mind is directed is different. However, in the end there is no diversity. Hence it is said, 'Given sincerity, there will be enlightenment, and given enlightenment, there will be sincerity.' "[74]

Since Yu Tso considered the matter from the aspects of the inside and outside and Yang Shih thought that sincerity and enlightenment were ultimately one, they were following Ch'eng I's doctrine in its essence. Nevertheless, Chu Hsi regarded them as not to the point. As he said,

> Lü Ta-lin was correct in the matters of nature and education, but in regarding sincerity as extremely simple and easy, and acting as if there is nothing, he seems not to have gotten the fundamental point. Furthermore, he talks about both nature and education arriving at the point of being concrete and unchanging, but "arriving at" does not describe nature, and "unchanging" does not amplify concreteness. However, he is far better than both Yu and Yang.[75]

Since Chu Hsi's emphasis was on investigating principle and fulfilling nature through watchfulness and care, naturally he did not approve of simplicity and easiness and acting as if there is nothing. On the point of being concrete and unchanging, however, his criticism seems to have gone too far, for more than once he himself asserted that principle is concrete and unchanging.

While firmly believing that a sage acts according to his nature, Chu Hsi's concern was chiefly with the learner, that is, the worthy. Thus his emphasis was on investigating principle and fulfilling nature. As he said, " 'Given enlightenment, there will be sincerity' is the result of giving it the fullest extension and development."[76] This refers to Mencius, who said, "All men have the Four Beginnings [of humanity, righteousness, propriety, and wisdom] and should know how to give them the fullest extension and development."[77]

Chu Hsi considered Ch'eng I's identification of sincerity with enlightenment to be wrong, but he did not explain himself. There is a conversation in the *Yü-lei* that may be taken as an answer. He said, "If we talk about enlightenment on the basis of sincerity, sincerity and enlightenment are combined as one. If we talk about sincerity on the basis of enlightenment, sincerity and enlightenment are separated as two."[78] This is the idea of "one is two and two are one." Therefore it is all right to say, as Ch'eng I did, that their destinations are the same; it is also all right to say, as Yang Shih did, that in the end there is no diversity. But to equate sincerity with enlightenment is to fail to distinguish between the sage and the worthy and between nature and education.

The fear is that the learner may tend to the side of sincerity and neglect the effort to proceed from enlightenment to sincerity. In the final analysis, the White Deer Hollow Academy was meant for the learner. That was why Chu Hsi put enlightenment ahead of sincerity in his prose-poem. But since sincerity and enlightenment are one-in-two and two-in-one, it is not surprising that Huang Tsung-hsi used both "enlightenment and sincerity" and "sincerity and enlightenment."

Wang Yang-ming also made the distinction between the sage and the worthy. He said,

> To be in accord with one's nature is the task of a sincere man. It is what is stated as "It is due to our nature that enlightenment results from sincerity." To cultivate the Way is the way of one who attains sincerity. It is what is stated as "It is due to education that sincerity results from enlightenment."[79] As the sage acts in accord with his nature, the Way obtains. People below the sage in moral qualities are not yet able to act in accord with the Way and at times deviate from the Mean. Therefore, they need to cultivate the Way. . . . Thus the Way is education.[80]

But since everyone has his innate knowledge of the good and can extend it, "If one does not deceive oneself, one's innate knowledge will have no falsehood and will be sincere. Given sincerity, there will be enlightenment. If one trusts oneself, one's innate knowledge will have no doubt and one will be enlightened. Given enlightenment, there will be sincerity."[81] In the final analysis, "If one is refined, one will be enlightened, single-minded, spiritual, and sincere, and if one is single-minded, one will be refined, enlightened, spiritual, and sincere. They are not two different things."[82] With Wang Yang-ming, sincerity and enlightenment are one, while with Chu Hsi they are one-in-two and two-in-one. The two men certainly differed on whether the chapter on investigation of things or that on sincerity of the will should come first in the *Great Learning*. It is no wonder they were also at odds with respect to enlightenment and sincerity.

## Knowledge and Action

On the relation of knowledge and action, or words and deeds, Chu Hsi adhered strictly to the Confucian tradition that they must correspond. The present study is not concerned with Chu Hsi's ideas about knowledge and action in general, but only with the way they anticipate Wang Yang-ming's doctrine of the unity of the two.

The *Yü-lei* records that a pupil asked, "Someone knows that it is this way, but in his action it is not this way. Why?" The Teacher said, "That is simply because his knowledge is not yet complete." Question: "Must he find out that all his acts are correct before he can verify his knowledge?" Answer: "You don't have to say it this way. If I say that your knowledge is not yet complete, you may not believe it. But suppose you devote your effort to investigating things and principles to the utmost, investigating again and again until finally realizing that this is good and that is evil, and are willing in your own heart not to do evil; only then can your will be sincere. If there is still the slightest doubt, it means your knowledge is not yet complete and you are not yet sincere, and after a long time you will do evil as usual. However, the learner cannot be like this [i.e., sincere] right away. He must extend his knowledge and accumulate his effort before his knowledge can be complete."[83] Here the emphasis is still on the attainment of complete knowledge. Yet Chu Hsi was careful not to say that knowledge must first be complete before the will can be sincere, for that would imply that the completion of knowledge and sincerity of the will are two different things. To him, if one knows but does not act, it is because one's knowledge is not yet complete. In this he anticipated Wang Yang-ming, who said, "There have never been people who know but do not act. Those who are supposed to know but do not act simply do not yet know."[84]

Chu Hsi said that it was not necessary to find out that all one's acts are correct in order to verify one's knowledge. Wang Yang-ming also said, "It is therefore necessary to talk about action to them before their knowledge becomes true. The ancient teachers could not help talking this way in order to restore balance and avoid defect."[85] Chu Hsi maintained that finally one realizes oneself that this is good and that is evil, and hence is willing in one's own heart not to do evil. He also said that one has to accumulate effort before one's knowledge can be complete, but that when one understands principle and attains complete knowledge, one's will will be sincere and one will naturally do good and avoid evil. He therefore said that one does not act simply because one's knowledge is not yet complete, but he did not say that one must find out that all one's acts are correct before one's knowledge becomes true. Wang Yang-ming also said, "The ordinary man is not free from the obstructions of selfish ideas. He therefore requires effort in the extension of knowledge and the investigation of things in order to overcome selfish ideas and restore principle. Then the mind's faculty of innate knowledge will no longer be obstructed and will be able to penetrate and operate everywhere. One's knowledge will then be extended. With knowledge extended, one's will becomes sincere."[86]

Chu Hsi's pupil Ch'en Ch'un (1159–1223) was even more explicit. In a letter to his own pupil, Ch'en Po-tsao, he said,

When I said that one can truly act if one truly knows, and that if one does not act diligently it is not the defect of action but the lack of relevance and truth of one's knowledge, I was being thorough about the investigation of things and wanted it related to action. . . . Essentially, in the ultimate sense, knowledge and action are in reality one thing, not two. Those who consider knowledge and action as two things, or either as more important or more urgent than the other, have not made a real effort that is relevant to the self; in short, they are superficial. He who has made a real effort to extend knowledge will in every instant of thought correspond with his action. If he knows but does not succeed in action, he will find out at every step what the obstacle is and will seek to know how to penetrate it. In that case, his knowledge will become more refined and his action more relevant. He who has made a real effort to act will correspond with his knowledge at every step. If he acts but does not know the reason why, his details must be negligent and will not conform to the established method of the sages and worthies. He must know the principle vividly before his eyes, and then his action will have no obstacle and his knowledge will be clear. . . . Knowledge and action always depend on each other and are not separated.[87]

He also said,

The essential points about one's effort do not go beyond the two tasks of extension of knowledge and diligence in action. The two tasks should be done together. They are not two distinct, different things—as if, after one extends knowledge, one can then act diligently; rather, they are the same task. He who knows truly will truly be able to act. If he does not act diligently, it is not the fault of his action but because his knowledge is not true and to the point. One must see the good just as one truly loves a beautiful color, and see evil just as one hates a bad smell. Only then can one's knowledge be called relevant, to the point, and complete. Then diligence in action is already in it.[88]

Wang Yang-ming said, "When only knowledge is mentioned, action is included."[89] Knowledge and action fit with each other like the two pieces of a tally.

Ch'eng I had said, "It is only difficult to know. . . . If one already knows, how can he fail to act?"[90] Commenting on this saying, Huang Tsung-hsi said, "Master I-ch'uan [Ch'eng I] already said that knowledge and action form a unity."[91] Chu Hsi went further than Ch'eng I, for Ch'eng I did not explain why knowledge and action are one, whereas Chu Hsi said that when one's knowledge is complete, one's will will be sincere, thus anticipating Wang Yang-ming. However, Wang's basic doctrine is that of innate knowledge. With innate knowledge, one will naturally act. One fails to act because one is obstructed by selfish desires—or, as Chu Hsi put it, one needs to make a special effort because one's natural endowment is partial. Thus, for Chu Hsi, the unity of knowledge and action is the result of effort, whereas for Wang, one is born to know and to act. Hence the peak of the doctrine of the unity of knowledge and action was not reached until Wang Yang-ming.

## The Four Beginnings and the Seven Feelings

This section is not strictly on the two-wheel pattern, though nature and feeling are indeed like two wheels of a vehicle or two wings of a bird. Instead, it is directed to the "four-seven" debate in Korea.

Chu Hsi said that the Four Beginnings (of humanity, righteousness, propriety, and wisdom)[92] are the expressions of principle, and that the seven feelings (of joy, anger, sorrow, fear, love, dislike, and desire)[93] are expressions of material force.[94] This led to a great debate in Korea that lasted for a long time. In his comments on Chŏng Ch'uman's (Chŏng Chiun) "Diagram of the Mandate of Heaven," Yi T'oegye (Yi Hwang, 1501–1570) quoted Chu Hsi's words and said that the Four Beginnings are all good but that the seven feelings are not definitely good or evil. His pupil Ki Kobong (Ki Taesŭng, 1527–1572) thought that, in so doing, T'oegye separated principle and material force in two. Thus the "four-seven" debate became a controversy over the unity or duality of principle and material force, and over their priority. Their dispute alone produced more than ten thousand words. Later, the debate was continued by Yi Yulgok (Yi I, 1536–1586) and others. The result was the most bitter confrontation in Korean Neo-Confucianism, far exceeding Chu Hsi's debate with Lu Hsiang-shan on the Great Ultimate, or with Ch'en Liang (1143–1194) on the issue of the sagely king and the powerful feudal lord. The period that the debate lasted was comparable to the long debate in the Ming and Ch'ing (1644–1911) dynasties over Wang Yang-ming's "Master Chu's Final Conclusions Arrived at Late in Life."

Neo-Confucians in Korea liked to oppose the seven feelings to the Four Beginnings, but that was not the case with Chinese Neo-Confucians. The two Ch'engs often talked about the Four Beginnings but seldom about the seven feelings. Although Wang Yang-ming talked about the seven feelings repeatedly in his Ch'uan-hsi lu, he did not oppose them to nature. Also, he talked about the perfect goodness of the original mind, but seldom about the Four Beginnings. Why did the traditions in the two countries differ in such a way? When Chu Hsi said that the Four Beginnings are the expressions of principle and that the seven feelings are expressions of material force, he definitely contrasted the seven feelings with the Four Beginnings, and it is obvious that the Korean "four-seven" debate can be traced to Chu Hsi. However, when Neo-Confucians in China talked about feelings, they always referred to the four feelings of joy, anger, sorrow, and pleasure in the *Doctrine of the Mean,* not the seven feelings mentioned in the "Evolution of Rites" of the *Book of Rites*. In addition, Chu Hsi talked often about the Four Beginnings but seldom about the seven feelings.

I believe the "four-seven" debate did not occur in Chinese Neo-Confucianism for two reasons. First, problems about nature and feelings such as those concerned with centrality (*chung*) and universality (*yung*), what has been aroused (*i-fa*) and what has not been aroused (*wei-fa*), and centrality (*chung*) and harmony (*ho*) are all derived from the first chapter of the *Doctrine of the Mean,* not from the "Evolution of Rites" chapter of the *Book of Rites*. Although the *Book of Rites* was one of the Six Classics[95] and the *Doctrine of the Mean* constitutes one of its chapters, the chapter began to assume importance only in the fifth century. Tai Yung (378–441) wrote the *Li-chi Chung-yung chuan* (Commentary on the *Doctrine of the Mean* chapter of the *Book of Rites*) in two chapters. Emperor Wu (*r.* 502–549) of the Liang dynasty wrote the *Chung-yung chiang-shu* (Explanation and commentary on the *Doctrine of the Mean*) in one chapter. Later, Li Ao (*fl.* 798) was the author of the *Chung-yung shuo* (Explanation of the *Doctrine of the Mean*) in one chapter, and his work on recovering one's nature was strongly influenced by the *Doctrine of the Mean*. When Chang Tsai went to see Fan Chung-yen (989–1052), Fan told him to study the *Doctrine of the Mean*.[96] By the time Chu Hsi grouped the *Great Learning,* the *Analects,* the *Book of Mencius,* and the *Doctrine of the Mean* as the Four Books in 1190, and wrote the *Chung-yung chang-chü* (Commentary on the *Doctrine of the Mean*), the *Chung-yung huo-wen* (Questions and answers on the *Doctrine of the Mean*), and the *Chung-yung chi-lüeh* (Selected commentaries on the *Doctrine of the Mean*), the tradition of the *Doctrine of the Mean* was firmly established in China. There was no such tradition in Korea, so the four feelings of the *Doctrine of the Mean* did not overwhelm the seven feelings of the *Book of Rites* in Korea.

Second, another tradition in China was that of matching. From the Han dynasty (206 B.C.–A.D. 220) on, the eight trigrams and the Five Agents[97] have been matched with many other sets of eight and five items. Therefore, Neo-Confucians liked to match the Four Beginnings with origination, flourishing, advantage, and firmness,[98] the four seasons, and so on. The seven feelings, however, are difficult to match. When Chu Hsi's pupil Liu Ch'i-fu (Liu Tzu-huan, 1217 *cs*) asked about matching the seven feelings with the Four Beginnings, Chu Hsi said, "Joy, anger, love, and dislike correspond to humanity and righteousness. Sorrow and fear belong to propriety. Desire has the quality of water and is therefore wisdom. I merely talk roughly in this way. The seven feeling are difficult to divide up."[99] Such matching is not only uneven but altogether too arbitrary. Another pupil commented, "The seven feelings are of course expressions of nature, but anger seems to come out of the sense of shame, and joy, anger, sorrow, and fear seem to come out of the sense of commiseration." Chu Hsi replied, "Where

have sorrow and fear come from? It seems they have come out of commiseration, for fear is also the extreme of alarm. But the seven feelings
cannot match the Four Beginnings, for they cut across them."¹⁰⁰ These
are the only two Chinese conversations concerning the Four Beginnings
and the seven feelings—a far cry from the Korean debate, which lasted
for almost a hundred years.

# Notes

1. *Wen-chi,* 33:2b, fourth letter in reply to Lü Po-kung (Lü Tsu-ch'ien).

2. *Ibid.,* 35:12b, second letter in reply to Liu Tzu-ch'eng. For the two sayings, see below, n. 5.

3. *Doctrine of the Mean,* ch. 27.

4. *Book of Changes,* commentary on the second hexagram, *k'un* (Earth,
female).

5. *I-shu* [Surviving works], 18:5b, in the *Erh-Ch'eng ch'üan-shu* [Complete
works of the two Ch'engs] (*SPPY* ed.).

6. *Wen-chi,* 63:19a, first letter in reply to Sun Ching-fu.

7. Wang Mao-hung, *Chu Tzu nien-p'u* [Chronological biography of Master
Chu] (*Ts'ung-shu chi-ch'eng* [Collection of series] ed.), *k'ao-i* [Investigation into
variants], ch. 1, p. 269.

8. See ch. 15 above.

9. See ch. 17 below.

10. See my *A Source Book in Chinese Philosophy* (Princeton, N.J.: Princeton
University Press, 1963), pp. 583–584.

11. *Book of Changes,* "Appended Remarks," pt. 1, ch. 1.

12. For an account of the meeting at the Goose Lake Temple, see ch. 26
below; the *Hsiang-shan ch'üan-chi* [Complete works of Lu Hsiang-shan] (*SPPY*
ed.), 34:24a–b, "Recorded Sayings," 36:8b–9b, "Chronological Biography";
and the discussion on the meeting in my *Chu-hsüeh lun-chi* [Studies on Chu Hsi]
(Taipei: Student Book Co., 1982), pp. 233–249.

13. *Wen-chi,* 54:5b–6a, second letter in reply to Hsiang P'ing-fu (Hsiang
An-shih).

14. *Hsiang-shan ch'üan-chi,* 36:11b, "Chronological Biography."

15. This saying also appears in the *Analects,* 2:11.

16. *Doctrine of the Mean,* ch. 27.

17. Chu Hsi, *Chung-yung chang-chü* [Commentary on the *Doctrine of the Mean*],
comment on ch. 27.

18. *Ibid.*

19. *Yü-lei,* ch. 64, sec. 131 (p. 2517).

20. *Ibid.,* sec. 150 (p. 2522).

21. *Analects,* 13:19.

22. *Ibid.,* 15:5.

23. *Yü-lei,* ch. 118, sec. 88 (p. 4568).

24. *Ibid.,* ch. 64, sec. 153 (p. 2524).

25. *Ibid.* sec. 155 (p. 2524).

26. *Ibid.,* sec. 152 (p. 2523).

27. *Ibid.*, sec. 140 (p. 2519).

28. *Ibid.*, sec. 151 (p. 2523), sec. 148 (p. 2521). See also Chu Hsi, *Chung-yung huo-wen* [Questions and answers on the *Doctrine of the Mean*] (*Chin-shih han-chi ts'ung-kan* [Chinese works in the recent period] ed.) pp. 48b–49a (p. 96–97).

29. *Ibid.*, sec. 159 (p. 2526).

30. *Ibid.*, sec. 149 (p. 2521). Also *Wen-chi*, 74:21a–b, "Yü-shan Lecture."

31. *Ibid.*, sec. 150 (p. 2522).

32. *Ibid.*, ch. 118, sec. 88 (p. 4569).

33. *Ibid.*, ch. 64, sec. 158 (p. 2525).

34. *Ibid.*, sec. 154 (p. 2524).

35. *Ibid.*, sec. 149 (p. 2521).

36. *Wen-chi*, 47:24a, twenty-fourth letter in reply to Lü Tzu-yüeh (Lü Tsu-chien).

37. *Yü-lei*, ch. 64, sec. 149 (p. 2522).

38. *Ibid.*, sec. 132 (p. 2517).

39. *Ibid.*, sec. 152 (p. 2523).

40. Yü-shan was a county in Kiangsi Province. For the Yü-shan lecture, see ch. 23 below.

41. *Wen-chi*, 74:21a–b, "Yü-shan Lecture."

42. *Yü-lei*, ch. 117, sec. 44 (p. 4504).

43. *Ibid.*, ch. 114, sec. 25 (p. 4397).

44. *Wen-chi*, 37:9b–10a, letter to Wang Kuei-ling (Wang Shih-p'eng).

45. *Yü-lei*, ch. 24, sec. 17 (pp. 918–919).

46. *Ibid.*, ch. 64, sec. 155 (p. 2524).

47. *Ibid.*, sec. 158 (p. 2525).

48. See nn. 1–2, above.

49. *Yü-lei*, ch. 64, sec. 149 (2522).

50. *Wu Wen-che'ng Kung ch'üan-chi* [Complete works of Wu Ch'eng] 1756 ed.), 22:1b, "Account of the Studio of Honoring the Moral Nature and Following the Path of Inquiry and Study."

51. Wang Yang-ming's "Master Chu's Final Conclusions Arrived at Late in Life" is appended to the end of his *Ch'uan-hsi lu* [Instructions for practical living], in the *Wang Wen-ch'eng Kung ch'üan-shu* [Complete works of Wang Yang-ming] (*SPPY* ed.). For an English translation of Wang's preface to the "Final Conclusions," see my *Instructions for Practical Living* (New York: Columbia University Press, 1963), pp. 264–267. See also ch. 27 below.

52. *Sung-Yüan hsüeh-an* [Anthology and critical accounts of Neo-Confucians of the Sung and Yüan dynasties] (*SPPY* ed.), 58:2a, chapter on Lu Hsiang-shan.

53. *Ibid.*, 58:3a.

54. *Wen-chi*, 1:2b, prose-poem for the White Deer Hollow Academy.

55. *Doctrine of the Mean*, ch. 21.

56. *I-shu*, 5:2b.

57. *Yü-lei*, ch. 95, sec. 141 (p. 3891). On "Master Ch'eng," see ch. 19 below, section on "Ch'eng Tzu" p. 293 ff.

58. See above, n. 4.

59. *Mien-chai chi* [Collected works of Huang Kan] (*Ssu-k'u ch'üan-shu chen-pen* [Precious works of the *Complete Collection of the Four Libraries*] ed.), 17:7a, letter to Huang Ch'ing-ch'ing.

60. Lo Ch'in-shun, *K'un-chih chi* [Knowledge painfully acquired] (1528 ed.), 1:9a, 16a, 35b.

61. *Ming-ju hsüeh-an* [Anthology and critical accounts of the Neo-Confucians of the Ming dynasty] (*SPPY* ed), 1:1a, 2a, chapter on Wu Yü-pi.

62. *Ch'uan-hsi lu,* sec. 171 (*Instructions for Practical Living,* p. 157).

63. *Doctrine of the Mean,* ch. 21.

64. *Chung-yung chang-chü,* comment on ch. 21.

65. *I-ch'uan wen-chi* [Collection of literary works of Ch'eng I], 4:1a, in the *Erh-Ch'eng ch'üan-shu.* Yen Hui was Confucius' favorite pupil. Confucius once remarked that Yen Hui loved to learn more than anyone else. See *Analects,* 6:2.

66. *I-shu,* 25:2a.

67. *Ibid.,* 25:6b.

68. *Chung-yung huo-wen,* p. 41a (p. 85).

69. *Chang Tzu yü-lu* [Recorded sayings of Master Chang Tsai] (*SPTK* ed.), pt. 3, p. 6b. The passage is also found in the *Chang Tzu ch'üan-shu* [Complete works of Master Chang Tsai] (*SPPY* ed.), 12:7a, selected sayings. It is also found in an abbreviated form in Chang Tsai's *Cheng-meng* [Correcting youthful ignorance], ch. 8, "Sincerity and Enlightenment."

70. *I-shu,* 23:3a.

71. See above, n. 68.

72. For acting according to one's nature and returning to one's nature, see the *Book of Mencius,* 7B:33.

73. Both quotations are from the *Doctrine of the Mean,* ch. 23.

74. The theories of Lü Ta-lin, Yu Tso, and Yang Shih are quoted in the *Chung-yung huo-wen,* 2:54a, in the *Ssu-shu ta-ch'üan* [Great collection of commentaries on the Four Books] (*Ssu-k'u ch'üan-shu chen-pen* ed.).

75. *Yü-lei,* ch. 64, sec. 43 (p. 2489).

76. *Ibid.,* ch. 64, sec. 44 (p. 2489).

77. *Book of Mencius,* 2A:6, where Mencius taught that "the feeling of commiseration is the beginning of humanity, the feeling of shame and dislike is the beginning of righteousness, the feeling of deference and compliance is the beginning of propriety, and the feeling of right and wrong is the beginning of wisdom."

78. *Yü-lei,* ch. 64, sec. 46 (p. 2489). For "one is two and two are one," see ch. 19 below, section on *"I-erh-erh, erh-erh-i,"* p. 311 ff.

79. Both quotations are from the *Doctrine of the Mean,* ch. 21.

80. *Ch'uan-hsi lu,* sec. 127 (*Instructions for Practical Living,* p. 84).

81. *Ibid.,* sec. 171 (*Instructions for Practical Living,* pp. 156–157).

82. *Ibid.,* sec. 153 (*Instructions for Practical Living,* p. 133).

83. *Yü-lei,* ch. 15, sec. 100 (pp. 482–483).

84. *Ch'uan-hsi lu,* sec. 5 (*Instructions for Practical Living,* p. 10).

85. *Ibid.,* (*Instructions for Practical Living,* p. 11).

86. *Ibid.,* sec. 8 (*Instructions for Practical Living,* p. 15).

87. *Pei-hsi ta-ch'üan-chi* [Complete collected works of Ch'en Ch'un] (*Ssu-k'u ch'üan-shu chen-pen* ed.), 28:7b–9b, letter to Ch'en Po-tsao.

88. *Ibid.,* 26:1b, letter in reply to Ch'en Po-tsao.

89. *Ch'uan-hsi lu,* sec. 5 (*Instructions for Practical Living,* p. 11).

90. *I-shu,* 17:5b–6a.

91. *Sung-Yüan hsüeh-an,* 15:9b, chapter on Ch'eng I.

92. *Book of Mencius,* 2A:2. See also n. 77 above.

93. *Li chi* [Book of rites], "Li-yün" [Evolution of rites], sec. 23.

94. *Yü-lei,* ch. 53, sec. 83 (p. 2060).

95. The Six Classics are the *Book of Odes,* the *Book of History,* the *Book of Changes,* the *Book of Rites,* the *Book of Music,* and the *Spring and Autumn Annals.* The *Book of Music* was lost before the third century B.C. and was replaced by the *Chou-li* (Book of Chou) during the Sung dynasty (960–1279).

96. *Chang Tzu ch'üan-shu,* 15:11a, "Biographical account."

97. The eight trigrams are eight combinations of continuous and broken lines that represent cosmological elements. The Five Agents (or Five Elements) are Metal, Wood, Water, Fire, and Earth.

98. These are the Four Qualities of the first hexagram, *ch'ien* (Heaven, male) in the *Book of Changes.*

99. *Yü-lei,* ch. 87, sec. 87 (p. 3559).

100. *Ibid.,* sec. 85 (p. 3558).

# – 17 –

# Chu Hsi and
# Quiet-sitting

W E do not have enough data to determine how often Chu Hsi practiced quiet-sitting, but it is safe to assume that he practiced it
often. In the *Yü-lei* there are two cases on record of his actually practicing quiet-sitting. Once he told a pupil, "After I read, I always sit quietly."[1] He told another pupil, "Although after quiet-sitting I have
understood principle, still I have not yet understood the way of moral
cultivation."[2] In the *Wen-chi*, we find three instances of actual quiet-sitting. In answer to a friend, he said in a letter, "Because of my poor eye-
sight, I dare not devote much energy to reading books. When I practice
quiet-sitting at leisure to collect my body and mind, it seems fairly effec-
tive."[3] To another friend, he wrote, "This year I suddenly feel weak
and tired, different from normal times. A hundred illnesses attack
simultaneously, leaving me no time even to speak haltingly. Medicine
shows no effect, either. I feel better only after one or two days of quiet-
sitting with no reading."[4] And he told his pupil Ts'ai Yüan-ting (1135–
1198), "I have recently felt that reading wears down my mind and eyes.
It is better to sit quietly to introspect. Please try it and you will see the
result."[5] These were not necessarily the only occasions when he practiced quiet-sitting. Daily activities like eating and sleeping generally go
unrecorded. Besides Chu Hsi said that he "always" sat quietly after
reading.

If Chu Hsi found quiet-sitting to be beneficial to himself, he probably
thought it beneficial as a matter of principle, although here it is difficult
to generalize. Once he told his students, "When you have time and do a
little quiet-sitting, there is no harm."[6] To pupil Huang Hsün (1147–
1212), he was more positive, teaching him "not to engage in thought
during illness but to leave everything alone and devote one's attention
solely to preserving the mind and nourishing the vital force. Merely

cross your legs and sit quietly, with your eyes on the tip of your nose, and concentrate your mind below the navel and the belly. In time you will feel warm, and gradually you will see the result."[7] When a Taoist priest built a library, Chu Hsi urged him to "learn quiet-sitting and read old texts at leisure."[8] However, when a pupil asked him if one's task includes quiet-sitting, he answered, "There are those who do not approve of quiet-sitting. For example, people like Kao-lao [Ta-hui P'u-chüeh Ch'an-shih, 1089–1163] strongly declared that meditation is wrong." The pupil said, "At present, when a student engages in meditation to the point of falling asleep, his mind is to a large extent calm." Chu Hsi replied, "It is no good to fall asleep."[9] There is no contradiction here, Chu Hsi was not commenting on whether or not quiet-sitting itself is good. Rather, he was giving advice to pupils according to their needs, very much like a physician prescribing different medicines for different illnesses.

His instructions to one of his pupils have caused a great deal of misunderstanding and controversy. The pupil was Kuo Yu-jen, whose courtesy name was Te-yüan; he was a native of Shan-yang County[10] in Ch'u-chou Prefecture in Kiangsu but a resident of Lin-an in Chekiang. There is no biographical data about him in books on Chu Hsi's pupils; the *Sung-Yüan hsüeh-an* (Anthology and critical accounts of the Neo-Confucians of the Sung and Yüan dynasties) does not even mention him except in its supplement, where Wang Tzu-ts'ai (1792–1851) added a brief comment that says, "The *Chu Tzu yü-lei* recorded that the Master [Kuo Yu-jen] has recorded: 'Question: You, my friend, formerly studied with Tseng Ta-ch'ing. What were his theories?', etc. Tseng Ta-ch'ing refers to Tseng Yüan-po, whose courtesy name was Nung-ch'ing."[11] Wang's research is generally most original and authoritative, but he is mistaken here. Sections 15 to 29 in chapter 118 of the *Yü-lei* are all Chu Hsi's instructions to Cheng K'o-hsüeh (1152–1212). The question in section 28 was addressed to Cheng, not to Kuo. Wang was misled because section 30 was recorded by Kuo. This oversight shows that information about Kuo is almost nonexistent.

For Kuo, we have to rely exclusively on the *Yü-lei*. There are eight sections, sections 48 to 55 in chapter 116, that are instructions to Kuo. One section says, "Your desire for the Way is very strong, and you have studied Ch'an [Meditation] Buddhism. . . . Since you have not studied literature extensively, you must get at the essentials of propriety. You have not devoted your efforts to investigating principle to the utmost. . . . You, Te-yüan, have understood principle in a vague way, but regrettably you have not read much. . . . You must now devote strenuous effort to reading books."[12] Another section says, "Sir, don't be in a hurry. Read only a small paragraph. If you don't get the point today, read it again tomorrow, and if you don't get it tomorrow, read it the day after tomorrow."[13] Most of the eight sections are devoted to how to read. The Teacher also said, "Sir, you must carefully understand every bit in detail. Don't be abrupt like this."[14] Again, "The reader should bury himself in the book. Whether he walks or stands still, sits down or lies down, his mind should be on it. He vows to understand it thoroughly. He is not concerned with anything outside; his mind is directed only to the book. Only then can he be considered skillful in reading."[15] Thus Chu Hsi taught Kuo how to concentrate. When Kuo came to say goodbye, he told him,

> If one refrains every day from saying one or two unnecessary words or seeing one or two fewer unnecessary guests, it will be helpful. If one's person is immersed in din and bustle, how can one read? If one is not bothered with affairs every day and is assured of one's daily food, if one devotes half a day to quiet-sitting and half a day to reading books, what worry is there that one will not improve in one or two years?[16]

Chu Hsi had many pupils, and he knew most of them intimately. He knew their backgrounds and their idiosyncrasies. For Kuo Yu-jen, his advice was to concentrate and read books. This contrasts sharply with his words to another pupil, Yang Tao-fu:

> Chung-ssu [courtesy name of Tao-fu], earlier you said that one should sit quietly and concentrate like the Buddha, sitting like an earthen idol doing nothing, and only then will it be all right. Our learning is precisely the opposite. When there is nothing to do, sit quietly. When there are books to read, then read. As to dealing with people and handling affairs, always keep your mind alert. That is the preservation of the mind. How can one leave all things alone and merely sit quietly?[17]

The instructions to both Kuo and Yang are to concentrate. But in one case the concentration takes place while handling affairs, and in the other while practicing quiet-sitting. The emphasis is different because their personalities were different.

Yen Yüan (1635–1704) reacted negatively to Chu Hsi's prescription of quiet-sitting for half a day and reading for half a day, maintaining that "Master Chu's quiet-sitting for half of the day means to be Bodhidharma [*fl.* c. 460–534], and his reading for half a day means to be scholars of the Han dynasty [206 B.C.–A.D. 220]. Let us ask: In the twelve time periods of the day, when is the moment for one to be like Yao, Shun, the Duke of Chou, and Confucius? Those who have followed Chu Hsi should think it over."[18] Seldom has an outstanding Chinese thinker twisted the facts to this extent. Chu Hsi only instructed Kuo Yu-jen to follow this schedule, not all his pupils. Even in his advice to Kuo, he told him to sit half the day and read the other half only when there was nothing else to do. Chu Hsi never meant to imply that people should cease dealing with their daily affairs in order to concentrate on quiet-sitting and reading books. But Yen Yüan suggested that Chu Hsi had indeed meant to imply this. Yen also asserted that by quiet-sitting Chu Hsi meant sitting facing a wall for a long time, as Bodhidharma did, and that by reading books he meant reading philological explanations, such as those that the Han scholars studied, to the total neglect of the worldly affairs to which sages like Yao, Shun, the Duke of Chou, and Confucius were devoted. Actually, Yen Yüan did not believe all this. His *Chu Tzu yü-lei p'ing* (Critique of the *Classified Conversations of Master Chu*) shows that he scrutinized Chu Hsi's work minutely. It was because he advocated a practical philosophy, in vehement revolt against the rationalism of Neo-Confucianism, that he purposely twisted the facts to attack Chu Hsi.

In their revolt against tradition over the last fifty years, Chinese intellectuals have loved to quote Yen Yüan when criticizing Chu Hsi. Professor Ch'ien Mu, however, regards Yen Yüan as having failed to read carefully:

In the *Yü-lei* there is only this one section mentioning quiet-sitting for half a day and reading books for half a day. But this was what Master Chu told Kuo Te-yüan himself, saying that if there is nothing to do and one is assured of one's daily food, it is all right to read books for half a day and sit quietly for half a day at home. After a year or two there will be progress. By then one should proceed to another task. Master Chu never taught people to close their doors at home and spend half a day sitting quietly and half a day reading books. Neither did he teach Kuo Te-yüan always to spend half a day sitting quietly and half a day reading. There is an essay entitled "Tu kao Kuo Yu-yen yü" [On reading what was told Kuo Yu-jen] in the *Lu Chia-shu wen-chi* [Collection of literary works of Lu Lung-chi]. It says that Yu-jen had studied Ch'an Buddhism, so that his record [of what Chu Hsi taught him] was probably not entirely correct. It also says that Ch'en Chi-t'ing [Ch'en Lung-cheng, 1585–1645] was the first to consider the two sayings as Master Chu's formula for teaching people. Now, in his *K'un hsüeh chi* [Records of painful learning], Kao Ching-i [Kao P'an-lung, 1562–1626] said that in a boat on the way to Chieh-yang,[19] he himself established strict rules and set aside half a day for quiet-sitting and half a day for reading. This was what he did on board for two months. In his "Tu-shu shuo" [Treatise on reading books], Liu Ch'i-shan [Liu Tsung-chou, 1578–1645] said, "Grand Master Chu once said, 'If a student devotes half a day to quiet-sitting and half a day to reading, in three or five years there will surely be impressive progress.' We should take this to be our model." All these events took place in the late Ming [1368–1644]. Yen Yüan did not go into the matter deeply enough and singled out these eight words to criticize Master Chu. This is a case of not reading books [carefully].[20]

Professor Ch'ien is too kind in describing Yen Yüan as "not reading books." In reality, Yen was quite familiar with Chu Hsi's works. His *Chu Tzu yü-lei p'ing* was intended primarily to attack Chu Hsi; therefore he was willing to lift Chu Hsi's saying out of context and take what Chu Hsi taught one person at one time as his regular formula. It may be argued that even before Yen Yüan's time, Ch'en Lung-cheng had misunderstood Chu Hsi's eight words as a standard teaching. However, Ch'en included an important condition, as did Chu Hsi—namely, to follow the regimen only when one is at leisure. He said, "Wen Kung [Chu Hsi] raised the point of quiet-sitting for half a day and reading for half a day. This is, of course, an important method of learning. However, only when one has nothing to attend to may one practice this. While in office or at home, it is difficult to fulfil this wish completely."[21] Although Ch'en and Yen both quoted Chu Hsi out of context, their attitudes were quite different. Ch'en's was one of admiration, while Yen's aimed chiefly at attack. Generally speaking, Ming Neo-Confucians honored Chu Hsi. This can be seen in Ch'ien Mu's references to Kao P'an-lung and Liu Tsung-chou.

Kao P'an-lung said, "In the autumn of *chia-wu* [1594], I went to Chieh-yang. . . . On board the boat I laid up a thick mat and quilt and set up strict rules. I devoted half a day to quiet-sitting and half a day to reading. . . . In the two months en route, fortunately there were no mundane affairs, but both mountain and river were clear and beautiful and master and servants clung to one another."[22] His "Recorded Sayings" also notes, "Master Chu said that if a student devotes half a day to quiet-sitting and half a day to reading, in three years he will never lack progress. I have experimented with this for one or two months, and what a difference!"[23] Chu Hsi's "one or two years" has become "three years" in Kao P'an-lung's account, which may have been merely a printing error. But in interpreting Chu Hsi's instructions for one pupil at one time as a regular teaching, Kao falsified Chu Hsi's idea. Kao not only accepted the formula as ideal for himself; he also advocated it for others.[24]

Liu Tsung-chou, too, considered it beneficial first to achieve a good effect in quiet-sitting and then to read. He said, "Grand Master Chu once said, 'If a student devotes half a day to quiet-sitting and half a day to reading, in three or five years there will surely be impressive progress.' We should take this to be our model. However, aside from the effort at quiet-sitting, there is no other way to read. Therefore, in reality they are not two different procedures."[25] Kao had extended the time to three years; Liu now extended it to three or five years. No wonder Yen Yüan compared the practice to Bodhidharma's facing the wall for a long time.

Lu Chia-shu (Lu Lung-chi, 1630–1693) went in a different direction;

he contended that the record was wrong. He wrote an essay entitled "On Reading What Was Told Kuo Yu-jen" in which he said, "My humble comment: Te-yüan once studied Ch'an. The saying was recorded by him. I am afraid he was not correct."[26] Following this remark, Lu cited two of Chu Hsi's letters to show that Chu Hsi taught seriousness (*ching,* reverence) but not quiet-sitting. Lu continued,

> I therefore say that what Te-yüan recorded was probably wrong. Ch'en Chi-t'ing was in error in considering these two sayings as Master Chu's method of teaching. . . . When did Ch'eng [Ch'eng I, 1033–1107] and Chu refrain from talking about tranquillity? However, we should remember that while Ch'eng and Chu did not refrain from talking about tranquillity, they never limited it to half a day. Furthermore, what they meant by tranquillity referred to seriousness, not to the tranquillity of Ch'an.

Surely Chu Hsi never limited seriousness to half a day, and surely Neo-Confucian tranquillity and seriousness are quite different from Ch'an meditation. But to say that Kuo Yu-jen's record was wrong is a feeble attempt at whitewashing. There is absolutely no need for that. The point is that Yen Yüan was wrong in turning what Chu Hsi told one pupil into a regular formula in order to attack Chu Hsi's teaching. There is no denying that Chu Hsi practiced quiet-sitting himself and taught his pupils quiet-sitting. But he enunciated no special doctrine on the subject and prescribed no particular formula.

The earlier reference to concentration on the tip of the nose may suggest that Chu Hsi was recommending a Taoist or Buddhist technique of meditation. Taoist or Buddhist influence on the Neo-Confucian practice of quiet-sitting cannot be denied. There is no hint, however, that Chu Hsi preferred any particular posture or procedure. From all his comments on the subject, we may say that he required two conditions—spontaneity, and reading books. When a pupil asked him about the method in one's effort at quiet-sitting, he said, "Quiet-sitting is simply quiet-sitting, without any unnecessary bother or thought. There is no method to speak of." Question: "During quiet-sitting, when one thinks of one thing, one's mind is attached to that thing. If one does not think, then the mind has nothing to attach to. How about that?" Answer: "There is no need for attachment. If so, it would be like the Taoist counting each inhalation and exhalation and directing his eyes to the shining tip of the nose. That is because his mind has nothing to abide by and therefore requires such an attachment. If one cannot cut off thought, one might as well leave the matter alone. There will be no harm."[27] Another pupil wanted particularly to engage in quiet-sitting. Chu Hsi admonished him "not to fall on that side. The only important point is that the mind must be open and free."[28] In other words, the mind should not be attached to anything but must be completely free and spontaneous.

One pupil acquired the habit of quiet-sitting and became tired of reading books. Chu Hsi warned him, "You should not go on like that. You should allow yourself some leisure. Still you must read."[29] This was why Chu Hsi advised Kuo Yu-jen to spend half a day on quiet-sitting and half a day on reading. In his opinion, quiet-sitting and reading were to be regarded as one task. He said,

> There are times when we sit quietly without any thought and there are times when we think of principles. How can we divide them into two paths and say that the task of quiet-sitting and the task of reading books are entirely different? . . . The defect of people today lies precisely in the fact that the task of quiet-sitting and the task of book reading are not unified. That is their mistake.[30]

Although the two tasks are emphasized equally, Chu Hsi seems to give priority to quiet-sitting. In reply to his friend Chou Shen-fu, he said, "If people want to read books, they must first collect their bodies and minds so that they become somewhat tranquil and peaceful before opening the books. Only then will it be beneficial. . . . Suppose you close your door and sit up straight, and after half a month or ten days you then begin to read books. You will believe that my words are not wrong."[31]

According to Chu Hsi, if one is skilful at quiet-sitting, it can, on the one hand, support one's effort at cultivation and on the other, help one understand principle. Once he told a pupil,

> Formerly, Master Ch'en Lieh suffered from poor memory. One day, when he read the passage from the *Book of Mencius* that says, "The way of learning is none other than finding the lost mind,"[32] he suddenly came to a realization and said, "I have not collected my mind. How can I remember?" Thereupon he closed his door and sat quietly without reading for more than a hundred days to collect his lost mind. He then went to read and totally understood without missing anything.[33]

On the subject of tranquillity, Chu Hsi said, "Only through quiet-sitting can one collect."[34] On the *ch'ien* (Heaven, male) hexagram[35] as the nature and feeling of Heaven, he said, "It is like a strong person. Although he sits quietly here, he is concentrated and is about to do something."[36] On Chang Tsai's (1020–1077) famous sayings, "At every moment something should be nourished, and in every instant something should be preserved,"[37] Chu Hsi said, "Although one may sit quietly, there must be the master to preserve before one can succeed. Otherwise one merely sits like an idol."[38] In these ways, collecting con-

centration, preservation, and nourishment all roll into one. Consequently, "With quiet-sitting, the source is stable and calm,"[39] and
"When quiet-sitting is free from unnecessary and mixed thought, one's
mind will be nourished healthily and smoothly."[40]

In a letter to a pupil, Chu Hsi said, "If one cannot avoid deliberation
while quiet-sitting, it means that one is not serious while quiet-sitting."[41] Thus quiet-sitting is also helpful to seriousness. As he said,
"People nowadays are not willing to try to understand the foundation.
Take seriousness. They only talk about it but do not practice it. Since
the foundation is not established, the other miscellaneous efforts do not
fall into place. . . . As we see it, one must practice quiet-sitting."[42] The
task of abiding in seriousness, he said, "consists only of collecting one's
mind in a general way and never letting it dissipate. When one investigates principle to the utmost in a refined manner, one's thought will
naturally not be active in a foolish way. All one does will be in accord
with the correct principle. In that case, why should abiding in seriousness necessarily be quiet-sitting like an idol?"[43]

If quiet-sitting is helpful to moral cultivation, it is also helpful to the
understanding of principle. Chu Hsi said, "One must have personal
experience in quiet-sitting before one can see the operation of the four
seasons and the beginning and end of all things."[44] He also said,
"When one is at leisure after reading, let him sit quietly to enable his
mind to be at peace and his vital force to be calm. He will gradually
understand principle."[45] A pupil once remarked that after sitting quietly and reading books, one arrives at the harmony of moral principles,
but after dealing with worldly things, moral principles seem strange,
and asked why this happens. To this, Chu Hsi just said, "You are simply not familiar with them."[46] To say that unless one avoids deliberation
one is not serious does not imply that one ought to avoid thought altogether, but only any thought that disturbs the mind. To avoid thought
altogether would be to act like an earthen idol, and that is not quiet-sitting. A pupil asked, "Every day when I am at leisure, I practice quiet-
sitting a little bit to nourish my mind, but I feel ideas naturally arising
in profusion. The more I want to be quiet, the more disquiet I become."
Chu Hsi answered, "Master Ch'eng [Ch'eng I] said that the mind is an
active thing.[47] How can it be stagnant and not think? The only thing is
not to think recklessly."[48] When Chu Hsi asked a pupil how he applied
his effort, the pupil replied, "I try to practice quiet-sitting and energetically suppress deliberative thought." The Teacher commented, "It will
not do to energetically suppress deliberative thought. Just let it go. If
one closes one's eyes and sits quietly, that means one still has deliberation." He added, "Not that there should be no thought whatsoever;
only no perverse thought."[49]

In addition to moral cultivation and understanding of principle, one must practice earnestly. This is a strong Confucian tradition for which quiet-sitting is merely a means. Someone asked: "After quiet-sitting for a long time, a thought inevitably arises. What should be done?" Answer: "It depends on the kind of work you are thinking of. If it is good and should be done, you must do it. If you have not thought it out, you must think it over thoroughly. If the thing should not be done, you must not do it."[50] Chu Hsi said,

> Since one is a human being, one must devote oneself to serving one's ruler and parents, associating with friends, giving comfort to wife and children, and directing servants. It will not do to give all this up, shut the door, sit quietly, and, when things happen, refrain from dealing with them, say "Wait for me to sit quietly," and not respond. Nor will it do to run after things in a confused manner. One must consider and make a decision between the two. Only then will it do. It is precisely here that one should devote one's effort.[51]

He also said, "One must penetrate and understand the ten thousand changes, and one's mind must always be clear on them. One must not close the door and sit quietly and hold onto oneself rigidly. When things happen, one must go forward to respond."[52] In short, "When there is nothing to do, practice quiet-sitting. When things occur, deal with them. One's body and mind must operate at all times and in all places."[53]

Although there seems to be an implication here that meditation takes precedence over action, Chu Hsi held that there is activity in tranquillity and action while sitting down. Question: "If in one's early stage of learning one's spirit is easily dissipated, how about quiet-sitting?" Answer: "This is also good. However, one should not concentrate one's effort on tranquillity. Activity, too, must be personally realized. Is the teaching of the sages and worthies entirely on meditation? One must devote one's effort wherever it may be, such as reading books, associating with people, and dealing with things. One's mind must be there, whether in activity or tranquillity, in speech or in silence."[54]

From the above, it is clear that the quiet-sitting Chu Hsi talked about is radically different from Ch'an meditation. Someone asked: "Regardless of quiet-sitting or dealing with things, should one concentrate?" Answer: "Quiet-sitting is not like Buddhist meditation, cutting off all thought. It is merely to collect the mind so it will not run after unnecessary thoughts. The mind will then be clear and free. It will naturally be concentrated. When things happen, one responds as they come. When things are over, the mind will again be clear and free."[55] Again, "The Buddhist concentration and meditation is to sit alone like an idol, with no response to anything. Only then will it be good. Our learning is the

exact opposite of this. Sit quietly when there is nothing to do. Read
when there is reading to do. In dealing with things and handling affairs,
always direct the mind to be alert. This means having presence of mind.
Why should one leave all things alone and only sit quietly?"[56] Someone
asked: "When one is tired, is it all right to sit quietly for a little while?"
Answer: "It is not necessary to meditate like a Ch'an Buddhist before it
can be considered quiet-sitting. It is enough just to let loose and be calm
in your thought."[57] Furthermore, Buddhist meditation is for its own
sake. "If you have nothing to do now, of course one may be quiet in
meditation. But if one purposely engages in quiet-sitting as a special
task, that would be Buddhist meditation."[58]

Where did Chu Hsi's doctrine of quiet-sitting originate? The natural
assumption is that it came from the Buddhist teaching of meditation, for
in his teens and early twenties, Chu Hsi was attracted to Ch'an Buddhism and had contacts with the Ch'an patriarch Ta-hui (1089–1163)
and his disciple Tao-ch'ien. The details of that story are given elsewhere.[59] Their brand of Ch'an Buddhism aimed at sudden enlightenment through *hua-t'ou* or catchwords, that is, a word or a phrase, however irrelevant or illogical, that could arouse the mind to intuit truth.
They did not approve of rigid meditation. Chu Hsi eventually rejected
Buddhism, inspired to do so by Li T'ung (1093–1163).

In 1153, Chu Hsi went to see Li T'ung at Yen-p'ing[60] on his way to
assume office as *chu-pu* (assistant magistrate) at T'ung-an in southern
Fukien. Chu Hsi was then twenty-four. Instead of Buddhist meditation,
which requires cessation of all activities, Li taught the Confucian doctrine of tranquillity. More specifically, he taught students to sit quietly
and see the disposition before the feelings of pleasure, anger, sorrow,
and joy have been aroused.[61] Chu Hsi did not accept without reserva-
tion the specific doctrine of practicing quiet-sitting to see the disposition
before the feelings are aroused. According to the *Yü-lei,* someone asked:
"Recently Liao Tzu-hui [Liao Te-ming, 1169 *cs*] said that this year he
saw your inquiry about Master Yen-p'ing's [Li T'ung] doctrine of
quiet-sitting, and that you disagreed to some extent. How about it?"
Chu Hsi replied,

This is hard to say. There is no harm if one sits quietly and understands
principle, but it will not do simply to insist on quiet-sitting. When one
understands principle clearly and thoroughly, one is naturally quiet. Nowadays, people generally insist on quiet-sitting in order to avoid things.
That will not do. Once I heard Master Li said that formerly he heard
Master Lo [Lo Ts'ung-yen, 1072–1135] expound on the *Spring and Autumn
Annals,* and at first he thought it was not very good and wondered how
much understanding [Master Lo] had achieved after he went to Lo-fou
Mountain [in Kuangtung] and became absolutely quiet. I have always

had my doubts about this, but as I see it now, it is true. If one's mind is excited, how can one perceive principle? One must be quiet before principle emerges. What is called quiet-sitting simply means not to have anything on one's mind. Only then will principle come out. When principle has come out, one's mind will be even clearer and more quiet.[62]

He also said, "Formerly, I saw that Master Li taught people quiet-sitting. Later, I came to see that that was wrong. Only the idea of seriousness is good."[63] A pupil asked: "Sir, in your 'Hsing-chuang' [Biographical account] of Master Li, you say [that he] 'sat sedately all day to examine the disposition before the feelings of pleasure, anger, sorrow, and joy were aroused in order to see what is called *chung* [the Mean, equilibrium].'[64] This seems to be different from I-ch'uan's [Ch'eng I] doctrine [that tranquillity involves both activity and principle]."[65] Answer: "In this case, my words at the time were too heavy. Now if we judge by the words of I-ch'uan, his effort is slightly one-sided. However, when Master Li remained quiet to the highest degree, there naturally was an enlightenment different from that of others. Now to sit sedately all day simply means to collect oneself right here, achieving results very quickly. If one keeps on like this, one would be like a Ch'an meditator who tranquilizes the body, speech, and mind."[66]

Although Chu Hsi saw merits and demerits in the doctrines of quiet-sitting of both Li T'ung and Ch'eng I, in the final analysis he preferred Ch'eng I's doctrine. His pupil Yang Tao-fu asked, "Li Yen-p'ing taught the student to see what the disposition is before the feelings of pleasure, anger, sorrow, and joy are aroused, while I-ch'uan said that thinking is the state of being aroused.[67] . . . Which doctrine of the two Masters should one follow?" Chu Hsi replied: "You will have to follow what Master Ch'eng said."[68] The above references to Ch'eng I all refer to his answers to questions from his pupil Su Chi-ming. Chi-ming asked whether the time of quiet-sitting means the state before the feelings are aroused. Ch'eng I answered by giving the example of covering the eyes and plugging the ears before a religious sacrifice.[69] Commenting on this, Chu Hsi said, "Covering the eyes and plugging the ears does not mean to see and hear nothing at all."[70] Chi-ming asked whether, before the feelings are aroused, there is activity or tranquillity. Ch'eng I answered, "It is all right to describe it as tranquil, but in tranquillity there must be something."[71] His pupil then said, "It is not all right to say that there is nothing, but naturally there is [only] consciousness." To this Ch'eng I responded, "Since there is consciousness, that means there is activity."[72] Commenting on this, Chu Hsi said, "I am afraid I-ch'uan has overstated here. . . . Now if one is not conscious of anything but is simply conscious, what is wrong with one's tranquillity? Does it mean that quiet-sitting is simply falling asleep?"[73]

From these comments we know that, as far as Ch'eng I's doctrine of activity and tranquillity is concerned, Chu Hsi approved in some respects but disapproved in others. On the doctrine of quiet-sitting, however, Chu Hsi generally agreed with Ch'eng I. In a reply to his pupil P'an Ping (b. c. 1168), Chu Hsi said, "You raised the question that I-ch'uan at times also taught people quiet-sitting. [That is true.] However, Confucius, Mencius, and the earlier sages did not have such a teaching. One must seek further to see that quiet-sitting and understanding principle are not incompatible. Only then can it be correct."[74] A pupil asked: "I-ch'uan once taught people quiet-sitting. How about it?" Chu Hsi replied, "That is because he noticed that people had too many deliberative thoughts, so he taught them to collect their minds. A beginning student should do this."[75] It is also recorded that when Ch'eng I saw anyone practice quiet-sitting, he readily praised him for knowing how to learn.[76] Commenting on this, Chu Hsi said, "This is the central point." He added, "Take the sentence, '[The education of the adult] lies in manifesting the clear character' in the *Great Learning*. This is where one must always be alert, and it is also where future progress lies. A person has only one mind as the foundation. This is where he must preserve it. If he understands its order and pattern, the whole system will be interpenetrated."[77]

From the above, it can readily be seen that Ch'eng I's teaching of quiet-sitting made a strong impression on Chu Hsi. But it does not follow that Chu Hsi was influenced only by Ch'eng I and not by his older brother Ch'eng Hao (1032–1085) as well, for the two brothers shared many ideas, including the doctrine of quiet-sitting. Chu Hsi said, "Both Ming-tao [Ch'eng Hao] and Yen-p'ing [Li T'ung] taught people quiet-sitting. As we see it, one must practice quiet-sitting."[78] He also said, "Ming-tao taught people quiet-sitting and Master Li also taught people quiet-sitting. For unless one's spirit is calm, principles will not be in place."[79] Why Ming-tao taught people quiet-sitting has not been made clear. However, in his answer to pupil Chang Hsia (1161–1237), Chu Hsi wrote, "Ming-tao taught people quiet-sitting because at the time many studied with him. They were in the school and were not involved with anything outside. That was why he taught this way."[80]

This was probably the practical situation at the time, but there was also another reason for Ch'eng Hao's teaching, as was true of Ch'eng I. This can be seen in Ch'eng Hao's instruction to Hsieh Liang-tso (1050–c. 1120). As Chu Hsi told the story, "Formerly, when Ming-tao was in Fu-k'ou,[81] he told his pupils, 'You people here only learn my words. Why not practice them?' When Hsieh Hsien-tao [Hsieh Liang-tso] asked for instruction, he merely said, 'Quiet-sitting.' "[82] In this brief answer, no reason is given for quiet-sitting, but it does not take much thought to realize that to understand why one must practice, one must understand principle, and to understand principle one must practice quiet-sitting. While in Fu-k'ou, Ch'eng Hao more than once told his pupils to put his words into practice. As related by Chu Hsi,

> When Ming-tao was in Fu-k'ou, Hsieh and Yu [Yu Tso, 1053–1123] were there to study with him. One day Ming-tao told them, "You gentlemen only learn my words here. Why not practice them?" The two gentlemen said, "We have nothing to practice." Ming-tao said, "When there is nothing to do, go ahead and sit quietly, for in quiet-sitting one can nourish the source so that it becomes somewhat calm. Although one cannot avoid chasing after external things, when one wakes up and collects one's mind in its home base, there is some resolution."[83]

Here Ch'eng Hao's portrayal of the efficacy of quiet-sitting is similar to that found in the teaching of Ch'eng I.

On another occasion, Chu Hsi related how Ch'eng Hao taught Hsieh Liang-tso quiet-sitting, saying, "At that time Ming-tao was in the county school of Fu-k'ou. He said, 'Gentleman, you merely listen to what I say but do not put it into practice.' Shang-ts'ai [Hsieh Liang-tso] responded that there was nothing to practice. Ming-tao taught him to practice quiet-sitting. If one has parents at home, one should serve and support them. When there is any affair, deal with it. One should not merely sit quietly and be through with it."[84] To concentrate correctly and thereby understand principle, and then to carry out the two in actual practice, is a major tenet in Confucianism. This is the sharp difference between Neo-Confucian quiet-sitting and Buddhist or Taoist meditation.

Yanagawa Takayoshi (*fl.* 1717) collected about thirty passages on quiet-sitting from the *Wen-chi* and the *Yü-lei* and entitled the collection *Seiza shūsetsu* (Collected passages on quiet-sitting).[85] The outstanding Japanese Neo-Confucian, Satō Naokata (1650–1719), wrote a preface for it in 1717. The collection includes Chu Hsi's most important sayings on quiet-sitting, but it is not complete. For example, the letters to Hsiung Meng-chao and Li Shou-yüeh,[86] and the ten or more passages on Li T'ung in the *Yü-lei*,[87] were not included. Nevertheless, since in China no similar work has been compiled, it indicates that Japanese Neo-Confucians have paid more attention to the subject of quiet-sitting. Along this line, Professor Okada Takehiko, in his *Zazen to seiza: Kusumoto Tanzan no seiza taininron* (Meditation and quiet-sitting: Kusumoto Tanzan's discussions on the personal experience of quiet-sitting), has devoted many pages to a discussion of Chu Hsi on quiet-sitting as practiced by Kusumoto Tanzan (1828–1883).[88] On the broader concept of tranquillity (*ching*), there is a most comprehensive study by Professor Ch'ien Mu in his *Chu Tzu hsin-hsüeh-an*[89] (New anthology and critical account of Master Chu), though the specific subject of quiet-sitting is dealt with only in passing.

## Notes

1. *Yü-lei,* ch. 116, sec. 28 (p. 4453).

2. *Ibid.,* ch. 9, sec. 32 (p. 241).

3. *Wen-chi,* 46:21b–22a, fifth letter in reply to P'an Shu-ch'ang (P'an Ching-yü).

4. *Ibid.,* separate collection, 4:14b, ninth letter to Lin Ching-po (Lin Ch'eng-chi).

5. *Ibid.,* supplementary collection, 2:13a, fifty-fourth letter in reply to Ts'ai Chi-t'ung (Ts'ai Yüan-ting).

6. *Yü-lei,* ch. 26, sec. 63 (p. 1054).

7. *Wen-chi,* 51:27a, ninth letter in reply to Huang Tzu-keng (Huang Hsün). This is the technique recommended in his "Poem in Praise of Regulated Breathing" in the *Wen-chi,* 86:6a.

8. *Ibid.,* 63:9b, letter in reply to Taoist priest.

9. *Yü-lei,* ch. 116, sec. 2 (p. 4441).

10. Present Huai-an County in Kiangsu.

11. *Sung-Yüan hsüeh-an pu-pi* [Supplement to the *Sung-yüan hsüeh-an*] (*Ssu-ming ts'ung-shu* [Ssu-ming series] ed.), 69:190a, biography of Kuo Yu-jen.

12. *Yü-lei,* ch. 116, sec. 50 (p. 4470).

13. *Ibid.,* sec. 54 (p. 4472).

14. *Ibid.,* sec. 48 (p. 4469).

15. *Ibid.,* sec. 53 (p. 4472).

16. *Ibid.,* sec. 55 (p. 4474).

17. *Ibid.,* ch. 115, sec. 14 (p. 4421).

18. Yen Yüan, *Chu Tzu yü-lei p'ing* [Critique of the *Classified Conversations of Master Chu*], p. 24a, in the *Yen-li ts'ung-shu* [Yen Yüan and Li Kung series] (*Ssu-ming ts'ung-shu* ed.), Bk. IV. Yao and Shu were legendary sage-emperors. The Duke of Chou (d. 1094 B.C.) founded ancient cultural institutions.

19. A county in Kwangtung Province.

20. Ch'ien Mu, *Chu Tzu hsin-hsüeh-an* [New anthology and critical accounts of Master Chu] (Taipei: San-min Book Co., 1971), vol. 2, p. 293.

21. *Chi-t'ing ch'üan-chi* [Complete works of Ch'en Lung-cheng] (1681 ed.), 5:15a.

22. *Kao Tzu i-shu* [Surviving works of Master Kao P'an-lung] (1876 ed.), 3:15a. "Records of painful learning."

23. *Ibid.,* 1:10b, "Sayings."

24. *Ibid.,* 8A:25b, first letter to Lu Ch'üeh-chai (Lu Chung-li); 8A:29b, first letter to An Wo-su (An Hsi-fan).

25. *Liu Ch'i-shan chi* [Collected works of Liu Tsung-chou] (*Ssu-k'u ch'üan-shu chen-pen* [Precious works of the *Complete Collection of the Four Libraries*] ed.), 11:29b, "Records of Reading."

26. *San-yü-t'ang wen-chi* [Collection of literary works of the Three-Fish Hall] (*Chia-hui-t'ang* ed.), 4:3b–4a.

27. *Yü-lei*, ch. 120, sec. 16 (pp. 4608–4609).

28. *Wen-chi*, 60:27a–b, fifth letter in reply to P'an Tzu-shan (P'an Shih-chü).

29. *Yü-lei*, ch. 113, sec. 41 (p. 4384).

30. *Ibid.*, ch. 12, sec. 142 (p. 347).

31. *Wen-chi*, 63:38a, letter in reply to Chou Shen-fu.

32. *Book of Mencius*, 6A:11.

33. *Yü-lei*, ch. 11, sec. 10 (p. 280).

34. *Ibid.*, ch. 12, sec. 137 (345).

35. *Ch'ien* is the first hexagram in the *Book of Changes*.

36. *Yü-lei*, ch. 68, sec. 23 (p. 2684).

37. *Cheng-meng* [Correcting youthful ignorance], ch. 12, "Possession of Virtue," sec. 6 in the *Chang Tzu ch'üan-shu* [Complete works of Master Chang Tsai] (*SPPY* ed.), 3:9a.

38. *Yü-lei*, ch. 118, sec. 40 (p. 4545).

39. *Ibid.*, ch. 12, sec. 140 (p. 345).

40. *Ibid.*, sec. 138 (p. 345).

41. *Wen-chi*, 55:24b, letter in reply to Hsiung Meng-chao.

42. *Yü-lei*, ch. 12, sec. 84 (p. 334).

43. *Wen-chi*, 55:8b, first letter in reply to Li Shou-yüeh (Li Hung-tsu).

44. *Yü-lei*, ch. 74, sec. 130 (p. 3022).

45. *Ibid.*, ch. 11, sec. 19 (p. 283).

46. *Ibid.*, ch. 117, sec. 27 (p. 4491).

47. *I-shu* [Surviving works], 5:1a, in the *Erh-Ch'eng ch'üan-shu* [Complete works of the two Ch'engs] (*SPPY* ed.).

48. *Yü-lei*, ch. 118, sec. 79 (pp. 4562–4563).

49. *Ibid.*, sec. 1, (p. 4525).

50. *Ibid.*, ch. 12, sec. 128 (p. 343).

51. *Ibid.*, ch. 45, sec. 54 (p. 1844). See also ch. 12, sec. 143 (p. 347).

52. *Ibid.*, ch. 115, sec. 35 (p. 4429).

53. *Wen-chi*, 61:12a, ninth letter in reply to Lin Te-chiu (Lin Chih).

54. *Yü-lei*, ch. 115, sec. 31 (p. 4427).

55. *Ibid.*, ch. 12, sec. 141 (pp. 345–346).

56. *Ibid.*, ch. 115, sec. 14 (p. 4421).

57. *Ibid.*, ch. 12, sec. 139 (p. 345).

58. *Wen-chi*, 62:6a, seventh letter in reply to Chang Yuan-te (Chang Hsia).

59. See ch. 29 below.

60. Present Nan-p'ing County, Fukien.

61. *Yen-p'ing ta-wen* [Li T'ung's answers to questions] (Pao-ku-t'ang [Hall of Precious Bestowment], *Chu Tzu i-shu* [Surviving works of Master Chu] ed.), 13b. The four feelings are taught in the *Doctrine of the Mean*, ch. 1.

62. *Yü-lei*, ch. 103, sec. 11 (pp. 4135–4136).

63. *Ibid.*, ch. 120, sec. 105 (p. 4654).

64. *Wen-chi*, 97:27b, biographical account of Li Yen-p'ing (Li T'ung).

65. *I-shu*, 18:15a.

66. *Yü-lei*, ch. 103, sec. 17 (p. 4139).

67. *I-shu*, 18:14b.

68. *Yü-lei*, ch. 115, sec. 11 (pp. 4418–4419).

69. *I-shu*, 18:15b.

70. *Yü-lei,* ch. 96, sec. 41 (p. 3920).

71. *I-shu,* 18:15b.

72. *Ibid.,* 18:15a.

73. *Yü-lei,* ch. 96, sec. 47 (pp. 3923–3924).

74. *Wen-chi,* 55:1a–b, second letter in reply to P'an Ch'ien-chih (P'an Ping).

75. *Yü-lei,* ch. 119, sec. 12 (p. 4588).

76. *Wai-shu* [Additional works], 12:9b, in the *Erh-Ch'eng ch'üan-shu.*

77. *Yü-lei,* ch. 11, sec. 19 (p. 283). See also ch. 96, sec. 57 (p. 3926).

78. *Ibid.,* ch. 12, sec. 84 (pp. 334–335).

79. *Ibid.,* sec. 137 (p. 345).

80. *Wen-chi,* 62:6a, seventh letter in reply to Chang Yüan-te (Chang Hsia).

81. Fu-k'ou was a county in Honan Province. Ch'eng Hao was magistrate there from 1176 to 1182.

82. *Yü-lei,* ch. 114, sec. 34 (p. 4401).

83. *Ibid.,* ch. 96, sec. 56 (p. 3926).

84. *Ibid.,* ch. 26, sec. 63 (p. 1054).

85. In the *Satō Naokata zensho* [Complete works of Satō Naokata], Bk. III.

86. See above, nn. 41 and 43.

87. See above, n. 77.

88. Okada Takehiko, *Zazen to seiza: Kusumoto Tanzan no seiza taininron* [Meditation and quiet-sitting: Kusumoto Tanzan's discussions on the personal experience of quiet-sitting] (Nagasaki: Educational Committee of Nagasaki County, 1972), pp. 32–34, 92–99.

89. Ch'ien Mu, *Chu Tzu hsin-hsüeh-an,* vol. 2, pp. 277–297.

# – 18 –

# Analogies and Diagrams

## Analogies

No one in Chinese history can surpass Chu Hsi in the number and variety of analogies he used, although in poetic imagination he must yield to Chuang Tzu. In chapter 41 of the *Yü-lei*, in his answer to pupils' questions on the Confucian aphorism, "To master oneself and return to propriety is humanity *(jen)*," five analogies are used in the first seven conversations. In explaining self-mastery, the Master employed the analogies of "a drop of ice in a red hot stove"; *jen* as "a current running in a blocked sewer"; "irrepressible fire"; "an isolated army surprised by the enemy, with nowhere to go but forward with all its might, to face death"; and "fighting fire with fire."[1] Once he called Ch'en Ch'un (1159–1223) into his bedroom and taught him the Confucian doctrine of studying things on the lower level and achieving understanding on the higher level. Chu Hsi compared this to the facts that one must first have seeds before farming, that one must first have cash before they can be strung together, and that water is water no matter whether it is in the bay or elsewhere.[2] To employ three analogies in one conversation is quite extraordinary. Once, the answer to a question consisted only of an analogy. Asked why the Four Beginnings of humanity, righteousness, propriety, and wisdom leave out faithfulness, Chu Hsi merely answered, "Sir, you have eaten the rice in the bowl but still try to pick some up on the back."[3]

Analogies are found mostly in the *Yü-lei*, since conversations lend themselves naturally to such usage. Chu Hsi applied them most effectively in his comments on historical persons. On Hsün Tzu's (313–238 B.C.?) theory of human nature, he said that the ancient philosopher "seems to let people eat coarse rice."[4] He criticized Su Tung-po (Su

271

Shih, 1036–1101) for mixing Confucianism with elements of Buddhism and Taoism "like shadow shows and fireworks."[5] He never excused Lu Hsiang-shan (1139–1193) and his follower, Yang Ching-chung (Yang Chien, 1141–1226), for teaching Confucianism but camouflaging it with Ch'an Buddhism, "like selling black-market salt in Fukien, and covering the illegal salt with fish so people won't see."[6] He had more favorable comments to make on Chuang Tzu, however: "Chuang Chou was a great talent . . . like saying that 'The *Book of Changes* talks about yin [passive cosmic force] and yang [active cosmic force], and the *Spring and Autumn Annals* talks about titles and functions.'[7] Who else after him was able to make such remarks? He seems to wield a cutting blade and a sharp axe to slice through, with every word well placed."[8]

There are about a thousand analogies of several hundred varieties in the *Yü-lei*. It was not necessary for Chu Hsi to think them out ahead of time, for he was able to use whatever he happened to see. It may be said that "he found the source whether he turns to the left or to the right,"[9] employing whatever came to mind. In terms of household articles, besides the house and the door,[10] he made analogies to the desk and the chair,[11] the tray, the pail, and the cooking pot,[12] the grindstone, the knife, and the balance.[13] The Chinese balance using dots to indicate the specific weight was used to show that Lu Hsiang-shan and his School ignored practical, specific, concrete affairs. Analogies were also made to money and the money bag,[14] clothing, straw sandals, and the fan,[15] the ink-slab and the incense burner,[16] each finding its appropriate application. Means of transportation that Chu Hsi compared things to included the road, the boat, and the carriage.[17] He also made references to grains, corn, the pear, the orange,[18] tea, soup, oil, and ginger,[19] and mentioned delicious dishes of meat and fish.[20] The animal kingdom was represented by the dog, the cat, the lion, and the fish.[21] Almost nothing was ignored.

In his conversations, Chu Hsi often turned to daily activities to clarify his teachings. He would point to cooking, drinking, and eating in general,[22] as well as eating rice, dumplings, and fruit; peeling fruit; eating coarse food, meat, and cold food;[23] steaming cakes and eating buns;[24] drinking tea; and making wine, drinking wine, and getting intoxicated.[25] In terms of movement, he talked about getting up and sitting down, walking on a road, riding in a boat, pushing a vehicle, riding on horseback, searching for a house, viewing a house, and entering a door.[26] He also talked about entering a den, digging a well, crossing a bridge, ascending a pagoda, and climbing a tree.[27] In the sphere of work, sweeping the floor, farming, drawing water, planting hemp, cutting grass, kindling fire, and stamping out fire were utilized.[28] In the area of handiwork, he turned to calligraphy, embroidery, carving, removing one's clothing, divination, and archery,[29] besides polishing jade, forging metal, alchemy, reciting chants, and repairing pots.[30] Even tightening a rope, lifting weight, pointing to one's palm, and spending money were not overlooked.[31] In addition, Chu Hsi used government service, lawsuits, and city defense for illustration,[32] not to mention catching thieves, chasing tigers, and capturing snakes, which are more exciting.[33] He made analogies to almost all daily activities so his students could easily make associations and remember them. Outside of ordinary matters, Chu Hsi employed several unusual analogies, such as the whole body being black, an ant trying to bore through a pearl, and a bottomless basket,[34] but such cases are few.

The analogies that have special significance are those involving water, the mirror, light, a precious pearl, medicine, rice, wood, and a pair of wheels. Of these, analogies to water outnumber the rest, perhaps by as many as ten times. At first sight, Chu Hsi's water analogy seems to have been derived from Mencius, who equated the downward tendency of water with the goodness of human nature, and from Ch'eng Hao (1032–1085), who equated the goodness of nature with the purity of water.[35] But Chu Hsi had criticized Ch'eng Hao for having said that by nature water runs downward, and also that water can be clear or turbid, which he thought was incompatible with the idea of its downward tendency. Therefore he said of Ch'eng Hao, "He drew the parallel again and again but always ended up in a defect."[36] Like Mencius and Ch'eng Hao, Chu Hsi loved to compare water with human nature, but his emphasis on its downward movement was slight,[37] whereas his emphasis on its clarity,[38] tranquillity,[39] and levelness[40] was quite substantial. In Chu Hsi's view, waves are like the disturbance of selfish desires,[41] while the wetness of water is like jen (humanity).[42] In its resemblance to the tranquillity of water, jen is substance, while in its resemblance to the flow of water, it becomes love and is function.[43] On the one hand jen can be compared to chung (being true to oneself, or conscientiousness), which is like water in a vase, and on the other hand to shu (extension of what is for the self to others, or altruism), which is like water overflowing from a vase.[44] The flow of jen is similar to the flow of water, which should not be obstructed[45] but should flow in a certain order and to a certain degree.[46] Besides, one must make effort to remove any possible obstruction,[47] as in overcoming fire with water.[48] Because of its nature of universality, jen is the same in the ocean, the stomach of a fish, a pond, a stream, or a cup of any size or shape.[49] It is still water when divided and contained in different bowls, very much like principle being one but its manifestations being many (li-i fen-shu).[50] Most important of all, living water comes from the source,[51] which reminds one of Chu Hsi's renowned poem on the subject.[52]

To use the mirror as an analogy of the mind originated with Chuang Tzu,[53] was continued through the Buddhists down to Ch'eng I (1033–

1107),[54] and thus became a tradition in Chinese thought. The emphasis was on the openness, clarity, and cleanliness of the mirror, coupled with one's effort to keep it clean. The analogy of a mirror occurs in the *Yü-lei* no less than ten times,[55] especially to explain the clear virtue of the mind. However, Chu Hsi made two points never touched on by Chuang Tzu, the Buddhists, or Ch'eng I—namely, that the human mind, like the mirror, can shine by itself;[56] and that in its operation its transforming influence follows, so that in its tranquillity its spiritual efficacy remains, which he compared to the fact that after a mirror has been used, it can be used again.[57] Thus Chu Hsi gave new meanings to an old analogy. In using light as an analogy, he also went beyond the Buddhists, who usually referred either to the light of the sun and the light of a lamp, for he made comparisons to the light of the sun and moon,[58] fire,[59] burning fuel,[60] a candle,[61] a lamp,[62] and a lantern.[63]

Like the Buddhists, who compared the Buddha and the Buddhist Law to a precious pearl, Chu Hsi compared *li* (principle) to this jewel, whereas *ch'i* (material force) he compared to water, which can be pure or turbid. Water does not change the nature of the pearl any more than *ch'i* changes the nature of *li*.[64] The pearl and the shell he compared to principle and selfish desire, respectively, pointing out that they are quite different even though both may be buried in the sand.[65] To Chu Hsi, the words of sages are like precious pearls, whose nature remains intact and is not affected by material desires.[66] The mind and the Way are also like precious treasures that must be closely guarded.[67] In his view, the Taoists originally possessed a precious treasure but abandoned it and took up the earthen dish of the Buddhists.[68] In place of the precious pearl, Chu Hsi sometimes referred to genuine gold instead.[69]

The analogy of medicine can be traced to the *Book of History*,[70] which Chu Hsi quoted.[71] The fact that he frequently resorted to this analogy is obviously related to his health, for he very often took medicine. He used the occasion of an ache in his arm,[72] for example, along with cooking medicine and taking medicine, to teach pupils a number of lessons, such as advancing gradually, mastering oneself, concentration, persistence, and putting ideas into actual practice.[73] He even equated medicine with the Three Bonds,[74] and held that the moral lesson to be drawn from medicine is that the effect depends on the person.[75]

In employing grain as an analogy both for *jen* and for the one foundation,[76] Chu Hsi had in mind Ch'eng I's famous saying, "*Jen* is comparable to seeds of grain."[77] Just as a tree trunk grows branches, so *jen* spreads from special affection for parents to loving all mankind.[78] Chu Hsi frequently used the two wheels of a carriage, two wings of a bird, and two legs of a person to illustrate the mutual dependence of knowledge and conduct, enlightenment and sincerity, and abiding in seriousness and investigating principle, none of which may be neglected.[79]

These analogies were not original with Chu Hsi, but no one else has developed such a well-balanced system.

If we follow the subjects in the *Yü-lei,* we find that the greatest number of analogies appear in chapters 8 to 13, on methods of learning—notably, those of building houses, eating fruit, alchemy, cooking, concocting herbal medicines, eating rice, and bathing in chapter 8;[80] raining, guarding the door, fighting a battle, walking on a road, learning archery, taking medicine, and accumulating wealth in chapter 9;[81] meting out punishment, catching thieves, operating an army, steering a sailboat, eating rice, watering plants, eating fruit, embroidery, drinking, and viewing a house in chapter 10;[82] wiping a desk, hearing a lawsuit, and supplying water to a farm in chapter 11;[83] the rising sun, planting, building a fire, precious pearls, entering a house, irrigating fields, weeding, and steering in chapter 12;[84] and ascending a pagoda, walking on a road, the ink-slab, clear water, and seeds in chapter 13.[85] By means of these analogies, numerous ways to study are set forth for the benefit of students.

The above cases, by no means complete, are drawn from the *Yü-lei.* Compared with the *Yü-lei,* the *Wen-chi,* the *Ssu-shu chang-chü chi-chu* (Collected commentaries on the Four Books), and the *Ssu-shu huo-wen* (Questions and answers on the Four Books) contain relatively few analogies. These works are expositions of principles or accounts of facts, unlike the *Yü-lei.* In the *Ta-hsüeh huo-wen* (Questions and answers on the *Great Learning*), we find only the mention of snow yielding to bare earth as an analogy for daily renewal in chapter 2; that of a wandering cavalry losing its way home[86] as an analogy for the investigation of things without examining the self in chapter 5; and the use of the traditional idioms of "the openness of a mirror and the levelness of a balance" to show how the mind should respond to things in chapter 7. There are also only three analogies in the *Chung-yung huo-wen* (Questions and answers on the *Doctrine of the Mean*): Ch'eng I's clear mirror and still water[87] as an analogy for the mind before feelings are aroused in chapter 1; Ch'eng I's story of someone listening to his son's reading in the next room[88] to illustrate splitting spiritual beings and their virtue into two things in chapter 16; and the fact that a tree must have a trunk before it has branches and leaves to explain that things must first exist before one can embrace them, in the same chapter.

Chapters 24 to 29 of the *Wen-chi* contain official documents that are completely free of analogies, as are the letters in the supplementary collection, chapters 1 to 11, and separate collection, chapters 1 to 6. There are some analogies in the letters in the regular collection, chapters 3 to 64, but very few. In his debate with Ch'en Liang (1143–1194), Chu Hsi just repeated Lu Hsiang-shan's analogy of a bed on top of a bed[89] and Ch'en's of forging iron into gold.[90] In these thirty-five chapters of correspondence, only twelve analogies are found, mostly in literary but idiomatic expressions, such as "entering a market of salted fishes,"[91] "incompatibility of ice and burning charcoal,"[92] "covering one's ears when stealing a bell,"[93] and "buying a box of pearls but returning the pearls."[94] Twice Chu Hsi used famous analogies by Ch'eng I, notably the wandering cavalry losing its way home[95] and supporting a drunkard.[96] Once he used Han Yü's (768–824) famous remark[97] about taking a bath together but deriding nudism.[98] But half of the ten are Chu Hsi's own analogies, making use of tradition, as in the cases of archery as an analogy for achieving equilibrium in the mind[99] and the mirror as an analogy for the mind.[100] In the three remaining cases, he compared the learning of Lu Hsiang-shan to a worn-out bloom,[101] the character of the mind of a man of humanity to the wetness of water and the heat of fire,[102] and compulsive behavior to children playing hide-and-seek.[103] Once he said that "Analogies are not very pertinent to the self."[104] He must have meant that analogies are merely teaching tools and do not substitute for the principles themselves.

## Diagrams

Analogies highlight a point in conversation. In contrast, diagrams present an outline of a basic doctrine in graphic form. Both serve the goal of an efficient methodology, which Chu Hsi brought to a very high degree of refinement.

The Five Masters of the Northern Sung (960–1126) were interested in the *Book of Changes*. Master Chou (Chou Tun-i, 1017–1073) transmitted the *T'ai-chi-t'u* (Diagram of the Great Ultimate) and wrote the "T'ai-chi-t'u shuo" (Explanation of the diagram of the Great Ultimate) to expound its metaphysics.[105] Because Master Shao's (Shao Yung, 1011–1077) philosophy is a system of forms and numbers, there are many charts in his *Huang-chi ching-shih shu* (Supreme principles governing the world), which take up almost a quarter of its pages. In contrast, Master Chang (Chang Tsai, 1020–1077) confined his discussions to ideas and did not resort to diagrams.[106] The two Masters Ch'eng (Ch'eng Hao, 1032–1085, and Ch'eng I, 1033–1107) interpreted the doctrines of the *Book of Changes* in terms of moral principles, without the aid of diagrams either. Ch'eng Hao did not write a book, but Ch'eng I wrote short essays on burial and sacrificial rites, which contain only two minor diagrams to illustrate the positions of burials and an ancestral tablet.[107]

With his keen sense of order and systematic approach, Chu Hsi employed diagrams on many occasions. He placed Chou Tun-i's "Explanation of the diagram of the Great Ultimate" at the head of his and Lü Tsu-ch'ien's *Chin-ssu lu* (Reflections on things at hand), the first

Neo-Confucian anthology and a model for later collections. His own diagrams cover not only the *Book of Changes* but his basic doctrines of *jen* (humanity), nature, and learning. Some of his diagrams are purely descriptive, such as the diagram of the "deep" garment and head-gear,[108] diagram of ancestral temples of the Chou dynasty (1111–249 B.C.),[109] diagrams of the system of temples past and present,[110] diagram of the Hall of Light,[111] and diagram of the method of the measuring square.[112] These give only the measurement, position, or direction of the object concerned and do not offer any explanation of a text or a doctrine. Chu Hsi also modified Yüan Shu's (1131–1205) diagram on the hexagrams.[113] The following nine diagrams, however, do elaborate on or supplement a conversation or a treatise.

### Diagram on the Evaluation of Change

There are two diagrams in the *Yü-lei* to explain the development of Change. When a pupil asked about the passage, "In the system of Change there is the Great Ultimate. It generates the Two Modes [yin, passive cosmic force, and yang, active cosmic force]. The Two Modes generate the Four Forms [major and minor yin and yang]. The Four Forms generate the Eight Trigrams,"[114] Chu Hsi replied,

> The Great Ultimate in the system of Change means that yin and yang are generated, which are the Two Modes, denoting a match or a pair. The Two Modes generating the Four Forms means that each yin produces a yang, resulting in the form of —; each yang in turn produces yin, resulting in the form of --; each yin in turn produces a yin, resulting in the form of --; and each yang in turn produces a yang, resulting in the form of —. These are called the Four Forms. The Four Forms generating the Eight Trigrams means that when the Four Forms produce the four yin, they become the four trigrams of *k'an* (pit), *chen* (activity), *k'un* (Earth), and *tui* (pleasure), and when the Four Forms produce the four yang, they become the four trigrams of *sun* (bending), *li* (brightness), *ken* (to stop), and *ch'ien* (Heaven).

Then he drew the following diagram to clarify his remark:

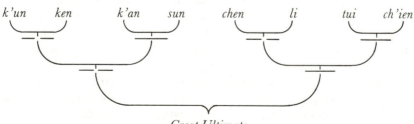

*Great Ultimate*

Each trigram combined with the eight to become sixty-four hexa-grams.[115]

## Diagram of Fingers

Although the preceding diagram is helpful, it does not really clarify the meaning of the process of Change. The same is true of the diagram of fingers. In answer to a pupil's question on the method of divination by sorting out divination stalks through the alternation of lefthand and righthand fingers, Chu Hsi said,

> Let us illustrate by using the numbers 7, 8, 9, and 6. The natural order is 6, 7, 8, 9. However, 7 is yang and cannot be subdued by 6 [which is yin] and has to rise [6 produces 7 above]. 7 gives rise to 8 and 8 to 9. 9 [being yang] also has to rise [that is, 9 remains above 8]. This is the system of one going up and one coming down, as in the following chart:[116]

| 9 | | 7 | |
|---|---|---|---|
| | 8 | | 6 |
| | | | |
| second | third | fourth | fifth |
| finger | finger | finger | finger |

## Diagram of the Great Ultimate

The diagram of fingers is not really self-explanatory but requires knowl-edge of the use of the fingers in sorting the stalks in divination. How-ever, the diagram of the Great Ultimate not only reveals ideas but even adds some new meaning. Chu Hsi said, "It is best to view the Great Ultimate, yin and yang, and the Five Agents[117] in terms of origination, flourishing, advantage, and firmness.[118] They are all present in the Great Ultimate. Advantage and firmness are yin, while origination and flourishing are yang. For the Five Agents, origination is wood, flourish-ing is fire, advantage is metal, and firmness is water." He then made the diagram that appears on the following page.[119]

   The diagram actually indicates more than what Chu Hsi said. He did not mention Wu-chi (Ultimate of Nonbeing), but the diagram shows that Wu-chi (the upper circle) is also the Great Ultimate because origi-nation, flourishing, advantage, and firmness are operating in both. In the diagram it is shown that advantage and flourishing are not only yin but the yin after the interaction of yin and yang, and that origination and firmness are not only yang but the yang after their interaction. Chu Hsi never mentioned earth in his remarks, but the diagram shows that earth exhibits its strength in fire, wood, water, and metal.

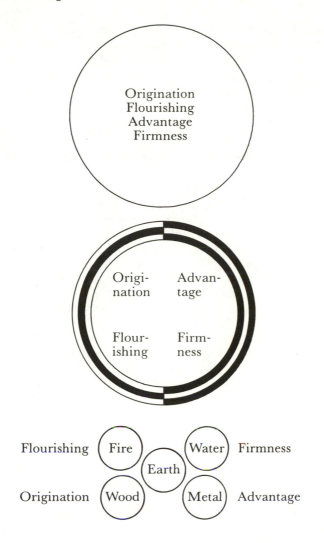

*Diagram on the Foundation of* Jen

Since *jen* (humanity) is the central virtue in Chu Hsi's philosophy, he used more diagrams to explain it than any other subject. For instance, Chu Hsi talked with Ch'en Ching-chih[120] for three or four days but could not make him understand about filial piety and brotherly respect being the root of *jen*.[121] He merely told him to read carefully but did not explain further. Several days later he drew a diagram to show him. In the innermost circle he wrote the word *jen*, in the intermediate circle he wrote "filial piety" and "brotherly respect," and in the outermost circle he wrote "being humane to all people and [having] love for all things."[122] The idea is that in the practice of humanity, one must start with filial piety and brotherly respect, and then gradually extend, through affection for kin and respect for elders, to loving all people— unlike the doctrine of universal love, in which there is no distinction between filial piety for one's parents and that for other people's parents.

### Diagram on the Extension of Jen

Discussing the same subject on another occasion, Chu Hsi said,

> Since filial piety and brotherly respect are not *jen,* what is it? The other day I joked with Chao Tzu-ch'in [Chao Yen-shu, 1165–1174] and said that we must draw a circle. There must be a series of circles within it. In the innermost circle, let us write the word "nature." In the second circle should be written "humanity," "righteousness," "propriety," and "wisdom," without separating them into four sections. Under "humanity" there should be written "commiseration" in the third circle, "serving parents" in the fourth, "humane to people" in the fifth, and "love for all things" in the last. Similarly, under "righteousness" there should be written "shame and dislike" in the third circle, "obeying the elder brother" in the fourth, "honoring the worthy" in the fifth, and "valuing virtue" in the last. Likewise, under "propriety" there should be written "compliance and humility" in the third circle, and "restraint by ornament" in the next. And finally, under "wisdom" there should be written "right and wrong" in the third circle and "examination and discrimination" in the next.[123]

On both diagrams on *jen,* Chu Hsi gave no further explanation and did not actually draw the diagrams.

### Diagram on the "Jen-shuo"

The most important, most detailed, and most complicated diagram is the *Jen-shuo t'u* (Diagram on the "Jen-shuo" [Treatise on humanity]). It should be considered together with the discussion of the treatise itself given in chapter 11 above. The diagram is translated and reproduced on the following page, with large Chinese characters in capital letters.

This diagram essentially reaffirms Mencius' doctrine that man is born with the feelings of commiseration, shame and dislike, respect and reverence, and right and wrong, which are the Four Beginnings of the Four Virtues of humanity, righteousness, propriety, and wisdom.[126] Here the doctrine of human nature is linked up with metaphysics, specifically with the Four Qualities of origination, flourishing, advantage, and firmness of the first hexagram, *ch'ien* (Heaven, male) in the *Book of Changes*. The diagram was probably drawn as a supplement after Chu

HUMANITY

is the mind of Heaven and Earth to produce things
and Origination, Flourishing, Advantage, and Firmness are the mind
of Heaven and Earth.

MAN
receives it to be his

MIND

BEFORE                              WHEN

MANIFESTATION

HAS TAKEN PLACE                    IS TAKING PLACE

THEREFORE          The Four Virtues    The Four Begin-     THEREFORE
humanity cherishes are present, but    nings are promi-    commiseration
and nourishes      only humanity       nent, but only      operates every-
completely without embraces all four.  commiseration       where and goes
any differentiation.                   penetrates all four. through every-
It unites and                                              thing. There is
commands all.                                              nothing it does not
                                                           penetrate.

SO-CALLED
                            inborn

NATURE
        feeling

LOVE
    manifestation        principle

HUMANITY
    function        substance

Collectively        the state before manifestation is        Humanity is

        SPEAKING                    SUBSTANCE

Separately          the state after manifestation is        Commiseration is

                            FUNCTION

IMPARTIALITY is the way personally to realize humanity, as in the saying, ''To
master oneself and return to propriety is humanity,''[124] for impartiality leads to humanity, and humanity leads to

LOVE

FILIAL PIETY and BROTHERLY RESPECT are the function of love and

ALTRUISM                                    is its application

CONSCIOUSNESS is a matter of wisdom[125]

Hsi's "Jen-shuo" was completed. The terms in large characters (capital letters in the translation) are probably meant to emphasize concepts not sufficiently stressed in the treatise, especially those of substance and function. As Chu Hsi wrote Chang Shih (1133–1180), "I made a mistake in a previous treatise in not distinguishing clearly between substance and function. . . . I have now corrected it."[127]

The virtues of filial piety, brotherly respect, and altruism are probably meant to underscore the practical search for humanity, an idea not explicit in the treatise. Ch'eng I's pupil Yang Shih (1053–1135) had propounded the theory that *jen* forms one body with Heaven and Earth, but Chu Hsi feared that this might lead people to ignore the distinction between the self and things. Another pupil of Ch'eng I, Hsieh Liang-tso (1050–c. 1120), had propounded the theory that *jen* means consciousness of other people's pain, but Chu Hsi feared that this might lead people to ignore the distinction between selfish desires and the Principle of Heaven.[128] Thus at the end of the diagram Chu Hsi simply added a note that consciousness is a matter of wisdom. He did not bring out the concept of forming one body with Heaven and Earth there. Instead, he mentioned impartiality twice, thereby implying the idea of unity with all things, but modifying it with the idea of actual practice—namely, altruism. In sum, the spirit of the diagram is directed to the practice of *jen,* clearly an effort to balance the theoretical nature of the treatise.

## Diagram on Nature

Similar to the foregoing diagram but much simpler is the following diagram on human nature, which is not a diagram to explain any conversation or treatise but an independent statement, as follows:

| | | |
|---|---|---|
| NATURE IS GOOD<br>  Nature is never evil | GOOD | When feelings are aroused and each and all attain due measure and degree, it is good wherever they may be found. |
| | EVIL | Evil cannot be said to come directly from goodness. There is evil when one fails to do good and falls on one side.[129] |

## Diagram on the Great Learning

Chapters 14 and 15 of the *Yü-lei* are devoted to the *Great Learning.* At the end of the second chapter is Chu Hsi's diagram on the *Great Learning,* which offers a graphic outline of the doctrines taught in the classic. Since the *Great Learning* is the most systematic of the classics, this diagram is the most systematic of Chu Hsi's charts. It is translated on the following page, with large Chinese characters in capital letters.

| INVESTIGATION OF THINGS | REGULATION OF THE FAMILY |
|---|---|
| EXTENSION OF KNOWLEDGE | ORDERING OF THE STATE |
| SINCERITY OF THE WILL | BRINGING PEACE TO THE |
| RECTIFICATION OF THE MIND | WORLD |
| CULTIVATION OF THE PERSON | |

| All these are matters of | Both manifesting the clear character and renewing the people should abide in the highest good. | All these are matters of |
|---|---|---|
| MANIFESTING THE CLEAR CHARACTER | | RENEWAL OF THE PEOPLE |
| KNOWING WHERE TO ABIDE | Kindness of the ruler, respect of the minister, affection of the father, filial piety of the son, and faithfulness of friends are its items. | BEING ABLE TO ATTAIN THE END |
| This means to know where the highest good is and to seek to abide in it. To be calm, tranquil, peaceful, and to deliberate lie between abiding and attaining. | | This means to attain where to abide. |

| INVESTIGATION OF THINGS | REGULATION OF THE FAMILY |
|---|---|
| EXTENSION OF KNOWLEDGE | ORDERING OF THE STATE |
| SINCERITY OF THE WILL | BRINGING PEACE TO THE |
| RECTIFICATION OF THE MIND | WORLD |
| CULTIVATION OF THE PERSON | |

| If one knows where to abide, one will find it anywhere. | If one can attain the end, one can attain anything.[130] |
|---|---|

It is significant that while in the *Great Learning,* manifesting the clear character, renewing the people, and abiding in the highest good have traditionally been regarded as the "three principles," Chu Hsi conceived abiding in the highest good as the central virtue to which all the rest are related. All ethical values and psychological factors are coordinated with the "eight items," from the investigation of things to bringing peace to the world.

In 1569, the outstanding Korean Neo-Confucian Yi Hwang (Yi T'oegye, 1501–1570) presented the *Sŏnghak sipto* (Ten diagrams for learning to be a sage)[131] to the Korean ruler. T'oegye was sixty-eight years old and had already lectured before the throne on Confucian classics eight times. The ten diagrams center on basic Neo-Confucian doctrines, especially those of Chu Hsi. Of the ten, the seventh was Chu Hsi's diagram on the "Jen-shuo"; the fourth consisted of Chu Hsi's "Article of Learning" for the White Deer Hollow Academy; and the ninth and tenth were based on Chu Hsi's admonition on seriousness (*ching,* reverence). The first, on the Great Ultimate, quotes Chu Hsi's commentary on it. The rest are on subjects Chu Hsi discussed frequently. It is not a distortion to say that the ten diagrams embody the complete teachings of Chu Hsi. T'oegye had devoted his life to studying the work of the Master, yet for the fourth diagram, on the *Great Learning,* he chose one by the Korean Neo-Confucian Kwŏn Kŭn (1352–1409) instead of Chu Hsi's. T'oegye was extremely familiar with Chu Hsi's works, including the *Yü-lei,* so he must have been aware of the existence of Chu Hsi's diagram. In 1983, the Institute for T'oegye Studies convened an international conference at Harvard University. Three papers dealt with the ten diagrams, but none mentioned Chu Hsi's diagram on the *Great Learning.*

Why would a loyal follower like T'oegye bypass Chu Hsi's diagram in favor of another?

A closer examination of T'oegye's presentation and a comparison of Chu Hsi's diagram and Kwŏn Kŭn's supply the answer. T'oegye's primary purpose was to offer guidance to the Korean ruler on how to become a sagely king. In short, his purpose was a practical one. Kwŏn Kŭn's diagram provides a procedure for doing precisely this, with four levels, each of which ends in results.

The first level consists of the "three principles" of the *Great Learning.* On the second level are the topics of knowledge, action, extension, beginning, and end, with the "eight items" and psychological factors in between. The "eight items" are repeated on the third level as the task, which finally ends up on the fourth level of results. The purpose of this diagram differs sharply from that of Chu Hsi's diagram, which offers an analysis and new structure of the teachings of the *Great Learning.* Since T'oegye's goal was a practical one, Kwŏn Kŭn's diagram met his need. T'oegye remained a loyal Chu Hsi follower. If Chu Hsi had been advising the Korean king, he would have emphasized the practical side, too. (Kwŏn Kŭn's diagram is on pp. 286–287.)

### Diagram on the "Eastern Inscription"

The preceding eight diagrams are Chu Hsi's own, whereas the remaining one is a pupil's treatment of an essay by Chang Tsai. Master Chang had written two inscriptions, one called "Correcting Obstinacy," to post on the right window of his study hall, and the other called "Puncturing Ignorance," to post on the left window.[132] When Ch'eng I saw them, he remarked, "This will cause controversy," and changed them to "Eastern Inscription" and "Western Inscription," respectively.[133] Chu Hsi highly praised the "Western Inscription" but rarely talked about the "Eastern Inscription." The latter is mentioned only once in the *Yü-lei* and one place (four times) in the *Wen-chi.* When his pupil Yang Tao-fu[134] asked about it, Chu Hsi replied, "It is precisely what present law books call *ku-shih* [purposely making a mistake]," and told Tao-fu to draw a diagram. Thereupon, Tao-fu copied the "Eastern Inscription" and wrote certain passages in large characters (capital letters in the following translation):

> Playful words come from thought. Playful acts come from deliberation. TO SAY that what we say and what we show in our bodily movements ARE NOT FROM OUR MIND IS UNINTELLIGIBLE, AND IT IS IMPOSSIBLE TO EXPECT OTHERS NOT TO SUSPECT THAT THEY ORIGINATE FROM OUR MIND. It is not our original mind that makes us err in speech, and it is not our sincere will that makes us err in action. To be mistaken in words and to be erroneous and deceived in action, and then TO SAY THAT IT IS NATURAL WITH US, IS TO SLANDER OURSELVES. AND TO EXPECT OTHERS TO THINK THE SAME WAY IS TO SLANDER THEM. SOME WILL SAY that although speech and action originate from our mind, any fault that there is lies not with it but with our playfulness, or that although we are wrong in thought, we are really sincere. SUCH PEOPLE DO NOT guard against what comes from within, and blame their mistakes on what does not come from within. Their pride will increase and, FURTHERMORE, they will finally be wrong. WHO CAN BE MORE STUPID?

In legal terms, "purposely making a mistake" means to mete out too heavy or too light a sentence. In Chu Hsi's view, the "Eastern Inscription" tends to emphasize thought and is deficient on the study of the lower level, that is, practical daily affairs. It is therefore comparatively inferior to the "Western Inscription," which starts from the lower level and reaches the higher. In his reply to Minister Wang (Wang Ying-ch'en, 1118–1176), Chu Hsi said,

> Although the "Eastern Inscription" and the "Western Inscription" were written at the same time, in what their terms are meant to indicate and in the extent of their prevailing spirit, they are radically different in dimension. That is why the School of the Ch'engs taught the students only the "Western Inscription" and remained silent on the "Eastern Inscription." If a student ponders the words of the "Western Inscription" again and again and obtains something for himself, his mind will be wide open and principle will be clear to him, and he will naturally get a unique taste of it. Although the "Eastern Inscription" makes it clear that the error of increasing pride and being wrong lies finally in an infinitesimal point, and therefore warns students of later generations in a personal and relevant way, its flavor is limited and it is deficient on the task of the lower level. How can it be spoken of in the same breath with the "Western Inscription," which penetrates both the higher and lower levels with one principle running through them?[135]

Tao-fu wrote "it is impossible" and "slander them" in large characters to show wherein "purposely making a mistake" lies. He deliberately

# Kwŏn Kŭn's Diagram of the *Great Learning**

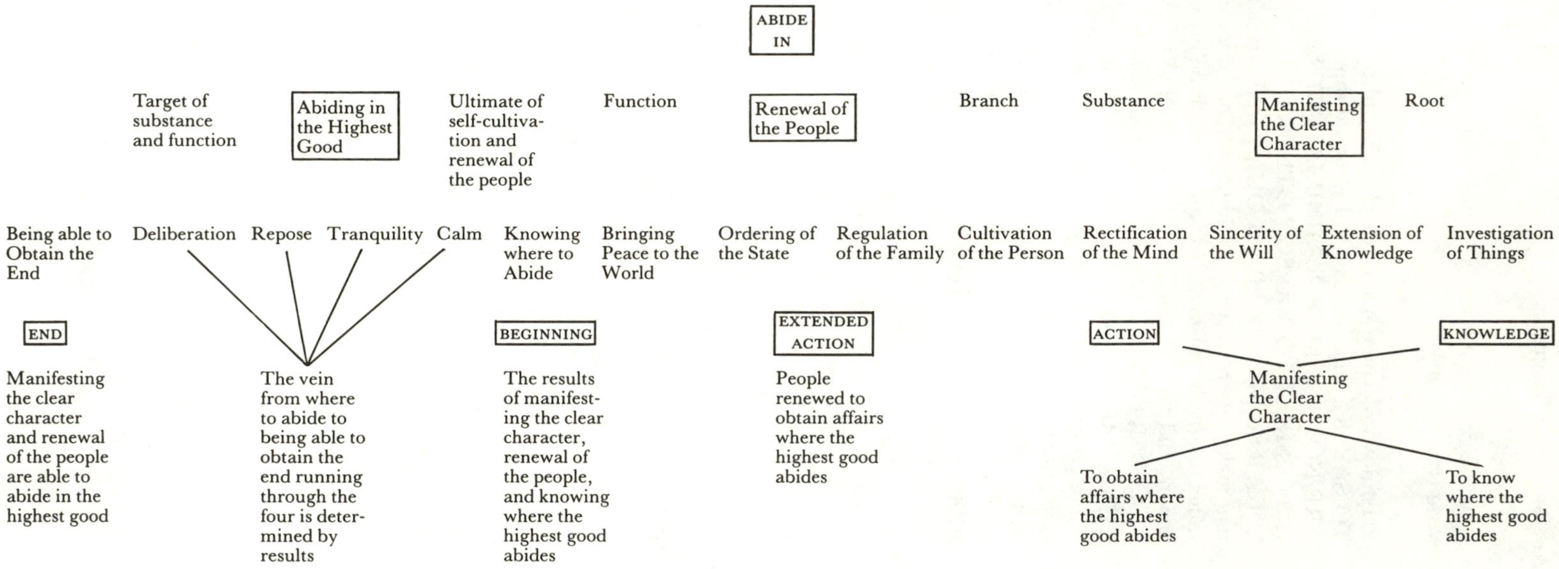

**Category labels (across):**
Target of substance and function · [Abiding in the Highest Good] · Ultimate of self-cultivation and renewal of the people · Function · [Renewal of the People] · Branch · Substance · [Manifesting the Clear Character] · Root

| Target of substance and function | Abiding in the Highest Good | Ultimate of self-cultivation and renewal of the people | Function | Renewal of the People | Branch | Substance | Manifesting the Clear Character | Root |
|---|---|---|---|---|---|---|---|---|
| Being able to Obtain the End / Deliberation / Repose | Tranquility | Calm / Knowing where to Abide | Bringing Peace to the World | Ordering of the State / Regulation of the Family | Cultivation of the Person | Rectification of the Mind | Sincerity of the Will / Extension of Knowledge | Investigation of Things |

Boxes along the top: [ABIDE IN]

---

**[END]**

Manifesting the clear character and renewal of the people are able to abide in the highest good

The vein from where to abide to being able to obtain the end running through the four is determined by results
*(connecting lines to: Deliberation, Repose, Tranquility, Calm)*

**[BEGINNING]**

The results of manifesting the clear character, renewal of the people, and knowing where the highest good abides

**[EXTENDED ACTION]**

People renewed to obtain affairs where the highest good abides

---

**[ACTION]**

To obtain affairs where the highest good abides

**[KNOWLEDGE]**

To know where the highest good abides

Manifesting the Clear Character
*(crossing lines connecting ACTION and KNOWLEDGE)*

EFFORT

Having things investigated    Knowing where to abide    Will is sincere    Mind rectified    Person cultivated    Family regulated    Order in the state    Peace in the world

Manifesting the Clear Character

Already know where the highest good abides

Already obtain order of abiding in the highest good

People renewed to obtain order of where the highest good abides

RESULTS

*From the *T'oegye chŏnsŏ*, bk. 1, p. 18a.

placed the word "further" between "pride will increase" and "will finally be wrong" to show that the slightest error can lead to a substantial mistake. There is no question that Chu Hsi was pleased with Tao-fu's diagram.[136]

# Notes

1. 41 (1661). The quotation is from the *Analects,* 12:1. The first number is the chapter number in the *Yü-lei.* Because there are many references to the *Yü-lei* in this chapter, the *Yü-lei* section numbers are omitted and the page numbers are put in parentheses.

2. 117 (4501). The Confucian doctrine refers to *Analects,* 14:37.

3. 53 (2060). The Four Beginnings refer to the *Book of Mencius,* 2A:6. See ch. 16 above, n. 77.

4. 137 (5256).

5. 137 (5262–5263).

6. 124 (4770).

7. *Chuang Tzu,* ch. 33, "Autumn Flood," (*SPTK* ed., *Nan-hua chen-ching* [True classics of Chuang Tzu] ed., 10:25b).

8. 125 (4790).

9. *Book of Mencius,* 4B:14.

10. House: 31 (1257–1261, 1267), 32 (1311), 33 (1359), 41 (1654), 118 (4525), 126 (4827). Door: 15 (477), 18 (686).

11. Desk: 21 (791), 95 (3841), 116 (4457), 126 (4849). Chair: 9 (248).

12. Tray: 1 (11). Pail: 27 (1079). Cooking pot: 1 (12).

13. Grindstone: 98 (3984). Knife: 6 (193), 15 (475), 28 (1160), 53 (2040), 63 (2446), 125 (4790). Balance: 16 (555), 19 (703), 126 (4839).

14. 27 (1074), 117 (4501).

15. Clothing: 19 (715). Straw sandals: 15 (487). Fan: 45 (1850), 98 (3986), 115 (4412).

16. 13 (356), 21 (787).

17. Road: 42 (1722). Boat: 12 (348), 34 (1406), 45 (1827). Carriage: 2 (26).

18. Grains: 28 (1145). Corn: 16 (525). Pear: 6 (182). Orange: 118 (4561).

19. Tea: 15 (486). Soup: 24 (929). Oil: 28 (1155). Ginger: 121 (4664).

20. 112 (4358), 121 (4706).

21. 31 (1279), 53 (2058), 130 (5010).

22. Cooking: 49 (1907). Drinking: 29 (1167). Eating: 24 (920), 31 (1263), 121 (4709).

23. Rice: 14 (450), 18 (680), 9 (697), 20 (728), 117 (4495), 120 (4627). Dumplings: 32 (1317), 114 (4407). Fruit: 18 (668), 117 (4494). Peeling fruit: 126 (4838). Coarse Food: 28 (1153). Meat: 79 (3224). Cold Food: 121 (4664).

24. 15 (486), 16 (528), 121 (4678).

25. Drinking tea: 123 (4738). Making wine: 41 (691). Drinking wine: 14 (450), 36 (1544). Getting intoxicated: 14 (417).

26. Walking: 16 (520). Road: 14 (440), 15 (471, 487), 16 (575), 18 (631), 52 (1964), 119 (4601). Boat: 114 (4395, 4402), 116 (4452), 117 (4499, 4510), 118 (4553), 120 (4628). Vehicle: 31 (1263, 1265). Horse: 94 (3770, 3773), 116

(4452), 121 (4692). Searching for a house: 121 (4681). Viewing a house: 20 (728), 28 (1152). Entering: 19 (690).

27. Den: 121 (4680). Well: 121 (4675). Bridge: 15 (4802). Pagoda: 15 (501). Tree: 125 (4789).

28. Floor: 118 (4561). Farm: 15 (488), 19 (691), 115 (4424), 117 (4501). Water: 120 (4632). Hemp: 16 (532). Grass: 44 (1775). Kindling: 17 (603), 43 (1751), 120 (4633). Stamping out fire: 15 (499).

29. Calligraphy: 36 (1547), 44 (1811), 53 (2056). Embroidery: 121 (4680). Carving: 33 (1369). Clothing: 29 (1208). Divination: 64 (2528). Archery: 113 (4375), 118 (4574).

30. Polishing: 121 (4693). Forging: 121 (4669). Alchemy: 114 (4407). Chants: 130 (4984). Repairing pots: 108 (4267).

31. 18 (677), 52 (1964), 121 (4668), 59 (2213).

32. 126 (4859), 44 (1798), 126 (4872).

33. Thieves: 15 (482), 35 (1508), 42 (1719), 43 (1751), 44 (1774, 1777). Tigers: 21 (782). Snakes: 15 (475).

34. 30 (1255), 26 (1053), 124 (4764).

35. *Book of Mencius,* 6A:2; *I-shu* [Surviving works], 1:7b, in the *Erh-Ch'eng ch'üan-shu* [Complete works of the two Ch'engs] (*SPPY* ed.).

36. 95 (3856–3857).

37. 4 (116), 58 (2145).

38. 4 (93), 12 (359), 16 (535), 18 (683), 59 (2218), 95 (3850–3851), 126 (4831).

39. 5 (151), 15 (490), 32 (1318), 53 (2042, 2062), 59 (2210).

40. 6 (188).

41. *Ibid.*

42. 23 (879), 95 (3900).

43. 6 (162).

44. 27 (1082).

45. 19 (704).

46. 20 (746).

47. 36 (1560), 41 (1703), 117 (4522).

48. 59 (2249).

49. 3 (62), 19 (689), 20 (752), 32 (1306), 33 (1359, 1362, 1365), 57 (2129), 117 (4502), 120 (4639).

50. 27 (1085–1086). For more on *li-i fen-shu,* see ch. 19 below, p. 297 ff.

51. 120 (4607).

52. *Wen chi,* 2:10b.

53. *Chuang Tzu,* ch. 7, "Fit to be Emperor or King" (*SPTK* ed.), 3:26a.

54. *I-shu,* 18:16a.

55. 2 (33), 11 (310), 14 (417, 426), 15 (472), 16 (552–554, 564), 17 (605), 18 (681), 28 (1158).

56. 31 (1253, 1262), 41 (1702).

57. 60 (2288).

58. 12 (320, 327), 32 (1325), 33 (1362), 34 (1407).

59. 4 (122), 6 (188), 7 (210), 15 (466, 467).

60. 12 (328).

61. 15 (483).

62. 5 (138), 15 (474), 20 (770), 23 (887), 101 (4125).

63. 64 (2498).

64. 4 (117–118), 12 (329), 17 (601).

65. 117 (4477).

66. 34 (1403, 1405), 48 (1895).

67. 59 (2218), 121 (4667, 4674, 4679, 4699), 126 (4824).

68. 126 (4820).

69. 16 (523, 535), 34 (1426), 50 (1996), 116 (4451).

70. *Book of History,* "Yüeh-ming" [Charge to Yüeh], pt. I, sec. 8.

71. 118 (4541).

72. 121 (4717).

73. Gradual advancement: 8 (220), 10 (259), 115 (4426). Mastery: 9 (240), 42 (1711, 1721). Concentration: 19 (709). Persistence: 10 (274), 35 (1490). Practice: 11 (287).

74. 15 (493). The Three Bonds are those binding ruler with minister, father with son, and husband with wife.

75. 20 (772), 22 (831), 28 (1142), 59 (2239).

76. 20 (763), 120 (4604).

77. *I-shu,* 18:2a.

78. 14 (413), 20 (747), 25 (980), 27 (1085), 43 (1762), 53 (2045), 55 (2087).

79. 9 (237, 238), 14 (449), 114 (4389). See also ch. 16 above.

80. 8 (209, 212, 220, 222, 223, 228).

81. 9 (238, 240, 241, 242, 244, 247, 250).

82. 10 (259, 260, 263, 265, 266, 269, 273, 275). Army also in 16 (529), 41 (1661, 1678), 116 (4469), 121 (4670, 4673, 4676, 4685).

83. 11 (289, 294, 309).

84. 12 (320, 326, 328, 329, 334, 341, 348).

85. 13 (355, 356, 359, 375).

86. *I-shu,* 7:3b.

87. *Ibid.,* 8:16a.

88. The source of this story has not yet been traced. Also in *Yü-lei,* 107 (4240).

89. *Wen-chi,* 36:9a, fourth letter in reply to Lu Tzu-ching (Lu Hsiang-shan). The analogy is found in the *Hsiang-shan ch'üan-chi* [Complete works of Lu Hsiang-shan] (*SPPY* ed.), 2:9a, second letter to Chu Yüan-hui (Chu Hsi).

90. *Wen-chi,* 36:27b, ninth letter in reply to Ch'en T'ung-fu (Ch'en Liang). Ch'en's analogy is found in the *Ch'en Liang chi* [Collected works of Ch'en Liang] (Beijing: Chung-hua Book Co., 1974), 20:290, letter to Chu Yüan-hui.

91. *Wen-chi,* 41:11a, third letter in reply to Ch'eng Yün-fu (Ch'eng Hsün). The common saying comes from the *Shuo-yüan* [Collection of discourses] (*SPTK* ed.), 17:22a, "Miscellaneous Sayings."

92. *Wen-chi,* 41:12a. Also in *Yü-lei,* 126 (4831). The common saying comes from the *Ch'u-tz'u* [Elegies of Ch'u] (*Wen-jui-lou* photocopy ed.), 12:8a, "Seven Admonitions."

93. *Wen-chi,* 44:45b, tenth letter in reply to Chiang Te-kung (Chiang Mo). The common saying comes from the *Lü-shih ch'un-ch'iu* [Mr. Lü's Spring and Autumn Annals] (*SPPY* ed.), 24:4b, "Understanding of words."

94. *Wen-chi,* 58:21a, letter in reply to Sung Tse-chih (Sung Chih-jun). The

common saying is from the *Han Fei Tzu,* ch. 32, "Explanations of Outer Collections" (*SPTK* ed.), 11:2b, pt. 1.

95. *I-shu,* 7:3b.

96. *Wen-chi,* 40:27b, thirteenth letter in reply to Ho Shu-ching (Ho Hao). Ch'eng I's saying is from the *I-shu,* 18:4b.

97. *Han Ch'ang-li ch'üan-chi* [Complete works of Han Yü] (*SPPY* ed.), 14:23b, letter in reply to Chang Chi.

98. *Wen-chi,* 54:8b, seventh letter in reply to Hsiang P'ing-fu (Hsiang An-shih).

99. *Ibid.,* 55:11b, eighth letter in reply to Li Shou-yüeh (Li Hung-tsu).

100. *Ibid.,* 49:9b, twelfth letter in reply to Wang Tzu-ho (Wang Yü).

101. *Ibid.,* 55:27b, letter in reply to Chao Jan-tao (Chao Shih-yung).

102. *Ibid.,* 60:18a, second letter in reply to Tseng Tse-chih (Tseng Tsu-tao).

103. *Ibid.,* 48:25a, forty-fifth letter in reply to Lü Tzu-yüeh (Lü Tsu-chien).

104. 74 (3018). For a penetrating study of Chu Hsi's use of the family, water, and the plant as metaphors, see Donald J. Munro, "The Family Network, the Stream of Water, and the Plant: Picturing Persons in Sung Confucianism," in Donald J. Munro, ed., *Individualism and Holism: Studies in Confucian and Taoist Values* (University of Michigan, 1985), pp. 259–292.

105. *Chou Tzu ch'üan-shu* [Complete works of Master Chou Tun-i], ch. 1.

106. See the *Chang Tzu ch'üan-shu* [Complete works of Master Chang Tsai], chs. 9 to 11, which contain the *I-shuo* [Explanation of the *Book of Changes*].

107. *I-ch'uan wen-chi* [Collection of literary works of Ch'eng I], 6:3b, 6a–b, in the *Erh-Ch'eng ch'üan-shu.*

108. *Wen-chi,* 68:7b–10a, "System of the Deep Garment."

109. *Ibid.,* 69:3a–5a, "Discussion on Imperial Sacrifices."

110. *Ibid.,* 15:19b–23a, "Statement on Imperial Temples."

111. *Yü-lei,* ch. 87, sec. 69 (p. 3553).

112. *Wen-chi,* 44:40b, third letter in reply to Chiang Te-kung.

113. *Ibid.,* 38:16a–b, seventh letter in reply to Yüan Chi-chung (Yüan Shu).

114. *Book of Changes,* "Appended Remarks," pt. 1, ch. 11.

115. *Yü-lei,* ch. 75, sec. 85 (pp. 3068–3069).

116. *Ibid.,* sec. 51 (pp. 3054–3055). In the process of using yarrow stalks for divination, the number of stalks remaining between one's fingers has the numerical value of either 9 or 6. If the number is 9, or "old yang" (an undivided line), it will be transformed into its opposite (a divided line). This means 9 going down to produce 8, the "young yin." If the number is 6, or "old yin" (a divided line), it will be transformed into its opposite (an undivided line). This means 6 going up to produce 7, the "young yang." In either case, a divided line or an undivided line is found. The same process repeated six times will result in six divided or undivided lines, thus forming a hexagram.

117. The Five Agents (or Five Elements) are Metal, Wood, Water, Fire, and Earth.

118. These are the Four Qualities of Change. See the *Book of Changes,* commentary on the first hexagram, *ch'ien* (Heaven, male).

119. *Yü-lei,* ch. 94, sec. 61 (p. 3776).

120. For Ch'en Ching-shih, see my *Chu Tzu men-jen* [Master Chu's pupils] (Taipei: Student Book Co., 1982), p. 223.

121. *Analects,* 1:2.

122. *Yü-lei,* ch. 20, sec. 77 (pp. 744–745).

123. *Ibid.,* sec. 122 (p. 764). For the various moral concepts, see the *Book of Mencius,* 2A:6, 4A:27, 7A:45.

124. *Analects,* 12:1.

125. *Yü-lei,* ch. 105, sec. 43 (p. 4185).

126. *Book of Mencius,* 2A:6, 6A:6. See n. 3 above.

127. *Wen-chi,* 32:17a, forty-second letter in reply to Chang Ch'in-fu (Chang Shih).

128. See chapter 11 above, pp. 168–169.

129. *Yü-lei,* ch. 55, sec. 10 (p. 2078).

130. *Ibid.,* ch. 15, sec. 157 (p. 502).

131. *T'oegye chŏnsŏ* [Complete works of Yi Hwang], Bk. I, 7:4b–35a (pp. 195–211), ten diagrams.

132. The two essays were originally part of ch. 17 of Chang Tsai's *Cheng-meng* [Correcting youthful ignorance] but have usually been printed separately as independent essays.

133. *Wai-shu* [Additional works], 11:6b, in the *Erh-Ch'eng ch'üan-shu.* The reason for the change is not clear and has been variously interpreted by writers. See my translation of Chu Hsi's and Lü Tsu-ch'ien's anthology, the *Chin-ssu lu,* entitled *Reflections on Things at Hand* (New York: Columbia University Press, 1967), p. 81, n. 236. For a description of Chang Tsai's window, see the *I-shu,* 2A:16b.

134. For Yang Tao-fu, see my *Chu Tzu men-jen,* pp. 272–273.

135. *Wen-chi,* 30:12a–b, seventh letter in reply to Minister Wang.

136. *Yü-lei,* ch. 98, sec. 107 (pp. 4016–4017).

# Clarification of
# Certain Expressions

Some Chinese philosophical terms are open to several interpretations and therefore present a great deal of difficulty in translation, such as *li* (principle, order, reason), *ch'i* (material force, vital force, ether, breath), and *wu-hsing* (five agents, five elements, five phases). I have discussed these in several places and need not deal with them here.[1] This chapter is concerned with expressions frequently encountered in Chu Hsi studies that have been controversial or misunderstood, especially in the West. These include *Ch'eng Tzu, li-i fen-shu, tzu-te, hsin-fa, huo-jan kuan-t'ung, mo,* and *i-erh-erh erh-erh-i.*

### "Ch'eng Tzu"

Chu Hsi quoted sayings by "Ch'eng Tzu" (Master Ch'eng) many times in his *Ssu-shu chang-chü chi-chu* (Collected commentaries on the Four Books).[2] This is also true of the material in the *Wen-chi* and *Yü-lei.* In other words, he sometimes referred simply to "Ch'eng Tzu" without specifying the elder Master Ch'eng (Ch'eng Hao, 1032–1085) or the younger Master Ch'eng (Ch'eng I, 1033–1107), thus leaving the reader wondering who is meant. In some cases the context indicates which of the two brothers Chu Hsi had in mind. For example, a pupil asked, " 'Heaven and Earth have their fixed positions and yet the system of Change operates in them.'[3] Why is it only seriousness (*ching*)?" Chu Hsi answered, "The system of Change is natural creation and transformation. The original idea of the Sage [Confucius] was to elucidate the operation of this natural process, but Master Ch'eng applied it to the human person."[4] We know that here Master Ch'eng means Ch'eng Hao, because those are his words.[5] In another case Chu Hsi said, "Yin Yen-ming [Yin T'un, 1071–1142] had to wait for half a year after he attended Master Ch'eng before he was given the *Great Learning* and the 'Western Inscription' to read."[6] Here we know that Master Ch'eng refers to Ch'eng I, because the *Wai-shu* (Additional works) clearly states that Yin Yen-ming studied under I-ch'uan (Ch'eng I).[7]

Chu Hsi often used the literary names of the brothers, especially when they differed on the point in question. In a conversation on nature, for instance, Chu Hsi said, "Here Ming-tao [Ch'eng Hao] was speaking from the point of view of the function of human nature, . . . while I-ch'uan [Ch'eng I] was speaking from the point of view of nature traced to the source of our being."[8] Sometimes he used "the elder Grand Master Ch'eng" and "the younger Grand Master Ch'eng." For example, he said, "If you think of the elder Grand Master Ch'eng, you should realize his easiness and mellowness. If you think of the younger Grand Master Ch'eng, you should realize his sternness in his younger years and his moderation, with broadness for peacefulness in his later years."[9] In such cases, the references are quite clear and there is no reason for misunderstanding. Other cases in which Chu Hsi specified "the elder Master Ch'eng," "the younger Master Ch'eng," "the elder Ch'eng," "the younger Mr. Ch'eng," and so on are also perfectly clear. Why did he fail to use such terms of address in some cases and merely say "Ch'eng Tzu" instead? There must be a reason when the speaker is a man with a logical mind such as Chu Hsi.

In 1168 Chu Hsi compiled the *I-shu* (Surviving works) of the two Ch'engs in twenty-five chapters, and in 1173 he compiled the *Wai-shu* in twelve chapters. These are sayings recorded by pupils of the two Ch'engs. Chu Hsi was careful in these selections. Chapters 11 to 14 of the *I-shu* are explicitly ascribed to Master Ming-tao, and chapters 15 to 25 to Master I-ch'uan. Aside from some cases where Chu Hsi used the names Ch'un or Po-ch'un (courtesy name of Ch'eng Hao) or Ming (for Ming-tao), and Cheng or Cheng-shu (courtesy name of Ch'eng I), the sayings in the first ten chapters of the *I-shu* are ascribed to "the two Masters," and those in the *Wai-shu* are unspecified.

Some scholars have felt uncomfortable with "the two Masters" and have attempted to ascribe each saying to one of the brothers. Ch'en Lung-cheng (1585–1645) compiled the *Ch'eng Tzu hsiang-pen* (Detailed compilation of Ch'eng Tzu) in fourteen chapters; he used the name Ming to designate Ming-tao, the name I to designate I-ch'uan, the word *ho* (combined) to designate both, and a circle to designate neither. Although the number of circles is still high, Ch'en ascribed many sayings assigned in the *I-shu* to "the two Masters" to either Ch'eng Hao or Ch'eng I. Ch'en did not explain the criteria he used. In some cases he is definitely wrong. For example, there are two entries attributed to both brothers in the *I-shu* 2A, on Hung-ch'ü's (Chang Tsai, 1020–1077) concept of purity, unobstructedness, oneness, and greatness; Ch'en Lung-cheng ascribed one to Ch'eng I and left the other unspecified.[10] Or take the saying, "Formerly, when we received instructions from Chou Mao-shu [Chou Tun-i, 1017–1073], he often told us to find out wherein Confucius and Yen Tzu [Yen Hui] found their happiness." This is ascribed to "the two Masters" in the *I-shu*,[11] but Ch'en arbitrarily assigned it to Ming-tao.[12] If it must be attributed to one of the brothers, it would be more logical to assign it to Ch'eng I. Both brothers studied under Chou Tun-i, but the essay "What Yen Tzu Loved to Learn" was written by Ch'eng I.[13] In his *Sung-Yüan hsüeh-an* (Anthology and critical accounts of the Neo-Confucians of the Sung and Yüan dynasties), Huang Tsung-hsi (1610–1695) also assigned it to Ming-tao without explanation. Professor Mou Tsung-san is not too harsh in observing that Huang lacked discriminating principles in his selection.[14]

However, Professor Mou himself also assigned most of the sayings of "the two Masters" to Ming-tao. According to Mou, first, "All sayings described as by 'the two Masters' may be considered as expressions of the early stage in their discussion of learning, and in this stage Ming-tao was the major figure." Second, "Among the sayings of 'the two Masters,' those that are light, free, refined, independent, straight from the heart, and conforming to moral principles, and at the same time possess the air of modesty and reserve are largely the utterances of Ming-tao." Third, "Ming-tao's sayings are simple, often proverbial, with deep and far-reaching understanding." Fourth, "Ming-tao loved to express himself smoothly, while I-ch'uan resorted to analysis." Finally, "The foregoing four points are the key to judging the wisdom of Ming-tao. Grasping this key, we know that the sayings described as by 'the two Masters' are largely by Ming-tao."[15] To assert that the sayings designated as by "the two Masters" are those of the early stage of their discussion, and to maintain that Ming-tao was the major figure, is pure speculation. Neither Chu Hsi nor Huang Tsung-hsi ever made such a suggestion. Mou's standard for the other three points is also subjective. Many scholars have regarded the sayings as belonging to either brother on the basis of similarity in thought or in expression, but Chu Hsi never did this. What was the reason?

It was a pleasant revelation to read the general preface of Lü Nan's (1479–1542) *Sung Ssu-tzu ch'ao-shih* (Selections of four masters of the Sung dynasty explained), which quotes Chu Hsi as saying, "The two Ch'eng brothers *(Ch'eng-shih)* shared their learning in common and their word did not differ. I have therefore generally called them 'Ch'eng Tzu.' " From this we see that Chu Hsi's use of "Ch'eng Tzu" was due not to carelessness or vagueness but to a desire to emphasize that their ideas were similar. I have checked, without success, Lü Nan's quotation against the twenty-five entries under *Ch'eng-shih* in the index of the *Yü-lei*[16] and the 105 entries under *Ch'eng-shih* in the index of the *Wen-chi*.[17]

Lü Nan compiled his anthology from the *Chu Tzu yü-lüeh* (Brief selection of Master Chu's sayings), now lost, by Chu Hsi's pupil Yang Yü-li (1193 *cs*). In all likelihood, the quoted saying now survives only in Lü Nan's work.

I can offer direct evidence to show that "Ch'eng Tzu" refers to the two brothers. In the *Yü-lei* it is said, "Heng-ch'ü compared to Ch'eng Tzu is similar to Po-i and I-yin[18] as compared to Confucius."[19] Here Chu Hsi meant that Master Ch'eng represented the completeness of Northern Sung (960–1126) Neo-Confucianism whereas Chang Tsai represented only part of it, just as Confucius was a sage in all respects but Po-i and I-yin were sages in only one respect. Chu Hsi surely would not have regarded only one of the Ch'eng brothers as representative of Northern Sung Neo-Confucianism. In his own system of the transmission of the Way, he considered both brothers to have continued the line directly from Mencius. He claimed that "Ch'eng Tzu did not transmit the diagram of the Great Ultimate to pupils."[20] He also said, "In the diagram of the Great Ultimate, the idea of forming the images was complete. Its analysis is both deep and refined. Master Chou [Chou Tun-i] could not help drawing it. Viewed from his idea of personal transmission, it must have been his idea that only Ch'eng Tzu could have received it. As to why Ch'eng Tzu kept it a secret and did not transmit it, I suspect that no one was qualified to receive it."[21] Leaving aside the questions of whether Chou Tun-i ever transmitted the diagram of the Great Ultimate to the Ch'eng brothers and whether they refused to pass it on because no one was qualified to receive it, here "Ch'eng Tzu" cannot refer to only one of the brothers, because both studied under Chou and there is no indication that Chou regarded one as superior to the other. Chu Hsi said, "Now the *T'ung-shu* [Penetrating the *Book of Changes*] is entirely an elucidation of the Great Ultimate.[22] Although the book is small, its system is perfect. The fact was that the two Ch'engs received the transmission from him."[23] Here Chu Hsi could easily have said "Ch'eng Tzu" instead of "the two Ch'engs."

There is another entry in the *Yü-lei* where both "Ch'eng Tzu" and "Erh-Ch'eng" (the two Ch'engs) are used—very solid evidence indeed. Chu Hsi said,

Mencius conceived that nature is good. He understood this merely from the angle of the fundamental, without any deliberative thought on how later differences in physical endowment give rise to good and evil. Later scholars failed to understand this and stirred up a great deal of controversy over whether good and evil were mixed. What Ch'eng Tzu said is more refined, namely, "Talk about nature but not about material force is incomplete, and talk about material force and not about nature is unintelligible. It is wrong to consider them as two."[24] We must talk about both nature and material before our discussion can be complete. In his [diagram of the] Great Ultimate, Lien-hsi [Chou Tun-i] said that yin [passive cosmic force], yang [active cosmic force], and the Five Agents[25] are uneven in some places.[26] Based on his doctrine, the two Ch'engs inferred the theory of physical nature. Had Ch'eng Tzu lived before Master Chou, Ch'eng Tzu might not have been able to make such a discovery.[27]

In this passage, Chu Hsi first uses "Ch'eng Tzu," then "Erh-Ch'eng," and then "Ch'eng Tzu" again, surely referring not to one but to both brothers.

Chu Hsi quoted the above saying on nature and material force numerous times. In chapter 6 of the *I-shu,* this saying is assigned to "the two Masters." In one place in the *Wen-chi*[28] and four places in the *Yü-lei,*[29] Chu Hsi quoted the saying without mentioning any speaker. In one place in the *Wen-chi*[30] and two places in the *Yü-lei,*[31] he assigned the saying to Ming-tao. Twice in the *Yü-lei,*[32] once in the *Meng Tzu chi-chu* (Collected commentaries on the *Book of Mencius*),[33] and once in the *Chin-ssu lu* (Reflections on Things at Hand),[34] Chu Hsi attributed it to I-ch'uan. But in eight places the utterance is ascribed to Ch'eng Tzu— once in the *Wen-chi*[35] and seven times in the *Yü-lei.*[36] Hence the number of times the saying is attributed to "Ch'eng Tzu" is twice as large as the number of times it is assigned to either brother individually. This is not the result of Chu Hsi's contradicting himself or having a poor memory; rather, it is due to the similar beliefs about nature and material force held by both brothers. Thus it is perfectly permissible to assign it to Ming-tao or I-ch'uan, and even better to assign it to Ch'eng Tzu (meaning both brothers). Therefore we may conclude that unless the context shows that the speaker is one or the other brother, all references to "Ch'eng Tzu" are identical in meaning to the *I-shu's* references to "the two Masters."

Scholars are not agreed as to who uttered the saying that it is incomplete to talk about nature without including material force and unintelligible to talk about material force without talking about nature. Sun Ch'i-feng (1585–1675)[37] and Ch'en Lung-cheng[38] attributed it to Ming-tao, while Huang Tsung-hsi[39] and Ch'ien Mu[40] attributed it to I-ch'uan. Mou Tsung-san does not know who the speaker was.[41] The *Hsing-li ching-i* (Essential meanings of nature and principle) compiled by Li Kuang-ti (1642–1718), simply says "Ch'eng Tzu."[42] I believe Li comes closest to Chu Hsi's idea.

### Li-i fen-shu

Ch'eng I was the one who made *li-i fen-shu* a cardinal concept in Neo-Confucian thought. In his famous "Western Inscription," Chang Tsai had said that "Heaven is my father and Earth is my mother. . . . All people are my brothers and sisters, and all things are my companions." Chang continued to give examples of ancient sages and worthies who took care of their parents and educated the young.[43] Ch'eng I's pupil Yang Shih (1053–1135) raised the question of whether or not Chang Tsai had been talking only about substance. In reply, Ch'eng I said, "The 'Hsi-ming' [Western inscription] makes it clear that principle is one (li-i) but is expressed or manifested in many ways (fen-shu). . . . You say that it talks only about substance and neglects function. He wants people to extend principle and practice it. That is basically for function."[44] This is the source of the famous doctrine of li-i fen-shu in Neo-Confucianism. The idea is reiterated in Ch'eng I's I chuan (Commentary on the Book of Changes).[45]

The person who led Chu Hsi to this idea of Ch'eng I's was Li T'ung (1093–1163), Chu Hsi's first teacher. Scholars generally contend that Li T'ung taught Chu Hsi the doctrine of observing the disposition of the mind before the feelings are aroused. This is perfectly true, but Li T'ung also taught Chu Hsi about Ch'eng I's doctrine of li-i fen-shu. We learn from Chu Hsi's Yen-p'ing ta-wen (Li T'ung's answers to question) that they discussed li-i fen-shu often and at great length.[46] As Chu Hsi told his pupil Chao Shih-hsia (1190 cs), "Yen-p'ing [Li T'ung] said that the difference between Confucianism and heterodox schools lies in the doctrine of li-i fen-shu."[47] Chu Hsi vigorously promoted this doctrine and made it a fundamental principle in his philosophy. As his pupil Yang Fang (1163 cs) put it, "In discussing the 'Western Inscription' with reference to one's name, there are differences (shu) in one's lot (fen). When one extends to include one's kind, the principle is one."[48] In the Chung-yung huo-wen (Questions and answers on the Doctrine of the Mean), Chu Hsi himself said, "The principle of the world is always one, but when we talk about its fen [lot, position, duty] there are many. This is the natural tendency. . . . With reference to fen, that is the work of Heaven and something beyond man."[49] In the Meng Tzu huo-wen (Questions and answers on the Book of Mencius), he also said, "The principle is one, but the manifestations (fen) are always many. Because the principle is one, one can extend to others what one wants for oneself, and because fen are many, in the demonstration of love, one must begin with one's parents."[50] Similar quotations may be found in many other places. Very often the phrase i-pen wan-shu (one foundation and many differentiations) is used. It means the same thing as li-i fen-shu.

As can readily be seen, fen is extremely difficult to translate. It means one's lot, duty, or position, like that of a son in relation to his parents. In other words, fen is principle as demonstrated, expressed, or manifested in individual cases. In the case of the son, it is filial piety, but in the case of brothers, it is respect. This is what Chu Hsi meant when he answered a question on *fen-shu,* "There is the father, the mother, the son in direct line of descent, the head of the family staff. These are *fen-shu.*"[51] The principle of love is one, but when love is applied to different people in the family, the expressions or manifestations are many and different. There is no difficulty in translating *li-i,* which simply means one principle, but there is no agreement among scholars in rendering *fen-shu.* It is sometimes translated as "many varieties," "differentiations into the many," and "diversification." These terms are possible, except that they may lead the reader to think that the word *fen* means "to divide." However, *fen* should not be read in the first tone, meaning to divide, but in the fourth tone, meaning name, lot, share, or duty. Two examples prove that this is the correct pronunciation. In the *Chung-yung huo-wen* just quoted, there is a punctuation mark at the upper right corner of *fen* to indicate that it is pronounced in the fourth tone. In fact, in the *Chung-yung ta-ch'üan* (Complete commentaries on the *Doctrine of the Mean*) edition of the *Chung-yung huo-wen,* there is a note under *fen* that says it is pronounced like *fu-wen* combined, that is, with the initial of *fu* (to support) and the ending of *wen* (to ask). This note shows indisputably that the word is pronounced in the fourth tone and does not mean "to divide." The other piece of evidence is that, in the above quotations from Chu Hsi, principle and *fen* are used as nouns that are parallel to each other. If *fen* were understood as the verb "to divide," these sentences would make no sense.

We cannot say that Chu Hsi never used the word *fen* to mean "to divide." In one conversation he did say that "principle is of course one. Separately speaking . . . ."[52] In this case he was not saying that principle is divided but was talking about the manner of speaking. In his introduction to the *Commentary on the Doctrine of the Mean,* Chu Hsi quotes Ch'eng Hao as saying that "the *Doctrine of the Mean* first speaks of one principle, next it spreads out to cover the ten thousand things."[53] But here *san* (spreads) does not mean that the principle is divided and scatters; rather, it means that the book spreads out to cover things.

After all this discussion, perhaps the only way out is to interpret rather than translate the term *li-i fen-shu.* I have been using "one principle and many manifestations." However, I won't argue against "oneness of fundamental principle and multiplicity of its concrete manifestation," "unity of principle and its diverse particularization," or similar interpretations, as long as the pronunciation of *fen* is correct.

Was the Neo-Confucian doctrine of *li-i fen-shu* the result of Buddhist influence? Chu Hsi quoted the "Yung-chia cheng-tao ko" (Song testifying the truth by Ch'an patriarch Hsüan-chüeh [665–713] of Yung Chia), which says, "One moon is reflected in all waters and every reflection involves the moon."[54] Chu Hsi was talking about Chou Tun-i's *T'ung-shu,* which expounds the theory that everything has its own principle but all principles come from the same source; thus Chu Hsi would have granted that Buddhists had also had this insight. Among Confucian sources of the idea of *li-i fen-shu,* Chu Hsi could have gone directly to Chou's *T'ung-shu,* where it is said that "the many are [fundamentally] one and the one is differentiated in the many. The one and the many each has its own correct state of being. The great and small each has its definite function."[55] In discussing this point, he said, "Like the moon in the sky, there is only one moon, but when it is spread out over rivers and lakes it can be seen everywhere. But it cannot be said that the moon has been split."[56] No one can deny Buddhist influence on Neo-Confucianism, but the impact was one of stimulation, not of a father-son relationship.

## *Tzu-te*

In the *Book of Mencius,* it is said, "The superior man steeps himself in the Way because he wishes to find it in himself. Having found it in himself, he abides in it at ease. Abiding in it at ease, he can draw deeply upon it. Drawing deeply upon it, he finds its source on the left and right. Therefore the superior man wishes to find it in himself."[57] The question here is not whether it is possible to find it in oneself *(tzu-te),* but how to find it. Two interpretations are possible, to find it naturally and to find it by or in oneself.

In his *Meng Tzu chi-chu,* Chu Hsi explains the passage this way: "This means that the superior man devotes himself to steeping but must follow the Way because he wants to have something to follow and to hold onto, so that he will silently and thoroughly understand and naturally get it in himself." He also quotes Master Ch'eng [Ch'eng Hao], who said, "If learning can be obtained without words by oneself *(tzu-te),* that is getting it in oneself *(tzu-te).* If there is any manipulation or arrangement, that is not getting it in oneself. One must, however, have a concentrated quiet mind and think for a long time, all the while leisurely digesting one's thought. Only then can one get it. If one anxiously seeks it, that is merely selfishness and in the end one will not be able to get it."[58] The emphasis here is clearly on being natural and at ease, not on acquiring it by oneself.

The explanation in the *Meng Tzu huo-wen* is even more elaborate. It says,

> If one studies a principle, one wants to make sure that one gets it in one's person. If one does not get it in one's person, it will be no more than a principle of the mouth and ear. However, one must not try to acquire it by force. One must steep himself in the Way. Only then can he hope to understand silently and thoroughly and get it naturally *(tzu-jan te-chih).*

One who does not steep himself in the Way but directs his effort to the superficial and expects immediate results, or one who does not follow the Way but devotes himself to the task of emptiness and foolishly tends to words and opinions, is not capable of achieving the wonder of understanding silently and thoroughly and being sure of getting it in the self *(tzu-te)*. If one devotes more of his effort and is not anxious for the result, and strictly follows a formula and does not skip the steps, then even though he does not expect to be sure to get it he will naturally get it, and there is nothing to stop him. What Master Ch'eng called being earnestly sincere and understanding principle clearly, having a concentrated quiet mind, thinking for a long time, cultivating at leisure, and deeply nourishing are all ways to reach the Way and how the superior man gets it in himself *(tzu-te)*. . . . If one gets it not in the natural way *(tzu-jan)*, even if there is somewhere to abide in, one will not be at ease. Only when one gets it in oneself *(tzu-te)* can one abide in the principle that is inherent in the self.[59]

Similar ideas are found in the *Yü-lei*, where Chu Hsi said, "When one steeps further, one will naturally *(tzu-jan)* get it. After one gets it by oneself *(tzu-te)* and it becomes one's own, one will abide in it at ease."[60] In the same vein, he elaborated on the saying by Ch'eng Hao and said, "Principle is naturally vast and great. If one only has a concentrated, quiet mind and thinks for a long time, and slowly keeps on cultivating, one will naturally *(tzu-jan)* be familiar with it. If one anxiously seeks it, that means one makes up one's mind to pursue it, and that is merely selfishness. How can one enter the Way?"[61]

The central point in these passages is to arrive at the Way in the self naturally. They leave no doubt that, in Chu Hsi's mind, *tzu-te* meant *tzu-jan te-chih* (to get it in the natural way). In this he differed from Chang Shih (1133–1180), who had another interpretation. The *Meng Tzu ta-ch'üan* (Complete commentaries on the *Book of Mencius*) edition of the *Meng Tzu chi-chu* quotes Ch'en Ch'un (1159–1223) as saying,

There are two interpretations of *tzu-te*. Master Chu understood it as getting it naturally *(tzu-jan)*. By quoting Master Ch'eng, he wanted to prove that his interpretation came from Master Ch'eng. The other interpretation understands *tzu-te* as getting it in the self by oneself *(tzu-te)*. As Nan-hsüan [Chang Shih] said, "Unless one gets it by oneself *(tzu-te)*, one cannot possess it. Only when one gets it oneself *(tzu-te)* does it become one's possession. The reason for this is that this is the knowledge of one's moral nature and is not something another person can give. Hence it is called *tzu-te*."[62] This is similar to what Chuang Tzu called "One gets what one has obtained and not what other people have obtained."[63] However, there is a defect in this interpretation. It is not as good as the theory that it means getting it naturally *(tzu-jan te-chih)*, which has the flavor of leisure and ease.[64]

The standard explanation of the *Book of Mencius* is that by Chao Ch'i (d. 201), who merely said, "The idea is to enable one to get at the source, that is, what is inherent in one's nature," without indicating whether this means getting it by being natural, as Chu Hsi understood it, or getting it by oneself, as Chang Shih understood it. Chiao Hsün's (1763–1820) *Meng Tzu cheng-i* (Correct meanings of the *Book of Mencius*) is quite extensive, but likewise leaves the term *tzu-te* unexplained. Traditional commentators have used *tzu-te* without explanation. Most Japanese annotators of the *Book of Mencius* have rendered the term as "getting it by oneself." The *Daikanwa jiten* (Great Chinese-Japanese dictionary), in citing the passage from the *Book of Mencius,* explains *tzu-te* as "obtaining understanding in the mind by oneself."[65] Scholars in the United States have followed this trend. Since both interpretations are possible, it is perfectly permissible to choose either one. However, as far as Chu Hsi is concerned, one must interpret *tzu-te* as Chu Hsi understood it, that is, "getting it in the natural way."

## Hsin-fa

*Hsin-fa* literally means "the method of the mind" or "the law of the mind." There is nothing wrong with a literal translation, but this one must be used with extreme care or it will lead to a serious misunderstanding of Chinese thought, especially that of Chu Hsi. The earliest occurrence of the term is in a poem by Po Chü-i (772–846), in which he mentions the method of washing the mind,[66] but the compound there is *hsi-hsin* (washing the mind), not *hsin-fa.* Thus most scholars have traced the first use of the term to Ch'eng I. As Yin T'un reported, "Master I-ch'uan once said that the *Doctrine of the Mean* is the *hsin-fa* in which the doctrines of the Confucian School are transmitted."[67] Chu Hsi quoted this saying twice, once in the introduction of his *Chung-yung chang-chü* (Commentary on the *Doctrine of the Mean*) and once in his "Epilogue on the *Doctrine of the Mean.*"[68] In his *Lun-yü chi-chu* (Collected commentaries on the *Analects*), commenting on Yen Yüan's (Yen Hui) question on *jen* (humanity), he said, "My humble opinion is that the question and answer in this chapter are important and relevant words about the *hsin-fa* in which the doctrines are transmitted."[69]

When James Legge (1815–1897) translated the *Doctrine of the Mean,* he rendered *hsin-fa* as "the law of the mind," and this has been followed by later translators. In recent years Western scholars have been greatly influenced by Japan, where Buddhism, with its doctrine of mind-to-mind transmission, has flourished. It is no wonder that the authoritative Japanese dictionary, the *Daikanwa jiten,* defines *hsin-fa* as "the method of cultivating the mind." It continues to say, "A term of the Neo-Confucians of the Sung dynasty (960–1279), it means the preservation and nourishment of the substance of the mind and the examination of the function of the mind." Finally, it cites the saying quoted in the *Chung-yung chang-chü*. Clearly, the compilers of the dictionary regarded *hsin-fa* as "the method of the mind." But there is no such word as *hsin* in the *Doctrine of the Mean*. Yen Yüan's question is on humanity, not on the mind. It is true that, in his commentary on the conversation, Chu Hsi said that "*jen* is the complete character of the original mind," but he was merely arguing for the close connection between *jen* and the mind, not that the *Doctrine of the Mean* or the *Analects* teaches doctrines on the mind. A Chinese dictionary, the *Tz'u-hai* (Sea of terms), defines *hsin-fa* as "essential method," and another dictionary, the *Tz'u-yüan* (Source of terms), defines it as "transmission from teacher to pupil." In neither case is the meaning confined to the mind.

I believe *hsin-fa* should be understood as it has been traditionally understood by Confucians themselves. Perhaps the first one to use the term was not Ch'eng I but Shao Yung (1011–1077), who said, "The learning of the primordial state *(hsien-t'ien)* is *hsin-fa*. Therefore all diagrams start from the center, because all transformations and all affairs arise from the mind. . . . All principles of Heaven, Earth, and the ten thousand things are in it." As Huang Yüeh-chou explained it, "The preceding second chapter on primordial forms and numbers is meant to develop and clarify the excellence and profundity of the diagrams. The impressive and uniform forms and numbers are united in the center. The center is the Great Ultimate; it is the human mind. The methods of the diagrams are the *hsin-fa*. The student may see the mind by means of the diagrams."[70] Although Huang's explanation seems to emphasize the role of the mind, Shao Yung's system is actually a system of principle, for as Huang put it, "Viewing things does not mean viewing them with one's physical eyes but with one's mind. Nay, not with one's mind but with the principle inherent in things."[71] As already indicated, Shao Yung's system is one of forms and numbers, the mechanical side of the *Li-hsüeh* (School of Principle). Surely it is absurd to maintain that the School of Principle centers on the mind. In his essay on "A New Explanation of Shao Yung's Primordial Learning," Professor N. Z. Zia maintains that in Shao Yung's view, *hsin-fa* corresponds to rationalism. Thus it amplifies the mathematical method, which exists a priori and which emphasizes reason: "It is not the ego-centric subjective method employed in general by Idealists, but is instead the logo-centric objective method."[72] This is a far cry from the cultivation of the substance and function of the mind as described in the *Daikanwa jiten*.

The case of Chu Hsi is similar. In establishing his own line of orthodox transmission *(tao-t'ung),* he quoted in his preface to the *Chung-yung chang-chü* the famous sixteen-word formula in four sentences from the *Book of History:* "The human mind is precarious. The moral mind is subtle. Have absolute refinement and singleness of mind. Hold fast to the Mean."[73] Chu Hsi took this formula to be the core of the Confucian transmission. Since it mentions the mind twice, it may be suggested that Chu Hsi's line of transmission was that of the mind. But in his new system of *tao-t'ung,* Chu Hsi was thinking not of the mind itself but of how, in one's self-cultivation and relations with others, one can transform selfish human desires to conform with the Principle of Heaven. This is perfectly clear from his use of the term *hsin-fa* in his comments on the *Analects,* where he was concerned with the importance of propriety for speech, hearing, seeing, and action.[74]

The *Lu-chai hsin-fa* (Method of the mind by Hsü Heng) is ascribed to the outstanding Neo-Confucian of the Yüan dynasty (1277–1368), Hsü Heng (1209–1281). In his preface to the book, Han Shih-ch'i said, "Man is honored in the world because of his mind, and the mind is honored among men because it has method. The transmission of the *hsin-fa* was started by Yao and expanded by Shun."[75] This refers to the sixteen-word formula just mentioned, which, according to tradition, the legendary sage-emperor Yao transmitted to sage-emperor Shun as the formula of transmission from mind to mind. But, in the first place, although the formula is called the method of the mind, it actually refers not just to cultivation of the mind but to cultivation of the whole person. In the second place, the book was not written by Hsü Heng himself but is a collection of his sayings compiled by someone else. It is not confined to the mind but deals with the sun and moon, principle, *jen,* extension of knowledge, literature, statecraft, and so on. Emperor Ch'eng-tsu (*r.* 1403–1424) of the Ming dynasty (1368–1644) also selected from the classics passages on the ways of ruler and minister, father and son, and other topics, and called it the *Sheng-hsüeh hsin-fa* (Method of the mind of the Confucian School). Like the *Lu-chai hsin-fa,* the *Sheng-hsüeh hsin-fa* involves the total learning of the Confucian School, and thus represents the essential method rather than the method of the mind alone.

Chan Jo-shui (1466–1560) wrote the "K'ung-men ch'uan-shou hsin-fa lun" (Essay on the transmission of the *hsin-fa* in the Confucian School). It begins by saying that "the mind is produced by Heaven. Since Heaven has neither internal or external, the mind also has neither internal or external. Whatever has internal or external is not mind. If it is not mind, it is not qualified to unite with Heaven."[76] At first glance, this seems to be a discussion on how to preserve the mind. But the essay continues,

> Man is the principle of production of Heaven, the mind is the principle of production of man, nature is the principle of production of the mind, and the Way is the principle of production of nature. . . . Therefore the mind must be preserved. When it is preserved, all four will be established. . . .

> Neither to go too far and nor not to go far enough—this is the *hsin-fa* of the *Doctrine of the Mean*. The mind embraces all affairs outside and affairs that operate in the mind. Thus the internal and the external are combined. This is the method. . . . This is the way to combine the internal and the external. Great is the *Doctrine of the Mean*. It is perfect.[77]

In the final analysis, what is called *hsin-fa* is the way of the Mean, which unites the internal and the external. It is, after all, the essential way in the transmission of the Confucian School.

Chu Ron-Guey has informed me that there is a book entitled *Cheng-i hsin-fa* (*Hsin-fa* of the correct *Book of Changes*) by the Buddhist monk Ma-i Tao-che of the early Sung dynasty, with an annotation by Ch'en T'uan (c. 906–989). The earliest preface, by Li Chi-tao (Li Ch'ien), is dated 1104 and says, "The term 'correct' refers to the trigrams, which are comparable to the texts of the classics. Commentaries [on the trigrams] by the Duke of Chou [d. 1094 B.C.] and Confucius are but footnotes. Each section [of this book] consists of four sentences. It is the *hsin-fa*."[78] Chu Ron-Guey has also observed that "the use of the term *hsin-fa* seems to be similar to Chu Hsi's usage. Probably early in the Sung dynasty the term was used as a book title. This fact may help scholars to understand the background of the term *hsin-fa*." His observation is both keen and correct. Although the preface is probably later than the time of Ch'eng I, it is obvious that *hsin-fa* does not mean the transmission of the mind but essential method. Regardless of the argument in the preface, the significant point is that the term *hsin-fa* is not confined to the Neo-Confucian School.

### Huo-jan kuan-t'ung

In his amended commentary on the fifth chapter of the *Great Learning*, Chu Hsi said, "After exerting himself in this way for a long time, the student will one day achieve a wide and far-reaching penetration. Then the qualities of all things, whether internal or external, refined or coarse, will be apprehended, and the mind, in its total substance and great functioning, will be perfectly intelligent." Western scholars have often translated *huo-jan kuan-t'ung* as "sudden penetration." More than once I have tried to correct them at conferences and seminars, but they have disagreed. There are two reasons why they have adhered firmly to their view. First, in the West religious consciousness is extremely strong, especially mysticism. One special characteristic of traditional Western mysticism is the idea of a sudden breakthrough. Thus it is natural that Western scholars have interpreted Chu Hsi's *huo-jan kuan-t'ung* as a sudden breakthrough. Second, when James Legge translated the *Great Learning* and rendered Chu Hsi's remark *i-tan huo-jan kuan-t'ung* as "he will suddenly find himself possessed of a wide and far-reaching penetration." His "wide and far-reaching penetration" for *huo-jan kuan-t'ung* was perfectly correct. Whether his rendering of *i-tan* as "suddenly" is acceptable deserves some consideration. Unfortunately, some Western scholars have thought that Legge translated *huo-jan* as "suddenly," and have concluded that Chu Hsi's theory of the investigation of things and the extension of knowledge results in a sudden breakthrough. This is, of course, diametrically opposed to Chu Hsi's doctrine of gradual understanding, but Westerners' views on religious consciousness make it too tempting to resist.

I do not deny for a moment that there is an element of mysticism in Chu Hsi's thought, whatever one may understand mysticism to be. In discussing *kuei-shen* (spiritual cosmic forces or spiritual beings), he said, "They suddenly come and suddenly go. As soon as they are this way, they are that way. The wonderful functioning of *kuei-shen* cannot be predicted."[79] This is mysticism. He also said, "Basically, is it that there is principle first and then material force, or that there is material force first and then principle? This cannot be inferred or investigated at all."[80] This, too, is mysticism. I merely maintain that Chu Hsi's mysticism is different from that of the West, and that *huo-jan kuan-t'ung* should not be understood as a mystic breakthrough.

*Huo-jan* is defined in various dictionaries as "open and great," "open and clear," and so on, but never as "sudden." In his *Ta-hsüeh huo-wen* (Questions and answers on the *Great Learning*), Chu Hsi said, "Therefore the mind of the superior man is broad and extremely impartial."[81] The idea here is the same. Surely Chu Hsi did not mean to say that the mind of the superior man is selfish and suddenly becomes extremely impartial. In the *Ta-hsüeh huo-wen,* he discussed the phrase *huo-jan kuan-t'ung* at great length. He quoted Ch'eng I as saying, "One must investigate one item today and another item tomorrow. When one has accumulated much knowledge, one will achieve a penetration *(kuan-t'ung)* without any restriction *(t'o-jan).*"[82] Ch'eng I is also quoted as saying, "If one understands much, from one's own person to the principles of the ten thousand things, one will naturally achieve an extensive understanding."[83] Again Ch'eng I is quoted as saying, "To devote oneself to investigating principle to the utmost does not mean that it is necessary to investigate the principle of all things in the world to the utmost, nor does it mean that principle can be understood merely by investigating one particular principle. One must accumulate much, and then one will naturally achieve an understanding without any restriction."[84]

To these quotations Chu Hsi added his own words, saying, "One must cover the internal and the external, the refined and the coarse, with nothing left behind, and, furthermore, infer in kind to see them through, so that one day one will achieve a penetration without any restriction."[85] Again, "Let the big and the small embrace each other, and let activity and tranquillity mutually nourish. Never make any distinction between the internal and external, the refined and the coarse. When one accumulates true effort for a long time and achieves a wide and far-reaching penetration, one will know that there is an undifferentiated unity and that there is really no internal and external or refined and coarse to speak of."[86] Again, "Be leisurely and ponder deeply. After accumulating for a long time, one will achieve a penetration. . . . When this happens, one will be free and untrammeled. One should then go forward step by step and investigate another item. After doing this for a long time, there will be much accumulation and in one's mind one will be naturally free and easy."[87] From these sayings, it is clear that progress is gradual and that the result is broad and wide penetration. Two more quotations reaffirm this point. Chu Hsi said, "In learning, there is only gradual advance and no such thing as learning in a hurry."[88] He also said, "As in the case of going forward with the left foot, one then goes forward with the right foot. As the right foot advances a step, the left foot then advances. When this continues without stop, one will naturally achieve a penetration."[89]

Both Ch'eng I and Chu Hsi used *t'o-jan* and *huo-jan* interchangeably. *T'o* means to cast off, but here it means getting rid of old ideas and preconceived opinions. But since *t'o* also means release, Western scholars have inevitably associated it with religious deliverance. Religious release is often a sudden affair, and this reinforces the misinterpretation of *huo-jan* as "sudden."

As to the term *i-tan*, which Legge rendered as "suddenly," no Chinese dictionary supports this interpretation. According to Chinese dictionaries, the term means "one morning," "one day," "some day," or "one time." Among the meanings given in the *Daikanwa jiten*, one is "sudden."[90] When Chu Hsi said, "One day there will be a penetration without any restriction,"[91] it is possible to understand this as implying a sudden penetration. Legge was not entirely wrong when he rendered *i-tan* as "suddenly." In matters like understanding, how can one determine whether it happens abruptly or gradually? But the methodological system of Chu Hsi is definitely gradual. Therefore, the *i-tan* in his commentary on the *Great Learning* should be understood as "one day," not as "suddenly."

In the winter of 1984, there was a symposium on Chinese intellectual history at Tsing-hua University in Taiwan. Among those present were Professor Yamanoi Yū and Professor Watanabe Hiroshi, both of Tokyo University. In my presentation, I discussed the translation of *huo-jan kuan-t'ung*. After Professor Watanabe returned to Japan, he wrote me and said,

Professor Yamanoi has shown me Chu Hsi's letter in reply to Shao Shu-i, in which Chu Hsi said, "In this learning one should . . . advance gradually following an order. Only then can one achieve something. Certainly learning cannot be attained by lamenting with a long sigh (*i-tan*) and skipping the steps, while sitting quietly and thinking far away."[92] "Advance gradually" and *i-tan* are clearly opposites. I am afraid that *i-tan huo-jan kuan-t'ung* cannot be free of the idea of being sudden.

I was thankful for this information, but I still believe that "advance gradually" is the antithesis of "skipping steps while sitting quietly and thinking far away." The *i-tan* in Chu Hsi's letter could mean "suddenly," it is true, but it could also mean "one day." I cannot deny that Chu Hsi never used the term *hu-jan* (suddenly). For example, he once said, "In reading, let one apply one's own effort. . . . In time, one will see by oneself. When one has accumulated a great deal and suddenly (*hu-jan*) exploded, one will naturally understand thoroughly."[93] Thus Chu Hsi did not completely refrain from talking about sudden understanding, but his prevailing method was accumulation and gradual improvement. In any case, neither *huo-jan* nor *t'o-jan* can be understood as *hu-jan*. *I-tan* can possibly be rendered as "suddenly," but its normal meaning is "one day" or "one morning." And Chu Hsi himself used "one day" in his conversation.

Professor Watanabe called my attention to another interesting fact. He pointed out that, in his *Lun-yü cheng-i* (Correct meanings of the *Analects*), Liu Pao-nan (1791–1855) quoted the outstanding Japanese thinker Ogyū Sorai (1666–1738). I asked him for further information, which he quickly supplied. In his comments on the *Analects* 7:27 and 9:13, Liu quoted from Sorai's *Rongochō* (Inquiry on the *Analects*). Sorai expressed the opinion that the fact that Confucius angled without using a net shows his reverential seriousness[94] and that the good price of the beautiful jade meant the price offered by the seller.[95] Although neither throws a new light on the study of the *Analects,* it is significant that more than a hundred years ago there was a Japanese imprint on Chinese thought.

## Mo

In Chu Hsi's official documents, does *mo* (with a component meaning evil spirits) refer to a demonic religion or to *Mo-ni-chiao* (Manichaeism)? This was an issue at an international seminar on Chinese thought held at Princeton University in 1984. In 1190, when Chu Hsi was sixty-one years old, he was appointed prefect of Chang-chou in southern Fukien. He took office in the fourth month and was in office for exactly a year. When he first arrived at Chang-chou, he issued a proclamation instructing citizens to observe the proper mourning rites. Then he prohibited men and women from gathering at the residences of Buddhist monks to receive transmissions of Buddhist scriptures, and female followers from establishing private nunneries. In his proclamations, he used the three terms *fo-fa mo-tsung* (the Buddhist Law and religion of demons), *mo-fo* (demonic Buddhism), and *mo-chiao* (religion of demons). *Mo* is the key word in all three. If it means demon, there is no problem, but if it means *MO* (with a component meaning the hand), it would refer to Manichaeism. In other words, it would indicate that Chu Hsi knew of Manichaeism and prohibited it. This point must therefore be clarified.

In November 1984, there was a conference on "Neo-Confucian Education: The Formative Stage" at the Princeton University Conference Center in Princeton, New Jersey. Although the conference was on Sung education, it centered on Chu Hsi, because it was an outgrowth of the workshop on education at the 1982 International Conference on Chu Hsi in Honolulu, Hawaii. Participants included twenty-three scholars from the United States, Asia, and Europe. Chu Ron-guey of Columbia University presented a paper on Chu Hsi's proclamations on education, in which he rendered *mo* as demon. While I maintained that he was correct, several Western scholars strongly opposed that interpretation. Professor Erik Zurcher of the Sinologisch Instituut, the Netherlands, a world-renowned authority on the history of foreign religions in China, said that during the Southern Sung (1127–1279), Manichaeism still existed in Fukien.

Manichaeism was founded by Mani in Iran in the third century. Its teachings are based on the Zoroastrian doctrine of the dualism of good and evil, mixed with certain elements of Christianity and Buddhism. It was introduced to Sinkiang in the sixth or seventh century, entered the Chinese capital, Ch'ang-an, in 694, and gradually spread over the Yangtze area. As a consequence of the persecution of Buddhism in 845, Manichaeism began to decline. However, there were still traces of it in Kiangsi and Fukien during the Southern Sung. In China it was mixed with the Buddhist and Taoist religions and was called *Ming-chiao* (Religion of light), *Mo-chiao* (Religion of demons), and *Ch'ih-ts'ai Shih-mo Chiao* (Religion of vegetarianism and the worship of demons).

The problem for us is not whether Manichaeism existed in Fukien during the Southern Sung, but whether the term *mo-chiao* in Chu Hsi's official proclamations refers to Manichaeism. In his "Proclamation Admonishing Female Seekers of the Law to Return to Lay Life," Chu Hsi said,

> As social instructions in late ages have not been prominent, the Buddhist Law and the religion of demons (*fo-fa mo-tsung*) seized the chance to develop secretly. It spread perverse doctrines to delude people's minds. It taught grown men and women not to marry, and called it leaving the fam-

ily to practice religion with the hope of blessings in a future life. . . . Isn't it better to let those who are still young and whose appearance has not yet faded return home and obey the order of their elders, openly engaging matchmakers and thus getting married, so as to revive the moral principles of the ancient kings and follow the normal course of human nature and feelings? Isn't it beautiful when the perverse words of demonic Buddhism *(mo-fo)* are stopped and the dirty custom of adultery is wiped out?[96]

In his "Proclamation of Instructions," he said,

Nor should they [members of the community] spread or practice demonic religion *(mo-chiao)*. . . . It is not permissible to keep the coffin at home or in a temple. . . . Never should one employ Buddhist monks, offer sacrifice to the Buddha, or make an extravagant display at funerals. . . . They [men and women] should not establish hermitages on their own under the pretext of engaging in religious practice. . . . Temples and people are prohibited from holding mixed gatherings of men and women during the day or in the evening under the pretext of worshiping the Buddha or transmitting the scriptures. . . . Towns and villages are prohibited from collecting money or donations, or making and parading figurines under the pretext of averting disaster or gaining fortune.[97]

Attention should be paid to two points in these documents: that they were directed entirely at Buddhism, and that they aimed primarily at social reform. There is nothing in them to suggest that Chu Hsi was trying to control religious beliefs. What he wanted was to have Buddhist nuns return to lay life and get married, and his prohibition was confined to private hermitages, some of which had been used for adultery. The practice of parading figurines to avert disaster and to gain good fortune was common to both Buddhism and Taoism. If it is argued that the phrases *mo-tsung* and *fo-fa mo-tsung* refer to *Mo-chiao* or Manichaeism, why was the Taoist religion not also attacked? Furthermore, although Manichaeism probably still existed in Fukien, it did not flourish to the extent of having private hermitages. Ch'en Ch'un, Chu Hsi's pupil, wrote extensively on popular religions in Fukien but made no mention of Manichaeism.[98] Hence *mo* in the phrases *fo-fa mo-tsung, mo-fo,* and *mo-chiao* means "demon." The phrase *fo-fa mo-tsung* does not refer to two different religions but is simply a four-word literary expression. Nor does *mo-fo* refer to two religions but only to "the demonic Buddhist religion." The same is true of *mo-chiao.* In no case does *mo* refer to Manichaeism.

Some may counter that when Shen Chi-tsu accused Chu Hsi of committing six major crimes and four evil deeds, they included "incorporating the perverse teachings of the Ch'ih-ts'ai Shih-mo religion in the unimportant doctrines of Chang Tsai and Ch'eng I,"[99] which clearly shows that Chu Hsi had a definite connection with Manichaeism. My response is that Shen's memorial is based almost entirely on fabrication and rumors.[100] Since Shen mentioned Manichaeism by name, the religion must have existed in Fukien and Shen must have learned of it through hearsay. But the teachings of Chang Tsai and Ch'eng I have not the remotest relation with Manichaeism. There is nothing in Shen's memorial, or anywhere else, to prove a connection between Chu Hsi and Manichaeism, much less any evidence that Chu Hsi prohibited it. In his *Chu Tzu nien-p'u* (Chronological biography of Master Chu), under the year 1190, Wang Mao-hung (1668–1741) said, "The customs [of Chang-chou] especially honor the religion of Buddhism. Men and women gather in monks' residences to transmit scriptures. Unmarried women secretly established hermitages to live in. All these were prohibited." Beyond doubt, only moral Buddhist practice was involved.

## *I-erh-erh, erh-erh-i*

One day, Professor Yang Lien-sheng of Harvard wrote me and said, "It is extremely reasonable to mention the two propositions *i-erh-erh, erh-erh-i* (one-is-two and two-are-one) at the same time. My Chinese friends often use them, but they do not necessarily know their origin. I have now found in the *Li-ch'i lei-pien* (Classified compilation on principle and material force), p. 8a, of the Korean author Master Ta-shan, a quotation from Chu Hsi which says, 'Nature is similar to the Great Ultimate, and the mind is similar to yin and yang. The Great Ultimate is in yin and yang and cannot be separated from them. However, in the perfect sense, the Great Ultimate is the Great Ultimate and yin and yang are yin and yang. The same is true of nature and the mind. This is the so-called *i-erh-erh, erh-erh-i*.' "[101] Although Professor Yang did not raise the question of whether or not Chu Hsi was the first to use the expression, I suspected that Chu Hsi often used it. However, a survey of both the *Wen-chi* and the *Yü-lei* shows that he used it on only two other occasions. In one case he said, "Generally speaking, the mind and nature seem *i-erh-erh, erh-erh-i*."[102] In the other case he remarked that "discussing what is manifested and what is hidden is similar to saying *i-erh-erh, erh-erh-i*."[103]

Since Chu Hsi described the expression as "so-called," it must be an idiom or be derived from an ancient text. But a search for it in the indexes of old texts and dictionaries of idioms has failed to locate it. The Buddhists are fond of saying "One is all and all is one," but this refers to the relationship between one and many, comparable to the Neo-Confucian doctrine of *li-i fen-shu* (principle is one but its manifestations are many), an idea different from *i-erh-erh, erh-erh-i*. The Ch'an patriarch Hui-chao (I-hsüan of Lin-chi, d. 867) uttered a well-known saying,

"One is three, and three is one."[104] But he did not say *i-erh-erh, erh-erh-i*. And no Buddhist writer is known to have used the phrase.

In his *Cheng-meng* (Correcting youthful ignorance), Chang Tsai said, "If the two [yin and yang] do not exist, the one [Great Ultimate] cannot be revealed. If the one cannot be revealed, then the function of the two will cease. Reality and unreality, motion and rest, integration and disintegration, and clearness and turbidity are two different substances. In the final analysis, however, they are one."[105] Here he practically said that one-is-two and two-are-one, although not in so many words. He also said, "Because of one, there is spirit [Original note:] (It is unpredictable because of the presence of the two), and because of two, there is transformation [Original note:] (They extend and operate in the one)."[106] Here the idea of *i-erh-erh, erh-erh-i* is even clearer, although Chang did not use the actual expression. Commentators on his *Cheng-meng,* however, have employed it. Commenting on the "Great Harmony" chapter, Kao P'an-lung (1562–1620) had this to say, "Master Chang made the clarification based on Change that concrete things are the Way. Therefore, he called Great Harmony the Way. The reason is that principle [the Way] and material force [concrete things] are *i-erh-erh, erh-erh-i.*"[107] In discussing "Because of one, there is spirit, and because of two, there is transformation," Yü Ch'ang-ch'eng (*fl.* 1700) also said, "One is united in two, but it also rides in two. . . . Because it is never separated from yin and yang, sincerity is embodied in things and is everywhere. Because it is not stagnated in yin and yang, sincerity operates in things without limit. Therefore it is said that the Way of Heaven and Earth is one-and-two, two-and-one."[108] The expression is slightly different in this case, but the meaning is the same.

Chang Tsai never used *i-erh-erh, erh-erh-i,* but Ch'eng I did use the expression. He once said, "Morning and evening are the way of death and life. If we know the way of life, we know death. If one completely fulfills the way of man, one can serve spiritual beings. Death and life, and man and spiritual beings, are *i-erh-erh, erh-erh-i.*"[109] Chu Hsi quoted this passage in full in his *Lun-yü chi-chu.*[110] It is also quoted three times in the *Yü-lei.*[111] As far as we know Ch'eng I was the first to use the expression, but it must have originated long before him.

Since the time of Ch'eng I and Chu Hsi, many Sung and Ming (1368–1644) Neo-Confucians have employed the expression. Ch'en Ch'un, commenting on the *Analects* chapter on self-mastery and returning to propriety,[112] said, "We must know that self-mastery and returning to propriety are *i-erh-erh, erh-erh-i.*"[113] The *Mu-chung chi* (Collection of wood and bell) of Ch'en Chih (*fl.* 1208) contains this conversation: Question, "Hui-weng [Chu Hsi] said that the hidden and the manifested, the beginning and the end, do not follow two different principles,[114] and Master Ch'eng said that morning and evening are the way of death and life.[115] I suppose that principle does not have two different directions, which is called *i-erh-erh*. The hidden and the manifested are explained in terms of beginning and end, which is called *erh-erh-i*." Answer: "When material force gathers, it begins and grows. When it is scattered, it ends and dies. . . . What is called *i-erh-erh* means that what gathers or scatters is but one material force. When divided, it can gather or scatter. What is called *erh-erh-i* means that although in its division it gathers and scatters, in reality it is one material force. Because it is *i-erh-erh*, whatever is born will die, and because it is *erh-erh-i*, we know life so as to know death."[116] In the words of Huang Kan (1152–1221), in his *Chung-yung tsung-lun* (General discussions on the *Doctrine of the Mean*), "If one knows that substance and function are two, one should apply one's effort to both preservation and examination. If one knows that substance and function are one, one can be at ease with the Mean and devotes one's effort to everything."[117]

These three thinkers were all Chu Hsi's pupils, which indicates that the idea was prevalent in the Chu Hsi School. They were followed by Ming Neo-Confucians. In his comments on Chou Tun-i's diagram of the Great Ultimate, Hsüeh Hsüan (1389–1464) said, "Although the Great Ultimate is not mixed with yin and yang, it is also not separated from them. The nature of Heaven and Earth and physical nature are *i-erh-erh, erh-erh-i*.[118] Lo Ch'in-shun (1465–1547) discussed Chang Tsai's saying, "Because of one, there is spirit, and because of two, there is transformation," and said, "When transformation is spoken of, spirit is in it, and when spirit is spoken of, transformation is in it. When yin and yang are spoken of, the Great Ultimate is in it, and when the Great Ultimate is spoken of, yin and yang are in it. *I-erh-erh, erh-erh-i*."[119] In answer to a question on Heaven and Earth not being of two minds and being unpredictable, Hao Ching (1558–1639) said,

Before the Great Ultimate assumes definite shape, it is undifferentiated and all merged as one. After it assumes definite shape, the one is divided into two and the two are embraced in the one. If you consider it as one, the two are already formed. If you consider it as two, the one embraces them. Thus it cannot be called one or two. Though [Heaven and Earth] are called two, they are neither one nor two. As yang is active and yin tranquil, opening and closing alternates. The one runs through them all. That is why it is called unpredictable. In the case of the human mind, the harmony that has been aroused and the equilibrium that has not been aroused are intertwined, being affected in ten thousand ways and responding to ten thousand things. This is called *i-erh-erh, erh-erh-i*.[120]

Both Hsüeh Hsüan and Lo Ch'in-shun were close to Chu Hsi in thought, and Hao Ching, a specialist on the classics rather than Neo-

Confucianism, also tended toward Chu Hsi. Thus it is generally correct to say that *i-erh-erh, erh-erh-i* is a basic concept in the Chu Hsi School. Wang Yang-ming (1472–1529) and his followers, in contrast, emphasized one and not two. Chu Hsi once said, "One must make the moral mind always the master of one's person and must make the human mind it."[121] To Wang Yang-ming this was splitting the mind in two[122] without realizing Chu Hsi's *i-erh-erh, erh-erh-i* philosophy. In commenting on Wang's criticism of Chu Hsi, Liu Tsung-chou (1578–1645) said,

> The Master [Wang Yang-ming] was entirely correct in saying that the human mind and the moral mind are really one. But when you look at the matter closely, he merely kept some remaining ideas of Ch'eng I and Chu Hsi. Mencius said, "*Jen* is man's mind."[123] The human mind is simply the human mind that Mencius mentioned, and the moral mind is *jen*. If we think of the matter this way, are they one or two? The human mind is simply man's mind. Why should it be described as the false mind or selfish mind? I wish to ask the Master about this.[124]

Of course, Liu's criticism is of Wang's view of the false mind or the selfish mind, not of Chu Hsi's view of *i-erh-erh, erh-erh-i*. Liu censored Wang Yang-ming in many places, but he loyally adhered to Wang's doctrine of oneness as opposed to duality. Wang Yang-ming himself said, "I feel fortunate that my ideas are not in conflict with those of Master Chu, and also am happy that he apprehended before me what our minds have in common."[125] Commenting on this, Shih Pang-yao (1585–1644) said, "Whether or not the Master [Wang Yang-ming] and Master Chu agreed can be seen in this remark."[126] Shih's idea was that Wang had wanted to be one with Chu Hsi. He will not be far amiss if we say that the School of Chu Hsi stands firm with *i-erh-erh, erh-erh-i*, while the School of Wang Yang-ming stands firm with one and one only. The leading Neo-Confucian in Korea, Yi Hwang (Yi T'oegye, 1501–1570), an ardent follower of Chu Hsi, strongly adhered to the doctrine of *i-erh-erh, erh-erh-i*. In his *Sohak chesa* (Introductory remarks on the *Elementary Education*), T'oegye wrote, "The *Hsiao-hsüeh* [Elementary education] and the *Ta-hsüeh* [Great learning] support and complete each other, and therefore they are *i-erh-erh, erh-erh-i*."[127] The proposition spread far indeed.

## Notes

1. See my *A Source Book in Chinese Philosophy* (Princeton, N.J.: Princeton University Press, 1963), pp. 783–791; my translation of Chu Hsi and Lü Tsu-ch'ien's compilation, the *Chin-ssu lu*, entitled *Reflections on Things at Hand* (New York: Columbia University Press, 1967), pp. 359–370; and my "Neo-Confucianism: New Ideas in Old Terminology," *Philosophy East and West*, vol. 17, nos.

1-4 (1967), pp. 15–35. In "Chu Hsi and World Philosophy," in G. J. Lareon and Eliot Deutsch, eds., *Interpreting Across Boundaries: New Essays in Comparative Philosophy* (Princeton, N.J.: Princeton University Press, 1988), pp. 230–264, I have offered some guidelines for the translation of certain terms.

2. The Four Books are the *Great Learning,* the *Analects,* the *Book of Mencius,* and the *Doctrine of the Mean.*

3. *Book of Changes,* "Appended Remarks," pt. 1, ch. 7.

4. *Yü-lei,* ch. 96, sec. 17 (p. 3911).

5. *I-shu* [Surviving works], 11:2a, in the *Erh-Ch'eng ch'üan-shu* [Complete works of the two Ch'engs] (*SPPY* ed.).

6. *Yü-lei,* ch. 85, sec. 176 (p. 3903). The "Western Inscription" or *Hsi-ming* was written by Chang Tsai. For an English translation, see *A Source Book in Chinese Philosophy,* pp. 497–500, or *Reflections on Things at Hand,* pp. 76–78.

7. *Wai-shu,* 12:13b, in the *Erh-Ch'eng ch'üan-shu.*

8. *Yü-lei,* ch. 95, sec. 46 (p. 3859).

9. *Ibid.,* ch. 93, sec. 75 (p. 3748).

10. In the *Ch'eng Tzu hsiang-pen* [Detailed compilation of Ch'eng Tzu] (1643 ed.), ch. 11, Ch'en Lung-cheng assigned the saying in the *I-shu* 2A:16a to Ch'eng I, but in ch. 1 he left the saying in the *I-shu* 2A:6b unspecified.

11. *I-shu,* 2A:2b.

12. *Ch'eng Tzu hsiang-pen,* ch. 2.

13. *I-ch'uan wen-chi* [Collection of literary works of Ch'eng I], 4:1a–2a, in the *Erh-Ch'eng ch'üan-shu.*

14. Mon Tsung-san, *Hsin-t'i yü hsing-t'i* [Substance of the mind and substance of nature] (Taipei: Cheng-chung Book Co., 1968), vol. 2, p. 9.

15. *Ibid.,* vol. 2, pp. 5–9.

16. *Chu Tzu yü-lei* (Taipei: Cheng-chung Book Co., 1970), index, p. 109.

17. Yamanoi Yū, ed., *Shushi bunshū koyū meishi sakuin* [Index to the proper names in the *Chu Tzu wen-chi*] (Tokyo: Tōhō Book Co., 1980), pp. 683–684.

18. According to tradition, when King Wu (r. 1121–1104 B.C.), founder of the Chou dynasty, launched an expedition against the Shang dynasty, Po-i and his younger brother, Shu-ch'i, out of loyalty to the Shang, pleaded with him not to do so. When King Wu finally conquered Shang, the brothers refused to eat the grain of Chou, lived on berries in the mountains, and eventually starved to death. I-yin, who was a minister of King T'ang (r. 1751–1739 B.C.?), founder of the Shang, helped him to bring about peace and prosperity, and later banished T'ang's successor when he failed in his duties, but restored him after he repented. See the *Book of Mencius,* 5B:1.

19. *Yü-lei,* ch. 93, sec. 88 (p. 3751).

20. *Ibid.,* ch. 94, sec. 109 (p. 3790).

21. *Wen-chi,* 31:9a, nineteenth letter in reply to Chang Ch'in-fu (Chang Shih).

22. For an English translation of the *T'ung-shu,* see *A Source Book in Chinese Philosophy,* pp. 465–480.

23. *Yü-lei,* ch. 93, sec. 52 (p. 3743).

24. *I-shu,* 6:2a.

25. The Five Agents (or the Five Elements) are Metal, Wood, Water, Fire, and Earth.

26. The "T'ai-chi-t'u shuo" [Explanation of the diagram of the Great Ultimate] is found in ch. 1 of the *Chou Tzu ch'üan-shu* [Complete works of Master Chou Tun-i]. For an English translation, see *A Source Book in Chinese Philosophy,* pp. 463–465, or *Reflections on Things at Hand,* pp. 5–7.

27. *Yü-lei,* ch. 59, sec. 44 (p. 2200).

28. *Wen-chi,* 41:6a, third letter in reply to Lien Sung-ch'ing.

29. *Yü-lei,* ch. 59, sec. 47 (p. 2202); sec. 49–51 (pp. 2202–2203).

30. *Wen-chi,* 44:19a, third letter in reply to Fang Po-mu (Fang Shih-yao).

31. *Yü-lei,* ch. 4, sec. 64 (p. 113); ch. 62, sec. 62 (p. 2370).

32. *Ibid.,* ch. 4, sec. 48 (p. 108); ch. 59, sec. 42 (p. 2195).

33. Chu Hsi, *Meng Tzu chi-chu* [Collected commentaries on the *Book of Mencius*], comment on 6A:6. Here Chu Hsi does not explicitly state that the saying was uttered by Ch'eng Tzu, but earlier in the commentary he quotes a saying from the *I-shu,* 18:17b, as that of Ch'eng Tzu. Since the sayings in ch. 18 of the *I-shu* are all by Ch'eng I, the earlier quotation must also mean Ch'eng I.

34. *Chin-ssu lu,* ch. 2, sec. 30. Under sec. 28, there is a note saying that "This and the preceding sections were uttered by Ming-tao." Sec. 43 is headed by "Master Ming-tao said." Hence secs. 29 to 42 must be sayings by I-ch'uan.

35. *Wen-chi,* 39:24b, second letter in reply to Hsü Yüan-p'ing.

36. *Yü-lei,* ch. 4, sec. 4 (p. 107), sec. 62 (p. 112); ch. 53, sec. 78 (p. 2059); ch. 59, sec. 44 (p. 2200), sec. 48 (p. 2202), sec. 55 (p. 2205); ch. 137, sec. 68 (p. 5256).

37. Sun Ch'i-feng, *Li-hsüeh tsung-ch'uan* [Orthodox transmission of Neo-Confucianism] (1666 ed.), 2:14a.

38. *Ch'eng Tzu hsiang-pen,* ch. 1.

39. *Sung-Yüan hsüeh-an* [Anthology and critical accounts of the Neo-Confucians of the Sung and Yüan dynasties] (*SPPY* ed.), 15:9a, chapter on Ch'eng I.

40. Ch'ien Mu, *Sung-Ming li-hsüeh kai-lun* [General account of Sung and Ming Neo-Confucianism] (Taipei: Chinese Cultural Publication Enterprises Committee, 1953), p. 72.

41. Mou Tsung-san, *Hsin-t'i yü hsing-t'i,* ch. 2, p. 308.

42. Lu Kuang-ti, *Hsing-li ching-i* [Essential meanings of nature and principle] (*SPPY* ed.), 9:2b.

43. *Chang Tzu ch'üan-shu* [Complete works of Master Chang Tsai] (*SPPY* ed.), ch. 1.

44. *I-ch'uan wen-chi* [Collection of literary works of Ch'eng I], 5:12b. See also his *Ts'ui-yen* [Pure words], 1:23b–24a. Both are in the *Erh-Ch'eng ch'üan-shu.*

45. *I chuan,* 3:3b, in the *Erh-Ch'eng ch'üan-shu.* Also in the *Ts'ui-yen,* 2:30a.

46. *Yen-p'ing ta-wen* (Pao-kao-t'ang [Hall of precious bestowment] ed. of the *Chu Tzu-i-shu* [Surviving works of Master Chu]), pp. 11a, 24a, 27a–b, supplement, p. 7a.

47. *Ibid.,* supplement, p. 9b.

48. *Yü-lei,* ch. 98, sec. 103 (p. 4014).

49. Chu Hsi, *Chung-yung huo-wen* [Questions and answers on the *Doctrine of the Mean*] (*Chin-shih han-chi ts'ung-k'an* [Chinese works of the recent period] ed.), p. 43b–44a (pp. 86–87), comment on ch. 22.

50. Chu Hsi, *Meng Tzu huo-wen* [Questions and answers on the *Book of Mencius*] (*Chin-shih han-chi ts'ung-k'an* ed.), 1:7a, comment on 1A:8.

51. *Yü-lei,* ch. 98, sec. 92 (p. 4010).

52. *Ibid.,* ch. 98, sec. 91 (p. 4009).

53. *I-shu,* 14:1a.

54. *Taishō daizōkyō* [Taishō edition of the Buddhist canon], vol. 48, no. 2014, p. 396.

55. *T'ung-shu,* ch. 22. See *A Source Book in Chinese Philosophy,* p. 474.

56. *Yü-lei,* ch. 94, sec. 203 (p. 3824).

57. *Book of Mencius,* 4B:14.

58. *I-shu,* 11:4a. Cf. 2A:2a.

59. *Meng Tzu huo-wen,* 8:4a–5a, comment on 4B:14.

60. *Yü-lei,* ch. 57, sec. 22 (p. 2131).

61. *Ibid.,* ch. 95, sec. 149 (p. 3894).

62. *Kuei-ssu Meng Tzu chieh* [Explanation of the *Book of Mencius* of 1173] (*Ssu-k'u ch'üan-shu chen-pen* [Precious works of the *Complete Collection of the Four Libraries*] ed.), 4:51a–b, commentary on the *Book of Mencius,* 4B:14.

63. Paraphrasing the *Chuang Tzu,* ch. 4, "Webbed Toes," (*SPTK* ed., *Nan-hua chen-ching* [True classic of Chuang Tzu], 4:10a).

64. This quotation by Ch'en Ch'un is not found in his works now extant. It might have come from his *Meng-Tzu k'ou-i* [Oral explanation of the *Book of Mencius*], which is lost.

65. *Daikanwa jiten* [Great Chinese-Japanese dictionary], vol. 9, p. 413.

66. *Pai Hsiang-shan shih-chi* [Collection of poems by Po Chü-i] (*Ssu-k'u ch'üan-shu chen-pen* ed.), 10:4b.

67. *Wai-shu,* 1:11b.

68. *Wen-chi,* 81:9a–b.

69. Chu Hsi, *Lun-yü chi-chu* [Collected commentaries on the *Analects*], comment on 12:1.

70. Shao Yung, *Huang-chi ching-shih shu* [Supreme principles governing the world] (*SPPY* ed.), 7A:34b–35a.

71. *Ibid.,* 7:26a.

72. *Chung-kuo che-hsüeh ssu-hsiang lun-chi* [Anthology on Chinese philosophical thought] (Taipei: Cowboy Press, 1976) pp. 94–95.

73. *Book of History,* "Counsels of Great Yü," sec. 15. See also ch. 20 below, especially pp. 321–322 and 332.

74. *Lun-yü chi-chu,* comment on 12:1.

75. *Lu-chai hsin-fa* [Method of the mind by Hsü Heng] (*Chih-shih han-chi ts'ung-k'an* ed.), preface, p. 1a.

76. *Chan Kan-ch'üan Hsien-sheng wen-chi* [Collection of literary works of Master Chan Jo-shui] (1580 ed.), 24:42b.

77. *Ibid.,* pp. 43b, 44b.

78. Ma-i Tao-che, *Cheng-i hsin-fa* [*Hsin-fa* of the correct *Book of Changes*], preface by Li chi-tao, p. 3a. The "four sentences" refer to the four sentences in the *Book of History* (see above, n. 73), which is often called *hsin-fa.*

79. *Yü-lei,* ch. 68, sec. 12 (p. 2680).

80. *Ibid.,* ch. 1, sec. 13 (p. 4).

81. Chu Hsi, *Ta-hsüeh huo-wen* [Questions and answers on the *Great Learning*] (*Chin-shih han-chi ts'ung-shu* ed.), p. 17b (p. 34), comment on ch. 5.

82. *I-shu,* 18:5b; *Ta-hsüeh huo-wen, ibid.*

83. *Ibid.*, 17:6a; *Ta-hsüeh huo-wen, ibid.*

84. *Ibid.*, 2A:22b; *Ta-hsüeh huo-wen*, p. 18a (p. 35), comment on ch. 5.

85. *Ta-hsüeh huo-wen*, p. 20b (p. 40), comment on ch. 5.

86. *Ibid.*, p. 21a (p. 41), comment on ch. 5.

87. *Ibid.*, p. 24b (pp. 47–48), comment on ch. 5.

88. *Yü-lei*, ch. 18, sec. 8 (p. 627).

89. *Ibid.*, sec. 12 (p. 629).

90. *Daikanwa jiten*, vol. 1, p. 41.

91. *Ta-hsüeh huo-wen*, p. 20b (p. 40), comment on ch. 5.

92. *Wen-chi*, 55:28b, letter in reply to Shao Shu-i.

93. *Yü-lei*, ch. 11, sec. 77 (p. 295).

94. Liu Pao-nan, *Lun-yü cheng-i* [Correct meanings of the *Analects*], (*Kuo-hsüeh chi-pen ts'ung-shu* [Basic sinological series] ed.), Bk. II, p. 49.

95. *Ibid.*, p. 96.

96. *Wen-chi*, 100:4a–5a, "Proclamation Admonishing Female Seekers of the Way to Return to Lay Life."

97. *Ibid.*, 100:6a–7a, "Proclamation of Instructions." The translation is by Chu Ron-Guey.

98. *Pei-hsi tzu-i* [Ch'en Ch'un's explanation of terms], pt. 2, sec. on spiritual beings. See my English translation entitled *Neo-Confucian Terms Explained* (New York: Columbia University Press, 1986), pp. 142–168.

99. Yeh Shao-weng, *Ssu-ch'ao wen-chien lu* [What was heard and seen in the four reigns] (*P'u-ch'eng i-shu* [Surviving works of P'u-ch'eng County] ed.), 4:10b, "Faction during the Ch'ing-yüan period (1195–1200)."

100. For more on Shen's memorial, see ch. 31 below.

101. *Yü-lei*, ch. 43, sec. 42 (pp. 141–142).

102. *Ibid.*, ch. 5, sec. 56 (p. 144).

103. *Ibid.*, ch. 74, sec. 126 (p. 3018).

104. *Lin-chi Hui-chao Ch'an-shih yü-lu* [Recorded sayings of Ch'an Patriarch Hui-chao of Lin-chi], in the *Taishō daizōkyō*, vol. 47, p. 499.

105. *Cheng-meng*, ch. 1, "Great Harmony," sec. 12, in the *Chang Tzu ch'üan-shu*, 2:4b. See also the *Sung-Yüan hsüeh-an*, 17:5b, chapter on Chang Tsai.

106. *Ibid.*, ch. 2, "Heaven and Earth," in the *Chang Tzu ch'üan-shu*, 2:5b.

107. *Cheng-meng shih* [Explanation of the *Cheng-meng*], comment on ch. 1, "Great Harmony," sec. 1.

108. Yü Ch'ang-ch'eng, *K'o-i-t'ang wen-chi* [Collection of literary works of the Hall of Proper Standard] (*Ts'ung-shu chi-ch'eng* [Collection of series] ed.), 1:16–17.

109. *Ts'ui-yen*, 1:7a.

110. *Lun-yü chi-chu*, comment on 11:11.

111. *Yü-lei*, ch. 39, sec. 20, 21 (p. 1614); ch. 96, sec. 82 (p. 3934).

112. *Analects*, 12:1.

113. *Pei-hsi ta-ch'üan-chi* [Complete collected works of Ch'en Ch'un] (*Ssu-k'u ch'üan-shu chen-pen* ed.), 7:7a.

114. *Wen-chi*, 43:15a–b, letter in reply to Wu Kung-chi (Wu Chi).

115. *Ts'ui-yen*, 1:7a.

116. Ch'en Chih, *Mu-chung chi* [Collection of wood and bell] (*Ssu-k'u ch'üan-shu chen-pen* ed.) 1:87b.

117. *Mien-chai chi* [Collected works of Huang Kan] (*Ssu-shu ch'uan-shu chen-pen* ed.), 3:39a.

118. Hsüeh Hsüan, *Tu-shu lu* [Records of reading] (*Chin-shih han-chi ts'ung-k'an* ed.), 2:15a–b (p. 106).

119. Lo Ch'in-shun, *K'un-chih chi* [Knowledge painfully acquired] (1528 ed.), 1:21a–b.

120. Quoted in the *Ming-ju hsüeh-an* [Anthology and critical accounts of Neo-Confucians of the Ming dynasty] (*SPPY* ed)., 55:8a, chapter on various scholars.

121. Chu Hsi, *Chung-yung chang-chü* [Commentary on the *Doctrine of the Mean*], preface.

122. Wang Yang-ming, *Ch'uan-hsi lu* [Instructions for practical living], sec. 10. See my translation, also entitled *Instructions for Practical Living* (New York: Columbia University Press, 1963), p. 17.

123. *Book of Mencius,* 6A:11.

124. *Liu Tzu ch'üan-shu i-pien* [Supplement to the complete works of Master Liu Tsung-chou] (1892 ed.), 13:4b.

125. Preface to Wang Yang-ming's "Chu Hsi's Final Conclusions Arrived at Late in Life" at the end of his *Ch'uan-hsi lu*. See *Instructions for Practical Living*, p. 266.

126. Shih Pang-yao, *Yang-ming Hsien-sheng chi-yao* [Anthology of important sayings of Master Wang Yang-ming] (1906 ed.), 4:91a–b.

127. *T'oegye chŏnsŏ* [Complete work of Yi Hwang (Yi T'oegye)], (*Taedong munhwa yon'gu wŏn* [Great Eastern Institute of Culture] ed.), Bk. I, p. 202.

# -20-

# The New *Tao-t'ung*

THE concept of the *tao-t'ung* (tradition of the Way) has had a long history. It developed from stage to stage until it reached its culmination in Chu Hsi. Since I have dealt with the subject elsewhere in great detail,[1] it is necessary here only to add new material and to emphasize Chu Hsi's contribution.

Mencius was the first to conceive of the idea. According to him, the tradition originated with the legendary sage-emperors Yao and Shun. It was transmitted every five hundred years, and was given successively to the sagely King T'ang (r. 1751–1739 B.C.?), King Wen (r. 1171–1122 B.C.?), and Confucius.[2] Han Yü (768–824) repeated this but said that the tradition was suspended after the death of Mencius because Hsün Tzu (313–238 B.C.?) and Yang Hsiung (53 B.C.–A.D. 18) were neither clear nor refined enough to receive it.[3] Ch'eng I (Ch'eng I-ch'uan, 1033–1107) declared that his elder brother, Ch'eng Hao (Ch'eng Ming-tao, 1032–1085), had acquired the "suspended learning" in the surviving classics.[4] Chu Hsi accepted this, but he also expanded it, modified it, and refined it to bring the whole tradition to its apex. In his time, it was generally accepted that the tradition originated with Yao and Shun, was transmitted to Confucius and Mencius, was suspended after Mencius, and was revived by the two Ch'engs. Hence in 1172, Li Yüan-kang drew up the following chart:[5]

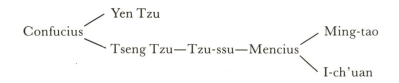

Yao—Shun—Yü—T'ang—Wen—Wu—Duke Chou—Confucius

Confucius 〈 Yen Tzu

Tseng Tzu—Tzu-ssu—Mencius 〈 Ming-tao

I-ch'uan

Chu Hsi was probably not aware of this diagram, but it reflects the general belief of the time, which Chu Hsi must have shared. In the *Yü-lei* it is recorded that he said, "The Way was successively perfected by sages and worthies. If after Yao and Shun there had been no Confucius, where could later generations have gone to seek to understand it? If after Confucius there had been no Mencius, there would be no understanding, either. Only several thousand years after Mencius did we have the Ch'eng brothers who expounded the principle."[6] But this does not tell the whole story. To get a complete picture of how Chu Hsi viewed the *tao-t'ung*, we have to see what contributions he made to it and how he gave the system an entirely new complexion.

There are four ways in which Chu Hsi introduced new elements into the prevailing concept of the tradition of the Way. First, he coined the term *tao-t'ung*. In the 1189 preface to his *Chung-yung chang-chü* (Commentary on the *Doctrine of the Mean*), he said, "The history of the *tao-t'ung* had its beginning," thus using the term for the first time. The two characters *tao* and *t'ung* had already appeared in Li Yüan-kang's diagram, but they had appeared separately, not as a compound. It has been maintained that the term appeared in an official document as early as 1136, but the source cited merely says, "Your servant humbly states that the Way of Confucius was transmitted to Tseng Tzu . . . Tzu-ssu . . . and Mencius, after whom it was not transmitted. More than a thousand years later, Ch'eng Hao and Ch'eng I passed on the Way. . . . Being a worthy, Hsieh Liang-tso [1050–c. 1120] personally transmitted the *tao-hsüeh* [Learning of the Way]. None in the world could match him."[7] This was written more than fifty years before Chu Hsi's preface to the *Chung-yung chang-chü*. However, it only mentions *tao-hsüeh*, not *tao-t'ung*, so although the idea was present, the term was not.

Second, Chu Hsi gave *tao-t'ung* a philosophical interpretation. Ever since, *tao-t'ung* has been a philosophical category. This was truly epoch-making. Chu Hsi's interpretation was arbitrary, but it introduced a new concept just the same. His preface says,

When the sacred sages of antiquity continued the work of Heaven and established the ultimate, the history of the tradition of the Way *(tao-t'ung)* had its beginning. As we learn in the classic, "Hold fast the Mean."[8] That is what Yao transmitted to Shun. "The human mind *(jen-hsin)* is precarious. The moral mind *(tao-hsin)* is subtle. Have absolute refinement and singleness of mind. 'Hold fast the Mean.' "[9] This is what Shun transmitted to Yü. . . . Since their time, one sage after another has handed down the tradition. King T'ang, King Wen, and King Wu [r. 1121–1116 B.C.] inherited and passed on the tradition as sovereigns, and Kao-yao,[10] I-yin,[11] Fu Yüeh,[12] Duke Chou (d. 1094), and Duke Shao (d. 1056 B.C.)[13] inherited and passed on the tradition as ministers. As to our Grand Master [Confucius], although he did not hold any official position, in the way

he continued the tradition of past sages and enlightened future generations, his accomplishment was superior to that of Yao and Shun. However, few understood him in his time. Only what was handed down by Yen
Hui and Tseng Shen was true to his fundamental principles. When it
came to the next generation, there was the person of Confucius' grandson
Tzu-ssu. . . . From Tzu-ssu the tradition was further transmitted to
Mencius. . . . When the Masters Ch'eng, the two brothers, appeared,
they had something to look into in order to continue the transmission that
had been interrupted for a thousand years.

The quotation on the human mind, the moral mind, refinement, singleness, and the Mean totals sixteen Chinese characters in four sentences,
and has come to represent the *tao-t'ung* as the "sixteen-word formula."

However, Chu Hsi's preface merely states the fundamental principle
without clarifying it. His disciple, Huang Kan (1152–1221), wrote the
"Sheng-hsien tao-t'ung ch'uan-shou tsung-hsü-shuo" (General treatise
on the transmission of the tradition of the Way of the sages and
worthies), in which he attempted to provide a detailed explanation.
Briefly, Huang thought that the tradition that Yü transmitted to King
T'ang consisted of rites and moral principles. The tradition that King
T'ang transmitted to King Wen was "to govern the mind with rites and
to govern affairs with moral principles."[14] The tradition that King Wen
transmitted to King Wu and Duke Chou was that "seriousness means
to straighten the internal life and righteousness means to square the
external life."[15] The tradition that Duke Chou transmitted to Confucius
was the doctrine of "extensive study of literature and restraining oneself
with rules of propriety" and "mastering oneself and returning to propriety," as taught in the *Analects,*[16] as well as the doctrines of the investigation of things, extension of knowledge, sincerity of the will, rectification of the mind, cultivation of the person, regulation of the family,
ordering of the state, and bringing peace to the world, as taught in the
*Great Learning.*[17] Yen Tzu inherited the teachings of the *Analects,* while
Tseng Tzu inherited those of the *Great Learning.* As to Tzu-ssu, first he
taught caution, apprehension, and being watchful over oneself when
alone; next he taught knowledge, humanity, and courage; and finally he
taught sincerity.[18] The tradition that Mencius received from Tzu-ssu
consisted of seeking the lost mind,[19] accumulating righteousness,[20] and
the fullest extension and development (of original goodness),[21] in that
order.[22] Huang Kan's account is no less arbitrary than Chu Hsi's, but
his attempt to bring out the philosophical nature of the tradition of the
Way must nevertheless be applauded.

Chu Hsi's third innovation was to extend the *tao-t'ung* to high antiquity. Because it was necessary to view the tradition from a philosophical

angle, he placed its origin earlier than the time of Yao and Shun. As his preface says, "The sacred sages of antiquity continued to do the work of Heaven and established the ultimate." By "sacred sages of antiquity," Chu Hsi meant the legendary sages Fu-hsi, Shen-nung, the Yellow Emperor, Yao, and Shun. This can be seen in his preface to the *Ta-hsüeh chang-chü* (Commentary on the *Great Learning*), where he says, "This is how Fu-hsi, Shen-nung, the Yellow Emperor, Yao, and Shun continued the work of Heaven and established the ultimate." He mentioned Fu-hsi in great seriousness, and did so repeatedly. He is quoted in the *Yü-lei* as saying,

"If Heaven had not produced Chung-ni [Confucius], it would have been an eternal night." T'ang Tzu-hsi [T'ang Keng] once saw this saying on the beam of a postal station. Chi-t'ung [Ts'ai Yüan-ting, 1135–1198] said, "It was impossible for Heaven, having produced Fu-hsi, Yao, Shun, and King Wen, not to produce Confucius, and later not to produce Mencius. Two thousand years later, it was impossible for Heaven not to produce the two Ch'engs."[23]

Chu Hsi also said, "The Way of the Masters [the Ch'engs] is the same as that of Fu-hsi, Yao, Shun, Yü, T'ang, Wen, Wu, Duke Chou, Confucius, and Mencius."[24] Again, he said, "The *tao-t'ung* is traced far back, to Fu-hsi and the Yellow Emperor, and was synthesized in the great completion [by Confucius]."[25] Thus Fu-hsi was invoked again and again. Chu Hsi did so because the philosophical foundation of the tradition of the Way based not only on the sixteen-word formula of the *Book of History* but also on the Great Ultimate (*T'ai-chi*) of the *Book of Changes*. According to this classic, "In the system of Change there is the Great Ultimate. It generates the Two Modes [yin, or the passive cosmic force, and yang, or the active cosmic force]. The Two Modes generate the Four Forms [major and minor yin and yang]. The Four Forms generate the Eight Trigrams."[26] According to tradition, Fu-hsi devised the Eight Trigrams,[27] which is why Chu Hsi said, "The Eight Trigrams were revealed when the diagram emerged from the Yellow River, and the Nine Categories were in order when the writing appeared in the Lo River."[28]

Chu Hsi's fourth innovation was to add Chou Tun-i (1017–1073) to the line of transmission. Because of Chu Hsi's philosophical emphasis, he strongly upheld the theory that the Ch'eng brothers continued the *tao-t'ung* that had been suspended after Mencius. Of the early Sung Neo-Confucians, he set aside both Chang Tsai (1020–1077) and Shao Yung (1011–1077), because he felt that the former's system of *ch'i* (material force) was one-sided and the latter's philosophy based on form and number was too mechanical. He did not even include his own teacher, Li T'ung (1093–1163), in his *tao-t'ung* system, probably because Li did not discuss principle *(li)* enough to suit his taste. And although Chu Hsi praised the Ch'eng brothers highly, he nevertheless considered them insufficient for transmitting the philosophical significance of the *tao-t'ung*, because they had not clarified the relationship between principle and material force. To do this himself, Chu Hsi adopted the philosophy of the Great Ultimate and yin and yang, and because the two Ch'engs had not talked about these topics, he turned to Chou Tun-i.

Chou was known for his *T'ung-shu* (Penetrating the *Book of Changes*), but he had also written a short treatise on the Great Ultimate, the "T'ai-chi-t'u shuo" (Explanation of the diagram of the Great Ultimate). This work remained obscure until Chu Hsi promulgated it vigorously and made it the foundation of his own philosophical system. In so doing he had to swallow his pride, because the diagram came from Taoism, which he denounced. Chou obtained the diagram from Mu Po-ch'ang, who had inherited it from the Taoist priest Ch'en T'uan (906–989). In this diagram, the *Wu-chi* (Ultimate of Nonbeing) is also the *T'ai-chi* (Great Ultimate). The *T'ai-chi* successively generates the two material forces, and through their interaction, the myriad things. Thus principle (the Great Ultimate) and material force (yin and yang) operate together. The significant point about Chou's diagram is that at the end of the universal operation, the sage finally settles affairs by the principles of the Mean, correctness, humanity, and righteousness. Thus Taoist metaphysics is made to serve Confucian ethics.[29]

Thus prior to Yao and Shun, Chu Hsi added Fu-hsi, Shen-nung, and the Yellow Emperor, and between the two Ch'engs and Mencius, he added Chou Tun-i. Chu Hsi said, "After more than a thousand years, the continuity was resumed. Chou and the Ch'engs received it and transmitted it. The ten thousand principles came from one source."[30] Here Chu Hsi did not mean to deny that Ch'eng Hao obtained the teaching of Mencius in the surviving classics. What he meant was that Chou Tun-i continued the tradition historically, by virtue of his explanation of the diagram, while the Ch'engs were instrumental in clarifying the tradition from the philosophical point of view. Since the Ch'eng brothers clarified the Way, it can be said that they derived the Way directly from Mencius. As Chu Hsi said, "Since the decline of the Chou dynasty [1111–249 B.C.], Mencius passed away and there was no one to transmit the Way. . . . Then the Master [Chou Tun-i] appeared. Without any help from a teacher, he quietly understood the substance of the Way. He drew the diagram and did the writing. He laid the foundation and advocated the essential. At that time the Ch'engs saw these and knew them. Thereupon they expanded and clarified them."[31]

Chu Hsi firmly believed that the Ch'engs had studied under Chou; that Chou transmitted the diagram to them; and that the brothers did not talk about the Great Ultimate simply because they found no one to whom they could transmit it.[32] These contentions have given rise to a great deal of controversy over the centuries. I have discussed the pros and cons elsewhere; there is no need to repeat them here.[33] The important point is that, in between Mencius and the two Ch'engs, Chu Hsi added Chou Tun-i. This is the most radical change he made in the system of the *tao-t'ung*. He said, "The Master's [Chou] learning of the Way is profound and excellent. It was transmitted from Heaven. Above, he continued it from Confucius and Yen Tzu, and below, he opened it up for the Ch'engs."[34] He also said, "The tradition of the two Ch'engs came from our Grand Old Man Chou."[35] He said further, "When the Master appeared, he elaborated and clarified the Way and transmitted it to the Ch'engs."[36] Again, he said, "The learning of the Grand Master Lien-hsi [Chou Tun-i] . . . was transmitted to the Masters Ch'eng of Honan."[37] Chu Hsi was so insistent about this because the theories of the Great Ultimate and yin and yang were woven into his philosophy. Therefore he traced the system all the way back to Fu-hsi and added Chou Tun-i ahead of the Ch'engs. Thus there is a logical connection between Chu Hsi's philosophy and his concept of the *tao-t'ung*.

In addition to coining the term, giving it a philosophical interpretation, tracing its source back to Fu-hsi, and adding the important link of Chou Tun-i, there is another point that Chu Hsi never explicitly claimed but that his pupils, friends, and later followers took for granted —namely, that Chu Hsi himself continued the *tao-t'ung*. Chu Hsi did hint as this idea more than once. In the preface of his *Ta-hsüeh chang-chü*, he said, "The two Grand Masters Ch'eng of Honan appeared and were able to continue the transmission from Mencius. . . . Although I am not bright, fortunately I was able to learn indirectly and heard from them." By what he had heard, Chu Hsi meant more than the basic doctrines of the classics: he meant the Confucian Way in general, that is to say, the transmission from Confucius and Mencius. Toward the end of his life, after he had built the Chu-lin Ching-she (Bamboo Grove Study) in K'ao-t'ing in Chien-yang County, Chu Hsi performed a religious ceremony before the portrait of Confucius in the Bamboo Grove Study and read the written report, in which he recounted the transmission of the Way from Fu-hsi through Confucius and Mencius to Chou and the Ch'engs, and pointed out that Shao Yung, Chang Tsai, and Ssu-ma Kuang (1019–1086) traveled on different roads but arrived at the same destination. He also said, "Although ordinary and ignorant, I received the right direction to moral principles at youth. I did not have a regular teacher in my middle years, but in later years I have encountered those who embodied the Way."[38]

This may well indicate that Chu Hsi thought he himself was in line to perpetuate the *tao-t'ung;* at any rate, that was the common belief among his pupils. In his narration of the transmission of the Way, after recounting the succession from Yao and Shun to Mencius, Chu Hsi's son-in-law Huang Kan said,

> When it came to Master Chou [Tun-i], he regarded sincerity as the foundation and desires as a warning,[39] and that was the tradition Master Chou continued from Confucius and Mencius. When it came to the two Ch'engs, they said, "Self-cultivation requires seriousness; the pursuit of learning depends on the extension of knowledge."[40] This is the tradition that the two Ch'engs continued from Master Chou. The learning of our late Teacher, Wen Kung [Chu Hsi], can be found in the Four Books,[41] but its essential lies especially in the *Great Learning,* which is the program for entering the Way. . . . This is the tradition our late Teacher continued from the two Ch'engs.[42]

In his "Record of the Chu Wen Kung Shrine at Hui-chou," Huang said, "The Way prevailed only because there were Yao, Shun, Yü, T'ang, Wen, Wu, and Duke Chou. The Way became clear only because there were Confucius and Mencius. It was continued by Masters Chou, the Ch'engs, and Chang [Tsai], and the Way of Masters Chou, the Ch'engs, and Chang was continued by Wen Kung Master Chu [Hsi]. This is the transmission of the Way through ten thousand generations beyond question."[43] In his "Chu Tzu hsing-chuang" (Biographical account of Master Chu), he also said, "I have heard that the correct tradition of the Way waited for the proper person before it was transmitted. . . . Since the time of Confucius, Tseng Tzu and Tzu-ssu continued the Way in its subtlety, but it didn't become prominent until Mencius. Since the time of Mencius, Masters Chou, the Ch'engs, and Chang continued the Way after its suspension, but it did not become manifest until our Master."[44] Here Huang Kan comes close to equating Chu Hsi with Mencius.

Huang Kan's schoolmate, Ch'en Ch'un (1159–1223), spoke in the same vein:

> From the very beginning, Fu-hsi created the Changes and opened up the universe. . . . Yao, Shun, Yü, T'ang, Wen, and Wu successively transmitted. . . . Confucius . . . became the teacher for ten thousand generations. . . . After Mencius, the transmission was lost. . . . Consequently Master Lien-hsi [Chou Tun-i] and the two Masters Ch'eng of Honan appeared one after the other with their outstanding quality of being the first to know and to awaken. . . . Proceeding from their subtle words and surviving principles, Chu Wen Kung refined them, clarified them, and made them crystal clear.[45]

That Chu Hsi inherited the *tao-t'ung* was not only a common belief among his pupils but also an accepted orthodoxy throughout the Yüan, Ming, and Ch'ing dynasties (1277–1911).[46]

Did Chu Hsi choose someone, or did he intend to choose someone, to continue the tradition? A great deal of misinformation has surrounded this controversial question. In its biography of Huang Kan, the *Sung shih* (History of the Sung dynasty) says, "When [Chu Hsi] was near death, he gave his "deep" garment[47] and the books he wrote to Kan. In his handwritten farewell letter, he said, 'Here I place my trust of the Way. I have no more regrets.' "[48] This has been repeated in two basic accounts of the Chu Hsi School, namely, the *K'ao-t'ing yüan-yüan-lu* (Source and development of the Chu Hsi School)[49] and the *Sung-Yüan hsüeh-an* (Anthology and critical accounts of the Neo-Confucians of the Sung and Yüan dynasties).[50] But the great authority on the biography of Chu Hsi, Wang Mao-hung (1668–1741), flatly denied it, saying, "As to the *Sung shih*'s claim that Kan was sent the 'deep' garment, there is not the slightest evidence [for this]. This is a secret borrowing of the doctrine of transmission of the Ch'an [Meditation] School symbolized by a monk's robe and bowl. Undoubtedly this is a farfetched story."[51]

Wang is correct. Neither the several chronological biographies *(nien-p'u)* of Chu Hsi nor the "Hsing-chuang" by Huang Kan mentions the gift of a robe. When Chu Hsi passed away, his pupils Ts'ai Ch'en (1167–1230) and Chu Mu (*fl.* 1200) were present. Both wrote detailed accounts of the Master's sickness and death, and no reference to the robe is made.[52] The letter to Huang Kan that Chu Hsi wrote the day before his death says, "I am writing you on this eighth day of the third month. . . . The messenger has returned with your letter, from which I know that you have gone back to San-shan.[53] . . . You should make more effort in everything. The trust of my Way lies with you. I have no more regrets."[54] Both Ts'ai Ch'en and Chu Mu witnessed Chu Hsi writing his last letters. Chu Mu said that the Teacher first wrote to his son Tsai and then to Huang Kan and Fan Nien-te asking them to continue his work on ritual texts. We know that Chu Mu is correct in this because both the available *nien-p'u* and Huang Kan's "Hsing-chuang" state that Chu Hsi wrote first to his son. Only in the *Nien-p'u* by Chu Yü, the sixteenth-generation descendant, is the order reversed, with the letters to Huang and Fan appearing before the one to Chu Hsi's son.[55] This *nien-p'u* may be based on the earliest *nien-p'u*, which is no longer extant. In any case, this is a minor matter, except that if Chu Hsi had Huang Kan in mind for continuing the transmission, he would probably have written Huang first.

Although Wang Mao-hung rejected the theory of the gift of the robe, he hinted that Chu Hsi did intend to transmit the Way and that Huang Kan hoped to assume the task. This matter merits examination. Wang said:

On his deathbed, Master Chu wrote Mien-chai [Huang Kan] and said, "The trust of my Way lies with you. I have no more regrets." Here he was talking only about the process of the transmission of learning, and I don't know whether he was equating Huang with Yen Tzu and Tseng Tzu of the Confucian School. However, in his letters to friends in later years, he often talked about the transmission of the Confucian Way hanging in the balance. And in talking about the followers of the Ch'eng brothers, he said none of them was capable of the transmission of the robe and the bowl. Here his subtle idea can be seen. In Mien-chai's last funeral address, he said, "In entrusting me in his last year and in his repeated injunctions on his deathbed, he was greatly worried about the discontinuance of his subtle words and the distortion of the great principles. What kind of a person am I to face up to such a great expectation?"[56] Upon examining this letter, we find no such idea [of transmission]. In the supplementary collection [of the *Wen-chi*] there is a letter to Chih-ch'ing [Huang Kan] that says, "Formerly, some of the elders of Ch'an worried about the lack of transmission of their learning and reached the point of shedding tears. Personally, I never expect to see this situation."[57] This letter was written between 1198 and 1199. His [Huang's] tomb address expressed the same sentiment, that is, he had great expectations but dared not say that he had actually received the transmission. Such is the great caution of people of the past.[58]

What Wang was saying was that Chu Hsi had the subtle idea of passing on the tradition to Huang Kan, and that Huang Kan was aware of this. To Wang, the references to the transmission in the Ch'eng School and to the robe and bowl tradition of Ch'an Buddhism made this all very clear.

Nevertheless, I am afraid that Wang's contention is farfetched and was influenced by the Ch'an tradition. He was correct in interpreting Chu Hsi's "trust of my Way" as referring to the transmission of learning, not of the *tao-t'ung* itself, and he was sound in being skeptical about Chu Hsi equating Huang Kan with Yen Tzu and Tseng Tzu. But to maintain that Huang Kan's profession of inability to bear the responsibility means that he expected to receive it is to misunderstand Huang Kan. By "Mien-chai's last funeral address" Wang meant Huang Kan's tomb address, from which Wang's quotation comes. But this tomb address was not written until twenty-one years after Chu Hsi's death, when Huang Kan was sixty-nine years old. As Huang said, "For several months sputum has arisen above and the abdomen has swelled below. I am afraid one day I shall disappear before the morning dew." Because of his declining health, Huang sent his son Lo to report to the tomb of the Teacher. In that address Huang exclaimed: "What kind of a person am I to be among the pupils?" "What kind of a person am I to receive personally the finest of the Way and virtue?" "What kind of a person am I to enjoy the gift of a lifetime?" "What kind of a person am I to face up to such a great expectation?"[59] All these are reflections of what Huang had received from Chu Hsi over the course of his life. Expressions like "entrusting," "injunctions," "subtle words," "great principles," and "expectation" refer to Chu Hsi's instruction for Huang's moral cultivation and learning, not to transmission of the *tao-t'ung*. If transmission had been in the mind of either Chu Hsi or Huang Kan, each should have expressed the wish much earlier, and Huang Kan would not have waited twenty-one years after the death of the Master to voice his expectation. In another funeral address, Huang said, "I received your letter that you sent when you were seriously ill. . . . I recall that you entrusted me with a very great responsibility, which my meagre ability was not adequate to bear."[60] Here "entrusted" can be taken to refer to entrusting Huang Kan either with the transmission of the Way or with the work on ritual texts. To interpret it in the sense of transmission, we must first determine that Chu Hsi definitely had that idea.

Wang is correct in saying that in his later years Chu Hsi repeatedly lamented the fact that the transmission of the Way hung in the balance. In a letter to Huang Kan, for example, Chu Hsi said, "I have not found among those who have come to study any who is outstanding enough to be entrusted with the transmission of the Way. Now that there is this additional handicap [the Court's attack on *tao-hsüeh* (Learning of the Way) as *wei-hsüeh* (false learning)], the situation is all the more insoluble. I never realized that the misfortune of our Way had reached this degree."[61] In another letter he said, "There are one or two scholars here in the midst of trouble in moving house. Although we have not been able to discuss matters thoroughly, generally speaking there is still none who can bear the responsibility. This is very worrisome."[62] In a letter to his pupil Yü Yü, he said, "Chih-ch'ing [Huang Kan] has returned here. This year about ten or twenty scholars have come and gone. In our discussions here, it is not that none can understand. But I don't see anyone who is totally and decidedly able to bear the responsibility. This is very worrisome."[63] And to his friend Chao Yen-shu (1165–1174 *cs*), Chu Hsi wrote, "There are several friends and scholars here, but in talking with them, I have often found them to be unsatisfactory. If I should suddenly pass away, there is no one to whom to entrust this matter. I cannot help worrying about this."[64]

All these worries prove that Chu Hsi had not settled on Huang Kan to carry on the *tao-t'ung*. If he had chosen Huang Kan, why was he looking for someone else, and continuing to worry? Moreover, Chu Hsi was concerned about the possible discontinuance of the *tao-hsüeh*, especially as a result of its persecution by the Court, not about the lack of a particular person to whom to pass on the robe and bowl. I believe that the laments of Buddhist elders over the suspension of their transmissions should also be interpreted in this light. It has been pointed out that Ch'eng I kept secret the diagram of the Great Ultimate because none of his pupils was capable of transmitting it. When Chu Hsi said that "The robe and bowl of the two Masters do not seem to have been passed on,"[65] he was talking about the inadequacy of the followers of the Ch'eng brothers, not about the absence of transmission of the *tao-t'ung*.

Similarly, none of Chu Hsi's discussions on the Ch'an Buddhist patriarchs mentioned the transmission of the lamp.[66] He did not believe that any of the twenty-eight Ch'an patriarchs could write rhymed poems.[67] Nor did he accept the stories that, after death, Bodhidharma (in China between 460 and 534) returned to India holding a single shoe, and that the Ch'an School grew into five schools like a flower with five petals.[68] And although Chu Hsi praised many Ch'an patriarchs as great, he questioned how many of those recorded in the *Ching-te ch'uan-teng lu* (Transmission of the lamp), compiled during the Ching-te period (1004–1007), had accomplished as much as Yao, Shun, Wen, Wu, and Confucius.[69] Thus there was no reason Chu Hsi should have emulated the Ch'an patriarchs in the matter of transmission. Many scholars have asserted that Chu Hsi's completion of the system of the *tao-t'ung* was influenced by Ch'an Buddhism. In my essay "Chu Hsi's Completion of Neo-Confucianism," I have provided ample evidence for rejecting this theory.[70]

The *Sung shih* states that Chu Hsi gave Huang Kan the books Chu Hsi himself had written. This is either a borrowing of the Buddhist idea of transmitting a scripture, or a misinterpretation of Chu Hsi's request for Huang Kan and others to continue his work on ritual texts. There is no mention of the gift of written works in the chronological biographies, the "Hsing-chuang" by Huang Kan himself, or the record of Chu Hsi's death by Ts'ai Ch'en. In this connection, the theory that Chu Hsi transmitted the classics to his pupils should be totally demolished. In his *Ching-i k'ao* (Investigation into the meanings of the classics), Chu I-tsun (1629–1709) listed 106 pupils as having inherited the *Book of Changes* (in chapter 283); 75 as having inherited the *Book of Odes* (in chapter 284); and 61 as having inherited the *Book of Rites* (in chapter 285), for a total of 139 students, since 103 of the names are duplicates. About thirty inherited three classics, more than seventy inherited two classics, and more than thirty inherited only one classic. Chu I-tsun selected the names from Chu Hsi's works on the Five Classics[71] and from the *Yü-lei*. Why the *Spring and Autumn Annals* was not transmitted has not been explained.

Although Chu I-tsun's work on the classics has been hailed universally as authoritative, his lists of Chu Hsi's pupils were extremely superficial. For example: (1) Chao Shih-kung asked only one question about a hexagram but is listed as having inherited the *Book of Changes;* (2) Ch'en Wen-wei just discussed the *Book of Odes* but is listed as having inherited it as well as the *Book of Rites*—the latter because the Teacher admonished him for turning his sleeve to one side; (3) Chiang Ch'ou is considered to have inherited the *Book of Odes* because he asked a question about it, although he also asked about the *Book of History* and is not among those who inherited that classic; (4) Chao Shih-yüan asked about the *Book of Rites* but is not among its inheritors; (5) Ch'en Ch'un is considered as having inherited the *Book of Changes,* the *Book of Odes,* and the *Book of Rites,* but in his *Pei-hsi ta-ch'üan chi* (Complete collected works of Ch'en Ch'un), there are no more than two pages on the *Book of Changes* and the rest is on basic concepts of Neo-Confucianism, which have nothing to do with any particular classic; and (7) Yü Cheng-fu, who assisted Chu Hsi in the compilation or ritual texts, discussing rites extensively both in the *Wen-chi* and the *Yü-lei,* was obviously an expert on rites and yet is absent from the list on the *Book of Rites.*

Chu I-tsun's careless selection is but a minor problem. The basic question is whether Chu Hsi ever had the idea of transmitting the classics. The doctrine of transmitting classics *(ch'uan-ching)* originated in the Han dynasty (206 B.C.–A.D. 220), when it was claimed that Confucius transmitted a certain classic to certain pupils. T'ao Ch'ien (372–427) formalized this notion and asserted that a particular classic was transmitted to a particular pupil.[72] Chu I-tsun's theory of the transmission of classics was derived from T'ao.

Chu Hsi had no interest in this, however. No trace of the doctrine can be found in his works or conversations. His interest in the *Book of Changes,* and in Han commentaries on it, was confined to divination. When asked about Ch'eng I's commentary on it in terms of moral principles, he replied, "If we read literature this way, what insight will there be?"[73] He considered the *Book of History* hard to read, did not believe it was the actual words of Confucius, and thought the preface was not the work of K'ung An-kuo (*fl.* 130 B.C.).[74] To him, the general preface to the *Book of Odes* was a later addition, and the individual prefaces were not reliable either.[75] Chu Hsi also believed that the *Book of Rites* was a compilation of the Warring States period (403–222 B.C.) and of Han times.[76] In short, he was skeptical about the authenticity of the classics. This being the case, there was really no impetus for him to transmit them. To Chu Hsi, the value of studying the classics was to find the principles behind them. "Once the principles are found, there is no need to depend on the classics."[77] He grouped the *Great Learning,* the *Analects,* the *Book of Mencius,* and the *Doctrine of the Mean* into the Four Books in 1190, not for purposes of transmitting them but for purposes of learning. He wanted "people first to read the *Great Learning* to determine the patterns, then read the *Analects* to establish the foundation, then read the *Book of Mencius* to see the elaboration, and then read the *Doctrine of the Mean* to find out the subtlety and profundity of the ancients."[78] All in all, the question of the transmission of the classics was far from his mind.

Because the sixteen-word formula mentions the mind twice, it has often been called *hsin-fa* (literally, the method of the mind), and because Chu Hsi had explained the *tao-t'ung* in terms of the sixteen-word formula, the *tao-t'ung* is often labeled *hsin-ch'uan* (transmission of the mind). Because of this connection, many writers have jumped to the conclusion that the whole tradition resulted from the influence of Buddhism. We are not opposed to the theory of Buddhist influence on Neo-Confucianism, of which there has been a good deal. But the *tao-t'ung,* is traced back to Mencius, and none of the paraphernalia of Ch'an—the transmission of the robe, the bowl, or the scripture—is present in the Confucian system.

We are not concerned here with the subject of the transmission of the mind, but two authorities should nevertheless be cited in this connection. In his essay on *hsin-hsüeh* (learning of the mind), Ku Yen-wu (1613–1682) vigorously attacked the theory that the mind can be transmitted. He took Ch'eng I to task for borrowing a Buddhist phrase, and insisted that the Way should not be equated with the mind.[79] Ch'ien Mu, however, entertained the opposite view. In his most thorough discussion on the *jen-hsin* and *tao-hsin,* he named a number of Neo-Confucians, including Chu Hsi, who used the term *ch'uan-hsin* to mean the transmission of the mind. However, Ch'ien made it clear that as far as the *tao-t'ung* is concerned, the transmission is that of the Way, not of the mind as understood in Buddhism. According to him, Ch'eng I used the term *hsin-fa* in a very narrow sense, though still with a Buddhist flavor. Ch'ien agreed with Ku Yen-wu that the learning of the mind is part and parcel of the learning of the Confucian School, because all things are principle and principle is embodied in the mind. He did not mind equating *hsin-hsüeh* with *li-hsüeh* (learning of principle), he said. But he felt that to label the school of Ch'eng I and Chu Hsi as *Li-hsüeh* and the school of Lu Hsiang-shan (1139–1193) and Wang Yang-ming (1472–1529) as *Hsin-hsüeh,* as many scholars have done, is grossly mistaken.[80]

## Notes

1. See my "Chu Hsi's Completion of Neo-Confucianism," in Françoise Aubin, ed., *Étude Song-Sung Studies in Memoriam Etienne Balazs,* Ser. II, no. 1, 1973, pp. 59–90, sec. 2, "Completion of the Concept of the Tradition of the Way," pp. 73–81; reprinted in my *Chu Hsi: Life and Thought* (Hong Kong: Chinese University Press, 1987), pp. 103–136; Chinese translation in my *Chu-hsüeh lun-chi* [Studies on Chu Hsi] (Taipei: Student Book Co., 1982), pp. 1–35.

2. *Book of Mencius*, 7B:38.

3. *Han Ch'ang-li ch'üan-chi* [Complete works of Han Yü] (*SPPY* ed.), 11:4b, "Yüan-tao" [Inquiry on the Way].

4. *I-ch'uan wen-chi* [Collection of literary works of Ch'eng I] 7:6a–6b, biographical account of Master Ming-tao, in the *Erh-Ch'eng ch'üan-shu* [Complete works of the two Ch'engs] (*SPPY* ed.).

5. *Pai-ch'uan hsüeh-hai* [Sea of learning from a hundred rivers] (1927 ed.), p. 1001.

6. *Yü-lei*, ch. 93, sec. 2 (p. 3731).

7. James C. T. Liu, "How Did a Neo-Confucian School Become the State Orthodoxy?" *Philosophy East and West,* vol. 23, no. 4 (October, 1973), pp. 490–491, n. 14. The source cited is the *Chien-yen i-lai hsi-nien yao-lu* [Important records chronologically interrelated from the Chien-yen period [1127–1130] onward] (*Ts'ung-shu chi-ch'eng* [Collection of series] ed.), ch. 101, pp. 1660–1661.

8. *Analects*, 20:1.

9. *Book of History,* "Counsels of the Great Yü," sec. 15. For more on this famous "sixteen-word formula" in four sentences, see ch. 19 above, pp. 303–304, and below, p. 332.

10. Kao-yao was minister of Shun.

11. I-yin was a minister who helped King T'ang found the Shang dynasty (1751–1112 B.C.?).

12. Fu Yüeh was a minister of Kao-tsung (r. 1304–1266 B.C.) of Shang.

13. Dukes Chou and Shao were ministers of King Ch'eng (r. 1104–1068 B.C.).

14. *Book of History,* "Announcement of Chung-hui," sec. 8.

15. *Book of Changes, k'un* (Earth, female) hexagram, "Commentary on the Text."

16. *Analects,* 6:27; 12:1, 15.

17. *Great Learning,* the text. See also ch. 18 above, section on "Diagram on the *Great Learning,*" p. 282 ff.

18. *Doctrine of the Mean,* chs. 1, 20, 21–26, 33.

19. *Book of Mencius,* 6A:11.

20. *Ibid.,* 2A:2.

21. *Ibid.,* 2A:6.

22. *Mien-chai chi* [Collected works of Huang Kan] (*Ssu-k'u ch'üan-shu chen-pen* [Precious works of the *Complete Collection of the Four Libraries*] ed.), 3:17a–20b, "General Treatise on the Transmission of the Tradition of the Way of the Sages and Worthies."

23. *Yü-lei,* ch. 93, sec. 3 (p. 3731).

24. *Wen-chi,* 60:21a, letter in reply to Li Ch'eng-chih (Li Ch'en).

25. *Ibid.,* 86:12a, "Report to the Ancient Sage at the Completion of the Ch'ang-chou Ching-she."

26. *Book of Changes,* "Appended Remarks," pt. 1, ch. 11.

27. *Ibid.,* pt. 2, ch. 2.

28. *Wen-chi,* 78:12b, "Record of the Reconstruction of Master Lien-hsi's [Chou Tun-i] Study Hall at Chiang-chou." The *Book of Changes,* "Appended Remarks," pt. 1, ch. 11, tells us that the diagram and the writing appeared in

the Yellow and Lo rivers. The Nine Categories refer to those in the "Great Norm" chapter of the *Book of History*, namely, the (1) Five Agents (Five Elements), (2) Five Activities, (3) Eight Government Offices, (4) Five Arrangements of Time, (5) Supreme Standard, (6) Three Virtues, (7) Examination of Doubts, (8) General Verification, and (9) Five Blessings.

29. For Chou Tun-i's treatise, the "T'ai-chi-t'u shuo" [Explanation of the diagram of the Great Ultimate], see the *Chou Tzu ch'üan-shu* [Complete works of Master Chou], ch. 1. For an English translation, see *A Source Book in Chinese Philosophy* (Princeton, N.J.: Princeton University Press, 1963), pp. 463–465. For the diagram, see ch. 18 above, p. 279.

30. *Wen-chi,* 86:12a, "Report to the Ancient Sage at the Completion of the Ch'ang-chou Ching-she."

31. *Ibid.,* 78:12b, "Record of the Reconstruction of Master Lien-hsi's Study Hall at Chiang-chou."

32. *Ibid.,* 31:9a, nineteenth letter in reply to Chang Ching-fu (Chang Shih).

33. See my "Chu Hsi's Completion of Neo-Confucianism," pp. 77–78, and *Chu-hsüeh lun-chi,* p. 16.

34. *Wen-chi,* 86:4b, "Essay Commemorating the Shrine of Master Lien-hsi at Feng-an."

35. *Ibid.,* 86:11b, "Essay in Homage to the Reconstructed Shrine for the Three Masters at Tao-chou."

36. *Ibid.,* 78:19a, "Essay Commemorating the Shrine of Master Lien-hsi at the Prefecture School of Lung-hsing."

37. *Ibid.,* 79:3a, "Essay Commemorating the Shrine of Three Masters at the Wu-yüan County School at Hui-chou."

38. *Ibid.,* 86:12a, "Report to the Ancient Sage at the Completion of the Ch'ang-chou Ching-she."

39. Chou Tun-i, *T'ung-shu* [Penetrating the *Book of Changes*], chaps. 1–4, 20.

40. *I-shu* [Surviving works], 18:5b in the *Erh-Ch'eng ch'üan-shu.*

41. The Four Books are the *Great Learning,* the *Analects,* the *Book of Mencius,* and the *Doctrine of the Mean.*

42. *Mien-chai chi,* 3:17a–20b, "General Treatise on the Transmission of the Tradition of the Way of the Sages and Worthies."

43. *Ibid.,* 19:19a–b, "Record of the Chu Wen Kung Shrine at Hui-chou."

44. *Ibid.,* 36:48a–b, biographical account.

45. *Pei-hsi ta-ch'üan chi* [Complete collected works of Ch'en Ch'un] (*Ssu-k'u ch'üan-shu chen-pen* ed.), 15:2b–3b, "The Source of Teachers and Friends."

46. See Chang Po-hsing, *Tao-t'ung lu* [Records of the transmission of the Way] (*Cheng-i-t'ang ch'üan-shu* [Complete library of the Hall of Rectifying the Way] ed.), pp. 4a–9b.

47. The "deep" garment was a long gown in which the jacket and the skirt are continuous.

48. *Sung shih* [History of the Sung dynasty] (Beijing: Chung-hua Book Co., 1977), ch. 430, biography of Huang Kan, p. 12778.

49. *K'ao-t'ing yüan-yüan lu* [Source and development of the Chu Hsi School] (*Chin-shih han-chi ts'ung-k'an* [Chinese works of the recent period series] ed.), 6:1b, biography of Huang Kan.

50. *Sung-Yüan hsüeh-an* [Anthology and critical accounts of the Neo-Confu-

cians of the Sung and Yüan dynasties] (*SPPY* ed.), 63:2a, chapter on Huang Kan.

51. Wang Mao-hung, *Chu Tzu nien-p'u* [Chronological biography of Master Chu] (*Ts'ung-shu chi-ch'eng* ed.), *k'ao-i* [Investigation into variants], ch. 4, p. 344, under the sixth year of Ch'ing-yüan (1200).

52. Ts'ai Ch'en, "Chu Wen Kung meng-tien chi" [Account of Chu Hsi's death], in the *Ts'ai-shih chiu-ju shu* [Works of nine Confucians in the Ts'ai family] (1868 ed.) 6:58b–61a; Chu Mu, "Chu Tzu i-tse ssu-i" [Humble opinion on Master Chu's passing away], in Tai Hsien, *Chu Tzu shih-chi* [True records of Master Chu] (*Chin-shih han-chi ts'ung-k'an* ed.), pp. 518–521.

53. San-shan is an elegant name for Min-hsien, Huang Kan's native county.

54. *Wen-chi*, 29:22a, letter to Huang Chih-ch'ing (Huang Kan).

55. *Chu Tzu wen-chi ta-ch'üan lei-pien* [Classified compilation of the complete collection of literary works of Master Chu] (1722 ed.), Bk. I, p. 47a, chronological biography.

56. *Mien-chai chi*, 39:23a–24b, "Tomb Address Bidding Farewell to Master Hui-an [Chu Hsi]."

57. *Wen-chi*, supplementary collection, 1:17a, sixty-third letter in reply to Huang Chih-ch'ing (Huang Kan).

58. Wang Mao-hung, *Chu Tzu nien-p'u*, *k'ao-i*, ch. 4, p. 344.

59. See above, n. 56.

60. *Mien-chai chi*, 39:6b, "Funeral Address for Master Chu Hui-an."

61. *Wen-chi*, supplementary collection, 1:7a, twenty-fifth letter in reply to Huang Chih-ch'ing.

62. *Ibid.*, 1:10a, thirty-second letter.

63. *Ibid.*, regular collection, 50:25b, letter in reply to Yü Chan-chih (Yü Yü).

64. *Ibid.*, 56:4a, seventh letter in reply to Chao Tzu-ch'ien (Chao Yen-shu).

65. *Yü-lei*, ch. 101, sec. 12 (p. 4063).

66. *Ibid.*, ch. 126, sec. 1 (p. 4817); sec. 68 (p. 4847); sec. 106 (p. 4861).

67. *Ibid.*, sec. 1 (p. 4817).

68. *Wen-chi*, separate collection, 8:3b, "On Buddhism," pt. 2.

69. *Ibid.*, regular collection, 43:11b–12a, first letter in reply to Li Po-chien (Li Tsung-ssu).

70. See above, n. 33.

71. The Five Classics are the *Book of Odes,* the *Book of History,* the *Book of Rites,* the *Book of Changes,* and the *Spring and Autumn Annals.*

72. T'ao Ch'ien, *Ch'ün-fu lu* [Record of group assistance] (1868 ed.), ch. 25, section on "Eight Confucians."

73. *Yü-lei*, ch. 67, sec. 76 (p. 2647).

74. *Ibid.*, ch. 78, sec. 25 (p. 3153).

75. *Ibid.*, ch. 80, sec. 26 (p. 3290); sec. 37 (p. 3295).

76. *Ibid.*, ch. 84, sec. 29 (p. 3470).

77. *Ibid.*, ch. 11, sec. 109 (p. 305).

78. *Ibid.*, ch. 14, sec. 3 (p. 397).

79. Ku Yen-wu, *Jih-chih lu* [Records of daily knowledge] (*Kuo-hsüeh chi-pen ts'ung shu* [Basic sinological series] ed.), ch. 18, p. 108.

80. Ch'ien Mu, *Chu Tzu hsin-hsüeh-an* [New anthology and critical accounts of Master Chu] (Taipei: San-min Book Co., 1970), vol. 2, pp. 99–106.

# -21-

# *Ching-she* and
# Pupils

## Life in the *Ching-she*

CHU Hsi built three studies *(ching-she)* in his lifetime: the Han-ch'üan Ching-she (Cold Spring Study), built in 1170; the Wu-i Ching-she (Mount Wu-i Study), in 1183; and the Chu-lin Ching-she (Bamboo Grove Study), in 1194. They are described in chapter 4 and below, together with a comparison between the *ching-she* and the *shu-yüan* (academy). What concerns us here is the life in the *ching-she*. There is hardly any material on the subject, and no writer has gone into the matter. What we have found is very little indeed, but it may prove to be helpful.

Of the three studies, the Wu-i Ching-she lasted for the longest time. Chu Hsi taught there for seven years, from its construction in the fourth month of the tenth year of Ch'un-hsi (1183) to his arrival in Chang-chou as prefect in the fourth month of 1189. This was longer than the five years and three months that he taught at the Chu-lin Ching-she. In terms of prominence, however, the Chu-lin outshone the other two. Most of the conversations recorded in the *Yü-lei* took place there, and there were more pupils at the Chu-lin than at either the Wu-i or the Han-ch'üan, including the most outstanding ones, such as Fu Kuang and Ch'en Ch'un (1159–1223).

Since the Hui-an (Secluded Cottage) in Cloud Valley (Yün-ku) on the peak of Mount Lu was no more than a thatched hut,[1] the nearby Han-ch'üan Ching-she could hardly have been elaborate. But it was by no means a quiet sanctuary. As Chu Hsi told his friend Ts'ai Yüan-ting (1135–1198), "As soon I arrived at the Han-ch'üan Ching-she, guests filled the hall."[2] In a letter to pupil Fang Shih-yao (1148–1199), he said, "At the beginning of the month I came to Han-ch'üan. Shu-ching [Ho Hao, 1128–1175] promised to come for about ten days of rendezvous. I wonder if you can invite like-minded friends to join us. What I worry is that the pupils here may neglect their work, which I don't want."[3] The Han-ch'üan Ching-she must have been a lively place if the gathering lasted for ten days. Chu Hsi's concern about causing his pupils to neglect their work suggests that there was some regular academic program. In 1175, when Lü Tsu-ch'ien (1137–1181) visited Chu Hsi at the Han-ch'üan to compile the *Chin-ssu lu* (Reflections on things at hand) with him and stayed for about ten days,[4] the regular academic work must have been suspended. The Han-chüan gained tremendous fame as a result of this visit, but it never matched that associated with the Wu-i and Chu-lin studies.

We do not know much about life at the Wu-i Ching-she, though the physical layout was well documented by Chu Hsi himself.[5] We know a little more about the Chu-lin Ching-she, but not much. After Chu Hsi left the prefectship at Chang-chou in 1191, he decided to settle in Chien-yang, and temporarily lived in the T'ung-yao Bridge area. Because the place was cramped, he had to meet with students in the Fo-ting Temple.[6] For this reason he built the Chu-lin Ching-she in 1194, to the east of his residence. When Ch'en Ch'un and his father-in-law, Li T'ang-tzu, came to study in 1199, they arrived at Chu Hsi's residence in the middle of the eleventh month. They saw the Teacher in the chamber below the library, and found that he was still strong in voice and spirit but seemed weak in general, and particularly in his feet. In the evening, they went over to stay at the Chu-lin Ching-she.[7] From this we learn that Chu Hsi lived on the ground floor because of a foot ailment, and that the *ching-she* was a separate building.

When Tseng Tsu-tao came to study with Chu Hsi in the third month of 1197 and told the Teacher that he had been following Lu Hsiang-shan (1139–1193), he was told to move into the *ching-she*.[8] In 1196, when Ts'ai Yüan-ting was about to be banished as a warning to Chu Hsi, the Teacher paced the ground floor several times after dinner and then sat down to meditate; Yeh Wei-tao (1220 *cs*) then withdrew to the *ching-she* to tell his fellow pupils.[9] When Chu Hsi was seriously ill in 1200 and pupils from the Chu-lin Ching-she came to call, he thanked them for coming from afar and urged them to make greater efforts.[10] All these situations indicate that the *ching-she* was primarily a dormitory. We have no information as to whether some pupils had their own lodges, though we know that T'ung Po-yü (1144–1190) had one in Cloud Valley[11] and that some pupils built their own cottages along the Wu-i River.

There is also the record of a Ching-hsiang-t'ang (Quiet Fragrance Hall), but we do not know where it was.[12] It could have been in Chu Hsi's residence or in the Chu-lin Ching-she, because it was mentioned in 1194, when the *ching-she* was completed. There are also repeated references to a *shu-yüan* (lecture hall). Once, in talking to his pupil Kuo

Yu-jen, Chu Hsi pointed to the *shu-yüan* to illustrate his point.[13] Since this was recorded in 1198, it must refer to the time of the Chu-lin Ching-she. Also, according to the records made by Wang Kuo after 1194, the Master rose very early each morning and all his pupils gathered in the *shu-yüan* before performing religious ceremonies.[14] A *shu-yüan* can be either a separate building or a hall in a building. When we read Ts'ai Ch'en's (1167–1230) "Chu Wen Kung meng-tien chi" (Account of Chu Hsi's death), we discover that the *shu-yüan* was in Chu Hsi's residence. We are told in the account that

> on the second day of the third month of 1200, the Master wrote to summon Yeh Wei-tao to K'ao-t'ing. In the evening, Wei-tao and I went to attend to the Master. That evening, the Master examined several tens of sections of my *Shu chi-chuan* [Collected commentaries on the *Book of History*] and talked about current affairs in detail. Fellow pupils from the *ching-she* were all present and did not leave until the fourth watch in the morning [about 2 a.m.]. I alone stayed and slept in the *shu-yüan* on the ground floor.[15]

Since this was just several days before Chu Hsi's death, he must have been in his residence. Probably the *ching-she* was where pupils lived, but the *ching-she* and the *shu-yüan* together were also called the *ching-she,* so two names could be interchangeable at times.

Unlike the regular *shu-yüan* or academies, the *ching-she* had no *t'ang-chang* (head of the academy). When the Chu-lin Ching-she was near completion, Chu Hsi wrote Huang Kan (1152–1221) and said that Huang might take over his lecture platform.[16] Huang Kan himself said, "After the Master returned from lecturing before the emperor, he daily discussed learning with students in the Chu-lin Ching-she. He ordered Shu-chung [Tung Chu, 1152–1214] to head up the affair and then arrive at the central core in accordance with the Teacher."[17] Tung was not the head of the *ching-she* but somewhat like a chairman. In all likelihood, there was no organization or curriculum at a *ching-she*. Aside from questions and answers from time to time, pupils took turns choosing topics for discussion. According to the *Yü-lei*, "When Pao Yang had fourteen of his own pupils come, for four days there was no assignment. The Teacher told [Huang] I-kang to ask Hsien-tao [Pao Yang] his purpose in coming. Thereupon, according to the regulations of the *ching-she*, the *Analects* were to be discussed." Seven pupils took turns speaking on one chapter, with comments by the Teacher afterward.[18]

Conversations and discussions usually took place in the evening. One frequently encounters expressions such as "one evening"[19] and "last evening,"[20] in the *Yü-lei*. We read in Ts'ai Ch'en's "Meng-tien chi," "On the third day [of the third month of 1120], the Teacher was on the ground floor. . . . That evening he spoke on several tens of sections of the *Book of History*. . . . On the fourth day, the Teacher was on the ground floor. . . . That evening he spoke on the 'T'ai-chi-t'u shuo' [Explanation of the diagram of the Great Ultimate]. On the fifth day, the Teacher was on the ground floor. . . . That evening he spoke on the 'Western Inscription.' "[21] Naturally, questions and discussions followed each presentation. Although "pupils assembled every evening,"[22] assemblies were not confined to the evening, for it is also recorded that "morning and evening there were discussions as usual."[23]

Aside from pupils taking turns at presentations, as already noted,[24] a speaker was occasionally appointed.[25] Sometimes there were guests in the group.[26] When pupils failed to ask questions, Chu Hsi angrily asked what they had come for.[27] One evening when the pupils had finished, he said, "None of you five this evening has accomplished much."[28] He had high hopes for his pupils and was happy when he found a promising one.[29] But as far as the perpetuation of the Way was concerned, he was disappointed.[30]

Pupils attended to Chu Hsi while he was sitting[31] and accompanied him while eating.[32] When he was sick, they came to inquire of his illness. On those occasions, he would always adjust his headgear and bow while sitting.[33] If anyone was disrespectful, by falling asleep while in attendance,[34] talking in a meeting,[35] or withdrawing his hand into his sleeve,[36] Chu Hsi would admonish him. Sometimes he called pupils into his bedroom.[37] Often he went to the *ching-she* to meet with them.[38]

There is no information to speak of regarding the total number of pupils in each *ching-she*. In his "Shumon deshi shiji nenkō" (Chu Hsi's pupils' years in attendance), Tanaka Kenji, on the basis of their participation in discussions recorded in the *Yü-lei*, has carefully determined the number of visits and the duration of each visit by every pupil.[39] However, many who were in attendance but not in group meetings were overlooked, so the survey is not complete. Although one could figure out the attendance at each *ching-she* by the years pupils were in attendance, Tanaka has not done so.

From Chu Hsi's words in the *Wen-chi* and the *Yü-lei*, we can learn something about each place. On Cloud Valley, for example, we read that "for the more than ten days we stayed here, friends congregated and had considerable discussion."[40] On the Han-ch'üan Ching-she we read, "I took my two sons to Han-ch'üan and called Chi-t'ung [Ts'ai Yüan-ting] to come for a visit. There were one or two more friends in the gathering, and we did not neglect discussion."[41] We also read, "The other day Po-chien [Li Tsung-ssu, 1163 *cs*] was here and Chi-t'ung also came. We discussed the difference between Confucianism and Buddhism."[42] Again, we are told that "in the beginning of the month I came to the Han-ch'üan and invited Shu-ching [Ho Hao] to come for a

ten-day visit."[43] About the Wu-i Ching-she, it is recorded that "fortunately, there are one or two friends here and so discussion will not be
discontinued,"[44] and that "friends from Kiangsi and Chekiang all gathered here."[45] In Chu Hsi's late years in K'ao-t'ing, and especially after
the construction of the Chu-lin Ching-she, his followers greatly increased in number, and yet there was a time "when discussions almost
stopped."[46]

When Chu Hsi was dismissed from the government and the persecution of his school as "false learning" was in full force, many followers
feared involvement, and "friends did not always frequent the *ching-
she.*"[47] Indeed, "those who departed outnumbered those who came,"[48]
and "although more than ten friends here are benefited from discussion, none can remain for long."[49] But "fortunately, there are still one
or two friends for discussion morning and evening,"[50] Chu Hsi noted,
so that "there are still several people gathering in the *ching-she,*"[51] and
"there are more than ten friends in the *ching-she* to discuss learning,
which is quite interesting."[52] We are also told that "this year, no friend
has come at all. Only recently one or two arrived. There is still no
harm. If more had arrived, I am afraid there would have been much
trouble,"[53] and "in the spring there were several in the *ching-she,* but
they have dispersed and only one or two have remained."[54] However,
although the persecution of "false learning" worsened, there were still
many loyal followers. As Chu Hsi said, "This year there were still ten
or twenty people who came over to study and discuss."[55]

This covers only what is recorded in the *Wen-chi* and the *Yü-lei.* Obviously, much of the activity in Chu Hsi's several studies has gone unrecorded. Life in the *ching-she* awaits further research that will inform us
about this topic, much as Tanaka Kenji's account of the years of pupils'
attendance and my *Chu Tzu men-jen* (Chu Hsi's pupils) add to our
knowledge about the individual pupils.

## The Ts'ang-chou Ching-she

It is generally accepted that the Chu-lin Ching-she was later called the
Ts'ang-chou Ching-she.[56] Because of this, the *Sung-Yüan hsüeh-an* (Anthology and critical accounts of the Neo-Confucians of the Sung and
Yüan dynasties) has called the Chu Hsi School "Scholars of Ts'ang-
chou."[57] No one has ever asked why the name was changed, when the
change was made, and who was responsible for it. My belief is that Chu
Hsi had nothing to do with it, that the change was made after his death,
and that the new name derived from one of his literary names. We shall
examine each of these issues.

According to the *Chu Tzu shih-chi* (True records of Master Chu) by
Tai Hsien (d. 1508), under the entry for the K'ao-t'ing Shu-yüan

(K'ao-t'ing Academy), because scholars came from all directions, in 1195 the Master erected a building to the east of his residence and called it Chu-lin Ching-she. Later, because the front of the building was surrounded by water, the name was changed to Ts'ang-chou Ching-she (Waterside Study).[58] The Chinese dictionary *Tz'u-hai* (Sea of terms), however, is much more elaborate. It says, "That term means a cove and is often used to denote the abode of a hermit. The place was originally called Lung-she-chou [Dragon-tongue Island], but Chu Hsi changed it to Ts'ang-chou. He further built the Ts'ang-chou Ching-she. He called himself the Sick Old Man of Ts'ang-chou and changed his literary name to Tun-weng [Old man in retirement] to indicate the idea of being a hermit."[59] The meaning of a place for a hermit and the meaning of a cove are not mutually exclusive. Whether either interpretation is correct will become clear when the questions of the time and people concerned are answered.

The various chronological biographies *(nien-p'u)* merely say that "later the name was changed to Ts'ang-chou Ching-she," without specifying the year. According to Huang Kan, in the beginning of the Ch'ing-yüan period (1195–1200), after the Master returned from lecturing before the emperor, he daily discussed learning with students in the Chu-lin Ching-she and ordered Tung Chu to head up the affair.[60] The early Ch'ing-yüan period may mean 1195 or 1196. In the *Yü-lei* there are several hundred conversations recorded by Tung Chu from 1196. This means that the *ching-she* was known as Chu-lin at least in that year. In Huang Kan's "Chu Tzu hsing-chuang" (Biographical account of Master Chu), he also said, "The Master daily discussed learning with pupils at the Chu-lin Ching-she. Some suggested that he dismiss pupils but the Master merely smiled and did not answer."[61] This too was in 1196, and is further evidence that the *ching-she* was still called Chu-lin at that time. If the purpose of the name change was to symbolize the idea of a hermit or retirement, why was it not changed in 1195, when Chu Hsi adopted the literary name Tun-weng? Recall Ch'en Ch'un's account of his second visit in the eleventh month of 1199, when he was accompanied by his father-in-law and stayed at the Chu-lin Ching-she.[62] Thus as late as 1199, five years after the study was built, it was still called the Chu-lin Ching-she, and this was only four months before Chu Hsi's death.

Moreover, Ch'en Ch'un's pupil, Ch'en I (*fl.* c. 1210), in his account of Ch'en Ch'un, said, "In the winter of 1199, they paid homage to Wen Kung [Chu Hsi] at K'ao-t'ing again. At that time, Wen Kung was seriously ill. They were invited into the bedroom. . . . Consequently, all that they heard at the Chu-lin was decisive and pertinent to the self."[63] Also, in Ch'en Ch'un's *Pei-hsi tzu-i* (Neo-Confucian terms explained), there is a note referring to "sayings of Wen Kung recorded by the Master [Ch'en Ch'un] at the Chu-lin Ching-she."[64] These sayings were recorded in 1190 and 1199, showing once more that the *ching-she* was still called Chu-lin in 1199. Besides, no pupil ever used the name Ts'ang-chou Ching-she. To argue that the *ching-she* was known by both names, or that Chu Hsi changed its name in the last four months of his life, is hardly convincing.

In the *Wen-chi* there is a poem on Chu Hsi's portrait painted ten years earilier than the date of the poem. At the end of the poem, Chu Hsi signed his literary name "Ts'ang-chou Ping-sou" (Sick old man of Ts'ang-chou) and dated it the eighth day of the second month of 1200.[65] It is most unlikely that, in the last month of his life and when seriously ill, Chu Hsi bothered to change the name of the Chu-lin Ching-she. As far as we know, he used this literary name only once. I believe he adopted it not because the name of the *ching-she* had been changed, but because looking at his portrait made him reflect on his declining years and his retirement; hence he applied the traditional terminology of a hermit and called himself "Ts'ang-chou ping-sou." This is similar to what he did earlier when he called himself "Yün-ku lao-jen" (Old man of Cloud Valley). We may conclude, therefore, that the name of the *ching-she* was not changed during Chu Hsi's lifetime. This being the case, the theory that he changed the name because of his retirement is definitely untenable. As to when after his death the name was changed, we can only speculate about that.

The name Chu-lin Ching-she does not appear in the contents of either the *Wen-chi* or the *Yü-lei,* which refer to the place simply as *ching-she.* Only in the titles of the essays in the *Wen-chi* is the name Ts'ang-chou mentioned three times.[66] All three cases occur only in the titles, and not in the essays themselves. I believe the editor of the *Wen-chi* used "Ts'ang-chou" simply because it had become popular. The *Wen-chi* was compiled several decades after Chu Hsi's demise. It is hard to say whether the editors changed the name to Ts'ang-chou or whether the name was already in common use. There is no evidence that Chu Hsi's pupils had changed the name, because none of them used it. My belief is that after Chu Hsi's death, the Chu-lin Ching-she became desolate. At the same time, Chu Hsi's poem about his portrait became popular, and along with it his literary name, Ts'ang-chou ping-sou, became well known. As a result, the name Ts'ang-chou Ching-she gradually came to replace Chu-lin Chang-she. In the interim, both names may have been in use. In the *Chien-yang hsien-chih* (Accounts of Chien-yang County), it is reported that in the K'ao-t'ing Shu-yüan, "There were two wings, called Chu-lin Ching-she and Ts'ang-chou Ching-she."[67] However, the county record includes an essay by P'eng Shih (1416–1475), which says that "a hall in front of the corridor was very wide. . . . It was changed to be Ts'ang-chou Ching-she and Han-ch'üan

Ching-she."[68] Thus by P'eng's time, the name Chu-lin had been forgotten. No wonder, when Huang Tsung-hsi (1610–1695) compiled the *Sung-Yüan hsüeh-an,* he called the Chu Hsi School "Scholars of Ts'ang-chou."

The gradual disappearance of the name Chu-lin may be due to the fact that it was originally a Buddhist term. Chu Hsi adopted it in spite of its Buddhist association, possibly because the place was indeed surrounded by bamboo. To later Confucians, however, the Buddhist association of Chu-lin was unacceptable, and the poetic image and tradition of retirement associated with Ts'ang-chou were too strong to resist.

## Characteristics of Pupils

There is no question that members of the Chu Hsi School outnumbered those of all other philosophical schools in Chinese history except the school of Confucius, which tradition says had three thousand pupils. Tai Hsien's *Chu Tzu shih-chi* lists 318 students of Chu Hsi; the *K'ao-t'ing yüan-yüan lu* (Records of the source and development of the Chu Hsi School) by Sung Tuan-i (1481 *cs*) lists 379; the *Ihak t'ongnok* (General record of the School of Principle) by the Korean Neo-Confucian Yi Hwang (Yi T'oegye, 1501–1570) lists 411; the *Ching-i k'ao* (Investigation into the meanings of classics) by Chu I-tsun (1629–1709) lists 139; the *Ju-lin tsung-p'ai* (Successive generations of the Confucian School) lists 433; the *Sung-Yüan hsüeh-an* lists 224; its supplement, the *Pu-i,* by Wang Tzu-ts'ai (1792–1851) and Feng Yün-hao (1834 *cs*), adds 298, for a total of 522; and the *Chu Tzu wen-chi ta-ch'üan lei-pien* (Classified compilation of the complete collection of literary works of Master Chu), by Chu Hsi's sixteenth-generation descendant, Chu Yü (*fl.* 1722), lists 442. These sources included 140 friends and correspondents who were not really pupils and in many cases overlooked the *Yü-lei,* in which conversations with pupils are recorded. By going through the *Yü-lei,* the *Ihak t'ongnok* found eight students not mentioned elsewhere, and by consulting many additional works, the *Pu-i* added thirty-one. By examining the *Yü-lei* closely and considering as a pupil everyone who received even the answer to a single question, I have discovered fifty-two new names, for a total of 467.[69]

The books just mentioned are highly confused and inconsistent about names of counties and prefectures. Some errors are obviously misprints. In many cases, elegant or ancient names are used, and the books do not agree on the native county or prefecture of many pupils. The same is true of the pupils' names. The matter is complicated by the fact that several pupils had the same courtesy or literary name, making it extremely difficult to identify the correct person in each case. I have tried to untangle the skein in my *Chu Tzu men-jen.*[70]

An illustration of the difficulty involved in discovering the name of a pupil is the case of Ting Fu-chih. We do not know whether his private name was Yao or K'e. In his funeral address, Huang Kan merely addressed him as Fu-chih.[71] In his tomb inscription, Chu Hsi told us that "Fu-chih, named Yao, studied with me for several years but unfortunately died young."[72] The name Yao has been repeated in the *Chu Tzu shih-chi,* the *K'ao-t'ing yüan-yüan lu,* the *Tao-nan yüan-wei* (Record of the promulgation of the Way southward) by Chu Heng (1512–1584), and the *Ju-lin tsung-p'ai.*[73] But the *Ihak t'ongnok* has K'e;[74] so does the *Sung-Yüan hsüeh-an pu-i,* and in its quotation from the *Ju-lin tsung-p'ai,* it has changed Yao to K'e.[75] The *Yü-lei* mentions neither Ting Yao nor Ting-K'e, but in the *Wen-chi* there are two poems and an essay commemorating the trip to Mount Lu in Nan-k'ang,[76] one of which uses K'e[77] while the other two use Fu-chih.[78] Therefore, Ting Fu-chih must be Ting K'e. Also, in his funeral address, Huang Kan said he was associated with Fu-chih for seven years. This jibes with Huang's trip in 1179 and Ting Fu-chih's death in 1185, and also agrees with Chu Hsi's "several years." Obviously, Fu-chih could not have been two different people. Since the *Analects* defines humanity (*jen*) as *k'e-chi* (self-mastery) *fu-li* (returning to propriety),[79] Fu-chi naturally goes with K'e, not Yao. The Yao in the tomb inscription in the *Wen-chi* is clearly a misprint that was then repeated in several later books. To his credit, Yi T'oegye was the first to use Ting K'e, in his *Ihak t'ongnok.*

Geographically, the greatest number of pupils came from Fukien—164 in all. This is perfectly logical because the three *ching-she* were located there and Chu Hsi lived and taught there most of his life. Fukien is followed by Chekiang, with 80 students; Kiangsi, with 79; Hunan and Anhui, with 15 each; Kiangsu and Szechuan, with 7 each; Hupei, with 5; Kwangtung, with 4; and Honan and Shansi, with 1 each. The statistic covers only those students whose native places are known, of course. It is significant that Fukien, although isolated and far from the political capital, should have become an intellectual center. It is also interesting that more pupils shifted from the Lu Hsiang-shan School in Kiangsi to the Chu Hsi School in Fukien than vice versa.

When pupils came, they brought gifts as tuition,[80] presented letters,[81] and offered poems.[82] Some performed formal ceremonies for becoming pupils.[83] Some came on foot, some gave up taking the civil service examinations, and some packed their own food.[84] Some waited for ten years before they succeeded in becoming pupils.[85] Some were boys, some were older than Chu Hsi, some sent their sons because of their own age or illness, some could learn only indirectly from community members who were pupils, and some were prevented from becoming pupils because of poverty, although there were also men of wealth and high station.[86] One brought his little boy.[87] There were nine cases of both father and son being students, twenty or thirty cases of brothers, and about ten cases of cousins studying under the Master.[88] One family sent pupils for three generations.[89] Several students came to visit six or seven times.[90] Many stayed for as long as ten years, or off and on for up to forty years.[91] Most left to devote themselves to scholarship or education, and only 133, or 28 percent, held government office.

## Conversations

Much is revealed in how conversations between Chu Hsi and his pupils were conducted. More than ten thousand conversations are recorded in the *Yü-lei*. The shortest consists of only sixteen words,[92] and the longest of 2,461 words, with notes,[93] or 2,454 without notes.[94] The shortest of Chu Hsi's sayings consists of only two words.[95] Recorders of the conversations number ninety-four, plus four whose names are unknown. Among them, Yeh Wei-tao recorded the most—more than 980 sections. In the chapters of "Instructions for Pupils," sections for Ch'en Ch'un outnumber the others.[96]

Conversations covered all kinds of subjects, from philosophy to literature and from geography to history. Some pupils seem to have asked questions chiefly on one subject, such as Tung Chu on rituals, Ch'en Hou-chih on the learning of the mind, Ch'iu Ying on Lao Tzu, Fan Yüan-yü on ancient sages and worthies, Chou Mu on principle and nature, Lin Chih on the learning of principle, and Lin Tzu-yüan on the investigation of things. Often several pupils jointly asked the same question,[97] and Chu Hsi frequently invited pupils to express their opinions.[98] He particularly encouraged pupils to ask questions and to doubt, welcoming differing opinions. One example is that when the Master criticized Wang An-shih (1021–1086) for imposing interest on loans, thereby violating the principle in the *Chou-li* (Rites of Chou), P'an Shih-chü countered with the statement, "How can that be avoided when the expenses of the nation depend on it?"[99] Fang Shih-yao once urged the Master not to write many books, and Ts'ai Yüan-ting had the same idea.[100] Many more examples can easily be found in the *Yü-lei*. The conversations were by no means a one-way indoctrination.

Chu Hsi's answers varied according to the needs of his pupils. For example, many asked about the doctrine of "where to abide" *(chih-chih)* as taught in the *Great Learning*.[101] To Hsü Yü, his answer was, "Truly to know how to arrive at the highest good"; to Ch'ien Mu-chih, "It is to know the principle where things and affairs should rest"; to Yu Tzu-meng, "It is like the archer aiming at the target"; to Lin Tzu-yüan, "The effort in knowing and action must both be exerted to the utmost"; and to Liao Te-ming, "It is like eating rice. It is simply to eat."[102] These pupils asked the same question at different times, but the variation in

Chu Hsi's response was due only to the interest and needs of the questioner.

Perhaps the best indication of Chu Hsi's attention to individual needs is the way he responded when a pupil came to say farewell. When Liao Te-ming came to say goodbye, the Master told him that "being cautious over what he did not see and apprehensive over what he did not hear[103] is an important task and is relevant to the self, and that he should concentrate on one book and then on another."[104] When Yü Ta-ya was about to leave and asked him for instruction, he said, "At present you must avoid unncessary affairs and direct your effort to the essential." He also told the pupil to seek the lost mind.[105] When Yeh Wei-tao begged leave and told the Master that he and Huang Hsien-tzu were returning home to take the civil service examinations, the Master said, "Who among the scholars in your community are not trying to buy their degrees? But you two gentlemen are returning home to take the examinations. This makes me very happy."[106] When Yang Tao-fu came to say goodbye, the Teacher simply told him to have a strong backbone.[107] When Hsü Yü begged to return home to perform a certain task, the Master said, "The task is right here."[108] As Shih Hung-ch'ing was about to return home, Chu Hsi called him in to tell him, "You must now first of all seek the source."[109] His advice to Huang I-kang before his departure was to ponder books and examine moral principles.[110] When Hsi Kai-ch'ing said farewell and asked for a word, the Teacher said, "After you return home, you should concentrate on concrete works."[111] As Tseng Tsu-tao bowed to say goodbye, the Teacher said, "After you leave, each of us should attend to our work, and later when we meet again we shall have something to talk about."[112] Before Kuo Yu-jen's departure, the Teacher told him, "You are strong in intelligence but weak in energy. You should not read much each day. Also, your memory is dull, but if you make effort without interruption, there will naturally be progress."[113] Chu Hsi's departing word for Wei Ch'un was to work hard,[114] while for Ch'en Ch'un, it was to travel more.[115] For Yang Fang (1163 *cs*), his advice was to "make effort at holding onto the self and investigating principle."[116] His farewell gift to Ch'en Chih was a copy of the *Chin-ssu lu,* adding, "This is very beneficial to the student."[117] Many more instances could be cited, but these are sufficient to show that Chu Hsi knew his pupils well and gave them advice pertinent to their individual cases.

## Personal Relations

The conversations reveal a high degree of intimacy between teacher and student. Chu Hsi visited many of the lodges where his students lived, toured many scenic spots with them, wrote numerous essays and prefaces for them, and exchanged poems with them. A great number of pupils treasured his calligraphy; perhaps the most famous case is that of Wu Shou-ch'ang, who requested the Teacher's calligraphy after he had drunk some wine.[118] Chu Hsi's affection for Ch'en Ch'un is well known, and Ch'en Ch'un fully reciprocated it.[119] He liked Huang Kan enough to give his daughter to him in marriage.[120] He also advised pupil Li T'ang-tzu to give his daughter in marriage to Ch'en Ssu-ch'ien,[121] and urged pupil Lü Huan to go home and get married.[122] When Ch'en Ch'un was going to return home, the Master gave him a farewell dinner.[123] In 1197, when Ts'ai Yüan-ting was banished to Tao-chou[124] as a warning to Chu Hsi for his "false learning," Chu Hsi also gave him a farewell banquet in a secluded Buddhist temple, which several hundred followers attended.[125]

Among the more than four hundred pupils, there were some disappointments. Perhaps the worst case was that of Yang Fang. Yang associated with Chu Hsi for almost fifty years but never saw eye to eye with the Teacher and would get angry whenever he disagreed with him.[126] Chu Hsi was not proud of Pao Yüeh, Hu Ta-shih, Hsü Chao-jan, and Ch'eng Yung-ch'i, either.[127] But most pupils were loyal. In 1196, when Chu Hsi was dismissed from his official post and temple superintendency as a result of giving offense to the Court, some pupils left him for fear of involvement. But pupils like Fu Kuang and Tung Chu stood firm.[128] Ch'ai Chung-hsing, Fu Po-ch'eng, and Wu Lieh protested,[129] and T'eng Lin, Wu Pi-ta, and Chin P'eng-yüeh resigned.[130] When Chu Hsi left the capital, most people avoided him, but Li Chi saw him off and Chang Tsung-yüeh accompanied him back to Fukien.[131] While Ts'ai Yüan-ting was en route to his banishment, Chan Yüan-shan protected him, and Liu Chih and his brother provided him with ample supplies.[132] Later, when Chu Hsi died, almost a thousand people attended his funeral.[133]

## Evening Seminars

One form of activity some pupils participated in may have been the forerunner of modern seminars or reading clubs. In his tomb inscription for fellow pupil Chou Mu (1141–1202), Huang Kan said,

> After the Teacher passed away, pupils dispersed, but in the K'ang-lu area,[134] Li Ching-tzu [Li Fan, 1190 *cs*], Yü Kuo-hsiu [Yü, Sung-chieh], Ts'ai Yüan-ssu [Ts'ai Nien-ch'eng], and Hu Po-liang [Hu Yung] and his brother led their pupils of several tens in number. They only read the works of the Master [Chu Hsi]. Every season they met, each one taking turns being the host. When the time came, they met at the host's home for discussion. The gentleman's [Chou Mu] son Yeh recounted his father's

life, bowed, and told me in tears, "Only after the Master became prefect in Nan-k'ang did our community know what learning was, and only after my father went to Fukien did scholars begin to travel a thousand *li*[135] to seek learning. The seasonal gatherings in our community were also started by my father." Is it not due to Shun-pi's [Chou Mu] effort that the Confucian culture did not disappear?[136]

## Pupils and Academies

Perhaps the most important movement carried on by the pupils was that of the *shu-yüan* (academies). At the beginning of Chu Hsi's reconstruction of the White Deer Hollow Academy, Yang Fang and Liu Ch'ing-chih contributed to the planning.[137] We do not know how many pupils studied under Chu Hsi at the academy, but there are records for sixteen.[138] In his later years, Li Lü saw Chu Hsi on Mount Lu, where the academy was located, and became friends with him; four of his sons and grandsons eventually became pupils.[139] While Chu Hsi was at the academy, his pupil Lin Yung-chung came to lecture.[140] Lin was followed by Huang Kan, Ch'en Mi (d. 1226), and Pao Ting.[141] Huang Kan's lecture on the *ch'ien* (Heaven, male) and *k'un* (Earth, female) hexagrams of the *Book of Changes* became most famous in Chinese history, perhaps ranking only after Lu Hsiang-shan's (1139–1193) lecture on righteousness versus profit, given earlier at the same academy. Huang said, "*Ch'ien* denotes task and virtue, while *k'un* denotes the principle of righteousness and seriousness (*ching*, reverence). Although they are different, they are mutually warp and woof. If one wants to advance in the virtue of *ch'ien*, one must base it on the seriousness of *k'un*, and if one undertakes the task of *ch'ien*, one must control it with the righteousness of *k'un*. Without righteousness, one's external life cannot be squared. How can the task be undertaken?"[142] As the *Sung shih* (History of the Sung dynasty) says of Huang, "He went to Lu-shan to visit his friend Li Fan. He and Ch'en Mi hovered around between Yü-yüan [Jade abyss] and San-hsia [Three gorges], reviewing the traces of their Teacher. He lectured on the *ch'ien* and *k'un* hexagrams at the White Deer Academy with scholars from north and south in the audience. His great reputation, which attracted scholars from north to south, has seldom been seen in history."[143]

Besides the White Deer Hollow Academy, we know of Hu An-chih lecturing at the Nan-hsüan Academy, Ch'en Chih at the Ming-tao Academy, and Huang Kan at the An-ch'ing-fu Academy.[144] According to the *K'ao-t'ing yüan-yüan lu*, Ch'en Chih was a professor at the Ming-tao Academy with "several hundred followers from all directions."[145] Seven other pupils headed academies. Of these, three had been *t'ang-chang* [academy head] of the White Deer Hollow Academy. As we read in the *Sung shih,* "After [Chu] Hsi died, the prohibition of his teachings was very severe. [Li] Fan led his schoolmates to attend the funeral and witnessed the lowering of the coffin without any fear. . . . The prefect invited him to be the *t'ang-chang* of the White Deer Academy. Scholars flocked together. The magnificence of their academic discussions could not be matched by other prefectures."[146] According to the *K'ao-t'ing yüan-yüan lu,* Huang I-yung "studied with Wen Kung [Chu Hsi] and finished his study under Huang Kan. When Ch'en Mi became prefect of Nan-k'ang Commandary, he selected Huang to be the *t'ang-chang* of the White Deer Academy."[147] In the biography of Chang Hsia (1161–1237) in the *Sung shih,* we read that "when he was invited to be the head of the White Deer Hollow Academy, he said, 'Alas! This was the position of our late Teacher. How can I decline?' When he arrived, he selected those students who loved learning and discussed with them daily."[148] Others were Lin Hsüeh-meng, who was the *t'ang-chang* of the Tao-nan Academy; Ts'ai Nien-ch'eng, who headed the Yen-p'ing Academy; Ts'ai Mu, who headed the Chien-an Academy; and Teng Pang-lao, who headed the Tao-nan Academy.[149] For three pupils to act as head of the most prestigious academy and four more to be head of three other outstanding academies reflects the extensive influence of the Chu Hsi School.

But their greater accomplishment lies in the establishment of new academies. The *Sung shih* says that Ch'en Mi "founded the Yen-p'ing Academy,"[150] and this is repeated in the *Sung-Yüan hsüeh-an.*[151] But in the biography of Lin Hsüeh-meng in the *K'ao-t'ing yüan-yüan lu,* it is said that "Ch'en Mi founded the Tao-nan Academy in Yen-p'ing[152] and invited Lin to be the *t'ang-chang.*"[153] As in some other cases, this academy was known by two names. According to the *Sung-Yüan hsüeh-an,* Fu Kuang "returned home with a temple superintendency and built the Ch'uan-i Academy to teach. Scholars came to call him Master of Ch'uan-i."[154] According to the *Sung-Yüan hsüeh-an pu-i,* Prefect Chao Shih-tuan "founded the Wen Kung Academy in the prefectural school and asked Mien-chai [Huang Kan] to write an account for it."[155] Huang Kan's account, however, is on the shrine for Chu Hsi, not on the academy.[156] The probability is that the prefect erected the shrine in part of the prefecture school and established the academy in another part. The *Pu-i* also tells us that "Chung Chen of Hsiang-t'an [Hunan] was a student of Hui-an [Chu Hsi]. He founded the Chu-i Academy to lecture on the Way and was respected by intellectuals of the community."[157] In addition, there were the Chao-wen Academy founded by Li Kuei-ch'en, the Yang-p'ing Academy founded by Wu Hsiung, the Chiu-i-shan Academy found by Liu Ch'ing-chih, and the Ho-shan Academy founded by Chu Hsi's indirect pupil, Wei Liao-weng (1178–1237), all in Hunan.[158] There were also the Yüeh-lin Academy, founded by the father of pupil P'an Yu-kung, and the Cheng-shan Academy, founded by the grandson of pupil Chao Shan-tai (1128–1188).[159]

Altogether, ten academies grew up through the efforts of Chu Hsi's pupils and their offspring. In virtually every case there was a shrine to Chu Hsi; his works, such as the *Chin-ssu lu* and the *Hsiao-hsüeh* (Elementary education), were studied; and his "Articles of Learning" for the White Deer Hollow Academy were promulgated as academy regulations. For example, the articles were adopted, promoted, and recommended by Ch'en Mi, Yeh Wu-tzu (1214 *cs*), and Liu Yüeh.[160] It is not an exaggeration to suggest that, as a group, Chu Hsi's pupils were the strongest constructive force in the development of the academy system in Chinese history.

## The Development of the Chu Hsi School

On the basis of the many academies founded by Chu Hsi's pupils, it might be presumed that the Chu Hsi School overwhelmed China. In fact, it did dominate Chinese thought from the Southern Sung (1127–1279) through the Yüan (1277–1368) to the Ch'ing dynasty (1644–1911). Even the predominance of the Wang Yang-ming (1472–1529) School during the Ming dynasty (1368–1644) may be regarded as a reaction against Chu Hsi. The Chu Hsi School has certainly reigned supreme in Chinese philosophy over the last seven hundred years, even though it compares unfavorably in some respects with the School of the two Ch'engs (Ch'eng Hao, 1032–1085, and Ch'eng I, 1033–1107). For instance, the earlier school produced the "Four Masters"—namely, Hsieh Liang-tso (1050–c. 1120), Yang Shih (1053–1135), Yu Tso (1053–1123), and Yin T'un (1071–1142)—whom none in Chu Hsi's group could match. Sun Ch'i-feng (1585–1675) argued that since there were two Ch'eng brothers but only one Chu Hsi, naturally the result of the former was doubled.[161] This is true enough, and we may add that the Ch'eng School was at the beginning stage of Neo-Confucian development, whereas Chu Hsi's thought was a mature system. But although Chu Hsi encouraged questions and doubts just as much as the Ch'eng brothers did, their early stage of development allowed more room for original thought. Consequently, their followers developed the doctrine of humanity *(jen)*, for example, in different directions, whereas Chu Hsi's fully developed system left little room for adventure. Finally, Chu Hsi was much more critical toward Buddhism and Taoism than the Ch'eng brothers were, so his school lacked true stimulation from differing ideologies.

Some even say that the Chu Hsi School lacked a prominent follower such as Yang Chien (1141–1226) of the Lu Hsiang-shan School. However, Yang Chien's reputation rests more on his high official position than on his intellectual originality. Yang, and therefore the Lu Hsiang-shan School, had practically no following, whereas the Chu Hsi School prevailed in China, Korea, and Japan for centuries. Unlike the followers of the Ch'eng brothers, who were usually identified with a particular doctrine, the followers of Chu Hsi have customarily been grouped geographically. As Huang Po-chia (*fl.* 1695) said, "Huang Mien-chai, Kan, received the orthodox tradition from Master Chu. He transmitted it to his pupil Ho Pei-shan, Chi [1188–1268], of Chin-hua,[162] who in turn transmitted it to Wang Lu-chai, Po [1197–1274]; Chin Jen-shan, Lü-hsiang [1232–1303]; and Hsü Pai-yün, Ch'ien [1270–1337]. He also transmitted it in Chiang-yu[163] to Jao Shuang-feng, Lu [*fl.* 1256], which led to Wu Ts'ao-lu, Ch'eng [1249–1333], who continued the learning of the classics. How magnificent!"[164]

Huang Kan also served as prefect of Han-yang Prefecture[165] and was thus instrumental in introducing the Chu Hsi School to the north under the Mongols. This does not mean, however, that the spread of the Chu Hsi School was due solely to Huang Kan. Fu Kuang also transmitted the teaching to Huang Chen (1213–1280), and Chan T'i-jen (1151 *cs*) transmitted it to Chen Te-hsiu (1178–1235), who passed it on to Wang Ying-lin (1222–1296). There is a chart in the *Ju-lin tsung-p'ai* showing the transmission of the Chu Hsi School for five generations.[166] Chu Hsi's own doctrines and scholarship; his grouping of the Four Books,[167] which eventually became the basic texts of Chinese education and civil service examinations; his school's promotion by the government in successive dynasties—all these increased the growth of the Chu Hsi School, although the contributions of his pupils must also be counted as an important factor.

## Notes

1. *Wen-chi,* 78:2a, "Account of Cloud Valley."
2. *Ibid.,* supplementary collection, 2:2b, sixth letter in reply to Ts'ai Chi-t'ung (Ts'ai Yüan-ting), repeated on p. 21a, ninety-third letter.
3. *Ibid.,* regular collection, 44:21b, seventh letter in reply to Fang Po-mu (Fang Shih-yao).
4. *Ibid.,* 81:6a, "Epilogue on the *Chin-ssu lu.*"
5. *Ibid.,* 9:3a, poems on Wu-i Ching-she, with an introduction.
6. *Ibid.,* 39:13a, eighth letter in reply to Hsü Shun-chih (Hsü Sheng). For this and the following pupils, see my *Chu Tzu men-jen* [Master Chu's pupils] (Taipei: Student Book Co., 1982).
7. *Pei-hsi ta-ch'üan chi* [Complete collected work of Ch'en Ch'un] (*Ssu-k'u ch'üan-shu chen-pen* [Precious works of the *Complete Collection of the Four Libraries* ed.), 10:3b, "Epilogue to the *Account of the Chu-lin Ching-she.*"
8. *Yü-lei,* ch. 116, sec. 33 (p. 4461).
9. *Ibid.,* ch. 107, sec. 22 (p. 4244).

10. Ts'ai Ch'en, "Chu Wen Kung meng-tien chi" [Account of Chu Hsi's death], in the *Ts'ai-shih chiu-ju shu* [Works of nine Confucians in the Ts'ai family] (1868 ed.), 6:59a.

11. Sung Tuan-i, *K'ao-t'ing yüan-yüan lu* [Records of the source and development of the Chu Hsi School] (*Chin-shih han-chi ts'ung-k'an* [Chinese works in the recent period series] ed.), p. 9a (p. 587), biography of T'ung Po-yü.

12. *Yü-lei*, ch. 118, sec. 89 (p. 4572).

13. *Ibid.*, ch. 116, sec. 50 (p. 4470).

14. *Ibid.*, ch. 107, sec. 54 (p. 4252).

15. "Chu Wen Kung meng-tien chi," in the *Ts'ai-shih chiu-ju shu,* 6:58b.

16. *Sung shih* [History of the Sung dynasty] (Beijing: Chung-hua Book Co., 1977), ch. 430, biography of Huang Kan, p. 12778.

17. *Mien-chai chi* [Collected works of Huang Kan] (*Ssu-k'u ch'uan-shu chen-pen* ed.), 38:17b, "Tomb inscription for Tung Chu." Yeh Kung-hui's *Chu Tzu nien-p'u* [Chronological biography] (*Chin-shih han-chi ts'ung-k'an* ed.), p. 226, and Tai Hsien's *nien-p'u* in his *Chu Tzu shih-chi* [True records of Master Chu] (*Chin-shih han-chi ts'ung-k'an* ed.), p. 193, both under the fifth year of Shao-hsi (1194). Both these sources overstated the fact and claimed that Tung was appointed *t'ang-chang* (head of the academy).

18. *Yü-lei*, ch. 119, sec. 7 (pp. 4578–4582).

19. *Ibid.*, sec. 25 (p. 4594).

20. *Ibid.*, sec. 26 (p. 4595).

21. *Ts'ai-shih chiu-ju shu,* 6:58b–59a.

22. *Yü-lei*, ch. 121, sec. 101 (p. 4713).

23. *Wen-chi*, 60:27a, fourth letter in reply to P'an Tzu-shan (P'an Shih-chü).

24. See above, n. 18, and *Yü-lei*, ch. 120, sec. 55 (p. 4634).

25. *Ibid.*, ch. 118, sec. 89 (p. 4574).

26. *Ibid.*, ch. 121, sec. 87 (p. 4707).

27. *Ibid.*, sec. 106 (p. 4716).

28. *Ibid.*, ch. 35, sec. 118 (p. 1498).

29. *Wen-chi*, 39:13a, eighth letter in reply to Hsü Shun-chih (Hsü Sheng).

30. *Ibid.*, 50:25b, fourth letter in reply to Yü Chan-shih (Yü Yü).

31. *Yü-lei*, ch. 117, sec. 49 (p. 4515); ch. 121, sec. 102 (p. 4714).

32. *Ibid.*, ch. 114, sec. 3 (p. 4385).

33. *Ibid.*, ch. 107, sec. 57 (p. 4253).

34. *Ibid.*, ch. 121, sec. 102 (p. 4714).

35. *Ibid.*, sec. 101 (p. 4713).

36. *Ibid.*, sec. 103 (p. 4715).

37. *Ibid.*, sec. 87 (p. 4707); ch. 117, sec. 43–45 (p. 4500–4507).

38. *Ibid.*, ch. 119, sec. 8 (p. 4583).

39. *Tōhō gakuhō* [Oriental journal], no. 44 (1973), pp. 147–209; no. 48 (1975), pp. 261–357.

40. *Wen-chi*, 44:23a, tenth letter to Fang Po-mu (Fang Shih-yao).

41. *Ibid.*, 39:44b, ninth letter in reply to Fan Po ch'ung (Fan Nien-te).

42. *Ibid.*, tenth letter, 39:45a.

43. *Ibid.*, 44:21b, seventh letter in reply to Fang Po-mu.

44. *Ibid.*, 50:28a, tenth letter in reply to Ch'eng Cheng-ssu (Ch'eng Tuan-meng).

45. *Ibid.*, 50:31b, eighteenth letter.

46. *Ibid.*, 39:15a, eleventh letter in reply to Hsü Shun-chih.

47. *Ibid.*, 59:32a, tenth letter in reply to Ch'en Ts'ai-ch'ing (Ch'en Wen-wei).

48. *Ibid.*, 60:27a, fourth letter in reply to P'an Tzu-shan.

49. *Ibid.*, 60:40b, eleventh letter.

50. *Ibid.*, 61:12a, tenth letter in reply to Lin Te-chiu (Lin chih).

51. *Ibid.*, 59:26a, fifth letter in reply to Fu Han-ch'ing (Fu Kuang).

52. *Ibid.*, 59:26b, seventh letter.

53. *Ibid.*, 50:25a, third letter in reply to Yü Chan-chih.

54. *Ibid.*, 60:27b, fifth letter in reply to P'an Tzu-shan.

55. *Ibid.*, 50:25b, fourth letter in reply to Yü Chan-chih.

56. Yeh King-hui, *Chu Tzu nien-p'u*, p. 226; Tai Hsien, *Chu Tzu shih-chi*, p. 193; Wang Mao-hung, *Chu Tzu nien-p'u* [Chronological biography of Master Chu] (*Ts'ung-shu ch'i-ch'eng* [Collection of series] ed.), p. 214, all under the fifth year of Shao-hsi (1194).

57. *Sung-Yüan hsüeh-an* [Anthology and critical accounts of the Neo-Confucians of the Sung and Yüan dynasties] chs. 69–70.

58. *Chu Tzu shih-chi*, p. 377, on academies.

59. *Tz'u-hai* [Sea of terms], *szu* [sixth section], p. 139.

60. See above, n. 17.

61. *Mien-chai chi*, 36:37b–38a, biographical account.

62. See above, n. 7.

63. *Pei-hsi ta-ch'üan chi*, separate collection, 10:11b, "Life account."

64. Ch'en Ch'un, *Pei-hsi tzu-i* [Neo-Confucian terms explained], twenty-third category on standard and expediency, sec. 6.

65. *Wen-chi*, 9:14b.

66. *Wen-chi*, 69:28a, 86:12a, and 74:22a.

67. *Chien-yang hsien-chih* [Accounts of Chien-yang County] (Shanghai: Hsin-ming Book Co., 1929), 8:54b.

68. *Ibid.*, 8:61b.

69. *Chu Tzu men-jen*, p. 9.

70. *Ibid.*, pp. 4–7.

71. *Mien-chai chi*, 39:2a–3a, funeral address for Ting Fu-chih.

72. *Wen-chi*, 94:27a, tomb inscription for Ting Fu-chih.

73. Tai Hsien, *Chu Tzu shih-chi*, p. 419, on Chu Hsi's pupils.

74. *Ihak t'ongnok* [General record of the School of Principle] (*T'oegye chōnsō* [Complete works of Yi Hwang (Yi T'oegye)]), Bk. III, 8:45a (p. 473).

75. *Sung-Yüan hsüeh-an pu-i* [Supplement to the *Sung-Yüan hsüeh-an*] (*Ssu-ming ts'ung-shu* [Ssu-ming series] ed.), 69:194a, chapter on the Chu Hsi School.

76. Present Hsing-tzu County, Kiangsi.

77. *Wen-chi*, separate collection, 7:10a.

78. *Ibid.*, regular collection, 84:29b.

79. *Analects*, 12:1.

80. *Yü-lei*, ch. 113, sec. 30 (p. 4376).

81. *Ibid.*, ch. 116, sec. 15 (p. 4447); ch. 118, sec. 12 (p. 4528); ch. 119, sec. 16 (p. 4589), sec. 36 (p. 4599), etc.

82. For example, *ibid.*, ch. 117, sec. 24 (p. 4488).

83. *Chu Tzu men-jen,* pp. 93, 229, 297, 325, etc., for more than thirty cases of pupils performing such ceremonies.

84. *Ibid.,* pp. 93, 149, 160, 333, 356, and p. 25, n. 63.

85. *Ibid.,* pp. 220, 361.

86. *Ibid.,* p. 25, nn. 58–64.

87. *Ibid.,* p. 100.

88. *Ibid.,* p. 25, nn. 52–54.

89. *Ibid.,* n. 55.

90. *Ibid.,* n. 56.

91. *Ibid.,* pp. 54, 276, 309; p. 25, n. 57.

92. *Yü-lei,* ch. 14, sec. 65 (p. 416).

93. *Ibid.,* ch. 90, sec. 42 (p. 3647–3654).

94. *Ibid.,* ch. 72, sec. 19 (pp. 2891–2899).

95. *Ibid.,* ch. 11, sec. 110 (p. 305).

96. *Ibid.,* ch. 117, secs. 24–57 (pp. 4489–4521).

97. *Ibid.,* ch. 40, sec. 45 (pp. 1651–1652); ch. 53, sec. 78 (pp. 2058–2059).

98. *Ibid.,* ch. 137, sec. 21 (pp. 5235–5236).

99. *Ibid.,* ch. 130, sec. 3 (pp. 4903–4904).

100. *Ibid.,* ch. 105, sec. 7 (p. 4175); ch. 121, sec. 76 (p. 4702).

101. *Great Learning,* the text.

102. *Yü-lei,* ch. 14, secs. 166, 163, 161, 169, 172 (pp. 446–450).

103. *Doctrine of the Mean,* ch. 1.

104. *Yü-lei,* ch. 113, sec. 12, 14 (pp. 4364–4365).

105. *Ibid.,* sec. 31 (p. 4377); sec. 38 (p. 4382). For seeking the lost mind, see the *Book of Mencius,* 64:11.

106. *Yü-lei,* ch. 114, sec. 27 (p. 4398).

107. *Ibid.,* ch. 115, sec. 19 (p. 4423).

108. *Ibid.,* sec. 37 (p. 4431).

109. *Ibid.,* sec. 41 (p. 4432).

110. *Ibid.,* ch. 116, sec. 9 (p. 4444).

111. *Ibid.,* sec. 7 (p. 4448).

112. *Ibid.,* sec. 37 (p. 4462).

113. *Ibid.,* sec. 56 (pp. 4471–4472).

114. *Ibid.,* ch. 117, sec. 18 (p. 4482).

115. *Ibid.,* sec. 54 (p. 4521).

116. *Ibid.,* ch. 119, sec. 5 (p. 4577).

117. *Ibid.,* sec. 21 (p. 4592).

118. See my *Chu Tzu men-jen,* p. 100. See also ch. 6 above, p. 92.

119. *Ibid.,* p. 220.

120. *Ibid.,* p. 261.

121. *Ibid.,* p. 218.

122. *Ibid.,* p. 106.

123. *Yü-lei,* ch. 117, sec. 53 (p. 4520).

124. Present Tao County in Hunan.

125. *Sung shih,* ch. 434, p. 12875, biography of Ts'ai Yüan-ting.

126. *Chu Tzu men-jen,* p. 268.

127. *Ibid.,* pp. 69, 167, 178, 242.

128. *Ibid.,* pp. 277, 302.

129. *Ibid.*, pp. 101, 166, 228.

130. *Ibid.*, pp. 90, 161, 325.

131. *Ibid.*, pp. 115, 190.

132. *Ibid.*, pp. 319, 332.

133. This is recorded in practically all biographies.

134. The K'ang-lu area refers to Mount Lu in Nan-k'ang.

135. A *li* is one-third of a mile.

136. *Mien-chai chi,* 38:20b, tomb inscription for Chou Shun-pi (Chou Mu).

137. *Wen-chi,* 1:2a, prose-poem on the White Deer Hollow Academy.

138. *Chu Tzu men-jen,* pp. 88, 102, 135, 136, 142, 169, 194, 195, 196, 233, 288, 314; *Sung-Yüan hsüeh-an,* 69:31a, biography of Ts'ai Nien-ch'eng.

139. *Chu Tzu men-jen,* p. 116.

140. *Sung-Yüan hsüeh-an pu-i,* 69:154b, biography of Lin Yung-chung.

141. *Pai-lu shu-yüan chih* [Account of the White Deer Hollow Academy] (1622 ed.), 5:7a–9a; *Chu Tzu men-jen,* p. 68.

142. *Mien-chai chi,* 1:23a–b, lecture at the White Deer Hollow Academy.

143. *Sung shih,* ch. 430, biography of Huang Kan, p. 12782.

144. *Chu Tzu men-jen,* pp. 168, 219, 261.

145. Sung Tuan-i, *K'ao-t'ing yüan-yüan lu,* p. 492, biography of Ch'en Chih.

146. *Sung shih,* ch. 430, biography of Li Fan, p. 12783.

147. *K'ao-t'ing yüan-yüan lu,* p. 478, biography of Huang I-yung.

148. *Sung shih,* ch. 430, biography of Chang Hsia, p. 12787.

149. *Chu Tzu men-jen,* pp. 156, 335, 336, 345.

150. *Sung shih,* ch. 408, biography of Ch'en Mi, p. 12312.

151. *Sung Yüan hsüeh-an,* 69:13a, biography of Ch'en Mi.

152. Present Nan-p'ing County, Fukien.

153. *K'ao-t'ing yüan-yüan lu,* p. 562, biography of Lin Hsüeh-meng.

154. *Sung-Yüan hsüeh-an,* 64:1b, chapter on Fu Kuang.

155. *Sung-Yüan hsüeh-an pu-i,* 69:169a–b, biography of Chao Shih-tuan.

156. *Mien-chai chi,* 19:21a, account of the Chu Wen Kung Shrine.

157. *Sung-Yüan hsüeh-an pu-i,* 69:173b, biography of Chung Chen.

158. Yang Jin-hsin, "Yüeh-lu shu-yüan and Chu Hsi," *Yüeh-lu shu-yüan t'ung-hsun* [Newsletter of the Yüeh-lu Academy] (No. 1, 1982), p. 27; and his unpublished manuscript, "Hunan Sung-tai shu-yüan kai-fang" [General condition of Hunan academies in the Sung period], pp. 3–5.

159. *Chu Tzu men-jen,* pp. 300, 326. See also pp. 156, 216, 297, 302, 355.

160. *Ibid.*, pp. 216, 279, 320.

161. Sun Ch'i-feng, *Li-hsüeh ts'ung-ch'uan* [Orthodox transmission of Neo-Confucianism] (1667 ed.), 17:21b.

162. A county in Chekiang.

163. The Kiangsi area.

164. *Sung-Yüan hsüeh-an,* 83:1b, chapter on Jao Lu.

165. The capital of Han-yang Prefecture is in present Han-yang County, Hupei.

166. Wan Ssu-t'ung (1638–1702), *Ju-lin tsung-p'ai* [Successive generations of the Confucian School] ch. 9.

167. The Four Books are the *Great Learning,* the *Analects,* the *Book of Mencius,* and the *Doctrine of the Mean.*

# – 22 –

# The *Chin-ssu lu*

THE *Chin-ssu lu* (Reflections on things at hand) was compiled by Chu Hsi in collaboration with Lü Tsu-ch'ien (1137–1181). It consists of 622 selections from four Northern Sung (960–1126) Neo-Confucian thinkers, namely, Chou Tun-i (1017–1073), Ch'eng Hao (1032–1085), his younger brother Ch'eng I (1033–1107), and Chang Tsai (1020–1077), in fourteen chapters. It is the first Chinese philosophical anthology, and became the model for the *Yü-lei*, the *Hsing-li ta-ch'üan* (Great collection of Neo-Confucianism), the *Chu Tzu ch'üan-shu* (Complete works of Master Chu), and the *Hsing-li ching-i* (Essentials of Neo-Confucianism). Either directly or indirectly, through these works, the *Chin-ssu lu* dominated Chinese thought for five hundred years and exerted a tremendous influence on Korean and Japanese philosophy for several centuries—accomplishments its two compilers could scarcely have imagined.

In 1967, I translated the *Chin-ssu lu* into English, under the title *Reflections on Things at Hand,* for the "Records of Civilization" series of Columbia University. Besides fully annotating proper names and technical terms, tracing or accounting for quotations, and providing dates and brief biographical accounts of major thinkers mentioned therein, I added comments on the passages by Chu Hsi and by later Chinese, Korean, and Japanese commentators; traced the sources of the 622 selections; described the *Chin-ssu lu* itself and sixty-two Chinese, Korean, and Japanese commentaries; and discussed the translation of certain Neo-Confucian terms.[1] What follows is additional material, covering three areas: the *Chin-ssu lu* in general, its order and titles of chapters, and what Chu Hsi said about the work.

## Supplements, Discoveries, and Problems

Reference has already been made to Chu Hsi's compilation "in collaboration with Lü Tsu-ch'ien." Most writers have ascribed the work to Chu Hsi alone, which is unfair to Lü, while some have asserted that the compilation was by both Chu and Lü, which is unfair to Chu. The fact is that Chu Hsi initiated the project, planned the outline, and laid down the fundamental principles. Most important of all, the work reflects the philosophy of Chu Hsi himself. There is no question that Lü performed a secondary, though important, role.[2]

With the exception of the Confucian classics, commentaries on and explanations of the *Chin-ssu lu* far exceed those written about any other Chinese work. In a recent study in Chinese, I have given an account of eighteen Chinese commentaries, eight Korean commentaries, twenty-two Japanese commentaries, two Western translations, and almost a hundred Japanese colloquial translations, lecture notes, annotations, and so on. Over the centuries, there have also been twenty-two Chinese and Korean supplements to the *Chin-ssu lu,* which contain selections from Chu Hsi and later Neo-Confucians and which are patterned after the *Chin-ssu lu* in fourteen chapters.[3] Since that study, I have learned of additional works. In the Beijing Library, there are preserved two manuscripts entitled the *Chin-ssu lu chi-chieh* (Collected commentaries of the *Chin-ssu lu*), compiled by Huang Shu-ching (K'ang-hsi period, 1662–1722, *cs*) in fourteen chapters in four stitched volumes, and the *Chin-ssu lu chi-shuo* (Collected explanations of the *Chin-ssu lu*), compiled by Huang Shih in fourteen chapters but in twelve stitched volumes. I have not seen the manuscripts and have no information on Huang Shih. There is also the *Chu Tzu wen-yü tsuan-pien* (Compilation of literary and conversational passages from Master Chu) by Yen Hung-k'uei, with a preface dated 1718. I have no information on Yen himself, but his work consists of 258 selections from the *Wen-chi* and the *Yü-lei* arranged according to the *Chin-ssu lu* in fourteen chapters, with similar chapter titles. Chapter 3 on the extension of knowledge is the longest, with 424 sections, while chapter 6 on the regulation of the family is the shortest, with only 29 sections. In the copy that I have, the preface, written by Minamoto Tadakiyo in 1856, says that it came from a merchant ship off the coast of Fukien and Chekiang. This anthology has not been mentioned in any Chinese or Japanese work, and I do not know whether another copy exists. It should be added that Ch'en Lung-cheng's (1585–1645) *Ch'eng Tzu hsiang-pen* (Detailed compilation of the Ch'eng Tzu), which consists of sayings by the Ch'eng brothers, is also patterned after the *Chin-ssu lu*. In Korea, there is Han Mongnin's *Sok kŭn-sarok* (Supplement to the *Chin-ssu lu* in fourteen chapters in three stitched volumes), with a preface dated 1819. There is also a *Sok kŭn-*

*sarok* by an unknown compiler at an unknown date, and there must be more supplements in Korea in addition to these.

The year before I translated the *Chin-ssu lu,* I spent a year in Japan. In the process of my studies there, I happened to make two discoveries in connection with the *Chin-ssu lu.* One was that of Ch'en Hang's (1785–1826) *Chin-ssu lu pu-chu* (Supplementary commentaries on the *Chin-ssu-lu*) in fourteen chapters. Ch'en's courtesy name was T'ai-ch'u and literary name, Ch'iu-fang. He was a native of Ch'i-shui County, Hupei Province. He was a compiler of dynastic history, was skillful in poetry, and had an interest in Neo-Confucianism. His work has not been mentioned anywhere and is most probably nonexistent in China. I happened to find it in the Room for Research in Chinese Philosophy at Tokyo University, and immediately had a microfilm made of it. Upon examination, I found that it is not outstanding. In terms of research, it is far inferior to Mao Hsing-lai's (1678–1748) *Chin-ssu lu chi-chu* (Collected commentaries on the *Chin-ssu lu*); in terms of elucidation, it is not as good as Chang Po-hsing's (1651–1725) *Chin-ssu lu chi-chieh* (Collected explanations of the *Chin-ssu lu*); and in terms of explaining Chu Hsi in his own words, it is nowhere comparable to Chiang Yung's (1681–1762) *Chin-ssu lu chi-chu* (Collected commentaries on the *Chin-ssu lu*). However, it is far superior to Yeh Ts'ai's (*fl.* 1248) *Chin-ssu lu chi-chieh* (Collected explanations of the *Chin-ssu lu*), which has been most popular in Japan. Ch'en Hang's anthology contains not only selections from Chu Hsi but selections from about fifty other Neo-Confucians as well. It also quotes the commentaries of Yeh Ts'ai, Chiang Yung, and Shih Huang (*fl.* 1705) from Shih Huang's *Wu-tzu chin-ssu lu fa-ming* (Exposition of the *Chin-ssu lu* of the five philosophers) but, curiously enough, not Chang Po-hsing. And with the exception of Nakamura Shūsai (1719–1799), in his *Kinshi roku kōsetsu* (Explanations of the *Chin-ssu lu*), Ch'en Hang is the only Chinese, Korean, or Japanese commentator to quote the comments made by Lü Tsu-ch'ien. Although Ch'en's work is not of the first quality, it deserves a place in its homeland.

The other discovery I made was Kaneko Sōsan's (1789–1865) *Kinshi roku teiyō* (Essentials of the *Chin-ssu lu*) in fourteen chapters. Sōsan was not outstanding, but his work was referred to frequently. Japanese scholars thought it had disappeared. One day in 1955, I happened to visit the library of Waseda University. Library officials showed me a manuscript on the *Chin-ssu lu* that the library had kept for several decades. It was written in Chinese characters and was entitled the *Chin-ssu lu t'ai-yao* (Essentials of the *Chin-ssu lu*); the compiler's name was Chin Chi-min. There was a preface dated 1846. As expected, it was in fourteen chapters, with annotations for most of the 622 sections and many quotations from Neo-Confucians of the Sung period (960–1279). At first I thought Chin Chi-min was a Korean writer whose Chinese name would be pronounced Kim Chemin in Korean. Eventually I found that Chin Chi-min (Kin Saimin in Japanese) was the Chinese name of Kaneko Sōsan. When I reported this to the Waseda librarians, they were overjoyed at finding that their manuscript was a real treasure and that a work thought to have been lost had been hiding in their preserve for years.

As I worked on the translation of the *Chin-ssu lu* itself, I made yet another discovery. Chapter 6, section 13 of the text runs as follows:

> *Question:* According to principle, it seems that one should not marry a widow. What do you think?
> *Answer:* Correct. Marriage is a match. If one takes someone who has lost her integrity to be his own match, it means that he himself has lost his integrity.
> *Further Question:* In some cases, widows are all alone, poor, and have no one to depend on. May they remarry?
> *Answer:* This theory has come about only because people of later generations are afraid of starving to death. But to starve to death is a very small matter. To lose one's integrity, however, is a very serious matter.

This passage is taken from Ch'eng I's *I-shu* (Surviving works).[4] Some Neo-Confucians have regarded Ch'eng I's answers as cruel to women, without realizing that Ch'eng I was reasoning on the basis of Mencius' injunction of sacrificing life over righteousness.[5] In his commentary, Chang Po-hsing deleted this passage from Ch'eng I and substituted another passage from the *I-shu* on brotherly love.[6] This substitution had never been noticed. Ch'eng I's opinion on the remarriage of widows is discussed in chapter 30 below. It suffices to point out here that Chang Po-hsing was not correct in altering the contents of the *Chin-ssu lu*.

A number of problems came up in the translation. In chapter 3, section 54, someone asked Ch'eng I about Master Hu's interpretation of the fourth, undivided line of a hexagram as that of the prince. Most commentators have not given the source of the passage but have said that Master Hu refers to Hu Yüan (993–1059), and that when Hu was director of the national university, Ch'eng I studied under him. Did Hu make the remark and Ch'eng I hear him personally, or is his remark written down somewhere? Ch'eng I can be said to have heard it personally from his teacher only if the remark cannot be found in one of Hu Yüan's works. It is known that Hu Yüan was the author of the *Chou-i k'ou-i* (Meanings of the *Book of Changes* orally explained), but this was extremely difficult to locate. Fortunately, the Cabinet Library of Tokyo kindly made a microfilm for me, and the reference is found in chapter 1.

Another problem concerns Chang Tsai's famous essay the "Western Inscription." It is well known that he wrote the "Eastern Inscription" and the "Western Inscription." These two essays are quoted in full in chapter 2, section 89 of the *Chin-ssu lu*. Commentators have merely noted that the essays were written on two windows in Chang's study, but never described how the windows looked or on what material the essays were written. It came to my attention that in the *I-shu* there is a description of the study of Chu Kung-yen (Chu Kuang-t'ing, 1037–1094) in Loyang, which had two windows, each with thirty-six panels. On one window he wrote the "Essentials of the Way of Heaven," and on the other he wrote "The Way of Humanity and Righteousness."[7] It is not clear how long these essays were and how the words were distributed among the panels. Chu Kuang-t'ing was somewhat later than Chang Tsai, and Chang did not live in Loyang. Furthermore, the "Western Inscription" is in 253 Chinese characters and the "Eastern Inscription" in 112 characters. Were Chang's windows divided into thirty-six panels? Were all the panels written on? Were the windows paneled with paper or with translucent tiles? These questions await answers from specialists.

Still another problem is the definition of the word *ts'ang* in chapter 4, section 20. The passage says, "One day, while Po-ch'un [Ch'eng Hao] was living in the *ts'ang* in Ch'ang-an, he was sitting at leisure. He looked at the columns in the corridor and counted them in his mind." Since the interest of Chinese commentators was in the moral meaning of such passages, they overlooked what kind of building a *ts'ang* was. Japanese commentators interpreted the word *ts'ang* as "temporary," "hastily," or as a storehouse. It would be most unusual for a storehouse to have columns, but in his *Kinshi roku rangaisho* (Notes on the *Chin-ssu lu*), Satō Issai (1772–1859) maintained that in the past Japanese storehouses had guest facilities, so that Ch'eng Hao could have stayed in them. It is true that in the Sung period there were granaries and yards. Were there guest facilities? Did Ch'eng Hao stay there? Was the granary in Ch'ang-an so magnificent as to have a long corridor with columns? Or did he temporarily stay somewhere? It is unlikely that he stopped there hastily, for then he would not have had the leisure to count the columns.

A similarly troublesome interpretation is that of the term *k'o-chiang* in chapter 10, section 50. Nakai Chikuzan (1730–1804), in his *Kinshi roku hyōki* (Selected comments on the *Chin-ssu lu* ), understood it to mean "a guest about to," which is meaningless in the context of the passage. Other Japanese annotators interpreted it as a military officer in charge of visits. I have found a conversation in the *Yü-lei* in which Chu Hsi said, "The *k'o-chiang* is next to the prefect. He had great power. All the troops in the prefecture were commanded by him."[8] But a different interpretation was offered by Mao Hsing-lai in his *Chin-ssu lu chi-chu;*

Mao said that the *k'o-chiang* was so called because he was in charge of reception of guests *(k'o)*.

Another instance occurs in chapter 3, section 16, where, in reply to a pupil's question on knowing nature and knowing Heaven, Chang Tsai said, "If *chu-kung* [several gentlemen] hold on without fail to what is discussed . . . ." Most annotators have taken the phrase to refer to Chang Ts'ai's pupils. I believe this is correct, and have translated the phrase accordingly. But some Japanese commentators have understood it to refer to the gentlemen in the Confucian School, to sages and worthies of the past, or to Neo-Confucians of the time. Should all these interpretations be ruled out?

Again, in chapter 4, section 11, the passage begins with "Hsing Ho-shu [Hsing Shu, *fl.* 1127] said." If this is correct, this would be the only passage in the *Chin-ssu lu* attributed not to one of the four Northern Sung Neo-Confucian thinkers but to Hsing Shu. Hsing was a pupil of the Ch'eng brothers but later turned away from them. It is most unlikely that Chu Hsi and Lü Tsu-ch'ien would have selected his saying and incorporated it in the *Chin-ssu lu*. Japanese commentators like Kaibara Ekken (1630–1714; *Kinshi roku bikō* [Notes on the *Chin-ssu lu* for further investigation]), Nakai Chikuzan (*Kinshi roku setsu* [*Chin-ssu lu* explained]), Satō Issai, Sawada Bukō (*fl.* 1720; *Kinshi roku setsuryaku* [Brief explanation of the *Chin-ssu lu*]), Higashi Masazumi (1832–1891; *Kinshi roku sankō* [An investigation on the *Chin-ssu lu*]), and Utsunomiya Ton'an (1634–1710; *Gōtō kinshi roku* [*Chin-ssu lu* annotated]) all cited T'ang Po-yüan's (1540–1598) *Erh-Ch'eng Hsien-sheng yü-lei* (Classified conversations of the two Masters Ch'eng), in which T'ang said that before the name Hsing Ho-shu there is the word *yü* (to give), that is, "Ch'eng Hao told Hsing Ho-shu and said," thus attributing the saying to Ch'eng Hao.[9] But the original passage in the *I-shu* does not have the word *yü*.[10] Besides, T'ang's compilation was not made until several hundred years after Ch'eng Hao's death. I believe most commentators are correct in maintaining that Hsing simply repeated what his teacher had said.

One more problem should engage our attention. In chapter 13, section 1, it is said, "Yang Chu's [440–360 B.C.?] egoism bears some vague resemblance to the doctrine of righteousness, while Mo Tzu's [468–376 B.C.?] universal love bears some vague resemblance to the doctrine of humanity." Certain editions have the words "righteousness" and "humanity" interchanged, because this saying was selected from the *I-shu*, chapter 13, where the two words are indeed the other way around.[11] But it makes no sense to say that egoism bears a resemblance to humanity, which means love for all, and that universal love bears a resemblance to righteousness, which means an appropriate virtue for an appropriate relation. That is why, in his *Meng Tzu chi-chu* (Collected commentaries on the *Books of Mencius*), Chu Hsi said, "Yang's egoism bears a vague resemblance to righteousness, and Mo's universal love bears a vague resemblance to humanity."[12] Ch'eng I himself once said, "Yang's egoism is also righteousness, and Mo's universal love is also humanity."[13] Hence we know that the *I-shu* is wrong in interchanging the two words. Mao Hsing-lai, Shih Huang, and Chiang Yung are correct in following the *Chin-ssu lu*. Yeh Ts'ai, however, has adhered to the passage in the *I-shu* and explained, "Yang Chu may be said to be selfish and not humane. Nevertheless, his doctrine still bears a vague resemblance to the doctrine of humanity, which is free from desires. Mo Tzu's universal love may be said to be reckless and devoid of righteousness. Nevertheless, it still bears a vague resemblance to the doctrine of righteousness, which is free from selfishness." Since Yeh's commentary has been popular in Japan, certain Japanese commentators have followed him. But such an interpretation is most arbitrary. Chang Po-hsing followed Yeh, but added a cautious note that "one edition has 'egoism bears a vague resemblance to righteousness, and universal love bears a vague resemblance to humanity,' . . . This makes much smoother reading." Yeh Ts'ai's error has been pointed out by the Korean commentator Kim Changsaeng (1548–1631; *Kŭnsarok sŏgŭi* [Doubts on the *Chin-ssu lu* removed]), but he has been overlooked by certain Japanese commentators.

The remaining point is not exactly a problem, but should nevertheless be noted. Chapter 1, section 32 of the *Chin-ssu lu* begins with "Empty and tranquil, and without any sign, and yet all things are luxuriantly present." This comes from the *I-shu* and is Ch'eng I's saying.[14] Almost all Japanese commentators have asserted that this saying originated in Buddhism, but no one has traced its source. Yamazaki Ansai (1618–1682) gathered all the sayings of Chinese and Korean Neo-Confucians that contain the phrase "Empty and tranquil, and without any sign" in his "Chubaku muchin setsu" (Treatise on "Empty and tranquil, and without any sign"), but he did not suggest that the saying is of Buddhist origin.[15] In their enthusiasm for Buddhism, Japanese scholars have the tendency to claim Buddhist origin for any Neo-Confucian thought or saying that has even a remote similarity to one in Buddhism. This is only one of many such instances. Another case is provided in chapter 3, section 49, where it is said, "Substance and function come from the same source, and there is no gap between the manifest and the hidden." This is a quotation from the preface of Ch'eng I's *I chuan* (Commentary on the *Book of Changes*). Kaibara Ekken, however, asserted that it is from Ch'eng-kuan's (c. 760–838) commentary on the *Hua-yen ching* (Flowery splendor scripture), but gave no specific section or page reference.[16] Many Japanese commentators and the *Daikanwa jiten* (Great Chinese-Japanese dictionary) have claimed that the first half of the saying comes from Ch'eng-kuan's commentary, but according to Ōta Kinjō (1765–1825), it does not appear in any of Ch'eng-kuan's works. Ōta added that the first half of the saying is quoted as Ch'eng-kuan's by Shang-chih in his *Kuei-yüan chih-chih* (Straight direction to return to the source), and that the second half originated with Fa-tsang (643–712).[17] Since Ōta gave no reference, it is impossible to check his statement. There is no question that Buddhism and Neo-Confucianism have exerted a strong influence on each other. By the eleventh century, the saying was common among both Buddhists and Neo-Confucians. As T'ang Shun-chih (1507–1560) said, "Both Buddhists and Confucians said the same thing, and none could tell whose words they were."[18]

## Chapter Titles and Sequence

In the original compilation of the *Chin-ssu lu,* there were no chapter titles. According to Chu Hsi's preface (actually postscript), "The essentials of the student's search for the beginning of things, exerting effort, conducting himself, and managing others, as well as the gist of understanding the heterodox schools and observing the sages and worthies, can be seen in rough outline." Consequently, for each chapter he merely provided a general statement. As he said later, "The outlines of the chapters in the *Chin-ssu lu* are: (1) the substance of the Way, (2) the essentials of learning, (3) the investigation of things and the investigation of principle to the utmost, (4) preserving [one's mind] and nourishing [one's nature], (5) correcting mistakes, improving oneself, self-discipline, and returning to propriety, (6) the way to regulate the family, (7) the principle of serving or not serving in the government, advancing or withdrawing, and declining or accepting, (8) the way of governing the state and bringing peace to the world, (9) systems and institutions, (10) the method for a gentleman to handle affairs, (11) the way to teach, (12) correcting mistakes and the defects of the human mind, (13) the learning of the heterodox schools, and (14) the disposition of sages and worthies."[19] As Huang Kan (1152–1221) told his fellow pupil Li Fang-tzu (1214 *cs*) in a letter:

> When the two Masters compiled the *Chin-ssu,* the original edition had no chapter titles. Originally they had the idea, of course, but they never had the titles. Later, friends in Chin-hua[20] coined the titles, either because they had heard the two Teachers talk about them or had invented them themselves. Now there are these titles, as if given by the two Teachers themselves. They are not good in spirit and not found in the original text. It is better to delete them and instead write a few words to include the

items, so that the reader will know what it is about and so as to retain the authenticity of the original text. Why don't you speak with Elder Chen [Chen Te-hsiu, 1178–1235] and see what he thinks?²¹

Both Huang Kan and Li Fang-tzu were outstanding pupils of Chu Hsi and knew the intentions of the Master well. Commentators like Miyake Shōsai (1662–1741; *Kinshi roku hikki* [Notes on the *Chin-ssu lu*]) and Nakamura Shūsai have contended that since Chu Hsi had written Lü Tsu-ch'ien to say, "We must have a few words from you to follow the table of contents,"²² there must have been chapter titles from the start. But what Chu Hsi referred to as the table of contents may have been simply the chapter numbers, or what Huang Kan suggested merely as an idea.

The titles that friends in Chin-hua gave to the chapters have never been known. The oldest titles are those used by Yeh Ts'ai (*fl.* 1248). They are: (1) On the Substance of Tao, (2) On Learning, (3) On the Extension of Knowledge, (4) Preserving One's Mind and Nourishing One's Nature, (5) On Self-discipline, (6) The Way of the Family, (7) On Serving or Not Serving in the Government, (8) The Substance of Government, (9) The Methods of Government, (10) Governmental Affairs, (11) On Teaching, (12) Caution, (13) Sifting the Heterodox Schools, and (14) Observing the Sages and Worthies.²³ Generally speaking, the titles are not greatly wrong, but they do not reflect Chu Hsi's original purpose. For example, he definitely said that chapter 5 deals with correcting mistakes, improving oneself, self-discipline, and returning to propriety, but Yeh Ts'ai mentioned only self-discipline. Unfortunately, many commentators in Japan, and Chang Po-hsing in China, copied him. It is far better to follow the examples of Mao Hsing-lai, Chiang Yung, and Ch'en Hang, who used Chu Hsi's own outline.

Yeh Ts'ai not only invented the chapter titles; he also arbitrarily created an outline for each chapter. In chapter 3, for example, he saw the first twenty-two sections as general discussions on the method of the extension of knowledge, and sections 22 through 33 as general discussions on the method of reading books. From section 34 to the end, Yeh said, the method of reading is discussed in specific terms, beginning with the *Great Learning* and followed by the *Analects,* the *Book of Mencius,* the *Book of Odes,* the *Book of History,* the *Doctrine of the Mean,* and the *Book of Changes.* As a rough order of the topics in the chapter, this is acceptable, but as a rigid demarcation, why is the *Doctrine of the Mean* placed between the *Book of History* and the *Book of Changes?* Because of Yeh's popularity, his aritificial sequence led to some farfetched analyses of the chapters. Yamazaki Ansai and his pupil Miyake Shōsai, for example, regarded the three items and the eight steps of the *Great Learning*²⁴ as the order of the chapters in the *Chin-ssu lu.* They considered chapters 3, 4, and 5 to be on self-cultivation, chapter 6 to be on the regulation of the family, and chapters 8, 9, and 10 to be on national order and world peace. As a general outline, there is nothing seriously wrong with this scheme, but the three items and the eight steps have not been matched with the chapters, chapters 13 and 14 are not accounted for, and chapter 12, on "correcting mistakes and the defects of the human mind," can hardly be considered not to belong to self-cultivation. Miyake Shōsai even said that the last sentence of each chapter is continued in the first sentence of the next. Another pupil of Yamazaki, Wakabayashi Kansai (1679–1732; *Kinshi roku kōgi: Jūshi moku* [Meanings of the fourteen chapter headings of the *Chin-ssu lu* discussed]), even said that the first and the last chapters echo each other and unite Heaven and man as one body.

Such interpretations go much further than anything Chu Hsi and Lü Tsu-ch'ien ever conceived of. Chinese commentators are not free from such wild flights of the imagination, either. Chou Kung-shu (*fl.* 1420; *Fen-lei chin-ssu lu chi-chieh* [Collected explanations of the *Chin-ssu lu* classified]), for instance, regarded chapter 10, on government, as pertaining to affairs in office, and saw chapter 11, on teaching, as pertaining to affairs after leaving office. But to Yin Hui-i (1691–1748; *Chien-yü Hsien-sheng wen-chi* [Collected literary works of Yin Hui-i]), chapter 11 should follow chapter 10 because a scholar, having had no opportunity to serve in the government, retires to teach.[25] It must be said that these commentators failed to understand the purpose of teaching in the Confucian School.[26]

## Chu Hsi's Comments on the *Chin-ssu lu*

In chapter 105, sections 22–23 of the *Yü-lei*, there are twelve comments by Chu Hsi on the *Chin-ssu lu*. They are as follows:

1. "The fundamentals of self-cultivation are completely covered in the *Hsiao-hsüeh* [Elementary education], while refined and subtle principles are fully treated in the *Chin-ssu lu*."

2. "The *Chin-ssu lu* is worth reading. The Four Books[27] are the ladder to the Six Classics.[28] The *Chin-ssu lu* is the ladder to the Four Books."

3. "The outlines of the chapters in the *Chin-ssu lu* are . . . [see above, p. 363]."

4. "Generally, the selections in the *Chin-ssu lu* are not systematic. Each chapter should not be considered to be dealing with one thing. For example, chapter 10 does not deal with serving the ruler alone, for there is a section on teaching boys."[29]

5. "Everything in the *Chin-ssu lu* is intimately connected with man's life and can save him from defects."

6. "Cheng[30] was commenting on how practical and close to human

life the sayings in the *Chin-ssu lu* are. The Teacher said, 'The Sage and the Worthy³¹ spoke of things plainly. For example, the *Doctrine of the Mean,* the *Great Learning,* the *Analects,* and the *Book of Mencius* are all plain and simple. The [contents of the] *Chin-ssu lu,* however, are words of men of recent times. They are more intimately connected with our lives.' "

7. "Someone asked about the *Chin-ssu lu.* The Teacher said, 'Suppose you read the *Great Learning* thoroughly, and then go right on to the *Analects* and the *Book of Mencius.* The *Chin-ssu lu* is difficult to read.' "

8. "The first chapter of the *Chin-ssu lu* is difficult to read. This is the reason I talked the matter over with Po-kung [Lü Tsu-ch'ien] and asked him to write a few words as a postscript. If one reads this chapter only, one will be unable to relate to life the principles one finds in it. Stopping there would be like halting one's troops outside the strong defenses of a city. It would be far better to read the *Analects* and the *Book of Mencius,* which are plain and straightforward and can be enjoyed."

9. "In reading the *Chin-ssu lu,* if the student does not understand the first chapter, he should begin with the second and the third. In time, he will gradually understand the first chapter."

10. "When Fei-ch'ing [T'ung Po-yü, 1144–1190?] was asked how he was getting along with the *Chin-ssu lu,* he said that there were many doubtful points. The Teacher said, 'If one hurriedly reads it for the first time, it is difficult—that is true. Sometimes it says something first this way but later that way, or says one thing here and a different thing there. However, if one reads it carefully again and again, one will find in it a certain direction. When a search has been made to understand forty or fifty sections, one will find that there is only one principle running through it all. I-ch'uan [Ch'eng I] said that principle cannot be investigated to the utmost in one day, but when one has investigated a great deal, one will thoroughly understand it.' "³²

11. "When discussing the *Chin-ssu lu,* the Teacher said, 'Selections should not be made from [Ch'eng I's] *I chuan* [Commentary on the *Book of Changes*].' When asked the reason, he said, 'You must find out for yourself.' His idea was that the *I chuan* itself constitutes a book."

*Note:* Although this concerns only one of the 622 sections in the *Chin-ssu lu,* 106 of its sections come from Ch'eng I's *I chuan,* more than from any other work. Chu Hsi insisted that the *Book of Changes* was for divination, and was strongly opposed to Ch'eng I's interpretation of it as referring to moral principles. The prominence of the *I chuan* in the *Chin-ssu lu* is no doubt due partly to Lü Tsu-ch'ien's insistence and partly to the fact that Chu Hsi himself, upon further thought, saw in Ch'eng I's commentary much that is pertinent to daily life.

12. "Speaking about the *Hsü chin-ssu lu* [Supplement to the *Reflections on Things at Hand*], the Teacher said, 'There are already too many books. We cannot manage to read if there are any more.' "

*Note:* Chu Hsi's friend, Liu Ch'ing-chih (1139–1195), selected sayings of the Ch'eng brothers' pupils for the *Hsü chin-ssu lu,* which has long been lost. Chu Hsi once said, "Tzu-ch'eng [Liu Ch'ing-chih] compiled the *Chin-ssu hsü-lu* [*Hsü chin-ssu lu*]. I urged him not to do so, for it is impossible to continue the thoughts of the two Ch'engs."[33] He also wrote Liu and said, "In a day or so, I shall have finished reading the *Chin-ssu hsü-lu* and I shall report to you. The third anthology is also good. However, aren't anthologies like these too hard on the mind? It does no harm to copy down [an excerpt] whenever one reads and feels one has found something, but purposely to collect, search, and arrange is a waste of mental effort and energy. It is better to save the trouble."[34] We have no information on the third anthology. Undoubtedly, the *Chin-ssu hsü-lu* showed some defects in its selection and arrangement.

Aside from the preceding twelve comments, which are largely on the nature of the *Chin-ssu lu* and the method of reading it, there are many more comments in the *Wen-chi* and the *Yü-lei* that are worth our attention, especially on the compilation and evaluation of the work:

13. "The *Chin-ssu lu* is a selection of the essential and important sayings of the several Masters, to show students of later generations the gate to enter into virtue. The first chapter shows people where the substance of the Way lies."[35]

14. "The *Chin-ssu lu* discusses very keenly the defects of the patterns of learning in recent times. It will be fine if one can read it along with [the Four Books]."[36]

15. "The writings of I-Lo[37] amount to a great deal. I am afraid it is difficult to read all of them. The important essentials may be found in the *Chin-ssu lu,* which I already reported to you. One might not even understand this book thoroughly. There is no need to read many others."[38]

16. "The *Chin-ssu lu* is fundamentally for the student who cannot read all the works of the several Masters. For this reason, the most important passages and those of immediate concern have been selected, so that the student can gradually enter into the Way. If he thoroughly understands these, he will extend, on the basis of similarity in kind, to understand the rest and thus achieve an extensive learning. If he does not read it thoroughly, he cannot understand even this book of several chapters. How can he have the energy or time to read all the works listed in the beginning of the book?"[39]

17. " 'The mind is the principle of production.'[40] This sentence was recorded by Chang Ssu-shu [Chang I]. I am afraid it is incomplete. It must be that, at the time, a literary rendering was substituted, so that the intended meaning was lost. Po-feng [Wu Pi-ta] said, 'Why then include it in the *Chin-ssu lu?*' The Teacher replied, 'How dare we not include it? I am only afraid that something is missing. The sense of the four words is incomplete.' "[41]

18. "Previously, when we compiled the *Chin-ssu lu,* I told Po-kung [Lü Tsu-ch'ien] that this passage [chapter 10, section 18, on the text of the lowest, undivided line of the *i* (increase) hexagram] need not be included, because there is not always such a case.[42] Po-kung said, ' "There is not always such a case" means that there sometimes is such a case. How can we not cite it as a warning?' When I thought about it later on, it proved to be true."[43]

19. "Ch'in-fu [Chang Shih, 1133–1180] sent the *Chin-ssu lu,* which he has published, and wanted me to add several sections on the civil service examinations. I have written them down and sent them to him."[44]

*Note:* These may be sections 33–35 of chapter 7. Chu Hsi also wanted to include several additional sections on the harmful influence of civil service examinations, but Lü Tsu-ch'ien objected. As Chu Hsi told Shih Yün, "Previously, we compiled the *Chin-ssu lu.* I wanted to add several sections on how civil service examinations spoil the human mind, but Po-kung refused."[45]

20. "Po-kung thought all things are included but law. We happened to have this passage, [in which Chieh-fu (Wang An-shih, 1021–1086) said that laws are comparable to the 'eighty percent script.'[46] This is his insight.][47] So we included it."[48]

21. "Ch'en Chih came to say goodbye and the Teacher gave him a copy of the *Chin-ssu lu,* saying, 'In serving your mother, you may look up the passage on dealing with one's mother[49] and you will see the princple.' Therefore, he said, 'The *I chuan* is a book in itself. Po-kung, however, used it as a model for women, and this passage is now included in the *Chin-ssu lu.* Orginally, I was not happy that he did so, but after careful examination, I realize that every paragraph is closely relevant to one's daily task and should not be omitted. It is of great benefit to the student.' "[50]

22. " 'My mind is the mind of Heaven and Earth, my principle is the principle of the myriad things, and the evolution of one day is the evolution of one year.'[51] This saying is very good. People can understand but not necessarily apprehend its real truth. When we compiled the *Chin-ssu lu,* I wanted to select this passage, but Po-kung was afraid that people would not understand it and that it might lead to trouble."[52]

23. "Asked about the saying, 'Because there is unity, there is the wonderful functioning of the spirit,'[53] the Teacher said, 'Heng-ch'ü [Chang Tsai] has said it very well. One must look at it carefully. But what has been included in the *Chin-ssu lu* is different from the book we are talking about.[54] At the time, Po-kung refused to select the whole passage from this book, so in the end it was not included. After the sentence "Because there is unity, there is the wonderful functioning of the spirit," Heng-ch'ü himself added a note that says, "Because of the presence of the two [yin, or passive cosmic force, and yang, or active cosmic

force], the change is unpredictable." There is only this one thing operating universally among the myriad things. . . . After the sentence
"Because of the two, there is therefore transformation," he added a
note that says, "promoting the operation of the one." Among the things
in the world, if they are one, they cannot change. Only when they are
two can they be transformed. . . . This theory is extremely refined. We
must look at it carefully.' " [55]

24. "K'ang-chieh [Shao Yung, 1011–1077] has some extremely good
sayings that were not included in the *Chin-ssu lu*. Recently, I have seen
the *Wen-chien* [Mirror of literature], in which K'ang-chieh's poems have
been compiled, but I don't know why his poetic lines, 'Facing toward
the one, Heaven spreads creation and transformation / Man in his
mind generates order and regulation,' [56] have not been included." [57]

*Note:* This was recorded by Huang I-kang after 1193, when Chu Hsi
was sixty-four years old, and eighteen years after the compilation of the
*Chin-ssu lu*. I have said that Shao Yung was excluded from the *Chin-ssu
lu* essentially because he was outside the orthodox transmission of the
tradition of the Way. That was the case because, on the one hand, he
seldom talked about the fundamental Confucian virtues like humanity
and righteousness and, on the other, because Shao's philosophy of number and form carried with it too much of a Taoist flavor. [58] Does Chu
Hsi's lament that the *Wen-chien* had excluded these poetic lines mean
that, in later years, he regretted that the *Chin-ssu lu* had excluded Shao
Yung?

25. "In part 2 of the 'Chao-shih k'o-yü' [What Chao's visitors said]
in the *I-shu*, Chang Ssu-shu recorded Master Ch'eng's [Ch'eng I] saying, 'When one wishes to investigate things, one is already near the
Way.' [59] This saying should have been included in the *Chin-ssu lu*." [60]

26. "The Teacher happened to mention Ming-tao's [Ch'eng Hao]
saying in the 'Tung-chien lu' [Records of seeing (the two Masters
Ch'eng) in the East], 'The student must first of all understand the
nature of *jen* [humanity]. The man of *jen* forms one body with all things
without any differentiation. Righteousness, propriety, wisdom, and
faithfulness are all [expressions of] *jen* . . . .' [61] It should have been
added to the *Chin-ssu lu*." [62]

*Note:* Quotations 25 and 26 were recorded by Shen Hsien after 1198.
Thus they were uttered after Chu Hsi was sixty-nine years old. They
truly represent his final conclusions, arrived at late in life. Of all the
Chinese, Korean, and Japanese commentators, Ch'en Hang alone
repeated them.

27. "I believe that the essentials of the student's search for the beginnings of things, exerting effort, conducting himself, and managing others, as well as the gist of understanding the heterodox schools and
observing the sages and worthies, can be seen in rough outline. Thus if

a young man in an isolated village, who has the will to learn but no enlightened teacher or good friend to guide him, obtains this volume and explores and broods over the material in his own mind, he will be able to find the gate to enter. He can then read the complete works of the four gentlemen, deeply sift their meanings and repeatedly recite their words, and absorb them at leisure, so as to achieve extensive learning and return to the simple truth. He can then acquire all the beauties of the ancestral temple and all the richness of the governmental offices.[63] Someone may shrink from effort and be content with the simple convenient, thinking that all he needs is to be found here, but this is not the purpose of the present anthology."[64]

28. "Previously, we disliked several passages because we thought they were too high-sounding, such as those on the Great Ultimate and Ming-tao's [Ch'eng Hao] discussion on human nature.[65] But now I think they should not be omitted. . . . I must ask you, my friend [Lü Tsu-ch'ien], to say a few words at the end of the table of contents to give careful instructions."[66]

29. "Some people believe that the doctrines of yin and yang, change and transformation, and the nature and destiny of man and things in chapter 1 are, generally speaking, not matters for the beginning student. I have had the opportunity of understanding the purpose of this compilation. Although a young man should not be allowed to go into the fundamentals of moral principles all of a sudden, nevertheless, if he is completely ignorant even of their outline, where would he be at the end? To include these doctrines at the beginning of the book is merely to enable the student to know their terms and have something to look forward to. As to the contents of the remaining chapters, dealing with methods of study and the concrete steps of daily application and personal practice, they involve definite steps. If the student proceeds accordingly, ascending from the low to the high and going from the near to the far, he will probably not miss the aim of this anthology. If, however, he disdains the low and the near and restlessly seeks the high and the far, skips over the steps and crosses the limits, he will be drifting in emptiness and vacuity, without anything to rely on. Can that be called reflecting on things at hand? The reader should thoroughly understand this idea."[67]

## Notes

1. See my translation of the *Chin-ssu lu* entitled *Reflections on Things at Hand* (New York: Columbia University Press, 1967), pp. 307–370. The term *chin-ssu* is here translated as "things at hand." It is derived from the *Analects,* 19:6. The term should not be translated as "self-reflection," because that would be insufficient to bring out Chu Hsi's idea that the book is "closely related to daily application," as he stated in his preface to the book, and would make Chu Hsi's phil-

osophical system too much like that of Lu Hsiang-shan (1139–1193), which is basically contemplative.

2. The question of Chu Hsi and Lü Tsu-ch'ien's collaboration is discussed in detail in *Reflections on Things at Hand*, pp. 325–326.

3. See my *Chu-hsüeh lun-chi* [Studies on Chu Hsi] (Taipei: Student Book Co., 1982), pp. 163–180.

4. *I-shu*, 22B:3a, in the *Erh-Ch'eng ch'üan-shu* [Complete works of the two Ch'engs] (*SPPY* ed.).

5. *Book of Mencius*, 6A:10.

6. *I-shu*, 18:45a.

7. *I-shu*, 2A:16b.

8. *Yü-lei*, ch. 83, sec. 33 (p. 3474).

9. *Erh-Ch'eng Hsien-sheng yü-lei* (1585 ed.), 8:26a.

10. *I-shu*, 1:8a.

11. *Ibid.*, 13:1a.

12. *Meng Tzu chi-chu*, comment on 3B:9.

13. *I-shu*, 15:21b.

14. *Ibid.*, 15:8b.

15. *Zoku Yamazaki Ansai zensho* [Supplement to the *Complete Works of Yamazaki Ansai*] (1937 ed.), pt. 2, pp. 78–86.

16. Kaibara Ekken, *Taigi roku* [Records of great doubt] (1766 ed.), pt. 2, p. 4b.

17. Ōta Kinjō, *Gimon roku* [Records of doubt] (1831 ed.), pt. 1, p. 6b.

18. *T'ang Ching-ch'uan chi* [Collected works of T'ang Shun-chih] (1573 ed.), 6:2b.

19. *Yü-lei*, ch. 105, sec. 24 (p. 4179).

20. Chin-hua was Lü Tsu-ch'ien's native county in Cheking Province.

21. *Mien-chai chi* [Collected works of Huang Kan] (*Ssu-k'u ch'üan-shu chen-pen* [Precious works of the *Complete Collection of the Four Libraries*] ed.), 8:19a–b, third letter in reply to Li Kung-hui (Li Fang-tzu).

22. *Wen-chi*, 33:28b, forty-first letter in reply to Lü Po-kung (Lü Tsu-ch'ien).

23. Yeh Ts'ai, *Chin-ssu lu chi-chieh* [Collected explanations of the *Chin-ssu lu*].

24. The three items of the *Great Learning* are: manifesting the clear character, renewal of the people, and abiding in the highest good. The eight steps are: investigation of things, extension of knowledge, sincerity of the will, rectification of the mind, cultivation of the person, regulation of the family, ordering of the state, and bringing peace to the world.

25. *Chien-yü Hsien-sheng wen-chi* [Collected literary works of Yin Hui-i] (*Ts'ung-shu chi-ch'eng* [Collection of series] ed.), ch. 9, p. 95.

26. The question of chapter titles and sequence is discussed in greater detail in *Reflections on Things at Hand*, pp. 326–330.

27. The Four Books are the *Great Learning*, the *Analects*, the *Book of Mencius*, and the *Doctrine of the Mean*.

28. The Six Classics are the *Book of Odes*, the *Book of History*, the *Book of Changes*, the *Book of Rites*, the *Spring and Autumn Annals*, and the *Book of Music*. The *Book of Music* was lost before the third century B.C., and was replaced by the *Chou-li* (Rites of Chou) during the Sung period (960–1279).

29. *Chin-ssu lu*, ch. 10, sec. 64.

30. Chu Hsi had ten pupils by the name of Cheng. Most probably this refers to Cheng K'o-hsüeh (1152–1212), because the remark was recorded by Yeh Ho-sun (Yeh Wei-tao) in 1191, and Cheng K'o-hsüeh attended the Master from 1190 to 1191.

31. The Sage was Confucius; the Worthy, Mencius.

32. Paraphrase of the *I-shu,* 18:5b.

33. *Yü-lei,* ch. 101, sec. 2 (p. 4061).

34. *Wen-chi,* separate collection, 3:12b, letter to Liu Tzu-ch'eng (Liu Ch'ing-chih).

35. *Ibid.,* regular collection, 61:26a, second letter in reply to Yen Shih-heng (Yen Shih-wen).

36. *Ibid.,* 59:12b, first letter in reply to Tou Wen-ch'ing (Tou Ts'ung-chou).

37. I-Lo refers to the I River and Loyang, where the Ch'eng brothers lived and taught.

38. *Wen-chi,* 26:32b, a separate note to Prime Minister Ch'en (Ch'en Chun-ch'ing).

39. *Ibid.,* 64:37a, tenth letter in reply to someone.

40. *I-shu,* 21B:2a.

41. *Yü-lei,* ch. 95, sec. 94 (p. 3874). In Chinese, the sentence contains four characters.

42. Ch'eng I's commentary on this part of the *i* hexagram in the *I-chuan,* 3:41b–42a, says, "A person in an inferior position should not assume an important undertaking. An important undertaking is a serious one. If it is delegated to him by a superior, he will bear a great responsibility and should try to accomplish such an important undertaking and obtain great fortune, and then there will be no error on his part. If he can obtain great fortune, the superior who gave him the responsibility will be considered to know him well, and he himself will be considered equal to the task he has assumed. Otherwise, both will be wrong."

43. *Yü-lei,* ch. 123, sec. 12 (p. 4747).

44. *Wen-chi,* 34:4b, fifty-sixth letter in reply to Lü Po-kung.

45. *Ibid.,* 54:25b, letter in reply to Shih Tzu-yü (Shih Yün).

46. "Eighty percent script" is a form of script consisting of 20 percent "bronze style" or "seal style," which is characterized by curved lines, and 80 percent "clerical style," which is characterized by angular lines.

47. *Chin-ssu lu,* ch. 9, sec. 20.

48. *Yü-lei,* ch. 96, sec. 66 (p. 3929).

49. The passage in the *Chin-ssu lu* on dealing with one's mother is in ch. 6, sec. 3.

50. *Yü-lei,* ch. 119, sec. 21 (p. 4592).

51. These are Ch'eng I's words in the *I-shu,* 2A:1b.

52. *Yü-lei,* ch. 97, sec. 22 (p. 3944).

53. *Cheng-meng* [Correcting youthful ignorance], ch. 2, "Heaven and Earth," sec. 2, in the *Chang Tzu ch'üan-shu* [Complete works of Master Chang Tsai] (*SPPY* ed.), 2:5b.

54. This refers to the *Chin-ssu lu,* ch. 1, sec. 49. This selection comes from Chang Tsai's *I shuo* [Explanation of the *Book of Changes*], comment on "Appended Remarks," pt. 1, ch. 10, in the *Chang Tzu ch'üan-shu,* 11:12b.

55. *Yü-lei*, ch. 98, sec. 33 (p. 3990).

56. Shao Yung, *I-ch'uan chi-jang chi* [Collection of striking an earthen musical instrument at the I River] (*SPTK* ed.), 15:1a.

57. *Yü-lei*, ch. 100, sec. 54 (p. 4057).

58. *Chu-hsüeh lun-chi*, p. 126.

59. This saying is not found in the *I-shu*, 21A or 21B, which were recorded by Chang I, or in the *Wai-shu* [Additional works], 12:17b–18a, "What Chao's Visitors Said," in the *Erh-Ch'eng ch'üan-shu*.

60. *Yü-lei*, ch. 18, sec. 63 (p. 651).

61. *I-shu*, 2A:3a, "Records of seeing (the two Masters Ch'eng) in the East."

62. *Yü-lei*, ch. 95, sec. 126 (pp. 3886–3887).

63. This is a reference to the *Analects*, 19:23.

64. Chu Hsi's postscript to the *Chin-ssu lu*, translated as "preface" in *Reflections on Things at Hand*, pp. 1–2. It is also found in the *Wen-chi*, 81:6a–b.

65. This probably refers to ch. 1, secs. 1 and 21, etc.

66. *Wen-chi*, 33:28a–b, forty-first letter in reply to Lü Po-kung (Lü Tsu-ch'ien).

67. This is Lü Tsu-ch'ien's postscript. It appears as his preface in *Reflections on Things at Hand*, p. 3, and is also found in the *Tung-lai Lü T'ai-shih wen-chi* [Collection of literary works of Lü Tsu-ch'ien, member of the Han-lin Academy], ch. 7.

# The *Yü-lei*,
# the Yü-shan Lecture,
# the *Meng Tzu chi-chu*,
# and the *Hsiao-hsüeh*

THIS chapter deals with some of Chu Hsi's works, not as representative of any particular aspect of his life or thought, but simply because information on them has thus far been unavailable in any language. Technically, the *Yü-lei* is not Chu Hsi's own work, but it contains his ideas just the same.

## Notes on the *Yü-lei*

In the study of Chu Hsi, scholars are almost entirely dependent on the *Yü-lei*. In the *Chu Tzu ch'üan-shu* (Complete works of Master Chu), the selections from the *Yü-lei* come first, and those from the *Wen-chi* come next. In the *Hsing-li ching-i* (Essentials of Neo-Confucianism), almost all the selections are from the *Yü-lei*, with very few from the *Wen-chi* and other writings. Chapters 48 and 49 of the *Sung-Yüan hsüeh-an* (Anthology and critical accounts of Neo-Confucians of the Sung and Yüan dynasties) begin with several essays from the *Wen-chi*, but in the selection of sayings that follows, those from the *Yü-lei* come first. In his *Chu Tzu hsin-hsüeh-an* (New anthology and critical accounts of Master Chu), Professor Ch'ien Mu made considerable use of the *Wen-chi*, but the majority of his selections is nevertheless from the *Yü-lei*.[1] Ch'ien Mu has pointed out that in ten areas—such as Chu Hsi's revision of his commentary on the *Book of Changes*, his new interpretations after the completion of his various commentaries, and his corrections of the two Ch'engs' (Ch'eng Hao, 1032–1085, and Ch'eng I, 1033–1107) explanation of the Confucian classics—the *Yü-lei* is indispensable in understanding Chu Hsi.[2]

In his *Chu Tzu nien-p'u* (Chronological biography of Master Chu),

Wang Mao-hung (1668–1741) differed from the above by relying on letters from the *Wen-chi* rather than sayings from the *Yü-lei*. The conversations in the *Yü-lei* were recorded by pupils whose interpretations were inevitably colored by their own levels of understanding. In some cases, two pupils gave different records of the same conversation. Materials in the *Wen-chi,* in contrast, come from Chu Hsi's own hand. The *Yü-lei* covers the period from 1170, when Chu Hsi was forty-one, to four days before his death in 1200. In comparison, the *Wen-chi* covers the period from 1153, when he issued proclamations at T'ung-an as *chu-pu* (assistant magistrate), at the age of twenty-four,[3] to the day before he passed away, when he wrote his last letter to his pupil and son-in-law Huang Kan (1152–1221).[4] Thus the *Wen-chi* represents Chu Hsi's thoughts throughout his lifetime, whereas the *Yü-lei* represents those of the second half of his life. However, most of the conversations recorded in the *Yü-lei* are his final conclusions, arrived at late in life. Moreover, they are classified, making them comparatively easy to trace. Therefore scholars have ample reason to make greater use of the *Yü-lei*. According to Li Hsing-ch'uan (Chia-ting period, 1208–1224, *cs*):

> I have humbly said that where the *Yü-lu* [Recorded sayings, i.e., the *Yü-lei*] and the *Ssu-shu* [*Ssu-shu chang-chü chi-chu* (Commentaries on the Four Books)] differ, the latter should be regarded as authentic, while the *Yü-lu* should be used as supporting material where the deliberations in his correspondence have left questions unanswered. In the cases where the *Shih* [*Shih chi-chuan* (Collected commentaries on the *Book of Odes*)] and the *I* [*Chou-i pen-i* (Original meanings of the *Book of Changes*)], etc., differ [from the *Yü-lu*], the letters before the completion of those works should be regarded as authentic, but the *Yü-lu* should be considered correct after their completion.[5]

I would add that where the *Yü-lei* and the *Wen-chi* differ, the *Wen-chi* should be followed, and where they agree, the later date should be followed.

The *Yü-lei* was compiled by Li Ching-te (*fl.* 1263) and printed in 1270. Li collected several tens of anthologies of conversations, "gathered what was overlooked, corrected what was in error, examined their similarities and differences, and eliminated more than 1,250 duplications."[6] Hu Shih (1891–1962) has written a definitive history of the *Yü-lei* that is most worthwhile.[7] The *Yü-lei* consists of 140 chapters in more than 14,200 sections. The longest chapter is the sixteenth, with 253 sections on the text of the *Great Learning;* the shortest is the eighty-eighth, with only eight sections on the *Ta-Tai li-chi* (Book of rites of the Elder Tai). There is a definite scheme of classification. As Huang Shih-i (*fl.* 1219) said,

We have adopted some principles and guidelines for the order of sequence. There must be the Great Ultimate before there can be Heaven and Earth, there must be Heaven and Earth before there are man and things, and there must be man and things before there are the terms of nature and destiny. The principles of humanity, righteousness, propriety, and wisdom are what constitute man's nature and destiny. The pursuit of learning is to learn these principles. Hence the book begins with the Great Ultimate and Heaven and Earth, followed by sources of the nature and destiny of man and things, and the definite order of ancient learning. Next come the various classics, whose purpose is to make principles manifest. Next come Confucius, Mencius, Master Chou [Chou Tun-i, 1017–1073], the Masters Ch'eng [Ch'eng Hao and Ch'eng I], and Master Chu, who have transmitted the principles. Then follow the heterodox schools, which obscure principle and must be rebuked by those who are responsible for the orthodox tradition of the Way. After this come the rulers, ministers, institutions, and personages and their discussions of the present and previous dynasties, all of which are to some extent provided for. This is where principles have been operating since the establishment of Heaven and Earth, and are manifested in order and disorder, rise and decline. The subjects that cannot be classified are grouped together as miscellaneous literature to conclude the book.[8]

This scheme of classification is neither clear nor systematic. For example, chapter 1 is supposed to be on the Great Ultimate, but the subject is discussed at greater length in chapter 94, in connection with Master Chou's work. For comments on humanity, propriety, and so on, one has to go to the chapters on the *Analects* and look up the sections concerned with the subject. What is badly needed, therefore, is a subject index to supplement the index of proper names in the 1970 edition published in Taipei.

Conversations and sayings in the *Yü-lei* were recorded by 101 pupils, including 94 whose names are known, three who recorded together with others, and four whose names are unknown. In the list of recorders at the head of the *Yü-lei,* family and private names are given, with courtesy names in smaller characters. The year in which—or after which—the records were made is also indicated. The earliest conversation was recorded by Yang Fang (1163 *cs*) in 1170. Chu Hsi was then forty-one years old. By that time his thought was already mature. We do not know when the last conversation was recorded or by whom. In his "Chu Wen Kung meng-tien chi" (Account of Chu Hsi's death), Ts'ai Ch'en (1167–1230) said that, four days before the Master died (the fifth day of the third month of 1120), he spoke on the "Western Inscription" and the essentials of learning.[9] There are more than thirty sections on the "Western Inscription" in chapter 98, but none deals with the essentials of learning. There are also more than ten sections in chapter 107 recorded after 1196, among which the latest was recorded by Hu Yung in 1198. However, several pupils heard the Master speak as late as 1199. Therefore it is impossible to determine who recorded the last conversation. At the end of each conversation or saying, the recorder's private name is given. The time of the record can be determined by referring to the list of recorders at the head of the work. In many cases, the note merely says "heard after such and such a year." Liao Te-ming (1169 *cs*), for example, recorded conversations covering more than twenty years. In such cases it is impossible to date the individual conversation.

When two pupils had the same private name, a distinction is made at the end of the recorded conversations. In the case of Hu Yung and T'ang Yung, those recorded by the former are noted as by Hu Yung, while those recorded by T'ang Yung are noted merely as by Yung.[10] Because this distinction is not explained in the *Yü-lei,* some scholars have mistaken "Yung" to mean "Hu Yung."[11] Equally unexplained is why recorders sometimes referred to other people by their private names, although the general practice was to refer to other people by their courtesy names and to oneself by one's private name. The private names of Liu Huai and Hsieh Chiao,[12] for instance, are obviously exceptional, but were they so addressed because they were young? When a conversation refers to a private name, that name may apply to two or more different people, for among Chu Hsi's pupils there were two Yen-chungs, two Ch'ien-chihs, two I-chihs, three Kuang-tsus, three Hsing-chihs, three Te-chihs, and four Shu-chihs. Thus it is extremely difficult to know whom is meant. In my *Chu Tzu men-jen* (Master Chu's pupils), I tried my best to distinguish them,[13] but much more work needs to be done. In a number of cases, a determination can be made from the context of the conversation or the time of the record.

When a conversation was recorded jointly by several pupils, this fact is stated in the list of recorders, as in the case of Yang Yü-li (1193 *cs*), Liu Fu, and Kung Li. The most interesting joint record is that of Wu Shou-ch'ang and his son Hao.[14] There are other conversations recorded by Hao, but Hao alone refers to Tsou Hao, not Wu Hao. The greatest number of records was made by Yeh Ho-sun (Yeh Wei-tao, 1220 *cs*), for a total of 980 sections. Of the more than fourteen thousand sections, the longest conversation is more than twenty-four hundred words,[15] the shortest is sixteen words,[16] and the shortest saying is only two words.[17] The longest discussion is on Mencius' doctrine of maintaining an unperturbed mind and nourishing the strong, moving power, which occupies 54 pages,[18] while conversations on the Confucian saying, "To master oneself and return to propriety is humanity," cover a whole chapter.[19] Among the recorded conversations, some are duplications,[20] some are recorded by two different pupils in greater or lesser length,[21] some differ from each other,[22] some are different in wording but similar in substance,[23] and some are contradictory.[24] Of all the recorders, Dr. Hu Shih praised most highly Ch'en Ch'un (1159–1223). Dr. Hu said, "In his records made at two different times, Ch'en Ch'un was the most careful, made the most effort, and was able to reveal the spirit of Chu Hsi's conversations to the highest degree."[25]

Sections in the *Yü-lei* are mostly questions and answers, but also include sayings of the pupils.[26] Generally speaking, a pupil would ask a question and the Teacher would give his answer. Occasionally, the question was written down[27] and the Teacher would give a written reply.[28] Sometimes three or five pupils engaged in discussion and came to the Teacher for an answer.[29] Often Chu Hsi asked pupils to speak.[30] He particularly wanted pupils to ask questions. Once he told his pupils, "Recently you people have not asked any questions at all. What are you doing here?"[31] When he was deeply affected, he would speak in a loud voice,[32] talk very fast,[33] wait for a long time before answering,[34] or simply smile without answering.[35] His answers differed according to the need of the questioner and were always relevant to the person.

Of the questions asked by pupils, those addressed by Huang Kan were the most distinguished. In his questions he cited the names of Neo-Confucians and their theories on the *Analects* discussed by Chu Hsi in his *Lun-yü chi-chu* (Collected commentaries on the *Analects*) and in his *Lun-yü chi-i* (Collected meanings of the *Analects*). In the *Yü-lei*, the theories of from five to nine commentators on a given passage of the *Analects* are subject to criticism by Chu Hsi.[36] Most likely he cited them from memory. If so, his memory was extraordinary, and Huang Kan had done his homework well. Discussions usually took place in the evening.[37] Once a lantern had to be used for light.[38] Sometimes there were guests present.[39]

The index of proper names referred to earlier was really a rough draft by Japanese scholars that was hastily published in Taipei, thus leaving a great number of mistakes uncorrected. It is better than nothing, although it needs to be revised without delay.[40] For many years Japanese scholars, under the leadership of Professor Okada Takehiko, have been rendering the *Yü-lei* into colloquial Japanese. So far, one volume, entitled *Shushi gorui* (Classified conversations of Master Chu), has been published in the *Shushigaku taikei* (Great Master Chu studies series).[41] Although the anthology is limited to one volume, it is punctuated and annotated, and as such is a great help to the study of Chu Hsi.

## The Yü-shan Lecture

In 1196, when Chu Hsi was sixty-five, he was lecturer-in-waiting and expounded on the *Great Learning* before the emperor. Because his memorial offended Han T'o-chou (d. 1207), who wielded all power in his own hand, Chu Hsi was dismissed in the intercalary tenth month. He was in court for only forty-six days. After thanking the emperor, he left for his home in Fukien. En route he arrived at Yü-shan County in Kiangsi on the eleventh day of the eleventh month. According to the oldest extant *Chu Tzu nien-p'u,* compiled by Yeh Kung-hui in 1431, "The magistrate Ssu-ma Fang asked him to lecture before the students. He begged to decline but the magistrate insisted. Thereupon, he took the seat of a guest at the county school to expound the essentials of the Way in response to the questions of scholars. His audience was aroused. Fang had the lecture printed so as to transmit it to the world. The lecture comprises instructions given from the heart of the Master in his late years. The reader should ponder it deeply."[42] This comment was repeated in full in the *nien-p'u* in Tai Hsien's (d. 1508) *Chu Tzu shih-chi* (True records of Master Chu) of 1513.[43] In his *Chu Tzu nien-p'u,* Wang Mao-hung quoted the same words from Hung Ch'ü-wu's *nien-p'u* of 1700, except that the name Fang is replaced by the name Mai.[44] The lecture may be found in the *Wen-chi.*[45]

When the chronological biographies state that Chu Hsi expounded the essentials of the Way in response to questions of scholars, they are true to fact. One scholar in attendance was Ch'eng Kung, whose courtesy name was Chung-pi and literary name, Liu-hu. He was a native of Po-yang County in Kiangsi.[46] Ch'eng asked two questions. One was about the fact that the *Analects* are concerned largely with *jen* (humanity), whereas Mencius discussed humanity and righteousness. In Ch'eng's opinion, the Grand Master of the *Analects* was talking about the original material force, whereas Mencius talked about the two material forces of yin (passive cosmic force) and yang (active cosmic force) and held that humanity was substance and righteousness was function. Ch'eng wanted to know whether his opinion was correct. In reply, Chu Hsi said, "Righteousness is included in humanity. In terms of substance and function, the two are substance and function to each other. If one recognizes this thoroughly and sees the matter through, then in one's daily life everything will be in place for devoting one's effort to understanding principle." Here Chu Hsi placed equal emphasis on substance and function. To understand principle and put it into concrete practice was the standard pattern of his teaching throughout his life. Chu Hsi himself tried to put this conviction into practice. Thus the various chronological biographies sound the right note when they say that the Yü-shan lecture was given from his heart late in life. Although Ch'eng Kung raised the question on humanity, Chu Hsi would have discussed it even if he had not, for the subject was his own chief concern. His "Jen-shuo" (Treatise on humanity) was a result of more than ten years of thought and deliberation with friends,[47] and *jen* occupied more of his attention than did the concepts of the Great Ultimate, principle, and material force.[48]

Ch'eng Kung also asked, "In the Three Dynasties[49] and before, the subjects of discussion were equilibrium *(chung)* and the ultimate *(chi)*. When it came to [members of] the Confucian School, all their discussions were on humanity. Why?" In his reply, Chu Hsi again dwelt on the importance of concrete practice. According to him, man's nature is originally good but is beclouded by his physical endowment. In order to return to our original nature, it is therefore necessary to do away with selfish human desires and recover the Principle of Heaven. Honoring the moral nature and following the path of inquiry and study mutually increase the beneficial effect of each other and develop each other.[50] This injunction indicates that, throughout life, Chu Hsi advocated the doctrine that substance and function operate together and that sincerity and enlightenment advance simultaneously. He neither emphasized following the path of inquiry and study one-sidedly, nor did he stress both honoring the moral nature and following the path of inquiry and study only after being accused of being one-sided by Lu Hsiang-shan (1139–1193) in 1175.

Wang Mao-hung thought that the statement in the chronological biography, "The lecture comprises instructions given from the heart of the Master in his late years. The reader should ponder it deeply," must have come from the earliest *Chu Tzu nien-p'u* by pupil Li Fang-tzu (1214 cs), which disappeared long ago. According to Wang,

> "Kuo-chai's [Li Fang-tzu] statement, 'In his later years he pointed out the original substance so people could think it over deeply and find out for themselves,'[51] refers to the Yü-shan lecture, letters to Ch'en Ch'i-chih [Ch'en Chih] and Lin Chiu-te [Lin Chih], and so forth. If we examine them, we will find that they all amplified the concept that human nature is good, bringing out its foundation and detailed items, as in the case of Master Han's [Han Yü, 768–824] 'Inquiry on Human Nature,' in which he maintained that what constituted human nature are five and what constituted feelings are seven.[52] The idea was not to point out the original substance for people to think over deeply and find out for themselves. Wang Yang-ming's [1472–1529] 'Chu Hsi's Final Conclusions Arrived at Late in Life' [in which he contended that Chu Hsi had shifted in his later years to the cultivation of the original substance (the mind) similar to what Wang himself advocated][53] had been anticipated in the Chu School for a long time. Master Chu said, 'The great principle had been twisted without waiting for the seventy pupils [of Confucius] to pass.'[54] Isn't it the truth!"[55]

Ch'en Ch'i-chih's letter was an inquiry on the Yü-shan lecture, which is why there is a note in the *Wen-chi* under the title of the letter from Chu Hsi to Ch'en indicating that it is a response to Ch'en's letter about the lecture.[56] In his reply, Chu Hsi strongly emphasized that nature is the substance of the Great Ultimate without any differentiation. Thus Chu Hsi did point out the original substance, and Li Fang-tzu was not baseless in his statement. However, Chu Hsi's remark on the original substance arose because Ch'en Ch'i-chih asked about it. The Teacher simply answered his question and was in no way deemphasizing the concrete effort he had stressed in his lecture. Wang Mao-hung never explained how Li Fang-tzu twisted the great principle of his Teacher. If it is contended that Li's statement that Chu Hsi pointed out the original substance prepared for Wang Yang-ming's claim that Chu Hsi talked about the original substance late in life, that obviously overlooks Ch'en Ch'i-chih's question on the original substance. Rather than viewing the matter from a partisan point of view, as Wang Mao-hung did, and denying that Chu Hsi talked about the original substance in the Yü-shan lecture, it is far better to point out that Chu Hsi's discussion on the original substance was in response to Ch'en's question, not a key point in the lecture.

In his reply to Lin Chiu-te, Chu Hsi said, "Recently I spoke to students of the county school at Yü-shan. Magistrate Ssu-ma had someone make a copy and send it to me. At the time, there was no thorough discussion and my talk was not to my heart's content. After I came home, I happened to be talking to a friend. Because he did not understand, I went over the points again and again. I spoke to the fullest extent. I am now sending you both versions. If you look at them, they ought to be helpful to your thoughts."[57] It is not known who the friend was or what they talked about, but the discussion must have been an elaboration of the lecture. In the *Wen-chi* there is a letter in reply to Ch'eng Kung, but that deals with the rectification of names and has nothing to do with the lecture at Yü-shan.[58] The *Sung-Yüan hsüeh-an* identified Ch'eng Kung as a pupil of Chu Hsi simply on the basis of the two questions Ch'eng asked at the Yü-shan county school.[59] This is hardly justified. The inquiry on the rectification of names does not seem to be a request from a pupil.[60]

As to the private name of the magistrate, some chronological biographies use Fang and some use Mai. A temple tablet inscription in the *Wen-chi* mentions the magistrate as Ssu-ma Fang,[61] but in his colophon on Ssu-ma Kuang's (1019–1086) compilation of recommendations of scholars, Chang Shih (1133–1180) said that Ssu-ma's main-line grandson showed the compilation to him.[62] Chang Shih could not have been mistaken about the name because he saw the grandson himself. There is no biography of Ssu-ma Fang or Ssu-ma Mai in the *Sung shih* (History of the Sung dynasty) or the *Sung-Yüan hsüeh-an*. In the Yü-shan lecture, Chu Hsi simply referred to him as a high officer of the county. Although he praised him as a "well-known personage of the present age," that was probably because he was a descendant of Ssu-ma Kuang. The magistrate was not really a famous person, since there is no biography of him anywhere. I believe his name was really Mai, as it appears in the *Nan-hsüan Hsien-sheng wen-chi* (Collection of literary works of Chang Shih), that the compilers of the *Wen-chi* probably mistook the name to be Fang because the simplified form of the character *mai* is *fang* minus a dot, and that this mistake was repeated in the subsequent chronological biographies. As defined in the *Yü-p'ien* (Book of jade), *fang* means "to walk quickly," whereas *mai* is defined in the *Shuo-wen* (Explanation of words) as "to travel afar." In the *Tso chaun* (Tso's commentary), *mai* is explained as "to denote effort."[63] Ssu-ma Kaung's name means bright; his son's name K'ang means good health. His nephews' names, Liang, Liang, and Fu, and Mai's grandfather's name, P'o,[64] all mean good virtue or happiness. *Mai,* with its meaning of making an effort to travel far, conforms to the Ssu-ma family tradition of having auspicious names. *Fang,* meaning to walk fast, suggests abruptness, hardly a name for the Ssu-ma family.

## The *Meng Tzu chi-chu*

In his *Gimon roku* (Records of questioning), part 2, in the section entitled "Errors in the *Commentary on the Book of Mencius,*" Ōta Kinjō (1765–1825) made the following criticism of Chu Hsi's *Meng Tzu chi-chu* (Commentary on the *Book of Mencius*):

> There are many, many inadequacies and oversights in Hui-an's [Chu Hsi] work. In the introduction of his *Meng Tzu chi-chu,* he quoted the *Shih chi* [Historical records], which says, "Mencius withdrew, and with pupils Wan Chang and others expounded the *Book of Odes* and the *Book of History* and gave an account of the ideas of Chung-ni [Confucius] to make the *Book of Mencius* in seven parts."[65] He also quoted Master Han [Han Yü], who said, "The book of Meng K'o [Mencius] was not written by himself. After his death, his pupils Wan Chang and Kung-sun Ch'ou together recorded what he had said, that is all."[66] Hui-an made the determination and said, "I humbly note that the two theories are different but the *Shih chi* is nearer the truth."[67] It is clear that he considered the *Book of Mencius* to be the work of Meng K'o himself. However, in his commentary on 3A:1, which says, "Mencius discoursed on the original goodness of human nature, and when he spoke, he always praised [sage-emperors] Yao and Shun," he noted, "Mencius' pupils could not remember the words but summarizd the general idea like this." Then in chapter 4, which says, "Yü opened a vent for the Ju and Han and regulated the course of the Huai and Ssu so that they all flowed into the Yangtze," he noted, "Here it says that all four rivers flow into the Yangtze, a mistake by the recorders."[68] It

is clear that in this case he considered the *Book of Mencius* to be the work of his pupils. In the same book, what is said earlier and what is said later are thus contradictory. It may be said to be inadequate and full of oversight. This is why people like Wu Po-feng [Wu Pi-ta] and Tung Shu-chung [Tung Chu, 1152–1214] of the Chu School all suspected that his theory was incoherent (*chih-li,* fragmentary). This can be seen in his letters in reply to Wu Po-feng and Tung Shu-chung in the *Wen-chi.* It is laughable.

In my opinion, there is no contradiction here at all. Chu Hsi clearly subscribed to the theory that Mencius withdrew, and with Wan Chang and others expounded and gave an account of Confucius' ideas. This means the *Book of Mencius* is not the product of one person. Assuming that Mencius directed the compilation and pupils made some mistakes in the records, one may criticize Mencius for his oversight but not for his contradiction or incoherence.

In the *Wen-chi,* there are ten letters to Tung Chu. The seventh one talks about nature, destiny, material force, and so on; the eighth talks about Mencius' study under Tzu-ssu (492–421 B.C.?). Neither has anything to do with the question under discussion. Only in the third letter did Chu Hsi say, "I believe a copy of the *Meng Tzu* [*chi-chu*] has been sent to you. But in your suspicion that I have the defect of being too hasty in searching [for explanations], I am afraid you are being too cautious. . . . The present revision concerns only lack of clarity and duplication, but the general idea remains the same."[69] Thus Tung Chu's suspicion involved haste in searching, not contradiction or incoherence, and even so, Chu Hsi said his pupil was being too cautious.

Letters to Wu Pi-ta total twenty-four. The fifth letter deals with Shen Ts'un-chung's (Shen Kua, 1029–1092) theory about regulating the course of the four rivers and has nothing to do with incoherence. In the sixteenth letter Chu Hsi said, "Please check and correct the mistaken characters of the *Meng Tzu* [*chi-chu*]. Recently I received a letter from Cheng-fu [Yü Cheng-fu] in which he raised the question of [my comments on] chapter 6A. . . . I have tried to straighten out the doubtful points. Both my mind and eyes have been dimmed and I am unable to examine the text thoroughly. If any passages are unsatisfactory, please go over them."[70] Chu Hsi always encouraged his pupils to raise questions, but it never crossed Wu Pi-ta's mind that his Teacher was incoherent. In a letter to him, Wu Pi-ta said, "The biography in the *Shih chi* regards the *Book of Mencius* as Mencius' own work, while Master Han said that it was not by him. You, Sir, said that the two theories are different but that the *Shih chi* is nearer to the truth. But in your commentary on 3A:1 you said that pupils did not remember all the words, while in chapter 4 you said the recorder was mistaken. How about this?"[71] In reply, Chu Hsi said, "The first opinion is correct and the subsequent two opinions are wrong. When you have read the seven parts [of the *Book of Mencius*] and observe the force of the style of writing of the work, you will find that it is the product of a mold and not patched together. The *Analects* is a patchwork of records and not the literary product of the same stroke."[72]

Here Chu Hsi admits his mistakes too quickly. Both the *Analects* and the *Book of Mencius* are patchworks. The *Shih chi* may be correct in stating that the *Book of Mencius* was compiled by Mencius and his pupils together. If Mencius was really the chief compiler, he may have made some mistakes, but he certainly was not incoherent. In one of his replies to Wu Pi-ta, the Teacher said, "Now you have read only one sentence in the *Great Learning,* and already you say that you tend in the same direction as the *Doctrine of the Mean.* In your fragmentation and your spreading out like this, you are beclouding one with the other and causing them to mutually damage each other. Not only will you fail to understand the *Great Learning;* you will lack the effort and ability to get at the *Doctrine of the Mean.*"[73] This being the case, any incoherence lay with Wu Pi-ta, not Chu Hsi.

## The *Hsiao-hsüeh*

Chu Hsi wrote the *I-hsüeh ch'i-meng* (Study of the *Book of Changes* for beginning students) in the third month of 1186, and the *Hsiao ching k'an-wu* (Corrections of misprints in the *Classic of Filial Piety*) in the eighth month of the same year. In the several years before this, he must have been greatly concerned with the education of children. Hence the desire to compile the *Hsiao-hsüeh* (Elementary education). He delegated the task to Liu Ch'ing-chih (1139–1195), with whom he had associated for years. In his letter to Liu, he talked about the *T'ung-chien kang-mu* (Outline of the *Comprehensive Mirror of Good Government*), the *Erh-Ch'eng i-shu* (Surviving works of the two Ch'engs), and the *Hu Tzu chih-yen* (Master Hu's understanding of words).[74] He also urged Liu not to compile the *Chin-ssu hsü-lu* (Supplement to the *Reflections on Things at Hand*).[75] The main reason for assigning the work to Liu was probably that Liu had compiled his own *Hsün-meng hsin-shu* (New book to instruct children) as well as the *Chieh-tzu t'ung-lu* (General accounts for the admonition of sons), so that he was an expert on this type of literature.[76]

According to the *Wen-chi,* the two friends discussed the project for quite a long while. In 1183, Chu Hsi wrote Liu to say,

> Have you put in order the *Hsiao-hsüeh?* Please do so soon and send it to me at your convenience and I will be most fortunate. In your letter yesterday, you merely wanted to keep what I have compiled, but now upon careful thought it is not as good a pattern as what you have described in your let-

ter. The present compilation consists completely of passages on regulations. I wish to add two categories of fine words and virtuous deeds. For these categories, selections should be made from the classics, histories, philosophers, and literary collections. Only then can the discussions be complete. The selections should be simple, and it is best that they not be overly extensive. The writing especially should not be overextended. As in the case of the *Li-sao* [Encountering sorrow], its sentiment of loyalty and integrity is praiseworthy, but the main text alone is already sufficient. Here a careful selection is particularly necessary. Also, the account of ancient primers is excessive, and is, furthermore, obscure, rugged, and difficult to read. I am afraid that it is not material for beginners. In contrast, the feeling of ancient lyrical ballads and the poems of Tu Fu [712–770] is excellent, and many of them are worth having. When young students are induced to love to recite and it is easy to make an impression, it will be most beneficial. In your letter, you also want to avoid the suspicion of advocating Ch'eng I. When did Ch'eng I have to depend on our advocacy? In the matter of instituting instructions for the education of later generations, it is something that has concerned us for a long period of time. Should we avoid any suspicion? Although the details [of not avoiding suspicion] can be found in the *Chin-ssu lu* [Reflections on things at hand],[77] every sentence and every phrase of it is brilliantly relevant to life, and students of the younger generation should not be prevented from learning them early and absorbing them first of all. Naturally, there is no harm in including the material in this book.[78]

In another letter, Chu Hsi said, "The *Hsiao-hsüeh* is not comparable to this [self-cultivation throughout life]. Please finish it soon."[79] In still another letter, he said, "The *Hsiao-hsüeh* is a different task. It should take only several days of work to finish. Please finish it and send it to me at your convenience."[80] In a letter dated the ninth day of the seventh month of 1185, he said, "The *Hsiao-hsüeh* is at present being revised here by adding stories of past and present. The first part has been shifted to the end so the beginning student readily receives some benefit as soon as he opens the book. In the last chapter, brief instructions for people by Master Chou [Chou Tun-i], the Ch'engs, and Chang [Chang Tsai, 1020–1077], as well as [Lü Ta-chün's, 1031–1082] "Hsiang-yüeh" [Community pact] and [Ssu-ma Kuang's] *Tsa-i* [Miscellaneous ceremonies] constitute the second part. These come definitely to six parts. It will take several more days before it is completed."[81] The last letter reads, "If the *Hsiao-hsüeh* can be printed for circulation, it will be nice, but it must be further readjusted before it can be all right."[82]

In all this correspondence, both the material and the structure were evidently in place and ready for publication. Probably Chu Hsi was not satisfied with Liu's publication, and so he published another edition. In his letter to pupil P'an Kung-shu, he said, "The *Hsiao-hsüeh* was not yet completed and was printed by Tzu-ch'eng. I am now revising it for publication and it should be finished momentarily. It should then be sent to the printer. When it is done, a copy will be sent to you. This book is greatly beneficial."[83] The book was finally completed in the third month of 1187. It consists of four inner chapters, namely "Establishment of Institutions," "Clarification of Human Relations," "Seriousness about the Person," and "Examining Antiquity," and two outer chapters, "Fine Words" and "Virtuous Deeds." Material was collected from thirty-two sources ranging from high antiquity to the Northern Sung (960–1126), in a total of 385 sections.

Ch'en Hsüan (1129–1486) of the Ming dynasty (1368–1644) wrote the *Hsiao-hsüeh chi-chu* (Collected annotations of the *Hsiao-hsüeh*). Commenting on it, the *Ssu-k'u ch'üan-shu tsung-mu t'i-yao* (Essentials of the contents of the *Complete Collection of the Four Libraries*) remarked, "Hsüan's annotation was for village and community schools. It amplified the meanings following the passages, aiming particularly at easy understanding. Its discussions are rather simple."[84] Chang Po-hsing (1651–1725) of the Ch'ing dynasty (1644–1911) thought that "the many tens of editions available in the market, in their compilation, annotation, and titles, aim only at enabling the reader to pick and steal for the purpose of civil service examinations, and seldom do they try to expound the subtlety of the passages and their intention of teaching people with personal concern. . . . I have therefore put together the explanations of various commentators from fine editions and synthesized and harmonized them."[85] This is from the preface to his *Hsiao-hsüeh chi-chieh* (Collected explanations of the *Hsiao-hsüeh*) in six chapters. The collected annotations of Ch'en Hsüan aim at clarifying the text, while Chang's explanations are directed at promoting Neo-Confucianism.

I have translated *hsiao-hsüeh* as "elementary education." Some scholars do not approve of this rendering, contending that Ch'en Hsüan mentions the titles of books from which the passages were selected. These books, they maintain, contain passages too difficult for young students to understand, and the book is not for the purpose of teaching children. Further, they add, the introduction to chapter 1 says that it enables the teacher to know how to teach and the pupil to know how to learn, so it is clearly a chapter for the teacher. In addition, the introduction to chapter 2 says that its purpose is to instruct the scholar *(shih);* therefore it is not aimed at popular education. My response is that while the difficult language of the *Hsiao-hsüeh* may be inappropriate for elementary education, in the traditional educational system, difficult texts were also used for children. Take the *San-tzu ching* (Three-character classic), for example. It contains the names of the different dynasties, the three commentaries of the *Spring and Autumn Annals,* and so on. It is no less difficult than the *Hsiao-hsüeh.* I myself began to recite the *San-tzu ching* at age five. Shall we say that the *San-tzu ching* was not intended for elementary education? Since the first chapter of the *Hsiao-hsüeh* is entitled "Establishment of Education," Chu Hsi said that "the chapter enables the teacher to know how to teach." The scholar referred to in chapter 2 means the beginning scholar—that is, a schoolchild.

Since the educational reform in China in the twentieth century, the *Hsiao-hsüeh* is no longer included in the curriculum. For centuries, however, Ch'eng Tuan-li's (1271–1345) *Tu-shu fen-nien jih-ch'eng* (Daily program of reading year by year) was regarded by Neo-Confucians as the golden rule for educating the young. According to it, before children went to school at age eight, they were to read the *Hsing-li tzu-hsün* (Explanation of words on nature and principle),[86] and upon beginning school, they were immediately to read the text of the *Hsiao-hsüeh:*

> In accordance with their effort and capability, they should gradually increase from one or two hundred words to six or seven hundred words. As they grow older and the days become longer, they may stop at nearly one thousand words. Each large paragraph is to be divided into small paragraphs. Each small paragraph must be read and recited one hundred times; recited from memory one hundred times, and the whole [large] paragraph recited from memory twenty or thirty times. . . . The teacher need not teach many books he himself has already read. First explain the *Hsiao-hsüeh*. Having done that, proceed to the *Great Learning* and then the *Analects*. Suppose one is to explain the *Hsiao-hsüeh*. First let the student generally explain each sentence. After he has understood Master Chu's basic annotations and Hsiung's explanation, together with his titles,[87] let him explain the text with the aid of their explanations of the terms and the meaning of the sentences. If their explanations do not cover a certain term, let him find out from rhymed dictionaries, but do not make up anything to mislead him. It does no harm to use popular language or simple explanations. When he has generally explained the basic meaning of each sentence and each paragraph, let him generally explain to himself again and again, until he can pass the examination in front of the teacher.[88]

This curriculum is no longer suitable for modern education, but was still applicable at the end of the Ch'ing dynasty. In 1899, when Dr. Hu Shih was eleven, he recited the *Hsiao-hsüeh* from memory.[89] Most probably he was not the only one to do so at the time.

The Neo Confucian thinker, Li Kung (1659–1733), in the preface of his *Hsiao-hsüeh ch'i-yeh* (Task of studying the *Hsiao-hsüeh*), had this to say about Chu Hsi's *Hsiao-hsüeh:* "Its accounts of the Way of Heaven, nature, and destiny are learning of the higher level. Personal receptions and audiences with the emperor are matters for the adult. From these to items like serving as prime minister and retirement are not matters for children. Besides, how is it different from *ta-hsüeh* [greater learning]?"[90] On the basis of this passage, one may argue that the *Hsiao-hsüeh* is not suitable for children and therefore should not be translated as "Elementary Education." Li Kung also said, "Someone may say, 'The object of primary education is to let children understand principle. Why is it necessary to deal with affairs?' I was terrified, stood up, and said, 'Are you rambling? This will do harm to learning. In the *Analects,* it is said, "Young disciples should sprinkle and sweep the floor, answer and reply to questions, and learn to advance or withdraw."[91] In the *Ta-Tai li-chi* it is said, "At eight, a boy enters primary school to learn minor skills and to practice minor matters."[92] It has never been said [that the purpose of elementary education is] merely to understand principle.' "[93]

From what Li Kung said, his objection to the *Hsiao-hsüeh* was twofold. First, the *Hsiao-hsüeh* teaches things on the higher level; second, it deals with principle. It is not clear what Li Kung had in mind when he referred to "the Way of Heaven, nature, and destiny." The opening chapter of the *Hsiao-hsüeh* begins with the excerpt from the *Doctrine of the Mean* that says, "What Heaven imparts to man is called human nature. To follow our nature is the Way. Cultivating the Way is called education."[94] Since the first chapter of the *Hsiao-hsüeh* is on education, the focus of this quotation is on education, not on nature or the Way of Heaven. The *Three-Character Classic* is undeniably a primer for children, but it teaches reverence on the part of the ruler, loyalty on the part of the minister, and so forth, which are certainly applicable to actual imperial audiences and official administrations. If one were to cite Li Kung's criticism of the *Hsiao-hsüeh* as not for children, shall we say that the *Three-Character Classic* is also not for children? While Li Kung limited his work to specific, practical behavior, the goal of Chu Hsi's *Hsiao-hsüeh* was "to nourish the root and to reach the branches."[95] Hence he said, in his "Note on the *Hsiao-hsüeh,*" "In ancient times, the *hsiao-hsüeh* taught children the items of sprinkling and sweeping the floor, replying and answering questions, and advancing and withdrawing, and the way of loving the parents, respecting the elders, honoring the teacher, and being intimate with friends. All this is to be the foundation of self-cultivation, family harmony, national order, and world peace. It is necessary to let them understand and practice in their youth."[96]

Chu Hsi carefully distinguished the *hsiao-hsüeh* and the *ta-hsüeh*. In the preface of his *Ta-hsüeh chang-chü* (Commentary on the *Great Learning*), he said,

Children—from sons of princes and dukes to those of the common people —entered the *hsiao-hsüeh* at eight and were taught the items of sprinkling and sweeping the floor and answering and replying to questions, as well as the arts of ceremonies, music, archery, carriage driving, writing, and mathematics. When they reached fifteen, the emperor's eldest son and his younger sons, the main-line sons of dukes, great officers, and virtuous gentlemen, and the talented children of the common people all entered the *ta-hsüeh* and were taught the principles of investigating principle, rectifying the mind, cultivating the self, and governing people. This is the distinction of school education and the major or minor items.[97]

In his "Instructions to Pupils," he said, "Students in ancient times entered the *hsiao-hsüeh* at eight and studied the matters of periods of the day and the various directions, and writing and arithmetic. At fifteen, they entered the *ta-hsüeh* to study the rites and music of ancient sages."[98] In his "Treatise on the Well-field System and the Like," he said, "When children entered the *hsiao-hsüeh* at eight to study the periods of the day, the four directions, the Five Agents,[99] writing and arithmetic, they began to know the order of the family and seniority. At fifteen, they entered the *ta-hsüeh* to study the rites and music of ancient kings and thereby knew the ceremonies of the Court and the relation between the ruler and the minister. Those with unusual talents would be promoted to the community school, and its superior students would be promoted to the national school."[100] This account is based on the "Records of Food and Commodities" of the *Han shu* (History of the Han dynasty).[101] Thus the distinction between the *hsiao-hsüeh* and the *ta-hsüeh* can be traced to ancient times, a fact well known to Chu Hsi.

However, Chu Hsi seems not to have been entirely consistent about which students were to enter the *hsiao-hsüeh* and the *ta-hsüeh,* and at what age. According to the preceding quotations, children entered the *hsiao-hsüeh* at age eight and the *ta-hsüeh* at fifteen. Chu Hsi also said this in his classics mat lecture before the emperor.[102] This ancient system is well described in the *Pai-hu-t'ung* (Comprehensive discussions in the White Tiger Hall). In its chapter on the national university, it says, "Why did students in ancient times enter the *t'ai-hsüeh* [national university] at fifteen? At eight, children replaced their teeth and began to have knowledge. They entered school to study writing and arithmetic. At fifteen, which is the combination of seven and eight, their correspondence to yang and yin is complete. Therefore at fifteen the purpose of the children was clear and they entered the *t'ai-hsüeh* to study the doctrines of the classics."[103] But in the *Yü-lei* it is said, "In ancient times, children went to the *hsiao-hsüeh* when very young. They were taught only things like ceremonies, music, archery, carriage driving, writing, and mathematics, and matters like filial piety, brotherly respect, loyalty, and faithfulness. When they entered the *ta-hsüeh* at sixteen or seventeen, they were taught principles, such as the extension of knowledge and investigation of things, and the reasons for loyalty, faithfulness, filial piety, and brotherly respect."[104] The ages of sixteen and seventeen do not seem to agree with the age of fifteen, but the *Ta-Tai li-chi* speaks of "bundling the hair and entering the *ta-hsüeh*."[105] This simply refers to a teenager;

one does not have to stick to any particular year. The same is true of the phrase "when very young."

There is also a seeming inconsistency about who went to school. In his preface to the *Ta-hsüeh chang-chü,* Chu Hsi said that children of princes, dukes, and the common people all went to the *hsiao-hsüeh,* and that sons of the emperor, main-line sons of dukes, high officials, and virtuous scholars, and the talented children of common people all entered the *ta-hsüeh.*[106] This is based on the "Wang-chih" (Royal regulations) chapter of the *Book of Rites.*[107] In his classics mat lecture, however, he merely said that at fifteen young men entered the *ta-hsüeh,* without mentioning the talented ones. This seems to be different from the ancient system.[108] However, even at present, when education is widespread, only the talented can get into good universities. There is no need to argue over minor literal discrepancies in ancient classics. Chu Hsi firmly believed in the existence of the work called the *Hsiao-hsüeh.* That is why, in his "Note on the *Hsiao-hsüeh,* " he declared, "Although the book cannot be seen today, many passages appear here and there in commentaries and accounts."[109] Chu Hsi's belief that the *Hsiao-hsüeh* had been lost in the burning of books during the Ch'in dynasty (221–206 B.C.) was similar to his belief in the loss of the commentary on the investigation of things in the *Great Learning,* which he undertook to amend. We do not doubt Chu Hsi's belief, but we do doubt whether the *Hsiao-hsüeh* really existed in ancient times, for there is not the slightest evidence of it.

Some scholars have contended that the *Hsiao-hsüeh* was compiled not by Chu Hsi but by Liu Ch'ing-chih. They quote the *Ssu-k'u ch'üan-shu tsung-mu t'i-yao,* which says, "The compilation of this book was really entrusted to Tzu-ch'eng."[110] We do not know what Chu Hsi turned over to Liu, or when. From his several letters to Liu, there can be no doubt that the initiative, the outline, and the guidelines for the work originated with Chu Hsi. What Chu Hsi entrusted to Liu and other friends must have been the fine words and virtuous deeds gathered from various sources for inclusion in the book. No one can belittle Liu's contribution, but to say that the work was his product is contrary to fact. In the *Yü-lei,* Ch'en Ch'un recorded a conversation in which pupils asked the Teacher why the *Hsiao-hsüeh* lacked a section on friends. In his reply, Chu Hsi said, "At the time, many shared in the compilation and classification. Accidentally, that section was not included."[111] Thus it is clear that more than one pupil assisted him and Liu, and that Wang Mao-hung was correct in asserting that "probably the compilation was not done by Liu alone."[112]

Such collaborations were not unusual at the time. For example, the *I-Lo yüan-yüan lu* (Record of the origin of the School of the Two Ch'engs) and the *Sung ming-ch'en yen-hsing lu* (Words and deeds of famous ministers of the Sung period) were both compiled under the direction of the Teacher. There is nothing wrong with specialists regarding them as the works of Chu Hsi. In the case of the *Chin-ssu lu* (Reflections on things at hand), compiled by Chu Hsi with the collaboration of Lü Tsu-ch'ien (1137–1181), people have regarded Chu Hsi as the author even though both wrote an epilogue for it, and Chu Hsi explicitly said in his that they had collaborated on the book. In contrast, Chu Hsi said nothing about collaboration in either the "Colophon on the *Hsiao-hsüeh*" of the "Note on the *Hsiao-hsüeh*," and Liu did not write a preface or an epilogue for the work. Furthermore, in a letter to Liu, Chu Hsi mentioned "the compilation in this place,"[113] thus showing that Liu was not the only compiler. Under such circumstances, how can it be maintained that Liu was the only compiler? In his letter to Prime Minister Ch'en (Ch'en Chün-ch'ing, 1113–1186), Chu Hsi told Ch'en that "recently the *Hsiao-hsüeh* has been compiled."[114] This was mentioned along with Chu Hsi's own *Ta-hsüeh chang-chü* and *Chung-yung chang-chü* (Commentary on the *Doctrine of the Mean*), so obviously he regarded it as his own work, and the *Ssu-k'u ch'üan-shu tsung-mu t'i-yao* is not mistaken in labeling it as such. However, it would be unfair to Liu to say that the *Hsiao-hsüeh* was compiled by Chu Hsi alone, just as it would be unfair to Chu Hsi to say that it was compiled by Liu alone. There is no need to quarrel over such trivial matters.

## Notes

1. Ch'ien Mu, *Chu Tzu hsin-hsüeh-an* [New anthology and critical accounts of Master Chu] (Taipei: San-min Book Co., 1971), in five volumes.

2. *Chu Tzu yü-lei* (Taipei: Cheng-chung Book Co., 1970), preface.

3. *Wen-chi*, 74:1b, instructions to pupils at T'ung-an County.

4. *Ibid.*, 29:22b–23a, letter to Huang Chih-ch'ing (Huang Kan).

5. *Yü-lei*, prefaces, pp. 5–6.

6. *Ibid.*, Li Ching-te's note following the table of contents.

7. *Ibid.*, preceding the table of contents.

8. *Ibid.*, prefaces, pp. 9–10.

9. Ts'ai Ch'en, "Chu Wen Kung meng-tien chi" [Account of Chu Hsi's death], in the *Ts'ai-shih chiu-ju shu* [Works on nine Confucians in the Ts'ai family] (1868 ed.), 6:59a. Also in Wang Mao-hung, *Chu Tzu nien-p'u* [Chronological biography of Master Chu] (*Ts'ung-shu chi-ch'eng* [Collection of series] ed.), ch. 4B, p. 227, under the sixth year of Ch'ing-yüan (1200). The "Western Inscription" was by Chang Tsai (1020–1077). It is found in the *Chang Tzu ch'üan-shu* [Complete works of Master Chang], ch. 1.

10. *Yü-lei*, ch. 121, sec. 12 (p. 4673); ch. 124, sec. 48 (p. 4772).

11. For example, Ch'ien Mu, *Chu Tzu hsin-hsüeh-an*, vol. 3, p. 356, mistook

T'ang Yung as Hu Yung. Wang Mao-hung, *Chu Tzu nien-p'u, k'ao-i* [Investigation into variants], ch. 3, p. 308, under the twelfth year of Ch'ün-hsi (1185) is correct in giving the name of T'ang Yung.

12. *Yü-lei,* ch. 120, sec. 99 (p. 4652); ch. 25, sec. 135 (p. 1023).

13. See my *Chu Tzu men-jen* [Master Chu's pupils] (Taipei: Student Book Co., 1982), pp. 6–7.

14. *Yü-lei,* ch. 107, sec. 52 (p. 4252).

15. *Ibid.,* ch. 90, sec. 42 (pp. 3647–3654).

16. *Ibid.,* ch. 14, sec. 65 (p. 416).

17. *Ibid.,* ch. 11, sec. 101 (p. 305).

18. *Ibid.,* ch. 52, secs. 2–152 (pp. 1951–2005). Mencius' doctrine is found in the *Book of Mencius,* 2A:2.

19. *Ibid.,* ch. 41. The reference is to *Analects,* 12:1.

20. *Ibid.,* ch. 119, sec. 22 (p. 4592), duplicating ch. 116, sec. 41 (pp. 4464–4465); ch. 121, sec. 64 (p. 4695), duplicating ch. 118, sec. 60 (p. 4558).

21. *Ibid.,* ch. 124, sec. 16 (p. 4758), sec. 36 (p. 4765).

22. *Ibid.,* ch. 123, sec. 12 (p. 4747); ch. 134, sec. 85 (p. 5163).

23. *Ibid.,* ch. 16, sec. 30 (p. 511).

24. *Ibid.,* ch. 133, sec. 18 (p. 5122).

25. See above, n. 7.

26. *Yü-lei,* ch. 87, sec. 6 (p. 3534); ch. 100, sec. 55 (p. 4057).

27. *Ibid.,* ch. 34, sec. 114 (p. 1413); ch. 73, sec. 64 (p. 2956); ch. 117, sec. 47 (p. 4512).

28. *Ibid.,* ch. 73, sec. 64 (p. 2956).

29. *Ibid.,* ch. 20, sec. 113 (pp. 760–761); ch. 40, sec. 45 (p. 1651).

30. *Ibid.,* ch. 75, sec. 17 (p. 3043).

31. *Ibid.,* ch. 97, sec. 9 (p. 3939).

32. *Ibid.,* ch. 90, sec. 42 (p. 3648).

33. *Ibid.,* ch. 120, sec. 15 (p. 4628).

34. *Ibid.,* ch. 64, sec. 204 (p. 2544); ch. 71, sec. 58 (p. 2856), sec. 98 (p. 2871); ch. 72, sec. 48 (p. 2909); ch. 74, sec. 158 (p. 3032); ch. 90, sec. 42 (p. 3651).

35. *Ibid.,* ch. 100, sec. 10 (p. 4042).

36. *Ibid.,* Five theories: ch. 31, sec. 54 (p. 1274). Six theories, ch. 32, sec. 50 (p. 1307); ch. 33, sec. 13 (p. 1331). Seven theories: ch. 31, sec. 4 (p. 1250); ch. 32, sec. 43 (p. 1304), sec. 67 (p. 1313), sec. 91 (p. 1334); ch. 33, sec. 47 (p. 1344), sec. 51 (p. 1347). Eight theories: ch. 30, sec. 62 (p. 1246); ch. 31, sec. 83 (p. 1285); ch. 33, sec. 11 (p. 1330), sec. 40 (p. 1340), sec. 90 (p. 1367). Nine theories: ch. 31, sec. 44 (p. 1267); ch. 32, sec. 40 (p. 1302).

37. *Ibid.,* ch. 64, sec. 49 (p. 2492), sec. 91 (p. 2501).

38. *Ibid.,* sec. 62 (p. 2497).

39. *Ibid.,* ch. 52, sec. 58 (p. 1969); ch. 90, sec. 29 (p. 3640).

40. *Chu Tzu yü-lei,* index.

41. *Shushi gorui* [Classified conversations of Master Chu] (Tokyo, 1976), vol. 6 in the *Shusigaku daikei* [Great Master Chu study series].

42. Yeh Kung-hui, *Chu Tzu nien-p'u* [Chronological biography of Master Chu] (*Chin-shih han-chi ts'ung-k'an* [Chinese works in the recent period series] ed.), p. 225, under the fifth year of Shao-hsi (1194).

43. Tai Hsien, *Chu Tzu shih-chi* [True records of Master Chu] (*Chin-shih han-chi ts'ung-k'an* ed.), p. 193, under the same year.

44. Wang Mao-hung, *Chu Tzu nien-p'u,* ch. 4A, p. 213, under the same year.

45. *Wen-chi,* 74:18a–22a, "Yü-shan Lecture."

46. *Chu Tzu men-jen,* p. 244, biography of Ch'eng Kung.

47. *Wen-chi,* 67:20a–21b, "Treatise on Humanity."

48. See ch. 11 above.

49. The Three Dynasties are Hsia (2183–1752 B.C.?), the Shang (c. 1751–1112 B.C.), and the Chou (1111–249 B.C.).

50. *Doctrine of the Mean,* ch. 27. See also ch. 16 above.

51. Wang Mao-hung, *Chu Tzu nien-p'u,* ch. 4B, p. 239, under the sixth year of Ch'ing-yüan (1120) quoting Li Kuo-chai's *Chu Tzu shih-shih* [Facts about Master Chu].

52. *Han Ch'ang-li ch'üan-chi* [Complete works of Han Yü] (*SPPY* ed.), 11:6a, "Inquiry on Human Nature."

53. Wang Yang-ming, *Ch'uan-hsi lu* [Instructions for practical living], pt. 2, appendix.

54. Chu Hsi, *Ta-hsüeh huo-wen* [Questions and answers on the *Great Learning*] (*Chin-shih han-chi ts'ung-k'an* ed.), p. 24a (p. 47).

55. Wang Mao-hung, *Chu Tzu nien-p'u, k'ao-i,* ch. 4, p. 335, under the first year of Ch'ing-yüan (1195).

56. *Wen-chi,* 58:21a–23a, second letter in reply to Ch'en Ch'i-chih.

57. *Ibid.,* 61:1b, second letter in reply to Lin Chiu-te.

58. *Ibid.,* 60:7b, letter in reply to Ch'eng Kung.

59. *Sung-Yüan hsüeh-an* [Anthology and critical accounts of the Neo-Confucians of the Sung and Yüan dynasties] (*SPPY* ed.), 69:15b, chapter on the Chu Hsi School.

60. See above, n. 46.

61. *Wen-chi,* 89:19a, temple tablet inscription for two heroic gentlemen.

62. *Nan-hsüan Hsien-sheng wen-chi* [Collection of literary works of Chang Shih] (*Chin-shih han-chi ts'ung-k'an* ed.), 34:4a (p. 1021), colophon on Ssu-ma Wen-cheng Kung (Ssu-ma Kuang's) compilation of recommendations of scholars.

63. *Tso chuan* [Tso's commentary] Duke Chuang, eighth year.

64. *Wen-chi,* 83:18a, epilogue on Ssu-ma P'o. See also the *Sung-Yüan hsüeh-an,* 8:30b, biography of Ssu-ma P'o.

65. *Shih chi* [Historical records], ch. 74, biographies of Mencius and Hsün Tzu.

66. *Han Ch'ang-li ch'üan-chi,* 14:23a, letter in reply to Chang Chi.

67. Note to the "Meng Tzu hsü-shuo" [Introduction to the *Meng Tzu chi-chu*].

68. Only the Han River flows into the Yangtze.

69. *Wen-chi,* 51:1b, third letter in reply to Tung Shu-chung (Tung Chu).

70. *Ibid.,* 52:17b–18a, fifteenth letter in reply to Wu Po-feng (Wu Pi-ta).

71. *Ibid.,* 52:19a, letter in reply to Wu Po-feng.

72. *Ibid.*

73. *Ibid.,* 52:1b, second letter in reply to Wu Po-feng.

74. *Ibid.,* 35:15b, 17b, fifth and sixth letters in reply to Liu Tzu-ch'eng (Liu Ch'ing-chih).

75. *Yü-lei,* ch. 101, sec. 2 (p. 4061).

76. *Sung shih* [History of the Sung dynasty] (Beijing: Chung-hua Book Co., 1977), ch. 437, p. 12957, biography of Liu Ch'ing-chih.

77. *Chin-ssu lu,* 6:12, the way to regulate the family.

78. *Wen-chi,* 35:17b–18a, seventh letter in reply to Liu Tzu-ch'eng.

79. *Ibid.,* 35:19b, ninth letter.

80. *Ibid.,* 35:21b, tenth letter.

81. *Ibid.,* 35:23b, twelfth letter.

82. *Ibid.,* 35:26b, fourteenth letter.

83. *Ibid.,* 50:19b, letter in reply to P'an Kung-shu.

84. *Ssu-k'u ch'üan-shu tsung-mu t'i-yao* [Essentials of the contents of the *Complete Collection of the Four Libraries*] (Shanghai: Commerical Press, 1922), p. 1904.

85. Chang Po-hsing, *Hsiao-hsüeh chi-chieh* [Collected explanations of the *Hsiao-hsüeh*] (*Chengi-i-t'ang ch'üan-shu* [Complete library of the Hall of Rectifying the Way] ed.), preface, p. 2a.

86. The *Hsing-li tzu-hsün* [Explanation of words on nature and principle] was written by Ch'eng Tuan-meng (1143–1191), Chu Hsi's pupil, and consists of only 428 words, each sentence with four words, to explain the basic Neo-Confucian terms. See my account of it in my *Chu-hsüeh hsin-t'an-so* [New investigations on Master Chu] (Taipei: Student Book Co., 1988), pp. 421–422.

87. This probably refers to Hsiung Chieh's (1199 *cs*) *Hsing-li ch'ün-shu chü-chieh* [Punctuation and annotation of Neo-Confucian works], which includes the *Hsing-li tzu-hsün* and is annotated by Hsiung Kang-ta.

88. Ch'eng Tuan-li, *Tu-shu fen-nien jih-ch'eng* [Daily program of reading year by year] (*Cheng-i-t'ang ch'üan-shu* ed.), 1:1a–4a.

89. Hu Sung-p'ing, *Hu Shih Hsien-sheng nien-p'u chien pien* [Brief chronological biography of Dr. Hu Shih] (Taipei: Continental Journal Press, 1971), p. 2. Hu Shih probably recited certain passages.

90. *Yen-Li i-shu* [Surviving works of Yen Yüan and Li Kung] (*Chi-fu ts'ung-shu* [Capital and surrounding series] ed.), vol. 13, p. 1a.

91. *Analects,* 19:12.

92. *Ta-Tai li-chi* [Book of rites of the Elder Tai], ch. 48, "Protector and tutor" (*SPTK* ed., 3:8b).

93. *Yen-Li i-shu,* vol. 13, p. 1a.

94. *Doctrine of the Mean,* ch. 1.

95. *Wen-chi,* 76:19a, "Colophon on the *Hsiao-hsüeh.*"

96. *Ibid.,* 76:19b, "Note on the *Hsiao-hsüeh.*"

97. *Wen-chi,* 76:20a, preface to the *Ta-hsüeh chang-chü* (Commentary on the Great Learning).

98. *Ibid.,* 74:2a, "Instructions to Pupils."

99. The Five Agents (or Five Elements) are Metal, Wood, Water, Fire, and Earth.

100. *Ibid.,* 68:28b, "Treatise on the Well-field System and the Like."

101. *Han shu* [History of the Han dynasty] (*SPTK* ed.), 24:4b, "Records of Food and Commodities."

102. *Wen-chi,* 15:1a, "Classics Mat Lecture."

103. *Pai-hu-t'ung* [Comprehensive discussions in the White Tiger Hall] (*SPTK* ed.), 4:16b, chapter on the national university.

104. *Yü-lei,* ch. 7, sec. 1 (p. 199).

105. *Ta-Tai li-chi,* ch. 48, "Protector and Tutor" (*SPTK* ed., 3:8b).

106. See above, n. 97.

107. *Book of Rites,* "Wang-chih" chapter, sec. 40.

108. See above, n. 102.

109. *Wen-chi,* 76:19b, "Note on the *Hsiao-hsüeh.*"

110. *Ssu-k'u ch'üan-shu tsung-mu t'i-yao,* p. 1904.

111. *Yü-lei,* ch. 105, sec. 20 (p. 4178). In their annotations, both Ch'en Hsüan and Chang Po-hsing claim that sec. 34 in the last chapter is on friendship, but it is actually on deference and integrity. Obviously, they watned to cover up Chu Hsi's oversight.

112. Wang Mao-hung, *Chu Tzu nien-p'u, k'ao-i,* ch. 3, p. 310, under the fourteenth year of Ch'un-hsi (1187).

113. *Wen-chi,* 35:17b–18a, seventh letter in reply to Liu Tzu-ch'eng (Liu Ch'ing-chih).

114. *Wen-chi,* 26:32b, a separate note to Prime Minister Ch'en.

# – 24 –

# Chu Hsi and
# Chang Shih

Few in Chinese history are as famous a pair of friends as Chu Hsi and Chang Shih (1133–1180). Chang is practically unknown in the West, because there is virtually nothing in English or any European language on him. Even in Chinese and Japanese, most of the information presented here is unknown. But Chu Hsi would have been utterly different in personality and thought had it not been for Chang Shih, as we shall see.

## The Relationship Between the "Two Worthies"

Chang Shih was a native of Kuang-han County in Szechuan but moved to Heng-yang County in Hunan. His courtesy name was Ching-fu— and also Ch'in-fu—and his literary name was Nan-hsüan, also pronounced Nan-hsien. The two men first met in 1163, when Chu Hsi was summoned to the capital in Hangchow for an audience on the sixth day of the eleventh month. According to the *Yü-lei,* "When the emperor intended to summon Wei Kung [Venerable Gentleman Wei],[1] he first called Nan-hsüan to come. I was also summoned to the temporary capital. I talked with Nan-hsüan . . . ."[2] Chu Hsi was thirty-four years old at the time; Chang Shih was thirty-one. In the following year, Wei Kung died: "On the twentieth day of the ninth month, I arrived at Yü-chang[3] and got on the boat that carried his coffin to mourn him. . . . From Yü-chang I sent him off to Feng-ch'eng.[4] In the boat I enjoyed the company of Ch'in-fu for three days."[5]

Three years later, in 1167, accompanied by his pupil Fan Nien-te, Chu Hsi visited Chang Shih at T'an-chou (Changsha), arriving there on the eighth day of the ninth month.[6] They stayed in Changsha for two months. On the sixth day of the eleventh month, Chu Hsi, Chang Shih,

and Chu Hsi's pupil Lin Yung-chung set off to tour the famous Mount
Heng. They ascended on the thirteenth day and began to descend on
the sixteenth; in the meantime, they had been joined by Hu Shih and
Fan Nien-te. The group left the mountain on the nineteenth and
arrived at Chu-chou[7] on the twenty-third, parting the next day. Chu
Hsi, Chang Shih, and Lin Yung-chung exchanged 149 poems as a
result, which are collected in the well-known *Nan-yüeh ch'ang-ch'ou chi*
(Collected poems on the trip to the southern mountain).[8] Chang Shih
was then lecturing at the Yüeh-lu Academy in Changsha. Some say he
was a government official there.

Chang Shih was a true and loyal friend, offering advice on Chu Hsi's
behavior and endeavors. Like Lü Tsu-ch'ien (1137–1181), Chang felt
that Chu Hsi suffered from impatience.[9] He once wrote,

> I feel that you, Yüan-hui [Chu Hsi], are respected by people for both your
> learning and deeds. You have produced many scholars who stand forth
> before our eyes. Ordinarily, you only admonish others. In most cases, you
> see where other people are wrong and feel you are right. Others, fearing
> your vigor in argument and seriousness in attack, dare not question you
> even when they have doubts. I am afraid flattering words may be frequent
> but criticism is rare. If by any chance you should lean to one side without
> realizing it, inevitably there will be harmful effects developing in the
> future. In my mind, among friends in the world, none is closer than you.
> We dare not fall behind others in our duty of polishing each other in order
> to improve ourselves.[10]

In another letter, Chang Shih said,

> In your letter to Kuang-chung [Hu Shih], your philosophical analysis is
> clear and excellent, and you may be said to be vigorous in correcting him.
> But it must be admitted that in your wording there are places lacking a
> sense of composure. I would say that you should follow the example of
> those previous to us who used simple words to express comprehensive
> ideas and to advise at a critical point. If the listener is willing to think, he
> may be in a receptive mood. Otherwise, the more you stress the point, the
> more it gets away from him.[11]

We do not know which of the six letters to Hu Kuang-chung preserved
in the *Wen-chi* Chang Shih was referring to. Possibly he was talking
about the fifth letter, on doubts about personal cultivation and the
extension of knowledge, or to a letter no longer extant. None of the
existing letters reveals a strong temper. However, Chu Hsi himself realized his defect of intolerance.[12]

In his letter, Chang Shih continued to say,

In the last few days, I inquired of Kung-fu [Liu Kung, 1122–1178] about your daily affairs in detail. Many of them, of course, led me to praise and admire you. But in my humble opinion, there have been instances in which you have not been able to transform completely an existing imbalance of material endowment. . . . I hope you will treat what you ordinarily regard as minor ills as a serious sickness and apply medicine accordingly. I am sure that when we meet again, we shall see the result of the transformation of physical endowment.[13]

In a letter to Liu Kung-fu, Chu Hsi had discussed the question whether the term *chih* (nephew) should be changed to *yu-tzu* (similar to a son), and remarked that Kung-fu held to his own position too strongly and took himself too seriously.[14] Chang Shih said, "In your letter to Kung-fu, what you said seems to anticipate an attempt to deceive you, as if predicting your being distrusted; it lacks a sense of broadmindedness and understanding, and gives the impression of great anger to the point of causing one's hair to go through one's hat." He added, "I hope you will calm your mind, ease your temper, and examine what is right and what is wrong."[15]

Chu Hsi took the matter of whether or not to serve in the government very seriously, and repeatedly declined appointments. Yet both Chang Shih, who "always had doubts about your accepting or declining an appointment," and Lü Tsu-ch'ien pleaded with Chu Hsi to serve in the government, thus fulfilling the good intentions of the Court.[16] In 1168, there was great starvation in Chien-ning Prefecture of Fukien. Chu Hsi, with the aid of local elders, established a public granary in Wu-fu Village, where he lived. This was an epoch-making innovation in local charity, setting a pattern for many areas and having special significance in Chinese history. When Chang Shih heard about it, he wrote Chu Hsi and said,

I have heard that, because of a shortage of grain in your local area, you have acquired rice from the government and stored it, to be loaned out in the spring and paid back in the autumn. The interest accrued is merely to make up for the loss. This measure is beneficial to the whole community and will, of course, do no harm. However, someone may erroneously deride you for spreading "rice seedlings." I have heard that you have written that, of all the measures carried out by [Prime Minister] Wang Chieh-fu [Wang An-shih, 1021–1086], only the spreading of rice seedlings [enabling farmers to get loans from the government when planting rice seedlings and pay them off with high interest after the harvest] was correct. With great dedication you wanted to write an account of the community granary to express this idea. To me, this will be too much. Chieh-fu stole the idea from the office of regulating commodities in the *Chou-kuan* [Rites of Chou][17] to force loans [on farmers] and reap profit, thus violat-

ing the universal principle. . . . It is clear that your intention for the community and Wang's measure represent the difference between righteousness and profit.[18]

What Chang Shih had heard was not entirely correct. In his
"Account of the Wu-fu Village Community Granary," Chu Hsi clearly
stated that "[Wang An-shih's] ever-normal charitable granaries . . .
were all stored in prefectural or county capitals, and benefit only lazy
people in the cities and towns. As for farmers who labor hard in faraway
mountains and valleys and who were almost starving to death, the distance was too great for the grain to reach them. Furthermore, the regulations were too severe, so that officials fearing the law and avoiding
trouble would not send out relief, knowing that people were starving."[19]
Chu Hsi understood perfectly well which system was more beneficial.
To him, the distinction was not merely whether the motive for establishing the granaries was to benefit the people or to reap a profit. Eleven
years later, in 1185, Lü Tsu-chien's pupil, P'an Ching-hsien, asked his
father to contribute grain to establish a community granary in Chin-
hua County, where they lived. In his account for the granary, Chu Hsi
said,

> People in popular society have considered this a defect, merely because
> they have regarded it as similar to Wang's system of rice seedlings. . . .
> The original idea of the institution of the rice seedlings system was really
> not bad. However, it gave the farmers money but not grain; it was admin-
> istered by the county, not by the community; it was staffed by government
> officials, not by scholars and gentlemen of the locality; and it was carried
> out with the purpose of a quick accumulation of profit, not with a mind of
> compassion or honest benefit. That was why Wang's measure could only
> prevail in one city and not throughout the country.[20]

This account may have been written as a response to Chang Shih's letter. However, Chu Hsi and Chang Shih knew each other very well.
What Chang Shih had heard must have been twisted.

Another piece of misinformation that Chang Shih received was a
report that Chu Hsi had burst into song in a heroic but mournful tone
after excessive drinking.[21] It is true that Chu Hsi would sing after enjoying some wine, but the report was definitely an exaggeration. Similarly,
because of poverty, Chu Hsi resorted to the business of printing books.
Chang Shih considered that unsatisfactory, but offered no help in meeting Chu Hsi's dire needs. These two matters are taken up in chapters 5
and 6 above, and need not detain us here.

Chang Shih's advice to Chu Hsi was offered with utter sincerity and
was accepted in the same spirit. Chu Hsi wrote to Chang Shih, "In
recent days I have a tendency to chase after external things. My mind

loves to do so and cannot stop itself. In all such cases I have followed the precedent of abstaining from alcohol. I have stopped the tendency completely and it seems an easy matter. . . . I have suffered from demanding too much and from petty language. Only recently have I realized my mistake."[22] After Chang Shih's death, Chu Hsi wrote Lü Tsu-ch'ien to say, "Today's request for a sinecure of a temple superintendency is the first priority of carrying out the admonitions Ching-fu left behind."[23] And after Lü died, he wrote Liu Ch'ing-chih (1139–1159), "In the past, I still had Ching-fu and Po-kung [Lü Tsu-ch'ien] to give me warnings and advice at all times, so I could keep myself alert. Now that these two friends have passed away, I no longer hear those words. . . . My greatest hope lies with my Tzu-ch'eng [Liu Ch'ing-chih]."[24] Chu Hsi once wrote Chang Shih, "Generally speaking, when one reads books, one should have an open mind and a calm disposition, so as to see in a leisurely way where moral principles may lie."[25] This was intended to admonish Chang Shih as well as himself.

Aside from mutual admonitions, the correspondence between the two men sometimes dealt with private matters, the printing of books, and association with friends, although there is much less of this sort of material than is found in Chu Hsi's correspondence with Lü Tsu-ch'ien. For one thing, Changsha, where Chang Shih lived, was much farther from Chu Hsi's home than was Lü's residence in Chin-hua. In addition, Chekiang, where Chin-hua is located, was the home of the national capital, where scholars gathered. Nevertheless, Chang Shih did not hesitate to write to Chu Hsi about his own decisions to abstain from alcohol[26] and to build a library.[27] He also wrote about Lü's refusal to accept more pupils.[28] Especially heartfelt were his telling Chu Hsi about his son's tuberculosis,[29] his reaction to Chu Hsi's wife's death, and his comment on Lü Tsu-ch'ien's wife's death.[30]

In the *Wen-chi,* the letters to Chang from Chu Hsi deal almost exclusively with philosphical matters. Only casually did Chu Hsi mention that some people thought that, being a high official in the national capital, he should not have too many pupils, a fact that did not bother Chu Hsi himself.[31] He also urged Chang Shih to use popular ceremonies in seasonal religious sacrifices.[32] The *Yü-lei,* however, contains several items that have nothing to do with ideas or moral admonitions. For instance, we learn that the only tablet in Chu Hsi's library was Chang Shih's calligraphy of the two characters *ts'ang-shu* (book collection).[33] When Chang Shih abolished religious sacrifices at popular festivals, Chu Hsi asked "if you could refrain from eating glutinous rice dumplings on the fifth day of the fifth month, and if you could refrain from drinking dogwood wine on the ninth day of the ninth month. And if you enjoyed those things without first offering them in a religious observance, whether you felt comfortable."[34] Chang Shih had once said that, according to Chu Hsi's fate, he would hold many offices but receive little in terms of emoluments. To this Chu Hsi replied, "In my life I have written a great deal to decline official appointments."[35] Chu Hsi also recalled that after Chang Shih's father returned home after some trouble in the government, Chang Shih and his younger brother always went in and out together in two sedan chairs.[36] All this goes to show that the two friends were quite intimate.

## Chu Hsi's Appraisal of Chang Shih

Since Chu Hsi and Chang Shih knew each other well, it is to be expected that Chu Hsi's attitude toward Chang Shih's character was both complimentary and critical. I have gathered from the *Wen-chi* and the *Yü-lei* Chu Hsi's evaluation of his friend. The latter records are Chu Hsi's answers to his pupils' questions after Chang Shih's death—answers that represent not only Chu Hsi's personal opinion but the final public judgment of Chang Shih as well.

Chu Hsi observed that Chang Shih composed very quickly. Sometimes he would write a draft on his lap and would finish it in a moment.[37] When Chang Shih was advised to revise an essay, Chu Hsi said, he would maintain that "it makes no difference, even with revision. It is even better if not elaborated."[38] As a consequence, his writing "is seldom revised, and often is not as good as before revision."[39] As a result of discussions with Chu Hsi, Chang Shih revised his *Lun-yü shuo* (Explanation of the *Analects*) in many places. However, he did not discuss his *Meng Tzu shuo* (Explanation of the *Book of Mencius*) with Chu Hsi.[40] Because of his superior intelligence, he made decisions quickly. Therefore he read books carelessly, as, for example, when he believed that the *Ma-i i* (Explanation of the *Book of Changes* by Ma-i) was really the work of a Taoist.[41] On another occasion, Chang Shih inscribed the two characters *tuan-chuang* (dignified) on a folio of bad calligraphy that he supposed was by Su Shih (1037–1101).[42]

Also, because Chang Shih was so brilliant, his deliberations on principle were too rapid for some people. Once he said something, he was through with it.[43] He would not ask whether or not his listeners had been able to follow his train of thought. Therefore the smartest of his pupils understood him, but those of lesser intelligence did not know where to start.[44] Chu Hsi said, "Ching-fu as a person was smart. When he talked with students, he poured everything out. This is all right. But when students who had not developed to an adequate level listened to him, they would no longer [be able to] think about it. This is very bad."[45] Chu Hsi also felt that, because of his brightness, Chang Shih did not scrutinize principles carefully. For example, when he explained the clarity of the mind as having been aroused, he went too far, for clarity refers to the substance of the mind. Sometimes the mind is spoken of in terms of its substance, and sometimes it is spoken of in terms of its function, so one should not confuse the two and regard clarity as having been aroused.[46] Or take his explanation of *Wu-chi erh T'ai-chi* (the Ultimate of Nonbeing and also the Great Ultimate) as that which is done without man's doing it. Here Chu Hsi said that Chang Shih had presented a preliminary observation as the final conclusion, for he did not deliberate any further and so come to realize that the Great Ultimate merely means the ultimate beyond which there is nothing else.[47] Hence Chu Hsi maintained that Chang Shih "drew his conclusions too quickly."[48] He also said, "Ching-fu's comments were expressed too early, and therefore there were many mistakes."[49] According to Chu Hsi, Chang Shih's theory about the clarity of the mind as having been aroused was an idea of his early years that he corrected when he realized his mistake. Unfortunately, his early theory had circulated, so some scholars never realized that Chang Shih later changed his mind.[50] Chu Hsi considered "Nan-hsüan to have understanding on a high level. It is like building a house. The main frames are in place but the minor structures are largely missing."[51] Chu Hsi probably meant that his friend lacked daily practice. One of his letters may be taken as his general criticism of Chang Shih. It says,

> In my humble view, your cultivation is generally dignified, but a calm and profound disposition is not enough. Consequently, your expression is long on frankness and short on reserve. This is probably due to the fact that the work of cultivating the source has not been accomplished. This being the case, I am afraid that one's seeing and listening cannot be intelligent and one's thought cannot be thorough. I have seen that your writings in recent years mostly lack rhythm and order, and you often speak to students about principles that they are not up to. All these are defects.[52]

Chu Hsi also compared Chang Shih with Lu Hsiang-shan (1139–1193), saying that "Tzu-ching's [Lu Hsiang-shan] learning contains some element of Ch'an [Meditation] Buddhism and also some elements of the school of schemes and tricks. Sometimes he will tell you what he wants to say, but sometimes he won't. Nan-hsüan, on the other hand, frankly and directly speaks his mind, and does so to everybody."[53] Again, "The learning of Chin-hsi [Lu Hsiang-shan] is truly Ch'an. Ch'in-fu [Chang Shih] and Po-kung [Lü Tsu-ch'ien] have not seen through Buddhism because they have not read Buddhist books. I alone understand it."[54] He further remarked that Chang and Lü told their students to read Ch'eng I's (1033–1107) *I chuan* (Commentary on the *Book of Changes*), but that more often than not the students did not get anything out of it.[55] Comparing them with each other, Chu Hsi thought that "Ch'in-fu's knowledge and experience were of the highest order, but he was impatient. In Po-kung's learning, he was patient, but he had defects."[56] He also said, "The learning of both tended to the higher level, and Po-kung's deficiency tended to the lower level."[57] In the end, however, Chu Hsi thought that "if the two, Po-kung and Ch'in-fu, were still living today, they would be shining in a big way."[58]

This final analysis outweighs all Chu Hsi's preceding criticisms. As Chu Hsi told a friend, "Ching-fu loves me deeply."[59] He told another friend, "The learning of Ch'in-fu is transcendental and very much at ease with itself. He has a clear vision and is not restricted by words, because his learning is immediately relevant to the self, wherever it leads. Although what he says today is not entirely free from slips of the tongue, still he is talented. We are not his equal."[60] And to his students he said, "Whenever Nan-hsüan saw what was right, he courageously went forward to do it. He never hesitated or manipulated. What needed to be done, he would do. People say he was brave. Certainly he was. We cannot measure up to him." Having said that, Chu Hsi sighed several times.[61] This was recorded by Yeh Wei-tao (1220 *cs*) after 1191, when Chang Shih had been dead for more than ten years.

When Chang Shih died, Chu Hsi suspended all feasting in order to mourn him and wrote two funeral addresses for him. One of them repeats twice, "Alas! Ching-fu has abandoned me and left the world!"[62] The other is a sort of litany in which Chu Hsi seems to be talking to his friend in person: "Your brightness . . . . My stupidity . . . . Your lofty background . . . . My humble station . . . . Your great heights and brilliance . . . . My narrow-mindedness . . . . You used to tell me . . . . I used to tell you . . . ."[63] The sincerity and intimacy of this address are indeed moving. It is clearly the most heartfelt funeral address Chu Hsi ever composed. Several months later, he wrote Lü Tsu-ch'ien, "Without my realizing it, Ch'in-fu has been dead for half a year. Whenever I think of it, I can't help the feeling of choking. Letters from like-minded friends all mourn him, which makes me sigh all the more. Not only does it indicate the decline of our Way; it also makes a great difference for the present age."[64] Chu Hsi also wrote a eulogy for Chang Shih's portrait in which he said, "You expand the beginning of humanity and righteousness until they fill the universe, and you are as serious about the distinction between the good and the profitable as if you were splitting a hair."[65] Chu Hsi was clearly as sincere in this eulogy as he was in his funeral addresses, and we do him a great injustice if we treat it as conventional literature.

Five or six years later, he even wrote a tomb inscription. Chang Shih's younger brother wrote Chu Hsi and said, "Many people knew my elder brother, but you knew him best." Thereupon Chu Hsi wrote an inscription for his tomb, which says in part:

As a man, the venerable gentleman was frank and plain, with both the internal and the external open and clear. His understanding of principle was excellent, and his belief in the Way was firm. He was glad to hear about his own mistakes and was brave in moving toward righteousness. In all these he was forceful and determined, without the slightest hesitation. In teaching others, he made sure that the students first of all distinguished between righteousness and profit, and then understood principle and abided by reverent seriousness to reach the limit. His analysis was clear-cut and he was totally devoted. He would not stop on any question until he went from one end to the other and exhausted it.[66]

To write two funeral addresses, a portrait eulogy, and a tomb inscription all for a single person is surely unique.

## Agreements and Differences in Thought

In his second funeral address, Chu Hsi also had this to say:

In our exchanges, you and I had the same purpose and a harmonious mind. When personal conversations did not exhaust the subject, we continued in correspondence without stop. Sometimes what I considered right you regarded as wrong, and what you approved of I objected to. There were also occasions when we both tended toward the same direction but finally realized that it was one-sided, as well as points that we both rejected at first but found interesting later on. Thus we tangled in arguments to and fro for more than ten years, but finally arrived at the same destination and reached agreement.[67]

The tangled arguments to which Chu Hsi refers are found in the *Wen-chi,* while the approvals and objections are found in the *Yü-lei.* The discussions in the latter are mostly concerned with the teachings of the *Analects* and the *Book of Mencius.* Disciples asked about Chang Shih's interpretations because they had doubts. This indicates that there were more differences than agreements between Chu Hsi and Chang Shih. The discussions in the *Wen-chi,* in contrast, deal with fundamental concepts. On these the two men engaged in lengthy debates but finally arrived at the same conclusions. Their agreements and differences are presented below.

In his *Lun-yü shuo,* Chang Shih would not accept Hu Yin's (1098–1156) interpretation of the *Analects.* On this Chu Hsi voiced disapproval, saying, "If his theory is correct, it should not be rejected."[68] Confucius taught that "if for three years one does not deviate from the way of his father, one may be called filial."[69] Chang Shih understood this to mean that one has not changed although he could do so. On this understanding, Chu Hsi commented, "If this interpretation is correct, one does not have to change at all throughout life."[70] On the aphorism "Confucius never discussed strange phenomena, physical exploits, disorder, or spiritual beings,"[71] Chang Shih thought that Confucius did not talk about spiritual beings because there were none, whereas Chu Hsi contended that spiritual beings surely exist and that Confucius merely refrained from talking about them.[72] Chang Shih understood "All under Heaven will return to humanity"[73] to mean one's embracing everything in the world. Chu Hsi at first agreed with him, but later shifted to the interpretation that if one can master oneself and return to propriety, then in all cases one will realize humanity.[74]

To Chang Shih, the Confucian saying "neither for anything nor against anything"[75] described the state of mind—"for" meaning to take a stand, and "against" meaning to take no stand. For Chu Hsi, however, the Confucian injunction merely meant neither taking a stand nor taking no stand.[76] Confucius said that the calf of a brindled cow could be used for religious sacrifice.[77] Chang Shih interpreted this as Confucius teaching his pupil how to employ people, which Chu Hsi saw as far-fetched.[78] Chang Shih thought that the joy of Confucius' most virtuous pupil, Yen Hui,[79] and the joy of Confucius[80] himself differed in nature, whereas Chu Hsi thought that they differed only in degree.[81] Chang Shih distinguished the Confucian saying, "Observing a man's errors, it may be known that he is a man of humanity,"[82] as two different things, but Chu Hsi thought that splitting the sentence in two was not quite satisfactory.[83] To Chang Shih, the Confucian pupil Tseng Shen's examining himself on three points every day[84] was the way he cultivated the virtue of humanity; Chu Hsi, however, felt that self-examination should be applied to everything, not just to the cultivation of humanity.[85] In Chang Shih's explanation, "Only the man of humanity knows how to love people"[86] meant that the man of humanity can master himself, but Chu Hsi looked at it as a matter of one becoming a man of humanity precisely because one can master oneself, rather than the other way around.[87]

In explaining "anticipating an attempt to deceive" and "not predicting one's being distrusted,"[88] Chang Shih thought that a worthy was one who was the first to understand people's feelings, but Chu Hsi held a different view. To him, the one who is the first to understand knows people's deceit and distrust but does not anticipate either one.[89] Chang Shih understood "The man of wisdom cultivates humanity for its advantage"[90] as being done for a purpose, but Chu Hsi saw the deed as merely following principle, and thought that Chang Shih's explanation meant manipulation.[91] According to Chu Hsi, Chang Shih mistakenly interpreted "not forgetting an objective" and "not helping it to grow" in the *Book of Mencius*[92] to mean that one should not forget or help it to grow; Chu Hsi felt that Chang Shih did not realize that both not forgetting and not helping merely indicate the operation of the Principle of Heaven.[93] Chang Shih emphasized "knows" in the saying, "One who knows how to give the beginning of virtue the fullest expansion and development,"[94] but Chu Hsi believed that the emphasis should be on "the fullest expansion and development" instead.[95] In the sentence, "The fundamental principle [of reasoning] from facts is to follow [their natural tendencies],"[96] Chang Shih explained *ku* (facts) as "what has originally existed." Again Chu Hsi objected, saying, "If so, there would be another 'what has originally existed' besides goodness." To him, *ku* is simply the trace of what has existed.[97]

These differences concern Chang Shih's *Lun-yü shuo* and *Meng Tzu shuo* only. Besides these, there are many more, which also extend to other classics. About the hawk flying and fish leaping in the *Doctrine of the Mean*,[98] Chang Shih brought out only the fact that they can do so; hence Chu Hsi felt that Chang failed to express the idea that the Way operates throughout the universe.[99] In explaining the *Book of Changes*, Chang Shih held that it was sufficient to rely on its "Appended Remarks," but Chu Hsi maintained that the "Appended Remarks" are intended to clarify the meaning of the *yao-tz'u* (explanations of the component lines of the hexagrams) and therefore cannot be comprehended without understanding the *yao-tz'u*.[100] Chang Shih followed his teacher, Hu Hung (1106–1161), and considered the centrality *(chung)* in the *Doctrine of the Mean*[101] as the common nature of man, and "the state of absolute quiet and inactivity"[102] as the moral mind *(tao-hsin)* of the sage. To Chu Hsi, however, the mind that is "in the state of absolute quiet and inactivity" is possessed by all people, whereas the mind that can "immediately penetrate all things when acted on"[103] is possessed only by the sage.[104] In interpreting the sentence, "If we investigate the cycle of things, we shall understand the concepts of life and death,"[105] Chu Hsi also differed from Chang Shih.[106] Chang Shih considered that the essence of yin and yang (passive and active cosmic forces) and the Five Agents (Metal, Wood, Water, Fire, and Earth) coming into mysterious union in Chou Tun-i's (1017–1073) "T'ai-chi-t'u shuo" (Explanation of the diagram of the Great Ultimate)[107] should not be taken together with the Great Ultimate. Chu Hsi replied that in that case the two cosmic forces and the Five Agents would have nothing to do with the Great Ultimate.[108]

When Chu Hsi compiled the *I-shu* (Surviving works) of the Ch'eng brothers (Ch'eng Hao, 1032–1185, and Ch'eng I, 1033–1107), he changed a number of words; Chang Shih regarded some of the changes as unnecessary, and others as unsuitable.[109] Chang Shih considered the traditional capping ceremony as difficult to practice, but Chu Hsi thought it was easy.[110] To Chu Hsi, Chang Shih's account of the execution of eunuchs in the Eastern Han dynasty (25–220) merely glossed over the facts and did not get at the truth of the matter.[111]

The differences between the two thinkers concerning the classics are many, but deal only with minor matters. Thus, we turn instead to areas of thought on which they disagreed in more fundamental ways. For instance, to Chang Shih, literature contains in it human nature and the Way of Heaven. To this, Chu Hsi said, "He is too smart. He just says so."[112] Moreover, Chang Shih did not see any difference between humanity and wisdom, a position that Chu Hsi regarded as unsatisfactory.[113] A pupil asked, "Ming-tao [Ch'eng Hao] said that what is inborn is nature. He had said that nature is good, but then also said that 'it cannot be said that evil is not one's nature.'[114] Here he was talking about physical nature, and does not seem to continue from the earlier passage." To this, Chu Hsi answered, "He was not talking about physical nature. . . . It is like water mixed with dirt and sand. One cannot say that it is no longer water." The pupil said, "What I have just asked about was the idea of Nan-hsüan [i.e., that Ch'eng Hao was talking about physical nature]." Chu Hsi said, "Ching-fu drew his conclusions too early. He made many mistakes."[115]

It has already been pointed out that Chu Hsi did not accept Chang Shih's description of the clarity of the mind as having been aroused.[116] To Chang Shih, the substance of the mind is always aroused. As it is aroused, the mind is preserved in dealing with things and becomes their master. Commenting on this, Chu Hsi asked, "Does the mind have to wait to be aroused to become the master?"[117] Chang Shih regarded the mind as empty and unobstructed at all times. Once the mind is understood, its exercise is always smooth. Chu Hsi looked upon this as too sweeping and as too easily drifting into Buddhism. To him, the mind is of course empty and unobstructed at all times, but it has been submerged in selfish human desires for a long time.[118] Chang Shih also said that one knows the mind only when one sees tranquillity in activity. Here Chu Hsi thought that Chang Shih turned the matter upside down, for according to the commentary on the *fu* (to return) hexagram in the *Book of Changes*,[119] one can see the mind of Heaven and Earth if one can see activity in tranquillity.[120] Again, Chang Shih held that although Confucius taught people about humanity, he developed the idea by proceeding from nature and destiny. To Chu Hsi, this meant that humanity is not sufficient in itself and has to depend on the assistance of nature and destiny.[121] Chang Shih maintained that self-mastery depends on the investigation of things and the extension of knowledge,[122] but Chu Hsi regarded self-mastery as overcoming one's selfishness. To him, Chang Shih "merely wrote offhand without much thought."[123] Finally, Chang Shih did not believe in *kuei-shen* (yin and yang, spiritual beings), while Chu Hsi regarded them as the traces of creation.[124]

From these examples, it is clear that Chu Hsi and Chang Shih disagreed on many issues. Because of their differences, their pupils raised questions, and they themselves corresponded in a sort of ongoing

debate. Thus the *Wen-chi* and the *Yü-lei* tell us more about their differences than their agreements. Yet it is not unreasonable to assume that
they agreed in more instances than those that have come down to us.
And some cases of agreement were recorded, of course. For example, as
Chang Shih understood it, Confucius told his pupils about Kuan
Chung's (d. 645 B.C.) accomplishments because they raised questions
about Kuan Chung's virtue of humanity,[125] and Chu Hsi approved of
this interpretation.[126] He also agreed with Chang Shih that after the
Han dynasty (206 B.C.–A.D. 220), the reign name should continue with
that of the state of Shu (221–263), which continued the Han.[127] Chang
Shih credited Hu Ming-chung (Hu Yin) with three achievements, and
Chu Hsi thought his observation good.[128] To Chang Shih, whether or
not Confucius served in the government was "the constant law of conducting oneself and the great expediency of the substance of the Way."
He also said, "When Confucius went on to serve, it was his humanity to
love people, and when he finally declined to go, it was the wisdom of the
man who knows." Chu Hsi thought these remarks made things very
clear.[129] Question: "How about Nan-hsüan's saying, '*Kuei-shen* can be
summed up in one word, namely, sincerity?' " Answer: "Sincerity is
the principle of realness, and *kuei-shen* are also real principles."[130] Someone said that Chang Shih explained the terms *chung* (conscientiousness,
loyalty) and *shu* (altruism, empathy) as Confucius' complete fulfillment
of the Way of Heaven. Chu Hsi responded, "It is well said."[131]

There are also cases where Chu Hsi expanded on the subject in addition to their essential agreement. For instance, Chang Shih described
K'ung-ming (Chu-ko Liang, 181–234) as correct and great in substance
but deficient in learning. Chu Hsi also appraised him as fundamentally
ignorant of learning and completely mixed in thought, but as having the
disposition of a Confucian scholar.[132] Chu Hsi said, "Nan-hsüan once
said that the concept of the Great Ultimate was to clarify the profound
nature of activity and tranquillity. He got the point."[133] When a pupil
asked about Chang Shih's opinion that the substance of the Great Ultimate is perfectly tranquil, Chu Hsi said it was incorrect,[134] but he himself said that "tranquillity is the substance of the Great Ultimate, and
activity is its function."[135] The contradiction is only apparent, however,
for Chu Hsi felt that Chang Shih only talked about substance and not
function. Chang Shih took "for oneself" in Confucian teachings to
mean "doing so without any calculation." Chu Hsi said, with admiration, "His idea is deep and to the point, an idea not expressed by previous scholars. If a student examines himself according to his idea, he
will be able to discriminate between the good and the profitable and will
not err in the slightest degree."[136]

According to Chang Shih, the Mean, correctness, humanity, and
righteousness in the "T'ai-chi-t'u shuo"[137] are characterized by both

activity and tranquillity. At first, Chu Hsi dismissed this as a superflu-
ous remark. Upon thinking it over more carefully, he said, "These four
virtues are equivalent to origination, flourishing, advantage, and firmness.[138] These four penetrate and return. How can they be without
activity and tranquillity?"[139] In writing to a friend, Chu Hsi said,
"Ch'in-fu's theory that in the state before the feelings are aroused
[there is nothing in the mind] certainly seems to go too far. But what he
meant by nothing does not mean that there is no principle inherent in
the feelings, but that when [selfish] material desires play havoc with
them, there is not yet time to purify or calm them."[140] Chang Shih held
that seriousness penetrates both activity and tranquillity but is fundamentally tranquil. Although Chu Hsi stressed actual practice, he also
said that there is no harm in quiet-sitting when one is at leisure.[141]
Chang Shih believed that when action reaches the limit, knowledge
becomes clearer, and that when knowledge becomes clear, action will go
further. Chu Hsi agreed, but added that the efforts should advance
together.[142] It was inevitable that, between the two friends, there were
such agreements and differences.

## Chu Hsi's Search for Equilibrium and Harmony

To appreciate the two friends' differences in small matters but agreement on basic issues, and differences at the outset but agreement at the
end, it is necessary to investigate the issues on which they conducted
sustained discussions. These fall into three areas: the question of equilibrium and harmony, the *Hu Tzu chieh-yen* (Master Hu's understanding
of words), and Chu Hsi's "Jen-shuo" (Treatise on humanity).

The beginning chapter of the *Doctrine of the Mean* teaches that "before
the feelings of pleasure, anger, sorrow, and joy are aroused, it is called
equilibrium (*chung,* centrality). When these feelings are aroused, and
each and all attain due measure and degree, it is called harmony *(ho).*"
But how to achieve equilibrium and harmony was an issue that troubled
Chu Hsi.

He was taught by Li T'ung (1093–1163) to sit quietly with a clear
mind to observe the disposition before the feelings are aroused *(wei-fa).*
Chu Hsi was not quite satisfied with this instruction. Chang Shih, in
contrast, perpetuated the learning of Hu Hung and became the leader
of the Hu-Hsiang (Hunan) School, whose cardinal doctrine was to
examine what has been aroused *(i-fa)* before preserving the mind and
nourishing nature. In an attempt to solve this troubling question, Chu
Hsi took a long journey to Changsha to discuss it with Chang Shih.
According to the traditional *nien-p'u* (chronological biography) of Chu
Hsi, his pupil Fan Nien-te said, "The two Masters discussed the meaning of the *Doctrine of the Mean* for three days and three evenings and

could not come to an agreement." In his later *nien-p'u,* Wang Mao-hung (1668–1741) maintained that Fan's remark had no basis.[143] However, Fan Nien-te was present at the discussion, so his remarks were not based on hearsay. The oldest existent *nien-p'u* is the one edited by Yeh Kung-hui in 1431. Under its entry for 1167, on Chu Hsi's visit to Changsha, it states that "they came to perfect agreement on the concept of the Great Ultimate after discussions." This is then followed by what Fan said. Wang did not see Yeh's *nien-p'u* but consulted the one revised by Hung Ch'u-wu in 1700. Hung also quoted Fan's remark, but Wang claimed that Hung had imagined what Fan was reported as saying on the basis of poems the several friends had composed on Mount Heng.[144] Wang's purpose was to stress Chu Hsi's agreement with Chang Shih that nature is before the feelings are aroused and that the mind is after they are aroused—a perfectly understandable motive. Nevertheless, the issue remains of how to achieve equilibrium before the feelings are aroused and harmony after they are aroused. Should examination precede cultivation, or vice versa? There was no conclusion after three days of discussion.

The concept of *jen* (humanity) was also a topic of conversation. According to the *Yü-lei,* a pupil asked, "Formerly, when you and Nan-hsüan deliberated on *jen,* did you come to an agreement?" Answer: "There were one or two points on which we differed. Ching-fu's theory is based on the doctrine of Hu Hung. Only Ching-fu understood it. The other pupils did not comprehend it, but merely said that they should adhere to the doctrines of their teacher. I went to Changsha precisely to discuss this topic with Ching-fu."[145] As to what theory each insisted on, we have no information on it.

While in Changsha, Chu Hsi wrote his friend Ts'ao Chin-shu and said,

> I arrived in Changsha on the eighth day of this month. It has already been half a month. Ching-fu loves me deeply. We engage in conversations on topics new to us, with benefit to our learning each day. This is most fortunate. Ching-fu's scholarship is on a high level, and his insight is outstanding. His discussions go beyond people's expectations. Recently, I read his *Yü-shuo* [Explanation of the *Analects*]. Without realizing it, my mind seems to be free. He is really admirable. The number of scholars at the Yüeh-lu [Academy] is gradually increasing. Some among them are of pure physical endowment and concrete interest, but they don't have a direction. They often chase after empty talk and keep a distance from concrete principles. The responsibility to warn them lies with Ching-fu, a responsibility which he cannot shirk.[146]

From this we know that Chang Shih was teaching at Changsha.

After he returned home from Changsha, Chu Hsi wrote his friend Shih Tun (1145 *cs*),

I went to Changsha in mid-autumn of last year. It took me a month to get there. I returned home after two months. On the way, I went here and there for more than fifty days. After I got home, fortunately I found the old folks in good health. Various conditions are roughly in order, but otherwise nothing is worth reporting. Ch'in-fu's outstanding insight cannot be matched. As I associate with him over time, I am much benefited from our discussions. However, his natural gifts are bright. He never had to go through the steps to obtain his achievement. Therefore, when he talks to people today, in most cases he makes the mistake of being too lofty. Scholars in the Hsiang [Changsha] area who have followed him have engaged in empty talk as a rule. The effects that have developed will be harmful. Recently, he has realized this defect. I hope he found a way to remedy the situation after I left. But among his pupils, it is extremely difficult to find one who can understand in a simple and concrete way. It can be seen that our Way is difficult to understand. Hu Hung's younger generation and pupils also talk about the Way, but none has been able to get at the truth in a concrete way. They make gestures of all kinds, as if they are talking about Ch'an. They are entirely opposed to the immediate followers of Wen-ting [Hu An-kuo, 1074–1138], and one cannot reason with them. Ch'in-fu alone has an insight that penetrates the inside and the outside. In the past, his preconceived opinions were slightly out of balance. After this meeting, they seem to have all disappeared. One can reason with him.[147]

Obviously, Chu Hsi's impression of Chang Shih at the meeting in Changsha was very favorable.

After returning home, Chu Hsi wrote four letters to Chang Shih to discuss the problem of equilibrium and harmony—that is, what occurs before *(wei-fa)* and after *(i-fa)* the feelings of pleasure, anger, sorrow, and joy have been aroused.[148] Wang Mao-hung dated these letters in 1166, when Chu Hsi was thirty-seven years old, which would place them before his visit to Changsha.[149] Ch'ien Mu, however, dated them in 1168.[150] I believe Ch'ien Mu is nearer the truth. The first letter says,

There is the undifferentiated total reality that responds to things indefinitely. This is the moving power of the process of unceasing production and reproduction *(sheng-sheng)* in the operation of the Mandate of Heaven. Although it rises and disappears ten thousand times in a single day, its absolutely silent original substance is never devoid of that tranquillity. What is called *wei-fa* is nothing but this. . . . Just as the buds and sprouts of the innate mind spring forth, it always reveals itself as it comes into contact with things. If at this point a learner can examine, control, and preserve his mind, he can penetrate the entirety of the great foundation and the universal path. He can then return to his original mind.[151]

This shows that Chu Hsi was getting away from Li T'ung's teaching of quiet-sitting to find equilibrium and tending toward the direction of the Hunan School of Hu Hung, which advocated examining the mind as one comes into contact with things. But this was not really the answer he was looking for, which is why he later added a note that "this letter is incorrect."

The second letter says, "I have been favored with your instruction, and learn that I still have the defect of regarding [substance and function] as two different things. . . . As I see it now, both substance and function are present in an instant of thought. As what has been aroused starts to go, what has not been aroused starts to come, without any gap or separation.[152] Chang Shih's letter is no longer extant. We do not know what he meant by two different things, but probably he was criticizing Chu Hsi for treating substance, or what has not been aroused, and function, or what has been aroused, as two separate states. That would explain why Chu Hsi subsequently emphasized the simultaneity of substance and function. But in so doing, he brought himself closer to Hu Hung's position on the identity of nature and the mind. As he thought it over more carefully, he became even more uncomfortable. Therefore, he added a footnote that "this letter is even more absurd."

The third letter says,

> Henceforth, I know that in the tremendous process of the great transformation, everyone has a peaceful abode in him. That is precisely where he brings peace to himself, establishes his destiny, becomes his own master, and sensitizes his consciousness. It is the axis that enables him to establish the great foundation and travel the universal path. What is meant by the saying, "Substance and function come from the same source, and there is no gap between the manifest and the hidden,"[153] lies right here. What I said previously about what is starting to go or to come shows that I was in a hurry with no place to settle.[154]

This letter, in which the self is the master, is an advance over the second, in which the self is passive in the great transformation. In the third letter, the self is an active participant in the great transformation and has a sense of direction.

In the fourth letter, Chu Hsi said,

> Throughout the universe there is only one dynamic operation of nature. Its operation and development do not stop for a moment. From the point of view of what has been aroused, and pointing to the fact of what has not been aroused, what has been aroused is the human mind and what has not been aroused is nature. . . . All daily affairs are merged into one body, like the running current without stop and the evolution of the sky with no end. That is why substance and function, the refined and the coarse, activity and tranquillity, the fundamental and the secondary are wide open with not even a hair in between. Wherever the hawk flies or the fish leaps, the atmosphere is clear. When we talk about preserving [the mind],

this is what we want to preserve, and when we talk about nourishing [nature], this is what we want to nourish. . . . In the past I resorted to some manipulation and could not settle down. But now I feel like a boat floating in ample water, free from restraints and guided by a rudder, sailing up or down as I please.[155]

The mind is now the master, and the effort of preserving and nourishing comes easily and naturally.

We have no information on Chang Shih's reaction to the four letters, except his cryptic comment on separation into two things. There are, however, two letters to Chu Hsi in his literary collection that include brief discussions on equilibrium. In one letter he said, "The idea of equilibrium is extremely complex, but to interpret abiding in equilibrium as the inside, as contrasted with something outside, is unsatisfactory. . . . If one speaks of it as an internal principle, then after the feelings have been aroused, will equilibrium cease to be there?"[156] In the other letter he wrote, "I am afraid that to say that equilibrium is the substance of nature and harmony the function of nature is unsatisfactory. Equilibrium describes both the whole and the parts of nature, and one should not say that equilibrium is the substance of nature. It will be all right to say that the substance of nature is in the state of equilibrium, but its function is in the state of harmony."[157]

With these exchanges of opinion, it was natural that Chu Hsi and Chang Shih should come to a general agreement. However, the agreement was by no means complete. In a reply to Ch'eng Hsün, Chu Hsi said, "Last winter, when I went to Changsha, the benefit resulting from our discussions was considerable. However, in this matter [the search for equilibrium and harmony], one must devote oneself to the task of daily matters such as walking, resting, sitting, and lying down before one can have an insight. From that point on, if one can control and preserve [the mind] to the limit, one can then claim it as one's own. Ching-fu's insight is superb and outstanding, beyond our ability to match."[158] In these words there is a hint of criticism of the Hunan School for its doctrine of internal examination to the neglect of daily practice. In a letter to Lin Tse-chih, Chu Hsi said, "Recently, I received a letter from Nan-hsüan. All his theories seem to be agreeable. But he still holds firmly to the idea of examining [the mind] first and then cultivating [nature]. The order of what has been aroused and what has not been is not quite clear, either. He has abruptly shifted from his old theory but still hangs onto something with which he is comfortable."[159]

In another letter to Lin, Chu Hsi said,

In reading Nan-hsüan's recent writing, I feel that, generally speaking, he lacks effort in daily matters. In general, the substance of the mind penetrates what is and what is not, and covers both activity and tranquillity. Therefore one's effort should also penetrate what is and what is not, and cover both activity and tranquillity before anything is left out. If one must wait for the feelings to have been aroused before examining, and wait for examination before preserving, the probability is great that one's effort will not reach its objective. One must cultivate oneself before the feelings are aroused. If so, what is aroused will attain due measure and degree in most cases, and will fail to attain it only in a few cases. At the time of examination, one is very clear and one's task is easy. This is vastly different from his earlier theory, which was baseless.[160]

Lin must have participated in the discussions at Changsha and understood the issues well.

Several years later, when Chu Hsi was forty years old, he wrote the scholars in Hunan to expound his theory of equilibrium and harmony. The letter says, in part,

Before there is any sign of thought or deliberation, and prior to the arrival of [the stimulus] of external things, there is the state before the feelings of pleasure, anger, sorrow, and joy are aroused. At this time, the state is identical with the substance of the mind, which is absolutely quiet and inactive, and the nature endowed by Heaven should be completely embodied in it. Because it is neither excessive nor insufficient, and is neither unbalanced nor one-sided, it is called equilibrium. When it is acted upon and immediately penetrates all things, the feelings are then aroused. In this state the functioning of the mind can be seen. Because it never fails to attain the proper measure and degree and has nowhere deviated from the right, it is called harmony. . . . However, the state before the feelings are aroused cannot be sought, and the state after they are aroused permits no manipulation. So long as in one's daily life the effort at seriousness and cultivation is fully extended and there are no selfish human desires to disturb it, before the feelings are aroused it will be as clear as a mirror and as calm as still water, and after the feelings are aroused it will attain due measure and degree without exception. . . . This is the reason why he [Ch'eng I] said . . . "Self-cultivation requires seriousness; the pursuit of learning depends on the extension of knowledge."[161]

This letter[162] summarized the strong points of the four letters to Chang Shih himself and added the concept of seriousness, thus establishing a well-organized system of equilibrium and harmony. From this point on, the two wheels of a vehicle, or the two wings of a bird— namely, seriousness and extension of knowledge—formed the basis of Chu Hsi's teaching, which remained firm for the next thirty years. Although this letter was not its final expression, the mutual support of seriousness and righteousness as the philosophy of life was thereby completed. Chu Hsi then sent a long letter of more than a thousand words to Chang Shih, to elaborate on the dual concept of cultivation and examination proceeding at the same time. "Seriousness in the state before the feelings are aroused," the letter said, "is, of course, the master of the reality of preserving the mind and nourishing nature. In the state after the feelings have been aroused, it also always operates in the process of examination." The letter also pinpoints the concept of *jen,* saying,

> What masters the person and leaves no gap in one's activity or inactivity, speech or silence, is the mind. *Jen* is the Way of the mind and seriousness is the firmness of the mind. This is the Way penetrating both the higher and lower levels and the basic system of the learning of the sages. If we understand this, the character of nature and feelings and the wonder of equilibrium and harmony can be fully understood in one word. . . . As to your statement that the learner must first examine the starting point of a clue before he can apply the effort of preserving the mind and nourishing nature, I cannot but have my doubts. Of course one should examine at the outset, but there are times when the feelings have not yet been aroused. One should preserve and nourish at this stage, and should not wait until after feelings have been aroused to examine, or until after one has examined to preserve. Furthermore, if one has not preserved and nourished from the beginning and tries to examine as things occur, I am afraid that in the vast arena one has no place to start.

And so, he concluded, "Movement and tranquillity alternate and become the root of each other"; moreover, "Seriousness and righteousness support each other, and no gap between them should be allowed."[163]

In 1172, Chu Hsi wrote the "Chung-ho chiu-shuo hsü" (Account of the old theory of equilibrium and harmony) to recall the steps through which he had sought the meaning of equilibrium and harmony. As he related,

> In my youth I studied under Master Li Yen-p'ing [Li T'ung]. He instructed me on the *Doctrine of the Mean* and told me to seek the fundamental idea before the feelings of pleasure, anger, sorrow, and joy are aroused. Before I understood the idea, the Teacher passed away. I was sad for my stupidity and felt like a pauper without a home. When I heard that Chang Ch'in-fu had acquired the learning of Master Hu of Heng-shan, I went to inquire of him. Ch'in-fu told me what he had heard, but I did not understand it. I withdrew to think deeply, almost forgetting food and sleep. One day I sighed heavily and said, "Although a person, from infancy to old age and death, is varied in speech and silence, activity and inactivity, for the most part all these are but the feelings having been aroused. What has not been aroused is only yet to be aroused. . . . I related this to my friend Ts'ai Chi-t'ung [Ts'ai Yüan-ting, 1135–1198] in the spring of 1169. In

the course of questioning and sifting through the matter with him, I suddenly raised a doubt in myself. . . . I again read the works of the Ch'eng brothers, slowly and with an open mind and a calm air. Before I had finished several lines, my doubt was completely dissolved. . . . I quickly wrote Ch'in-fu to tell him and the others who shared the same opinion. Only Ch'in-fu replied with profound approval. The others half believed and half doubted, or have not been able to decide after a number of years.[164]

These "others" refer to the gentlemen of Hunan. Although Chang Shih profoundly approved of Chu Hsi's conclusion, he still held that one should first examine and then preserve and nourish. Some scholars have asserted that Chang Shih changed his position and followed Chu Hsi, but this is not exactly correct.

## Discussions on the *Hu Tzu chih-yen*

Hu Hung's most important philosophical work is the *Hu Tzu chih-yen* (Master Hu's understanding of words). Since Chang Shih inherited the doctrines from Hu, it may be expected that he shared Hu's views in this work. But Chu Hsi strongly objected to certain of Hu's tenets, and wrote the "*Hu Tzu chih-yen* i-i" (Doubts on *Master Hu's Understanding of Words*) to dispute him paragraph by paragraph. Through correspondence he also debated points with Lü Tsu-ch'ien and Chang Shih.[165] In the *Hu Tzu chih-yen* it is said, "The mind is that which knows Heaven and Earth and masters the ten thousand things to complete nature." This is what Chu Hsi called "the mind completely viewed as function," one of the eight doubts he raised about the *Chih-yen*.[166] Feeling that Hu Hung confused the mind and nature as one, Chu Hsi wanted to change Hu's *hsin i ch'eng-hsing* (the mind to complete nature) to *hsin t'ung hsing-ch'ing* (the mind unites and commands nature and the feelings). Chang Shih suggested "the mind masters nature and the feelings," a suggestion Chu Hsi did not accept.

Hu Hung had said, "To love or to hate is nature. The inferior man loves and hates for himself, but the superior man loves and hates according to the Way." To Chu Hsi, "This meant that nature is neither good nor evil. If so, nature simply loves or hates without any principle." Chang Shih did not see any difficulty in Hu Hung's formulation but proposed the revision, "To love or to hate is nature. This is the impartiality of the Principle of Heaven. The superior man follows his nature, but the inferior man confuses his mind with selfish human desires and thus loses its principle." Refuting him, Chu Hsi said, "It is incorrect simply to call love or hate nature, for love and hate have to do with material things, whereas to love good and hate evil have to do with principle. . . . I am afraid it will do harm to concentrate on things and leave out principle in talking about nature." The *Chih-yen* also says, "The Way of man is perfectly great and perfectly good." Chu Hsi questioned this, saying, "If nature is really neither good nor evil [as Hu Hung maintained], how can it be like this?" Chang Shih wrote at length trying to explain Chu Hsi's misunderstanding. Chang Shih said, "Nature is purely good and not evil. Its activity is feeling. . . . Evil emerges because of feeling. Is it nature as it originally is? The saying [by Ch'eng Hao], 'It cannot be said that evil is not man's nature,'[167] describes how nature has drifted to that state, but nature as it originally is still remains." However, as Chu Hsi pointed out, this saying by Ch'eng Hao refers to physical nature, as the preceding and following sections in Ch'eng Hao's passage show. Chu Hsi did not elaborate, and his statement here that Ch'eng Hao was indeed referring to physical nature seems to contradict the one quoted above on p. 407. Actually, Ch'eng Hao's saying can be interpreted both ways, just as water mixed with dirt and sand is still water, whether contaminated or not.

On the remainder of the *Chih-yen,* Chang Shih agreed with Chu Hsi in some cases, or said that the original passage in the *Chih-yen* could be deleted. None of these cases deals with an important issue. Generally, Chang Shih expressed more opinions than did Lü Tsu-ch'ien. According to the *Yü-lei,*[168] he strongly adhered to his teacher's belief that "what is called good in nature is an expression of praise and is not opposed to evil."[169]

## The Debate on the Doctrine of Humanity

In his funeral address for Chang Shih, Chu Hsi said, "We tangled in arguments to and fro for more than ten years." This remark may well refer specifically to their debate on Chu Hsi's "Jen-shuo" (Treatise on humanity).[170] Chu Hsi discussed this treatise with his friends over a long period of time, and talked about it with Chang Shih more than anyone else. Four letters on it are preserved in the *Wen-chi,* and two in the *Nan-hsüan Hsien-sheng wen-chi.*[171] The letters are quite detailed. They are dealt with at length in connection with the "Jen-shuo" itself and need not be described here.[172] Suffice it to say that in their discussions Chang Shih yielded more to Chu Hsi than vice versa, although Chu Hsi's "Jen-shuo" was also modified as a result. Chang Shih also wrote his own "Jen-shuo," which has been confused with Chu Hsi's. Chang's treatise, too, is discussed extensively in chapter 11 above and need not engage our attention here.

Chang Shih also collected the sayings of Confucius and Mencius on *jen,* explained them according to the interpretations of the Ch'eng brothers and others, and entitled the anthology *Chu-Ssu yen-jen* (Confucius and Mencius on humanity). This work has been lost, with the exception of its preface. Chu Hsi did not approve of this work. He felt that other subjects that Confucius and Mencius talked about were also useful, and that Chang's compilation might provide a shortcut for students, who would thereby fall into inhumanity.[173] Both men, however, regarded *jen* as the zenith of morality and taught people to seek it eagerly. In the end, the two arrived at the same destination.

## Note on Chang Shih's Divination

Ch'en Chi-ju (1558–1639) related the following anecdote: "Chang Nan-hsüan was an expert in divination. His judgment on Chu Hsi was, 'Many official posts but not much emolument.' Hui-weng [Chu Hsi] nodded his head and said, 'This old man *(lao-han)* in his life has written many pieces to decline an official post.' "[174] This story is based on the *Yü-lei,* already quoted above,[175] and is obviously an embellishment. There is no evidence that Chang Shih was an expert of divination; indeed, he once wrote Chu Hsi advising him not to believe in a diviner.[176] Chang's remark was about Chu Hsi's fate in general, not his fortune. Chu Hsi himself never said that Chang Shih was a specialist in divination, and he never used the term *lao-han.* Moreover, before Chu Hsi visited Chang Shih in Changsha in 1167, he had declined official posts only three times—in 1159, 1163, and 1165. From 1167 to Chang Shih's death in 1180 the two scholars never met again, so there could not have been a conversation about declining many posts. The *Yü-lei* remark was recorded by Chu Hsi's pupil Wang Kuo after 1194, long after Chang Shih's death. By that time Chu Hsi had indeed declined office many times. Ch'en Chi-ju simply wanted to show how well the two friends knew each other and how seriously Chu Hsi took an official post.

## Notes

1. This refers to Prime Minister Chang Chün (1096–1164), Chang Shih's father.

2. *Yü-lei,* ch. 103, sec. 50 (p. 4146).

3. Present Nan-ch'ang, Kiangsi Province.

4. Southwest of Nan-ch'ang.

5. *Wen-chi,* supplementary collection, 5:11b, letter in reply to Counselor Lo (Lo Po-wen).

6. *Ibid.,* regular collection, 24:14b, letter to Ts'ao Chin-shu.

7. A city in present T'an-hsiang County, Hunan Province.

8. For Chang Shih's preface, see the *Nan-hsüan Hsien-sheng wen-chi* [Collection of literary works of Master Chang Shih] (*Chin-shih han-chi ts'ung-k'an* [Chinese works of the recent period series] ed.) 15:1a–3b (pp. 505–510).

9. *Ibid.,* 22:10a (p. 709), forty-third letter in reply to Chu Yüan-hui (Chu Hsi).

10. *Ibid.*, 20:11a–b (pp. 659–660), eleventh letter in reply to Chu Yüan-hui.

11. *Ibid.*, 20:8b (p. 654), tenth letter.

12. *Wen-chi*, 31:15b, twenty-seventh letter in reply to Chang Ching-fu (Chang Shih).

13. *Nan-hsüan Hsien-sheng wen-chi*, 20:8b (p. 654), tenth letter to Chu Yüan-hui.

14. *Wen-chi*, 37:14a, first letter to Liu Kung-fu (Liu Kung).

15. *Nan-hsüan Hsien-sheng wen-chi*, 21:2b–3a (pp. 668–669), fifteenth letter in reply to Chu Yüan-hui. The reference on anticipating deceit is to the *Analects* 14:33, and the reference on anger is to the *Shih chi* [Historical records] (*SPTK* ed.), 81:1b, biography of Lin Hsiang-ju.

16. *Ibid.*, 20:2 (p. 641), second letter; 21:8a (p. 679), twenty-first letter.

17. *Chou kuan* [Rites of Chou], Office of the Earth, "Ch'üan-fu."

18. *Nan-hsüan Hsien-sheng wen-chi*, 20:9b (p. 656), eleventh letter in reply to Chu Yüan-hui.

19. *Wen-chi*, 77:24b–25a, "Account of the Wu-fu Village Community Granary in Ch'ung-an County, Chien-ning Prefecture."

20. *Ibid.*, 79:16b, "Account of the Community Granary of Chin-hua County, Wu-chou Prefecture."

21. *Nan-hsüan Hsien-sheng wen-chi*, 21:11a (p. 659), eleventh letter in reply to Chu Yüan-hui.

22. *Wen-chi*, 31:14b–15a, twenty-seventh letter in reply to Chang Ching-fu.

23. *Ibid.*, 34:8b, eighty-fourth letter in reply to Lü Po-kung (Lü Tsu-ch'ien).

24. *Ibid.*, 35:17a, seventh letter in reply to Liu Tzu-ch'eng (Liu Ch'ing-chih).

25. *Ibid.*, 31:9b, twentieth letter in reply to Chang Ching-fu.

26. *Nan-hsüan Hsien-sheng wen-chi*, 21:4b (p. 672), twentieth letter in reply to Chu Yüan-hui.

27. *Ibid.*, 21:8a (p. 679), twenty-fourth letter.

28. *Ibid.*, 21:12a (p. 688), thirty-first letter.

29. *Ibid.*, 23:8a (p. 728), fifty-third letter.

30. *Ibid.*, 23:12a (p. 735), fifty-sixth letter; 24:11a (p. 757), seventy-first letter.

31. *Wen-chi*, 31:4b, fifteenth letter in reply to Chang Ching-fu.

32. *Ibid.*, 30:27b, eighth letter in reply to Chang Ch'in-fu (Chang Shih).

33. *Yü-lei*, ch. 107, sec. 61 (p. 4254).

34. *Ibid.*, ch. 90, sec. 132 (p. 3684).

35. *Ibid.*, ch. 107, sec. 70 (p. 4257).

36. *Ibid.*, ch. 103, sec. 50 (p. 4149).

37. *Ibid.*, ch. 140, sec. 54 (p. 5350).

38. *Ibid.*, sec. 94 (p. 5358).

39. *Ibid.*, ch. 139, sec. 50 (p. 5313).

40. *Ibid.*, ch. 103, sec. 45 (p. 4143).

41. *Ibid.*, ch. 125, sec. 62 (p. 4811). See also ch. 67, sec. 161, 169–174 (pp. 2669, 2672–2675); *Wen-chi*, 81:11b–13b, epilogues on the *Ma-i i* [Explanation of the *Book of Changes* by Ma-i]. Chu Hsi contended that the work was not by a Taoist but a forgery by Tai Shih-yü.

42. *Yü-lei*, ch. 140, sec. 95 (p. 5359).

43. *Ibid.*, ch. 44, sec. 97 (p. 1811).
44. *Ibid.*, ch. 103, sec. 35 (p. 4140).
45. *Ibid.*, sec. 36 (p. 4141).
46. *Ibid.*, ch. 62, sec. 133 (p. 2401).
47. *Ibid.*, ch. 94, sec. 18 (p. 3762).
48. *Wen-chi,* 38:38b, letter in reply to Chan T'i-jen (Chan I-chih).
49. *Yü-lei,* ch. 95, sec. 39 (p. 3851).
50. *Wen-chi,* 56:15a, fifth letter in reply to Fang Pin-wang (Fang I).
51. *Yü-lei,* ch. 93, sec. 60 (p. 3744).
52. *Wen-chi,* 25:2b, first letter in reply to Chang Ching-fu (Chang Shih).
53. *Yü-lei,* ch. 124, sec. 54 (p. 4777).
54. *Ibid.*, sec. 25 (p. 4762).
55. *Wen-chi,* 50:23b, first letter in reply to Cheng Chung-li.
56. *Yü-lei,* ch. 103, sec. 32 (p. 4140).
57. *Ibid.*
58. *Ibid.*, ch. 31, sec. 66 (p. 1279).
59. *Wen-chi,* 24:14b, letter to Ts'ao Chin-shu.
60. *Ibid.*, 40:24a, eleventh letter in reply to Ho Shu-ching (Ho Hao).
61. *Yü-lei,* ch. 108, sec. 44 (pp. 4271–4272).
62. *Wen-chi,* 87:8b, funeral address for Chang Shih.
63. *Ibid.*, 87:9b, second funeral address for Chang Shih.
64. *Ibid.*, 34:25a, eighty-third letter in reply to Lü Po-kung (Lü Tsu-ch'ien).
65. *Ibid.*, 85:10a, eulogy for Chang Shih's portrait.
66. *Ibid.*, 89:8b, tomb inscription for Chang Shih.
67. *Ibid.*, 87:9b, second funeral address for Chang Shih.
68. *Yü-lei,* ch. 19, sec. 67 (p. 705).
69. *Analects,* 1:11.
70. *Yü-lei,* ch. 22, sec. 29 (p. 825); sec. 30 (p. 827).
71. *Analects,* 7:20.
72. *Yü-lei,* ch. 83, sec. 99 (p. 3438).
73. *Analects,* 12:1.
74. *Yü-lei,* ch. 41, sec. 90 (p. 1702).
75. *Analects,* 4:10.
76. *Yü-lei,* ch. 26, sec. 97 (p. 1066); ch. 113, sec. 32 (p. 4378).
77. *Analects,* 6:4.
78. *Yü-lei,* ch. 31, sec. 7 (p. 1251).
79. *Analects,* 6:9.
80. *Ibid.*, 7:15.
81. *Yü-lei,* ch. 31, sec. 65 (p. 1278).
82. *Analects,* 4:7.
83. *Wen-chi,* 31:5b, sixteenth letter in reply to Chang Ching-fu.
84. *Analects,* 1:4.
85. *Wen-chi,* 31:10a, twenty-first letter in reply to Chang Ching-fu.
86. *Analects,* 4:3.
87. *Wen-chi,* 31:24b, "Discussion with Chang Shih on his *Explanation of the Analects.*"
88. *Analects,* 14:33.
89. *Yü-lei,* ch. 44, sec. 76 (p. 1802).

90. *Analects,* 4:2.

91. *Yü-lei,* ch. 26, sec. 9 (p. 1032).

92. *Book of Mencius,* 2A:2.

93. *Yü-lei,* ch. 63, sec. 75 (p. 2437).

94. *Book of Mencius,* 2A:6.

95. *Yü-lei,* ch. 53, sec. 63 (p. 2051).

96. *Book of Mencius,* 4B:26.

97. *Yü-lei,* ch. 57, sec. 59 (p. 2145).

98. *Doctrine of the Mean,* ch. 12.

99. *Yü-lei,* ch. 63, sec. 80 (p. 2439).

100. *Ibid.,* ch. 67, sec. 73 (p. 2646). See also ch. 72, sec. 80 (p. 2917); ch. 70, sec. 133 (p. 2809); ch. 60, sec. 7 (p. 2578); *Nan-hsüan Hsien-sheng wen-chi,* 23:2b (p. 716), forty-fourth letter in reply to Chu Yüan-hui.

101. *Doctrine of the Mean,* ch. 1. It is said here, "Before the feelings of pleasure, anger, sorrow, and joy are aroused, it is called equilibrium (*chung,* centrality, Mean)."

102. *Book of Changes,* "Appended Remarks," pt. 1, ch. 10.

103. *Ibid.*

104. *Yü-lei,* ch. 95, sec. 2 (pp. 3383–3384).

105. *Book of Changes,* "Appended Remarks," pt. 1, ch. 4.

106. *Yü-lei,* ch. 94, sec. 106 (p. 3789).

107. In the *Chou Tzu ch'üan-shu* [Complete works of Master Chou Tun-i] (*Kuo-hsüeh chi-pen ts'ung-shu* [Basic sinological series] ed.), ch. 1, p. 14.

108. *Wen-chi,* 31:2b–3a, twelfth letter in reply to Chang Ching-fu.

109. *Nan-hsüan Hsien-sheng wen-chi,* 21:2a (p. 667), fifteenth letter in reply to Chu Yuan-hui; *Wen-chi,* 30:23a, letter to Chang Ch'in-fu on changing some words in the *I-shu* [Surviving works].

110. *Yü-lei,* ch. 89, sec. 3 (p. 3603).

111. *Ibid.,* ch.135, sec. 69 (p. 5186).

112. *Ibid.,* ch. 44, sec. 97 (p. 1811).

113. *Wen-chi,* 31:6a, seventeenth letter in reply to Chang Ching-fu.

114. *I-shu,* 1:7b, in the *Erh-Ch'eng ch'üan-shu* [Complete works of the two Ch'engs] (*SPPY* ed.).

115. *Yü-lei,* ch. 95, sec. 39 (p. 3851).

116. See above, n. 46.

117. *Yü-lei,* ch. 100, sec. 46 (p. 4054).

118. *Wen-chi,* 30:18a–b, second letter in reply to Chang Ch'in-fu.

119. *Fu* (to return) is the twenty-fourth hexagram in the *Book of Changes.*

120. *Yü-lei,* ch. 103, sec. 43 (p. 4142).

121. *Wen-chi,* 30:28b, ninth letter in reply to Chang Ch'in-fu.

122. *Nan-hsüan Hsien-sheng wen-chi,* 36:2a (p. 1055), "K'o-chi ming" [Inscription on self-mastery].

123. *Yü-lei,* ch. 41, sec. 17 (p. 1665).

124. *Ibid.,* ch. 3, sec. 19 (p. 58).

125. *Analects,* 14:17, 18.

126. *Yü-lei,* ch. 44, sec. 54 (p. 1793).

127. *Ibid.,* ch. 105, sec. 55 (p. 4190).

128. *Ibid.,* ch. 101, sec. 144 (p. 4103).

129. *Ibid.*, ch. 47, sec. 23 (p. 1881).

130. *Ibid.*, ch. 63, sec. 130 (p. 2462).

131. *Ibid.*, ch. 27, sec. 83 (p. 1114).

132. *Ibid.*, ch. 136, sec. 6 (p. 5192).

133. *Wen-chi,* 45:11a, letter in reply to Wu Te-fu (Wu Lieh).

134. *Yü-lei,* ch. 94, sec. 43 (p. 3771).

135. *Ibid.*, sec. 29 (p. 3766).

136. Chu Hsi, *Ta-hsüeh huo-wen* [Questions and answers on the *Great Learning*] (*Chin-shih han-chi ts'ung-k'an* ed.), p. 9a–b (pp. 17–18), comment on the text. See also the *Yü-lei,* ch. 17, sec. 45 (p. 616).

137. *Chou Tzu ch'üan-shu,* ch. 2, p. 23, "T'ai-chi-t'u shuo."

138. These are the Four Qualities of the *ch'ien* (Heaven, male) hexagram in the *Book of Changes*.

139. *Wen-chi,* 31:5b–6a, sixteenth letter in reply to Chang Ching-fu.

140. *Ibid.*, 42:1a, first letter in reply to Hu Kuang-chung (Hu Shih).

141. *Yü-lei,* ch. 26, sec. 63 (p. 1054).

142. *Ibid.*, ch. 103, sec. 39 (p. 4141); ch. 9, sec. 5 (pp. 235–236).

143. Wang Mao-hung, *Chu Tzu nien-p'u* [Chronological biography of Master Chu] (*Ts'ung-shu chi-ch'eng* [Collection of series] ed.), p. 258, under the third year of Ch'ien-tao (1167).

144. *Ibid.*, p. 257, under the same year.

145. *Yü-lei,* ch. 103, sec. 41 (p. 4142).

146. *Wen-chi,* 24:14b–15a, letter to Ts'ao Chin-shu.

147. *Ibid.*, 42:22b–23a, fifth letter in reply to Shih Tzu-chung (Shih Tun).

148. *Doctrine of the Mean,* ch. 1.

149. Wang Mao-hung, *Chu Tzu-nien-p'u,* ch. 1A, pp. 23–25, under the second year of Ch'ien-tao (1166).

150. Ch'ien Mu, *Chu Tzu hsin-hsüeh-an* [New anthology and critical accounts of Master Chu] (Taipei: San-min Book Co., 1971), vol. 2, pp. 134, 140, 160.

151. *Wen-chi,* 30:19a–b, third letter to Chang Ch'in-fu.

152. *Ibid.*, p. 20b, fourth letter.

153. Ch'eng I, preface to his *I chuan* [Commentary on the *Book of Changes*].

154. *Wen-chi,* 32:4a–b, thirty-third letter in reply to Chang Ching-fu.

155. *Ibid.*, p. 5a–b, thirty-fourth letter.

156. *Nan-hsüan Hsien-sheng wen-chi,* 20:4a–b (pp. 645–646), fifth letter in reply to Chu Yüan-hui.

157. *Ibid.*, p. 5b (648), sixth letter.

158. *Wen-chi,* 41:17a–b, fifth letter in reply to Ch'eng Yün-fu (Ch'eng Hsün).

159. *Ibid.*, 43:18a, third letter in reply to Lin Tse-chih (Lin Yung-chung).

160. *Ibid.*, p. 30b, twenty-second letter.

161. *I-shu,* 18:5b.

162. *Wen-chi,* 64:28b–29a, "First letter to the Gentlemen of Hunan on Equilibrium and Harmony." For an English translation, see my *A Source Book in Chinese Philosophy* (Princeton, N.J.: Princeton University Press, 1963), pp. 600–602. The "I-fa wei-fa chi" [Account of what has been aroused and what has not been aroused], in the *Wen-chi,* 67:10a, is the draft of the letter.

163. *Ibid.*, 32:25a–26b, forty-seventh letter in reply to Chang Ch'in-fu. Ths

first concluding quotation comes from Chou Tun-i's "T'ai-chi-t'u shuo" (Diagram of the Great Ultimate); the second is from the Ch'eng brothers, in the *I-shu*, 5:2b.

164. *Wen-chi*, 75:22b–23b.

165. *Ibid.*, 73:40a–47b. What Hu Hung said and what Chu Hsi quoted here is not included in the present edition of the *Hu Tzu chih-yen* [Master Hu's understanding of words], which is in six chapters. Chang Shih and Lü Tsu-ch'ien's comments are not found in their literary collections, either.

166. *Yü-lei*, ch. 101, sec. 154 (p. 4104).

167. *I-shu*, 1:7b. The saying is generally ascribed to Ch'eng Hao.

168. *Yü-lei*, ch. 103, sec. 42 (p. 4142).

169. *Wen-chi*, 73:44a, "*Hu Tzu chih-yen* i-i" [Doubts on *Master Hu's Understanding of Words*].

170. *Ibid.*, 67:20a–21b. See n. 67, above, for Chu Hsi's remark in his funeral address.

171. *Ibid.*, 32:16b–21b, forty-second through forty-fifth letters in reply to Chang Ch'in-fu on the "Jen-shuo"; *Nan-hsüan Hsien-sheng wen-chi*, 20:7b (p. 652), ninth letter in reply to Chu Yüan-hui; 21:5b (p. 674), twenty-first letter.

172. See ch. 11 above.

173. *Wen-chi*, 31:7b, eighteenth letter in reply to Chang Ching-fu; *Yü-lei*, ch. 103, sec. 48 (p. 4142); ch. 118, sec. 47 (p. 4552).

174. *T'ai-p'ing ch'ing-hua* [Light comments on time of peace] (*Pao-yen-t'ang pi-chi* [Treasures of the Hall of Precious Appearance] ed.), 1:8a.

175. See above, n. 35.

176. *Nan-hsüan Hsien-sheng wen-chi*, 23:12a (p. 735) fifty-third letter in reply to Chu Yuan-hui.

# Chu Hsi and
# Lü Tsu-ch'ien

Lü Tsu-ch'ien's (1137–1181) courtesy name was Po-kung. He was a native of Wu-chou.[1] Because an ancestor of his was made Duke of Tung-lai in the Lai-chou Prefecture[2] during the Han dynasty (206 B.C.– A.D. 220), he was honored as Master of Tung-lai. His family had been prominent for generations. His grandfather, Lü Pen-chung (1084– 1145), was the first to be called Master of Tung-lai. Therefore he was called the Senior Tung-lai and Tsu-ch'ien the Junior Tung-lai. The Lü family not only served as high officials for generations, ranking as departmental ministers and lecturers before the emperor; they also passed on a traditional scholarship. The *Sung-Yüan hsüeh-an* (Anthology and critical accounts of Neo-Confucians of the Sung and Yüan dynasties) devotes four chapters to the Lü family, which boasted seventeen thinkers in seven generations.[3]

Tsu-ch'ien's learning was based on this family tradition. When he grew up, he studied with Lin Chih-ch'i (1112–1176), Wang Ying-ch'en (1118–1176), and Hu Hsien (1086–1162), but in interest and spirit he remained strictly in the family tradition. He studied documents extensively and scrutinized history. He did not attack heterodox schools but preferred compromise and harmony. He was particularly interested in rituals, agriculture, and similar practical arts that can be applied to ordering the state and society. Although this interest gave his work a utilitarian flavor, he was able to avoid the extremes of Chekiang utilitarians like Ch'en Fu-liang (1137–1203) and Ch'en Liang (1143–1194), while absorbing their good points. Thus he became the founder of the Chekiang historical school. As many as three hundred scholars gathered around him.[4]

In his later years, Tsu-ch'ien taught at the Li-tse Academy in Chin-hua City, a center for scholars in Chekiang.[5] As Chu Hsi wrote, "Po-kung said that when he was young, he had a bad temper. If he did not like the food, he would throw the dishes to the ground. Later, when he became ill and lay in bed for a long time, he read the *Analects* day and night. He suddenly calmed down, and throughout his life he was never angry again."[6] Chu Hsi also said, "[Confucius said], 'He who requires much from himself and little from others will stay clear of resentment.'[7] In the past, Venerable Lü had a quick temper. When he read the *Analects* during an illness, he was inspired by this aphorism. Ever since, he became good like this."[8] As Chu Hsi recalled, "Lü was not a good talker. He was difficult to understand. Even his greeting was unintelligible, because his accent was hard to follow."[9] Chang Shih (1133–1180) also mentioned that Lü's dress was untidy and his movements careless.[10] According to Chu Hsi, Lü "read during illness late into the night."[11] The three knew one another well. They were fast friends, since they were outstanding scholars of the time.

Chu Hsi and Lü Tsu-ch'ien first met about 1156. When Chu Hsi was *chu-pu* (assistant magistrate) at T'ung-an in southern Fukien from 1153 to 1156, Lü's father went to Foochow to serve as an official and Tsu-ch'ien accompanied him. It is likely that Chu Hsi met him at that time, because he later wrote Lü that "it has been several years since we parted in San-shan [Foochow]."[12] Twenty years later, in 1175, Lü visited Chu Hsi at his Han-ch'üan Ching-she (Cold Spring Study) in northern Fukien. Together they compiled the *Chin-ssu lu,* which I have translated as *Reflections on Things at Hand.*[13] Lü also arranged for Chu Hsi and Lu Hsiang-shan (1139–1193) to become acquainted. In journeying to the Cold Spring Study, he left Chin-hua on the twenty-first day of the third month, and on the first day of the fourth month arrived at Wu-fu Village, where Chu Hsi lived, and stayed in the study.[14] After compiling the *Chin-ssu lu* in the fifth month, Chu Hsi, Lü, and some pupils and friends toured Mount Wu-i on the twenty-first day, on the way to Ch'ien-shan County in present Kiangsi Province for the famous meeting at the Goose Lake Temple in the sixth month.[15] In the third month of the following year, Chu Hsi went to Wu-yüan[16] to visit his ancestral graves. Since he was going to pass through Ch'ü-chou,[17] he asked Lü to meet him nearby. Lü did so, and they spent several days together.[18]

The two friends corresponded frequently. In the *Wen-chi,* 104 letters in reply to Lü Po-kung are preserved, more than to anyone else.[19] In the *Tung-lai Lü T'ai-shih wen-chi* (Collection of literary works of Lü Tsu-ch'ien, member of the Han-lin Academy), there are 67 letters to Chu Hsi,[20] more than double the number to anyone else. Their correspondence naturally dealt with philosophical subjects, but they also discussed personal matters, such as requests for a sinecure or a temple superintendency, whether or not to serve in the government, Chu Hsi's printing enterprise, and the situations of their friends. The meeting at the Goose Lake Temple had ended with displeasure for both Chu Hsi and Lu Hsiang-shan. Neither Chu Hsi nor Lü Tsu-ch'ien could get the matter off his mind. Therefore, in their correspondence, the two repeatedly talked about the Lu brothers. To Chu Hsi, Lu Hsiang-shan was too self-confident, and there was little hope that his attitude would change.[21] Lü, however, only talked about Lu Hsiang-shan's good points, for his purpose was to patch up their differences.[22]

From letters between Chu Hsi and Lü, we learn about the education of Chu Hsi's eldest son, their concern for each other's families, their mutual admonitions, and their cooperation on social institutions. Chu Hsi's eldest son, Shu, had been born in 1153. When Shu reached twenty-one, Chu Hsi felt that he was too lazy to accomplish anything in his studies[23] and could not concentrate because of distractions. There were not many friends around, and Chu Hsi himself did not want to supervise him day and night.[24] Therefore he sent Shu to Chin-hua to study with Lü. Lü arranged for the young man to live and board with his pupil P'an Ching-hsien (1137–1193). Three or four years later, P'an gave his eldest daughter to Shu in marriage. When Shu went to Chin-hua, Chu Hsi gave him a letter in which he instructed him to keep daily records, not to be lazy, not to go out without permission, not to associate freely with people, not to make fun or too much noise, and not to drink. Details were also given on how to act and what to say when Shu arrived in Chin-hua.[25] In the several years after Shu's arrival, Chu Hsi wrote Lü seven or eight times to ask Lü to discipline his son severely.[26] Lü obliged. He told Chu Hsi in a letter that "every day, when Shu comes to my place, he comes with Shu-tu [P'an Ching-hsien] and his brother. Shu is not allowed to go to other pupils' lodges. Even when he comes to my place, he is not allowed to come alone. Such strict measures are necessary in the city."[27] Under such a discipline, Shu's schoolwork was bound to show progress. During his six years at Chin-hua, Shu returned home four times, once to mourn the death of his mother and three times to take the local civil service examinations. The last time, in 1180, he took his wife and child home to stay. As for the examinations, he failed every time.

Chu Hsi showed great concern for his own and Lü's families. More than once he wrote Lü about Shu's marriage.[28] He also told Lü about his search for a bride for his second son, Yeh.[29] He expressed sorrow to Lü upon the death of Lü's aunt.[30] In 1176, when his own wife died, Chu Hsi wrote Lü and said, "I cannot stand the bitterness of my sorrow."[31] He also inquired repeatedly about Lü's wife's illness. When she finally passed away, he conveyed to Lü his sadness and urged Lü to "control your feelings for the sake of propriety." "Since your health is not yet fully recovered," he added, "you should greatly restrain your sorrow."[32] At the death of Lü's father, Chu Hsi's poverty precluded his offering libations in the form of money, a fact that deepened his sorrow.[33] When Lü's younger brother passed away, he also extended condolences.[34] On his part, Lü showed much interest in Chu Hsi's choice of a burial plot for his wife.[35] All these concerns indicate the intimate feeling between the two friends.

Because they were very close, it is to be expected that they were frank in admonishing each other. As Chu Hsi wrote Chang Shih, "Since Po-kung stoops to ask me questions, I dare not keep my thoughts to myself."[36] He therefore advised Lü on the importance of self-cultivation and the pursuit of knowledge, as well as on correcting mistakes. In response, Lü said, "You have pinpointed my great defect and I shall never forget it when I reflect, day or night."[37] And just as Chu Hsi admonished Lü, so Lü warned Chu Hsi. He told Chu Hsi that "in your readiness to be aroused, you seem to lack an air of broadness and warmth."[38] Actually, each lacked a certain balance. That is why Chu Hsi said,

Perhaps, you, Po-kung, have the natural gift of warmth and generosity, and that is why what you say is calm, considerate, and accommodating, but I suffer from being irascible, and therefore in what I say, I always show the force of going forward and striving to succeed. In my humble opinion, when judged according to the Principle of Heaven, I am afraid neither is the Mean. The way I express myself is enough to hurt myself and injure others, and that is particularly detestable. At the same time, you, Po-kung, should not regard your imbalance as perfectly correct.[39]

Several days after he received Lü's obituary, Chu Hsi composed a poem in which he said, "I am thinking of my man of simple character and mind."[40] The two men understood each other and seemed to continue to communicate in spirit.

With regard to their cooperation in undertakings, three are worth mentioning, namely, those concerning the *Chin-ssu lu,* the White Deer Hollow Academy, and the community granary. All were important undertakings in Chu Hsi's career, exerted a tremendous influence on Chinese history and thought, and benefited from Lü Tsu-ch'ien's contributions. The *Chin-ssu lu* was the model for later Neo-Confucian anthologies and exercised a strong influence on Chinese thought for several hundred years. In the introduction to my translation of this work, I quoted what Chu Hsi had to say about it, fully explained its impact in China, Korea, and Japan, provided the sources of the passages it quotes, and described all the Chinese, Korean, and Japanese commentaries on it.[41] The White Deer Hollow Academy also served as the standard for Neo-Confucian academies throughout the centuries.

Chu Hsi asked Lü to write an account of the academy to emphasize its educational significance and historical importance. They took the account so seriously that they discussed it paragraph by paragraph.[42] In 1171, Chu Hsi established a community granary in Wu-fu Village. It inaugurated the system of local granaries—an epoch-making innovation. When Lü saw it during his trip to the Cold Spring Study, he was so impressed that he wanted to establish one in Chin-hua. But he died before his dream came true. Later, his pupil P'an Ching-hsien persuaded his father to donate rice to establish the Chin-hua Community Granary.[43] Thus the institution of community granaries spread from Fukien to Chekiang.

Although Chu Hsi and Lü Tsu-ch'ien were congenial, they often disagreed on ideas. Chu Hsi considered the *Book of History* hard to read, but Lü thought otherwise, only to share Chu Hsi's viewpoint some years later.[44] To Chu Hsi, Lü's explanation of the *Book of Odes* was too detailed and rigid, and did not see through the individual prefaces, which Chu Hsi said turn the love poems into moral injunctions.[45] However, he praised Lü's comments on a particular ode[46] as showing profound insight,[47] and gave Lü special credit for separating the text and the commentary in the *Book of Odes*.[48] In addition, Lü loved to discuss the *Tso chuan* (Tso's commentary on the *Spring and Autumn Annals*) with students. Chu Hsi criticized this and said, "He did not talk about the many principles in the *Analects*, the *Book of Mencius*, and the Six Classics, but liked to talk about this book. Even if it offers some miscellaneous principles, what good does it do?"[49] Previously, he had written Lü to say, "I have seen that you discussed with your students Tso's commentary in a thorough and extensive way. However, in your words and ideas, you suffer from a certain degree of ingenuity."[50] Moreover, Lü considered Hu Hung's (1106–1161) *Hu Tzu chih-yen* (Master Hu's understanding of words) to be superior to Chang Tsai's (1020–1077) *Cheng-meng* (Correcting youthful ignorance), whereas Chu Hsi regarded the scope of the *Cheng-meng* as large and that of the *Chih-yen* as small.[51] Chu Hsi also pointed out that both Lü and Chang Shih taught their students to read Ch'eng I's (1033–1107) *I chuan* (Commentary on the *Book of Changes*). In most cases, he said, the students did not learn anything, for they had no doubts and did not do their own thinking. There are many questionable points about the component lines of the hexagrams and the text, Chu Hsi noted, and one must understand their principles before they become relevant to daily practice.[52]

Another point of difference was that Chu Hsi vigorously attacked Su Hsün (1009–1066), his eldest son Su Shih (1037–1101), and his second son Su Ch'e (1039–1112). Su Shih wrote the *I chieh* (Explanation of the *Book of Changes*), which Chu Hsi considered to embody the doctrines of the Buddha and Lao Tzu. Su Ch'e wrote the *Lao Tzu chieh* (Explanation of the *Lao Tzu*), which Chu Hsi considered to be an "interpretation of Confucianism in the light of Taoism, and moreover, a cover-up with Buddhism."[53] To Lü, however, their doctrines were not like those of Yang Chu or Mo Tzu (whom Mencius strongly attacked), and hence did not need to be disputed at any length.[54] But Chu Hsi persisted in his opposition and wrote Lü to say, "You, Po-kung, still want to accommodate them. Have you not thought the matter over?"[55] He also wrote Chang Shih and said, "He [Lü] has for a long time been interested in the literary composition of the civil service examinations. Having gone in and out of the current of ingenuity of the Su father and sons, he has sought an ingenuity of his own. Consequently, he has damaged his thinking and all along has not considered the Su learning to be wrong. He covers it up from left and right, and rejects it openly but aids it secretly. This makes people feel disappointed all the more."[56] Chang Shih sought a compromise and wrote Chu Hsi, "Recently Po-kung likes to talk. He knows well the mistakes of the Su father and sons. As I see him, he is not aiding the Su family. . . . He merely does not want to criticize them openly."[57]

To seek compromise and harmony was characteristic of the learning of the Lü family. Therefore Lü did not speak out vigorously on the dispute between Confucianism and Buddhism.[58] As Chu Hsi said, "He is deathly afraid to talk about the errors of the heterodox schools and vulgar learning. He especially defends the Su father and sons. He thinks that instead of engaging in controversy, it is better to confine oneself to cultivation."[59] To Lü, Chu Hsi's concentrated effort on attacking other schools, as if engaging in battle to win or lose, "seems to lack broadmindedness."[60] Chu Hsi, however, was "afraid that Po-kung is not free from secretly upholding Buddhist ideas in what he says, but because of the depth and vastness of his moral nature, he does not want to say it out loud."[61] We can readily see that the personalities of the two friends were different, and that both lacked what Chu Hsi himself referred to as the Mean.

Indeed, the starting points of the two scholars were different, so it is not surprising that their views were not the same. Chu Hsi emphasized the moral principles of the mind and nature; Lü seldom talked about these. For Chu Hsi, the basis was the Confucian classics; for Lü, it was history.[62] Chu Hsi laid special emphasis on the *Analects;* Lü did not teach his students to read this classic.[63] Chu Hsi held that only with the pursuit of learning can one transform physical nature; Lü held that only after one has transformed one's physical nature can one pursue learning.[64] From Chu Hsi's standpoint, "Tung-lai's merit lies in extensive learning and much information, but he has yet to hold on to simplicity. . . . His defect lies entirely in ingenuity."[65] He also said, "Po-kung's defect lies in [explaining] too much, while Tzu-ching's [Lu Hsiang-

shan] defect lies in [explaining] too little,"[66] and "Lü is extremely inge-
nious in fabrication, while Lu loves agreement and is impulsive."[67] As
to Lü's effort toward extensive and miscellaneous learning, attention to
civil service examinations, confused discussions and complicated conversations, these were but minor matters.[68]

Since the opinions of the two thinkers were in many instances diametrically opposed, and since their personal characters were vastly different, it is surprising that they nevertheless agreed in many respects.
Despite their differences, they succeeded in producing the *Chin-ssu lu*.
Chu Hsi conducted an extensive correspondence with both Lü Tsu-
ch'ien and Chang Shih on two of his major treatises, namely, the "*Hu
Tzu chih-yen* i-i" (Doubts on *Master Hu's Understanding of Words*)[69] and the
"Jen-shuo" (Treatise on humanity).[70] In both cases, Chu Hsi took
many years to think about and accept suggestions from various scholars. Yet in a letter to Lü, he said, "Although I have differed from you in
many places, the time is not far off when our discussions will reach an
agreement, for the divergence of our views is but infinitesimal."[71]

Chu Hsi and Lü Tsu-ch'ien were bound to reach an agreement
because they were outstanding thinkers in the Learning of the Way *(tao-
hsüeh)*. Their differences were minor, their agreements major. Although
their personalities and viewpoints were not the same, that did not prevent them from acting with cooperation and mutual respect. In the *Sung
shih* (History of the Sung dynasty), the biography of Lü Tsu-ch'ien is in
the *Ju-lin chuan* (Biographies of Confucians) but not in the *Tao-hsüeh
chuan* (Biographies of the Learning of the Way). This is sheer partisanship and would not have been sanctioned by Chu Hsi. In characterizing
Lü's formulation of theories, Chu Hsi said,

> He synthesized various doctrines and left out nothing. He pointed out the
> main points so that there is a penetrating comprehensiveness from the
> beginning to the end. He settled disputes in a satisfactory manner. In his
> own style of writing, harmonious synthesis is so penetrating that it is
> merged as if it were his own school of thought. He was always careful in
> acknowledging the source of the explanation of a single word or the mean-
> ings of a single event. If at times he went beyond what previous thinkers
> had considered in making his own judgment, he would decline credit and
> never intended to criticize even slightly thinkers who went before him.[72]

Therefore, Chu Hsi characterized Lü as "warm, tender, honest, and
sincere,"[73] and also as "kind and tolerant, with a compassionate
heart."[74]

When Lü died, in 1181, Chu Hsi set up an altar to mourn him and
sent an offering of libations to his family. His funeral address begins by
saying,

How severely has Heaven cut off this cultural tradition! Last year, Heaven took away my Ching-fu [Chang Shih]. Why now is Po-kung not spared? Who is going to promote the Learning of the Way? Who is going to restore the virtue of the ruler? Who is going to teach the rising generation? Who is going to benefit the people? Who is going to continue the explanation of the classics? And who is going to carry on the recording of events? As to my stupidity, who is going to admonish me on my defects and reprove me for my mistakes? This being the case, how can your death, Po-kung, not compel me to weep aloud and cry to Heaven in sorrow?[75]

Chu Hsi wrote over a hundred funeral addresses. This and his second funeral address for Chang Shih are the most moving of them all.
  Chu Hsi continued,

Your moral capacity is vast and your intellectual ability extensive. You received from various sources like an ocean and gathered like a river. You purified the water and avoided the impurity. You submerged yourself in the instructions and literature of your family. Making your teacher prominent and associating intimately with friends, you extended your inquiry to every corner. As your endowment was rich and your cultivation profound, what you acquired is extensive and what you completed is pure. Thus what you established is high and what you sought is complete. Consequently, just as you discussed learning at home, there is the transforming influence by the timely rain. As you went forward to serve in the government, your high position was exemplary.[76]

This is not a conventional eulogy but a speech from Chu Hsi's heart. Lü's pupil, P'an Shu-tu, painted his portrait. Chu Hsi's inscription for it says, "When he extended what he had, it was enough to honor the ruler and benefit the people. When he offered his surplus, it was enough to become a model for society and a heritage for generations."[77] There were certainly more than sufficient reasons for Chu Hsi to honor and respect his friend.

## Notes

  1. Present Chin-hua County, Chekiang Province.
  2. Present Yeh County, Shantung Province.
  3. *Sung-Yüan hsüeh-an* [Anthology and critical accounts of the Neo-Confucians of the Sung and Yüan dynasties] (*SPPY* ed.), chs. 23, 31, 36, and 51.
  4. *Tung-lai Lü T'ai-shih wen-chi* [Collection of literary works of Lü Tsu-ch'ien, member of the Han-lin Academy] (*Hsü Chin-hua ts'ung-shu* [Supplement to the *Chin-hua Series*] ed.), separate collection, 9:8a, letter to Liu Tzu-ch'eng (Liu Ch'ing-chih).

5. *Sung shih* [History of the Sung dynasty] (Beijing: Chung-hua Book Co., 1977) ch. 434, biography of Lü Tsu-ch'ien, p. 12874.

6. *Wen-chi,* 54:22a, fourth letter in reply to Lu Te-chang.

7. *Analects,* 15:14.

8. *Yü-lei,* ch. 122, sec. 8 (p. 4720).

9. *Ibid.,* ch. 95, sec. 177 (p. 3905).

10. *Nan-hsüan Hsien-sheng wen-chi* [Collection of literary works of Chang Shih] (*Chin-shih han-chi ts'ung-k'an* [Chinese works of the recent period series] ed.), 25:4a (p. 765), second letter to Lü Po-kung (Lü Tsu-ch'ien).

11. *Wen-chi,* 82:2a, inscription of Lü Po-kung's folio.

12. *Ibid.,* 33:1a, first letter in reply to Lü Po-kung.

13. For the *Chin-ssu lu,* see ch. 22 above. My translation, entitled *Reflections on Things at Hand,* was published by the Columbia University Press of New York in 1967.

14. *Tung-lai Lü T'ai-shih wen-chi,* ch. 15, "Records of Arrival in Fukien."

15. See ch. 26 below.

16. A county in Wu-chou in Anhui in Chu Hsi's time, but now in Kiangsi.

17. Ch'ü County in Chekiang.

18. *Wen-chi,* 33:31a, 33b, forty-fifth and forty-eighth letters in reply to Lü Po-kung.

19. Of Chu Hsi's 104 known letters to Lü Tsu-ch'ien, 3 are in the *Wen-chi,* ch. 25; 100 are in chs. 33–35; and 1 is in the supplementary collection, ch. 5.

20. *Tung-lai Lü T'ai-shih wen-chi,* separate collection, chs. 7 and 8.

21. *Wen-chi,* 34:4b, fifty-sixth letter; p. 17a, seventy-seventh letter; p. 23b, eighty-first letter; 26a, eighty-second letter; p. 32a, ninetieth letter; p. 33a, ninety-second letter; p. 34a, ninety-third letter.

22. *Tung-lai Lü T'ai-shih wen-chi,* separate collection, 8:1b, twenty-second letter; p. 11b, fifty-fourth letter; p. 12b, fifty-fifth letter; p. 15a, sixty-second letter.

23. *Wen-chi,* 33:12a, eighteenth letter in reply to Lü Po-kung.

24. *Ibid.,* supplementary collection, 8:7a, letter to the eldest son Shou-chih (Chu Shu).

25. *Ibid.,* pp. 6a–8b. See also ch. 3 above.

26. *Ibid.,* regular collection, 33:13b, twentieth letter in reply to Lü Po-kung; p. 14b, twenty-second letter; p. 15b, twenty-third letter; p. 18b, twenty-seventh letter; p. 26b, thirty-ninth letter; p. 30a, forty-second letter; 34:10a, sixty-seventh letter; p. 16b, seventy-sixth letter.

27. *Tung-lai Lü T'ai-shi wen-chi,* separate collection, 7:16b–17a, twentieth letter to Lecturer-in-waiting Chu.

28. *Wen-chi,* 33:26a, thirty-eighth letter in reply to Lü Po-kung; 34:1a, fiftieth letter; p. 1b, fifty-first letter.

29. *Ibid.,* 33:26a, thirty-eighth letter.

30. *Ibid.,* p. 10b, fifteenth letter.

31. *Ibid.,* 34:2a, fifty-second; p. 2b, fifty-third letter.

32. *Ibid.,* 34:11b, sixty-ninth letter; p. 13b, seventieth letter; 33:8a, ninth letter; 34:16a, seventy-sixth letter.

33. *Ibid.,* 33:10a, thirteenth and fourteenth letter.

34. *Ibid.,* p. 26a, thirty-ninth letter.

35. *Tung-lai Lü T'ai-shih wen-chi,* separate collection, 8:5b, thirty-third letter; p. 6a, thirty-fifth letter.

36. *Wen-chi,* 31:3a, twelfth letter in reply to Chang Ch'in-fu (Chang Shih).

37. *Tung-lai Lü T'ai-shih wen-chi,* separate collection, 7:7a, third letter; p. 10b, seventh letter, 8:6b, thirty-seventh letter.

38. *Ibid.,* 7:6b, second letter.

39. *Wen-chi,* 33:6b, seventh letter in reply to Lü Po-kung.

40. *Ibid.,* 8:1b.

41. *Reflection on Things at Hand,* pp. 309–358. See also ch. 22 above.

42. *Ibid.,* 34:12a–23a, letter to Lü on the White Deer Hollow Academy.

43. *Ibid.,* 79:15b–17a, "Account of the Community Granary at Chin-hua, Wu-chou Prefecture." See also ch. 24 above.

44. *Yü-lei,* ch. 79, sec. 18, 19 (p. 3150); sec. 140 (p. 3270); *Wen-chi,* 83:7b, inscription on Lü Po-kung's *Explanation of the Book of History.*

45. *Yü-lei,* ch. 81, sec. 106 (p. 3364); ch. 122, sec. 9 (p. 4720).

46. Ode no. 164 in the *Book of Odes.*

47. *Yü-lei,* ch. 81, sec. 97 (p. 3361).

48. *Ibid.,* ch. 80, sec. 100 (p. 3326).

49. *Ibid.,* ch. 121, sec. 75 (p. 4699–4700). See also ch. 83, sec. 32 (p. 3407). The Six Classics are the *Book of Odes,* the *Book of History,* the *Book of Changes,* the *Book of Rites,* the *Spring and Autumn Annals,* and the *Book of Music.* The latter was lost before the third century B.C. and replaced with the *Chou-li* (Rites of Chou) during the Sung dynasty (960–1279).

50. *Wen-chi,* 33:6a, sixth letter in reply to Lü Po-kung.

51. *Yü-lei,* ch. 101, sec. 153 (p. 4104).

52. *Ibid.,* ch. 67, sec. 21 (p. 2626); *Wen-chi,* 50:23b, first letter in reply to Cheng Chung-li.

53. *Wen-chi,* 72:22b, "The *I chieh* by Su," p. 23b, "The *Lao Tzu chieh* by Vice Prime Minister Su [Su Ch'e]."

54. *Tung-lai Lü T'ai-shih wen-chi,* separate collection, 7:7b, third letter to Lecturer-in-waiting Chu. For Mencius' attack on Yang and Mo, see the *Book of Mencius,* 3B:9.

55. *Wen-chi,* 33:5a, fifth letter in reply to Lü Po-kung.

56. *Ibid.,* 31:4a, thirteenth letter to Chang Ching-fu (Chang Shih).

57. *Nan-Hsuan Hsien-sheng wen-chi,* 22:3b (p. 696), thirty-fifth letter in reply to Chu Yüan-hui (Chu Hsi).

58. *Wen-chi,* 25:15a, letter to Lü Po-kung.

59. *Ibid.,* 39:45b, eleventh letter in reply to Fan Po-ch'ung (Fan Nien-te); 33:3a, forty-fourth letter in reply to Lü Po-kung.

60. *Tung-lai Lü T'ai-shih wen-chi,* separate collection, 7:6b, second letter to Lecturer-in-waiting Chu; p. 9b, sixth letter.

61. *Wen-chi,* 47:22a, nineteenth letter in reply to Lü Tzu-yüeh (Lü Tsu-chien).

62. *Yü-lei,* ch. 122, sec. 10 (p. 4720); sec. 14 (p. 4721); sec. 15 (p. 4722); *Wen-chi,* 33:33a, forty-seventh letter in reply to Lü Po-kung.

63. *Yü-lei,* ch. 122, secs. 6, 7 (pp. 4720–4721).

64. *Ibid.,* sec. 5 (p. 4719).

65. *Ibid.,* sec. 2 (p. 4719); sec. 19 (p. 4725).

66. *Ibid.*, sec. 4 (p. 4719).

67. *Ibid.*, sec. 3 (p. 4719).

68. *Wen-chi,* 31:3b, 4a, thirteenth letter to Chang Ching-fu (Chang Shih); separate collection, 6:10a, fifteenth letter to Lin Tse-chih (Lin Yung-chung).

69. *Wen-chi,* 73:40b–47b. For a fuller discussion on the *Hu Tzu chih-yen* [Master Hu's understanding of words], see ch. 24 above.

70. *Ibid.*, 33:7b, eighth letter in reply to Lü Po-kung; p. 12a, eighteenth letter; p. 15a, twenty-fourth letter; p. 18a, twenty-seventh letter; p. 20b, thirtieth letter; *Tung-lai Lü T'ai-shih wen-chi,* separate collection, 7:14b, fifteenth letter to Lecturer-in-waiting Chu; p. 15b, seventeeth letter; p. 17a, nineteenth letter. For a fuller discussion on the "Jen-shuo," see ch. 11 above.

71. *Wen-chi,* 33:9b, twelfth letter in reply to Lü Po-kung.

72. *Ibid.*, 76:6b, epilogue to the Lü family school's account of reading the *Book of Odes.*

73. *Ibid.*

74. *Wen-chi,* supplementary collection, 5:1b, letter in reply to Lü Tung-lai (Lü Tsu-ch'ien).

75. *Ibid.*, regular collection, 87:12b, funeral address for Lü Po-kung.

76. *Ibid.*, p. 13a.

77. *Ibid.*, 85:10a, eulogy for Lü's portrait.

# – 26 –

# Chu Hsi and
# Lu Hsiang-shan

Few scholars have been presented as so opposed to one another as Chu Hsi and Lu Hsiang-shan (1139–1193). Literature abounds on the subject of Chu-Lu. No writer can afford to write on Neo-Confucianism without discussing Chu-Lu. They have been regarded as philosophical antagonists. The more I have delved into the subject, however, the more I am convinced that they had a great deal in common and that their personal relationship was quite cordial, although philosophically they refused to compromise. Here I offer new and revealing material on their meeting at the Goose Lake Temple in 1175, on Lu's visit to the White Deer Hollow Academy in 1181, on Chu Hsi's comments on Lu's character, on their personal relationship, on Chu Hsi's much misunderstood remark upon Lu's death, and on Lu's supposed "final conclusion late in life." In this study, I am not concerned with a comparison of their thought, since much has been written about this in more than one language. My discussion is directed to those areas that have heretofore been overlooked.

## The Meeting at the Goose Lake Temple

This meeting was arranged by Lü Tsu-ch'ien (1137–1181). In a long article on the subject published in Chinese, I gathered a great deal of hidden material that led me to conclude that the meeting was not one of confrontation but for purposes of becoming acquainted.[1] I shall now reiterate the essential points in this argument and add some new information.

### The Place

The Goose Lake Temple is located on O-hu (Goose Lake) Mountain, about 15 $li^2$ northeast of the capital of Ch'ien-shan County.[3] Originally called Ho-hu (Lotus Lake) because lotuses flourished here, it was renamed O-hu because, during the Eastern Chin (317–420), a gentleman by the name of Kung raised geese there.[4] Originally, the lake was on a plain about halfway up the mountain; by the T'ang dynasty (618–907), it had become rice fields, and at present its exact location is not to be found. The temple, founded in the Ta-li period (766–769) of the T'ang dynasty, is at the foot of the mountain near a public road. When the temple was rebuilt in the Ch'ing-li period (1041–1048), it was reported that the central hall cost ten million cash, that the library for imperial books had twelve columns, and that images were gilded with gold. There is no information about the temple at the time of the 1175 meeting, but Chu Hsi's contemporary, Yü Liang-neng (1157 *cs*), described it in extravagant terms.[5] According to the *Hsiang-shan ch'üan-chi* (Complete works of Lu Hsiang-shan), Yang Ju-li, prefect of Hsin-chou, built a shrine for the Four Masters (Chu Hsi, Lü Tsu-ch'ien, Lu Hsiang-shan, and his brother Lu Chiu-ling, 1132–1180) by the side of the temple.[6] We do not know when this was done, but we do know that in 1250 the shrine was renamed, with imperial permission, Wen-tsung Shu-yüan (Hsiang-shan Academy).[7] Later it was called O-hu Shu-yüan (Goose Lake Academy). The compound was quite large.

In the 1940s, the academy was still intact. It consisted of three halls in a row, separated by courtyards. The halls at the rear were the shrine for the Four Masters, with their tablets in the main section. In the compound was the Half Moon Pond with a stone bridge. There used to be a decrepit pagoda to the left of the academy, but by the 1940s only some fallen bricks remained. The Republican government used the compound for a school, with accommodations for a thousand students. At that time, there were still a hundred Buddhist monks in the temple on top of the mountain.[8] The academy has now been restored and is open to visitors. The temple was a logical location for the meeting because it was roughly equidistant from the homes of the participants.

## The Dates

Two dates for the meeting are well known. Most writers know that Chu Hsi's epilogue to the *Chin-ssu lu* (Reflections on things at hand), which he and Lü Tsu-ch'ien compiled at the Han-ch'üan Ching-she (Cold Spring Study), is dated the fifth day of the fifth month of 1175.[9] They also know that the Goose Lake meeting dispersed on the eighth day of the sixth month.[10] But few know that on a cliff at the sixth turn of Wu-i River on Mount Wu-i is carved Chu Hsi's calligraphy, in which the names of Lü Po-kung (Lü Tsu-ch'ien) and P'an Shu-ch'ang are mentioned. The date is the twenty-first day of the fifth month. Few writers know, too, that by Lü's own account, he and P'an Shu-ch'ang left Chin-hua, his home in Chekiang, on the twenty-first day of the third month and arrived at Wu-fu Village on the first day of the fourth month, where they stayed in Chu Hsi's study.[11] With these four definite dates, we can reasonably determine that Chu Hsi and Lü spent about a month compiling the *Chin-ssu lu,* then toured Mount Wu-i, and finally arrived at the Goose Lake Temple at the end of the fifth month. The meeting at the temple lasted for ten or twelve days at the most, and may have lasted only five or six days, depending on how much time was spent on the journey from Mount Wu-i to the temple.[12]

## The Participants

Most accounts have repeated the names mentioned in the *Hsiang-shan ch'üan-chi,* that is, Chu Hsi, Lu Hsiang-shan, his brother Lu Tzu-shou (Lu Chiu-ling), Lü Tsu-ch'ien, Chao Ching-ming, Chao Ching-chao, and Liu Tzu-ch'eng.[13] But I would add three more, namely Chu Fu, Chu T'ai-ch'ing, and Tsou Pin, all Lu Hsiang-shan's pupils. According to the *Sung-Yüan hsüeh-an* (Anthology and critical accounts of Neo-Confucians of the Sung and Yüan dynasties), they all attended the meeting at the Goose Lake Temple.[14] In addition, Professor Chang Li-wen of People's University, Beijing, has reminded me in a letter that P'an Shu-ch'ang, who accompanied his teacher to the Cold Spring Study and Mount Wu-i, must have been at the meeting.

Professor Ch'eng Chao-hsiung has suggested that several of Chu Hsi's pupils whose homes were near Goose Lake Mountain could have attended the meeting.[15] Maybe they were what the *Hsiang-shan ch'üan-chi* refers to as "friends from Kiangsi and Chekiang at the meeting."[16] These may also include Chan I-chih, courtesy name T'i-jen, a native of Chekiang, who, according to one source, "was prefect of Hsin-chou when Chu and Lü discussed learning at O-hu and came to ask questions every day,"[17] and Liu Yü, courtesy name Man-weng, a native of Kiangsi, who came to present some poems.[18] If Chan was the prefect of Hsin-chou, where the meeting took place, he should have been the host, but the *Hsiang-shan ch'üan-chi* does not even mention him or Liu.

Of the principal participants, Chao Ching-ming, whose literary name was Cho-chai, was a native of K'ai-feng.[19] Being a magistrate of Lin-ch'uan,[20] he probably acted as host, because he invited his elder brother Ching-chao and Liu Tzu-ch'eng.[21] He had been in contact with Chu Hsi before, but his brother, a follower of Lu Hsiang-shan,[22] met Chu Hsi for the first time at the Goose Lake Temple. Liu Tzu-ch'eng (1139–1195), whose private name was Ch'ing-chih, was a native of Lin-chiang County.[23] He was an associate of both Chu and Lu, though closer to Chu. Among the seven principal participants, Chao Ching-ming was neutral, Chao Ching-chao closer to Lu, and Liu closer to Chu. The three Lu pupils were probably too young to be principal participants. Therefore the composition was quite balanced, perhaps by

the design of Lü Tsu-ch'ien, a well-known compromiser. The main
point is that none of Chu Hsi's pupils were present. Several took part in
the tour of Mount Wu-i, and their names are included in the calligraphic carving on the cliff, but they did not proceed to the Goose Lake
Temple. If the meeting was a confrontation, as has usually been
portrayed, Chu Hsi should have had more representation on his side.[24]

## Topics of Discussion

There was no theme or agenda for the meeting. The participants talked
about anything that came to their minds at any given time. This reinforces the impression that the meeting was for the purpose of getting
acquainted rather than resolving any intellectual conflicts. The records
of the discussion are limited to two passages in the *Hsiang-shan ch'üan-
chi*.[25] The speakers were the Lu brothers and Chu Hsi, followed by Lü
Tsu-ch'ien. The rest merely listened.

From the two passages, we know that the idea paramount in the
minds of the Lu brothers was that Chu Hsi paid too much attention to
books and writing commentaries. They thought that Chu Hsi stressed
extensive learning to the neglect of simplicity. They wrote poems to this
effect just before the meeting, and at the meeting Lu Hsiang-shan asked
Chu Hsi what books there were to read before the time of legendary
sage-emperors Yao and Shun, in the third millenium B.C. We also learn
that when Chu and Lu discussed the order of the hexagrams in the *Book
of Changes,* Lu Hsiang-shan went into a long oration on the important
role of the original mind. According to the record, both Chu Hsi and
Lü Tsu-ch'ien were convinced. It must be remembered that the record
reflects the point of view of the Lu School, and was probably written
some years following the meeting, after partisan spirit had already
arisen in this regard. Hence the customary contrast between the Chu
Hsi School as advocating "following the path of inquiry and study"
and the Lu Hsiang-shan School as advocating "honoring the moral
nature"[26]—a contrast that has been overblown, as if it constituted the
key issue to be resolved at the Goose Lake Temple meeting. However,
as already discussed in chapter 16 above, it is unfair to describe Chu
Hsi as neglecting the mind, for since 1170 he had placed equal emphasis
on cultivating seriousness (*ching,* reverence) and pursuing study, comparing them to the two wings of a bird or two wheels of a vehicle.

Besides simplicity versus extensive learning and the order of the hexagrams, I have found other topics that were discussed at the gathering.
It is recorded in the *Yü-lei* that Lü Tsu-ch'ien was writing a commentary on the *Book of History.* Asked if the classic was difficult to understand, Lü replied that it was not, only to admit several days later that
there were passages difficult to understand.[27] Chu Hsi also asked him if
there were missing words or doubtful interpretations.[28] This seems to

have nothing to do with the meeting and has never been mentioned in connection with it, but it is very significant for the meeting in several ways: it proves that the meeting lasted for several days and that Lü had the leisure to do his own writing; it is the only record of a dialogue between Chu and Lü at the meeting; and, most important of all, it shows that discussions were not limited to the two items reported in the account of the Lu School.

In addition, Lu Chiu-ling presented Chu Hsi with his new essay at the meeting.[29] We do not know what the composition was, because Lu Chiu-ling's collection of literary works was no longer extant by the middle of the eighteenth century.[30] The Lu brothers also praised Ts'ao Chien (1147–1183), who first studied with Lu Hsiang-shan but later shifted to Chu Hsi,[31] much to Lu's disappointment. From Chu Hsi's own recollection, we know that he also talked with Lu Hsiang-shan about the interpretation of the *ch'ien* (Heaven, male) hexagram in the *Book of Changes* as easy and the *k'un* (Earth, female) hexagram as simple.[32]

All these details seem trivial, but they do underscore the point that there was no central issue at the meeting, much less an effort to resolve philosophical differences. Unfortunately, pupils who moved between the two Masters distorted their ideas, and this led to the emergence of the partisan spirit that was to last for several hundred years thereafter.

## The Lecture at the White Deer Hollow Academy

In 1181, Lu Hsiang-shan, accompanied by six pupils, went to visit Chu Hsi at Nan-k'ang,[33] where Chu Hsi was prefect. Lu came to ask Chu Hsi to pen the tomb inscription for his elder brother Chiu-ling that Lü Tsu-ch'ien had composed. While Lu was there, Chu Hsi invited him to give a lecture at the White Deer Hollow Academy.[34] According to Chu Hsi's own account,

> In the second month of the spring of the *hsin-ch'ou* year [1181], my friend Lu Tzu-ching [Lu Hsiang-shan], accompanied by his pupils Chu K'e-chia, Lu Lin-chih, Chou Ch'ing-sou, Hsiung Chien, Lu Ch'ien-heng, and Hsü Hsün-shih,[35] came from Chin-ling.[36] On the tenth day, *ting-hai,* I led colleagues, friends, and pupils to go together to the lecture hall of White Deer Hollow Academy. I asked him for a word to admonish the students. . . . None in the audience was not aroused with awe. Fearing that in time people may perhaps forget it, I asked Tzu-ching to write it down for preservation.[37]

The chronological biographies *(nien-p'u)* of Chu Hsi and of Lu give slightly different reports of the occasion. According to Wang Mao-hung's (1668–1741) *Chu Tzu nien-p'u* (Chronological biography of Master Chu), "Tzu-ching came to visit and ask [Chu Hsi] to write his professor brother's tomb inscription. The Master led friends and pupils and together went to the White Deer Hollow Academy. He asked [Lu] to ascend the lecture platform. Tzu-ching orated on the chapter that the superior man or the inferior man understands righteousness or profit."[38] The *nien-p'u* in the *Hsiang-shan ch'üan-chi* put it this way: "He requested the Master [Lu] to ascend the lecture platform at the White Deer Hollow Academy. The Master spoke on the chapter that says, 'The superior man understands righteousness. The inferior man understands profit.'[39] . . . He also asked the Master to write down the lecture, which he did. Later, [Chu Hsi] had the lecture carved on stone. . . . The lecture was very moving, to the point that some of the audience wept. Yüan-hui [Chu Hsi] was much aroused. The weather was somewhat cool but he sweated and had to fan himself."[40] The fact that Lu moved people to tears was confirmed by Chu Hsi himself, for he spoke to his pupils in words to that effect when he recalled the event,[41] although to have to use a fan in a cold month sounds like an exaggeration.

This meeting stands in sharp contrast to that at the Goose Lake Temple. First of all, the earlier meeting was arranged by Lü Tsu-ch'ien, whereas this time Lu Hsiang-shan came on his own initiative. Second, although the earlier meeting was not meant to be a debate, it was concerned with philosophical matters, whereas this time the matter was purely personal. Also, Chu Hsi had no pupils with him at the Goose Lake Temple, but here both Chu and Lu had a number of pupils, although the exact number Chu Hsi had at the White Deer Hollow Academy is not known. The more important point is that Lu chose to speak on the Confucian aphorism that "the superior man understands righteousness. The inferior man understands profit." On this Confucian doctrine, the two scholars were in perfect agreement. We may say that the gathering at the Goose Lake Temple was distinguished by the difference between them, whereas this meeting was characterized by their agreement.

Their agreement was not really perfect, however. When he was asked about Lu's lecture in 1181, Chu Hsi answered,

Tzu-ching was out of order. I-ch'uan [Ch'eng I, 1033–1107] had said, "Only when one understands deeply can one love earnestly."[42] Tzu-ching, however, insisted on saying that only after one loves can one understand. With regard to righteousness and profit, most people understand them before liking or disliking them. If one does not understand at all, how can one love? If one loves, one will understand. In the final analysis, I-ch'uan's words are nearer to the truth.[43]

Several months after the meeting at Nan-k'ang, Chu Hsi wrote Lü Tsu-ch'ien and said, "Tzu-ching's former pattern [at the Goose Lake Temple] still remains [at Nan-k'ang]. The trouble with his learning is that he considers people's ideas as mere opinions."[44]

The greatest contrast between the two meetings was that the first ended with displeasure on all sides and the latter with great pleasure. Chu Hsi asked Lu to write down his lecture and had it carved on stone. Since then, the lecture has been reproduced in various forms in many places. In 1983 I saw a tablet of the lecture beside a tablet of Chu Hsi's "instructions" for the White Deer Hollow Academy in its compound. Regrettably, these were the only two occasions on which Chu and Lu met. If they had come together more often, they might have ironed out whatever differences they had, so that philosophical partisanship would have had no chance to develop in China.

## Chu Hsi on Lu Hsiang-shan's Character

Chapter 124 of the *Yü-lei* is devoted to Lu Hsiang-shan and his school. Of its 68 sections, 58 are on Lu and the rest are on his followers. Ninety percent of the material is critical, equating Lu's views with Ch'an (Meditation) Buddhism. In the letters in the *Wen-chi,* the attack is even stronger. Generally, Chu Hsi attacked Lu more than Lu attacked Chu. However, Chu Hsi's accusations were directed only at Lu's philosophy. When we read Chu Hsi's comments on Lu, we must distinguish those on Lu's thought from those on his character. Having made this distinction, it becomes clear that although philosophically they were in direct opposition to each other, personally they remained true friends. The following excerpts from the *Wen-chi* and the *Yü-lei* are listed chronologically to let Chu Hsi speak for himself.

1. 1176: In a letter to Chang Shih (1133–1180), Chu Hsi said,

> The disposition of Tzu-shou [Lu Chiu-ling] and his brother [Lu Hsiang-shan] is very good. Their defect lies in completely discarding study and devoting themselves solely to practice. In the matter of practice, they even want people to be alert and intuit their original mind. This is their great defect. However, essentially they conduct themselves carefully and simply. In them the internal and the external are one. In this they really surpass others. Unfortunately, they are too self-confident, and their scope is narrow. They do not learn from the good points of others. Without realizing it, they will drift into heterodox learning.[45]

This is Chu Hsi's first comment on Lu in writing. It was made a year after the Goose Lake Temple meeting. In Chu Hsi's opinion, because of Lu's excessive self-confidence, it was difficult to bridge their differences in thought.

2. 1179: In a letter to Lü Tsu-ch'ien, Chu Hsi said, "Tzu-ching [Lu Hsiang-shan] was not willing to turn around and admit that today he was right but yesterday he was wrong. He still covers up here and conceals there, trying to be clever in expression. It seems to me that this disposition is no good."[46]

3. 1180: In another letter to Lü he said, "Is it easy to find people today like the brothers? However, Tzu-ching still retains some of his old ideas. According to his pupil, Tzu-shou said he [Hsiang-shan] has turned around a bit, but not completely. It is inevitable that he will do so in time. What an air he showed in the discussion at the Goose Lake Temple! At present, has he not reduced it by seventy or eighty percent?"[47]

4. In a letter to his pupil Lin Yung-chung, Chu Hsi said, "In their recent discussion, Lu Tzu-shou and his brother surprisingly turn to understanding through study. The disposition of their pupils who visit here is very good, though they sometimes still have their old defect [of overemphasizing intuition]."[48]

5. In a letter to Wu Ying, Chu Hsi said, "In their recent discussions, Lu Tzu-shou and his brother differ greatly from the past. Surprisingly, they insist on understanding what study means."[49]

6. This remark was recorded by Wan Cheng-ch'ün (Wan Jen-chieh) after 1180: "Lu Tzu-ching has underestimated the Ch'eng brothers [Ch'eng Hao, 1032–1085, and Ch'eng I, 1033–1107]. I am afraid he has not understood their ideas thoroughly. It is like saying that a piece of pure gold is not perfect. There is nothing wrong with the gold. What is wrong is one's ignorance about it."[50]

7. 1181: In a letter to Lü Tsu-ch'ien, Chu Hsi said, "Tzu-ching was here for several days. I have seen your tomb inscription for Tzu-shou. Your account and elaboration are a great contribution. Your profound intention is especially seen in the subtlety of your last paragraph. How great is my admiration! Tzu-ching's discussion in recent days differs from the past, but at bottom he is not entirely correct. Fortunately, we can talk over the matter, which will be beneficial to both of us."[51]

8. In his next letter to Lü he said, "Tzu-ching's past pattern is still there. His defect is that, in discussing learning, he always says this is merely an opinion or that is merely a theory. . . . His defect is not necessarily looking at a person and not looking at principle. His trouble is that he has some Ch'an idea all the time. Moreover, he insists on his own ideas, and has to say that he is not Ch'an. His pupils have failed to understand him and have therefore drifted to this degree."[52] In the *Yü-lei*, recorded by Kan Chieh after 1193, Chu Hsi said, "Formerly, I talked with Tzu-ching. He regarded what I said as mere opinion. I said to him, 'One should not have incorrect opinions but should have correct

opinions.' Tzu-ching thought that was idle discussion. I said, 'Idle discussions should not be discussed, but correct discussions should be discussed.' "[53] This remark was made more than ten years after the letter. Chu Hsi's impression must have been very deep.

9. Chu Hsi wrote to Liu Ch'ing-chih in 1181 and said, "Tzu-ching is completely Ch'an. Nevertheless, he does not have a high degree of utilitarianism or schematization. At present, he is not without success in teaching pupils to control their bodies and minds. However, they have nothing to base themselves on and that, I am afraid, will lead to trouble."[54]

10. This remark was recorded by P'an Ping after 1183: Someone asked about the learning of Lü Tsu-ch'ien and Lu Hsiang-shan. Chu Hsi answered, "Po-kung's defect lies in [explaining] too much, while Tzu-ching's defect lies in [explaining] too little."[55]

11. About the same year, Chu Hsi wrote Chan I-chih and said, "It is very good that Professor Kao[56] pays attention to the school. He once studied under Lu Tzu-ching. Since he made up his mind to improve himself, I am sure Tzu-ching will lead and develop him."[57]

12. 1184: In a letter in reply to Hu Ta-shih, Chu Hsi said, "Yüan-shan [Chan T'i-jen, 1143–1206] has written me and said that his meeting with Tzu-ching was very cordial. I do not know what his ideas are. Generally speaking, the great defect of scholars today is to aim at quick results and to love a shortcut."[58]

13. 1185: Chu Hsi told Liu Tzu-ch'eng in a letter, "Tzu-ching has sent me his answers to questions by the throne.[59] His words are very smooth and satisfactory, strong and powerful, completely merged in a unified harmony, and without any impediment. This is the effect of his achievement. Nevertheless, he is not free from some sort of Ch'an thinking. In my letter in reply, I jokingly said, 'I am afraid this has been imported across the Himalayas.' He will surely not be pleased. However, it is really true. It is no use to cover it up."[60]

14. 1188: In a letter to Chao Yen-shu, Chu Hsi said, "Tzu-ching's later letters were even worse. By and large, his learning is not without insight as far as the work of the mind is concerned. But if he wants to rely on this to stay on top of past and present, and no longer makes any careful effort to investigate principle, in the end he will lose what he has already got. When human selfish desires run wild, one is not aware of it oneself but talks freely and in a high-souding manner, thinking that the Principle of Heaven lies completely therein. In that case, where is the so-called effort of the mind?"[61]

15. In 1188, Huang Hsün heard and recorded this remark: "Lu knows how to talk. His spirit can inspire people. Once one is aroused by him, one's mind readily becomes clear and bright. But the whole thing

is empty, like a bottomless basket. 'He who thinks but does not study is in danger.'[62] This says precisely that a bottomless basket is dangerous.''[63]

16. As recorded by Ch'en Wen-wei (1154–1239) after 1188, in talking about Lu Hsiang-shan, the Master remarked that south of the Yellow River, there has never been a person with his feet so firmly on the ground.[64]

17. Also recorded after 1188 by Li Hung-tsu (1211 *cs*): "Tzu-ching should 'have no attachment to external things and in this way let his mind grow.' ''[65]

18. 1189: In answer to Lu Hsiang-shan's letter of 1188 strongly challenging Chu Hsi's interpretation of the Great Ultimate, Chu Hsi replied, "In all discussions one must be calm, careful, and thorough. One must exchange views again and again, seeking to find out the truth, and only then can there be a conclusion. Otherwise, if, in a great hurry and under heavy pressure, one merely indulges in rash and inordinate words to give vent to one's anger and excited air, I am afraid it is far better to follow so-and-so's words and to be calm, peaceful, broad, and sustaining—qualities expected of a gentleman or elder. . . . Now, if one starts with a crude and shallow mind, assumes an angry air, is not willing to lay aside temporarily the selfishness of considering oneself to be right and others to be wrong, and wishes to judge the right or wrong according to moral principles, even if the case is clear-cut, like black and white, and can easily be seen, one may still make a mistake. How much more so when the difference is extremely small: who is going to make the adjustment without falling into error? . . . Your honorable brother, Tzu-mei [Lu Chiu-shao, *fl.* 1150], is of course endowed with rich and solid qualities. When he did not see the principle completely, he failed to investigate carefully before setting up a theory. Consequently, he was too self-confident to turn back. Although his views are defective, his intention was not wrong. But you, my friend, draw a conclusion beforehand. . . . Without exception, you go out of the way to find fault, insisting on looking for what is wrong. Even if your deliberation is perfectly faultless, your intention is already wrong. How much more so when your words are crude and not free from defect?"[66] This letter is easily the strongest outburst of Chu Hsi's life.

19. Chu Hsi said in a letter in reply to Shao Shu-i, "I have received a letter from Tzu-ching. It is quite unreasonable. Ordinarily, he hides things and dares not broadcast them. I never realized that he exposes himself like this. . . . He has also made copies of letters to his associates. I imagine he feels good. Perhaps he has written a good deal and spreads it all over, fearing that people do not know about it. This is his normal manner. We should not regard it as very strange."[67]

20. In the *Hsiang-shan ch'üan-chi,* it is recorded: "A scholar wrote [Chu Hsi] to censure the Master [Lu Hsiang-shan] for the debate on the Great Ultimate [between Lu and Chu]. In his reply, Hui-an [Chu Hsi] said, 'Since we moved south of the Yellow River, only Lu Tzu-ching and I have stood firmly on the ground and understood what concrete effort means. I really respect him. You, my friend, should not lightly criticize him.' "[68]

21. This was recorded by Huang Ch'iao-chung (Huang Tao-fu, 1183 *cs*) after 1189: "The spirit of Po-kung's pupils is very strong. They have become a splinter group, each one propounding his own theory. In time, the school will disappear. It is different in the case of Tzu-ching. His spirit is alert and his doctrine is clear. He can transform people, so that they change from morning to late afternoon. His long accumulated harmful effect knows no end."[69]

22. One item recorded by Yeh Ho-sun (Yeh Wei-tao, 1220 *cs*) after 1191 says, "Although Tzu-ching chooses to be treacherous and does not speak plainly, he sees a thing as a concrete unit, and therefore there are visible traces in what he says. Only people do not understand him and therefore fail to see [those traces]. Nevertheless, they can easily be seen. If a person does not agree with him, he will not talk. When a person has been prevailed upon, he will talk right away, and then he will reason with you."[70]

23. Another item says, "P'an Kung-shu [P'an Yu-kung] said that in spite of what Hsiang-shan says, when it is time to respond to things, he responds in the wrong way. [The Master] said, 'From this we know that his learning and his doctrines are all false. None of it is in conformity with established standards. His response to things is also false. How can it be correct?' "[71]

24. Still another item says, "I can hardly say whether he [Lu Hsiang-shan] has a lot or a little. I dare not talk about him. But I cannot refrain from talking because you gentlemen have asked me about him. He only goes in one direction. No one can turn him back. He does not believe in people. What can be done with him?"[72]

25. 1193: In a letter in reply to Chan T'i-jen, Chu Hsi said, "I have heard that Tzu-ching's coffin has been well attended to on its way [home]. This is most worrisome. I saw that he ordinarily slapped his head strongly and shouted wildly. Why has he suddenly come to this point [of passing away]? As his doctrines prevail in the river and lake area,[73] weakening the resolve of the virtuous and enhancing the errors of the stupid, I don't know when its damage will end."[74]

26. According to what P'an Chih heard in 1193, Chu Hsi said, "Lu Tzu-ching said that Kao Tzu [420–350 B.C.?] was lofty because he himself did not measure up to him. Kao Tzu rigidly controlled his mind so

it could be unperturbed.[75] When Lu encountered things, it was not always certain that he would remain unperturbed."[76]

27. One item recorded by Huang I-kang after 1193 says, "Take Lu Tzu-ching. How high and brilliant was his natural talent! But he did not teach following the Mean, and his learning later did damage to people. I have always said that in his discussions, Tzu-ching had a black belt around his waist. In the beginning, he would speak with numerous twists and turns. It was extremely impressive. After a little while, when a critical point was reached, he would conceal it and would not talk. He would then find another lead that would give rise to more twists and turns. That is why people could not get at his critical point."[77]

28. Another item says, "Lu Tzu-ching was clearly Ch'an. However, since he has become an establishment, you can still get hold of him."[78]

29. Still another item says, "Shu-ch'i [Hu An-chih] asked about Hsiang-shan's succession of teachers. Answer: 'Their natural gifts were great. I don't know who he studied under. But there is no need to ask about his heritage from any teacher. Most scholars act according to their physical endowment. Consequently, their understanding is partial.' "[79]

30. This was heard and recorded by Wang Kuo in 1194: "Our Master once said that Lu Tzu-ching and Yang Ching-chung [Yang Chien, 1141–1226] are of course a hundred percent good people, but they seem to suffer from an obsession with cleanliness. Also, their discussion of principles is like that of the salt smugglers in Fukien. They put the contraband salt at the bottom and cover it with dried fish so people will not notice it. What I mean is that their learning is fundamentally Ch'an, but they cover it up with our Confucian teachings."[80]

31. This was recorded by Fu Kuang after 1194: "Tzu-ching's discussion was always bright at both ends but dark in the middle. That was where he would not speak plainly. The fact that he did not speak plainly shows he was Ch'an."[81]

32. As recorded by Shen Hsien after 1198, Chu Hsi said, "From what I have seen in recent times, among those who can speak in a sonorous voice and can arouse people, none can surpass Lu Tzu-ching."[82]

33. According to what Lü T'ao heard in 1199, Chu Hsi said, "Wang Chieh-fu [Wang An-shih, 1021–1086] and Lu Tzu-ching were simply arbitrary in what they said."[83]

34. Recorded by Yang Jo-hai, date unknown: "Nature [Original note:] (Lu Tzu-mei). Spirit [Original note:] (Tzu-ching)".[84] Chu Hsi was probably thinking of Tzu-mei's [Lu Chiu-shao] devotion to community affairs and Lu Hsiang-shan's brilliance.

35. Recorded by Liao Te-ming (1169 cs) after 1173: "Lu Tzu-ching and Yang Ching-chung have made an effort for the self. If they had been willing to investigate principle, the result would have been very

impressive. Unfortunately, they have not changed."[85] Liao attended Chu Hsi's teachings six times between 1173 and 1199. Since the record also involved Lu's pupil, it was probably fairly late.

## Chu and Lu: Their Personal Relations

To date, scholars have concentrated on the thought of Chu Hsi and Lu Hsiang-shan, to the almost total neglect of their personal relationship. Because they were opposed to each other in ideas, they have been regarded as rivals. Although that was largely true, their personal relations remained friendly and cordial. They were blunt and forthright in their criticisms but also treated each other with consideration and respect. I have selected pertinent passages from their literary collections and recorded conversations and arranged them in chronological order below. One cannot help but be impressed by their genuine friendship despite their philosophical differences.

1. 1173: Lü Tsu-ch'ien wrote Chu Hsi and said, "Lu Chiu-ling of Fu-chou[86] is genuine, filial, and brotherly. He and his younger brother [Lu Hsiang-shan] have firmed up their character. In the past, their learning was somewhat unbalanced. Recently, they came here for several days and expressed the desire to consult with scholars everywhere."[87] This indicates that Tzu-shou and Tzu-ching wanted to meet Chu Hsi.

2. 1174: In a letter in reply to Lü Tsu-ch'ien's brother, Lü Tsu-chien (d. 1196), Chu Hsi said, "Recently I have heard one or two things about the style and ideas of Lu Tzu-ching. They are entirely the learning of Ch'an under a different name. But [his pupils] compete to follow it. I am afraid it will harm the coming generation. I regret I do not know him and have not been able to inquire deeply into his doctrine and ask him some questions."[88]

3. 1175: After the Goose Lake Temple meeting, Chu Hsi wrote Lu Hsiang-shan, "It is regrettable that we parted in a hurry. Both of us felt that we missed something. I admire, and shall not forget, your instructions, which are admonitory and to the point."[89]

4. 1177: Chu Hsi told Yeh Wei-tao (1200 cs) in a letter, "When their stepmother passed away, Lu Tzu-shou and his brother [Tzu-ching] [wrote] to ask me [how to proceed]. At that time, I told them to set up an altar [for sacrificial offerings] after burial. But Tzu-ching did not approve. He wanted to remove the sacrificial offerings after wailing and burial. Tzu-shou was skeptical and asked me again. I told them that . . . to remove the offerings right after wailing does not express the mind of a filial son. In that case, the great foundation of ritual is already lost. To the end, Tzu-ching did not regard that as correct, although Tzu-shou was convinced. He wrote to thank me and went as far as to

say that he should carry a rod to ask for punishment [i.e., to apologize]."[90]

5. 1180: Chu Hsi said in a letter in reply to Lü Tsu-ch'ien, "I have heard from Tzu-shou and his brother. Tzu-ching suggested coming and touring Mount Lu [with me] in the summer, when it is cooler, but I am afraid by that time the host will be replaced."[91] Chu Hsi's term as prefect of Nan-k'ang, about 15 *li* from Mount Lu, was soon to be up. Hence the remark about the host.

6. In his next letter to Lü, Chu Hsi said, "I have not heard from the Lu brothers again. Famine relief measures are now proceeding at a rapid pace, and I have had no opportunity to send a messenger to inquire of them. Tzu-ching wants to come and tour the mountain. Now that he has heard about the drought conditions, I don't know whether he will come."[92]

7. In still another letter to Lü he wrote, "For a long time I have not heard from Tzu-shou and his brother. Tzu-ching wants to come, but because of the drought he may not be able to do so. In a day or so I shall send a messenger to inquire of them."[93]

8. Chu Hsi told Fu Meng-ch'üan in a letter, "The year drew to a close soon after Ching-chou's[94] [Chang Shih] death, and now I have received the obituary of my dear friend, the professor from Ch'ing-t'ien[95] [Tzu-shou]. The misfortune of our Way has reached such a degree! When I think of it, my bitter sorrow knows no end. I especially cannot bear the thought when I think of his significance as a teacher."[96]

9. In reply to a letter from Lü Tsu-ch'ien, Chu Hsi said, "Tzu-ching has written to say that he has already asked you to compose the tomb inscription [for Tzu-shou] and has asked me to write it. I dare not decline this request. However, his biographical account *(hsing-chuang)* [of his brother][97] is not satisfactory at all. I am afraid special thought must be given it before [Tzu-shou's career] can be made prominent."[98]

10. 1181: When Lu Hsiang-shan visited Chu Hsi at Nan-k'ang, according to the *Hsiang-shan ch'üan-chi*, "He and the Master [Hsiang-shan] enjoyed a boat ride and [Chu Hsi] declared, 'The mountain and stream have been here since the universe existed. Has there ever been a distinguished guest like you?' "[99]

11. 1183: In a letter to Lu Hsiang-shan, Chu Hsi said briefly, "Recently, I made an appointment with Chu-ko Ch'eng-chih [Chu-ko Ch'ien-neng, Ch'un-hsi (1174–1189) *cs*] to meet in my study. It has been most beneficial. Virtuous scholars in Chekiang have all been drawn to your seat of learning, in especially large numbers in recent times. This is our fortune." In another letter he said, "My arm hurt after I returned home. During this illness, I have given up study and left books alone. I feel that my body and mind are under control and there seems to be some progress. Hitherto, I have spread myself too

thin. It really has not helped matters. I regret not to have had an opportunity for a hearty talk, to receive your instruction, and to express all that is in my mind."[100]

12. In a letter to Commissioner of Tribute Grain Yu Yen-chih (Yu Mao), Lu Hsiang-shan said briefly in a letter, "Chu Yüan-hui [Chu Hsi] gained a reputation in Nan-k'ang as being too severe. His governmental measures surely have some defects, but I am afraid he should not be criticized generally as being severe. If the punishment suits the crime, the punishment should not be reduced. Should we find fault with him for being severe? . . . From the letters that I have received from many friends and relatives and also from hearsay, I know a little about Yüan-hui's drought relief in East Chekiang. People there have been greatly benefited. His action of [presenting a petition requesting the ministry of personnel] to censure him[101] is particularly appropriate."[102]

13. 1184: In a letter to Lu Hsiang-shan, Chu Hsi said briefly, "I do not know when you are going to appear in Court to offer your recommendations. As you have a chance to see the enlightened ruler, it is better to say a few words on important issues. It is not worthwhile to talk about trivial matters."[103]

14. People could not agree on what Lu Hsiang-shan had said in his memorials in answer to the emperor's question. Chu Hsi asked for a copy, and Lu sent one to him. Upon receipt of it, Chu Hsi wrote, "I have received your memorials and have learned of your perfect ideas. I am greatly satisfied. Your scope is vast and your source deep and remote. How can rotten scholars or worthless pedants imagine them? I don't know when you answered and elaborated, what utterances did the emperor understand? . . . Only in your tendency toward the transcendental [the concentration on the mind], from which you have not turned around, you still make people skeptical. I am afraid that this has been brought in across the Himalayas."[104] This letter is also included in the *Hsiang-shan ch'üan-chi,* but with the last sentence omitted, obviously because of its suggestion of Buddhism.[105]

15. 1186: In answer to Chu-ko Ch'ien-neng, Chu Hsi wrote, "Tzu-ching has personally dedicated his life to leading students to identify themselves with the Principle of Heaven, without being mixed with an iota of selfish human desire. I am certain that he has not come to the point [of indignation] as you have suspected."[106] Chu Hsi had written a tomb inscription for Ts'ao Chien in which he said that Ts'ao first studied with the Lu brothers and then went to Chang Shih, implying that Ts'ao finally came to him.[107] Lu's pupils were indignant, and Chu-ko Ch'ien-neng had written to Chu Hsi that he suspected that Lu Hsiang-shan felt the same.

16. 1187: In a letter to Chu Hsi, Lu Hsiang-shan said, "Because of serious drought, the Court has given you a commission that you more

than deserve. If you see fit to accept it, how fortunate are the people of Chiang-hsi.[108] In the beginning of winter, the gentleman Hsü came. Only then did I receive your letter of the eighth day of the fifth month. From it I learned that your good little girl has passed away. I am sure of your sadness and grief. A month ago I received your letter of the second day of the fifth month, in which you greatly comforted me. I, being unworthy, have also suffered from a great calamity. In the middle of summer, my second brother, Tzu-i, did not survive his illness. Only toward the end of last month were the funeral arrangements carried out. At the end of the seventh month I lost a child of three, who was to succeed my [late] elder brother the professor [Lu Chiu-ling]. Recently, I also lost a grandniece. My niece's husband, Chang Fu-chih, who had been sick for months, also passed away after my brother's funeral. Ah, me! There have never been calamities piling up to this extent. I cannot stand the sorrow accumulating in me. I have had blood trouble for some time. It has become serious in the last two or three years. Recently, it was transformed into hemorrhoids that were very painful and took several days to heal."[109]

17. In another letter, Lu said, "Your appointment outside the national capital is probably meant to put your advanced virtue in the proper place. It is probably an omen of the new policy of recruiting worthy scholars. . . . I imagine your petition to decline will probably not be accepted. I hope you will try your best in medication and graciously fulfill the wishes of the people. Even if your energy is not strong enough, if you make a great effort to rest and recuperate, your fighting spirit will rise to no small degree."[110]

18. In a letter to Wang Lin-shih, Lu said, "I have heard that Yüan-hui has left [for the capital] to report to the throne. It may be said that lucky stars have gathered in Chiang-hsi."[111]

19. 1188: In a letter to Chu Hsi, Lu said, "I have heard that you have gone to the capital to report to the throne. When will the interview be? I believe you will amply express your long-cherished ideas and give the enlightened ruler your sincere advice so as to arouse his profound thought and benefit the empire. I regret that I have not been able to learn of your details right away so as to quench my thirst. There is a report that you will remain in Court to lecture and discuss. Is that true? If that is so, it will be something worthy of congratulations. A fellow community person, P'eng Shih-ch'ang,[112] acquired a hill in the western region of Hsin-chou only two houses from my lodge. The hill is really the starting point of Dragon and Tiger Mountain. Rising conspicuously, it is big and seems about to strike like an elephant. It is called Elephant Mountain. . . . My friend P'eng built a hall there and extended an invitation to me [to lecture]. I myself also built a study by its side. In the spring I will take a nephew and two sons to read in it. I also got a nice place for a small lodge (*fang-chang*) in which to live."[113]

20. In his reply, Chu Hsi said, "This past summer I happened to receive your letter at Yü-shan.[114] At the time I was on the way to the capital. Then I returned home. Because of illness and many other matters, and also because of the lack of a courier, I could not reply to you immediately. But your kindness and the excellence of the scenery at Elephant Mountain have lingered in my mind, and I cannot help facing west and sighing in lamentation. . . . Now I have been summoned again. . . . I have sent someone to petition to Court to be excused."[115]

21. Lu said in another letter, "Your letter of the eighth day of the eleventh month explains fully your movement [with regard to the appointment]. It is a great comfort to me. From an official gazette, I have learned that by an imperial edict your resignation has been refused. Don't you feel you should serve once more? Whether to advance forward to serve or to withdraw should be a matter of fundamental principle. Shall we merely avoid suspicion or ward off criticism?"[116]

22. 1192: Chu Hsi told Lu in a letter, "When I returned to Chienyang,[117] I did not plan well and built a small house. It has been a year but it is not yet finished [because of poverty]. There has been all sorts of trouble. When I wish to give up, I cannot do so."[118]

23. This was recorded by Yeh Ho-sun after 1191: Question: "In Lu Tzu-ching's family, there are more than a hundred people at dinner." Master Chu answered: "Recently, I received a letter from him in which he said he has built a separate house. That is because there are too many people and there is no way to achieve order. . . . Lu Tzu-ching was at first the manager. The family regulations were in perfect order. All uncles eat in one place, aunts in one place, sons in one place, daughters-in-law in one place, grandsons in one place, granddaughters-in-law in one place, and small children in one place."[119]

24. 1193: In reply to Chao Shih-yung (1187 *cs*), Chu Hsi said, "When I heard of the death of Ching-men[120] [Lu Hsiang-shan], I was extremely sad. When an old friend falls, I cannot help being sorrowful. I can no longer figure out whether ordinarily we are in agreement in our discussions or not."[121]

## "It is regrettable that Kao Tzu has passed away"

It is recorded in the *Yü-lei* that when "Hsiang-shan died,[122] the Master led pupils to a temple to mourn him. When they had finished, after a long pause he said, 'It is regrettable that Kao Tzu has passed away.' " An original note adds, "This story was obtained from Wen-ch'ing [Tou Ts'ung-chou]."[123]

The first question that comes to mind is why Chu Hsi compared Lu Hsiang-shan to Mencius' opponent Kao Tzu [420–350 B.C.?]. From Chu Hsi's discussion of Lu in connection with Kao Tzu, we can discern four criticisms of both men. The first is that they failed to understand physical nature *(ch'i-ping)*. As recorded in the *Yü-lei,* Chu Hsi said,

> From Tzu-ching's letter, I can see that he has very much an air of rude-ness. It is terrible. His pupils are all like this. As soon as they say a few words, so long as they flow out of their minds, they are all the Principle of Heaven, regardless of whether things are big or small, and regardless of whether there is a father or an elder brother. They completely ignore actual practice. As I see it, their mistake lies precisely in not knowing that there is such a thing as physical nature. . . . Mencius did not discuss material force *(ch'i)*. That is why in his lengthy talks with Kao Tzu and others, he could not make them understand.[124] Since Kao Tzu's time, Hsün Tzu (313–238 B.C.?), Yang Hsiung [53 B.C.–A.D. 18], and the like have all taken material force to be nature.[125]

The second criticism was that they did not teach people to read books. A pupil asked, "Lu's learning does not teach people to read books or to pursue literature. Was he similar to Kao Tzu?" Chu Hsi answered, "That is it."[126]

The third criticism concerns the doctrine that righteousness is exter-nal. In his letter in reply to Hsiang An-shih (d. 1208), Chu Hsi said,

> Kao Tzu did not know [that righteousness is internal] and considered it to be external. In that case, when his mind was not disturbed, he merely for-cibly controlled it so it would be dull and not moved. It was not that he had this vital force [strong moving power] and was naturally undisturbed. Hence [Mencius] further said, "I therefore said that Kao Tzu did not know righteousness because he made it something external."[127] However, Kao Tzu's trouble lay in the fact that he failed to realize that when the mind feels satisfactory [about one's conduct], that is where righteousness comfortably lies, and if the mind does not feel satisfactory, that means that one's conduct does not comply with righteousness. Consequently, he immediately considered righteousness to be external and did not seek for it. Because of what Mencius said, people nowadays understand this idea and know that righteousness is internal, but they do not know that whether or not [one's conduct] is satisfactory to one's own mind still depends on study and investigation before one can examine the essential and the subtle. Therefore, they regard all that one has obtained from accumulation through study and sifting through inquiry as external, and do not regard them as where righteousness is to be found. Therefore, they have rejected all of that and would not do anything of that sort. Although this is somewhat different from what Kao Tzu taught, in reality it is some-where between a hundred paces and fifty paces.[128]

Here Lu Hsiang-shan is not explicitly mentioned, but most letters to Hsiang An-shih deal with him. In the *Yü-lei,* it is clearly said, "Now Lu only considers what he sees in his own mind as internal. Whatever others say is wrong. As soon as others say something, he considers it to be righteousness that is external. This is the doctrine of Kao Tzu."[129]

The fourth criticism focuses on Kao Tzu's theory that "what is not attained in words is not to be sought in the mind."[130] Chu Hsi said,

> To say "what is not attained in words is not to be sought in the mind" means that the mind and words are not related. . . . This is Kao Tzu's theory. Kao Tzu merely wanted to control his mind so it would be calm. He paid no attention to things outside. He did not care whether they were right or wrong. Mencius' idea is that if one's mind is wrong, one's words will reveal it, just as an ailment of the liver is seen in the eye. Lu Tzu-ching said that Kao Tzu had some good points and that people today not only fail to understand Mencius but also do not understand Kao Tzu. As in the case of what is not attained in words, Lu Tzu-ching has contended that Kao Tzu relied only on the outside and paid no attention to the inside. In my view, Kao Tzu merely held onto the inside and paid no attention to the outside.[131]

When Yang Chih asked about Kao Tzu's doctrine, the Master replied, "If Kao Tzu did not understand [the words], he would not return to the mind and seek the principle there. I once heard Lu Tzu-ching discuss Kao Tzu's sayings. On the whole he praised Kao Tzu's view as lofty. Of course Kao Tzu's view was lofty, but Master Lu was in favor of Kao Tzu because his own learning resembled his. But Lu's learning is especially mixed up, like that of Kao Tzu."[132] According to P'an Chih,

> When Chih-chih [Yang Chih] asked about Kao Tzu's saying, the Master said, "Lu Tzu-ching had no use for words. His learning is precisely like that of Kao Tzu. That is why he always avoided the subject." Chih-chih said, "Lu once said, 'People not only do not know the lofty points of Mencius; they do not know the high points of Kao Tzu, either.' You said to Lu, 'Please explain.' Lu merely responded in a confused manner." Thereupon the Master told the pupils, "Lu Tzu-ching said that Kao Tzu was lofty because he himself did not measure up to him. Kao Tzu rigidly controlled his mind so it could be unperturbed. When Lu encountered things, it was not always certain that he would remain unperturbed."[133]

The third and fourth criticisms are really two sides of a single coin, for not to seek righteousness outside and not to seek in the mind what one cannot attain in words were both Kao Tzu's way of maintaining an unperturbed mind. In the eyes of Chu Hsi, both Kao Tzu and Lu Hsiang-shan lacked the unperturbed mind that Mencius possessed due to his strong moving power and remained undisturbed only through forceful control. Lu, in fact, could not even maintain an unperturbed mind in this way.

From the foregoing, it is clear that when Chu Hsi lamented the death of Lu as comparable to that of Kao Tzu, he was thinking their similar

approaches to calming the mind. He could not have been thinking of
their doctrines of human nature or their failure to teach people to read,
because these first two criticisms were mentioned only incidentally,
whereas the third and fourth were mentioned repeatedly. In other
words, from the standpoint of doctrine, Chu Hsi and Kao Tzu never
agreed.

Chu Hsi's frankness on matters of doctrine can be seen in his remark
upon the death of Lü Tsu-chien, Lü Tsu-ch'ien's younger brother. He
had corresponded frequently with Chu Hsi on philosophical issues.
There are 49 letters in the *Wen-chi* to Lü Tsu-chien,[134] more than to
anyone else except Chang Shih and Lü Tsu-ch'ien. Yet they never came
to an agreement. Chu Hsi once said, "It is a pity that Tzu-yüeh [Lü
Tsu-chien] worked hard at reading throughout life, but in the end I
could not agree with him."[135] When Tsu-chien died, Chu Hsi said,
"Tzu-yüeh has gone and taken many confused principles with him."[136]

No one has ever quoted Chu Hsi's remark on Lü Tsu-chien's death
in a discussion of his equally frank remark on Lu Hsiang-shan's death.
Thus there has been a general failure to realize that the remark about
Lu Hsiang-shan was made from a purely philosophical point of view.
Instead, the impression has been that Chu Hsi failed to show any sorrow but derided Lu instead—in short, that he was unkind, if not cruel.
Hence the episode was not included in either the *Hsiang-shan ch'üan-chi*
or in Wang Mao-hung's *Chu Tzu nien-p'u*. Moreover, some have taken
Chu Hsi's failure to write a funeral address for Lu as a sign of disrespect. But Chu Hsi did lead pupils to a temple to mourn him. Could
that have been mere pretense? As has already been pointed out, there is
a note at the end of the statement in the *Yü-lei* that the story was
obtained from Wen-ch'ing (Tou Ts'ung-chou). Yet Wang Mao-hung
observed,

> This affair is not included in Ts'ung-chou's record [of Chu Hsi's conver-
> sations in the *Yü-lei*]. I am afraid it is a mistake in hearsay. The *Hsien-p'i lu*
> [Refutation of heterodoxy] says, "To mourn him is an expression of per-
> sonal friendship, but to deride him is a matter of public discussion in the
> Confucian tradition."[137] This is correct. However, while it is all right to
> say that his learning is similar to that of Kao Tzu and to refute him, to say
> that it is regrettable that Kao Tzu has passed away is too lighthearted an
> utterance. Surely these were not Master Chu's words.[138]

Ch'ien Mu, too, has maintained that "since the recorder did not hear
these words personally, the report may not be reliable."[139] Both Wang
and Ch'ien seemed to feel that the purported saying is unkind and
hence tried to vindicate Chu Hsi.

Wen-ch'ing became Chu Hsi's pupil in 1185, at the late age of fifty,[140]
and must have participated in the mourning. Wang Mao-hung is cor-

rect in saying that there is no other record of the event by Tou in the *Yü-lei*, but one cannot therefore conclude that the event did not take place. Tou recorded over thirty conversations, all of which concern ideas. It is not reasonable to say that this matter was not within his interest. Tou was not only a mature pupil; he was noted for self-discipline.[141] He was not the kind of person who repeated unfounded stories or believed in hearsay. The event was recorded by T'ang Yung in 1195, two or three years after Lu's death. It is possible that the true facts were lost in hearsay, but it is far more probable that Tou actually participated in the mourning. If we remember Chu Hsi's saying after Lü Tsu-chien's death, any doubt about his saying after Lu Hsiang-shan's death should be dispelled. If we deny Chu Hsi's saying about Lu, shall we deny the mourning also? The fact is that Chu Hsi was frank and blunt. He simply spoke his mind. He had enjoyed a friendly personal relation with Lu. It is unimaginable that he would have deliberately derided a friend at his death. As far as we know, he never derided anyone.

At the bottom of the section in the *Yü-lei* in which Chu Hsi's remark is recorded, there is the name Yung. Ch'ien Mu took it to refer to Hu Yung, but Wang Mao-hung thought it referred to T'ang Yung. According to the style of the *Yü-lei*, those sections recorded by Hu Yung bear his full name, while those recorded by T'ang Yung bear only the name Yung. This was a slip on the part of Professor Ch'ien; Wang was right.

## Lu Hsiang-shan's "Final Conclusion"

Professor Huang Chang-chien has propounded the theory that just before Lu Hsiang-shan died, he expressed agreement with Chu Hsi. Professor Huang has determined the dates of Sun Ying-shih's (1154–1206) twenty-one exchanges of letters with Chu Hsi and three with Lu.[142] His research is excellent and correct, a valuable supplement to Wang Mao-hung's standard chronological biography. One letter addressed to Chu Hsi in Sun Ying-shih's *Chu-hu chi* (Collected works of Sun Ying-shih) said, "Master Lu of Ching-men ended this way. How sorrowful! I hear that when he was about to pass away, he told his pupils to follow only your [Chu Hsi's] teachings and regretted that he was too self-confident."[143] On the basis of this statement, Professor Huang decided that Lu had finally agreed with Chu Hsi. He also determined that Sun Ying-shih was a pupil of both Chu and Lu. The latter conclusion is partly true, but the former is unwarranted.

With reference to the latter point, Professor Huang said, "Huang Tsung-hsi (1610–1695), in his *Sung-Yüan hsüeh-an*, ch. 77, said, 'Sun sought learning from both Chu and Lu but followed Lu,'[144] and Mr. Wing-tsit Chan in his *Chu Tzu men-jen* (Chu Hsi's pupils) considers Huang to be correct.[145] Neither has seen the precious material in the *Chu-hu chi*."[146] Both the *Sung-Yüan hsüeh-an* and my *Chu Tzu men-jen* agree that Sun was a pupil of both Chu and Lu. As to whether Sun ended up following Lu or Chu, I confess I cannot say because I have not yet seen the *Chu-hu chi*. However, based on the letters reproduced in Professor Huang's article, I still believe that Huang Tsung-hsi was correct in contending that Sun followed Lu. In the letters between Sun and Lu, there is no discussion of philosophical ideas, so it is impossible to determine whether Sun's thoughts agreed with those of Lu. In Sun's correspondence with Chu Hsi, however, the two are opposed time and time again. Sun raised doubts about Chu Hsi's commentaries on the *Great Learning,* the *Doctrine of the Mean,* and the "T'ai-chi-t'u shuo" (Explanation of the diagram of the Great Ultimate).[147] For example, Chu Hsi maintained that the brief introductions in the *Book of History* were not authentic and that the preface by K'ung An-kuo ( *fl.* 130 B.C.) was not the writing of his time, but Sun refused to accept these conclusions. Chu Hsi insisted that the *Book of Changes* was intended for divination, but Sun held that it was for teaching moral principles.[148] Thus it can hardly be argued that Sun was a follower of Chu Hsi.

With regard to Lu's so-called final conclusion, I have three difficulties. One is that Sun's report is based on hearsay, not firsthand information. The second is that neither Lu's biographical account written by his star pupil Yang Chien nor his chronological biography mentions Lu's saying that he agreed with Chu Hsi. And the third is that if Lu did utter such words, Chu Hsi's pupils would have been jubilant and would have talked about it a great deal. But in all the recorded conversations, there is no hint that Lu Hsiang-shan finally shifted to Chu Hsi's point of view. The fact that Chu Hsi compared Lu with Kao Tzu is sufficient evidence that Lu remained opposed to Chu Hsi's thought to the end.

## Notes

1. See my *Chu-hsüeh lun-chi* [Studies on Chu Hsi] (Taipei: Student Book Co., 1982), pp. 233–249.

2. A *li* is one-third of a mile.

3. A county in Hsin-chou Prefecture, Kiangsi.

4. *Ch'ien-shan hsien-chih* [Accounts of the Ch'ien-shan County] (1871 ed.), 3:1a.

5. *Ibid.,* 7:4a.

6. *Hsiang-shan ch'üan-chi* [Complete works of Lu Hsiang-shan] (*SPPY* ed.), 36:9a, chronological biography.

7. *Ch'ien-shan hsien-chih,* 9:67a.

8. Ch'eng Chao-hsiung, *I O-hu* [Recollecting the Goose Lake Temple] (Taipei: Mu-ts'ai Press, 1954), pp. 21–22, 29. Professor Ch'eng was head of an agricultural college there in the 1940s and lived near the academy.

9. *Wen-chi,* 81:6b, "Epilogue of the *Chin-ssu lu.*"

10. *Ibid.,* 49:1a, first letter to Wang Tzu-ho (Wang Yü).

11. *Tung-lai Lü T'ai-shih wen-chi* [Collection of literary works of Lü Tsu-ch'ien, member of the Han-lin Academy] *Hsü Chin-hua ts'ung-shu* [Supplement to the Chin-hua series] ed.), 15:9a, "Entrance to Fukien."

12. For more details, see my *Chu-hsüeh lun-chi*, pp. 236–237.

13. *Hsiang-shan ch'üan-chi*, 36:8b–9b, chronological biography.

14. *Sung-Yüan hsüeh-an* [Anthology and critical accounts of the Neo-Confucians of the Sung and Yüan dynasties] (*SPPY* ed.), 77:7a, 11a, chapter on the Lu School.

15. Ch'eng Chao-hsiung, in *Central News,* Taipei, April 19, 1977, sec. 3.

16. *Hsiang-shan ch'üan-chi*, 36:9a, chronological biography.

17. *Wan-hsing t'ung-p'u* [Records of ten thousand families] (1579 ed.), 67:19a.

18. *Ibid.,* 59:24a.

19. A county in Honan.

20. *Sung-Yüan hsüeh-an pu-i* [Supplement to the *Sung-Yüan hsüeh-an*] (*Ssu-ming ts'ung-shu* [Ssu-ming series] ed.), 58:33b, biography of Chao Ching-ming. Lin-ch'uan is a county in Kiangsi.

21. *Hsiang-shan ch'üan-chi*, 36:8b–9a, chronological biography.

22. *Ibid.,* 36:9b; *Sung-Yüan hsüeh-an pu-i,* 58:34a, mistaking Ching-chao for Ching-ming.

23. Present Ch'ing-chiang County in Kiangsi.

24. For more information on the participants, see my *Chu-hsüeh lun-chi,* pp. 237–241.

25. *Hsiang-shan ch'üan-chi*, 34:24a–b, 36:8b–8b, recorded sayings.

26. Both quotations are from the *Doctrine of the Mean,* ch. 27. For more on this topic, see ch. 16 above.

27. *Yü-lei,* ch. 78, sec. 50 (p. 3160).

28. *Wen-chi,* 83:7a–b, "Epilogue to Lü's Explanation of the *Book of History.*"

29. *Ibid.,* 87:11a, funeral address for Lu Tzu-shou (Lu Chiu-ling).

30. *Sung-Yüan hsüeh-an,* 57:7b, chapter on Lu Chiu-ling.

31. *Wen-chi,* 90:7a–b, tomb tablet for Ts'ao Li-chih (Ts'ao Chien).

32. *Yü-lei,* ch. 16, sec. 52 (p. 516). For more details on topics of discussion at the Goose Lake Temple meeting, see my *Chu-hsüeh lun-chi,* pp. 241–245.

33. Both Nan-k'ang, which is present Hsing-tzu County, and Chin-hsi, Lu Hsiang-shan's home, are in northeastern Kiangsi, about 150 miles apart.

34. *Wen-chi,* 81:25a, epilogue to Lu Hsiang-shan's lecture notes at the White Deer Hollow Academy.

35. Lu Lin-chih was Lu Hsiang-shan's nephew. Lu Ch'ien-heng's courtesy name was Yen-pin, and Hsü Hsün-shih's courtesy name was Pi-hsien. According to the *Ju-lin tsung-p'ai* [Confucian schools and their generations] (*Ssu-ming ts'ung-shu* [Ssu-ming series] ed.), 11:10a, Chou Ch'ing-sou's courtesy name was Lien-fu. For Hsiung Chien, see the *Sung-Yüan hsüeh-an,* 77:3b, and for Lu Lin-chih, Chou Ch'ing-sou, Lu Ch'ien-heng, and Hsü Hsün-shih, see the *Sung-Yüan hsüeh-an pu'i,* 58:36b, 77:15b, 22a, chapter on Lu Hsiang-shan and the Lu School.

36. I believe that Chin-ling should here be read as Chin-hsi, the home of the Lu family.

37. *Wen-chi,* 81:25a, epilogue to Lu Hsiang-shan's lecture.

38. Wang Mao-hung, *Chu Tzu nien-p'u* [Chronological biography of Master Chu] (*Ts'ung-shu chi-ch'eng* [Collection of series] ed.), p. 96.

39. *Analects*, 4:16.

40. *Hsiang-shan ch'üan-chi*, 36:10b, chronological biography.

41. *Yü-lei*, ch. 119, sec. 17 (4590).

42. *Ts'ui-yen* [Pure words], 2:34a, in *Erh-Ch'eng ch'üan-shu* [Complete works of the two Ch'engs] (*SPPY* ed.).

43. *Yü-lei*, ch. 124, sec. 8 (p. 4755). See also ch. 78, sec. 222 (p. 3203).

44. *Wen-chi*, 34:34b, ninety-third letter in reply to Lü Po-kung (Lü Tsu-ch'ien).

45. *Wen-chi*, 31:15b–16a, twenty-seventh letter in reply to Chang Ching-fu (Chang Shih).

46. *Ibid.*, 34:17b, seventy-seventh letter in reply to Lü Po-kung.

47. *Ibid.*, p. 26a–b, eighty-third letter.

48. *Ibid.*, 43:31b, forty-sixth letter in reply to Lin Tse-chih (Lin Yung-chung).

49. *Ibid.*, 44:30b, first letter to Wu Mou-shih (Wu Ying).

50. *Yü-lei*, ch. 80, sec. 88 (p. 3321).

51. *Wen-chi*, 34:33a, ninety-second letter in reply to Lü Po-kung.

52. *Ibid.*, p. 34a–b, ninety-third letter.

53. *Yü-lei*, ch. 124, sec. 21 (p. 4759).

54. *Wen-chi*, 35:22a, eleventh letter to Liu Tzu-ch'eng (Liu Ch'ing-chih).

55. *Yü-lei*, ch. 122, sec. 4 (p. 4719).

56. We have no information on who Professor Kao was.

57. *Wen-chi*, 27:18a, third letter to Chan T'i-jen (Chan I-chih). The earlier part of the letter refers to a work by Ch'in-fu (Chang Shih) that was finally published in 1184. Hence this letter is placed in 1183.

58. *Wen-chi*, 53:22a, ninth letter in reply to Hu Chi-sui (Hu Ta-shih). The letter is undated, but the eighth letter, on p. 21b, mentions the *Nan-hsüan chi* [Collected works of Chang Shih], the preface of which is dated 1184. Hence the ninth letter is dated the same year.

59. In 1184, Lu Hsiang-shan was summoned to the palace to answer questions by the emperor. He presented them in five notes, which are found in the *Hsiang-shan ch'üan-chi*, 18:1a–3b, memorials.

60. *Wen-chi*, 35:24b, ninth letter to Liu Tzu-ch'eng. "This has been imported across the Himalayas" refers to Buddhism, which spread from India to China via Central Asian trade routes.

61. *Ibid.*, 56:2b–3a, fourth letter in reply to Chao Tzu-ch'in (Chao Yen-shu).

62. *Analects*, 2:15.

63. *Yü-lei*, ch. 124, sec. 33 (p. 4764).

64. *Ibid.*, sec. 6 (p. 4754).

65. *Ibid.*, sec. 40 (p. 4769). The quotation is from the *Diamond Scripture*, sec. 10.

66. *Wen-chi*, 36:11a–15b, sixth letter in reply to Lu Tzu-ching (Lu Hsiang-shan).

67. *Ibid.*, 55:29b, fourth letter in reply to Shao Shu-i.

68. *Hsiang-shan ch'üan-chi*, 36:21a, chronological biography.

69. *Yü-lei*, ch. 122, sec. 39 (p. 4731).

70. *Ibid.*, ch. 123, sec. 2 (p. 4739).

71. *Ibid.*, ch. 124, sec. 32 (p. 4764).

72. *Ibid.*, sec. 57 (p. 4780).

73. This refers especially to Kiangsi and Chekiang.

74. *Wen-chi*, 46:18a, third letter in reply to Chan Yüan-shan (Chan T'i-jen).

75. *Book of Mencius,* 2A:2.

76. *Yü-lei*, ch. 124, sec. 14 (pp. 4757–4758).

77. *Ibid.*, ch. 64, sec. 141 (p. 2520).

78. *Ibid.*, ch. 123, sec. 22 (p. 4750).

79. *Ibid.*, ch. 124, sec. 7 (p. 4754).

80. *Ibid.*, sec. 46 (p. 4770).

81. *Ibid.*, ch. 104, sec. 38 (p. 4165).

82. *Ibid.*, ch. 95, sec. 177 (p. 3905).

83. *Ibid.*, ch. 139, sec. 17 (p. 5303).

84. *Ibid.*, ch. 124, sec. 1 (p. 4753).

85. *Ibid.*, sec. 58 (p. 4781).

86. A prefecture in Kiangsi.

87. *Tung-lai Lü T'ai-shih wen-chi,* separate collection, 8:1b, twenty-second letter to Lecturer-in-waiting Chu (Chu Hsi).

88. *Wen-chi*, 47:20b–21a, seventeenth letter in reply to Lü Tzu-yüeh (Lü Tsu-chien).

89. *Hsiang-shan ch'üan-chi,* 36:9b, chronological biography. This letter is not found in the *Wen-chi.*

90. *Wen-chi*, 58:25a, second letter in reply to Yeh Wei-tao. The story of apology refers to the *Shih chi* [Historical records] (*SPTK* ed.), 81:6a, biography of Lin Hsiang-ju.

91. *Ibid.*, 34:26a, eighty-third letter in reply to Lü Po-kung (Lü Tsu-ch'ien).

92. *Ibid.*, p. 28a, eighty-fourth letter.

93. *Ibid.*, p. 29b, eighty-fifth letter.

94. Ancient name for Heng-yang, Chang Shih's place of residence.

95. In eastern Chin-hsi, the home of the Lu family.

96. *Wen-chi*, 54:16a, first letter in reply to Fu Tzu-yüan (Fu Meng-ch'üan).

97. *Hsiang-shan ch'üan-chi,* 27:1a–4b, biographical account of Lu Chiu-ling.

98. *Wen-chi*, 34:32a, ninetieth letter in reply to Lü Po-kung.

99. *Hsiang-shan ch'üan-chi,* 36:10b, chronological biography.

100. *Ibid.*, p. 11b. The two letters are not found in the *Wen-chi.*

101. In the tenth month of the 1179, Chu Hsi petitioned to have himself censured for demanding taxes too vigorously.

102. *Hsiang-shan ch'üan-chi,* 36:12a, chronological biography.

103. *Ibid.*, p. 12b.

104. *Wen-chi*, 36:6a, first letter to Lu Tzu-ching.

105. *Hsiang-shan ch'üan-chi,* 36:13b, chronological biography. See also n. 60 above.

106. *Wen-chi*, 54:4b, first letter in reply to Chu-ko Ch'eng-chih (Chu-ko Ch'ien-neng).

107. *Ibid.*, 90:7a–9b, tomb inscription for Ts'ao Li-chih (Ts'ao Chien).

108. The western route to Chiang-nan, an area that is roughly equivalent to present-day Kiangsi.

109. *Hsiang-shan ch'üan-chi,* 13:7a–b, first letter to Chu Yüan-hui (Chu Hsi).

110. *Ibid.*, p. 7b, second letter.

111. *Ibid.*, 9:1a, first letter to Wang Ch'ien-chung (Wang Lin-shih).

112. P'eng Shih-ch'ang's private name was Hsing-tsung. For him, see the *Sung-Yüan hsüeh-an,* 77:3b–4a, chapter on the Lu School; *Hsiang-shan ch'üan-chi,* 36:15b, chronological biography; and *Yü-lei,* ch. 124, sec. 68 (p. 4783).

113. *Hsiang-shan ch'üan-chi,* 2:5a, first letter to Chu Yüan-hui.

114. A county in Kiangsi.

115. *Wen-chi,* 36:7b, fifth letter in reply to Lu Tzu-ching (Lu Hsiang-shan).

116. *Hsiang-shan ch'üan-chi,* 2:7b, second letter to Chu Yüan-hui.

117. A county in northern Fukien.

118. *Hsiang-shan ch'üan-chi,* 36:23b, chronological biography. This letter is not found in the *Wen-chi.*

119. *Yü-lei,* ch. 90, sec. 64 (pp. 3663–3664).

120. A commandary in Hupeh where Lu Hsiang-shan was a prefect.

121. *Wen-chi,* 55:27b, letter in reply to Chao Jan-tao (Chao Shih-yung).

122. Lu Hsiang-shan died on the fourteenth day of the twelfth month of the third year of the Shao-hsi period, which corresponds to January 10, 1193.

123. *Yü-lei,* ch. 124, sec. 48 (p. 4772).

124. *Book of Mencius,* 6A:1–6.

125. *Yü-lei,* ch. 125, sec. 38 (pp. 4768–4769).

126. *Ibid.,* ch. 52, sec. 28 (p. 1960).

127. *Book of Mencius,* 2A:2.

128. *Wen-chi,* 54:8a–b, sixth letter in reply to Hsiang P'ing-fu (Hsiang An-shih). "Between a hundred paces and fifty paces" refers to the *Book of Mencius,* 1:3, about those who run fifty paces laughing at those who run a hundred paces.

129. *Yü-lei,* ch. 124, sec. 37 (pp. 4766–4767).

130. *Book of Mencius,* 2A:2.

131. *Yü-lei,* ch. 52, sec. 27 (p. 1959).

132. *Ibid.,* sec. 28 (pp. 1959–1960).

133. *Ibid.,* ch. 124, sec. 14 (pp. 4757–4758).

134. There are 48 letters from Chu Hsi to Lü Tsu-chien in chs. 47 and 48 of the *Wen-chi* and one in the separate collection, ch. 1.

135. *Yü-lei,* ch. 122, sec. 33 (p. 4729).

136. *Ibid.,* sec. 37 (p. 4731).

137. The *Hsien-p'i lu* [Refutation of heterodoxy] was written by Ch'eng T'ung of the Ming dynasty (1368–1644).

138. Wang Mao-hung, *Chu Tzu nien-p'u, k'ao-i* [Investigation into variants], ch. 3, p. 309.

139. Ch'ien Mu, *Chu Tzu hsin hsüeh-an* [New anthology and critical accounts of Master Chu] (Taipei: San-min Book Co., 1971), vol. 3, p. 456.

140. For Wen Ch'ing (Tou Ts'ung-chou), see my *Chu Tzu men-jen* [Master Chu's pupils] (Taipei: Student Book Co., 1982), pp. 360–361, and the *Sung-Yüan hsüeh-an,* 69:16a, chapter on the Chu Hsi School.

141. *Yü-lei,* ch. 114, sec. 36 (p. 4404).

142. Huang Chang-chien, "Hsiang-shan ssu-hsiang lin-chung t'ung-yü Chu Tzu" [Lu Hsiang-shan agreed with Chu Hsi in thought just before Lu died], *Ta-lu tsa-chih* [Continental journal], vol. 69, no. 1 (July, 1984), pp. 32–42.

143. *Ibid.,* p. 38.

144. *Sung-Yüan hsüeh-an,* 77:6a, chapter on the Lu School.

145. See my *Chu Tzu men-jen,* p. 176.

146. Huang Chang-chien, "Hsiang-shan ssu-hsiang lin-chung t'ung-yü Chu Tzu," p. 42.

147. *Ibid.,* pp. 33, 36.

148. *Ibid.,* p. 37.

# -27-
# What Wang Yang-ming Thought of Chu Hsi

WANG Yang-ming (1472–1529) became chief minister of the court of state ceremonials *(hung-lu ssu-ch'ing)* in 1514, at the age of forty-three. He attracted many followers, and the atmosphere of learning and discussion was extremely exciting. During this period, he selected a paragraph each from thirty-four letters in the *Wen-chi*. These he entitled "Master Chu's Final Conclusions Arrived at Late in Life," to suggest that, at the end of his life, Chu Hsi shifted from a lifelong emphasis on writing commentaries to Wang's own emphasis on personal cultivation. In the preface to this work, which Wang wrote in the eleventh month of 1515, he said:

> Later, when I was banished to become an official in Lung-ch'ang,[1] I lived among the barbarians [1508–1509] and in the midst of great difficulties. As a consequence of stimulating my mind and hardening my nature, I seemed to have rapidly awakened. I searched and made an effort at personal realization for another year. . . . There was absolutely no more doubt left in my mind. Only in Master Chu's doctrines did I find some disagreement, for which I felt sorry for a long time. I was wondering whether, with his wisdom and virtue, Master Chu could still have failed to understand. When I was an official in Nanking [1514], I got hold of his works and searched through them. Only then did I find that in his later years he clearly realized the mistakes of his earlier doctrines. He regretted them so deeply as to say that he "cannot be redeemed from the sin of having deceived others as well as himself."[2] His [*Ssu-shu*] *chi-chu*[3] and [*Ssu-shu*] *huo-wen,*[4] which have been transmitted from generation to generation, represent the tentative conclusions of his middle age. He blamed himself for not having been able to correct the mistakes of the old texts *(chiu-pen)* [of his commentary on the *Great Learning*], much as he had wanted to.[5]

After writing the preface, Wang had to suppress a rebellion, so the treatise was not published until 1518. Its publication immediately created an intellectual storm that was to last for 150 years and generate a partisan spirit that strongly opposed Wang's doctrine of mind as identical with principle, later called *Hsin-hsüeh* (School of Mind), to Chu Hsi's doctrine of nature as identical with principle, later called *Li-hsüeh* (School of Principle). We shall recount first the sharp reaction to the treatise and then its various aspects, to show what Wang Yang-ming thought of Chu Hsi.

The first to criticize Wang was the most prominent Neo-Confucian of his time, Lo Ch'in-shun (1465–1547). In his letter to Wang Yang-ming in 1520, he pointed out that Wang's selection of Chu Hsi's letter to Ho Shu-ching (Ho Hao, 1128–1175), as a final conclusion arrived at late in life was wrong, for Ho died in 1175 and the *Chi-chu* and *Huo-wen,* which Wang had regarded as writings of Chu's middle age, were not finished until 1177. Lo also told Wang that in Chu Hsi's letter to Huang Chih-ch'ing (Huang Kan, 1152–1221), Chu Hsi merely said "former mistakes," whereas Wang had changed it to read "former mistakes of the final text *(ting-pen),* " and had also changed *ting-pen* to *chiu-pen* (old text), to indicate that Chu Hsi had regretted the mistakes in his earlier writings. Lo therefore concluded that Wang had selected the excerpts from the *Wen-chi* merely for the sake of supporting his own high-sounding doctrines.[6]

Several years later, in 1524, Ku Lin (1476–1545) wrote Wang to say, "I have heard that you told students that to follow the theory of investigating the principle of everything with which we come into contact[7] is to trifle with things and lose one's purpose, and that you have also selected Chu Hsi's doctrines of rejecting the complex and preferring the simple, cultivating the fundamental, and so forth to show to students, labeling them as Chu Hsi's final conclusions arrived at late in life. I am afraid that is also wrong."[8] Ku may have gone on to explain why it was wrong, but the part of his letter quoted by Wang does not say anything more.

Several decades later, in 1548, Ch'en Chien (1497–1567) published his *Hsüeh-pu t'ung-pien* (General critique of the obscuration of learning) to attack Lu Hsiang-shan (1139–1193), Wang Yang-ming, and Ch'an (Meditation) Buddhism, with Wang as the chief target. According to Ch'en, Wang had followed in the footsteps of Chao Fang (1319–1369) and Ch'eng Min-cheng (1466 cs). Chao had written the "Essay on the Six Gentlemen of Chiang-yu"[9] to assert that because Chu Hsi had intended to reject shortcomings and accumulate merit,[10] he would have come to agree with Lu Hsiang-shan's point of view had Lu not died before him. This, Ch'en Chien said, was the beginning of the theory that Chu and Lu at first differed but finally agreed.[11] According to Ch'en, Ch'eng Min-cheng, in his *Tao-i pien* (Compilation on the One-

ness of the Way), first presented the opposition between Chu Hsi and
Lu Hsiang-shan, then their hesitation, and finally their compatibility,
thus cementing the theory that Chu Hsi finally agreed with Lu.[12] Following Ch'eng, who contended that Chu Hsi regretted the mistakes of
his fragmentation and his failure to understand Lu, Wang declared in
his preface that Chu Hsi regretted the errors of his earlier doctrines.

Ch'en Chien also pointed out that one of Chu Hsi's letters to Ho
Shu-ching mentioned Chu's serving his mother, who died when he was
forty, so that the opinions it expressed could hardly be considered those
of Chu Hsi's later years. But in Wang's excerpt from this particular letter, he had omitted the reference to Chu Hsi's mother. In fact, said
Ch'en, all four letters to Ho were written before Chu Hsi met Lu
Hsiang-shan in 1175.[13] Ch'en went on to say that Chu Hsi's letter to
Chang Ching-fu (Chang Shih, also called Chang Ch'in-fu, 1133–1180)
was written before the completion of the *Chi-chu* in 1177, and therefore
could not be taken as a product of Chu Hsi's last years. Wang had omitted the section of this letter in which Chu Hsi mentioned the revision of
his commentaries on the *Great Learning* and the *Doctrine of the Mean*—
undoubtedly, Ch'en thought, because this would have contradicted
Wang's contention that Chu Hsi had wanted to revise his commentaries
but had not had time to do so.[14] Moreover, in excerpting Chu Hsi's letter to Lü Tzu-yüeh (Lü Tsu-chien, d. 1196), Wang had selected only
the part on seeking the lost mind, Ch'en said, without realizing that the
entire letter aimed at Lü's defect of burying himself in books.[15] Ch'en
repeated Lo Ch'in-shun's criticism of misinterpreting *ting-pen* to mean
old text. He then added that Wang had selected the letter to Huang
Chih-ch'ing from the supplementary collection of the *Wen-chi,* in which
the term *ting-pen* appears, rather than the letter to him from the regular
collection, in which it does not, and reiterated that *ting-pen* has nothing
to do with editions of books.[16] Ch'en quoted Chu Hsi's sayings that "in
teaching people, one must first set up a firm foundation *(ting-pen),*"[17]
and that "in learning, one simply must first establish a foundation
*(pen),*"[18] to show that by *ting-pen* Chu Hsi meant "a firm foundation."[19]

After Ch'en Chien came Feng K'o (*fl.* 1562). One of the sixty-eight
chapters of his *Ch'iu-shih pien* (Searching for truth) is devoted to refuting
Wang Yang-ming's treatise on Chu Hsi's final conclusions. Feng
pointed out that after Ch'eng Min-cheng had dated the letters as
belonging to Chu Hsi's middle age or old age, Wang had reversed the
periods. To Feng, Chu Hsi was engaged in writing the *Chi-chu* and the
*Huo-wen* throughout his adult life, so they could not be described as
works of either his middle or old age. Chu's works also involved both
complexity and simplicity, Feng said, so one should not isolate one
statement of his about simplicity or complexity as a doctrine he arrived
at late in life. As Feng K'o saw it, Wang Yang-ming had entertained no

idea of compromise from the outset but had merely slandered Chu Hsi for his own selfish purposes.[20]

Several decades after Feng K'o, Sun Ch'eng-tse (1592–1676) wrote the *K'ao-cheng wan-nien ting-lun* (Investigation into the correctness of *Master Chu's Final Conclusions Arrived at Late in Life*) in two chapters. As the *Ssu-k'u ch'üan-shu tsung-mu t'i-yao* (Essentials of the contents of the *Complete Collection of the Four Libraries*) describes it,

> This work regards Wang as unreliable because he did not specify when Chu Hsi's late life began but merely employed Chu Hsi's own words to attack him. Sun Ch'eng-tse therefore made selections from the [*Chu Tzu*] *nien-p'u* [Chronological biography of Master Chu], the "[Chu Tzu] hsing-chuang" [Biographical account of Master Chu], the *Wen-chi,* the *Yü-lei,* and so on, investigated the correct situation, and found that none of what Chu Hsi said after he was forty-five agreed with Lu Hsiang-shan or expressed regret.[21]

According to Ku Yen-wu (1613–1682), Sun compared Wang Yang-ming's doctrine of innate knowledge with the "light conversation" of Wang Yen (1156–1211) and the New Laws of Wang An-shih (1021–1086), and considered the great damage done by the three Wangs worse than that done by ancient wicked and cruel kings.[22]

The attack on Wang's work continued from the Ming dynasty (1368–1644) into the Ch'ing period (1644–1911). Citations from two thinkers will be sufficient to make the point. One was Lu Lung-chi (1630–1693), who said, "Wang Yang-ming spread the doctrine of innate knowledge under the name of Confucianism, although it is in reality Ch'an Buddhism, and wrote 'Master Chu's Final Conclusions Arrived at Late in Life' to show that his learning was not different from that of Master Chu. Followers like Lung-hsi [Wang Chi, 1498–1583], Hsin-chai [Wang Ken, 1483–1541], Chin-hsi [Lo Ju-fang, 1515–1588], and Hai-men [Chou Ju-teng, 1547–1629] have expanded it, and Wang's learning has spread all over the world."[23] Lu Lung-chi regarded Wang Yang-ming as "utilizing the words of Ch'eng-Chu [Ch'eng I, 1033–1107, and Chu Hsi] whenever they agreed with him to confirm his own ideas, and claiming that those he could not utilize were [Chu Hsi's] tentative conclusions in middle age, thus confusing falsehood and truth."[24] In short, in Lu Lung-chi's opinion, Wang Yang-ming made use of Chu Hsi to disguise Ch'an Buddhism under the name of Confucianism. By this time, Wang was being attacked not only for his distortion of Chu Hsi but for his own philosophy, regardless of its merit.

Later, Juan Yüan (1764–1849) wrote an epilogue to Ch'en Chien's *Hsüeh-pu t'ung-pien* in which he cited Chu Hsi's letters to various pupils,[25] as well as his letter to his pupil and son-in-law Huang Kan just before he died,[26] to show that in his later years Chu Hsi devoted much time and thought to ritual texts. As Juan Yüan observed, "If we follow Wang Yang-ming's slandering of Master Chu's final conclusions arrived at late in life, it would mean that in his later years Master Chu got tired of and rejected commenting on the classics, ignored teachings of social decorum, and merely devoted himself to the simple and quiet life of the Ch'an Buddhists, with no need to toil or to be sad."[27] Juan Yüan thought that Ch'en Chien had been unfair to portray Lu Hsiang-shan as mad, but he also regarded Ch'en as upholding correct learning and removing the injustice done to Chu Hsi.[28]

In this long period of controversy, most writers attacked Wang Yang-ming; only Liu Tsung-chou (1578–1645) and Li Fu (1637–1750) said a few good words about him. As Liu commented on Wang Yang-ming's preface, "The Master [Wang Yang-ming] was based on indisputable solid evidence in whatever he attributed to himself or to others. In the final analysis, Master Chu heard the Way in his late years."[29] Liu's own philosophy was derived from Wang Yang-ming. He elaborated on Wang's idea of innate knowledge as the knowledge known only to the self, and expounded his own doctrine of being watchful over oneself when alone. Consequently, Liu said,

> When Master Chu explained the *Great Learning,* he placed the investigation of things and extension of knowledge first and then taught the doctrine of the sincerity of the will. When the Master [Wang Yang-ming] explained the *Great Learning,* the sincerity of the will takes place at the same time as the investigation of things and the extension of knowledge. They do not seem to agree on [the procedure of] the task. But the most important part in the teaching of the two Masters does not go beyond the critical point of being watchful over oneself when alone. Their teachings are the same as what is called proceeding from enlightenment to sincerity in order to enter the way of the Sage [Confucius]. That is why the Master wrote "Master Chu's Final Conclusions Arrived at Late in Life."[30]

Liu seems to be saying that Chu Hsi not only agreed with Wang Yang-ming late in life but even agreed with Liu himself!

Following Liu, Li Fu wrote the *Chu Tzu wan-nien ch'üan-lun* (Complete discussion of *Master Chu's Final Conclusions Arrived at Late in Life*) in eight chapters, with more than 370 selections from the *Wen-chi.* As the *Ssu-k'u ch'üan-shu tsung-mu t'i-yao* said, "Li selected from the regular, the supplementary, and the separate collections [of the *Wen-chi*] what Master Chu had written from the age of fifty to seventy-one. . . . This work is entirely devoted to Master Chu's regret. In addition, whatever Master Chu said about effort that is concrete and close to principle is reduced to [Wang's] learning of the mind."[31] In emphasizing Chu Hsi's late age, Li Fu seemed to correct Wang Yang-ming's mistakes in selecting Chu Hsi's letters of his middle age, but his real aim was to avenge Ch'en Chien's criticisms of Wang, for Li's own method and goal did not differ from Wang's.[32]

From the preceding accounts, criticisms of Wang Yang-ming may be grouped under four headings. First, he wrongly regarded Chu Hsi's letters of middle age as written late in life. Second, he was mistaken in taking the *Chi-chu* and the *Huo-wen* as tentative conclusions of Chu Hsi's middle age. Third, he selected passages out of context, confining his choices to those stating a preference for simplicity to complexity and those conforming to his own theories. Fourth, he misunderstood *ting-pen* to mean "final edition" and substituted *chiu-pen* (old text) for *ting-pen*. In his reply to Lo Ch'in-shun, Wang Yang-ming defended himself by saying that although he did go into Chu Hsi's age, most, if not all, of the letters which he excerpted belonged to his old age;[33] however, he remained silent on the points of being out of context and misunderstanding *ting-pen*. Those who defended Wang simply repeated his errors. Liu Tsung-chou's claim that Chu and Wang agreed on proceeding from enlightenment to sincerity, for example, overlooks the fact that for Chu Hsi "Enlightenment and sincerity advance together."[34] Li Fu made the same mistake by selecting only from the *Wen-chi*, not from the *Chi-chu* or *Huo-wen* to which Chu Hsi devoted his entire life, and then only passages suggesting regret.

I believe that Wang honestly understood *ting-pen* to mean "final edition" and *chiu-pen* to mean "old text." If so, no one can blame him for taking the *ting-pen* in Chu Hsi's letter to Huang Kan to mean *chiu-pen*. In answering a question by his pupil Yang Shih-te (Yang Chi), Wang expressed the idea that late in life Chu Hsi regretted his earlier views. In the conversation, Yang Chi quoted Chu Hsi's statement about "former mistakes of the *chiu-pen*."[35] Surely Wang would not have consciously twisted the meaning of the term in a conversation with his pupil. There can be no excuse for Wang's misunderstanding, but his sincerity cannot be doubted. He definitely knew about Chu Hsi's concern with ritual texts and his revision of his commentary on the *Great Learning*, but from Wang's point of view these were minor matters, whereas Chu Hsi's abandonment of complexity in favor of simplicity was a major turning point in his philosophy. I prefer to think that Wang honestly believed this and did not consciously distort matters for a selfish purpose.

Most of his critics concentrated on Wang's treatment of letters that Chu Hsi wrote when middle-aged as final conclusions that he arrived at late in life. As Lo Ch'in-shun pointed out, all four letters to Ho Shu-ching were written before Chu Hsi was forty-six; Ch'en Chien has also noted that the letter to Chang Ching-fu was written before the *Chi-chu* was completed in 1177. However, Ch'en's assertion that the letter to Lü Tzu-yüeh[36] and the one to Lin Tse-chih (Lin Yung-chung) belonged to

Chu Hsi's middle age rather than his old age lacks evidence.[37] If we consider Chu Hsi's old age to begin after he turned forty-eight (1178–1200), most of the 34 letters Wang selected do belong to this period. Careful scrutiny of the contents of the letters shows that five definitely belong to Chu Hsi's early or middle life, while ten definitely belong to his late life and eight possibly so. For eleven there is no historical context to tell when in Chu Hsi's life they were written. All in all, Wang's claim that most of the letters were written late in Chu Hsi's life can be defended.[38]

Furthermore, since Chu Hsi expressed his ideas more fully in letters than in conversations, Wang's selection from the *Wen-chi* rather than the *Yü-lei* cannot be considered a defect. His greatest defect lay in taking a passage or an idea out of context. The 34 letters Wang excerpted represent only 23 correspondents out of some 430 to whom Chu Hsi wrote, or about 5 percent. Thus it is obvious that they are not in any sense representative of Chu Hsi's thought. The *Wen-chi* contains more than sixteen hundred letters. If several scores of letters could represent Chu Hsi's doctrine, almost any doctrine could be thus presented as his final conclusion. Chu Hsi's letters to Chang Ching-fu (Chang Shih) preserved in the *Wen-chi* number 47, and these are among the most important because Chang Shih was his close friend and the leader of a competing school.[39] Yet Wang selected only a small portion of one of them, the portion suggesting his regret. Besides, this letter says that Chu Hsi wanted to write a commentary on the *Book of Mencius* but due to his declining energy had not done so.[40] This shows that it was written before the completion of *Chi-chu* in 1177—hardly late in life. There are 101 letters to Lü Po-kung (Lü Tsu-ch'ien) preserved in the *Wen-chi*.[41] From these Wang selected only six lines from one, which include the words, "I realize that hitherto I have not devoted enough effort to cultivation."[42] Although this letter is not dated, it mentions the correction of many mistakes in the *Chin-ssu lu* (Reflections on things at hand), so it must be within one or two years after the compilation of the *Chin-ssu lu* in 1175. This means that the letter was written in Chu Hsi's middle years rather than late in life.

As to Wang's motive, different critics have had different interpretations. Aside from mentioning Wang's attempt to prove his high-sounding theories, Lo Ch'in-shun did not go into Wang's motive. But Ch'en Chien accused Wang of "using Master Chu's words to bring out Chu's own errors and Lu Hsiang-shan's correctness. . . . For one thing, he made use of Master Chu to praise Hsiang-shan, and for another, he presumed upon Master Chu's name to influence students of later generations."[43] In his opinion, Wang was "outwardly Chu but secretly Lu"[44] and "put Chu Hsi's ideas into Lu's mouth."[45] Ch'en added, "Knowing that people believe in Master Chu, Yang-ming selected passages from

Master Chu to induce them, without mentioning Lu at all, so that people think those are only the words of Master Chu. Why should they
have any doubt and not follow them?"[46] In Ch'en's view, Wang's aim
was to promote Lu by using the name of Chu. To Feng K'o, Wang was
promoting Mo Tzu (468–376 B.C.?)—a strange interpretation indeed.
Feng wrote that Wang "felt fortunate that his theories were not in conflict with those of Master Chu. His purpose was to put Confucian ideas
into the mouth of Mo Tzu, and to push Moism and get it under the protection of Confucianism."[47] Sun Ch'eng-tse believed that Wang's aim
was to attack Chu Hsi by using Chu's words, and Lu Lung-chi also said
that Wang pretended to be quoting Chu Hsi while outwardly promoting
Confucianism but secretly promoting Ch'an Buddhism. To all Wang's
critics, Lu Hsiang-shan and Ch'an Buddhism meant the same thing. In
sum, his critics accused Wang of slandering Chu Hsi in order to praise
Lu and put Chu Hsi's words into Lu's mouth. This is pure partisanship, accompanied by not a little emotional outburst.

Did Wang Yang-ming really try to overthrow Chu Hsi and put Lu
Hsiang-shan on his pedestal? Writers on Confucian learning in the
Sung (960–1279) and Ming (1368–1644) dynasties were fond of grouping Lu Hsiang-shan and Wang Yang-ming together and calling their
system *Hsin-hsüeh* (School of Mind), in sharp distinction to the system of
Ch'eng I and Chu Hsi, which they call *Li-hsüeh* (School of Principle)—
and this despite the fact that both mind and principle are basic tenets of
each system. Regardless of the appropriateness or inappropriateness of
such labels, it is definitely wrong to suppose that Wang's philosophy
was derived from Lu or that Wang was enthusiastically promoting Lu.
Wang praised Lu but also criticized him, and his original doctrines of
the extension of innate knowledge and the unity of knowledge and
action were not inspired by Lu. Wang was banished to Lung-ch'ang in
1508 at the age of thirty-seven. In 1509, Assistant Superintendent of
Education Hsi Shu asked him to be the head of the Kuei-yang Academy. When Hsi Shu asked Wang about the similarities and differences
between the systems of Chu and Lu, Wang did not answer but instead
told Hsi Shu about his own intuition of the unity of knowledge and
action. The next day, Hsi Shu asked again. Thereupon Wang told him
that "both Chu and Lu have their merits and demerits, and there is no
need to argue about them. One will naturally understand if one
searches one's own nature."[48]

Clearly, Wang had no interest in the Chu-Lu controversy but was
primarily interested in his own theories. In the *nien-p'u* (chronological
biography) on Wang, we find no concern on Wang's part over that issue
before his meeting with Hsi Shu, who may even have been the first to
introduce him to the subject. Eleven years later, in 1520, when Wang
was pacification commissioner in the Kiangsi area, he wrote the preface

to the *Hsiang-shan wen-chi* (Collection of literary works of Lu Hsiang-shan), in which he said that since the time of Mencius scholars had bifurcated mind and principle as two, with a consequent decline in the learning of refinement and singleness.[49] Only after the appearance of Chou Tun-i (1017–1073) and the Ch'eng brothers (Ch'eng Hao, 1032–1085, and Ch'eng I, 1033–1107), Wang maintained, did the Confucian School rediscover its origin: "After that, there was Lu Hsiang-shan. Although his purity and calmness did not measure up to the two Masters, his simplicity, directness, and decisiveness truly enabled him to receive the transmission from Mencius."[50] Wang also said, "People have criticized Lu for being different from Master Chu and have slandered him as a Ch'an Buddhist. This is no more than using psychology to win an argument, for it is not necessary to debate whether Chu and Lu are similar or different, right or wrong."[51]

Thus Wang was not particularly promoting Lu. His complaint about splitting the mind and principle into two is his own criticism of Chu Hsi, not a promotion of Lu.[52] In 1521, Wang ordered that the Lu descendants be exempt from military service and that talented youths of the Lu clan be sent to government schools. That year, too, Hsi Shu sent him the *Ming-yüan lu* (Complaining against injustice), in which Hsi defended Lu. In reply, Wang said that "the simple, direct, and decisive learning of Hsiang-shan is the best since Mencius," but that "his doctrine of the extension of knowledge and the investigation of things is not free from the defect of imitation."[53] Wang's attitude toward Lu was still neutral, but he must have been stimulated by Hsi's effort on behalf of Lu. Therefore in 1522, in letters to Hsü Ch'eng-chih, he said that "[Hsi Shu] was willing to endure the criticism of the world to expose Lu's doctrine" because it was a great injustice to Lu for scholars to label him as a Ch'an Buddhist.[54] Wang still thought that both Chu and Lu had been true followers of Confucius, with their own merits and demerits, and that one should therefore not be partisan toward either of them.[55] According to Wang's outstanding pupil Ch'ien Te-hung (1497–1574), "Our Teacher felt that inasmuch as people had for a long time concluded that Chu Hsi was right and that Lu Hsiang-shan was wrong, it was difficult to reverse the trend overnight. The two letters were meant as a compromise so that people could think for themselves and reach their own conclusions."[56] As late as 1524, Wang still advised his pupil Chou Tao-t'ung (Chou Meng) "not to discuss the right and wrong of Chu and Lu."[57] Two years later, in 1526, he even took Lu to task. In a letter in reply to a friend, he said, "In the doctrines of the extension of knowledge and the investigation of things, Confucians hitherto have followed each other. Therefore Hsiang-shan has also followed. It cannot be denied that Hsiang-shan failed to see the meaning of refinement and singleness."[58]

In a conversation with his pupil Ch'en Chiu-ch'uan (1495–1562), Wang said, "Since the time of Lien-hsi [Chou Tun-i] and Ming-tao [Ch'eng Hao], there has been only Lu Hsiang-shan. But he was still somewhat crude."[59] He never explained what he meant by "crude," and later writers have not been of much help. T'ang Chün-i thought that Lu Hsiang-shan was crude in Wang's eyes because he subordinated the task of equilibrium and harmony of the mind to clear discrimination of the Way.[60] Judged by what Wang wrote to Hsi Shu about Lu's imitation, and what he said to his friend about Lu's deficiency in refinement and singleness, Professor T'ang has a point. Furthermore, when Lu Ch'eng asked him about Lu's doctrine that "one should devote one's effort to the area of human feelings and affairs,"[61] Wang answered, "The important point is to achieve the state of equilibrium and harmony."[62] This may be taken as a criticism of Lu's lack of equilibrium and harmony. Professor Tu Wei-ming offers another explanation. According to him, Wang perhaps felt that Lu was deficient in deep human experience to support his doctrine, and is therefore regarded him as crude.[63] In reply to a pupil, Wang said, "[Lu Hsiang-shan] had made some effort in his mind and was of course different from those who imitated others, depended on others, or sought only literal meanings. However, if you scrutinize his doctrines carefully, you will find there are crude spots. You will see it if you continue your effort long enough."[64] Here the word "effort" is used twice, indicating that Lu had not made sufficient effort. Commenting on Lu's famous statement that "the affairs in the universe are my own affairs. My own affairs are affairs of the universe,"[65] Wang said, "Unless one devotes a concrete effort, what is called great in only an abstract view."[66] This surely reinforces Wang's emphasis on effort. To Professor Yamada Jun, Lu was crude because in his theory of the investigation of things, knowledge and action are still separate, although just why this made him crude is not explained.[67] I believe the word "crude" should be considered along with its opposite, namely, "refinement." This is clear from Wang's evaluation of Lu as failing to attain refinement and singleness of mind.

In his teachings, Wang stressed the quality of refinement and singleness of mind. In the *Book of History*, it is taught that "the human mind is precarious and the moral mind is subtle. Have absolute refinement and singleness of mind. Hold fast the Mean."[68] Refinement and singleness are the means for transforming the human mind that is liable to make mistakes into the moral mind that follows the Way. Again and again, Wang returns to this point. To him, all cultivation of the person, rectification of the mind, sincerity of the will, and investigation of things taught in the *Great Learning* are but one thing: the learning of refinement and single-mindedness.[69] The doctrine of refinement and single-mindedness is to be understood in terms of principle.[70] Wang also said,

"Here is our innate knowedge today. We should extend it to the utmost according to what we know today. As our innate knowledge is further developed tomorrow, we should extend it to the utmost according to what we know then. Only this can be said to be the task of refinement and single-mindedness."[71] In short, one should "put the Mean into application and extend its refinement and singleness to the moral mind," which is innate knowledge.[72] Thus refinement and singleness form the basis of Wang's major doctrines of the extension of innate knowledge and the unity of knowledge and action.

From the above it is clear that Wang was more interested in propounding his own doctrines than in promoting Lu. If he did not exalt Lu, did he denounce Chu? Or did he outwardly praise him but secretly denounce him? In his preface, Wang said, "I am happy that Master Chu apprehended before me what our minds have in common."[73] In his letter to Lo Cheng-an (Lo Ch'in-shun), he said, "My chief idea was that it was important to compromise."[74] In his letter to An-chih, he said, "When I was in the capital, I talked too much and aroused a great deal of comments. People from all directions attacked me. I selected Master Chu's expressions of regret to be his final conclusions in order to resolve the dispute."[75] And in his second letter to Lu Yüan-ching (Lu Ch'eng, 1517 *cs*), he said, "The numerous troubles today are not easily resolved."[76] From all these utterances, we know that Wang was facing a great crisis and making a desperate effort to find a solution. He was trying to bring about a compromise that had nothing to do with praising Lu or promoting Ch'an Buddhism.

There is a positive element in this whole affair, however—Wang's search for unanimity with Chu Hsi. Wang valued unanimity highly. As he wrote Chan Jo-shui (1466-1560), "From now on, the learning in our movement will result in unanimity. This is my fortune and the fortune of the later generations."[77] To repeat his words, already quoted in part, "I feel fortunate that my ideas are not in conflict with those of Master Chu, and also am happy that Master Chu apprehended before me what our minds have in common."[78] Commenting on this remark, Shih Pang-yao (1585-1644) said, "Whether or not the Master [Wang Yangming] agreed with Master Chu can be seen in this saying."[79]

Unanimity with Chu Hsi did not mean however, that Wang accepted the system of orthodox transmission of the Way *(tao-t'ung)* established by Chu Hsi. Wang generally accepted the lineage of transmission up to Chu Hsi's time, but had the ambition to replace Chu Hsi with himself. When he departed for Lung-ch'ang, he sent a poem to Chan Jo-shui in which he said that the lineage from Confucius to the Ch'eng brothers was hanging in the balance, that the several gentlemen since then had had their shortcomings, and that he himself, despite his limited ability, entertained high hopes.[80] Here Wang was suggesting that Chu Hsi was not qualified to continue the *tao-t'ung*. He himself was then thirty-four. By the time he was forty-one, he had gone a step further and treated himself as an indirect pupil of the Ch'eng brothers, who thus replaced Chu Hsi in that capacity. In a reply to Ch'u Ch'ai-hsü, Wang said, "I have always thought that there have been in the world the several gentlemen Chou [Chou-Tun-i] and Ch'eng [the Ch'eng brothers]. I can of course serve as their disciple, in which case it is my great fortune."[81] In the same year, he wrote a farewell essay for Chan Jo-shui in which he said, "Two thousand years after the learning of the Sage was suspended after Mencius, it was continued by Chou and Ch'eng. Ever since then, learning has been fragmented. . . . With divine help from Heaven, I achieve some awakening. I then searched among the doctrines of Chou and Ch'eng and seem to have found something."[82] Yet Wang still had not assumed a role in the *tao-t'ung*. (It should be noted, too, that he was following Chou and Ch'eng, not Lu Hsiang-shan.) By 1525, when he reached fifty-four, however, he frankly put himself in the *tao-t'ung*. As he said, "Since the passing away of Confucius and Mencius, this learning was suspended for a thousand and hundreds of years. With the divine help of Heaven, I happen to have an insight. This is the joy of a long, long time."[83] Here it might even appear that Wang was bypassing Chou and Ch'eng. However, in the following year, his pupil Nieh Pao (1487–1563) said that in Wang he "unexpectedly found Tzu-ssu (492–431 B.C.?), Mencius, Chou, and Ch'eng in this late generation."[84] The pupil was virtually saying that Wang had replaced Chu Hsi in the *tao-t'ung*.

Wang honored Chou and Ch'eng as highly as did Chu Hsi, but the two men differed in which of the Ch'eng brothers they preferred, and why. For Wang the preferred Ch'eng was Ch'eng Hao rather than Ch'eng I. When Wang was thirty and toured Chiu-hua Mountain, he called on a strange person in a cave, who told him that there had been two talented Confucians, namely, Chou Lien-hsi (Chou Tun-i) and Ch'eng Ming-tao (Ch'eng Hao).[85] This left a deep impression that grew deeper over the years, culminating in the opening statement of Wang's preface to his "Final Conclusions," which says, "The transmission of the teachings of Confucius terminated with Mencius. It was not until one thousand five hundred years later that Lien-hsi and Ming-tao began to search again for its clues."[86] For Chu Hsi, Chou Tun-i's "T'ai-chi-t'u shuo" (Explanation of the diagram of the Great Ultimate) provided the basis for his own philosophy. But the Great Ultimate did not interest Wang at all; it is mentioned only once in the *Ch'uan-hsi lu,* and the emphasis there is on activity and tranquillity.[87] For Wang, the attraction of Chou's "explanation" lay not in its metaphysical discussion of the Great Ultimate but in the ethical doctrine that "the sage settles these affairs by the principles of the Mean, correctness, humanity, and righteousness, regarding tranquillity as fundamental,"[88] which he quoted with admiration.[89] Likewise, his exaltation of Ch'eng Hao was due to his doctrine of calmness. Wang said,

> The doctrine of settling by humanity, righteousness, the Mean, and correctness, and regarding tranquillity as fundamental, and Ch'eng Hao's doctrine that 'One's nature is calm whether it is in a state of activity or in a state of tranquillity. One does not lean forward or backward to accommodate things, nor make any distinction between the internal and external,'[90] are virtually the basic principles of refinement and single-mindedness.[91]

Wang's admiration for Ch'eng Hao can be seen in his sixteen quotations of him in the *Ch'uan-hsi lu,* and seven in the *Complete Works.*[92] Since Chu Hsi also honored Ch'eng Hao, Wang's respect for Ch'eng Hao amounts to respecting Chu Hsi.

Wang's exposure to Chu Hsi's thought took place fairly late in his education. When he was seventeen, he was still primarily interested in the Taoist technique of nourishing life. In 1489, when Wang was eighteen, he visited Lou Liang (1422–1491), who told him about the doctrine of the investigation of things of the Sung Neo-Confucians, thereby linking him directly with Chu Hsi. Undoubtedly, Wang read Chu Hsi's commentaries on the Four Books soon afterward. In 1492, when he was twenty-one, he searched for Chu Hsi's works to read, and was ready to put what he believed to be Chu Hsi's doctrine of the investigation of things into actual practice. He and his friend Ch'ien meditated and tried to investigate the principle of bamboos in front a pavilion, only to get sick after seven days.[93] Evidently Wang did not quite understand either Chu Hsi's commentary on the *Great Learning,* which says that "the first step in the education of the adult is to instruct the learner in regard to all things in the world, to proceed from what knowledge he has of their principle, and to investigate further until he reaches the limit,"[94] or his lengthy discussions on the investigation of things in the *Ta-hsüeh huo-wen* (Questions and answers on the *Great Learning*).

It is also possible that Wang ignored all these deliberations and approached the matter with an independent spirit, as was his wont. According to his chronological biography, in 1498, at the age of twenty-seven, when he read Chu Hsi's memorial to the emperor that says, "The foundation of book reading is to abide in seriousness *(ching)* and to hold the will firm, and the method of book reading is to follow an order in order to achieve excellence,"[95] Wang was deeply impressed. Yet after trying out the method, he still thought that the principle of things and the mind were split in two, a frustration that resulted in illness. At this time he still wanted to pursue the Taoist way of nourishing life.[96] In other words, he had become skeptical of Chu Hsi's doctrines. Thus for almost twenty years he really did not study Chu Hsi's thought thoroughly.

It was not until 1514, when he was forty-three, that Wang again searched for Chu Hsi's works and studied them diligently. He quoted Chu Hsi twenty times in the *Ch'uan-hsi lu,* including eleven quotations from the *Ssu-shu chi-chu,* six from the *Ssu-shu huo-wen,* two from the *Wen-chi,* and one from the *Yü-lei.* These excerpts are not confined to the questions of simplicity and personal cultivation, as his quotations in the "Final Conclusions" are, but cover the topics of the Principle of Heaven versus selfish human desires, the relation of the mind and principle, honoring the moral nature, innate knowledge, nature, and material force.

In almost all cases, however, Wang stood in direct opposition to the position put forth in his quotation by Chu Hsi. Chu Hsi had said that "all events and things possess in them a definite principle,"[97] but Wang considered this to be "regarding righteousness as external."[98] Chu Hsi had said that "the moral mind is always the master of the person, and the human mind always obeys the moral mind,"[99] but Wang said, "There is only one mind. Before it is mixed with selfish human desires, it is called the moral mind, and after it is mixed with human desires contrary to its natural state, it is called the human mind. . . . The Principle of Heaven and selfish desires cannot coexist. How can there be the Principle of Heaven as the master and at the same time selfish human desires to obey it?"[100] Chu Hsi had said that "evil [revealed in the classics] can serve to correct one's idolence,"[101] but Wang dismissed this idea as "making an excuse after having failed to find a satisfactory explanation."[102]

Chu Hsi had said, "Man's objective of learning is simply mind and principle,"[103] but Wang thought this was interpreting mind and principle as two different things.[104] About Chu Hsi's statement, "Split [principle] and you will find it extremely refined and not confused; then put it together again and you will find it extremely great and all inclusive,"[105] Wang asked, "Does principle permit any splitting up? And what is the need of putting it together again?"[106] About Chu Hsi's statement, "Learning is following the conduct of those who are the first to be enlightened,"[107] Wang said, "That is to mention only one item of the process of learning."[108] Chu Hsi had considered Tseng Tzu (Tseng Shen, 505–436 B.C.?) as "having carefully examined matters as they came along and practiced them vigorously,"[109] but Wang thought that "He was not in complete accord with truth."[110]

To Chu Hsi, education as cultivating the Way meant that the Sage (Confucius) regulated and restricted the nature with which we are originally endowed,[111] but to Wang there was no need for the Sage to regulate and restrict.[112] Chu Hsi considered Confucius' remark on government in the *Analects* 15:10 as "setting up the system for ten thousand generations to follow";[113] Wang disagreed.[114] To Wang, Chu Hsi's statement that "although the mind is the master of the body, . . . actually it controls all principles in the world"[115] "opened the way to the defect among scholars of regarding the mind and the principle as two separate things."[116] For Chu Hsi, exerting the mind to the utmost, preserving the mind, and so forth were matters pertaining to the sage,[117] but for Wang, they pertain to the worthy.[118] Chu Hsi had explained the investigation of things as "investigating the principles of everything with which we come into contact,"[119] but Wang also took this as splitting mind and principle in two.[120] Chu Hsi had contended that as soon we talk about nature, there is already material force mixed in it,[121] but Wang refused to accept the bifurcation of nature and material force.[122]

To Chu Hsi's theory that quickness of apprehension, intelligence, insight, and wisdom are physical nature,[123] Wang was directly opposed.[124] Chu Hsi had grouped together examining one's subtle thoughts, searching for principles, testing them in activities, and discovering them in discussions,[125] but Wang considered this as lacking a sense of relative importance.[126] Wang also accused Chu Hsi of separating honoring the moral nature and following the path of inquiry and study,[127] for in his view, following the path of inquiry and study is the way to honor the moral nature.[128]

In the above cases, Chu and Wang stood in direction opposition and there was no possibility of compromise. However, in a few instances Wang did give Chu Hsi qualified approval. Wang said that when Chu Hsi wrote in his commentary on the *Great Learning* that "[manifesting the clear character is] the realization of the Principle of Heaven to the fullest extent without an iota of selfish human desires,"[129] he got the point.[130] Wang also approved of the idea of all parts of the body obeying the command of the original mind[131] as though having a master.[132] Perhaps Chu Hsi's statement that "what people do not know but I alone know"[133] was most agreeable to Wang, for he said that that is indeed "exactly the innnate knowledge in our mind."[134] Likewise, he welcomed Chu Hsi's opinion that reviewing the old amounts to honoring the moral nature,[135] for that fit well with his doctrine of the unity of knowledge and action.[136]

Wang also criticized Chu Hsi for what he called Chu Hsi's fragmentation, but in this case he really could not make up his mind. When he said that since the time of Chou Tun-i and Ch'eng Hao, Confucian teaching had "gradually tended to be fragmented,"[137] and that "since the time of Chou and Ch'eng, learning has become increasingly fragmented,"[138] he probably had Chu Hsi in mind. However, Chu Hsi had divided his "Instructions for Learning" for the White Deer Hollow Academy into five sections.[139] Wang thought that the five seemed unrelated. Though Wang conceded that Chu Hsi probably had one thread running through all of them, he quickly added that "scholars of the world often make the mistake of fragmentation."[140] Again and again he complained of this.[141] In his second letter in reply to Hsü Ch'eng-chih on the agreements and disagreements between Chu Hsi and Lu Hsiang-shan, Wang said, "Throughout his life Master Chu dedicated his time to commentaries. . . . Scholars of the world have missed many points . . . and have criticized him for being fragmentary. They don't realize that this is the defect of later scholars. In what Hui-an [Chu Hsi] did at the time, did he reach that point?"[142] It was not Chu Hsi, then, but scholars of the world that were fragmentary.

In reviewing Wang's criticisms of Chu Hsi, I have quoted his *Ch'uan-hsi lu* many times. The date of its compilation is difficult to determine. The first part was printed in 1518, definitely earlier than the "Final Conclusions." In the "Final Conclusions," Wang wanted to agree with Chu Hsi, but in the *Ch'uan-hsi lu* he differed from him. Did Wang himself regret his own mistakes late in life and seek unanimity with Chu Hsi? Or did he contradict himself? Neither is necessarily the case, for their thoughts are similar in certain respects and different in others. Wang could not accept Chu Hsi's doctrine of the investigation of things that he had inherited from Ch'eng I, but he welcomed Chu Hsi's theories of mind and nature that he had received from Ch'eng Hao. Clearly Wang was selective. Thus the final conclusions were not actually Chu Hsi's but Wang's. Wang depended on Chu Hsi for his final conclusions because he wanted to arrive at unanimity with him.

When Wang was thirty-seven, he did not agree with Chu Hsi's bifurcation of the mind and the principle as two, a frustration that caused him to become ill, but he "was happy with Chu Hsi's teaching of moral cultivation."[143] When he disagreed with Chu Hsi, he nevertheless protested that "my ultimate purpose and that of Hui-an are not different."[144] When he was criticized, he said, "Even I-ch'uan [Ch'eng I] and Hui-an were not immune from criticism in their time."[145] In defending his disagreement with Chu Hsi on the theory of the investigation of things, he declared, "Even with Master Chu, while he respected and believed in Master Ch'eng [Ch'eng I], he would not carelessly follow him whenever he came to something he could not understand."[146] In short, Wang looked upon Chu Hsi as his model. Consequently, despite his original theories, his philosophy seldom went beyond the confines of Sung Neo-Confucianism. For example, when he instituted the principles of the investigation of things and the extension of knowledge at Lung-ch'ang, Wang had to find support and proof in the Five Classics.[147] Although his theory of the investigation of things differed radically from that of Chu Hsi, he still relied on the old text of the *Great Learning* for his argument, unable to go beyond Chu Hsi's standpoint that the *Great Learning* provides the key to the investigation of things. Wang had copied the old text of the *Great Learning* at Lung-ch'ang in 1516.[148] He waited for two years before writing the preface for it,[149] and his short introductions were revised three times.[150] These hesitations can be clearly seen in his letter to Lo Ch'in-shun.[151] All this shows both his eagerness to follow Chu Hsi and his adherence to Sung Neo-Confucianism. Wang criticized Lu Hsiang-shan for imitating and for being crude, but he could also have applied these criticisms to himself.

That Wang did indeed submit to Chu Hsi is perhaps best expressed by Liu Tsung-chou, Wang's faithful follower. Liu's comments on the *Ch'uan-hsi lu* are most poignant. On Wang's passage, "To set one's purpose earnestly on the Way is of course sincerity of the will, but if one presses too hard, it becomes selfishness instead,"[152] Liu commented, "This saying naturally coincides with that of Ch'eng and Chu."[153] Liu also said, "The Master has already said that the investigation of things is the same as the task of making goodness manifest as taught in the *Doctrine of the Mean,* and is not separate from study, inquiry, thinking, sifting, and practice.[154] What is the difference from the doctrine of Master Chu?"[155] He added, "The concepts of the Principle of Heaven and selfish human desires are the same in Chu and Wang. What is the need for the 'Final Conclusions'?"[156] Again, Liu remarked,

> In the recorded sayings of the Master, it is said more than once to eliminate human desires and preserve the Principle of Heaven. It also says, "The highest good is the original substance of the mind. . . . And yet it is not separated from events and things,"[157] and "Realize the Principle of Heaven to the fullest extent."[158] Thus the teachings the Master [Wang Yang-ming] followed in his mind unexpectedly remain within the framework of Sung Neo-Confucians, except that the Master made the points clearer.[159]

Wang had interpreted equilibrium to mean not leaning on one side. To Liu, "This is the same as Master Chu's doctrine of equilibrium as not leaning to one side but holding tranquillity as fundamental, but the Master shot through it with his doctrine of innate knowledge."[160] Generally speaking, Liu Tsung-chou's thoughts were derived from Wang Yang-ming, and he supported Wang's assertion that Chu Hsi's final conclusions were arrived at late in life. Yet Liu pointed out that Wang had been inspired by Chu Hsi in more than one respect. Professor Ch'ien Mu also observed, "From the beginning to the end, Shou-jen's [Wang Yang-ming] doctrines cannot be freed from the confines of Chu Hsi," although he did not go into details.[161]

In addition to Liu Tsung-chou's observations, I may add three points concerning Wang's major doctrines. One is that Wang repeatedly declared that the highest good is the original substance of the mind. To support his theory, he quoted from Chu Hsi, who said, "[Manifesting the clear character is] the realization of the Principle of Heaven to the fullest extent without an iota of selfish human desires."[162] Second, in saying that "what people do not know but I alone know is exactly the innate knowledge in our mind,"[163] Wang was actually quoting Chu Hsi.[164] Third, and most important of all, Wang said, "The original mind is vacuous [devoid of selfish desires], intelligent, and not beclouded. All principles are contained therein and events proceed from it. There is no principle outside the mind; there is no event outside the mind."[165] He also said, "The clear character is the nature given by the Mandate of Heaven. It is intelligent, shining, and not beclouded, and all principles proceed from it."[166] In his commentary on the *Great Learning,* Chu Hsi said,

> The clear character is what man receives from Heaven. It is vacuous, intelligent, and not beclouded. It embraces all principles and responds to all events. However, because it is restricted by physical endowment and beclouded by human desires, it is sometimes darkened. But the brilliance of its original substance has never ceased. Therefore the student should follow its disclosure and make it manifest so that it resumes its original state.[167]

Similarly, Wang said, "When it is sometimes beclouded, that is because of selfish desires. To manifest the mind is simply to eliminate the beclouding of selfish desires and preserve the brilliance of the original substance."[168] The idea is practically the same, and the language is almost identical.

In the three basic tenets of his thought—namely, the mind of the highest good, innate knowledge, and manifesting the clear character— Wang Yang-ming depended on Chu Hsi for support. No wonder he declared, "Hui-an has been infinitely kind to me."[169] He also said, "All my life, Master Chu's doctrine has been a revelation to me, as though from the gods."[170] Once Wang asked, "All my life, what has Hui-an meant to me?"[171] The answer is obvious.

## Notes

1. In modern Kuei-chou. Wang Yang-ming presented a memorial in defense of Policy Review Adviser Tai Hsien and thus angered the powerful eunuch Liu Chin, was beaten forty strokes, and was banished to Lung-ch'ang.

2. *Wen-chi,* 40:27a, thirteenth letter in reply to Ho Shu-ching (Ho Hao).

3. Chu Hsi, *Ssu-shu chi-chu* [Collected commentaries on the Four Books]. The Four Books are the *Great Learning,* the *Analects,* the *Book of Mencius,* and the *Doctrine of the Mean.*

4. Chu Hsi, *Ssu-shu huo-wen*, [Questions and answers on the Four Books].

5. At the end of Wang Yang-ming's *Ch'uan-hsi lu* [Instructions for practical living], in the *Wang Wen-ch'eng Kung ch'üan-shu* [Complete works of Wang Yang-ming] (*SPPY* ed.), 3:63b–64b; 7:21a–22b. For an English translation of the *Ch'uan-hsi lu,* see my translation, also entitled *Instructions for Practical Living* (New York: Columbia University Press, 1963).

6. Lo Ch'in-shun, *K'un-chih chi* [Knowledge painfully acquired] (1528 ed.), 5:4a–6a. I had thought Ku Tung-ch'iao (Ku Lin) was the first to criticize Wang Yang-ming, but Dr. Irene Bloom has pointed out to me that Lo wrote Wang in 1520, whereas Ku's letter was written in 1524. I am grateful for this correction.

7. This is Chu Hsi's theory in his *Ta-hsüeh chang-chü* [Commentary on the *Great Learning*] comment on ch. 5.

8. *Instructions for Practical Living,* sec. 135.

9. Present Kiangsi Province.

10. Chu Hsi stated this intention in a letter to Hsiang P'ing-fu (Hsiang An-shih) in the *Wen-chi,* 54:6a.

11. Ch'en Chien, *Hsüeh-p'u t'ung-pien* [General critique of the obscuration of learning] (*Cheng-i-t'ang ch'üan-shu* [Complete library of the Hall of Rectifying the Way] ed.), introduction, p. 1a. Also 2:10b. On Chu Hsi and Lu Hsiang-shan, see ch. 26 above.

12. *Ibid.,* introduction, p. 1a; 1:3a; 2:3b.

13. *Ibid.,* 1:3a, 4a.

14. *Ibid.,* 2:3a.

15. *Ibid.,* 2:3b–4a.

16. *Ibid.,* 2:5b.

17. *Wen-chi,* 34:34a, ninety-third letter in reply to Lü Po-kung (Lü Tsu-ch'ien).

18. *Ibid.,* supplementary collection, 1:3b, eighteenth letter in reply to Huang Chih-ch'ing (Huang Kan).

19. Ch'en Chien, *Hsüeh-pu t'ung-pien,* 2:5b.

20. Feng K'o, *Ch'iu-shih pien* [Searching for truth], 4:4b, in the *Cheng-pai wu-shu* [Five works of Feng K'o] (*Ssu-ming ts'ung-shu* [Ssu-ming series] ed.).

21. *Ssu-k'u ch'üan-shu tsung-mu t'i-yao* [Essentials of the contents of the *Complete Collection of the Four Libraries*] (Shanghai: Commercial Press, 1936), p. 1999.

22. Ku Yen-wu, *Jih-chih lu* [Record of daily acquisition of knowledge], ch. 18 (*Kuo-hsüeh chi-pen ts'ung-shu* [Basic sinological series] ed., p. 121).

23. Lu Lung-chi, *San-yü-t'ang wen-chi* [Collection of literary works of the Three-Fish Hall] (1868 ed.), 2:1b–2a.

24. *Ibid.,* 2:1b.

25. *Wen-chi,* 38:40b–41b, third and fourth letters in reply to Li Chi-chang (Li Pi); 54:12b, sixth letter in reply to Ying Jen-chung (Ying Shu); 58:27a, fourth letter in reply to Yeh Wei-tao (Yeh Ho-sun).

26. *Ibid.,* 29:23a, letter to Huang Chih-ch'ing.

27. Juan Yüan, *Yen-ching-shih hsü-chi* [Supplementary collection of the Hall of the Investigation of the Classics] (*SPTK* ed.), 3:5b–6a.

28. *Ibid.,* 3:7b.

29. Liu Ts'ung-chou, *Liu Tzu ch'üan-shu i-pien* [Surviving works of the complete works of Master Liu Tsung-chou] (1850 ed.), 12:12b.

30. Liu Tsung-chou, "Shih-shuo" [What my teacher said], quoted in the beginning of Huang Tsung-hsi's *Ming-ju hsüeh-an* [Anthology and critical accounts of Neo-Confucians of the Ming dynasty] (*SPPY* ed.), p. 4b.

31. *Ssu-k'u ch'üan-shu tsung-mu t'i-yao*, p. 2023.

32. See discussion on this point by Ch'ien Mu in his *Chu Tzu hsin-hsüeh-an* [New anthology and critical accounts of Master Chu] (Taipei: San-min Book Co., 1971), vol. 1, pp. 231–232. Fei Hsi's (1795–1852) "Chu Tzu wan-nien ting-lun p'ing-shu" [Critical account of *Master Chu's Final Conclusions Arrived at Late in Life*] is included in the *Fei Tao-feng i-shu* [Surviving works of Fei Hsi] (1894 ed.), but it has not been available to me.

33. *Instructions for Practical Living*, sec. 176, in the *Wang Wen-ch'eng Kung ch'üan-shu*, 2:63b, 47:31a.

34. *Wen-chi*, 1:2b, prose-poem on the White Deer Hollow Academy.

35. *Instructions for Practical Living*, sec. 100, in the *Wang Wen-ch'eng Kung ch'üan-shu*, 1:47b.

36. Ch'en Chien, *Hsüeh-pu t'ung-pien*, 2:3b.

37. *Ibid.*, 1:6a.

38. I have examined each of the letters and arrived at this statistic. See my *Wang Yang-ming Ch'uan-hsi lu hsiang-chu chi-p'ing* [Full annotation and collected commentaries of Wang Yang-ming's *Ch'uan-hsi lu*] (Taipei: Student Book Co., 1983), pp. 444–445.

39. *Wen-chi*, 30:17a–38:26b.

40. *Ibid.*, 31:15a, twenty-seventh letter in reply to Chang Ching-fu (Chang Shih).

41. *Ibid.*, 33:1a–35:11a; supplementary collection, 5:10b.

42. *Ibid.*, 33:33b, forty-eighth letter in reply to Lü Po-kung (Lü Tsu-ch'ien).

43. Ch'en Chien, *Hsüeh-pu t'ung-pien*, 1:7b–8a. On Chu Hsi and Lu Hsiang-sha, see ch. 26 above.

44. *Ibid.*, 3:15b.

45. *Ibid.*, 11:2b.

46. *Ibid.*, 12:10b.

47. Feng K'o, *Ch'iu-shih pien*, 4:5b.

48. *Wang Wen-ch'eng Kung ch'üan-shu*, 32:15a–b, chronological biography, under the year 1509.

49. Qualities of the mind as taught in the *Book of History*, "Counsels of Great Yü," sec. 15. See the quotation in the text preceding n. 68.

50. *Wang Wen-ch'eng Kung ch'üan-shu*, 7:29a–b.

51. *Ibid.*, 7:30a.

52. *Instructions for Practical Living*, sec. 33.

53. *Wang Wen-ch'eng Kung ch'üan-shu*, 5:4a–b, letter to Hsi Yüan-shan (Hsi Shu).

54. *Ibid.*, 21:15a, second letter to Hsü Ch'eng-chih.

55. *Ibid.*, 21:10a–11b.

56. *Instructions for Practical Living*, p. 89.

57. *Ibid.*, sec. 149.

58. *Wang Wen-ch'eng Kung ch'üan-shu*, 6:14a–b.

59. *Instructions for Practical Living*, sec. 205.

60. T'ang Chün-i, "Yang-ming yü Chu-Lu i-t'ung ch'ung-pien" [Further

critique on Wang Yang-ming in relation to the agreement and disagreement between Chu and Lu], *Hsin-ya hsüeh-pao* [New Asia journal], vol. 8, no. 2 (1968), p. 126.

61. *Hsiang-shan ch'üan-chi* [Complete works of Lu Hsiang-shan] (*SPPY* ed.), 34:5a.

62. *Instructions for Practical Living*, sec. 37.

63. Tu Wei-ming, *Neo-Confucian Thought in Action: Wang Yang-ming's Youth (1472–1509)* (Berkeley: University of California Press, 1976), p. 158.

64. *Instructions for Practical Living*, sec. 205.

65. *Hsiang-shan ch'üan-chi*, 22:5a.

66. *Wang Wen-ch'eng Kung ch'üan-shu*, 4:44a, letter to Fang Shu-hsien (Fang Hsien-fu).

67. Yamada Jun, *Riku Shōzan, Ō Yōmei* [Lu Hsiang-shan, Wang Yang-ming] (Tokyo: Iwanami Book Co., 1923), p. 100.

68. *Book of History*, "Counsels of Great Yü," sec. 15.

69. *Instructions for Practical Living*, sec. 174.

70. *Ibid.*, sec. 153.

71. *Ibid.*, sec. 225.

72. *Ibid.*, sec. 140.

73. *Ibid.*, p. 266.

74. *Ibid.*, sec. 176.

75. *Wang Wen-ch'eng Kung ch'üan-shu*, 4:40b, letter to An-chih. We have no information on who An-chih was.

76. *Ibid.*, 5:15b, second letter to Lu Yüan-ching (Lu Ch'eng).

77. *Ibid.*, 4:41a–b, first letter to Chan Kan-ch'üan (Chan Jo-shui).

78. *Instructions for Practical Living*, p. 266.

79. Shih Pang-yao, *Yang-ming Hsien-sheng chi-yao* [Anthology of important sayings of Master Wang Yang-ming] (1906 ed.), 4:91a–b.

80. *Wang Wen-ch'eng Kung ch'üan-shu*, 19:26b.

81. *Ibid.*, 21:20a, letter in reply to Ch'u Ch'ai-hsü.

82. *Ibid.*, 7:7a–8a, "Farewell to Chan Kan-ch'üan."

83. *Ibid.*, 8:17a, "Written for Wei Shih-meng's Folio."

84. *Instructions for Practical Living*, sec. 178.

85. *Wang Wen-ch'eng Kung ch'üan-shu*, 32:9a, chronological biography.

86. See above, n. 5.

87. *Instructions for Practical Living*, sec. 157.

88. *Chou Tzu ch'üan-shu* [Complete works of Chou Tun-i] (*Kuo-hsüeh chi-pen ts'ung-shu* ed.), ch. 2, p. 23, "Explanation of the diagram of the Great Ultimate."

89. *Wang Wen-ch'eng Kung ch'üan-shu*, 7:29b, preface to the *Hsiang-shan wen-chi* [Collection of literary works of Lu Hsiang-shan].

90. *Ming-tao wen-chi* [Collection of literary works of Ch'eng Hao), 3:1a, letter in reply to Master Hung-ch'ü's (Chang Tsai) letter on calming human nature, in the *Erh-Ch'eng ch'üan-shu* [Complete works of the two Ch'engs] (*SPPY* ed.).

91. *Wang Wen-ch'eng Kung ch'üan-shu*, 7:29b, preface to the *Hsiang-shan wen-chi*.

92. *Instructions for Practical Living*, secs. 23, 28, 72, 89, 93, 121, 136, 145, 149, 156, 163, 167, 201, 202, 235, 330: *Wang Wen-ch'eng Kung ch'üan-shu*, 4:1b, 5:19b, 20b, 27a; 6:26a, 33a; 22:14a. I have gone into the details of Wang Yang-

ming's attitude toward Ch'eng Hao in my *Chu-hsüeh lun-chi* [Essays on Chu Hsi studies] (Taipei: Student Book Co., 1982), pp. 452–454.

93. *Instructions for Practical Living,* sec. 319.

94. Chu Hsi, *Ta-hsüeh chang-chü* [Commentary on the *Great Learning*], comment on ch. 5.

95. *Wen-chi,* 14:11a, memorial of 1194.

96. *Wang Wen-ch'eng Kung ch'üan-shu,* 32:7b–8a, chronological biography.

97. Chu Hsi, *Ta-hsüeh huo-wen* [Questions and answers on the *Great Learning*] (*Chin-shih han-chi ts'ung-k'an* [Chinese works of the recent periods] ed.), p. 6a (p. 11), comment on the text.

98. *Instructions for Practical Living,* sec. 2.

99. In the preface in his *Chung-yung chang-chü.*

100. *Instructions for Practical Living,* sec. 10.

101. Chu Hsi, *Lun-yü chi-chu* [Collected commentaries on the *Analects*], comment on 2:2.

102. *Instructions for Practical Living,* sec. 14.

103. *Ta-hsüeh huo-wen,* p. 20b (p. 40), comment on ch. 5.

104. *Instructions for Practical Living,* sec. 33.

105. *Ta-hsüeh huo-wen,* p. 8a (p. 15), comment on the text.

106. *Instructions for Practical Living,* sec. 35.

107. *Lun-yü chi-chu,* comment on 1:1.

108. *Instructions for Practical Living,* sec. 111.

109. *Lun-yü chi-chu,* comment on 4:15.

110. *Instructions for Practical Living,* sec. 112.

111. Chu Hsi, *Chung-yung chang-chü* [Commentary on the *Doctrine of the Mean*], comment on ch. 1.

112. *Instructions for Practical Living,* sec. 127.

113. *Lun-yü chi-chu,* comment on 15:10.

114. *Instructions for Practical Living,* sec. 128.

115. *Ta-hsüeh huo-wen,* p. 20b (p. 40), comment on ch. 5.

116. *Instructions for Practical Living,* sec. 133.

117. *Lun-yü chi-chu,* comment on 7:1.

118. *Instructions for Practical Living,* sec. 134.

119. *Ta-hsüeh chang-chü,* comment on ch. 5.

120. *Instructions for Practical Living,* sec. 135.

121. *Wen-chi,* 61:22b, letter in reply to Yen Shih-heng.

122. *Instructions for Practical Living,* sec. 150.

123. *Chung-yung chang-chü,* comment on ch. 31.

124. *Instructions for Practical Living,* sec. 165.

125. *Ta-hsüeh huo-wen,* p. 20a (p. 39), comment on ch. 5.

126. *Instructions for Practical Living,* sec. 234.

127. *Wen-chi,* 54:5b, letter in reply to Hsiang P'ing-fu.

128. *Instructions for Practical Living,* sec. 325. On this topic, see ch. 16 above.

129. *Ta-hsüeh chang-chü,* comment on the opening sentence of the *Great Learning.*

130. *Instructions for Practical Living,* sec. 2.

131. Chu Hsi, *Meng Tzu chi-chu* [Collected commentaries on the *Book of Mencius*], comment on 6A:15.

132. *Instructions for Practical Living,* sec. 104.

133. *Ta-hsüeh chang-chü*, comment on ch. 6.

134. *Instructions for Practical Living*, sec. 318.

135. *Yü-lei*, ch. 64, sec. 149 (p. 2522).

136. *Instructions for Practical Living*, sec. 140.

137. *Ibid.*, p. 265.

138. *Wang Wen-ch'eng Kung ch'üan-shu*, 7:7a, "Farewell to Chan Kan-ch'üan."

139. *Wen-chi*, 74:16b–17b, announcement for the White Deer Hollow Academy.

140. *Wang Wen-ch'eng Kung ch'üan-shu*, 7:20b, "Preface to the Collection of the Tzu-yang Academy."

141. See *ibid.*, 7:34a, account of a Taoist priest; and 46a, account of a library.

142. *Ibid.*, 11:13b–14a, second letter in reply to Hsü Ch'eng-chih.

143. *Ibid.*, 6:18b, second letter in reply to Nan Yüan-shan (Nan Ta-chi).

144. *Instructions for Practical Living*, sec. 98.

145. *Wang Wen-ch'eng Kung ch'üan-shu*, 5:15b, second letter in reply to Lu Yüan-ching.

146. *Instructions for Practical Living*, sec. 6.

147. The Five Classics are the *Book of Odes*, the *Book of History*, the *Book of Rites*, the *Book of Changes*, and the *Spring and Autumn Annals*.

148. *Wang Wen-ch'eng Kung ch'üan-shu*, 32:57a, chronological biography.

149. *Ibid.*, 7:25a, "Preface to the Old Text of the *Great Learning*."

150. *Ibid.*, 5:21a, letter to Huang Mien-chih (Huang Hsing-tseng). See also *ibid.*, 27:27a, letter to Lu Ch'ing-po (Lu Ch'eng).

151. *Instructions for Practical Living*, sec. 173.

152. *Wang Wen-ch'eng Kung ch'üan-shu*, 4:2b, letter to Hsü Ch'eng-chih.

153. *Liu Tzu ch'üan-shu i-pien*, 11:2b, "Yang-ming ch'uan-hsin lu" [True transmission of Wang Yang-ming], I. In his selection of the "Yang-ming ch'uan-hsin lu" in the *Ming-ju hsüeh-an*, 10:5b, Huang Tsung-hsi omitted this comment.

154. As taught in the *Doctrine of the Mean*, ch. 20.

155. *Liu Tzu ch'üan-shu i-pien*, 11:4b, "Yang-ming ch'uan-hsin lu," I.

156. *Ibid.*, 13:1b, "Yang-ming ch'uan-hsin lu," III.

157. *Instructions for Practical Living*, sec. 2.

158. *Ibid.*

159. *Liu Tzu ch'uan-shu i-pien*, 13:5a, "Yang-ming ch'uan-hsin lu," III.

160. *Ibid.*, 13:8a–b. This comment is also deleted from the *Ming-ju hsüeh-an*, 10:15b.

161. Ch'ien Mu, *Chu Tzu hsin-hsüeh-an*, vol. 1, pp. 210–211.

162. *Ta-hsüeh chang-chü*, comment on the opening sentence of the *Great Learning*.

163. *Instructions for Practical Living*, sec. 318.

164. *Ta-hsüeh chang-chü*, comment on ch. 6.

165. *Instructions for Practical Living*, sec. 32.

166. *Wang Wen-ch'eng Kung ch'üan-shu*, 7:37b, "Account of the Hall of Loving the People."

167. *Ta-hsüeh chang-chü*, comment on the opening sentence.

168. *Wang Wen-ch'eng Kung ch'üan-shu,* 7:38b, "Account of the Hall of Loving the People."

169. *Ibid.,* 21:15b, second letter in reply to Hsü Ch'eng-chih.

170. *Instructions for Practical Living,* sec. 176.

171. *Wang Wen-ch'eng Kung ch'üan-shu,* 21:17a, second letter in reply to Hsü Ch'eng-chih.

# 28

# Chu Hsi and Taoism

N EO-CONFUCIANS regarded Buddhism and Taoism as heterodox traditions. They vigorously attacked them, and Chu Hsi, who went
much further than his predecessors, was especially devoted to doing so.
In the *Chin-ssu lu* (Reflections on things at hand)[1] that he and Lü Tsu-
ch'ien (1137–1181) compiled, there is a special chapter entitled "Sifting
the Heterodox Doctrines," in which sayings of four Northern Sung
(960–1126) Neo-Confucians are cited to criticize Buddhism and Taoism. In the *Yü-lei* there are special chapters devoted to Buddhism and
Taoism, which are almost totally critical. That Chu Hsi attacked them
has been fully discussed by various writers, past and present. Yet few, if
any, have pointed out that Chu Hsi was also complimentary to Lao Tzu
and Chuang Tzu. We propose to tread this untraveled ground. We shall
first discuss Chu Hsi's criticism of Lao Tzu, then his comparison
between Confucianism and Taoism, his favorable comments on Lao
Tzu, his praise of Chuang Tzu, and, finally, his association with Taoist
priests.

## Criticism of Lao Tzu

Chu Hsi's attack on Lao Tzu was painstaking. This can be seen in the
compilation of the *Chin-ssu lu*. Of its 622 passages, only one is from
Shao Yung (1011–1077), and this is a quotation of Shao by Ch'eng Hao
(1032–1085), not a direct citation from Shao Yung.[2] Chu Hsi omitted
Shao Yung from the Northern Sung Neo-Confucian masters simply
because Shao's metaphysics of numbers and forms was too reminiscent
of Taoism for Chu Hsi's taste. This can also be seen in another place in
the *Chin-ssu lu*, where Chu Hsi altered the text. In his selection from
Ch'eng I's (1033–1107) essay "What Yen Tzu[3] Loved to Learn,"[4] Chu
Hsi deleted the sentences, "This is therefore called turning feelings into

nature" and "This is therefore called turning nature into feelings." The former sentence came from Wang Pi's (226–249) commentary on the first hexagram of the *Book of Changes*. Chu Hsi probably omitted it because it was influenced by the Taoist theory that nature is good but feelings are evil. He also changed the original phrase, "to be clear in one's mind and to know what to nourish," to read "to be clear in one's mind and to know where to go," thus substituting the activism of Confucianism for the quietism of Taoism.

Chu Hsi attacked Taoism from both the philosophical and ethical points of view. Philosophically, he criticized the Taoist concept of Tao (the Way) and also the separation of Tao and virtue. Lao Tzu said, "Being comes from nonbeing."[5] All Neo-Confucians were strongly opposed to this concept. Chang Tsai (1020–1077) said, "The *Book of Changes* does not discuss being or nonbeing. Doctrines of being and nonbeing are vulgar views of the various philosophers."[6] Following him, Chu Hsi said, "The *Book of Changes* does not discuss being and nonbeing. Lao Tzu is wrong in saying that being comes from nonbeing."[7] He further elaborated on Chang Tsai's words, saying, "Nonbeing means that there is not a thing but there is principle. As there is principle, it is being. But Lao Tzu said that '[all things in the world] come from being, and being comes from nonbeing.' As being comes from nonbeing, even principle is nonbeing. That is wrong."[8] However, Chu Hsi did not consider Lao Tzu to hold to the doctrine of nonbeing absolutely. When asked about the difference between Buddhist and Taoist doctrines of nonbeing, Chu Hsi said, "To Lao Tzu, there is still being. This can be seen from his saying, 'Therefore, let there always be nonbeing, so we may see its subtlety. And let there always be being, so we may see its outcome.'[9] The Buddhists consider Heaven and Earth to be illusory and false and the Four Great Elements [Earth, Water, Fire, and Wind] as temporary combinations. Thus everything is completely nonbeing."[10]

In Lao Tzu's philosophy Tao is nonbeing, belonging to the realm of what exists before physical form, whereas *te* (virtue) is being, belonging to the realm of what exists after physical form. In this way, Tao and virtue are completely distinguished, a position Chu Hsi strongly opposed. He said,

> According to [Lao Tzu], "When Tao is lost, only then does the doctrine of virtue arise."[11] He was ignorant and separated the two as two different things, and therefore looked upon Tao as something empty. To us Confucians, Tao and virtue are only one thing. We call it Tao because it is the same thing past and present and is not tied to the human person, and virtue *(te)* because Tao is achieved *(te)* in the self. He said, "When Tao is lost, only then does the doctrine of virtue arise. When virtue is lost, only then does the doctrine of humanity arise. When humanity is lost, only then

does the doctrine of righteousness arise." How can there be moral principles aside from humanity and righteousness? And how can there
be Tao?[12]

In other words, for the Confucian School, substance and function come
from the same source, whereas in Taoism they are distinguished as two
separate entities. Actually, Lao Tzu's distinction between Tao and *te* is
not as complete as Chu Hsi claimed. Lao Tzu said, "Being and nonbeing produced each other,"[13] "The all-embracing quality of the great
virtue follows alone from the Tao,"[14] and "Tao produces them, virtue
fosters them."[15] Thus substance and function are not completely distinguished in Taoism after all.

Concerning virtue itself, Chu Hsi's onslaughts were even more inten-
sive. Lao Tzu said, "In order to grasp, it is necessary first to give."[16]
He also said, "[In ancient times, those who practiced Tao well] sought
not to enlighten the people, but to make them ignorant."[17] Commenting on this passage, Ch'eng I said, "The doctrines of Lao Tzu are even
more treacherous [than those of the Buddhists]. Take his words about
giving in order to grasp, expanding in order to contract, and making
the people ignorant in order to be clever himself. That being the case,
the various schemes of the Ch'in dynasty [221–206 B.C.] to keep the
people ignorant were derived from this philosophy."[18] Following
Ch'eng I, Chu Hsi concentrated on attacking Lao Tzu's ethics. Many
of the conversations recorded in chapter 125 of the *Yü-lei* are on this
topic. Chu Hsi thought that Lao Tzu "merely took a step backward in
order to take an advantageous position and did not want to deal with
things. 'To rule people and to serve Heaven there is nothing better than
to be frugal,'[19] to act only when he was forced to, and to move forward
only when he could not help it are all expressions of this idea. Consequently, many of those who pursued Taoism ended up in schemes and
tricks. People like Shen [Shen Pu-hai (d. 337 B.C.)] and Han Fei Tzu
[d. 233 B.C.] are like this."[20] Chu Hsi even went a step further and said
that "Lao Tzu was one who did not want to take responsibility but only
to take advantage. He held onto himself and would not care if Heaven
and Earth turned upside down."[21] To him, Lao Tzu's doctrine of
"keeping the spirit," "embracing the one," and "concentrating the
vital force and achieving the highest degree of weakness" is nothing but
"collecting and keeping and not dispersing."[22] According to Chu Hsi,
Lao Tzu loved to live; all of his ideas were directed to preserving his
person.[23]

But Chu Hsi did not stop there. He went on to assert that the Taoist
doctrine of trickery produced not only Legalists like Shen and Han, but
also Chang Liang (d. 189 B.C.) of the Western Han dynasty (206
B.C.–A.D. 8):

> The learning of Lao Tzu requires you only to retreat and lie low, and not to compete with anybody. . . . He would let you remain in a high place while occupying a low place and not competing with you. . . . But while he shows no sign, he is irresistible. For instance, he said, "Govern the state with correctness. Marshal the army with surprise maneuvers. Administer the empire by engaging in no activity."[24] Here this method is used. All Tzu-fang's [Chang Liang] devices are like these. In the battle of Yao-kuan, he had enticed the Ch'in generals with advantages and made peace with them, but then he turned his army around to extinguish them.[25] . . . From the very beginning to the end, the Han dynasty controlled the empire entirely by employing this method.[26]

It is not surprising to hear Chu Hsi condemning Chang Liang, but he also compared Shao Yung to Chang, which is really beyond imagination. He considered the learning of Shao Yung to "resemble that of Lao Tzu. All Lao Tzu wanted was to be at leisure and happy and that others could not hurt him. Later, Chang Tzu-fang was like that."[27] He also thought that Shao Yung "basically wanted to accomplish something but was not willing to bother much about it. In everything, he wanted to make sure that it could be done before he tried to do it. As soon as there seemed to be some difficulty, he would give up. He was truly the Chang Tzu-fang type."[28] It is true that Shao Yung seldom talked about humanity and righteousness, and it is understandable that Chu Hsi did not like him. Nevertheless, Shao Yung was content with poverty and personally farmed his land. He was not at all like Chang Liang, who coveted power and manipulated for advantage. It is unfair to equate them.

Ch'eng I had merely criticized Lao Tzu for trickery, but Chu Hsi compared Chang Liang with Lao Tzu and even compared Shao Yung with Chang Liang. Chu Hsi also regarded Lao Tzu as selfish and unwilling to exert effort. In all these opinions, he went far beyond those expressed by Ch'eng I. Probably because Buddhism, but not Taoism, flourished in Loyang, where Ch'eng I lived, Ch'eng I's reaction to Taoism had been mild. But Taoism was prominent in Chu Hsi's province of Fukien, so his reaction to it was severe.

## Comparison of Confucianism and Taoism

Given Chu Hsi's evaluation of Lao Tzu, it is obvious that his comparison of Confucianism and Taoism would favor Confucianism. The following is but a succinct introduction to the various subjects addressed by Chu Hsi. Both the *Wen-chi* and the *Yü-lei* contain many comparisons between the two systems of thought, covering philosophy, ethics, and the theory of knowledge. But most of the comments are brief, and sometimes occur only in relation to other subjects. Aside from Chu Hsi's essay on Chuang Tzu's treatise on nourishing life,[29] which is very short, there is no systematic discussion of any Taoist subject comparable to his "Kuan-hsin shuo" (Treatise on the examination of the mind) and "Shih-shih lun" (On Buddhism).[30] The following twenty-seven selections should be of interest to students of comparative thought:

1. *Concreteness versus emptiness.* "The distinction between Confucianism and Buddhism lies only in emptiness versus concreteness. As Lao Tzu said, 'Vague and elusive, there is in it the form. Elusive and vague, in it are things. Deep and obscure, in it is the essence.'[31] What are called things and essence are empty. Although we have in our system 'the state of absolute quiet and inactivity,'[32] in that state there is something bright and brilliant. All things take place there."[33]

2. *The Tao in Confucianism and Taoism.* "Should we regard Tao as high, distant, mysterious, and not susceptible to being learned? In fact, Tao is so called precisely because it is the unchanging principle of everyday life, like the road that should be traveled by millions and millions of people throughout the world. It is not like the so-called Tao in Taoism and Buddhism, which is empty, quiet, and has nothing to do with mankind."[34]

3. *Being and nonbeing.* Asked about Heng-ch'ü's (Chang Tsai) saying, "Doctrines of being and nonbeing are vulgar views of the various philosophers,"[35] the Master said, "Nonbeing means that there is not a thing but there is principle. As there is principle, it is being. But Lao Tzu said that '[All things in the world] come from being, and being comes from nonbeing.'[36] As being comes from nonbeing, even principle is nonbeing. That is wrong."[37]

4. *Without any sign but having principle.* "As there is this thing, there is this principle. The refined and the coarse form one thread and are basically not two different things. Nowadays, people only see what is in front of them, without any omen or sign, and say it is completely empty. They don't realize that it is 'Empty and tranquil, without any sign, and yet all things are luxuriantly present.'[38] The Buddhists only talk about emptiness, and the Taoists only talk about nonbeing."[39]

5. *Being and nonbeing as one or two.* "In my interpretation, in their discussion of being and nonbeing, the Taoists consider them as two. In his discussion of being and nonbeing, however, Master Chou [Chou Tun-i, 1017–1073] considered them as one. The two views are opposed like north and south, or like water and fire."[40]

6. *Being deep and profound and being concrete.* Question: "What is the difference between the idea of 'the operation of Heaven has neither sound nor smell'[41] and what Lao Tzu called 'deeper and more profound'[42] and what Chuang Tzu called 'unseen' and 'silent'?"[43] The Teacher did not answer. After a long time, he said, "This is naturally clear by itself. You may carefully look into it. . . . Take Confucius' saying, 'Does Heaven

say anything? The four seasons run their course and all things are produced.'⁴⁴ . . . His words are concrete like this."⁴⁵

7. *One and many.* "Although the ten thousand principles are one, the
student must go into the ten thousand principles, understand every one
of them, and then put them together. He will naturally see that they are
but one principle. . . . The learning of the Sage [Confucius] and the
Worthy [Mencius] is not equivalent to that of Lao Tzu. He claimed that
when the one penetrates all, all things will cease to be [individual enti-
ties]. That is all he said. Before long, he would prefer seeing the one
cease to be."⁴⁶

8. *The hidden versus the manifest.* "*Ch'ien* and *k'un* [male and female cosmic forces] are never destroyed, and this means that the process of
Change will never cease. I am afraid the last sentence is not what you
have quoted as resembling Lao Tzu's saying, 'It reverts to nothing-
ness.'⁴⁷ The last sentence of the *Doctrine of the Mean,* 'have neither sound
nor smell,' follows the preceding phrase, 'the operation of Heaven.'
Although there is neither sound nor smell, the operation of Heaven is
manifest. . . . Personally, I have heard that the difference between the
learning of the Sage and that of the followers of Taoism and Buddhism
lies in the fact that the refined and the coarse, the hidden and the manifest, and substance and function are all merged in [Confucianism]. All
of them are the norm of great centrality and perfect correctness, and
none has the defect of being one-sided, excessive, or deficient."⁴⁸

9. *Substance and function.* "The Sage became a sage solely because his
activity or inactivity was timely. When it was time to stop, he would
stop. When it was time to go, he would go." Thereupon, Chu Hsi cited
Lao Tzu's words, "Cautious, like crossing a frozen stream in the winter. Being at a loss, like one fearing danger on all sides. Reserved, like
one visiting. Supple and pliant, like ice about to melt,"⁴⁹ . . . [and
said], "All these have substance but no function."⁵⁰

10. *Two and three.* "In number, there are only two [yin and yang, the
active and passive cosmic forces]. Only the *Book of Changes* is correct.
Lao Tzu talked about three. That is also two. The two together produce
the three, the three being the one. 'The three produce the ten thousand
things.'⁵¹ From here it leads to infinity."⁵²

11. *One and two.* "As there is principle, there must be material force
(*ch'i*). In the case of material force, there must always be two. That is
why the *Book of Changes* says, 'The *T'ai-chi* [Great Ultimate] generates
the Two Modes [yin and yang].'⁵³ But Lao Tzu said that Tao first
produces the one and then the one produces the two.⁵⁴ He was not
refined in his examination of principle."⁵⁵

12. *Investigation of things.* "We must seek [principle] in what we come
into contact with. When we find the principle but have not reached the
limit of the thing, the principle of that thing has not been exhausted and

one's knowledge is not complete. That is why one must reach the limit before one stops. This is what is called the investigation of things until the thing is reached and the principle of the thing is exhausted. . . . In their learning, the Taoists and the Buddhists wish to extend their knowledge but do not know that the investigation of things is the way to extend it. Therefore, their knowledge cannot be free from the defects of blocking one's understanding, leading to degeneration, getting away from daily life, and coming to a dead end. As such, it does not deserve to be called knowledge."[56]

13. *The activity and tranquillity of the hexagram* fu *(to return)*. Question: "[Master Ch'eng I said,] 'In the *fu* hexagram, we see the mind of Heaven and Earth in the state of activity.'[57] How about those who hold that *fu* is seen in the state of tranquillity?"

Answer: "*Fu* is of course activity. To hold tranquillity as fundamental is the way to nourish one's activity. . . . What has been accumulated today will become the activity of tomorrow, and what has been accumulated tomorrow will become the activity of the day after, and so on. 'See the return [of things]' is a Taoist term, which Confucians do not utter. Lao Tzu liked to talk about activity and tranquillity. 'All things come into being, and I see thereby their return.'[58] He meant that all things return to their root. I merely see their return."[59]

14. *Spirit and material force*. Question: "The material force [nourishing air] of the calm morning that Mencius talked about is very small and subtle.[60] How can one nourish it to perfection?"

Answer: "Let one augment it in the daytime, and let one increase it in the nighttime. Increase it again and again, and the material force will be strong." Thereupon, Chu Hsi quoted Lao Tzu, who said, "To rule people and to serve Heaven, there is nothing better than to be frugal. Only by being frugal can one recover quickly. To recover quickly means to accumulate virtue heavily. By the heavy accumulation of virtue one can overcome everything."[61] He then commented, "The general idea is similar to that of Mencius. However, Lao Tzu was talking about the nourishment of the spirit, and his idea is naturally different. The material force of the calm morning seems to be performing its task in the morning. In one's daily affairs, one must direct one's mind to it."[62]

15. *The mind and its traces (effects)*. "They [the Buddhists] don't care about Heaven, Earth, or the four directions. They only think of the mind. As in the case of Lao Tzu, he also merely wanted to preserve the spirit and the vital force *(ch'i)*. Ch'eng I said, 'We can only go by the traces [of the mind].'[63] I don't know what the use is of [the Taoists] doing this."[64]

16. *Embracing the One and finding the lost mind*. "The Teacher asked the people: 'Buddhists talk about herding an ox, Lao Tzu talked about embracing the One,[65] and Mencius talked about seeking the lost

mind.[66] They are talking about the same thing. Why are they different?' Thereupon Chieh [Kan Chieh][67] asked, 'Isn't it because [the Buddhists and the Taoists] lack principle?' The Teacher said, 'They lack principle and harm things.' "[68]

17. *Four "don'ts" and shunning external things.* "I-ch'uan [Ch'eng I] only said that in looking, listening, speaking, and acting, one should not contravene propriety.[69] People nowadays are more abstract. Before long they go beyond the norm, like the Buddhists and Taoists, and shun external things."[70]

18. *Abiding seriousness* (ching, *reverence) and acting simply.* " '[One should] abide by seriousness in daily life but be simple in action.'[71] Lao Tzu was one of those who are merely devoted to simplicity in action. That is the way not to be simple."[72]

19. *Nonaction.* "When Lao Tzu talked about taking no action *(wu-wei),* he meant not to do anything at all. When the Sage talked about taking no action, he never meant doing nothing. He still wanted [the ruler to] do nothing but make himself reverent and correctly face south [in his royal seat as the ruler]."[73]

20. *Activity and tranquillity.* "Generally speaking, the Taoists and the Buddhists advocate tranquillity and wish there were no activity in the world. This is like sleeping all the time without waking and abandoning what is useful to something useless. The Sage and the Worthy do not do this."[74]

21. *Not being recognized.* " '[The superior man] does not feel hurt even though he is not recognized.'[75] The purpose of pursuing learning is of course neither to seek recognition nor to avoid recognition. Therefore one should not feel happy when one is recognized or hurt when one is not. This is the correct moral principle expounded in the Confucian School. But Lao Tzu said, 'Few people know me, and therefore I am highly valued.'[76] This is a selfish and heterodox view. It is entirely different from the prevailing spirit of the Confucian School."[77]

22. *Repaying virtue.* " 'Repay hatred with virtue'[78] is Lao Tzu's saying. To repay hatred with virtue is of course generous to the one who hates, but then there is nothing with which to repay virtue. Isn't that to slight the one who performs virtue? . . . The words of Lao Tzu are static, whereas the words of Confucius, '[Repay hatred with uprightness and repay virtue with virtue],'[79] are dynamic. They can fit either situation."[80]

23. *Fame.* "The learning of Lao Tzu and Chuang Tzu is not concerned with whether or not a thing is correct according to moral principles. They merely wanted to agree with people in order to avoid personal harm. The Way of the Sage and the Worthy is only to teach people to practice the good diligently in a concrete way. They did not teach people to seek or avoid fame."[81]

24. *Rules of propriety.* "Followers of Lao Tzu and Chuang Tzu aban-
don rules of propriety. . . . In talking about propriety, Confucius said,
'Be thrifty rather than extravagant'[82] and 'Be obstinate rather than disrespectful.'[83] It was well said."[84]

25. *Equally honored.* "I would humbly question whether it is correct to
call both Confucius and Lao An [Lao Tzu] sages."[85]

26. *Slightly similar.* "Po-i[86] slightly resembles Lao Tzu."[87]

27. *Dealing with events.* "The *Book of Changes* of course does not deal
with practical events but talks about a kind of principle up in the air. It
is unlike the other classics, every one of which talks about specific
events. That is why the Taoist School later adopted it and treated it as of
a kind with the *Lao Tzu,* for Lao Tzu did not say things in relation to
particular events."[88]

## Favorable Comments on Lao Tzu

Despite Chu Hsi's generally critical attitude toward Taoism, there are
conversations in the *Yü-lei* in which he made complimentary remarks
about Lao Tzu. Such passages are not many, but there are several, as
quoted below, one of which is philosophically very significant but has
hitherto been unnoticed. These few passages are enough to show that
Chu Hsi was not biased, although his philosophy dictated the general
view he entertained. He once said,

> Master Ch'eng [Ch'eng I] said that "there is something good in philoso-
> pher Chuang's [Chuang Tzu] description of the substance of Tao.[89] Lao
> Tzu's chapter, "The spirit of the valley never dies,"[90] is excellent."[91]
> Chuang Tzu said, "Those who indulge in many desires have very little of
> the secret of Nature."[92] This saying is very good. . . . "The superior man
> does not reject his words because of the man."[93] If someone's words are
> acceptable, how can I not accept them?[94]

This broad-minded spirit is well illustrated in the following selections.

1. "Humanity (*jen*) is a quality of warmth, peace, and tenderness. As
Lao Tzu said, 'The stiff and the hard are companions of death. The
tender and the weak are companions of life.'[95] His view is correct. As
you can see, what kind of thing can grow on a piece of rock?"[96] In Chu
Hsi's theory, *jen* is the character that generates all virtues. Because *jen* is
tender and weak, it can produce, as Lao Tzu had said.

2. In speaking about life, Chu Hsi said, "It is material force, but
material force has a great deal of principle in it. In the production of
man and things, there is first this thing [material force and principle],
which is endowed by Heaven from the beginning. As there is this thing,
a physical form is provided at birth, with a covering to embrace it. . . .

Now, the Confucians only understand this, and want to obey the principles of nature and life. The Buddhists and Taoists also understand this. However, the Taoists wants always to hold on to the material force and not allow it to disperse. One can then 'enjoy everlasting life.'[97] I don't see the possibility of an everlasting life, but if one makes sufficient effort, one may not die [prematurely]."[98] Both the Taoist theory and technique of nourishing the material force are far superior to those of Confucianism. It is no wonder that here Chu Hsi gave the Taoists the credit they deserve.

3. Question: "Chuang Tzu said, 'Lord Wen-hui heard Cook Ting's explanation of how to cut up an ox and learned how to nourish life.'[99] How can one nourish life?"

Answer: "Simply follow principle. Do not depend on any deliberation or thought. And do not harm life. In this way one can nourish life."

Further remark: "[Cook Ting] did not see the whole ox. He only saw [principle] and the frame of the body naturally fell into place."

Question: "What does Chuang Tzu mean?"

Answer: "It was the case that he understood principle to be like this."

Further question: "Lao Tzu said, 'Thirty spokes are united around the hub to make a wheel. . . . Therefore turn being into advantage, and turn nonbeing into utility.'[100] Is the idea the same?"

Answer: "I was about to say that they are similar. It is the case that he was able to see this point."[101] Here "this point" refers to principle. When principle is understood, the whole ox becomes nonexistent. The Confucians were most afraid of Taoist emptiness, but here emptiness leads to concreteness, for Cook Ting did not hurt the frame of the ox's body.

4. "Nothing in the world is more serious than military operations and the imposition of punishment, and these should not be taken lightly. How many lives have been sacrificed when there is confusion in approaching the battlefront? Therefore Lao Tzu said, 'Fine weapons are instruments of evil. It is only when he cannot avoid them that the sage uses them.'[102] In trials and lawsuits, when things are clear right from the start, it is easy. But when truth or falsehood is difficult to discern, evidence is lacking, each side insists on its own claim, and people's lives are at stake, one must think very hard. Even then there may still be a mistake."[103] This passage clearly shows that the Taoists' strong opposition to war and punishment had a sobering effect on Chu Hsi.

5. "Wen-chung Tzu [Wang T'ung, 584–617] occasionally had an insight. He was really a Taoist."[104] Chu Hsi did not explain what these insights were. But in thus calling Wen-chung Tzu a Taoist, Chu Hsi must have considered Lao Tzu to have had some insight, too.

6. "Lao Tzu said, 'If Tao is employed to rule the empire, spiritual beings will lose their supernatural power.'[105] If the kingly Way is culti-

vated, this kind of perverse force will disappear."[106] Here Chu Hsi was talking about the Confucian kingly Way. Nevertheless, Lao Tzu is quoted to show that if the Way prevails, perverse spirits will disappear. Obviously, this is indirect praise for Lao Tzu.

7. Chu Hsi also commented at length on Lao Tzu's notion of "life and more life" (sheng-sheng). In a letter to his pupil Ch'iu Ying,[107] Chu Hsi said, "Commentators on Lao Tzu's chapter on coming in to life and going out to death are all unsatisfactory. I am afraid they all have missed the original idea of Lao Tzu. If one reads from 'And for what reason?' the intent of the passage will be naturally clear. It says that man comes in to life but hastens to death because his effort at life and more life is too intense. Sound, color, smell, and taste; living at home and supporting parents; power, profit, and desires—all contribute to life. Only when one goes at it too intensely can things harm him. Those who are skillful at caring for life keep a distance from this trouble and will never get into that situation. These are matters of daily life that are right before our eyes and can be handled. Since the rest [of the chapter] is difficult to understand, it seem one does not need to probe it deeply."[108]

To understand fully Chu Hsi's remarks, it is necessary to quote Lao Tzu's chapter in its entirety:

> Man comes in to life and goes out to death.
> Three out of ten are companions of life.
> Three out of ten are companions of death.
> And three out of ten in their lives lead from activity to death.
> And for what reason?
> Because of man's intensive striving after life.
> I have heard that he who is a good preserver of his life will not meet
>     tigers or wild buffalo.
> And in fighting will not try to escape from weapons of war.
> The wild buffalo cannot butt its horns against him,
> The tiger cannot fasten its claws in him,
> And weapons of war cannot thrust their blades into him.
> And for what reason?
> Because in him there is no room for death.[109]

Past and present annotators have advanced all kinds of theories on the meaning of "three out of ten," from 30 percent to the four limbs and nine external cavities of the human body, to the Ten Evils and Three Karmas of Buddhism.[110] Chu Hsi told Ch'iu Ying to ignore all such ideas. What is striking is that he stressed the positive aspect of sheng-sheng. He also emphasized that one should not strive after life too much, which is of course the typical Confucian doctrine of the Mean. What is even more surprising is that although a great deal of superstititon and occultism has grown up around this chapter, Chu Hsi chose to see its contribution to the Confucian idea of *sheng-sheng*. This must be considered a large bouquet for Lao Tzu.

The Neo-Confucian concept of *sheng-sheng* also found strong support in Lao Tzu's chapter on the spirit of the valley. When asked about "the spirit of the valley never dies,"[111] Chu Hsi said, "The valley being empty, when sound reaches it, it responds with an echo. This is natural in the process of wonderful transformation. [The chapter goes on to say], 'It is called the subtle and profound female.' Being profound means to be mysterious, and the female is that which receives something and then can produce life. The most mysterious principle contains in it the idea of *sheng-sheng*. This is the theory Master Ch'eng accepted *(ch'u).*"[112] To say that Ch'eng I's theory of *sheng-sheng* came from Lao Tzu is truly shocking. *Sheng-sheng* is a basic concept of Neo-Confucianism, and it was given a new interpretation in Neo-Confucian thought. To say that it originated with Lao Tzu amounts to saying that the Taoism of quietude, silence, and taking no action should be considered the spring of dynamic Neo-Confucianism.

Ch'eng I did say, "Lao Tzu's chapter, 'The Spirit of the Valley Never Dies,' is excellent,"[113] and Chu Hsi said that Ch'eng I "accepted" *(ch'u)* this theory. Perhaps *ch'u* should be understood in the sense of praise rather than adoption. After all, Ch'eng I's idea of *sheng-sheng* comes from the *Book of Changes,* where it is said, "*Sheng-sheng* is called Change"[114] and "The great virtue of Heaven and Earth is *sheng.*"[115] The *Book of Changes* is really the source of the idea, which is why Ch'eng I said, "The mind is comparable to seeds of grain. The nature of *sheng* is *jen.*"[116] But Ch'eng I never explained why Heaven and Earth can produce life and more life. Chu Hsi filled this gap. According to him, Heaven and Earth, being vast and empty, can receive and produce indefinitely. Thus the reason why Heaven and Earth can produce and reproduce indefinitely is very similar to why the empty valley can continuously receive and produce life. Although the doctrine of *sheng-sheng* became prominent with Ch'eng I, its explanation had to wait until Chu Hsi. And Chu Hsi got it from Lao Tzu.[117]

## Praise of Chuang Tzu

Although Chu Hsi could be generous in praising Lao Tzu, his praise of Chuang Tzu was far more frequent. Of course, all Neo-Confucians, and especially Chu Hsi, were hostile toward Taoism. Chu Hsi's good friend Lü Tsu-ch'ien once warned him against "wholeheartedly attacking opposite schools and perhaps lacking in selfcultivation,"[118] but his attacks on Buddhism and Taoism never abated. And since Lao Tzu and Chuang Tzu were synonymous with Taoism, the two were often mentioned together. In the *Wen-chi,* their doctrines are regarded as "non-sensical,"[119] "entirely calculated to avoid personal harm,"[120] "lacking in concreteness,"[121] and "one-sided."[122] Similar characterizations abound elsewhere in the *Wen-chi.* But whereas Lao Tzu and Chuang Tzu are mentioned in the same breath in many places in the *Wen-chi,* they are seldom cited together in the *Yü-lei.* In chapter 125 of the *Yü-lei* there is of course a section on Lao-Chuang, but it consists of only three passages, and there are also only three passages in the section on Lao-Chuang-Lieh.[123]

Moreover, although Chu Hsi's attack on Lao Tzu was unreserved, his criticism of Chuang Tzu was limited to the latter's unwillingness to undertake activity. Chu Hsi said, "Lao Tzu still wanted to do something, whereas Chuang Tzu was unwilling to do anything at all."[124] He also said, "Essentially, his trouble was that when he understood something, he did not want to do it."[125] Nevertheless, Chuang Tzu did at least understand, and Chu Hsi gave him credit for that.

In addition to mentioning Lao Tzu and Chuang Tzu together, the *Wen-chi* mentions Chuang Tzu alone in more than twenty places. These passages deal with facts or with Chuang Tzu's literary writings and do not praise him for his ideas. In the *Yü-lei,* however, such praises occur many times. The reason for the difference is probably that the essays and letters in the *Wen-chi* aimed at defending the Way, so that an offensive posture was taken, whereas the *Yü-lei* contains discussions of ideas, and since Chuang Tzu "understood" in many respects, Chu Hsi accepted his words and praised him.

The *Yü-lei* quotes the *Chuang Tzu* twenty or thirty times. In a minority of cases, Chuang Tzu is quoted to amplify Confucian doctrines. For example, Chu Hsi said, "If the Mean[126] is supported by calmness and the knowledge of what to abide in,[127] it will naturally be brilliant. This is what Chuang Tzu meant in his saying, 'When one's moral being is serenely calm, he will send forth a Heavenly light.' "[128] However, the great majority of quotations are of Chuang Tzu's ideas that Chu Hsi considered acceptable and praiseworthy. For example, he said, "Chuang Tzu remarked, 'Everything has its norm and specific principle. This is called its nature.'[129] To say that each has its norm and specific principle is similar to [the Confucian saying] that 'as there are things, so there are their specific principles.'[130] Compared to the various thinkers, he is somewhat better."[131] Chu Hsi then cited Tung Chung-shu (176–104 B.C.), who had said, " 'Nature means primitive stuff. It cannot be perfected *(ch'eng)* without the transforming influence of education.'[132] Nature is perfect by itself. To say that it needs to be perfected by education is to injure principle very much."[133] Elsewhere,[134] Chu Hsi quoted Ch'eng Hao's praise of Chuang Tzu as "having important thoughts"[135] and "having some good points in describing the substance of Tao."[136] Like Ch'eng Hao, Chu Hsi regarded Chuang Tzu as having had some insight into the substance of Tao.

Of all Chu Hsi's complimentary remarks about Chuang Tzu, four seem especially significant for Neo-Confucianism. One is Chuang Tzu's statement that "the *Book of Changes* talks about yin and yang, and the *Spring and Autumn Annals* talks about titles and function."[137] Chu Hsi said, "Chuang Tzu clearly said that the *Book of Changes* talks about yin and yang. If you want to study the *Book of Changes,* you must look at things this way, that they are all produced by [the interaction of] yin and yang."[138] Again, he said, if Chuang Tzu "did not understand clearly, how could he have dared to say so?"[139] He even said, "Who else after Chuang Tzu was able to make remarks like 'The *Book of Changes* talks about yin and yang, and the *Spring and Autumn Annals* talks about titles and functions?' He seems to wield a cutting blade and a sharp ax to slice through things, with every word well placed."[140] Such high praise is quite exceptional for Chu Hsi.

The second passage that impressed Chu Hsi deeply was this: "To speak of Tao and not its sequence is not the Way."[141] He quoted this remark twice[142] and declared, "This is well said."[143] A third passage from the *Chuang Tzu* was very attractive to Chu Hsi. About the movement of the sky, the sun and the moon, Chuang Tzu asked,

Who masterminds this? Who manipulates this? Who, resting inactive himself, pushes them into circulation? I wonder, is there a mechanism that cannot stop? I wonder, do they revolve and cannot stop themselves? Do the clouds make the rain? Or does the rain make the clouds? Who showers them down so generously like this? Who, resting inactive himself, has the lascivious joy[144] to encourage all this?[145]

Commenting on this passage, Chu Hsi said, "He also understood this principle."[146] He quoted the passage once more and said, "These sayings of Chuang Tzu are very good. He could make utterances like these because he had insight."[147]

These three passages should be viewed together because they form a system. In the process of Change, there must be yin and yang before there can be Heaven, Earth, man, and things. There must be an order for yin and yang, and an order requires a director. To the Neo-Confucians, this director is the mind of Heaven and Earth to produce things, although this mind is not like the supreme deity of Taoism, the Jade Emperor, who, ruling from on high, personally and directly controls everything. Instead, the mind of Heaven and Earth is none other than principle, and principle operates by itself. We do not mean to assert that

Chu Hsi actually expounded this system in conversations with pupils. We merely suggest that there is such a system in Chu Hsi's thought, and that he found strong support for it in Chuang Tzu.

But the passage that meant the most to Chu Hsi is the one about Cook Ting cutting the ox:

> Cook Ting was cutting up an ox for Lord Wen-hui. At every touch of his hand, every shift of his shoulder, every tread of his foot, and every lift of his knee, the sound of the separation of bone and flesh resounded, and the swinging of his knife echoed more loudly. All was in perfect rhythm. . . . [Ting said,] "When I first began cutting up oxen, I could see nothing but the ox itself. After three years, I no longer saw the whole ox. . . . I have had this knife for nineteen years and I have cut up thousands of oxen with it. . . . There is plenty of room for the swinging knife."[148]

In conversations with his pupils, Chu Hsi referred to this story six times. He used it to explain how principle got its name, how principle penetrates all things, how to observe the many principles gradually, how to proceed according to order, how to take care of life, and how to meet with humanity and righteousness everywhere. Whether it was the concept of principle, the way to learn, or the method of self-cultivation, one could always find it in this story. He said, "This is why principle got its name. What the eye sees is no longer the whole ox. What familiarity!"[149] He also said,

> As in the case of Cook Ting cutting up the ox, whenever he came to a complicated joint, he would strike in the big hollows and guide the knife through the big openings. This is to find the principle that penetrates through the spots where tendons and bones come together. That is why after nineteen years his knife was still as sharp as when it first came from the grindstone. If one does not try to understand the point where principle and things meet, and sees only one side, how will that do?[150]

One could also take a lesson from Cook Ting on the method of study. As Chu Hsi told his pupils, "Generally speaking, when we study the words of the Sage and the Worthy, one must take time to wait. When one comes to a doubtful point, one can then raise a question. In the case of Cook Ting cutting up the ox, he merely located the cracks and swung his knife toward them, and all principles fell into place. His sharp knife did not become dull."[151] "When the student first studies some writing," he added elsewhere, "what he sees is something merged and indistinct. In time, he will see two or three pieces, and so on until he sees ten pieces or more. Only then can he achieve progress. This was the case with Cook Ting. When he cut up the ox, his eyes did not see the whole ox."[152]

As to nourishing life, a pupil asked: "Chuang Tzu said that [when Lord Wen-hui] heard Ting's description of cutting an ox, he learned how to nourish life. How can one nourish life?"

The Master answered: "Cook Ting did not see the whole ox. He only saw how the frame of the body is opened up by itself."

Question: "What did Chuang Tzu mean?"

Answer: "He also understood that the principle is like this."

Question: "He basically destroyed principle. How could he have any insight?"

Answer: "That is because he understood that this is so from the point of view of his principle." Thereupon he lamented, "The principles of the world are understood by people differently. When they are cut up, split, and wide open, what a joy it is! If one is confused about it, one is cheating oneself—that is all."[153]

The most important lesson to be derived from Cook Ting is that no matter what his hand or foot touches, it is in perfect rhythm; he finds his source whether he turns to the left or to the right. As Chu Hsi put it,

> If he is a ruler, he will encounter the principle of humanity. If he is a minister, he will encounter the principle of reverence. If he is a son, he will encounter the principle of filial piety. If he is a father, he will encounter the principle of deep love. And in dealing with the people of the country, he will encounter the principle of faithfulness.[154] It will be the same no matter where he turns.[155]

For a strong defender of Confucianism to draw support from a heterodox system is unusual indeed. This shows that there is a common element between Confucianism and Taoism, and that this common element is found in Chuang Tzu, not Lao Tzu.

Chu Hsi's theory about the origin of Chuang Tzu's ideas is even more startling, for he maintained that the source of Chuang Tzu's philosophy was the Confucian School. He said,

> I do not know who transmitted the doctrine to Chuang Tzu, but he himself understood the substance of Tao. After Mencius' time, gentlemen like Hsün Ch'ing [Hsün Tzu, 313–238 B.C.?] could not measure up to him. He said, for example, "To speak of Tao and not its sequence is not the Way"![156] Doctrines of this sort are excellent. I believe he must have received instructions from a follower of the Confucian School. There is a source for his ideas. Later, whenever the Buddhists had something good to say, it was all derived from Chuang Tzu. However, Chuang Tzu's knowledge did not reach the limit, because it lacked the work of refinement. Before long, his doctrines drifted away too far. This is what is called "The worthy goes beyond the Mean."[157]

True to the Confucian tradition, Chu Hsi adhered to the doctrine of the Mean. Such a correction of Chuang Tzu is to be expected. What is surprising is his lavish praise of the Taoist thinker.

## Association with Taoist Priests

On the practical side, we find Chu Hsi's association with Taoists to have been more extensive than that of Chou Tun-i, Chang Tsai, and the Ch'eng brothers before him, his contemporary Lu Hsiang-shan (1139–1193), and Wang Yang-ming (1472–1529) after him. The *Wen-chi* contains references to about ten cases of contact with Taoists, and actual meetings throughout his life must have been far more numerous. However, Chou Tun-i's metaphysical theory was greatly influenced by a Taoist diagram of the Great Ultimate, and Wang Yang-ming spent his wedding night talking with a Taoist priest about the technique of nourishing life that he later practiced. No such influence has been found in the case of Chu Hsi. When he was ten, a Taoist priest gave him a charm, but when his elders saw it, they burned it.[158] Whether this episode had anything to do with his later attitude toward Taoism, we do not know. In any event, it did not prevent him from frequent association with Taoist priests.

For the most part, such associations took the form of literary compositions. Chu Hsi wrote a colophon for the priest of Ch'ung-yu Temple at Mount Wu-i in Fukien; he also wrote an epilogue for the poem of priest Ch'en Ching-yüan.[159] These were but social dealings and do not indicate any particular friendship. His poems for the Taoist priest Ch'en, the Ching-hui Hall of the Hsien-ch'ing Ching-she, and priest Chou of Ch'ing-chiang all express some degree of admiration, however. Priest Chou, in particular, came to visit with a lute, but since Chu Hsi was in mourning, he could not listen to music.[160] In his farewell poem for priest Li, who was returning to Yu-ssu, Chu Hsi asked Li to reserve a bed for him. He also enjoyed drinking wine and composing poems with several priests at the Ch'ung-yu Temple.[161] All this shows a high degree of friendship. He wrote a poem to thank priest I Wei-na for some medicine to cure his mother's hardness of hearing,[162] and to thank a priest who had used acupuncture to relieve the pain in his feet.[163]

In his travels, Chu Hsi often stopped at Taoist cottages or temples, especially at Mount Lu in Kiangsi and Mount Wu-i in Fukien.[164] At Mount Wu-i, there had been a T'ieh-ti (Iron flute) Pavilion. Once Chu Hsi and several friends, including several Taoist priests, searched for and found its original site. It happened that the sound of an iron flute came from across the forest, so Chu Hsi had a new pavilion built at the spot to commemorate the occasion.[165]

We have no record, however, of Chu Hsi's discussing philosophical doctrines with Taoist priests. In a reply to the Taoist priest Kan, he merely said, "It is better to learn to sit quietly and to read old books at leisure, and rinse the mind of popular and mundane interests. Only then does one find a solution."[166] He also said, in reply to the Taoist priest Ch'en, "[Taoist occult] poems, Taoist charms, fame, profit, and other material attractions should all be rejected, and then there will be a place to start. I do not know if you can really make the discrimination in this matter."[167] In both cases, he was advising the priests to be true Taoists.

When Chu Hsi built the Wu-i Ching-she (Wu-i Study) in 1183, among the buildings was the Han-hsi Kuan (Lodge to Rest in the Cold), which he named after a phrase in the Taoist book *Chen-kao* (True exhortation) and built to house "followers of the Taoist School *(tao-liu)*."[168] There were many Taoist temples, cottages, and lodges on Mount Wu-i. The special building in the Wu-i Study may have been intended for the convenience of Taoists or to facilitate them in discussions on Neo-Confucianism. I believe *tao-liu* meant *tao-jen* (seeker after Tao), which may be used for both Taoist and Buddhist priests. Because Chinese monks are vegetarians and many Taoists are also, a separate building may have been necessary to meet their dietary needs.

Among Chu Hsi's 460-odd pupils, only one was a Taoist priest. He was Wu Hsiung,[169] courtesy name Po-ying, a native of P'ing-chiang County in Hunan. When he was twenty, he studied with Chu Hsi through the introduction of Ts'ai Yüan-ting (1135–1198). His side interests included astrology, divination, and military strategy. In his ten or more conversations with the Master, and in the four instructions the Master gave him, as recorded in the *Yü-lei,*[170] Chu Hsi taught him to abide by seriousness and to read books. The other mentions of Wu Hsiung concern topics in the *Analects,* except for one reference on Ch'eng I's theory of the standard and expediency. It is interesting that they did not talk about Taoist doctrines, and that Chu Hsi did not criticize Taoism to his face. Whether there were other Taoist followers is not known. It is not unreasonable to suppose that there were, since a building was erected to accommodate a number of Taoists.

## Notes

1. For an English translation of the *Chin-ssu lu,* see my *Reflections on Things at Hand* (New York: Columbia University Press, 1967).

2. This is in the *Chin-ssu lu,* 5:15. Shao Yung's comment is not found in any of his own works. Most probably Ch'eng Hao heard it from Shao personally. See n. 34 to the *Chin-ssu lu,* ch. 5, sec. 15, in *Reflections on Things at Hand.*

3. Yen Tzu's private name was Hui (c. 521–490 B.C.), and his courtesy name was Tzu-yüan, so he was often called Yen Yüan. He was Confucius' favorite pupil and was well known for his virtue.

4. This essay is found the the *I-ch'uan wen-chi* [Collection of literary writings

of Ch'eng I], 4:1a–2a, in the *Erh-Ch'eng ch'üan-shu* [Complete works of the two Ch'engs] (*SPPY* ed.).

5. *Lao Tzu,* ch. 40.

6. *Cheng-meng* [Correcting youthful ignorance] ch. 14, "Great Book of Changes," sec. 14, in the *Chang Tzu ch'üan-shu* [Complete works of Master Chang Tsai] (*SPPY* ed.), 3:11b.

7. *Yü-lei,* ch. 125, sec. 41 (p. 4803).

8. *Ibid.,* ch. 98, sec. 124 (p. 4022).

9. *Lao Tzu,* ch. 1.

10. *Yü-lei,* ch. 126, sec. 12 (p. 4826).

11. *Lao Tzu,* ch. 38.

12. *Yü-lei,* ch. 13, sec. 62 (p. 368).

13. *Lao Tzu,* ch. 2.

14. *Ibid.,* ch. 21.

15. *Ibid.,* ch. 51.

16. *Ibid.,* ch. 36.

17. *Ibid.,* ch. 65.

18. *I-shu* [Surviving works], 15:7b, in the *Erh-Ch'eng ch'üan-shu.*

19. *Lao Tzu,* ch. 59.

20. *Yü-lei,* ch. 125, sec. 37 (p. 4802).

21. *Ibid.,* ch. 137, sec. 9 (pp. 5222–5223).

22. *Ibid.,* ch. 87, sec. 160 (p. 3585), referring to *Lao Tzu,* ch. 10.

23. *Ibid.,* ch. 126, sec. 13 (p. 4326).

24. *Lao Tzu,* ch. 57.

25. This story is told in the *Shih chi* [Historical records], ch. 55, biography of Chang Liang.

26. *Yü-lei,* ch. 125, sec. 36 (p. 4801).

27. *Ibid.,* ch. 100, sec. 11 (p. 4042).

28. *Ibid.,* sec. 12 (p. 4044).

29. *Chuang Tzu,* ch. 3, "Fundamentals on Nourishing Life." Chu Hsi's treatise is found in the *Wen-chi,* 67:23a–24b.

30. *Wen-chi,* 67:23b–24b, and separate collection, 8:1a–4a, respectively.

31. *Lao Tzu,* ch. 21.

32. *Book of Changes,* "Appended Remarks," pt. 1, ch. 10.

33. *Yü-lei,* ch. 124, sec. 35 (p. 4765).

34. *Wen-chi,* 38:26b–27a, third letter in reply to Chou I-kung.

35. See above, n. 6.

36. *Lao Tzu,* ch. 40.

37. *Yü-lei,* ch. 98, sec. 124 (p. 4022).

38. This is Ch'eng I's saying, found in the *I-shu,* 15:8a.

39. *Yü-lei,* ch. 95, sec. 77 (pp. 3868–3869).

40. *Wen-chi,* 36:11b–12a, sixth letter in reply to Lu Tzu-ching (Lu Hsiang-shan).

41. *Doctrine of the Mean,* ch. 33, quoting ode no. 235 from the *Book of Odes.*

42. *Lao Tzu,* ch. 1.

43. *Chuang Tzu,* ch. 11, "Let It Be" (*SPTK* ed. entitled *Nan-hua chen-ching* [True classic of Chuang Tzu] 3:35a).

44. *Analects,* 17:19.

45. *Yü-lei,* ch. 64, sec. 201 (pp. 2543–2544).

46. *Ibid.,* ch. 117, sec. 42 (pp. 4498–4500).

47. *Lao Tzu,* ch. 14.

48. *Wen-chi,* 38:35a–b, first letter in reply to Chiang Yüan-shih (Chiang Yung).

49. *Lao Tzu,* ch. 15.

50. *Yü-lei,* ch. 120, sec. 111 (pp. 4656–4657).

51. *Lao Tzu,* ch. 42.

52. *Yü-lei,* ch. 65, sec. 37 (p. 2558).

53. *Book of Changes,* "Appended Remarks," pt. 1, ch. 11.

54. *Lao Tzu,* ch. 42.

55. *Wen-chi,* 37:32a, third letter in reply to Ch'eng K'o-chiu (Ch'eng Ch'iung).

56. *Ibid.,* 44:37a–38a, second letter in reply to Chiang Te-kung (Chiang Mo).

57. *I-shu,* 18:15a.

58. *Lao Tzu,* ch. 16.

59. *Yü-lei,* ch. 71, sec. 55 (p. 2855).

60. *Book of Mencius,* 6A:8.

61. *Lao Tzu,* ch. 59.

62. *Yü-lei,* ch. 59, sec. 71 (pp. 2212–2213).

63. *I-shu,* 15:10a.

64. *Yü-lei,* ch. 126, sec. 17 (p. 4827).

65. *Lao Tzu,* ch. 10.

66. *Book of Mencius,* 6A:11.

67. Kan Chieh's courtesy name was Chi-fu. He recorded about 300 conversations in the *Yü-lei* from 1193 on. For more on him, see my *Chu Tzu men-jen* [Master Chu's pupils] (Taipei: Student Book Co., 1982), p. 71.

68. *Yü-lei,* ch. 126, sec. 38 (p. 4832).

69. This refers to Ch'eng I's "Four Admonitions" in the *I-ch'uan wen-chi,* 4:4a–b. Ch'eng I was elaborating on the *Analects,* 12:2.

70. *Yü-lei,* ch. 73, sec. 58 (p. 2953).

71. *Analects,* 6:1.

72. *Yü-lei,* ch. 30, sec. 17 (p. 1226).

73. *Ibid.,* ch. 23, sec. 20 (p. 868), referring to *Analects,* 15:4.

74. *Wen-chi,* 54:35a–b, fourth letter in reply to Hsü Yen-chang.

75. *Analects,* 1:1.

76. *Lao Tzu,* ch. 70.

77. *Wen-chi,* 70:19b, "Account of Shang-ts'ai's [Hsieh Liang-tso] *Doubts on the Analects.*"

78. *Lao Tzu,* ch. 63.

79. *Analects,* 14:36.

80. *Yü-lei,* ch. 44, sec. 83 (pp. 1805–1806).

81. *Wen-chi,* 67:23b–24a, "Treatise on Nourishing Life."

82. *Analects,* 3:4.

83. *Ibid.,* 8:35.

84. *Yü-lei,* ch. 40, sec. 57 (p. 1730).

85. *Wen-chi,* 72:26a, "Treatise on Su Ch'e's Explanation of the *Lao Tzu.*"

86. According to tradition, when King Wu (r. 1121–1104 B.C.) conquered the Shang dynasty (1751–1112 B.C.) and founded the Chou dynasty (1111–249 B.C.), Po-i, out of loyalty to Shang, refused to eat the grain of Chou, lived on berries in the mountains, and eventually starved to death. Confucians have honored him as a sage.

87. *Yü-lei,* ch. 101, sec. 90 (p. 4091).

88. *Ibid.,* ch. 67, sec. 74 (p. 2646).

89. *Chuang Tzu,* ch. 2, "Equality of Things" (*SPTK* ed., *Nan-hua chen-ching,* 3:35b).

90. *Lao Tzu,* ch. 6.

91. *I-shu,* 3:4b.

92. *Chuang Tzu,* ch. 6, "Great Teacher" (*SPTK* ed., *Nan-hua chen-ching,* 3:3b).

93. *Analects,* 15:22.

94. *Yü-lei,* ch. 97, sec. 95 (p. 3968).

95. *Lao Tzu,* ch. 76.

96. *Yü-lei,* ch. 6, sec. 87 (p. 185).

97. *Lao Tzu,* ch. 59.

98. *Yü-lei,* ch. 16, sec. 13 (pp. 506–507).

99. *Chuang Tzu,* ch. 3, "Fundamentals of Nourishing Life" (*SPTK* ed., *Nan-hua chen-ching,* 2:4b).

100. *Lao Tzu,* ch. 11.

101. *Yü-lei,* ch. 103, sec. 47 (pp. 4145–4146).

102. *Lao Tzu,* ch. 31.

103. *Yü-lei,* ch. 110, sec. 31 (p. 4315).

104. *Ibid.,* ch. 137, sec. 44 (p. 5247).

105. *Lao Tzu,* ch. 60.

106. *Yü-lei,* ch. 3, sec. 83 (p. 88).

107. Ch'iu Ying's courtesy name was Tzu-fu. Chu Hsi discussed the *Lao Tzu* more with him than with any other pupil. For Ch'in Yung, see my *Chu Tzu men-jen,* pp. 67–68.

108. *Wen-chi,* 45:8a, third letter in reply to Ch'iu Tzu-fu (Ch'iu Ying).

109. *Lao Tzu,* ch. 50.

110. For the various interpretations, see my translation, *The Way of Lao Tzu* (New York: Bobbs–Merrill, 1963) n. 3, p. 189.

111. *Lao Tzu,* ch. 6.

112. *Yü-lei,* ch. 125, sec. 31 (p. 4799).

113. *I-shu,* 3:4b.

114. *Book of Changes,* "Appended Remarks," pt. 1, ch. 5.

115. *Ibid.,* pt. 2, ch. 1.

116. *I-shu,* 18:2a.

117. For a fuller discussion on this subject, see my *Chu-hsüeh lun-chi* [Studies on Chu Hsi] (Taipei: Student Book Co., 1982), pp. 99–121.

118. *Tung-lai Lü T'ai-shih wen-chi* [Collection of literary works of Lü Tsu-ch'ien, member of the Han-lin Academy] (*Chin-hua ts'ung-shu* [Chin-hua series] ed.). 7:9a, sixth letter to Lecturer-in-waiting Chu (Chu Hsi).

119. *Wen-chi,* 46:16b, second letter in reply to Chan Yüan-shan (Chan T'i-jen).

120. *Ibid.*, 67:23b. "Treatise on Nourishing Life."

121. *Ibid.*, 38:35a, first letter in reply to Chiang Yüan-shih.

122. *Ibid.*, 44:18a, second letter in reply to Fang Po-mu (Fang Shih-yao).

123. I have spotted the following joint references to Lao Tzu and Chuang Tzu in the *Yü-lei:* ch. 40, sec. 17 (p. 1637); ch. 125, sec. 54 (p. 4807); ch. 126, secs. 1, 2 (pp. 4817–4818); sec. 22 (p. 4828), sec. 23 (p. 4829).

124. *Yü-lei*, ch. 125, sec. 18 (p. 4790).

125. *Ibid.*, sec. 54 (p. 4807).

126. As taught in the *Doctrine of the Mean,* ch. 1.

127. The text of the *Great Learning* says, "Only after knowing what to abide in can one be calm."

128. *Yü-lei*, ch. 73, sec. 50 (p. 2944). The quotation is from the *Chuang Tzu,* ch. 23, "Keng-seng Ch'u" (*SPTK* ed., *Nan-hua chen-ching,* 8:9b).

129. *Chuang Tzu,* ch. 12, "Heaven and Earth" (*SPTK* ed., *Nan-hua chen-ching,* 5:9a).

130. *Book of Mencius,* 6A:6, quoting the *Book of Odes,* ode no. 260.

131. *Yü-lei*, ch. 125, sec. 51 (p. 4806).

132. *Ch'un-ch'iu fan-lu* [Luxuriant gems of the *Spring and Autumn Annals*] ch. 36, "Concrete Nature" (*SPTK* ed., 10:8b).

133. *Yü-lei*, ch. 125, sec. 52 (p. 4806).

134. *Ibid.*, ch. 40, sec. 16 (p. 1636).

135. *I-shu,* 7:2a.

136. *Ibid.*, 3:4b.

137. *Chuang Tzu,* ch. 33, "The Universe" (*SPTK* ed., *Nan-hua chen-ching,* 10:25b).

138. *Yü-lei*, ch. 74, sec. 196 (p. 3014).

139. *Ibid.*, ch. 125, sec. 54 (p. 4807).

140. *Ibid.*, sec. 19 (p. 4790).

141. *Chuang Tzu,* ch. 13, "The Way of Heaven" (*SPTK* ed., *Nan-hua chen-ching,* 5:27b).

142. *Yü-lei*, ch. 16, sec. 252 (pp. 590–591); ch. 84, sec. 8 (p. 3459).

143. *Ibid.*

144. Here "lascivious joy" refers to the idea that the interaction of yin and yang finds its expression in the union of man and woman.

145. *Chuang Tzu,* ch. 14, "Evolution of Heaven" (*SPTK* ed., *Nan-hua chen-ching,* 5:35b).

146. *Yü-lei*, ch. 68, sec. 11 (p. 2679).

147. *Ibid.*, ch. 125, sec. 54 (p. 4807).

148. *Chuang Tzu,* ch. 3, "Fundamentals on Nourishing Life" (*SPTK* ed., *Nan-hua chen-ching,* 2:2b–4a).

149. *Yü-lei*, ch. 125, sec. 50 (pp. 4805–4806).

150. *Ibid.*, ch. 75, sec. 10 (p. 3042).

151. *Ibid.*, ch. 20, sec. 55 (pp. 735–736).

152. *Ibid.*, ch. 10, sec. 15 (p. 257).

153. *Ibid.*, ch. 103, sec. 47 (pp. 4145–4146).

154. These five moral qualities refer to the *Great Learning,* ch. 3.

155. *Yü-lei*, ch. 57, sec. 24 (p. 2133).

156. See above, n. 141.

157. *Yü-lei,* ch. 16, sec. 252 (pp. 590–591), quoting the *Doctrine of the Mean,* ch. 4.

158. *Ibid.,* ch. 3, sec. 80 (p. 87).

159. *Wen-chi,* 76:27a–b, 83:24a–b.

160. *Ibid.,* 6:22; 1:12a–b; 76:14b.

161. *Ibid.,* separate collection, 7:2b; regular collection, 9:4b.

162. *Ibid.,* separate collection, 7:1a. I Wei-na must be a surname plus a private name, and therefore not a Buddhist name, which includes no family name.

163. *Ibid.,* regular collection, 9:10b.

164. *Ibid.,* 7:12b, 16a; 84:30a; 6:22b; 2:3b.

165. *Ibid.,* 9:4a.

166. *Ibid.,* 63:9b, letter in reply to Taoist Kan.

167. *Ibid.*

168. *Ibid.,* 9:3a.

169. For an account of Wu Hsiung, see my *Chu Tzu men-jen,* p. 99.

170. *Yü-lei,* ch. 120, secs. 43–46 (pp. 4627–4628).

# 29

# Chu Hsi and
# Buddhism

Our approach to this subject is utterly different from that of the typical study, which usually concentrates on Chu Hsi's criticisms of Buddhism. Along this line, there is excellent material in Japanese and French.[1] In *A Source Book in Chinese Philosophy,* I have translated fourteen selections from the *Yü-lei* and the *Wen-chi* that give an overview of Chu Hsi's thoughts on Buddhism. I also point out that although Chu Hsi's knowledge of Buddhism was very superficial, his attack on Buddhism was more comprehensive than that of his predecessors, for he criticized it from all points of view—ethical, theoretical, practical, historical, and textual—and concentrated on the Buddhist division of the mind into two, so that one examines the other and identifies the mind with nature, thus leading to the erroneous conclusion that the world is empty.[2] The present chapter investigates the source of his information on Buddhism, namely, his contact with Buddhist monks, his knowledge of Buddhist texts, and the Buddhist sayings he quoted.

## Association with Buddhist Monks

### Ch'an Master Ta-hui

When Chu Hsi was a young teenager, he studied under Liu Tzu-hui (1101–1147), often called Ping-weng (Sick old man), in Wu-fu Village in northern Fukien, where they both lived. As Chu Hsi himself recalled,

> When I was fifteen or sixteen, I was interested in this [i.e., Ch'an (Meditation) Buddhism, pronounced Zen in Japanese]. One day I met a monk at Ping-weng's place and talked with him. He merely repeated what I said

and did not say yes or no. Instead he talked to Liu. I did understand the theory of the brilliance and spiritual efficacy of the mind. Liu later told me [what the monk told him]. I therefore thought the monk had something wonderful with him, and I went to ask him. What he said was very good. Later, when I went to take the civil service examination [1148], I used his ideas and talked nonsense. At that time the examination essays were not as refined as they are now, and candidates were free to write crude essays. The examiner was moved by what I said. I passed.[3]

Chu Hsi was then nineteen.

The episode of his meeting the monk is not recorded in the earliest existent chronological biography *(nien-p'u)* of Chu Hsi, the *Chu Tzu nien-p'u* compiled by Yeh Kung-hui in 1431, but is related in Tai Hsien's (d. 1508) *Chu Tzu nien-p'u* of 1513. Wang Mao-hung's (1668–1741) *Chu Tzu nien-p'u* omits the story also. In Japan there has been a persistent tradition that may imply that the monk Chu Hsi met was Ta-hui. According to this tradition, when Chu Hsi went to take the civil service examination, Liu Tzu-hui searched his luggage and found a copy of the *Ta-hui yü-lu* (Recorded sayings of Ta-hui). This story is based on Yu Yü's preface in *Ta-hui P'u-chüeh Ch'an-shih yü-lu* (Recorded sayings of Ta-hui, Ch'an Master P'u-chüeh). The preface says,

> As a youth, Chu Wen Kung [Chu Hsi] did not like to read essays from civil service examinations of the time. When he heard an elderly master speak on the Ch'an doctrine of directly pointing to the mind, he readily understood the point of the brilliance and spiritual efficacy of the mind. When he was eighteen, he took the civil service examination. At the time he was a student of Liu P'ing-shan [Liu Tzu-hui]. P'ing-shan, believing that Chu Hsi was interested in the civil service examinations, opened his traveling chest and found a copy of the *Ta-hui yü-lu*. He passed the examination the next year.

The *Ta-hui yü-lu* is found in the *Taishō daizōkyō* (Taishō edition of the Buddhist canon),[4] but Yu Yü's preface is not there. Tokiwa Daijō (1870–1945) gave an account of Liu Tzu-hui's discovery of the *Ta-hui yü-lu* but dismissed it as "an irrelevant episode" and made no mention of Yü Yü's preface.[5] Yasuoka Masahiro quoted the preface but did not indicate where it could be found.[6] It is contained in another Buddhist canon,[7] but this does not answer the question of whether the monk Chu Hsi talked to was Ta-hui.

Ta-hui's private name was Tsung-kao, and his posthumous title was Miao-hsi (1089–1163). He was the direct spiritual descendant of Ch'an Master I-hsüan (d. 867) of Lin-chi. According to the pagoda inscription of Ta-hui written by Chang Chün (1096–1164),

In the first year of Lung-hsing [1163], on the tenth day of the eighth month, Ch'an Master Ta-hui Tsung-kao passed away in the Ming-yüeh-t'ang [Hall of the Bright Moon] in Ching-shan.[8] When the emperor heard about his death, he was extremely sad and decreed that the Ming-yüeh-t'ang be called the Miao-hsi-an [Wonderful and Happy Temple], conferred on him the posthumous title P'u-chüeh, and gave the pagoda the name Pao-kuang. . . . The Master's private name was Tsung-kao. He was a native of Ning-kuo County of Hsüan-chou.[9] His family name was Hsi. He became a Buddhist monk at seventeen. He did not want to remain in the village but wanted to follow masters of Buddhist scriptures, and he therefore started traveling. . . . He met with many scholars. Because of disorder, he traveled to Hunan, turned to Chiang-yu [Kiang-si], and entered Fukien. He built a small monastery on the island of Ch'ang-lo by the sea. He attracted fifty-three followers, and within fifty days, thirteen were converted to join the order of the Law of the Buddha. . . . When I arrived at Court [as prime minister], I invited him to Ching-shan in Lin-an [Hangchow]. The flourishing of Buddhism reached its zenith. . . . People he associated with numbered more than two thousand, all outstanding and fine. A famous high official of the time, the Honorable Vice Minister Chang Tzu-shao [Chang Chiu-ch'eng, 1092–1159], was a close friend. This friendship led to the Master's tragedy, for people in power hated him because they were afraid he might criticize them. Having abandoned his clerical robes and burned his credentials, he lived in exile at Heng-chou.[10] After ten years, he was transferred to Mei-chou.[11] Although Mei-chou was desolate and disease ridden, his followers packed their own food to accompany him. . . . Five years later, the emperor's father, in an expression of unusual kindness, recalled him. The following year, he resumed his attire as a monk. . . . In another two years, he moved to Ching-shan. . . . The Master lived to be seventy-five years old.[12]

Chang Ch'ün's inscription has no date. According to the chronological biography of Ta-hui, he arrived in Ch'ang-lo County in Fukien in the third month of 1134. In 1137, Prime Minister Chang Ch'ün invited him to Ching-shan. In 1141, Vice Minister Chang Chiu-ch'eng spoke from the altar of Ching-shan. At that time, Ch'in Kuei (1091–1155) was in power. It was said that Chang Chiu-ch'eng criticized the Court and thereby involved Ta-hui, with the result that the latter was banished to Heng-yang. He arrived there in the seventh month. He was ordered to go to Mei-chou in 1150. In 1156 he returned to Chekiang from Mei-chou, and in 1158 moved to Ching-shan.[13] This account is repeated in the *Fo-tsu li-tai t'ung-tsai* (General accounts of Buddhist patriarchs throughout the generations), except that the move to Mei-chou is one year later and the return to Chekiang is one year earlier.[14]

Based on the dates in the above accounts, Professor Tomoeda Ryūtarō believes that it was impossible for Chu Hsi to have met Ta-hui at Liu Tzu-hui's place in northern Fukien, because Ta-hui was then in exile in Heng-chou in Hunan Province.[15] He thinks that probably when Ta-hui was returning to Chekiang (1155), he passed through T'ung-an, in Ch'üan-chou in southern Fukien, and met Chu Hsi, who was then *chu-pu* (assistant magistrate) there. To Professor Tomoeda, the Buddhist monk whom Chu Hsi saw at age fifteen or sixteen was not Ta-hui but Tao-ch'ien,[16] who is discussed in the next section. As for the idea that Chu Hsi met Ta-hui at T'ung-an, this could not have occurred according to the chronological biography, because both in going from Heng-chou to Mei-chou and in returning from Mei-chou to Chekiang, Ta-hui went by land across Kiangsi, not by sea by way of Fukien.

In the *Yü-lei,* there is a passage that proves conclusively that Ta-hui and Liu Tzu-hui did meet. Chu Hsi said,

> One day, Ping-weng [Lin Tzu-hui] saw Miao-hsi [Ta-hui], who indulged in egotistic talk in front of him. He ascended the altar in the K'ai-shan Temple[17] and declared, "Yen-ch'ung [Liu Tzu-hui] cultivates his person but does not understand Ch'an, while Pao-hsüeh [Liu Tzu-yü, Tzu-hui's older brother, 1097–1146] understands Ch'an but does not cultivate his person. As the saying goes, Chang San has money but does not know how to spend it, while Li Ssu knows how to spend money but has none." Everything Ta-hui said was nonsense.[18]

Chu Hsi's recollection proves that Ta-hui and Liu Tzu-hui met in Wu-fu Village—a meeting that must of course have occurred before Liu's death in 1147. In all probability, Ta-hui visited Wu-fu Village during the several years he lived in Fukien after arriving there in 1134. At that time, the Liu brothers were in their prime, thirty or forty years old. Ta-hui meant to admonish them in typical Ch'an fashion. We do not know Liu Tzu-hui's reaction, but the episode must have made an impression, because he related it to Chu Hsi many years later. By the time Chu Hsi recounted the story, he himself regarded Buddhism as a perverse doctrine that was nothing but nonsense.

Chu Hsi had another memory which proves that he and Ta-hui met. He said,

> Take Kao-lao's [Venerable Kao, Ta-hui] doctrine of what is beyond speech and thought, etc. When he came to a difficult point, he did not speak plainly but dwelt on irrelevant matters. When I talked about self-mastery, for instance, he would say that it was obstruction from the outside. But if he talked about it, he would say it was an obstruction from the inside. He did not like me because I caught him at the critical moment. Those who did not understand Ch'an were disdained by him, but I understood Ch'an, and I therefore saw through him.[19]

This passage was recorded by Chu Hsi's pupil Huang I-kang after 1193. Although the recollection occurred several decades after the event, the fact that Chu Hsi and Ta-hui met cannot be doubted. The question is when and where. Ta-hui probably traveled from Ch'ang-lo in southern Fukien to Wu-fu Village in northern Fukien, but we must rule out the possibility of his meeting Chu Hsi then, because Chu Hsi and his widowed mother had not moved to Wu-fu when Ta-hui was in Ch'ang-lo. We must also rule out Ta-hui's meeting Chu Hsi in T'ung-an on his way back from Mei-chou because he did not travel by sea.

It is possible, however, that Ta-hui visited Wu-fu Village while Chu Hsi was studying with Liu Tzu-hui, because some of Ta-hui's Ch'ang-lo followers had presided over temples in northern Fukien. It is not unreasonable to suppose that one or two years before Liu died in 1147 —say in 1145—Ta-hui visited his pupils in northern Fukien, including Wu-fu Village. At that time Chu Hsi was sixteen, which was the year he said he met a Buddhist monk at Liu's place. Three years later, in 1148, when he took the civil service examination, he had a copy of Ta-hui's recorded sayings in his travel chest. The great difficulty with this theory is that Ta-hui was in exile in Heng-chou at the time, so it is unlikely that he would have taken a long trip to northern Fukien even if he had been allowed to so do. Nor is there any record in his chronological biography that he made such a journey. Rather, the *nien-p'u* says for the year 1142 that "after his arrival in Heng-yang, he declined to receive guests and suspended his correspondence."

The remaining possibility is that Chu Hsi and Ta-hui met in Mei-chou. This is a bold assumption, but it is supported by clear evidence. There can be no doubt that Chu Hsi visited Ch'ao-chou in Kwangtung Province. There are poems in the *Wen-chi* that show he was personally in Ch'ao-chou.[20] Additional evidence is supplied by the recent discovery of an essay he wrote for a local building in Chieh-yang County, Ch'ao-chou Prefecture.[21] I would suggest that Chu Hsi went there during his T'ung-an days, most likely in 1156, when he was twenty-seven years old. Since Ta-hui was in Mei-chou from 1150 to 1156, and Mei-chou is adjacent to Ch'ao-chou, either Chu Hsi traveled to Mei-chou or Ta-hui traveled to Ch'ao-chou. This theory supports Professor Tomoeda's timing. It is true that the chronological biography of Ta-hui makes no mention of their meeting in either place, but such an event is not comparable to a trip from Heng-chou to northern Fukien. The silence of the *nien-p'u* does not invalidate this theory. By the time of his meeting with Ta-hui, then, Chu Hsi had already visited his teacher Li T'ung (1093–1163), who influenced him to swing from Buddhism to Confucianism. I suggest that at this meeting Chu Hsi spoke of the Confucian doctrine of self-mastery in opposition to the Buddhist doctrine of the examination of the mind, as indicated in his recollection just quoted.

All agree that Chu Hsi had read the recorded sayings of Ta-hui. We
may cite additional support from the *Yü-lei*. Chu Hsi once told a pupil,
"If one reads books without finding out the meaning, no matter how
one searches, one cannot form any opinion. This is precisely what the
Buddhists call observing the catchword in recent years. There is the *Ta-
hui yü-lu* in popular society, which goes into the theory in detail. If you
take a look, you will know the whole story."[22] Chu Hsi also wrote the
"Chang Wu-kou Chung-yung-chieh" (Chang Chiu-ch'eng's *Explanation of the Doctrine of the Mean*), describing Vice Minister Chang as running away from Confucianism to join Buddhism. In it, Chu Hsi said
that Chang's Buddhist teacher had told him, "If you control the handle
in both hands when you explain, you should change what appears on
the surface and preach the Law in an expedient way, so that different
views may arrive at the same conclusion and the mundane will be
agreeable with the supramundane. However, what I have just said
should not be told to ordinary people, for they may believe what they
have heard to be really the case."[23] In a footnote, Chu Hsi added, "This
instruction appeared in Ch'an Master Ta-hui's letter to Vice Minister
Chang. It is omitted from the *Yü-lu* because Ta-hui's followers considered it taboo."[24] It can readily be seen that Chu Hsi had read Ta-hui's
*Yü-lu* with care and remembered it well.

Chu Hsi was not only familiar with Ta-hui's writings, he also knew
about Ta-hui's associates. He said, "Venerable Kao [Ta-hui] once said
that when he was young he saw Chang T'ien-chüeh."[25] He also said,
"Chang Wu-kou paid homage to Venerable Kao. Wang Yü-shan
[Wang Ying-ch'en, 1118–1176] was attracted by him and eventually
came to love Buddhism."[26] On another occasion, Chu Hsi remarked,
"The type of people Venerable Kao liked are crude and careless, like
Chang Tzu-shao and T'ang Li-fu. Wang Sheng-hsi [Wang Ying-
ch'en], Lü Chü-jen [Lü Pen-chung, 1084–1145], etc., were somewhat
prudent and sincere, and were greatly slighted by him. . . . Venerable
Wang once told me, 'The Ch'an learning of Venerable Kao really has
some good points.' I asked him, 'Have you, Vice Minister, ever gone
into his good points?' He said he hadn't."[27] Chu Hsi also related that
Wang Tuan-ming (Wang Ts'ao, 1079–1154) went to study Ch'an
under Ta-hui[28] and that Ta-hui "was appreciated by Chang Wu-
chin."[29] The fact that Chu Hsi was able to appraise their relationship
shows he had a profound knowledge of Ta-hui.

Chu Hsi could also tell one or two anecdotes about Ta-hui. Chu Hsi
thought that what people regarded as Buddhist lamps were nothing but
lights emitted by rotting leaves or fireflies. In that connection he said,
"When Miao-hsi [Ta-hui] once saw a light in some place, he ordered
someone to extinguish it. What he got was a small worm like a snake,
but very little, no larger than a thread."[30] Chu Hsi also "remembered

that when Venerable Kao was banished to Heng-yang, someone wrote a farewell poem with the words 'Whenever [you] meet people, you close your mouth tightly. When there is nothing to do, [you] try to comb your hair.' The lines are most interesting and can make one laugh, but one should not treat it as merely a laugh."[31] These lines ridicule Ta-hui's indulgence in egotistic talk, like a Buddhist monk with a shaved head trying to comb his hair.

There are only two cases in the *Yü-lei* where Chu Hsi commented on Ta-hui's thought. In one case, he said, "In the past, Venerable Liao [Liao-lao, Ch'en Kuan, 1057–1122?][32] concentrated on teaching people to sit in Ch'an meditation. Venerable Kao did not approve of that, and wrote the 'Cheng-hsieh lun' (Treatise to correct a perverse doctrine) to attack him. Later, when Kao preached at the T'ien-t'ung Temple, Liao-lao bowed to him as a teacher. As a result, Kao came to agreement with him. When he died, Venerable Kao wrote an inscription for him."

Question: "Since he wanted quiescence aiming at Nirvana, why couldn't he sit in meditation?"

Answer: "He wanted to achieve enlightenment. Formerly, Kao liked Tzu-shao very much. When he returned from the south, he wrote Tzu-shao to reprimand him, believing he had changed. Now Ta-hui's pupils have compiled his writings, but have omitted his 'Cheng-hsieh lun' and also deleted his letter to Tzu-shao."[33]

On another occasion, a pupil asked, "Kuei-feng [Tsung-mi, 780–841] said, 'To commit an act of righteousness means that the mind is awakened. To commit an act contrary to righteousness means that the mind is wild and confused. . . . The righteousness here is not that of humanity and righteousness but the righteousness of moral principles.' This is very ludicrous."

Answer: "He considered humanity and righteousness as kindness and love [in human relations]. That is why he said so. Although he spoke of moral principles, when did he ever dream of them? Later, Venerable Kao thought he was wrong, saying, 'The righteousness of moral principles is the same as the righteousness of humanity and righteousness. Why break emptiness into two sections?' "[34] Chu Hsi was opposed to Ta-hui at almost every turn, but here is a point on which they agreed. When Tokiwa Daijō asserted that Chu Hsi's idea of moral principles and the unity of humanity and righteousness was inspired by Ta-hui,[35] however, he certainly went too far.

### Monk Tao-ch'ien

The conclusion that Chu Hsi read Ta-hui's recorded sayings at age nineteen but did not meet Ta-hui until he was twenty-seven does not answer the question of who the monk was whom he saw at Liu Tzu-hui's place when he was fifteen or sixteen. I believe that monk was Tao-ch'ien. In a letter to Lo Po-wen (1116–1168), grandnephew of Lo Ts'ung-yen (1072–1135), Li T'ung said, "Originally, [Chu Hsi's] effort was made at Ch'ien-k'ai-shan's [Tao-ch'ien] place. Hence all his personal realization was internal. After discussions and debates [with me], he understands the Confucian line of thought and can definitely point out his errors."[36] Since Chu Hsi had achieved some personal realization under the guidance of Tao-ch'ien, the Buddhist monk must have made a deep impression on him; hence discussions and debates were needed before Li T'ung was able to turn him away from Buddhism.

This letter is quoted in Tai Hsien's chronological biography of Chu Hsi under the year 1153, when Chu Hsi was twenty-four.[37] It is also quoted in the *nien-p'u* written by Wang Mao-hung, but under the year 1160, when Chu Hsi was thirty-one.[38] Tao-ch'ien was Ta-hui's pupil. According to the *Yün-wo chi-t'an* (Recorded talks of one who makes clouds his bed), Tao-ch'ien "eventually returned to Chien-yang, where he built a temple on Hsien-chou Mountain. There were those who heard of his teachings, were attracted to them, and flocked to him, such as . . . Judicial Intendant Chu Yüan-hui [Chu Hsi], who repeatedly wrote to ask questions and often visited the temple."[39] The *Ch'ung-an-hsien hsin-chih* (New accounts of Ch'ung-an County) tells us that Tao-ch'ien's lay family name was Yu, that he was a native of Wu-fu Village, and that he built the Tzu-hsin Temple on Hsien-chou Mountain.[40] His name does not appear in the *Wen-chi* but occurs once in the *Yü-lei,* where Chu Hsi recalled his words that "it is said in the *Ta-tsang-ching* [Buddhist canon] that when a Buddhist had stomach trouble, he would be cured if only he meditated for six or seven days and reduced his amount of food."[41] Chu Hsi was not appointed judicial intendant until 1182. The use of this title in the *Yün-wo chi-t'an* may be explained by the fact that it was Chu Hsi's title at the time the story was written.

The *Yün-wo chi-t'an* also contains a letter by Tao-ch'ien in reply to Chu Hsi. In this letter, Tao-ch'ien said,

> During the twelve time periods of the day, if you are engaged in something, deal with it as the situation calls for. If you are not engaged in anything, turn your mind away from everything and chew on this one thought: Does a dog have the Buddha nature? Chao-chou [Ch'an Master Ts'ung-shen, 778–897] said, "Wu."[42] Just take this "public case" and chew on it. Don't deliberate or give any farfetched explanation. And don't offer any ingenious ideas or accept any conclusion with reluctance. Imagine you are going to close your eyes and jump across the Yellow River. Don't ask if you can jump across it or not. Just jump with all your might. If you can jump across it, everything will be settled, but if you cannot, just jump. Don't figure on whether you are going to succeed or fail, and don't mind any danger. Just be brave and go forward and stop any calculations.

If you hesitate and give rise to all kinds of thoughts, you won't be able to deal with the situation.[43]

The *Wen-chi* contains no letter to Tao-ch'ien. The *Yün-wo chi-t'an* was compiled in 1189; we do not know whether it is reliable.

There is a letter from Chu Hsi to Tao-ch'ien in the *Fo-fa chin-t'ang pien* (Stronghold of the Law of the Buddha) compiled by the monk Tai-tsung Hsin-t'ai (1327–1415). According to this account, Chu Hsi wrote Tao-ch'ien and said, "Formerly, I was enlightened by Miao-hsi [Ta-hui]. He was correct. I used to adhere strictly to the written word and ponder without allowing even the slightest bit to enter the mind. At all times I only chewed on the catchword about the dog. May I have a word from you to correct my defects." In the same account there is also a funeral address written by Chu Hsi for Tao-ch'ien in which Chu Hsi said, "The Teacher [Tao-ch'ien] lived in Hsien-chou and I in a village. We were separated by a hill. I would only look in his direction. In the fall of 1146, the Teacher came to the Kung-ch'en Cave and I got to meet him. Our smiles and conversations drew us closer every day. . . . I saw the Teacher three times. . . . After three months, . . . the Teacher passed away."[44] Neither the letter nor the funeral address is found in the *Wen-chi*.

Hu Shih has found that both the letter and the funeral address are derived from the *Shih-shih tzu-chien* (Mirror for Buddhism) compiled by Hsi-chung (*fl.* 1336). While Hu doubts the authenticity of the letter, he is inclined to accept the credibility of the funeral address.[45] The fact that the letter asserts that Chu Hsi's meeting with Ta-hui occurred before his association with Tao-ch'ien makes it suspect.

There is no doubt that Chu Hsi was influenced by Tao-ch'ien in his youth. Professor Tomoeda thinks that after he received instructions from Tao-ch'ien at fifteen or sixteen, Chu Hsi shifted from quietistic meditation to the dynamic technique of *hua-t'ou* ("public case" or catchword; *koan* in Japanese). Professor Satō Hitoshi shares this conclusion.[46] This observation is not unreasonable, for when Chu Hsi was fifteen or sixteen, Tao-ch'ien was in his thirties. He may even have been preaching in the K'ai-shan Temple of Wu-fu Village, for he was called K'ai-shan Ch'ien. Later, he probably built a temple called Mi-an on Hsien-chou Mountain, across the valley from Wu-fu Village. Because of its proximity, Chu Hsi visited Mi-an many times throughout his life. There are at least six poems and an essay on his visits to this temple. In 1181, Chu Hsi even built a pavilion on the mountain,[47] so he must have had some emotional attachment to it apart from its scenery. In a letter to his friend Lü Tsu-ch'ien (1137–1181), Chu Hsi said, "The chief monk at Mi-an, Ts'ung-mu, has recently passed away. His follower, Fa-chou, is temporarily in charge. . . . But the income of this temple is very small. The situation is nothing like the days of Ch'ien-lao [Venerable Ch'ien, Tao-ch'ien]."[48] In another letter he complained that the monk "Ching-sheng is increasingly impolite. . . . Will you ask your uncle, the prefect, to give me a letter or send another monk to take over the documents from Ching-sheng? Otherwise, the matter will be out of hand and the temple will be in danger. That will be most regrettable."[49] We do not know what the trouble was, but the letter shows that Chu Hsi was involved in the affairs of Mi-an. This indicates a lifelong relationship with the temple founded by Tao-ch'ien.

## Other Monks

Two more monks figured in Chu Hsi's life before his return to Confucianism. One was Yüan-wu, (literary name K'eng-an), a native of Chien-an. According to the records of the Ch'ung-an County, he lived in the K'ai-shan Temple in Wu-fu Village. He wrote an inscription for Chu Hsi's portrait, and when he died Chu Hsi wrote a poem of condolence.[50] The K'u-yai man-lu (Random notes of K'u-yai Yüan-wu) also says, "Ch'an Master Yüan-wu lived on Mount Wu-i for more than ten years. . . . He taught Hui-an Chu Wen Kung [Chu Hsi] Confucian learning."[51] We do not know if the two Yüan-wus just mentioned were the same person, and there is no support to either claim anywhere else. He could not have been Yüan-wu K'e-ch'in (1063–1135), the famous author of the Pi-yen lu (Records of the blue cave), who died when Chu Hsi was only six years old. However, Kusumoto Bun'yū believed that Chu Hsi studied with Yüan-wu K'e-ch'in in his last year of life, when Chu Hsi was six.[52] Since Chu Hsi did not move to northern Fukien until he was fourteen, he obviously could not have studied at Mount Wu-i at that time.

The other monk was Master Wei-k'o. As Chu Hsi recalled, in the winter of 1160, when he went to visit Li T'ung, he was a guest of Wei-k'o at the Hsi-lin Temple. He stayed there for several months and saw Wei-k'o morning and evening. When Wei-k'o built a room to the left of his house and called it Ta-kuan-hsüan, Chu Hsi wrote a poem to celebrate the occasion and showed it to the priest. Two years later, when he went to see Li T'ung again, he was Wei-k'o's guest for almost a month. The priest asked him to write down the story of his visit so he could hang it on the wall. Thereupon Chu Hsi wrote both a poem and an inscription for him, which are found in the Wen-chi.[53]

The fact that Chu Hsi was twice a houseguest of Wei-k'o reveals a friendly feeling between them. This friendly attitude toward Buddhist monks was evident throughout Chu Hsi's life and was expressed in two different directions, namely, in his travels and in his exchange of poems.

In terms of numbers, his association with Buddhist monks was roughly equal to that with Taoist priests. In both cases they exchanged poems and minor gifts. In his travels, however, Chu Hsi visited or stayed in more Buddhist than Taoist temples. Not counting mentions of *yüan* and *an,* which could be either Buddhist or Taoist, those establishments that can be identified as Buddhist far outnumber the Taoist ones, probably because there were more Buddhist temples, they offered better facilities, and they were situated in more scenic spots. We know of about twenty Buddhist temples that Chu Hsi visited—far more than the number visited by any of the other Sung Neo-Confucians. It may not be an exaggeration to say that the number of Buddhist temples Chu Hsi visited throughout his life exceeded a hundred. In these visits, he may have stayed overnight, enjoyed the scenery, viewed calligraphy and stone rubbings, written poems with friends, or had discussions.

The most famous of Chu Hsi's meetings at a Buddhist temple is undoubtedly the one at Goose Lake Temple in Kiangsi in 1175, when he, Lu Hsiang-shan (1139–1193), and others met to discuss various issues.[54] After he visited Chang Shih (1133–1180) in 1167, they and others ascended Mount Heng and toured the famous mountain for a week, stopping at at least four Buddhist temples where they composed poems and in one case held a farewell banquet.[55] In 1181, after his term as prefect of Nan-k'ang in Kiangsi was up, Chu Hsi and some of his pupils and friends toured scenic Mount Lu. His poems and travelogue about the trip mention twelve Buddhist temples.[56] On this trip, a Buddhist priest accompanied him, but on another, this time in Fukien, two monks did not appear as promised.[57] We also know of Chu Hsi's sojourns to other temples, where he wrote poems and epilogues, played host at dinners, and gathered like-minded friends for meetings.[58]

In all these cases Chu Hsi's acquaintance with the resident Buddhist priests may have been no more than casual, but in other instances the friendship was quite strong. In 1187, Chu Hsi and several pupils, accompanied by the monk Tuan-yu, called on Ch'an Master Yüan-ssu (Chih-an Ho-shang) at the Yung-ch'üan Temple on Ku-shan (Drum Mountain) in Foochow. They missed him, but Chu Hsi commemorated the event by having his own writing about the visit carved on a cliff nearby—an inscription that is still a tourist attraction.[59] He also corresponded with at least two Buddhist monks.[60] In one case a monk sent him some medicine and he reciprocated with tea and stone rubbings.[61] Another monk was reputed to be able to diagnose a patient's illness simply by looking at him, without feeling his pulse or even hearing about his condition. Chu Hsi not only believed in this monk but praised him for his utter sincerity, which Chu Hsi thought provided him with the power of telepathy.[62]

We know of no case in which Chu Hsi discussed Buddhist doctrines with a monk after the time of his youth. He did send two monks poems, which may suggest that they had discussed ideas.[63] On one occasion he and a monk talked about fate and seemed to agree.[64] To another monk, who he had not seen for years and who had once gone to a pavilion to welcome him, Chu Hsi sent a poem which says that there are divergent roads, some long and some short, and that if the priest had any new thoughts, he would like to hear them.[65] Clearly they had not come to an agreement. He even criticized a monk who claimed that whenever a worshiper came, the wooden ball in the central hall would become hot. He asked, "Why are you so attached to the wooden ball? Why do you want it to be hot?"[66] All in all, although Chu Hsi was socially amiable toward Buddhist priests, philosophically he remained critical of them.

## Acquaintance with Buddhist Literature

Like Chu Hsi's acquaintance with Buddhist monks, his knowledge of the Buddhist canon was quite limited, although much more extensive than that of other Sung Neo-Confucians. We shall first inquire into how many scriptures and treatises he mentioned. We shall then ask whether he read them or had simply heard of their titles, and how well he understood them.

As far as we know, the *Yü-lei* mentions fourteen Buddhist works by name: the *Ssu-shih-erh chang ching* (Forty-two chapter scripture), the *Ta-pan-jo ching* (Great wisdom scripture, *Mahāprajñāpāramitā sūtra*); the *Hua-yen ching* (Flowery splendor scripture, *Avataṁsaka sūtra*); the *Fa-hua ching* (Scripture of the Lotus of the Wonderful Law, *Saddharmapuṇḍarīka sūtra*); the *Leng-yen ching* (Strong character scripture, *Sūraṅgama sūtra*); the *Yüan-chüeh ching* (Scripture of perfect enlightenment); the *Chin-kang ching* (Diamond scripture); the *Kuang-ming ching* (Scripture of enlightenment and emancipation); the *Hsin ching* (Heart scripture, *Prajñāpāramitā-hri-daya sūtra*); the *Wei-mo ching* (Scripture spoken by Vimalakīrti, *Vimala-kīrti-nirdeśa sūtra*); the *Chao-lun* (Seng-chao's treatise); the *Hua-yen ta-chih* (Fundamental principles of Hua-yen); the *Hua-yen ho-lun* (Collected discussions on Hua-yen); and the *Ching-te ch'uan-teng lu* (Records of the transmission of the lamp completed during the Ching-te period [1004–1007]). Mention is also made of "Buddhist scriptures," "Buddhist books," "commentaries on Buddhist scriptures," "the Buddhist canon," "Buddhist classics," and so on.[67] The number of works cited is small, but those mentioned do represent the basic Buddhist schools, such as Hua-yen (Flowery splendor), T'ien-t'ai (Heavenly terrace), Ching-t'u (Pure land), San-lun (Three treatises), Wei-shih (Consciousness only), and Ch'an (Meditation).

The *Wen-chi* mentions only specific works: the *Forty-two Chapter Scripture*, the *Fa-hua ching*, the *Chin-kang ching*, the *Kuang-ming ching*, the *Leng-*

*yen ching,* the *Yüan-chüeh ching,* and the *Ching-te ch'uan-teng lu.* The *Yü-lei* does not mention the *Ta-hui yü-lu* (Recorded sayings of Ta-hui), but the *Wen-chi* mentions it three times.[68] There is a great deal of criticism of Buddhism in the letters in the *Wen-chi,* but these deal with general Buddhist doctrines, not specific scriptures, whereas in the *Yü-lei* specific Buddhist works are often discussed.

The number of Buddhist works is so huge that no one can read them all. Chu Hsi probably read a great number, for he quoted many Buddhist sayings. Although many were popular Buddhist aphorisms of the time that he could have picked up from hearsay, many must have come from his reading, for which there is concrete evidence. For example, he said, "In the beginning paragraph of chapter two of the *Leng-yen ching,* it is said that not only are there changes in the year; there are also changes in the month. There are not only changes in the month; there are also changes in the day. There are not only changes in the day; there are also changes in the time period. It is only that people are not aware of it. This theory is correct."[69] He also said, "The first and last parts of the *Leng-yen ching* only talk about chants. The middle part was added later, for those Chinese who loved Buddhism added it because they thought the chants were vulgar."[70] We shall not discuss his theory of the Chinese addition, but it is evident that he had read the scripture with care. Commenting on the *Hua-yen ho-lun,* he remarked, "In the thirteenth chapter, the Buddha basically said to reject mundane affairs completely, but later clever people appeared and said that one should not pick up even a speck of dust although one is actually buried in the ground, and in the arena of ten thousand affairs, one should not discard a single *dharma* [element of existence]."[71] Chu Hsi could hardly have specified the chapter number without having read the book.

His appraisal of the *Lotus Scripture* is another case in point: "If you look at the *Lotus Scripture,* you will readily know its absurdity. All it talks about is the number of grains of sand in the Ganges River over thousands and tens of thousands of infinitely long periods of time. There is nothing about recent periods."[72] Clearly, Chu Hsi could not have made such a statement without having read the text. Also, he once recalled a Buddhist scripture he had read in which it was said that on top of Kunlun Mountain there is Anu Pool, from which water runs in all directions.[73] And in talking about the turbans the people of the late T'ang dynasty used to wear, he remarked, "Once I saw in a Ch'an recorded dialogue that Emperor Chuang-tsung [r. 923–925] of [the late] T'ang told a monk, 'I acquired a treasure from the Central Plan and no one has appraised its value.' The monk said, 'May I see your treasure, Sir?' Chuang Tsung used his hand to unfold the two tassels to show him."[74] In each case his impression from his reading must have been very deep.

In criticizing the *Heart Scripture,* he said, "The Buddhists merely want to see emptiness in every form. In general, they want to confuse people. They say that, in reality, not a single *dharma* is set up, but at the same time they say that not a single *dharma* is rejected."[75] In his criticism of the *Scripture of Perfect Enlightenment,* he said, "Only the first couple of chapters are good. The rest is nonsense."[76] Both cases show his familiarity with the text.

In his appraisal of Buddhist works, Chu Hsi was ambivalent. For a Neo-Confucian, he may be considered impartial. He regarded the words of the *Forty-Two Chapter Scripture* as "very vulgar,"[77] but its doctrines as "fair and truthful."[78] Likewise, his attitude toward the *Leng-yen ching* was both positive and negative. In his opinion, the *Leng-yen ching* arbitrarily sets forth one or two ideas, keeps repeating them, and becomes meaningless after several sections.[79] However, "The *Leng-yen ching* was very well done."[80] In the case of the *Yüan-chüeh ching,* "Originally it amounts to something, but it is very vulgar because of farfetched additions."[81] To him, both scriptures are praiseworthy in some respects but should not be taken as an assistance to Confucian learning.[82] As to the *Hua-yen ho-lun,* its words were so vulgar and nonsensical that he could not understand what its good points were and why Ch'en Liao-weng (Ch'en Kuan) scrutinized it all his life without tiring of it. Chu Hsi felt sad that such a talented person was attracted to it in this way.[83] He was also ambivalent about Ch'en Liao-weng's fondness for the *Hua-yen ta-chih.* Question: "Why did people like Liao-weng like the *Hua-yen ta-chih* so much?" Answer: "They felt it was good because they failed to understand thoroughly. As we see it today, it had some good points; it can arouse people."[84]

Chu Hsi's evaluated Buddhist texts both from the standpoint of philosophical criticism and from that of historical research. From the point of view of Neo-Confucianism, Buddhism is of course a perverse doctrine. As he put it,

> Ch'in-fu [Chang Shih] and Po-kung [Lü Tsu-ch'ien] have not seen through Buddhism because they have not read Buddhist books. I alone understand it. Take scriptures like the *Leng-yen* and the *Yüan-chüeh.* If you look at them, you will roughly get the fundamental ideas. In the learning of Buddhism, it generally says that if you understand thoroughly, all the thousands of sins become extinct. If so, this type of learning is but the hideout of rebellious ministers and undutiful sons of the world.[85]

Such an explanation is too simplistic, for it is not true that Buddhism overlooks moral cultivation, just that the sphere of its moral cultivation is different from that of Confucianism. Or take Chu Hsi's comment on the *Transmission of the Lamp.* He asked how many of the patriarchs could have become Confucian sages like Yao, Shun, Yü, Chi, King Wen,

King Wu, the Duke of Chou, and Confucius. He then demanded concrete evidence[86]—the evidence of personal cultivation, regulation of the family, and ordering of the states, all of which are naturally different from the Buddhist goal of spiritual salvation. Among the patriarchs in the *Transmission of the Lamp,* there were not a few with deep insight and strong character.

When Chu Hsi said that the main idea of the *Diamond Scripture* lies in Subhuti, however, he was correct.[87] Subhuti was one of the ten disciples of the Buddha. The Buddha taught him not to give rise to any thoughts by being free from all attachments. Subhuti understood the doctrine of emptiness and preached it. This is the doctrine Confucians are most afraid of. However, in the Buddhist belief, every color and every fragrance is nothing but the Middle Way. Thus emptiness is not as nihilistic as Confucians tend to think it is.

Chu Hsi once said, "In a certain scripture, it is said that in the last infinitely long period of time, there will be few people. They will be burned into ashes. When the ashes are blown by wind and swept by water, they will become suds. Grains of all sorts will grow by themselves on the ground. People will fly from Heaven above to come and eat them and there will be the world again. The Buddhists do not understand the operation of yin and yang [passive and active cosmic forces] and therefore talk nonsense like this."[88] This passage was recorded by Cheng K'o-hsüeh (1152–1212) in 1191. From the standpoint of the Confucian theory of the rise and fall of yin and yang, the Buddhist account of the world is of course absurd. Chu Hsi also said that in the latter part of the *Leng-yen ching,* after the great calamity, "People in the world will all die and there will no longer be humankind. Instead, all kinds of grains will grow, each about a foot or more in height. Immortals from Heaven above will come to eat them. As the grains will seem to be good, they will keep on eating. As a result, their bodies will become heavy and they will be unable to rise. Thus the world will once more have humankind. This scenario is certainly laughable."[89] This passage was recorded by Huang I-kang after 1193. Huang attended the Master until 1199, and this passage could have been recorded then. If so, this account was written down eight or nine years after that of Cheng K'o-hsüeh. I believe that Chu Hsi incorrectly attributed this account to the *Leng-yen ching.* In the scripture's description of transmigration, it says that a plant became man and that when man dies he becomes a plant again. It does not say that all humankind will die and then all kinds of grains will grow. In chapter 8, several kinds of immortals are described, but the main idea is to show that they still have not left the realm of desire and therefore cannot transcend the cycle of transmigration. Confucians do not believe in transmigration, so it was natural that Chu Hsi looked upon it as an absurdity.

He fared much better with the *Chao-lun*. He said, "The *Chao-lun* that has been transmitted to the present age is said to have been written by Chao, Master of the Law [Seng-chao, 384–414]. It has the theory of Fourfold Immutability, which says, 'The sun and the moon traverse the sky but do not circulate. Rivers and streams compete to run to the sea but do not flow. Floating air whirls about but does not move. And mountains and peaks lie on their backs but are always quiet.' These four sentences have the same meaning, that is, there is tranquillity in activity."[90] The four sentences come from the first of four essays in the *Chao-lun,* that on "The Immutability of Things." In this essay, the general idea is that activity and tranquillity are not different and that *dharmas* neither come nor go. Therefore one must seek tranquillity in activity and activity in tranquillity. Chu Hsi's summary may be said to have hit the nail on the head.

On the history of Buddhist texts, Chu Hsi stubbornly held to his own theories. He said, "When Buddhism first entered China, it taught religious practice, as in the case of the *Forty-Two Chapter Scripture,*"[91] and "At first there was only the *Forty-Two Chapter Scripture.*" Elsewhere he said, "By the time of the Chin [265–420] and [Liu] Sung [420–479] dynasties, they began to talk about philosophy. In this respect, all their ideas were stolen from Lao Tzu and Chuang Tzu, and especially from Lieh Tzu. Later, Bodhidharma [c. 460–534 in China] came and talked about meditation [Ch'an]."[92] He explained, "At first there was only the *Forty-Two Chapter Scripture.* There weren't many others. By the Eastern Chin [317–420], there were philosophical discussions. There were lecturers like those today, who used to summarize their discussions in an essay. As time went on, they got tired of these discussions. At that point, Bodhidharma arrived. He taught only meditation, which provided some benefit."[93]

Chu Hsi thought that the transition from religious discipline to philosophical discussion had been the work of Master of the Law Hui-yüan (334–417) and Chih Tao-lin (Chih Tun, 314–366), who had merely stolen ideas from Chuang Tzu.[94] He therefore insisted that before the time of Chin and Sung, the talks of Hui-yüan and others did not go beyond Chuang Tzu and Lieh Tzu.[95] As he reiterated

When it came to the time of Chin and Sung, Buddhism gradually flourished. However, its literature at the time was merely an elaboration of the doctrines of Lao Tzu and Chuang Tzu. As in the case of Master Yüan's [Hui-yüan] treatises, every piece is completely the idea of Lao Tzu and Chuang Tzu. Only after Bodhidharma arrived during the P'u-t'ung period [520–526] of the Liang dynasty did he wipe out all [philosophical discussions]. He did not set up a body of writing but directly pointed to the human mind.[96]

In short, in Chu Hsi's opinion, "Only the *Forty-Two Chapter Scripture* is an old Buddhist text; the rest were all completed by Chinese writers, who polished them."[97]

For example, Chu Hsi thought that the *Vimalakīrti Scripture* had been written during the Southern and Northern Dynasties (420–589), although he admitted he was not quite sure about this: "I heard from the son of Li Po-chi that the *Vimalakīrti Scripture* was written by a noble man, perhaps a follower of Hsiao Tzu-liang. Li's son said the fact is recorded in the official history, but I have failed to locate it."[98] He was on a firmer ground when he said that Yang Ta-nien had revised the *Transmission of the Lamp*. In his words, "The *Transmission of the Lamp* is very crude. It was written by a monk during the reign of Chen-tsung [*r.* 998–1022]. When he presented it to the emperor, the emperor ordered Yang Ta-nien to revise it. Hence it was under Yang Ta-nien's name, although Yang Ta-nien himself did not understand it."[99] Yang Ta-nien was Yang I (974–1020), and the author was the monk Tao-yüan. Emperor Chen-tsung ordered Yang and others to edit the book with final authority. In Yang I's preface, he explicitly stated that the author was Tao-yüan, but it was published in Yang's name, probably to take advantage of his prestige as a member of the Han-lin Academy.

According to Chu Hsi,[100] the doctrine of "hearing oneself" in the *Leng-yen ching*[101] is Chuang Tzu's idea,[102] and the adage in the *Scripture of Perfect Enlightenment*, "When all the Four Great [Elements of Earth, Water, Fire, and Wind] have departed [from the body], where is the illusory body then?"[103] is the same as Lieh Tzu's saying, "When the spirit goes home and bones and limbs return to their roots, where will I be?"[104] Such contentions are farfetched, to say the least. Chu Hsi even said, "Buddhist scriptures originally came from a foreign country far away. The language was different. There were many strange words unintelligible to people. They therefore wrote many chants in a great variety of fashions for people to recite."[105] Obviously, he had no idea of the religious function of chants.

Chu Hsi's misunderstanding of Buddhist works is most unfortunate. But it is not really surprising, because he merely reflected the general situation of his time. Few Neo-Confucians cared to read Buddhist books. Certainly Chu Hsi read many more than his contemporaries, including Lu Hsiang-shan and Ch'en Liang (1143–1194).

At the end of many Buddhist scriptures—the *Heart Scripture,* for example—there is a chant, *"Gate gate . . . ."* This is a Sanskrit mantra that is meant to be recited over and over again, although some devotees take the word (which literally means "go") to refer to crossing the sea of suffering to the Other Shore. The Chinese Buddhists simply transliterated *gate* with two Chinese characters that literally mean "to announce" and "the emperor." According to Chu Hsi, Wang An-shih

(1021–1086) "interpreted *gate gate* as announcing what the emperorship should be, without knowing that it is a foreign term."[106] Chu Hsi did not go that far. Wang's interpretation vividly reveals the Neo-Confucian ignorance of Buddhist literature. The situation was not much different from that of today, when many Chinese intellectuals talk about Communism although few have actually read the works of Marx, Lenin, or Mao Tse-tung.

## Buddhist Sayings Quoted by Chu Hsi

Chu Hsi referred to about as many Buddhist sayings as he did scriptures, but few of the sayings are from the particular works he mentioned. Thus the sum total of scriptures and sayings that Chu Hsi cited shows that he was quite familiar with Buddhist literature.

Chu Hsi quoted Buddhist aphorisms several times as often as did the Ch'eng brothers (Ch'eng Hao, 1032–1085; Ch'eng I, 1033–1107) but less often than Wang Yang-ming (1472–1529). In his *Ch'uan-hsi lu* (Instructions for practical living) alone, Wang quoted Buddhist sayings about forty times.[107] In addition, Wang sometimes employed Ch'an techniques. For example, he once told a pupil, "Give me your selfish desires. I shall overcome them for you."[108] This is a borrowing from Bodhidharma, for when a monk came to him and said, "My mind is not calm. Please settle it for me," Bodhidharma replied, "Give me your mind and I shall pacify it for you."[109] Chu Hsi never used such methods.

This section lists sixty-one sayings quoted by Chu Hsi. Fifteen appear in the *Wen-chi,* forty three in the *Yü-lei,* and three (1, 9, and 14) in both. Thus the *Wen-chi* does not contain as many Buddhist sayings as the *Yü-lei,* since Chu Hsi quoted Buddhist sayings only in letters, not in official documents, essays, or inscriptions. Even in the *Yü-lei,* he seldom had occasion to quote Buddhist sayings in discussions on the Mandate of Heaven, nature, feelings, the investigation of things, or the Four Books and the Five Classics.[110]

Since the source of a quotation is seldom cited and the number of Buddhist works is vast, it is exceptionally difficult to locate the source of each saying. I have spent a great deal of time on this and have been able to locate hardly half the sources. Moreover, it is not easy to determine whether a saying is really a Buddhist one. Many terms have been taken to be Buddhist that are not. An example is *ch'iang-tzu.* As Chu Hsi said, "*Ch'iang-tzu* simply means the body. It is a common term and not a Ch'an expression."[111] In many cases, only a Buddhist term is used, not a Buddhist saying; examples include *cheng-chüeh* (correct awakening) and *Neng-jen* (the Buddha).[112]

Another example is *ch'ing-hsü-i-ta* (pure, vacuous, one, and great), which some scholars have regarded as Chang Tsai's (1020–1077) saying. Although Chang Tsai expounded these concepts,[113] he did not coin this saying in so many words. Because the Ch'eng brothers said he taught people a reality that is "pure, vacuous, one, and great,"[114] scholars have ascribed this saying to Chang Tsai, but they are actually the words of Seng-chao.[115] According to Chu Hsi, the Ch'eng brothers criticized Chang Tsai for expounding the ideas of purity, vacuity, oneness, and greatness, but not for quoting a Buddhist saying.[116] Thus we do not regard this expression as a Buddhist saying because Neo-Confucians did not consider it as such.

The oft-quoted saying, "Substance and function come from the same source and there is no gap between the manifest and the hidden," comes from the preface of Ch'eng I's *I chuan* (Commentary on the *Book of Changes*) and is cited frequently in the *Wen-chi* and the *Yü-lei*.[117] Japanese annotators of the *Ch'uan-hsi lu* have asserted that the saying comes from Ch'eng-kuan's (c. 760–838) commentary on the *Hua-yen ching*, but none of them has specified its location.[118] Since the eleventh century, Neo-Confucians have often quoted it. As T'ang Shun-chih (1507–1560) observed, "Confucians say that substance and function come from the same source, and Buddhists also say that substance and function come from the same source. Confucians say that there is no gap between the manifest and the hidden, and Buddhists also say that there is no gap between the manifest and the hidden. Who can distinguish which is correct?"[119] Chu Hsi also quoted Ch'eng I's saying, "Empty and tranquil, and without any sign."[120] Japanese scholars contend that it is of Buddhist origin, but again have not given a source. Yamazaki Ansai (1618–1682) listed its quotation by Chinese and Japanese Neo-Confucians but did not allude to its Buddhist origin.[121]

The Buddhist sayings that Chu Hsi quoted are mostly Ch'an utterances. His aim was to criticize Buddhism, unlike his quotations from the *Chuang Tzu*, which were for the purpose of supporting Neo-Confucian ideas.

1. "Old Master, be always alert." (The second half appears in *Wen-chi*, 15:15a. The whole utterance is found in the *Yü-lei*, ch. 12, sec. 15 [p. 318]. The saying belongs to Ch'an Master Jui-yen [c. 850–c. 910], in the *Wu-teng hui-yüan* [Convergence of the essentials of the five lamps], 7:120b, in the *Hsü-tsang-ching* [Supplement to the Buddhist canon], first collection, pt. 2, B, case 11.)

2. "The news like fire from kindling stone or lightning." (Quoted in the *Wen-chi*, 30:18b, the second letter to Chang Ch'in-fu [Chang Shih]. The source is the *Wu-teng hui-yüan*, 7:127a.)

3. "Only enlighten the mind; the mind gives rise to the ten thousand *dharmas*." (*Wen-chi*, 30:29a, ninth letter in reply to Chang Ch'in-fu. This may be a statement of general Buddhist ideas.)

4. "Empty without a single *dharma,* and yet all principles are completely present." (*Ibid.,* 31:2a, eleventh letter in reply to Chang Ch'in-fu. This may also be a general statement of Buddhist teachings.)

5. "All living beings with a generous heart." (Quoted in *ibid.,* 32:3a, thirty-second letter in reply to Chang Ching-fu [Chang Shih].)

6. "What ordinary people know, the innate original mind knows right away. When the innate original mind knows right away, ordinary people do not know." (Quoted in *ibid.,* 38:17b, ninth letter in reply to Yüan Chi-chung [Yüan Shih].)

7. "A Buddhist Master asked his pupil, 'Where did you come from?' 'Yu-chou,' came the reply. 'Do you think of it?' Answer: 'I always do.' 'What do you think of?' Answer: 'I think of its mountains and rivers, cities and towns, and the abundance of people, things, vehicles, and horses.' The Master said, 'Suppose you reflect: Are there still many things you are thinking about?' " (*Wen-chi,* 41:4a, third letter in reply to Hu Kuang-chuang [Hu Shih].)

8. "There are no obstacles to either affairs or principles." (*Ibid.,* 43:15a, letter in reply to Wu Kung-chi [Wu Chi]. A general statement on the third realm of Law of the Hua-yen School.)

9. "Every beating on the body will leave a scar and every slap on the face will fill the palm with blood." (Quoted in *ibid.,* 45:14a, fourth letter in reply to Yang Tzu-chih [Yang Fang]. Also in the *Yü-lei,* ch. 10, sec. 24 [p. 259]. The quotation comes from the *Ta-hui p'u-shuo* [Ta-hui's general discourse], ch. 2. Also in the *Pi-yen lu,* sec. 78.)

10. "Principle must be suddenly understood; it does not depend on gradual cultivation." (*Wen-chi,* 45:15b, first letter in reply to Liao Tzu-hui [Liao Te-ming], quoting this as "what the Buddhists have said," although it sounds more like a general statement of Buddhist teachings.)

11. "A pure man who transcends and is no longer attached to any class of Buddhas or sentient beings." (*Ibid.,* 45:42b, eighteenth letter in reply to Liao Tzu-hui. See below, no. 33.)

12. "Immature Suchness; ignorant Buddha nature." (*Ibid.,* 47:27b, twenty-fifth letter in reply to Lü Tzu-yüeh. Saying by Ssu-hsin Hsin-ho-shang, in the *Hsü-tsang-ching,* first collection, pt. 2, B, case 23, *Hsü-ku-tsun-su yü-yao* [Supplement to the *Important Sayings of Ancient Esteemed Elders*], ch. 1, p. 431. Also said by Ch'an Master Chan-t'ang-chuen of Le-t'an, in the *Chia-t'ai p'u-teng lu* [Universal lamp of the Chia-t'ai period (1201–1204)], ch. 26, p. 184, in the *Hsü-tsang-ching,* first collection, pt. 2, case 10.)

13. "Should understand the nature of the Realm of Law. All things are but the creation of the mind." (*Wen-chi,* 49:6b, ninth letter in reply to Wang Tzu-ho [Wang Yü].)

14. "Fetching water or moving firewood are all spiritual operations

and wonderful functioning." (*Ibid.*, 59:27b, first letter in reply to Ch'en Wei-tao. Also in the *Yü-lei*, ch. 62, sec. 72 [p. 2378]. The saying comes from the *P'ang Chü-shih yü-lu* (Recorded sayings of layman P'ang Yün], ch. 1, p. 28a, in the *Hsü-tsang-ching,* first collection, pt. 2, case 25; quoted in the biography of Layman P'ang Yün, *Ching-te ch'uan-teng lu,* 8:18a.)

15. "When the *liu-yung* [Six Organs] are not in operation, the self-nature will be revealed by itself." (*Wen-chi,* 59:28b, second letter in reply to Ch'en Wei-tao. *Liu-yung* refers to the operation of the ear, eye, nose, tongue, body, and mind.)

16. "Sudden spiritual awakening." (*Ibid.*, 70:24a, "Records of Doubts." Chu Hsi's remark: "This is a saying of the heterodox school.")

17. "Have you not seen a cat catching a rat? Its four feet are anchored on the ground, and the head and tail form a straight line. Its eyes do not wink. Its mind has no other thought. It does not move at all. Once it moves, there is no escape for the rat." (*Ibid.*, 71:6b, "Random Notes from Casual Reading." A paraphrase of what Ch'an Master Huang-lung [1002–1069] told his pupils in the *Wu-teng hui-yüan,* 17:335a, in the *Hsü-tsang-ching,* first collection, pt. 2, B, case 11).

18. "When all the Four Great [Elements] have departed [from the body], where is the illusory body then?" (*Wen-chi,* separate collection, 8:3a, "Treatise on Buddhism," pt. 2. See above, p. 525.)

19. "If the iron wheel revolves above one's head, the perfect brilliance of calmness and wisdom will never be lost." (*Yü-lei,* ch. 7, sec. 59 [p. 219].)

20. "Cut off the old monk's head." (*Ibid.*, sec. 90 [p. 275]. A saying by Chao-chou Ho-shang [Ch'an Master Ts'ung-shen, 778–897].)

21. "A monk, reading a tomb rubbing with someone, said, 'What you read are nothing but characters, but what I read is nothing but Ch'an.' " (*Ibid.*, ch. 11, sec. 83 [p. 297].)

22. "Because of a great event, the Buddha appeared in this world." (*Ibid.*, ch. 13, sec. 60 [p. 365]. The saying comes from the *Lotus Scripture,* sec. 2.)

23. "That there is the Twelve-fold Chain of Causation is due to the stirring of the mind." (*Ibid.*, ch. 16, sec. 107 [p. 540]. The twelve links in the Chain of Causation are ignorance, aggregates, consciousness, name and form, the six sense organs, contact, sensation, craving, grasping, coming into being, birth, and old age and death.)

24. "Ch'an Master Kuei-shan said, 'I have searched for enlightenment by meditation for a number of years, but even now I have not been able to cut off drifting thoughts.' " (*Ibid.* The saying is not found in the *Ching-te ch'uan-teng lu,* ch. 9, *Kuei-shan Ling-yu Ch'an-shih yü-lu* [Recorded sayings of Ch'an Master Ling-yu of Kuei-shan].)

25. "One moon universally shines on all rivers. The moons in all the rivers are the same moon." (*Ibid.*, ch. 18, sec. 29 [p. 640]. The quotation comes from the *Yung-chia cheng-tao ko* [Ch'an Master Hsüan-chüeh's (665–713) song testifying to the truth] in the *Taishō daizōkyō*, vol. 48, no. 2014, p. 396. Also in the *Ching-teng ch'uan-teng lu*, 30:11b.)

26. "Even in a small hamlet of three families, there is a Buddist monastery." (*Yü-lei*, ch. 22, sec. 103 [p. 851].)

27. "As in pointing to the moon, although the moon is at the fingertip, there is still the desire to see the moon by following the finger." (*Yü-lei*, ch. 33, sec. 83 [p. 1360].)

28. "Formerly, someone asked a monk something. The monk, pointing to the flower in front of him, asked, 'What is this?' The man answered, 'It is a flower.' The monk said, 'I conceal nothing from you.' " (*Ibid.*, [p. 1361]. The monk's quotation is from the *Analects*, 7:23.)

29. "Lay down the butcher's knife and become a Buddha where you are." (*Ibid.*, ch. 42, sec. 30 [p. 1721]. A popular Ch'an dictum.)

30. "It's not that one should do nothing, but it is wrong to have preconceptions." (*Ibid.*, ch., 52, sec. 180 [p. 2013].)

31. "To make a living and to engage in productive activity is not opposed to true reality." (*Ibid.*, sec. 192 [p. 2018]. The saying is that of Ch'an Master Wen-yen of Yün-men [864–949] in the *Wu-teng hui-yüan*, 15:280b.)

32. "The ten thousand affairs of the world are not as they always are; they do not surprise people and they last for a long time." (*Ibid.*, ch. 62, sec. 14 [p. 2351].)

33. "Over a lump of reddish flesh there sits a pure man who transcends and is no longer attached to any class of Buddhas or sentient beings. He comes in and out of your sense organs all the time." (*Ibid.*, [p. 2377]. The saying is by Ch'an Master Hui-chao [d. 850] in the *Taishō daizōkyō*, vol. 47, *Lin-chi Hui-chao Ch'an-shih yü-lu* [Recorded sayings of Ch'an Master Hui-chao of Lin-chi], p. 496. See above, no. 11.)

34. "The evergreen bamboo is none other than Suchness, and the sparkling flowers are none other than Wisdom." (*Ibid.*, ch. 63, sec. 72 [p. 2436]. The saying is quoted in the *Shen-hui Ho-shang i-chi* [Anthology of Monk Shen-hui's surviving writings], ed. by Hu Shih [Shanghai: Ya-tung Library, 1930], p. 139.)

35. "In the house of Buddhist affairs, not a single *dharma* is left out." (*Ibid.*, sec. 83 [p. 2442]. See below, no. 49.)

36. "Totally view the nature of the Realm of Law." (*Ibid.*, ch. 101, sec. 53 [pp. 4076–4077]. See below, no. 57.)

37. "An inch of iron can be used to kill people." (*Ibid.*, ch. 115, sec. 1 [p. 4411]. See also ch. 8, sec. 62 [p. 219].)

38. "I have already aroused the mind of Wisdom. What deeds must I perform to become a Buddha?" (*Ibid.*, ch. 118, sec. 15 [p. 4529].)

39. "The only fear is that one does not become a Buddha. There is no fear that one does not know what to say after becoming a Buddha." (*Ibid.,* ch. 119, sec. 20 [p. 4592].)

40. "Eat the rice of Ku-shan and exude the excrement of Ku-shan. All I see is white water over the head." (*Ibid.,* ch. 121, sec. 25 [p. 4679]. The words are Ku-shan's own.)

41. "During the twelve time periods, aside from wearing clothes and eating rice, to what other things do you apply your mind?" (*Ibid.,* sec. 60 [p. 4694].)

42. "A dried human-excrement-removing stick." (*Ibid.,* ch. 124, sec. 25 [p. 4761]. This was Ch'an Master Hui-chao's answer to a monk's question about the pure man. See above, no. 33.)

43. "One should have no attachment to external things and in this way let the mind grow." (*Ibid.,* sec. 40 [p. 4769]. The saying is found in the *Diamond Scripture,* sec. 10.)

44. "Bright and silently shining, penetrating everything. Without carrying on any activity at the site of religious rituals, prevail all through the worlds as numerous as the sands in the Ganges River." (*Ibid.,* ch. 125, sec. 4 [p. 4786]. A Buddhist saying.)

45. "Don't bother to walk at night. You will get to the destination at dawn." (*Ibid.,* sec. 17 [p. 4789].)

46. "As in the case of a man climbing a tree, he holds the tree branches in his mouth with both hands and feet in the air. And yet he has to answer a question." *(Ibid.)*

47. "Not having been affected by a speck of dust, the sense organs will have nothing to attach to. To reverse the current while preserving unity, the Six Sense Organs will not operate." (*Ibid.,* ch. 126, sec. 7 [p. 4823].)

48. Matter is emptiness, and emptiness is matter." (*Ibid.,* sec. 11 [p. 4826]. The saying is found in the *Heart Scripture.*)

49. "Although one is actually buried in the ground, one should not pick up even a speck of dust. In the midst of ten thousand activities, one should not discard a single *dharma.*" (*Ibid.,* sec. 42 [p. 4832]. The utterance comes from the *Ching-te ch'uan-teng lu,* 9:3a, *Kuei-shan Ling-yu Ch'an-shih yü-lu.*)

50. "There is something before Heaven and Earth. Without physical form, it is basically quiet. It can be the master of the ten thousand phenomena, and it does not trail the fading four seasons." (*Ibid.,* sec. 43 [p. 4834].)

51. "Struck down, it is not another thing. Going to the left and to the right, and going up and down, it is not a speck of dust. Mountains and rivers, and the great Earth, all reveal the presence of the King of the Law." *(Ibid.)*

52. "If people understand the mind, there is not an inch of land in the great Earth." *(Ibid.)*

53. "Three catties of hemp." (*Ibid.,* [p. 4835]. No. 12 in the *Pi-yen lu,* being Ch'an Master Tsung-hui of Tung-shan's answer to the question, "What is the Buddha?")

54. "If one does not go down into the pit, one cannot destroy the path of reason." *(Ibid.)*

55. "The king of a certain state asked a certain venerable monk, 'What is the Buddha?' Answer: 'One becomes a Buddha when one sees his nature.' Question: 'What is nature?' Answer: 'Function is nature.' A clever man said, 'When the venerable monk answered the king, why didn't the king ask him where nature is before it functions?' " (*Ibid.,* sec. 58 [p. 4841]. This was the answer by Bodhidharma's pupil to a question by a king in southern India. See the *Ching-te ch'uan-teng lu,* 3:4b.)

56. "For the eye, it is seeing. For the ear, it is hearing. For the nose, it is smelling the fragrance. For the mouth, it is discussion. For the hand, it is grasping. And for the foot, it is running." (*Ibid.,* sec. 60 [p. 4842]. A saying by Bodhidharma's pupil in the *Ching-te ch'uan-teng lu,* 3:5a.)

57. "Universally manifested, it includes the whole Realm of Law. Collected and grasped, it is a single speck of dust. Those who know realize that it is the Buddha nature. Those who do not know call it the spirit." (*Ibid.* A saying by Bodhidharma's pupil in the *Ching-te ch'uan-teng lu,* 3:5a.)

58. "Directly pointing to the human mind, see nature and become a Buddha." (*Ibid.* Comment on no. 1 in the *Pi-yen lu,* quoting Bodhidharma's *Treatise on Understanding Nature.*)

59. "Silently shining, the light spreads over all the sands in the [Ganges] River. Ordinary and saintly people, and all sentient beings, are in my family." (*Ibid.* A saying by Chang Cho [618–907].)

60. "The oak tree [in the front garden]." (*Ibid.,* sec. 80 [p. 4853]. Ch'an Master Ts'ung-shen of Chao-chou's answer to the question, "What was the purpose of the patriarch [Bodhidharma] coming from the West?" in *Wu-men-kuan* [Gate of Monk Wen-men], no. 37.)

61. "Chang San has money but does not know how to spend it, while Li Ssu knows how to spend money but has none." (*Ibid.,* sec. 85 [p. 4856]. See above, p. 512.)

## Notes

1. Tokiwa Daijō, *Shina ni okeru Bukkyō to Jukyō Dōkyō* [Buddhism in relation to Confucianism and Taoism in China] (Tokyo: Tōyōbunko, 1930), pp. 335–385; Galen Eugene Sargent, *Chou Hi contre le Bouddhisme* (Paris: Imprimerie nationale, 1955), pp. 1–156.

2. See my *A Source Book in Chinese Philosophy* (Princeton, N.J.: Princeton University Press, 1963), pp. 646–653.

3. *Yü-lei*, ch. 104, sec. 38 (p. 4166).

4. *Taishō daizōkyō* [Taishō edition of the Buddhist canon], vol. 47, no. 1998, pp. 836–837.

5. *Shina ni okeru Bukkyō to Jukyō Dōkyō* (Tokyo: Tōyōbunko, 1930) p. 379.

6. In Morohashi Tetsuji, ed., *Shushigaku nyūmon* [Introduction to the study of Master Chu] (Tokyo: Meitoku shuppansha, 1974), p. 41.

7. In the *Taishō daizōkyō*, case 31, vol. 4, at the head of the *Ta-hui P'u-chüeh Ch'an-shih yü-lu* [Recorded sayings of Ta-hui, Ch'an Master P'u-chüeh], p. 349.

8. A mountain in present Hangchow.

9. In present Anhui Province.

10. Heng-yang County in Hunan Province.

11. Present Mei County in Kwangtung Province.

12. *Ta-hui P'u-chüeh Ch'an-shih yü-lu*, ch. 6, in the *Taishō daizōkyō*, vol. 47, no. 1998, pp. 836–837.

13. *Ta-hui P'u-chüeh Ch'an-shih nien-p'u* [Chronological biography of Ta-hui, Ch'an Master P'u-chüeh], in the *Chung-hua ta-tsang-ching* [Chinese Buddhist canon], second collection, pp. 1707–1715. For an informative account in English, see Chün-fang Yü, "Ta-hui Tsung-kao and Kung-an Ch'an," *Journal of Chinese Philosophy*, vol. 6, no. 2 (June, 1979), pp. 211–235. I am grateful to Dr. Yü for duplicating the *nien-p'u* of Ta-hui for me.

14. *Taishō daizōkyō*, vol. 49, no. 2036, pp. 687–690.

15. Tomoeda Ryūtarō, *Shushi no shisō keisei* [Formation of Master Chu's thought] (Tokyo: Shunjūsha, 1979), pp. 44–45.

16. *Ibid.*, p. 45.

17. According to the *Fu-chien t'ung-chih* [General account of Fukien] (1922 ed.), ch. 34, p. 1b, the K'ai-shan Temple was in Wu-fu Village in Ch'ung-an County, where Liu Tzu-hui and Chu Hsi lived. In the *Yü-lei*, however, *k'ai-shan* was misprinted as *k'ai-hsi*. Ch'ien Mu, in his *Chu Tzu hsin-hsüeh-an* [New anthology and critical accounts of Master Chu] (Taipei: San-min Book Co., 1971, vol. 3, p. 11), changed the *Yü-lei* passage to read, "He ascended the altar of Miao-hsi," obviously a mistake.

18. *Yü-lei*, ch. 126, sec. 85 (p. 4856).

19. *Ibid.*, ch. 41, sec. 59 (p. 1687).

20. *Wen-chi*, 2:17a.

21. The discovery of the lost essay was reported in the *People's Daily News* for October 10, 1985.

22. *Wen-chi*, 60:5a, letter in reply to pupil Hsü (Hsü Chung-ying).

23. *Ibid.*, 72:27a. Also found in 63:20b–21a, fourth letter in reply to Sun Ching-fu (Sun Tzu-hsiu).

24. *Ibid.*

25. *Ibid.*, 50:32a, twentieth letter in reply to Ch'eng Cheng-ssu (Ch'eng Tuan-meng).

26. *Yü-lei*, ch. 126, sec. 117 (p. 4867).

27. *Ibid.*, ch. 124, sec. 25 (p. 4761).

28. *Ibid.*, ch. 132, sec. 52 (p. 5095).

29. *Ibid.*, ch. 130, sec. 134 (p. 5012). Chang Wu-chin was Chang Shang-ying.

30. *Ibid.*, ch. 126, sec. 108 (p. 4862).

31. *Wen-chi,* supplementary collection, 6:6a, letter to Chang Meng-yüan.

32. I am not sure that Liao-lao was Ch'en Kuan, but in the *Yü-lei,* ch. 126, sec. 118 (p. 4867), Chu Hsi mentioned both Venerable Kao and Ch'en Kuan and said that Ch'en loved Buddhism.

33. *Yü-lei,* ch. 126, sec. 80 (p. 4853).

34. *Ibid.,* sec. 83 (p. 4855).

35. *Shina ni okeru Bukkyō to Jukyō Dōkyō,* p. 379.

36. *Li Yen-p'ing chi* [Collected works of Li T'ung] (*Cheng-i-t'ang ch'üan-shu* [Complete library of the Hall of Rectifying the Way] ed.), 1:5a.

37. Tai Hsien, *Chu Tzu shih-chi* [True records of Master Chu] (*Chin-shih han-chi ts'ung-k'an* [Chinese works of the recent period series] ed.), 2:6b.

38. Wang Mao-hung, *Chu Tzu nien-p'u* [Chronological biography of Master Chu] (*Ts'ung-shu chi-ch'eng* [Collection of series] ed.), ch. 1A, p. 16.

39. *Yün-wo chi-t'an* [Recorded talks of one who makes clouds his bed], pt. 2, p. 18a, in the *Hsü-tsang-ching* [Supplement to the Buddhist canon], first collection, pt. 2, B, case 21.

40. *Ch'ung-an-hsien hsin-chih* [New accounts of Ch'ung-an County] (1941 ed.), 20:5a, 7b.

41. *Yü-lei,* ch. 126, sec. 109 (p. 4863).

42. *Wu-teng hui-yüan* [Convergence of the essentials of the five lamps], 4:66a, in the *Hsü-tsang-ching,* first collection, pt. 2, B, case 11.

43. *Yün-wo chi-t'an,* pt. 2, p. 18a, in the *Hsü-tsang-ching,* first collection, pt. 2, B, case 21.

44. *Fo-fa chin-t'ang pien* [Stronghold of the Law of the Buddha], 15:484b, and *Shih-shih tzu-chien* [Mirror for Buddhism], ch. 11, p. 118, both works in the *Hsü-tsang-ching,* first collection, pt. 2, case 21.

45. Hu Shih, *Hu Shih shou-kao* [Hu Shih's manuscripts], seventh collection, ch. 3, pp. 584, 586. Thanks to Professor Yü Ying-shih for this information.

46. Tomoeda Ryūtarō, *Shushi no shiso keisei,* pp. 45, 47; Satō Hitoshi, *Shushi* (Tokyo: Shūeisha, 1985), p. 57.

47. *Wen-chi,* 6:5a–6a; 8:31b; 84:30a, account of visit to Mi-an.

48. *Ibid.,* 33:12a, seventeenth letter in reply to Lü Po-kung (Lü Tsu-ch'ien).

49. *Ibid.,* 34:5a–b, fifty-eighth letter in reply to Lü Po-kung.

50. *Ch'ung-an-hsien hsin-chih,* (1941 ed.), 20:5b.

51. *K'u-yai man-lu* [Random notes of K'u-yai Yüan-wu], pt. 2, p. 81b, in the *Hsü-tsang-ching,* first collection, pt. 2, B, case 21.

52. Kusumoto Bun'yū, *Sōdai Jugaku no zen shisō kenkyū* [A study of Zen (meditation) thought in Confucianism of the Sung dynasty] (Nagoya: Nisshindō, 1980), pp. 333–334.

53. *Wen-chi,* 2:11a–b.

54. For the Goose Lake Temple meeting, see ch. 26 above.

55. *Wen-chi,* 5:5a, 6a, 7a; 79:11a.

56. *Wen-chi,* 7:12a–14b; 17a–b, separate collection, 7:9a.

57. *Ibid.,* regular collection, 84:30a, account of visit to Mi-an.

58. *Ibid.,* 6:18b, 82:6b, 1:9a, 2:3a, 5a; 2:3a, 9:8a, 2:4b, 39:13a.

59. The carving is in five lines totaling 50 Chinese characters and mentioning the names of the six visitors.

60. *Wen-chi,* 8:6b, 10:7b–8a; 81:24b–25a.

61. *Ibid.,* separate collection, 5:10b–11a.

62. *Yü-lei,* ch. 44, sec. 115 (p. 1817).

63. *Wen-chi,* 7:1a, 12a.

64. *Ibid.,* 10:3b.

65. *Ibid.,* 10:8a.

66. *Yü-lei,* ch. 3, sec. 80 (p. 87).

67. *Ibid.,* ch. 126, sec. 3 (p. 4819); ch. 125, sec. 72 (p. 4813); ch. 101, sec. 77 (p. 4082); ch. 126, sec. 106 (p. 4861); ch. 116, sec. 50 (p. 4470); ch. 91, sec. 11 (p. 3695). For individual works, consult the index in the 1970 edition of the *Yü-lei* published by the Cheng-chung Book Co. of Taipei.

68. *Wen-chi,* 60:5a, 63:21a, 72:27a. For individual works, consult Yamanoi Yū, ed., *Shushi bunshū koyū meishi sakuin* [Index to the proper names in the *Chu Tzu wen-chi*] (Tokyo: Tōhō Book Co., 1980).

69. *Yü-lei,* ch. 71, sec. 34 (p. 2846).

70. *Ibid.,* ch. 126, sec. 68 (p. 4847).

71. *Ibid.,* sec. 72 (p. 4848). See below, section on "Buddhist Sayings Quoted by Chu Hsi," no. 49.

72. *Ibid.,* sec. 128 (p. 4870).

73. *Ibid.,* ch. 2, sec. 74 (p. 44).

74. *Ibid.,* ch. 91, sec. 11 (pp. 3695–3696).

75. *Ibid.,* ch. 126, sec. 71 (pp. 4847–4848).

76. *Ibid.,* sec. 76 (p. 4851).

77. *Ibid.,* sec. 6 (p. 4822).

78. *Ibid.,* sec. 7 (p. 4823).

79. *Ibid.,* sec. 6 (p. 4822).

80. *Ibid.,* sec. 69 (p. 4847).

81. *Ibid.,* sec. 6 (p. 4822).

82. *Wen-chi,* 30:4a, second letter in reply to Minister Wang (Wang Ying-ch'en).

83. *Yü-lei,* ch. 126, sec. 74 (p. 4849).

84. *Ibid.,* sec. 75 (p. 4850).

85. *Ibid.,* ch. 124, sec. 25 (p. 4762).

86. *Wen-chi,* 43:11b, first letter in reply to Li Po-chien (Li Tsung-ssu).

87. *Yü-lei,* ch. 126, sec. 74 (p. 4849).

88. *Ibid.,* sec. 70 (p. 4848).

89. *Ibid.,* ch. 94, sec. 70 (pp. 3779–3780).

90. *Ibid.,* ch. 126, sec. 5 (p. 4821).

91. *Ibid.,* sec. 114 (p. 4864).

92. *Ibid.,* sec. 126 (p. 4869).

93. *Ibid.,* sec. 3 (p. 4819).

94. *Ibid.,* sec. 5, (p. 4821).

95. *Ibid.,* sec. 128 (p. 4870).

96. *Ibid.,* sec. 7 (p. 4824). See also ch. 137, sec. 16 (p. 5223).

97. *Ibid.,* sec. 21 (p. 4828).

98. *Ibid.,* and sec. 78 (p. 4852).

99. *Ibid.,* sec. 79 (p. 4852).

100. *Wen-chi,* separate collection, 8:3a, "Treatise on Buddhism," pt. 2.

101. *Leng-yen ching* [Strong character scripture], ch. 3, teaches that what one

hears from the outside is false and illusory, for it is not based on a primary cause or a secondary cause and thus has no self-nature. See the *Taishō daizōkyō,* vol. 19, no. 945, p. 115.

102. *Chuang Tzu,* ch. 8, "Webbed Toes" (*SPTK* ed. *Nan-hua chen-ching* [True classic of Chuang Tzu], 4:10a).

103. *Yüan-chüeh ching* [Scripture of perfect enlightenment], ch. 1, in the *Taishō daizōkyō,* vol. 17, no. 842, p. 914.

104. *Lieh Tzu,* ch. 1 (*SPTK* ed., *Ch'ung-hsü chih-te chen-ching* [True classic of the perfect virtues of simplicity and vacuity], 1:4a).

105. *Yü-lei,* ch. 125, sec. 26 (p. 4793).

106. *Ibid.,* ch. 130, sec. 17 (p. 4969). The modern pronunciation of the two Chinese characters is *chieh-ti.*

107. See my *Wang Yang-ming yü Ch'an* [Wang Yang-ming and Ch'an] (Taipei: Student Book Co., 1984), p. 75.

108. See my translation of Wang Yang-ming's *Ch'uan-hsi lu* entitled *Instructions for Practical Living* (New York: Columbia University Press, 1983), p. 79.

109. *Ching-te ch'uan-teng lu* [Records of the transmission of the lamp completed during the Ching-te period (1004–1007)] (*SPTK* ed.), 3:7a.

110. The Four Books are the *Great Learning,* the *Analects,* the *Book of Mencius,* and the *Doctrine of the Mean.* The Five Classics are the *Book of Odes,* the *Book of History,* the *Book of Rites,* the *Book of Changes,* and the *Spring and Autumn Annals.*

111. *Wen-chi,* 58:33b, first letter in reply to Teng Wei-lao (Teng Chiung).

112. *Ibid.,* 43:9a, first letter in reply to Li Po-chien (Li Tsung-ssu).

113. *Cheng-meng* [Correcting youthful ignorance], ch. 1, "Great Harmony," secs. 2–3, 8; ch. 4, "Spirit and Transformation," sec. 2, in the *Chang Tzu ch'üan-shu* [Complete works of Master Chang Tsai] (*SPPY* ed.), 1:2a, 3b; 2:13a.

114. *I-shu* [Surviving works], 2:6a, 16a, in the *Erh-Ch'eng ch'uan-shu* [Complete works of the two Ch'engs] (*SPPY* ed.).

115. Seng-chao, *Pao-tsang lun* [Treatise on the precious treasure], in *Taishō daizōkyō,* vol. 45, no. 1857, p. 145.

116. *Wen-chi,* 42:3b, second letter in reply to Hu Yen-chung.

117. For example, *Wen-chi,* 30:12b, seventh letter in reply to Minister Wang (Wang Ying-ch'en) and *Yü-lei,* ch. 67, sec. 36 (p. 2631).

118. See my *Wang Yang-ming Ch'uan-hsi lu hsiang-chu chi-p'ing* [Full annotation and collected commentaries on the *Instructions for Practical Living*] (Taipei: Student Book Co., 1983) p. 219. See also Chu Hsi and Lü Tsu-ch'ien, compilers of the *Chin-ssu lu,* in my translation of this work entitled *Reflections on Things at Hand* (New York: Columbia University Press, 1967), p. 109, n. 106.

119. T'ang Shun-chih, Preface to the *Chung-yung chi-lüeh* [Selected commentaries on the *Doctrine of the Mean*].

120. *I-shu,* 15:8a. Quoted in the *Wen-chi,* 48:17a, fourth letter in reply to Lü Tzu-yüeh (Lü Tsu-chien); *Yü-lei,* ch. 95, sec. 80 (p. 3869), etc.

121. *Zoku Yamazaki Ansai zensho* [Supplement to the *Complete Works of Yamazaki Ansai*] (1937 ed.), pt. 2, pp. 78–86.

# 30

# Chu Hsi's Treatment
# of Women

THERE is some, though not much, material on Chu Hsi's ideas about marriage and the regulation of the family, but practically nothing on his treatment of women—that is, how he handled practical problems like people's marriages and the like. What follows is information gathered from the *Wen-chi* and the *Yü-lei,* although much more work needs to be done.

Chu Hsi laid strong emphasis on human relations, and his actions largely matched his words. In his biographical account *(hsing chuang)* of Chu Hsi, his pupil and son-in-law Huang Kan (1152–1221) wrote, "In behavior at home, he was most filial in serving his parents and most loving in bringing up the children. In his married life, both husband and wife were dignified, and in their depth of gratitude toward each other, they were contented."[1] This is a general statement, and perhaps an idealized one. On Chu Hsi's practical relationship with his mother, the various *nien-p'u* (chronological biographies) of his life concur that in 1169, when his mother died, he built a study beside her grave and lived there for some time. We know he also wrote a biography of his mother.[2] We know very little about his wife, although it appears that the marriage was a happy one.[3]

As to Chu Hsi's feeling toward the female sex in general, there are several bits of information worth mentioning. In 1187, when his infant daughter died, he told Lu Hsiang-shan (1139–1193) about it in a letter. In reply Lu said, "In the beginning of winter, the gentleman Hsü came. Only then did I receive your letter of the eighth day of the fifth month. From it I learned that your good little girl has passed away. . . . I am sure of your sadness and grief. . . . I, being unworthy, have also suffered from a great calamity. . . . I lost a grandniece."[4] The two thinkers engaged in heated philosophical debates but informed each other of the death of a child. Their grief must have been deep and their mutual sympathy sincere. Also, when his friend Lü Tsu-ch'ien's (1137–1181) wife died, Chu Hsi wrote Lü and said, "I believe your sorrow must be unbearable, as the meaning of marital relationship is very deep. However, I hope you can restrain your feelings to comply with proper ceremony."[5]

Chu Hsi had five daughters, nine granddaughters, and seven great-granddaughters. I have gathered information about the five daughters and a grandchild that need not be repeated here, except to note that Chu Hsi was chiefly concerned about their marriages.[6] His concern extended not only to his own children but to his pupils as well. According to the *Sung-Yüan hsüeh-an* (Anthology and critical accounts of Neo-Confucians of the Sung and Yüan dynasties), "Ch'en Ssu-ch'ien, whose courtesy name was T'ui-chih, was a native of Lung-hsi [Fukien]. His learning was extensive and he taught students of the later generation. He was the first among recommended scholars of his community. He was the author of the *Ch'un-ch'iu san-chuan hui-t'ung* [Agreements of the three commentaries on the *Spring and Autumn Annals*] and the *Lieh-kuo lei-pien* [Classified compilation of the feudal states]. Chu Wen Kung [Chu Hsi] liked him and advised his pupil, Li T'ang-tzu [*fl.* 1199] to give his daughter in marriage to him."[7]

In another case, pupil Lü Huan, who attended the Master's teachings with his elder brothers Yen and T'ao, came to say goodbye in 1199 and told Chu Hsi, "I am going to get married and plan to return home on a certain day." When the time came, his elder brothers said, "We have discussed the matter with our younger brother. Let us receive your instructions for one more month and then return home." Chu Hsi said, "You, Sir, are going to get married. Why do you say such a thing? This is an important matter and should not be treated this way. I believe your family has made all the arrangements and is waiting for you. You should not do this." Lü left for home that very day.[8] In still another case, Chu Hsi wrote Kung Feng (1184 *cs*) and said, "Ssu-yüan [Hsü Wen-ch'ing][9] lost his wife and there was no one to assist him in his home. His plan for remarriage is uncertain. There is a desire to arrange the marriage quickly, but no one knows where to look for [a bride]. I wonder if among your relatives and friends anyone can look for him."[10] Such was Chu Hsi's concern with the marriage of his pupils.

In some instances Chu Hsi seems to have had great sympathy for women. There was a woman in a certain county whose husband could not support her. Her parents wanted to take her home, and the *chu-pu* (assistant magistrate) gave them permission. Chu Hsi's pupil Chao Shih-hsia (1190 *cs*) objected, saying, "The relationship between husband and wife should not be abandoned because of poverty, and the official should not have granted the request." Chu Hsi said, "A case like this should not be viewed from only one side. If the husband is incapable of supporting the wife and the wife has no way of supporting herself, what can be done? It seems that in a case like this one should not be bound by great moral principles. One should investigate only if the woman wants to leave her husband, or if there is some other complication."[11]

The marriage system that Chu Hsi followed was of course the traditional Confucian system. The right to choose a spouse rested with parents. In this respect, Chu Hsi's comment on the twentieth ode in the *Book of Odes* is enlightening: "In this ode, the woman talks about her own choice in marriage. As we see it, this is naturally not the correct principle. However, human feeling is sometimes like this. . . . If parents examine the matter in this situation, they surely will enable her to make the choice in time."[12] This was a very liberal opinion at a time when free choice in marriage was not yet dreamed of.

Traditionally, however, Confucianism regarded sons as superior to daughters, and Chu Hsi was not entirely free from this view. One day, when he was visiting the family of Ts'ai Yüan-ting (1135–1198), a son was born. Chu Hsi then remarked that since he had been thirty or so, whenever he visited a family, the newborn baby had been a girl, which he thought was unlucky.[13] This may have been uttered in jest, but it cannot be denied that Chu Hsi agreed with the tradition of the superiority of sons.

Moreover, he subscribed to the ancient doctrine that a wife could be expelled for any of seven reasons—for not obeying her husband's parents, having no sons, adultery, jealousy, an incurable disease, talking too much, or theft. However, she could not be expelled if she had no home to return to, if she had performed three years of mourning, or if the family had risen from poverty and a low station in life to wealth and a high station.[14] When a pupil asked about this, Chu Hsi replied that it was a correct principle; it was not just an expediency.[15] Judged by twentieth-century standards, such a doctrine is ridiculous, although jealousy or talking too much, like today's "incompatibility," could be simply a device to mask a much more serious situation. Fundamentally, we should judge Chu Hsi by the standards of his time, although we can also demand that, as a great thinker, he ought to have been a revolutionary or a reformer.

Chu Hsi also believed that a woman should have one husband all her life. He said, "A woman follows one husband all her life, with obedience as the correct principle,"[16] and "A husband may have a wife and concubines, but a woman is not allowed to have two husbands."[17]

Moreover, Chu Hsi generally adhered to the custom of not approving of remarriage for widows, although he was by no means of one mind on this. Ch'eng I (1033–1107) was once asked, "According to principle, it seems that one should not marry a widow. What do you think?" Ch'eng I answered, "Marriage is a match. If one takes someone who has lost her integrity to be his own match, it means he himself has lost his integrity." The questioner then asked, "In some cases the widows are all alone, poor, and with no one to depend on. May they remarry?" He answered, "This theory has come about only because people of later generations are afraid of starving to death. To starve to death is a very small matter but to lose one's integrity is extremely grave."[18] During the Chinese social revolution earlier in the twentieth century, and especially in the last thirty years on the Mainland, Ch'eng I has been condemned as being cruel to women by thinkers who seem to have forgotten the doctrine advocated by Mencius that, under special circumstances, one should sacrifice life for righteousness.[19] His critics also ignore the fact that in his biography of his father Ch'eng I noted that his father had arranged for his widowed niece to remarry.[20] If this had been a dishonorable thing to do, Ch'eng I would not have mentioned it. One of Chu Hsi's pupils thought that there was a contradiction between Ch'eng I's statement that a widow should not remarry and his account of his father's arrangement for a widowed niece to do so. Chu Hsi replied, "The general principle is like this, but sometimes people are unable to fulfill it to the fullest extent."[21] Thus Chu Hsi was still bound by the old morality, although capable of sympathy in special situations.

When the younger sister of a pupil, Ch'en Shou, became a widow, Chu Hsi wrote him and said,

> From friends I have learned that your younger sister is very virtuous. I am sure she will be able to honor and serve the aged and to bring up the orphans, thereby perfecting the integrity of the "Cypress-boat."[22] This matter depends especially on the wife of the prime minister [Ch'en Shou's father, Ch'en Chün-ch'ing, 1113–1186] encouraging and supporting her in order to bring it to realization, so that Tzu-ming [Cheng Chien] will remain a royal minister in death and his spouse a woman of integrity in life. This will be a beautiful thing in human relations, and I am sure you and your brothers will lose no time in favoring it. In the past, Master I-ch'uan [Ch'eng I] once discussed this matter. He considered that to starve to death is a very small matter but to lose one's integrity is a very serious matter. From the popular point of view, this is truly unrealistic, but in the eyes of a gentleman who knows the classics and understands the principle, this is something unalterable. What is more, the prime minister is a veteran statesman of the generation who is looked up to for teachings on social relationships. Whatever steps he takes should be carefully thought out. Since I have been privileged to be an old friend of his, according to principle I should not remain silent. However, I dare not speak directly to him and hope that you will tell him privately, and that I may be excused for being too presumptuous and abrupt.[23]

The fact that Chu Hsi dared not speak to Ch'en Chün-ch'ing directly probably indicates that Ch'en Chün-ch'ing wanted his daughter to remarry. In this case, Chu Hsi, adhering to the Confucian doctrine on social relations, would have felt duty-bound to echo Ch'eng I's opinion on the subject. However, Chu Hsi was not entirely unfair to widows. He disapproved of the regulation that required a widow's consent to sell family property even when she had left the family, considering that to be contrary to principle.[24] Presumably, when the widow had remained in the family, according to principle her permission would be required.

Turning to the moral qualities of men and women, Chu Hsi believed that there is no difference in what they have been endowed with by Heaven, for humanity, righteousness, propriety, and wisdom are common to both sexes, except that their expressions in feelings are different. Take, for example, humanity (jen). A pupil once remarked, "Most women are scared when they face certain problems, and that is due to their endowment in material force being unbalanced." Chu Hsi responded, "The humanity of women flows in the direction of love."[25] He also said, "The humanity of women cannot be restrained in love."[26] In terms of love, then, women are superior to men; in terms of capability, however, they are inferior. As Chu Hsi saw it, the popular songs of the states (kuo-feng) in the Book of Odes "probably came from the mouths of women and little men," unlike those that come after the hsiao-ya (lesser courtly songs), in which the language is of "those who understand moral principles."[27] This amounts to saying that women do not understand moral principles. He also said, "Among women of this dynasty, only Li I-an [Li Ch'ing-chao, 1084–c. 1156] and Madame Wei can write. Li has a poem that says . . . This type of language is [generally] beyond women."[28] To consider Li I-an an exception is tantamount to saying that, as poets, women do not measure up to men.

However, like Ch'eng I, Chu Hsi thought that women understood the mind. In the Yü-lei it is recorded that the daughter of Fan Tsu-yü (1041–1098) said that the mind does not come in or go out.[29] Commenting on this remark, Chu Hsi said, "I-ch'uan [Ch'eng I] said that although this woman did not understand Mencius, she could understand the mind.[30] . . . The mind is easy to understand. Only she did not understand the intention of Mencius."[31] Although Chu Hsi and Ch'eng I differed in many places, in this instance they both regarded women as able to understand the mind—that is, as not mentally inferior to men.

Chu Hsi also paid much attention to education for women. A pupil asked, "Women also should receive education. How about teaching them those parts of the Analects that can be understood right away, in addition to the Classic of Filial Piety?" Chu Hsi replied, "This is good. It is also good to teach them Great Lady Ts'ao's [Pan Chao, 52?–125] Nü-

*chieh* [Admonitions for women] and Wen Kung's [Ssu-ma Kuang, 1019–1086] *Chia-fan* [Models for the family]."[32] He took energetic steps to circulate the *Nü-chieh.* He once asked Prefect Fu (Fu Tzu-te, 1116–1183) of Chien-ning Prefecture in Fukien to print the *Ti-tzu chih* (Duties of youngsters) and the *Nü-chieh* together in one book, and append to them the *Tsa-i* (Miscellaneous ceremonies) of Ssu-ma Kuang, "for although the education for boys and that for girls are different, these works are what all of them should know, and to enable these works to circulate would be a feat of supporting and completing the moral teachings of the world."[33] When these works were printed in a single volume, a copy was sent to Liu Ch'ing-chih (1139–1195) with a note saying, "If convenient, please let the children of families each acquire a copy to read."[34] In a letter to Lü Tsu-ch'ien, Chu Hsi also said,

> The *Ti-tzu chih* and the *Nü-chieh* have been appended with Wen Kung's *Chia-i* [*Chia-fan*]. Before it was printed at Yu-hsi,[35] it was taken away by the prefect [of Chien-ning]. Now it has been printed, and I am sending you a copy. Originally, I wanted to send it to all friends, but copies have been exhausted and this is the only one left. If you can have a bookstore reprint it to extend its circulation, it will greatly help the moral teachings of the world. It will be a good fortune for me if you perhaps say a few words at the end.[36]

We do not know whether Lü did reprint the book. Our regret is that Chu Hsi himself was too poor to undertake the task.

Besides promoting Pan Chao's *Nü-chieh,* Chu Hsi wanted to compile another book similar to his own *Hsiao-hsüeh* (Elementary education). In a letter to Liu Ch'ing-chih he said,

> When I read the *Nü-chieh,* I found it incomplete and in some places superficial. Po-kung [Lü Tsu-ch'ien] also considered it defective. When I was at leisure, I wanted to select ancient sayings in another anthology like the *Hsiao-hsüeh,* in several parts, with items like "Correctness and Tranquillity," "Humility and Weakness," "Filial Piety and Love," "Peace and Cordiality," "Diligence and Carefulness," "Thrift and Simplicity," "Generosity and Charity," and "Discussion and Learning." Whatever of Pan Chao's book is worth including will be selected. . . . Being ill and tired, I cannot gather and inspect the material. Kindly review these items thoroughly to see if anything is missing, and if so, please supply it. If such a book can be compiled, it will be something.[37]

Chu Hsi had delegated the compilation of the *Hsiao-hsüeh* to Ch'ing-chih, and now he wanted to delegate this work to him. The *Hsiao-hsüeh* was completed in 1187, and Liu Ch'ing-chih died in 1195. Why the second anthology was not compiled in the interim remains a mystery. The item of "Discussion and Learning" was Chu Hsi's innovative idea; no previous book for women had ever included it. Did Chu Hsi intend to attract women to Neo-Confucian learning?

When Chu Hsi was superintendent in charge of affairs of ever-normal granaries, tea, and salt in Chiang-nan West[38] in 1182, he memorialized to impeach the former prefect T'ang Chung-yu, reporting that T'ang "liked the military barracks prostitute Yen Jui and wanted to take her home. He told her to lie that she was old and helped her get discharged. He gave a liberal amount of money and goods to her mother and brothers for compensation. . . . In broad daylight, he publicly rode in a sedan chair to go in and out of the house of prostitution." He also said that "Yen Jui was fairly well known for beauty, and Chung-yu fornicated with her. Even at public banquets, he was unrestrained. He publicly had her discharged, and sent his cousin, a dignitary for propagation of teachings, to take her in an official sedan chair with money and goods to go to live in a special mansion in Wu-chou.[39] At the time of Yen Jui's departure, it was Chung-yu's grandmother's death anniversary. He dared to arrange a banquet with public money in an official residence to bid Yen Jui farewell."[40] The *Ch'i-tung yeh-yü* (Rustic talks from eastern Shantung) claims that Chu Hsi "wanted to gather Yücheng's [T'ang Chung-yu] crimes, and forthwith accused him of illicit relations with Jui, who was imprisoned for over a month. Although Jui received a great deal of beating, she did not say a word about T'ang."[41] According to this account, the information was acquired from a family with illustrious ancestors in T'ien-t'ai.[42] Since Yen Jui was sent to live in Wu-chou with a farewell banquet, the tale of imprisonment is obviously unreliable.

Another account in the *Ch'i-tung yeh-yü* adds that Ch'en Liang (1143–1194) also liked Yen Jui and wanted her for himself but T'ang dissuaded her. When Ch'en saw Chu Hsi, Ch'en told Chu Hsi that T'ang had considered Chu Hsi illiterate. The account states further that when Chu Hsi arrived at T'ai-chou, T'ang, who was prefect there, was too slow to welcome him. Thereupon Chu Hsi impeached T'ang.[43] In his chapter on T'ang in the *Sung-Yüan hsüeh-an* (Anthology and critical accounts of the Neo-Confucians of the Sung and Yüan dynasties), Huang Tsung-hsi accepted these stories and said that because of bad temper, Chu Hsi had slandered T'ang.[44] Japanese scholars have also accepted them—for example, Ōta Kinjō (1765–1825).[45] There is no question that the case of Yen Jui is controversial. Ch'en Liang himself told Chu Hsi that "the case of T'ai-chou had elicited both praise and blame but it surely has excited people."[46] As for the other crimes T'ang was accused of committing, there were simply too many witnesses for them to be ignored.

As prefect of Chang-chou in 1190, Chu Hsi prohibited men and women from gathering in Buddhist monks' residences for "transmission of scripture meetings," and also forbade unmarried women to build huts to live in. In his proclamation, he said, "Isn't it better to let those who are still young and whose appearance has not yet faded return home and obey the order of their elders, openly engaging matchmakers and thus getting married, so as to revive the moral principles of the ancient kings and follow the normal course of human nature and feelings? Isn't it beautiful when the perverse words of the demonic Buddhism are stopped and the dirty custom of adultery is wiped out?[47] Evidently he achieved some success in this reform, because according to the *Yü-lei,* "Those who ordinarily followed Buddhism to attend meetings to transmit scriptures, to pay homage to pagodas, and to ascend mountains have in every case stopped. . . . Girls from good families who joined nuneries have closed their huts and in some cases returned to the normal life of sexual union."[48]

In 1196, when the Court attacked Chu Hsi and his followers, one Shen Chi-tsu memorialized to accuse him of six major crimes and other evil deeds. Among the items having to do with women, Shen blamed Chu Hsi for supplying his mother with coarse rice instead of refined rice, and said that Chu Hsi had taken two nuns to be his concubines.[49] The falsehood of Shen's statements is too obvious to engage our attention.

One thing that remains a bit of a mystery, however, is that moments before Chu Hsi died in 1200, he waved his hand to tell the women in the room to withdraw. According to Wang Mao-hung's (1668–1741) *Chu Tzu nien-p'u* (Chronological biography of Master Chu), "He was laying his head on the pillow but struck his headgear. He gazed at his pupils to correct the position of the headgear. He waved his hand to tell the women not to be near him. The pupils bowed and withdrew."[50] It is interesting that Wang did not relate this episode in the regular *nien-p'u* under the year 1200, but only in the *k'ao-i* (Investigation into variants), where he discussed various problems. He probably thought that since neither Huang Kan's (1152–1221) "Chu Tzu hsing-chuang" nor Ts'ai Ch'en's (1167–1230) "Chu Wen Kung meng-tien chi" (Account of Chu Hsi's death) mentions it, the story was questionable. Furthermore, Chu Hsi was already unable to speak and could not correct his headgear. How was he able to wave his hand? Yet the episode is recorded in Tai Hsien's (d. 1508) *nien-p'u* in his *Chu Tzu shih-chi* (True records of Master Chu), a work unknown to Wang Mao-hung. This indicates that the tradition is an old one. We also know that when Chang Shih's (1133–1180) father, Chang Chün (1096–1164), was about to die, he told the women present to leave the room.[51] This indicates that it was an old Confucian practice.

The question is why women were told to go away. Certainly it was not that Confucians believed women to be evil, for they never entertained such a belief. If it is argued a woman's attribute is yin (passive cosmic force), so that her presence may weaken the future life of the deceased, it can be countered that neither Chu Hsi nor other Neo-Confucian thinkers believed in an afterlife. One may also suggest that the practice was a result of Taoist influence. The *Chuang Tzu* recounts that when Tzu-lai was about to die, his wife and sons surrounded him and cried, but he told them to go away so as not to disturb his transformation into another being;[52] but again, Neo-Confucians did not believe in such a transformation. A clue is found in Ssu-ma Kuang's *Shu-i* (Documentary forms and ceremonies), which says, "To cry and wail will hurt the mind of the sick. To scream in sorrow is worse. To startle the sick person so that he will shake his head and die is to cut off his natural span of life. It is better to be calm and silent and wait for his breath to stop naturally. That will be best."[53] Chu Hsi's understanding of a woman's humanity as flowing in the direction of love, and his advice to Lü Tsu-ch'ien to restrain his sorrow when his wife died, support this interpretation.

A note should be added about feminine temptation. As Professor Yü Ying-shih has informed me, Chu Hsi once wrote a poem to warn himself about this. In his poem, Chu Hsi said that after ten years of living a pure life, he was affected by women's smiles, and that there is no greater danger than selfish desires.[54] As Professor Yü has observed, Chu Hsi must sometimes have found it difficult to resist the temptation of the opposite sex, and such a self-revelation is indeed rare in a Confucian philosopher.

## Notes

1. *Mien-chai chi* [Collected works of Huang Kan] (*Ssu-k'u ch'üan-shu chen-pen* [Precious works of the *Complete Collection of the Four Libraries*] ed.), 36:41b, biographical account.

2. See ch. 3 above, pp. 36–37.

3. See ch. 3 above, p. 37.

4. *Hsiang-shan ch'üan-chi* [Complete works of Lu Hsiang-shan] (*SPPY* ed.), 13:7a, first letter to Chu Yüan-hui (Chu Hsi).

5. *Wen-chi*, 33:8a, ninth letter in reply to Lü Po-kung (Lü Tsu-ch'ien).

6. See ch. 3 above, pp. 39–40.

7. *Sung-Yüan hsüeh-an*, (*SPPY* ed.), 70:7b, the Chu Hsi School.

8. *Yü-lei*, ch. 120, sec. 125 (p. 4662).

9. Hsü Wen ch'ing was one of Chu Hsi's pupils. For him, see my *Chu Tzu men-jen* [Master Chu's pupils] (Taipei: Student Book Co., 1982), p. 177.

10. *Wen-chi*, 64:8a, eighth letter in reply to Kung Chung-chih (Kung Feng).

11. *Yü-lei*, ch. 106, sec. 21 (pp. 4201–4202).

12. *Ibid.*, ch. 81, sec. 50 (p. 2341).

13. *Wen-chi,* 44:10b, eighth letter in reply to Ts'ai Chi-t'ung (Ts'ai Yüan-ting).

14. In the *Ta-Tai li-chi* [*Book of Rites* of the elder Tai] ch. 80, "Basic destiny," (*SPTK* ed. 13:6a).

15. *Yü-lei,* ch. 13, sec. 78 (p. 372).

16. *Ibid.,* ch. 72, sec. 28 (p. 2901).

17. *Wen-chi,* 62:27b, seventh letter in reply to Li Hui-shu (Li Hui).

18. *I-shu* [Surviving works], 22A:2b, in the *Erh-Ch'eng ch'üan-shu* [Complete works of the two Ch'engs] (*SPPY* ed.).

19. *Book of Mencius,* 6A:10.

20. *I-ch'uan wen-chi* [Collection of literary works of Ch'eng I], 8:4b, biography of his father, in the *Erh-Ch'eng ch'üan-shu.*

21. *Yü-lei,* ch. 96, sec. 60 (p. 3928).

22. In the forty-fifth ode, entitled "Cypress-boat," in the *Book of Odes,* the poetress, who had just been widowed, vows never to remarry.

23. *Wen-chi,* 26:26b–27a, letter to Ch'en Shih-chung (Ch'en Shou).

24. *Yü-lei,* ch. 128, sec. 56 (p. 4937).

25. *Ibid.,* ch. 4, sec. 9 (p. 91).

26. *Ibid.,* ch. 45, secs. 64–65 (p. 1849).

27. *Ibid.,* ch. 80, sec. 67 (p. 3310).

28. *Ibid.,* ch. 140, sec. 63 (p. 5352). See also ch. 81, sec. 33 (p. 3335). Madame Wei's name is unknown. She was the wife of Tseng Pu (1035–1107).

29. This refers to the *Book of Mencius,* 6A:8.

30. *Wai-shu* [Additional works], 11:4b, in the *Erh-Ch'eng ch'üan-shu.*

31. *Yü-lei,* ch. 59, ch. 119 (p. 2229).

32. *Ibid.,* ch. 7, sec. 18 (p. 204).

33. *Wen-chi,* 25:12a, note to Prefect Fu of Chien-ning. The *Ti-tzu chih* [Duties of youngsters] was originally the fifty-ninth treatise in ch. 19 of the *Kuan Tzu.*

34. *Ibid.,* separate collection, 3:13b, letter to Liu Tzu-ch'eng (Liu Ch'ing-chih).

35. A county in Fukien.

36. *Wen-chi,* regular collection, 33:21b, thirty-first letter in reply to Lü Po-kung (Lü Tsu-ch'ien).

37. *Ibid.,* 35:27b, fifteenth letter to Liu Tzu-ch'eng.

38. Eleven prefectures in Anhui and Chekiang.

39. Present Chin-hua County, Chekiang.

40. *Wen-chi,* 18:20a, 27b, third official document to charge T'ang Chung-yu.

41. *Ch'i-tung yeh-yü* [Rustic talks from eastern Shantung] (*Ts'ung-shu chi-ch'eng* [Collection of series] ed.), ch. 20, p. 264, "Prostitute Yen Jui."

42. T'ien-t'ai County in Chekiang.

43. *Ch'i-tung yeh-yü,* ch. 17, p. 226, "The Whole Story of Chu and T'ang Accusing Each Other in Memorials."

44. *Sung-Yüan hsüeh-an,* 60:1a–2a.

45. *Gimon roku* (Records of questioning) (1831 ed.), pt. 2, p. 29a.

46. *Ch'en Liang chi* (Collected works of Ch'en Liang) (Beijing: Chung-hua Book Co., 1974), letter to Chu Hsi of 1183, p. 277.

47. *Wen-chi,* 100:5a, "Proclamation Admonishing Female Seekers of the

Way to Lay Life." For more on this topic, see ch. 19 above, section on *"Mo"* (p. 308 ff.).

48. *Yü-lei,* ch. 106, sec. 36 (p. 4218).

49. See below, chap. 31, for Shen Chi-tsu's accusations.

50. Wang Mao-hung, *Chu Tzu nien-p'u* [Chronological biography of Master Chu], *k'ao-i* [Investigation of variants] (*Ts'ung-shu chi-ch'eng* ed.) ch. 4, p. 343, under the sixth year of Ch'ing-yüan (1200).

51. *Wen-chi,* 95B:37a, biographical account of Chang Chün.

52. *Chuang Tzu,* ch. 6, "Great Teacher" (*SPTK* ed., *Nan-hua chen-ching* [True classic of Chuang Tzu], 3:16b–17a).

53. Ssu-ma Kuang, *Shu-i* [Documentary forms and ceremonies] (*Ts'ung-shu chi-ch'eng* ed.), ch. 5, p. 47, "Funeral ceremonies."

54. *Wen-chi,* 5:9b.

# 31

# Shen Chi-tsu's Accusations
# against Chu Hsi

THE story begins with Hu Hung (1163 *cs*). According to the *Sung shih* (History of the Sung dynasty), before he became a prominent official, he paid a visit to Chu Hsi at Chien-an.[1] The *Sung shih* is misinformed in one respect, for Chu Hsi never taught at Chien-an. Yeh Shao-weng (c. 1175–1230) tells us in his *Ssu-ch'ao wen-chien lu* (What was heard and seen in the four reigns) that the visit took place in the Wu-i Ching-she (Wu-i Study),[2] probably soon after 1183, when Chu Hsi built the *ching-she* on Mount Wu-i in northern Fukien. Yeh continues,

> In treating scholars, the Master merely served coarse staple food. When eggplants were ripe, he would soak three or four in ginger sauce to eat together. When Hu came, Master K'ao-t'ing [Chu Hsi] could not make an exception in etiquette. Hu was not pleased. When he left, he told people, "This is not hospitality. A head of chicken or a bottle of wine is not lacking on the mountain."

After repeating Hu Hung's complaint, the *Sung shih* says, "He readily left. When he [became an investigating censor], he memorialized to attack [Prime Minister] Chao Ju-yü [1140–1196], even slandering him for introducing Chu Hsi and using him as the ringleader of false learning *(wei-hsüeh)*. As a result, Ju-yü was banished to Yung-chou."[3]

It should be pointed out that Chu Hsi, being poor, lived very frugally. In his letter to an old friend, Liu Ch'ing-chih (1139–1195), he said, "You lingered here for the whole day without tiring of conversation. Though we shared only coarse rice and vegetable soup, you showed not the slightest feeling of dissatisfaction."[4] Singing the praises of the beauty of Mount Wu-i, Chu Hsi wrote a poem in which he said, "If old friends are willing to visit / We shall live together in a straw hut /

Mountain and river will entertain you / There is no need to provide chicken and millet."[5] Hu Hung probably wouldn't understand that.

Seldom in human history has a personal grudge led to a political crisis, but such a crisis was already brewing. As Wang Mao-hung's *Chu Tzu nien-p'u* (Chronological biography of Master Chu) tells us,

> For some time, Court censors had been attacking "false learning." They had already sent notice to the Court. Before long, Chang Kuei-mu pinpointed [what he considered to be] the errors of the "T'ai-chi-t'u shuo" [Explanation of the diagram of the Great Ultimate, by Chou Tun-i (1017–1073), which Chu Hsi promoted], and the departments heard about it. Examination administrators Yeh Chu, Ni Ssu, Liu Te-hsiu, and others memorialized the emperor to tell of the defects of the compositions of the time. They also asserted that the leader of "false learning" [Chu Hsi], as a commoner, was trying to steal the power of the ruler and was agitating the world, which was why the literary atmosphere could not change for the better. They begged to have the *Yü-lu* [Recorded sayings of Ch'eng Hao (1032–1085) and Ch'eng I (1033–1107)] and the like completely destroyed. Among the candidates of the current class of civil service examinations, those who touched on Neo-Confucian thought were all rejected. The Six Classics,[6] the *Analects,* the *Book of Mencius,* the *Great Learning,* and the *Doctrine of the Mean* [which Chu Hsi had published as the Four Books in 1190] were strongly prohibited in the world. Scholars avoided trouble, and the literary spirit gradually declined. In their remonstrations, the censors were tumultuous, competing to get the Master [Chu Hsi] as a valuable catch. Upon hearing that people in remote areas aiming at profit often manufactured facts to suit the purpose of the censors, pupil Yang Tao-fu hurriedly wrote to tell the Master. The Master replied and said, "I have for a long time put life and death, and catastrophe and blessing, out of my mind. Please don't bother to worry too much."[7] After some time, wicked people looked at one another and dared not start. Hu Hung alone drafted a memorial, and when he was about to present it, he was transferred outside the capital. Because of his attack on I-ch'uan [Ch'eng I], Shen Chi-tsu was able to become an investigating censor. Hung gave him the draft. Chi-tsu was a go-getter, thinking that he could immediately achieve wealth and high position. He forthwith memorialized to dismiss [Chu Hsi] from his position [as lecturer-in-waiting] and to terminate his temple superintendency. His recommendations were accepted.[8]

The earliest record of Shen Chi-tsu's memorial is found in Yeh Shao-weng's *Ssu-ch'ao wen-chien lu.* Yeh lived somewhat later than Chu Hsi. His work is not easily available to scholars, and few have read the memorial firsthand. It is translated in full as follows:

> In the third year of Ch'ing-yüan [1197], in the second month of spring, on the ninth day [February 27, 1197], departmental official communica-

tion. Your servant humbly observes that Chu Hsi, grand dignitary for court service, compiler of the Imperial Library, and superintendent of the Hung-ch'ing Temple, is basically twisted in natural endowment and, in addition, is jealous and merciless. At first he played the bully and insisted on arbitrary decisions. Later, realizing that these tactics do not work in this sagely generation, he changed his practice. He has stolen the remnant theories of Chang Tsai [1020–1077] and Ch'eng I, and has concealed them in the evil schemes of [the cult of] vegetarianism and the worship of demons[9] to agitate students of the later generation. He exaggerates and excels in nonsense, and privately sets up slogans. He has recruited immoral people from all directions to augment his clique. Together they eat coarse and simple food and wear filthy clothing and broad sashes. He gathered his followers at the Goose Lake Temple of Kuang-hsin[10] or presented himself in the hall of reverence and simplicity [Confucian temple].[11] He hid his presence and concealed his shadow like a ghost and a demon. Scholar-officials who were fishing for fame and profit and believed he would be of help have proceeded to praise and recommend him. As his roots and branches are firm and his arms and elbows have been formed, he, as a commoner, forthwith stole the power of the ruler and exercised it in his private chamber. His letters and memorials have flown all around and have met with a response wherever they went. Minor figures have obtained profit and major figures have obtained fame. Not only did his followers fulfill their wishes; Hsi himself has become wealthy and honorable.

Your servant humbly declares that Hsi has committed six major crimes, and these do not include other evil deeds. Sons should serve their parents with the best food. Hsi lost his father early, and there was only his mother surviving. The rice of Chien-ning Prefecture is white, the best in Fukien, but Hsi did not supply his mother with this; instead, he daily served her with the granary rice that he bought. His mother could not stand it and often told people about it. Once she was invited by a neighbor and returned to tell Hsi, "Theirs is also a family, but they have such refined rice." Those who heard the story pitied her. Formerly, Mao Jung [of the Later Han dynasty, 25–220] butchered a chicken to feed his mother and shared with his guest a vegetarian dinner.[12] Now Hsi ate coarse meals to fish for fame and had no pity for his mother's suffering. Isn't that too atrocious? Hsi's unfilial behavior toward his mother is great crime number one.

During the reign of Hsiao-tsung [r. 1163–1189], he was repeatedly called to serve in office but would rest and stay put and would not proceed forward. When a commissioner or a prefect invited him, he would hurry to go in a vehicle. People theorize that he declined appointments for the purpose of giving up a lower position for a higher one, and that he hurried to answer invitations because he expected gifts in the evening if he arrived in the morning. A scholar in his community with the same family name wrote to criticize him severely, but he had nothing to say. Later, when he was appointed to be an executive in the ministry of the army [in 1188], he refused to assume office, feigning a foot ailment as a means to force a demand on the ruler. This can be seen in the official document of Vice Minister Lin Li [1142 cs]. Hsi's disrespect for the ruler is great crime number two.

When Hsiao-tsung passed away, the opinion of the whole country was that, according to rites, he should be buried on K'uai-chi Mountain[13] along with [other emperors]. But Hsi, on his own initiative, spread a different opinion. He memorialized first of all and begged to summon the common people from Kiangsi and Fukien, plotting to find another place through divination. His purpose was to find an official position for the evil person Ts'ai Yüan-ting [1135–1198], with whom he had been very friendly, and to support Chao Ju-yü's proposal of burial in another place. He paid no heed to the ritual institutions of the ancestors and did not care for the benefit or harm of the country. If it had not been for the sagely understanding of Your Majesty and the firm opinion of the Court, a great event would have been jeopardized. Hsi's disloyalty to the country is great crime number three.

Formerly, when Ju-yü ruled the government, he conspired to do something illegal. He wanted to utilize Hsi's hollow fame to recruit his treacherous gang and rely on them as brain and muscle. Hsi was suddenly elevated to be lecturer-in-waiting and acquired, out of order, a personal interview with the emperor [in 1194]. Once Hsi was appointed, according to law, out of imperial kindness titles should be conferred on his parents, his children should be recommended, and his regalia should be changed. But he suddenly presented a document pretending to decline the appointment. How could he resign from the office when all the amenities were granted because of that office? There is no greater offense to the Court than this. If this can be tolerated, what cannot be tolerated? This is Hsi's great crime number four.

After Ju-yü died, both the Court and people in the nation were jubilant. Hsi led more than a hundred of his followers to mourn Chao's death in the countryside. Although Hsi was thinking of the personal feeling of their mutual benefit and protection, could he be oblivious to the great principle of the Court? But he remained a member of the gang of diehards and had no scruples about what people would say. He even went as far as to write a poem to match that of Ch'u Yung,[14] in which he said, "Unless there is another Heaven in the world." Can there be another Heaven in the human world? Is the idea of what he said limited to a sigh? This is Hsi's great crime number five.

Having believed in the perverse theory of the evil person Ts'ai Yüanting, who said that, according to geomancy, the site of the Chien-yang county school will produce dukes and princes, Hsi wanted to acquire it. Ch'u Yung accommodated his wishes and moved the county school to the Hu-kuo Temple so that Hsi could acquire the county school site some other time and so that the county school [at the temple] would not fall into private hands. Thereupon, during the busy months for farmers, hills were cut and rocks were bored. Groups of workers pulled and pushed to make shortcuts. The move created a disturbance along the path and destroyed farmland. The school was thus shifted to the lower section of the county.

The image of the Grand Master [Confucius] was even relocated in the hall of the Buddha. Scaffolds were set up, and huge boards and large ropes were used to wrap around the sacred image. As it shook while passing through the broad boulevards and busy streets, the four limbs were damaged. Onlookers were alarmed and sighed. To the people of the county, the Grand Master is the sovereign of humanity, righteousness, rites, and the music of ten thousand generations. He has now suddenly met with the punishment of removal and, what is more, has suffered from broken limbs. The harm to mores is indeed great. This is Hsi's great crime number six.

As to his desire to repay Ju-yü's kindness in recruiting him, he was the matchmaker of Ju-yü's son Ch'ung-hsien. He himself married the daughter of Liu Kung [1122–1178] and hoped suddenly to inherit millions of cash after Liu's death. He also induced two nuns to be his pet concubines. Wherever he went to assume office, he would take them along. Can he be said to cultivate the person? His daughter-in-law became pregnant without a husband, and his sons stole oxen to butcher. Can he be said to regulate the family? When he was prefect of Nan-k'ang [Kiangsi, in 1179], he arranged for the marriage of several couples by mistake and then corrected them. When he was pacification commissioner of Changsha [Hunan, in 1194], he secretly concealed the imperial edict of amnesty and executed many prisoners. As prefect of Chang-chou [Fukien, in 1190], he searched for ancient texts and foolishly carried out the redefining of land boundaries. People over a thousand *li*[15] were disturbed, and all were harmed. When he was supervisor [of affairs of ever-normal granaries, tea, and salt] in Chekiang East[16] [in 1181], he distributed liberally to his pupils government relief food and all the money, which never reached the people. Can he be said to govern the people? Or take the case of Fan Jan.[17] Hsi took possession of Fan's ancestral hill to expand his own residence, and turned around and accused Fan of crime. He dug up the grave of an archer of Ch'ung-an[18] to bury his mother and did not mind the exposure of the dead. Can he be said to extend altruism to others? In the marriage of his children, he always chose wealthy families for the benefit of their ample dowries and gifts. When he opened his school doors to receive pupils, he always induced youngsters from wealthy families and required them to pay a substantial tuition. Gifts came from all directions, one after another. In a year he would receive more than ten thousand cash. Can he be said to have a sense of integrity and to have disciplined himself? The sense of integrity, altruism, cultivation of the self, regulation of the family, and governing the people are doctrines that Hsi has stolen from the *Doctrine of the Mean* and the *Great Learning* in the course of his life in order to fool the world. Now his words are like that, but his deeds are like this. Isn't he a great crook and a wicked person? Formerly, Shao-cheng Mao was "dishonest but argumentative in words" and "perverse but firm in deeds."[19] The Grand Master executed him within seven days after he became acting prime minister of the state of Lu. The Grand Master was a sage without the [king's] position, and yet he could get rid of him quickly like this. How much more so in the case of Your Majesty, who occupies the position of kingly government and wields the power of life and death? Hsi's crime is much greater than that of Shao-cheng Mao. Should he not be executed quickly? Your servant wishes and hopes that in your sagely mercy you will especially grant your wise decision, dismiss Chu Hsi from his office, and terminate his temple superintendency as a warning to those who cheat the ruler, deceive the world, defile their conduct, and steal their fame. Ch'u Yung should be demoted and never allowed to take office along with good citizens. I beg that Ts'ai Yüan-ting be taken to Chien-ning to be sent to another prefecture for supervision. In this way wicked people will know what to fear and the kingly way will again be manifest. From now on, scholars in the world will look upon Confucius and Mencius as teachers, and evil and small people will no longer be able to depend on them as a pretext for behaving tyranically at this clear and bright time. This will surely be of no small help.[20]

Several points need to be clarified in this infamous memorial. The first is its date. The memorial is dated the second month of the third year of Ch'ing-yüan. According to various *Chu Tzu nien-p'u,* Chu Hsi's dismissal took place in the twelfth month of the second year. Obviously, it makes no sense for Shen Chi-tsu to have asked for his dismissal after the fact. The earlier date almost agrees with the note in the *Ssu-ch'ao wen-chien lu* that says, "In the Ts'ai edition, the date [of the memorial] was the tenth month of the second year." Thus, two months after the memorial, its request was carried out.

The second point is the number of crimes of which Chu Hsi was accused. The memorial clearly lists six crimes, but the *Sung shih* says that Shen accused Chu Hsi of ten crimes.[21] This caused Wang Mao-hung (1668–1741) to remark, "The memorial mentions six great crimes, which does not agree with the *Sung shih,* but the *Hsü [tzu-chih] t'ung-chien* [Supplement to the *Comprehensive Mirror for the Aid of Government*] casually adopted it [ten crimes], and the Fukien editions of the *Nien-p'u* made the correction according to the *Hsü-t'ung-chien.*"[22] We do not know which Fukien edition Wang had in mind. One edition—the one in the first volume of Chu Yü's *Chu Tzu wen-chi ta-ch'üan lei-pien* (Classified compilation of the *Complete Collection of Literary Works of Master Chu*), of 1772—also states that there were ten crimes. This suggests that all Fukien editions used the same figure. But the *Sung shih* is not mistaken in using the figure of ten, because in addition to the six great crimes enumerated by Shen, Chu Hsi was accused of five more evil deeds—failure to cultivate the person, regulate the family, govern the people, extend altruism, and have a sense of integrity—for a total of eleven. The *Sung shih* may have used the round number of ten, or it may have combined the lack of altruism and integrity into one.

The third point is that the *Sung shih* also recorded that Yü Che, an alternate to an office, memorialized to have Chu Hsi executed.[23] Commenting on the two memorials, Wang Mao-hung said, "We don't know what the two memorials of Shen Chi-tsu and Yü Che are based on. I suspect that followers of Wang Yang-ming [1472–1529] copied or invented the story to slander Master Chu. Recent writers, being ignorant, have carelessly incorporated it into the *Nien-p'u*. Their stupidity and meanness have reached this point. It is pitiful."[24] Wang was a painstaking scholar, and his chronological biography of Chu Hsi is definitive. Unfortunately, he was not entirely free from partisan spirit. Evidently he had not seen Shen's memorial in the *Ssu-ch'ao wen-chien lu*. He should have realized that although the followers of Wang Yang-ming were relentless in criticizing Chu Hsi's thought, they never attacked his character.

Shen Chi-tsu did invent many stories. He claimed that Chu Hsi gathered followers at the Goose Lake Temple. The fact is that, of the seven participants mentioned in the *Hsiang-shan ch'üan-chi* (Complete works of Lu Hsiang-shan), not one was Chu Hsi's pupil.[25] One of the seven, Liu Tzu-ch'eng (Liu Ch'ing-chih), was only a friend. Besides the seven, I have found three more participants, all pupils of Lu Hsiang-shan.[26] Shen said that Chu Hsi's poetic line about another Heaven in the human world was a match to Ch'u Yung's poem. When Shen said that Chu Hsi's idea was not limited to a sigh, he was hinting that Chu Hsi believed there should be another Son of Heaven (i.e., emperor) in the world. Shen may be excused for his ignorance of Chu Hsi's ten poems glorifying the beautiful scenery of Mount Wu-i, one of which includes the line in question,[27] but his insinuation is inexcusable. Shen accused Chu Hsi of marrying the daughter of Liu Kung for his wealth. The fact is that Chu Hsi married the daughter of Liu Mien-chih (1091–1149), not Liu Kung. Liu Kung was indeed a rich man, but Mien-chih was well-to-do at best. According to his tomb inscription, written by Chu Hsi, "His wife's family was rich but there was no son. The family wanted to leave the wealth to the daughter but Mien-chih declined. He selected the virtuous relatives of his wife's family and gave the wealth to them."[28] Thus Chu Hsi did not inherit any wealth from his own wife's family, and his poverty is well known.[29]

Shen accused Chu Hsi of having concealed the amnesty edict and executed many prisoners. Whether Chu Hsi did execute the prisoners at Changsha is still a controversial subject. It is not mentioned in Huang Kan's (1152–1221) "Chu Tzu hsiang-chuang" (Biographical account of Master Chu), in any of the *nien-p'u*, or in the *Sung shih*. Perhaps this was like the case of Confucius executing Shao-cheng Mao, which is omitted from most biographies of the Sage because of its controversial character. Until recently, scholars in Mainland China liked to cite this as an example of Confucius' suppression of peasant revolt. Lu

Hsiang-shan had said that, at Nan-k'ang, Chu Hsi's administration of the law was too severe,[30] and Chu Hsi himself admitted that sometimes he was too harsh.[31] It is possible, therefore, that he did execute the prisoners at Changsha. According to the *Changsha hsien-chih* (Accounts of Changsha County),

> When Chu Hui-weng [Chu Hsi] was commander at Changsha, he received a letter from Prime Minister Chao [Ju-yü] telling him that Prince Chia would become the emperor and that his first appointment would be to invite Chu Hsi as lecturer-in-waiting. Hui-weng concealed the letter in his sleeve, went to the prison right away, and took eighteen prisoners and executed them. As soon as the executions had taken place, the imperial edict for amnesty arrived. He acted immediately for fear that had the edict arrived first, the great criminals would have escaped punishment.[32]

Whether the executions did take place and whether they were justified are irrelevant to our discussion. The point is that Shen twisted the facts to show Chu Hsi's disloyalty, for what Chu Hsi concealed in his sleeve was Chao's letter, not the imperial edict.

Shen condemned Chu Hsi for digging up the grave of a Ch'ung-an archer in order to bury his mother, but Chu Hsi's mother was laid to rest in Chien-yang, far from Ch'ung-an. Shen said that, in marrying off his daughters, Chu Hsi always chose rich families, yet the poverty of his son-in-law Huang Kan is proverbial. As to selecting pupils for their tuition, of the 467 pupils in my statistics, only 133 held an official position, hardly 28 percent. There were pupils from rich families, of course, but they were in the minority.[33] Shen asserted that Chu Hsi received tens of thousands of cash every year, but Chu Hsi lived largely on the meager salary of a temple directorship.[34] In 1173, when he was appointed to such a directorship, even the imperial edict publicly acknowledged that "Chu Hsi was at peace with poverty and adhered to the Way."[35] About the image of Confucius, Chu Hsi wrote to his pupil P'an Shih-chü that "Recently, in moving the new school, monks damaged the sculptured image, destroying the important limbs. This makes people heartbroken."[36] Whether Shen's account was the product of his imagination or based on rumor is difficult to say.

Chronologically, Shen presented his memorial in the tenth month of 1196, and two months later, in the twelfth month, Chu Hsi was dismissed from his lecturership as well as from the superintendency of a Taoist temple. In the following month, that is, the first month of 1197, he presented a memorial to the emperor giving thanks for the dismissal and the termination. In this memorial, Chu Hsi explicitly stated that at first he was not aware of the accusations of his so-called grave misdeeds,

but that later he "was deeply doubtful and afraid."[37] In his memorial to
the emperor to express thanks for his dismissal as compiler at the Imperial Library, he wrote,

> They said *(wei-ch'i)* that I recited the evil words of a demonic cult and
> practiced the dirty deeds of vulgar people; that feeding my mother with
> coarse food shows that my love for her declined; that, as an inferior, for
> me to harbor the mind of not serving the government clearly indicates my
> lack of propriety; that I even went as far as to take the wealth of old friends
> as my own and to take in the nuns; and that I plotted to acquire the site of
> a government school and changed it into a Buddhist square. I believe all
> this is an attempt to slander me and take my life without regret. Surpris-
> ingly, your kindness has spared me and let me avoid the virtuous officials
> to some extent but still retain an insignificant title in rank.[38]

Because of the falsehood of Shen's memorial, until recently no historians had given it any credence. But in the early 1970s, when the anti-
Lin Piao campaign was at its height, writers in Mainland China
emphasized the story of Chu Hsi's making nuns his concubines. Several
writers overlooked the words *wei-ch'i* and interpreted Chu Hsi's memorial of thanks as a confession of sins. One writer even added that the
nuns were seventeen and eighteen years old.[39] Fortunately, in more
recent years, Mainland writers have tried to be fair. They have given
Chu Hsi the credit that he deserves, although they still criticize him for
supporting feudalism. The fortunes of Chu Hsi have definitely taken a
turn for the better, far from the dark days of Shen Chi-tsu.[40]

## Notes

1. *Sung shih* [History of the Sung dynasty] (Beijing: Chung-hua Book Co.,
1977), ch. 392, p. 12023, biography of Hu Hung. Chien-an is now Chien-ou
County, Fukien Province.
2. Yen Shao-weng, *Ssu-ch'ao wen-chien lu* [What was heard and seen in the
four regions] (*P'u-ch'eng i-shu* [Surviving works of the P'u-ch'eng County] ed.),
4:16a, on Hu Hung.
3. See above, n. 1. The capital of Yung-chou was in present Ling-ling
County in Hunan Province.
4. *Wen-chi,* 35:12a, first letter in reply to Liu Tzu-ch'eng (Liu Ch'ing-chih).
5. *Ibid.,* 9:4a.
6. The Six Classics are the *Book of Odes,* the *Book of History,* the *Book of Changes,*
the *Book of Rites,* the *Spring and Autumn Annals,* and the *Book of Music.* The *Book of
Music* was lost before the third century B.C. and was replaced with the *Chou-li*
(Rites of Chou) during the Sung dynasty (960–1279).
7. This letter is not among the four in reply to Yang Chung-ssu (Yang Tao-
fu) in the *Wen-chi,* 58:2b–3b.
8. Wang Mao-hung, *Chu Tzu nien-p'u* [Chronological biography of Master

Chu] (*Ts'ung-shu chi-ch'eng* [Collection of series] ed.), ch. 48, p. 218, under the second year of Ch'ing-yüan (1196). Wang Mao-hung was quoting from Li Mo's *Chu Tzu nien-p'u* of 1552 and Hung Ch'u-wu's *Chu Tzu nien-p'u* of 1700. The same account was given earlier in Yeh Kung-hui's *Chu Tzu nien-p'u* of 1431 and Tai Hsien's *nien-p'u* in his *Chu Tzu shih-chi* [True records of Master Chu] of 1517.

9. On "the worship of demons," see ch. 19 above, section on *"Mo"* (p. 308 ff.).

10. This refers to the 1175 meeting of Chu Hsi, Lu Hsiang-shan (1139–1193), and others at Goose Lake Temple in Hsin-chou Prefecture in Kiangsi. See ch. 26 above.

11. For reverence and simplicity, see the *Analects*, 6:2. Chu Hsi was prefect in Changsha in 1194.

12. For Mao Jung, see the *Hou-Han shu* [History of the Later Han dynasty] (*SPTK* ed.), 98:2a, biography of Mao Jung.

13. An area in eastern Chekiang and western Anhui.

14. Ch'u Yung's courtesy name was Hsing-chih. He was *chu-pu* (assistant magistrate) of Chien-yang County.

15. A *li* is one-third of a mile.

16. Seven prefectures in Chekiang.

17. We do not know who Fan Jan was.

18. A county in northern Fukien where Chu Hsi lived.

19. *K'ung Tzu chia-yü* [School sayings of Confucius], sec. 2, "Official in the State of Lu" (*SPTK* ed., 1:5a).

20. *Ssu-ch'ao wen-chien lu,* 4:10b, on factions during the Ch'ing-yüan period (1195–1200).

21. *Sung shih,* ch. 429, biography of Chu Hsi, p. 12767.

22. Wang Mao-hung, *Chu Tzu nien-p'u, k'ao-i* [Investigation into variants], ch. 4, p. 337, under the second year of Ch'ing-yüan (1196).

23. *Sung shih,* ch. 429, biography of Chu Hsi, p. 12768.

24. *Chu Tzu nien-p'u, k'ao-i,* ch. 4, p. 337.

25. *Hsiang-shan ch'üan-chi* [Complete works of Lu Hsiang-shan] (*SPPY* ed.), 36:9a, chronological biography.

26. For the participants in the meeting at the Goose Lake Temple, see ch. 26 above.

27. *Wen-chi,* 9:6a.

28. *Wen-chi,* 90:21a, tomb inscription for Liu Mien-chih.

29. For Chu Hsi's poverty, see ch. 5 above.

30. *Hsiang-shan ch'üan chi,* 36:12b, chronological biography, under the tenth year of Ch'un-hsi (1183). For the Nan-k'ang case, see the *Yü-lei,* ch. 106, sec. 7 (p. 4195).

31. *Wen-chi,* 36:19b, seventy-ninth letter in reply to Lü Po-kung (Lü Tsu-ch'ien).

32. *Changsha hsien-chih* [Accounts of Changsha County] (1868 ed.), 36:6a, "Recovered Passages."

33. For Chu Hsi's pupils, see ch. 21 above, and my *Chu Tzu men-jen* [Master Chu's pupils] (Taipei: Student Book Co., 1982), pp. 1–27.

34. For Chu Hsi's acceptance of gifts, see ch. 5 above.

35. *Wen-chi*, 22:4b–5a, "Official Document on Resigning from the Director-ship of a Taoist Temple."

36. *Wen-chi*, 60:27b, fifth letter in reply to P'an Tzu-shan (P'an Shih-chü).

37. *Ibid.*, 85:17b–18a, "Memorial to Express Thanks for the Dismissal and Termination."

38. *Ibid.*, 85:18b–19a, "Memorial to the Emperor upon Dismissal as Compiler in the Imperial Library."

39. *Chu Hsi ti ch'ou-o mien-mao* [Chu Hsi's ugly face] (Kiangsi Political Propaganda Department, 1975), pp. 7, 35.

40. For Chu Hsi's new fortunes and for more recent Mainland Chinese writers, see my *Chu Hsi: Life and Thought* (Hong Kong: The Chinese University Press, 1987), p. 32.

# – 32 –

# Chu Hsi and
# Chin-men (Quemoy)

I N the *Chin-men ts'ung-shu* (Chin-men series) there is a volume entitled *Chu Hsi yü Chin-men* (Chu Hsi and Chin-men).[1] The introductory chapter contains an undated portrait of Chu Hsi, drawn by Hu Mei-ch'i, that is a copy of a portrait preserved in the National Palace Museum at Taipei. The copy is perfect, almost like a photograph. There is also a stone rubbing of the couplet carved on Ku-shan (Drum Mountain) in Foochow.[2] The portrait and the rubbing hang in the main hall of the Wu-chiang Academy, which was reconstructed in 1968.

The first chapter of the book is also entitled "Chu Tzu yü Chin-men" (Master Chu and Chin-men). Its first section, "The Educational Transformation of Chin-men," has the following account concerning Chu Hsi:

At the time of the Sung dynasty [960–1279], Chin-men was Hsiang-feng Village, Sui-te Township, T'ung-an County. Master Chu was *chu-pu* [assistant magistrate] of T'ung-an for five years. Judged by the fact that when he was prefect of Nan-k'ang [Kiangsi] and Chang-chou [Fukien], he inspected schools in the jurisdiction, he must have inspected Chin-men regularly or irregularly more than once during the five years. Based on the local histories of Chin-men, we have recorded his political and educational measures in Chin-men and his direct or indirect influence on it to serve as important evidential material on Chin-men.

(1) As Master Chu was an expert on the *Book of Changes,* he must have paid close attention to mountains and rivers and the natural environment. An old record of Chin-men says: "The mountain range of Chin-men . . . goes through Hung-chien Mountain. . . ." A common saying is, "From far corners of the sky, the dragon has crossed the river. Isn't the Hung-chien Mountain far corners of the sky?" Once Chu Wen Kung [Chu Hsi]

came to the mountain and sighed, "The head of Hung-chien has already crossed the river [to Chin-men]." He also said, "Hung-chien backs T'ung-an and faces Chin-men." The *K'ang-hsi yü-ti chih* [Geographic record of the K'ang-hsi period] says, "Hung-chien is the highest of the mountains. It is particularly beautiful when viewed from Chin-men across the river." Therefore it has been said in Chin-men that any community that corresponds to Hung-chien Mountain will flourish in culture.

(2) When Master Chu inspected schools in Chin-men, he visited the Ch'en Yüan Temple in Chin-men, which had been established in the T'ang dynasty [618–907]. The temple was in front of the monastery in the Chin-ch'eng Garrison, which was also the ground where Ch'en Yüan pastured horses. The *Fu-chi Miao chi* [Record of the Fu-chi (Ch'en Yüan) Temple], written by the defender of the Chin-men Garrison, Chieh-chih, in 1318, contains a poem by Master Chu entitled "Tz'u Mu-ma-wang Temple" [Poem on the temple of the prince of pasturing horses], which says, "Today I see the wind rushing across the sea / Courteous elders follow me from afar. . . ." From this poem we know that Wen Kung must have been to Chin-men and was enthusiastically welcomed by elders who accompanied him to visit the Ch'en Yüan Temple. From this we can also imagine the beauty of the scenery and the abundance of the forest in the area of the Feng-lien Mountain, which was in front of the monastery at the time. According to the tradition of the elders of Chin-men, Master Chu said after his visit to Chin-men, "The forest today will be the forest of scholars tomorrow." He was prophesying the flourishing of humanistic culture of Chin-men in the future.

(3) When Master Chu was *chu-pu* at T'ung-an, he also promoted education. He established the Yen-nan Academy in Chin-men. According to the *Ts'ang-wu so-lu* [Miscellaneous records of Chin-men], "When Master Chu was *chu-pu* of the county, he surveyed the customs of the island and led people with ceremony. Chin-men having been transformed, he established the Yen-nan Academy on Yen-nan Mountain. From then on, every family was devoted to music and literature, was at leisure with correct moral principles, and cherished the Confucian classics. Social mores greatly changed."[3]

In this account, four items are presented as historical facts: (1) Chu Hsi inspected Chin-men regularly or irregularly more than once during his five years as *chu-pu* at T'ung-an; (2) Chu Hsi once visited Hung-chien Mountain and sighed, "The head of Hung-chien has already crossed the river"; (3) Chu Hsi once visited the Ch'en Yüan Temple in Chin-men, as evidenced by the poem he wrote; and (4) Chu Hsi founded the Yen-nan Academy. All deserve careful scrutiny by historians.

Chu Hsi's term as *chu-pu* lasted for only three years, from the seventh month of 1153 to the seventh month of 1156. After his term was up, he visited the neighboring prefectures for several more months. It is possible that, during these three years or more, he paid a visit to Chin-men. Neither Hung-chien Mountain nor the poem for Mu-ma Wang Temple appears in the *Wen-chi* or any of the *nien-p'u* (chronological biographies). The story of his visit to Hung-chien is based on an old account of Chin-men; that of the visit to the Ch'en Yüan Temple is based on the *Fu-chi miao-chi,* written more than a hundred years after Chu Hsi's death. It is not clear what evidence there was for these accounts. Tai Hsien (d. 1508) gave brief accounts of all the academies with which Chu Hsi was associated in chapter 7 of his *Chu Tzu shih-chi* (True records of Master Chu), but the Yen-nan Academy is not among them. If we say the academy had disappeared by Tai Hsien's time, the fact remains that it is not mentioned in the *Yü-lei* or the *Wen-chi.* Chu Hsi built several studies *(ching-she)* and reconstructed both the White Deer Hollow Academy on Mount Lu and the Yüeh-lu Academy in Changsha, but he never founded an academy, although he visited, lectured at, and wrote plaques for many of them. His pupils founded or headed a number of academies, but not Yen-nan.[4]

Section 4 of chapter 9 of the *Chu Hsi yü Chin-men* mentions a number of outstanding men of Chin-men throughout the ages. Among them, Ch'en Kang, Ch'en T'ung, Ch'en Yu, Ch'en Ch'ang-hou, Ch'en Liang-ts'ai, and Ch'en Yü of the Sung period[5] are not found in the *Wen-chi* or the *Yü-lei.* Ch'en Yü (1196 *cs*) was a contemporary of Chu Hsi, but we do not know whether they were aware of each other because he was not a pupil of Chu Hsi and did not correspond or exchange poems with him. Chu Hsi's pupils Wang Li-hsing, Hsü Sheng, and Ch'en Ch'i-chung, as well as his friend Su P'in, were natives of T'ung-an, but we do not know their village or township.[6] We are sure, however, that they were not natives of Chin-men. The people of T'ung-an built a Chu Tzu Temple to the east of the county school, with Hsü Sheng, Wang Li-hsing, Lü Ta-k'uei, and Ch'iu K'uei accompanying Chu Hsi at the altar. Lü was a native of T'ung-an and a fourth-generation pupil of Chu Hsi, since he was a third-generation pupil of Ch'en Ch'un (1159–1223).[7] Ch'iu was a native of Hsiao-teng Township, Chin-men, and was also a fourth-generation pupil of Chu Hsi.[8] The list of outstanding men of Chin-men in section 4 of chapter 9 includes only Ch'iu K'uei, thus indicating that the other T'ung-an natives were not from Chin-men.

In short, we do not rule out the possibility of Chu Hsi's visit to Chin-men. More than one poem not in the *Wen-chi* has been recovered.[9] The literary style and the language in general of the poem quoted above indicate it could possibly be one of those. The exclamation about Hung-chien Mountain is based on tradition, but since the mountain is not mentioned in the *Wen-chi* or the *Yü-lei,* the account can be neither proved nor disproved. The most questionable record is that concerning the Yen-nan Academy. Many places have established academies to commemorate Chu Hsi and claim that Chu Hsi himself founded them. Can the Yen-nan Academy be one of these?

## Notes

1. *Chu Hsi yü Chin-men* [Chu Hsi and Chin-men] was compiled by Kuo Yaoling in 1979 and published by the Documents Committee of Chin-men County. Its nine chapters in 130 pages deal with (1) Chu Hsi and Chin-men, (2) Chu Hsi's life and works, (3) Chu Hsi's educational thought, (4) Chu Hsi's political thought, (5) Chu Hsi and the Four Books, (6) the Chu Hsi School and its influence, (7) brief accounts of important events in his life, (8) his official documents as *chu-pu* (assistant magistrate), and (9) the Master Chu Temple at Chin-men.

2. *Chu Hsi yü Chin-men*, p. 109.

3. *Ibid.*, pp. 5–6.

4. See ch. 21 above.

5. *Chu Hsi yü Chin-men*, pp. 113–114.

6. See my *Chu Tzu men-jen* [Master Chu's pupils] (Taipei: Student Book Co., 1982), pp. 29, 200, 223, 362.

7. *Sung-Yüan hsüeh-an* [Anthology and critical accounts of Neo-Confucians of the Sung and Yüan dynasties] (*SPPY* ed.), 68:12b, chapter on Ch'en Ch'un.

8. *Chu Hsi yü Chin-men*, p. 2; *Sung-Yüan hsüeh-an*, 68:13a, chapter on Ch'en Ch'un.

9. See my *Chu Tzu hsin-t'an-so* [New investigations on Master Chu] (Taipei: Student Book Co., 1988), pp. 668–671.

# Hu Shih and
# Chu Hsi

Hu Shih (1891–1962) was born and raised in a traditional Chinese family imbued with the ideals of Neo-Confucianism. When he was five years old, his father died and he began to study with his fourth uncle. By the age of nine, he was reciting from memory passages from the *Hsiao-hsüeh* (Elementary education), a work compiled by Chu Hsi's pupils under his direction. When he came to the passage quoted from Ssu-ma Kuang's (1019–1086) *Shu-i* (Documentary forms and ceremonies), "When a man dies, his physical form is destroyed and his spirit is also scattered,"[1] he was elated. This statement became the foundation of Hu Shih's atheism, which was firmly established by the time he was eleven or twelve.[2]

From 1895 to 1904, from the age of five to fourteen, Hu Shih studied at the family school. Besides the *Hsiao-hsüeh,* he studied Chu Hsi's *Ssu-shu chang-chü chi-chu* (Collected commentaries on the Four Books), including the annotations. Although he only recited the texts of Chu Hsi's *Shih chi-chuan* (Collected commentaries on the *Book of Odes*) and his *Chou-i pen-i* (Original meanings of the *Book of Changes*), he had already absorbed Chu Hsi's basic ideas. When he entered Ch'eng-chung School in Shanghai in 1905, his elder brother urged him to read the *Chin-ssu-lu* (Reflections on things at hand), compiled by Chu Hsi and Lü Tsu-ch'ien, which introduced him to the original works of Neo-Confucians. Of all the selections in the anthology, Ch'eng I's (1033–1107) saying, "The source of learning is thought,"[3] left the deepest impression. As Dr. Hu recalled, "That sentence, which I read in the *Chin-ssu lu* at Ch'eng-ch'ung School, attraced my attention. Later, when my line of thought followed the direction of Huxley and John Dewey, that was precisely because when I was a teenager I was devoted to the method of thinking."[4] What is significant is that the saying was uttered by Ch'eng I, not Chu Hsi, and that what influenced Hu Shih was not Neo-Confucian thought but Neo-Confucian methodology. Although the *Chin-ssu lu* made him interested in Ch'eng I and Chu Hsi, he did not read very much of their work,[5] for by that time books such as the *T'ien-yen lun* (Essay on evolution) and *Ch'ün-chi ch'üan-chieh* (Rights between society and the self), by Yen Fu (1853–1921), occupied the minds of China's youth.[6]

In the following years, Hu Shih studied and taught in Shanghai and did not come into contact with Chu Hsi's work. There was even less opportunity to do so in the United States, where he studied from the age of twenty to twenty-seven. After his return to China, he became a leader in literary reform and the new thought movement. In the sphere of thought, he promoted pragmatism and the philosophy of Tai Chen (1724–1777), while intellectually he focused almost entirely on evidential research in the Ch'ing dynasty (1644–1911). In August of 1919, he began to write "The Methodology of Ch'ing Scholars' Pursuit of Learning," in which he praised the spirit of the inductive method in Ch'eng I's interpretation of the *ko* in *ko-chih* (investigation of things) as *chih* (to reach), and of Chu Hsi's *chi* in "We must investigate the principle of everything with which we come into contact *(chi).*"[7] However, to Dr. Hu, "Their trust in the absolute wisdom of 'one day achieving wide and far-reaching penetration . . . lacked an emphasis on hypothesis" and was therefore "definitely devoid of science."[8] At the same time, he cited two sections from the *Yü-lei* to show Chu Hsi's spirit of the investigation of things—Chu Hsi's remark that mountain ranges are in the shape of waves because they were originally water that coagulated to become mountains, and his observation in the high mountains of the imprints of conch shells, which also led him to conclude that mountains were originally the sea.[9] Dr. Hu said, "These two sections show that Master Chu did put his investigation of things into actual practice. This type of observation is certainly incorrect but is quite praiseworthy. Geologists in the West observed similar phenomena; in addition, they made daring postulations and engaged in systematic studies that then became epoch-making geology."[10]

This conclusion is reasonably fair. When the anti-Confucian movement was at its height, it was not easy to make a favorable remark about Chu Hsi. Dr. Hu did his best to be objective. Nevertheless, the atmosphere among Chinese intellectuals at the time was extremely opposed to Ch'eng I and Chu Hsi. Hu particularly promoted the philosophy of Tai Chen, which is vigorously critical of Chu Hsi. His *Tai Tung-yüan ti che-hsüeh* (Philosophy of Tai Chen) appeared in 1927, betraying Tai's influence on him. In 1928 he wrote "Several Anti-Neo-Confucian Thinkers." In the section on Tai Chen, he repeatedly quoted Tai's words that the Neo-Confucians of the Sung period (960–1279) "killed people with principle *(li).*" Although he took care to point out that this was Tai's own, partial opinion, he also said that "the defect of the Sung

Neo-Confucians foolishly aimed at the highest level of 'wide and far-reaching penetration.' "[11] He also quoted Ch'eng I's words, "Self-cultivation requires seriousness *(ching);* the pursuit of learning depends on the extension of knowledge," and "To starve to death is a very small matter but to lose one's integrity [as when a widow remarries] is extremely grave."[12] In the section on Yen Yüan (1635–1704), he also quoted Yen's words, "We must demolish a bit of Ch'eng-Chu [Ch'eng I and Chu Hsi] before we can enter a bit into Confucius and Mencius."[13] The quotations were popular slogans in the anti-Neo-Confucian movement, and Dr. Hu was swept along by the strong current of the time.

Dr. Hu's learning was both deep and extensive, but Sung Neo-Confucianism was outside his specialty and Chu Hsi did not especially engage his attention. In the following twenty-five years, he hardly paid heed to this Neo-Confucian thinker. It is true that in 1933, when he lectured at the University of Chicago on "The Tendency of Chinese Culture," he mentioned that Chu Hsi had discovered the nature of fossils three hundred years before Leonardo da Vinci did so in the West.[14] Here he did not refer to the weakness of Chu Hsi's doctrine of the investigation of things but strongly emphasized his positive contribution. Although the tone of the comment was radically different from his earlier ones, it does not necessarily indicate a change of attitude toward Chu Hsi.

In the 1950s, however, his viewpoint changed fundamentally. Dr. Hu was then residing in the United States, leading a somewhat leisurely life. He had also acquired a complete set of the *Yü-lei,* which permitted him to do a systematic study of Chu Hsi. A direct result is the excellent history of the *Yü-lei* that he wrote in August of 1950. This was his first essay on Chu Hsi. It has yet to be surpassed in terms of thoroughness and refinement, and heads the 1962 and 1970 editions of the *Yü-lei* published by Cheng-chung Book Company in Taipei. In 1950 he selected six passages from the *Yü-lei* and three from the *Wen-chi* on Chu Hsi's criticism of the system of honoring the ruler and subordinating the minister. In 1952 he made sixteen selections from the *Wen-chi* and the *Yü-lei* to show Chu Hsi's view on life and death and spiritual beings, and also a number of sayings on the methods of Ch'an (Meditation) Buddhism. His research on Chu Hsi's view on life and death led him to a thorough research on the date of Chu Hsi's last letter to his pupil Liao Te-ming (Liao Tzu-hui, 1169 *cs*),[15] in which he corrected the date proposed by Wang Mao-hung (1668–1741). In 1961, Dr. Hu's sustained interest in Chu Hsi produced a twenty-chapter work entitled the *Chu Tzu yü-lüeh* (Brief anthology of Master Chu's sayings), a manuscript now preserved in the National Central Library in Taipei. It is remarkable, given his voluminous production on various sinological subjects and time-consuming duties as president of the Academia Sinica, that he could still make these selections. In pursuing his abiding interest in the

Neo-Confucian thinker, he must have felt quite differently from the time when he was following Yen Yüan and Tai Chen.

Dr. Hu's most important essay, as far as his study of Chu Hsi is concerned, was presented at the Third East-West Philosophers Conference in Honolulu, Hawaii, in 1959. During the previous ten years, I had occasionally visited him in his apartment in New York City and knew that he had a keen interest in the *Yü-lei*. For the month of the conference, our contact was even more frequent. I knew that although Dr. Hu would never become a follower of Chu Hsi, he had great understanding of him. The title of his eleven-thousand-word essay was "The Scientific Spirit and Method in Chinese Philosophy." Almost half of it was devoted to the spirit and method of Chu Hsi's investigation of things and pursuit of principle to the utmost. According to Dr. Hu, beginning with his collection of commentaries on the *Great Learning,* Chu Hsi devoted his whole life to the *Ssu-shu chang-chü chi-chu,* thereby inaugurating a new era in the study of the Confucian classics. Dr. Hu described Chu Hsi's spirit, methods, and procedures in this study.

One of these methods is to doubt. Dr. Hu quoted Chang Tsai (1020–1077), who said, "In the pursuit of learning, the first thing is to learn to doubt. In the pursuit of learning, one must doubt where there is no doubt. Only then can progress be achieved."[16] He then quoted Chu Hsi's words, "When one has no doubt in reading books, one must be taught to doubt. One's doubts must then be eliminated. Only at this point can progress be made."[17] Following this, he quoted Chu Hsi's injunction that the learner seek to doubt, doubt when he has learned something, and doubt when he encounters some obstruction.[18]

Another method is to have an open mind, that is, "to take a step backward to think."[19] He further quoted Chu Hsi's words, "One must read with an open mind and not have a preconceived opinion. After one is satisfied with the first paragraph, then read the next. One must follow the example of the judge, who listens to every word before making a judgment,"[20] and "Only in this way can one rinse away old opinions to allow new opinions to come in."[21] To Dr. Hu, this was Chu Hsi's method of "hypothesis and verification by evidence." Applying this spirit and methodology to the study of the *Analects,* the *Book of History,* and the *Book of Odes,* Chu Hsi prepared the way for the field of evidential research, which was pioneered by such outstanding scholars as Ku Yen-wu (1613–1682), Yen Jo-ch'ü (1636–1704), Chiang Yung (1681–1762), Tai Chen, Tuan Yü-ts'ai (1735–1815), and Wang Nien-sun (1744–1832). In this connection, Dr. Hu supplied many examples of both Chu Hsi's evidential research and that of scholars of the Ch'ing dynasty. He pointed out that Chu Hsi's method of hypothesis and verification by evidence had to wait for several centuries before it reached its zenith in the Ch'ing period. He regretted that Ch'ing scholars had directed their spirit and method to the study of ancient texts while Western scholars were applying theirs to physical phenomena, thus leading to the development of science and the New World in the West but not in China.[22]

I have always regarded this essay as the most important statement in Dr. Hu's study of Chu Hsi. For one thing, it was the longest article on Chu Hsi's thought in English up until that time. For another, despite its title, the essay is wholly about Chu Hsi, mentioning Ch'eng I only in passing. In addition, it gives a rational explanation of why modern science failed to develop in China. Many explanations have been offered, but they are mostly speculations, whereas Dr. Hu gave a historical and factual reason for China's failure. Finally, he emphasized Chu Hsi's methodology. Previously, Dr. Hu had asserted that there had been no postulation in Neo-Confucianism, but he now recognized that Chu Hsi's great contributions were his hypothesizing and evidential research. In his famous Chinese essay "The Methodology of Ch'ing Scholars' Pursuit of Learning," written four decades before, Dr. Hu had already stated that Chu Hsi's two outstanding characteristics were "daring hypothesis and careful evidence." But in his 1959 essay, almost all the quotations from Chu Hsi are from the *Yü-lei,* chapter 11, on the method of reading, not from the amended commentary on the fifth chapter of the *Great Learning,* in which the goal was a "wide and far-reaching penetration"—a phrase that Dr. Hu no longer repeated, much less condemned. However, Dr. Hu's 1959 essay does say that Chu Hsi's spirit and methodology can both be traced to his investigation on the *Great Learning.* This being the case, having doubts and having an open mind are both matters of the investigation of things, and a wide and far-reaching penetration to seek absolute wisdom is not inconsistent with the scientific spirit.

During his sojourn in the United States, Dr. Hu lectured in many places, and his admirers often requested his calligraphy. Many times he happily wrote, "Rather be full than brief, rather be low than lofty, rather be near than far, and rather be clumsy than clever," and then added, "Chu Hsi's words."[23] To him, this was a proverb. The Hu Shih Memorial Institute of the Academia Sinica at Taipei has issued a number of postcards of proverbs in Dr. Hu's handwriting. My favorite is this sixteen-character saying by Chu Hsi, because it was also the formula of Dr. Hu.

## Notes

1. *Hsiao-hsüeh* [Elementary education], ch. 5 "Fine Words" pt. 2, sec. 14. The *Hsiao-hsüeh* consists of passages of fine words and good deeds from various sources, as examples for young students.

2. Hu Shih, *Ssu-shih tzu-shu* [Self-reflections at forty] (Shanghai: Ya-tung Library, 1933), pp. 41–42.

3. *Chin-ssu lu* [Reflections on things at hand], ch. 3, sec. 6. See my translation, *Reflections on Things at Hand* (New York: Columbia University Press, 1967), p. 90. Ch'eng I's saying originally comes from the *I-shu* [Surviving works], 6:1a, in the *Erh-Ch'eng ch'üan-shu* [Complete works of the two Ch'engs] (*SPPY* ed.).

4. *Ssu-shi tzu-shu*, pp. 61, 73–74.

5. *Ibid.*, p. 61.

6. Hu Sung-p'ing, *Hu Shih Hsien-sheng nien-p'u ch'ang-p'ien ch'u-kao* [Preliminary draft of the full-length chronological biography of Dr. Hu Shih] (Taipei: Ching-lien Press, 1984) p. 60.

7. Ch'eng I, *I-shu*, 22A:1a; Chu Hsi, *Ta-hsüeh chang-chü* [Commentary on the *Great Learning*], comment on ch. 5.

8. *Hu Shih wen-ts'un* [Preserved writings of Hu Shih] (Taipei: Yüan-tung Book Co., 1953), first collection, p. 386.

9. *Yü-lei*, ch. 94, secs. 16–17 (pp. 3759–3761).

10. *Hu Shih wen-ts'un*, first collection, p. 387.

11. *Ibid.*, third collection, pp. 76–77, 82.

12. *Ibid.*, pp. 71, 76. The first quotation is from the *I-shu*, 18:5b, and the second from *ibid.*, 22B:3a. See ch. 30 above, p. 540.

13. *Ibid.*, p. 63. The quotation is from the *Yen-Li i-shu* [Surviving works of Yen Yüan and Li Kung] (*Chi-fu ts'ung-shu* [Capital and its surroundings series] ed.), vol. 2, chronological biography, pt. 2, p. 25b.

14. Hu Shih, *The Chinese Renaissance* (Chicago: University of Chicago Press, 1934), p. 59.

15. *Hu Shih Hsien-sheng nien-p'u ch'ang-pien ch'u-kao*, pp. 2201–2217. See also *The Bulletin of the Institute of History and Philosophy, Academia Sinica* (in Chinese), vol. 34, *In Memory of the Late Dr. Hu Shih*, pt. 2 (1963), pp. 802–803. These manuscripts are now preserved in the *Hu Shih shou-kao* [Hu Shih's manuscripts], ninth collection, pp. 79–137.

16. As pointed out by Dr. Yü Ying-shih (*Hu Shih in Modern History of Chinese Thought* [in Chinese] [Taipei: Lien-ching Publishing Enterprises, 1984], p. 45, n. 56), this saying is not found in the *Chang Tzu ch'üan-shu* [Complete works of Master Chang Tsai]. Dr. Yü is correct. However, in the *Chang Tzu ch'üan-shu* (*SPPY* ed.), ch. 6, "Moral Principles," p. 4a, there is the saying, "The reason for reading books is to dispel one's doubts and to clarify what one has not understood. Each time one sees that one's knowledge has increased, there will be progress. One must doubt where there is no doubt. Only then can progress be achieved." Dr. Yü probably had this passage in mind when he said that Chang Tsai had a similar saying.

17. *Yü-lei*, ch. 11, sec. 78 (p. 296).

18. *Ibid.*, sec. 76 (p. 295).

19. *Ibid.*, sec. 30 (p. 285).

20. *Ibid.*, sec. 36 (p. 284).

21. *Ibid.*, sec. 32 (p. 286).

22. Charles Moore, *The Chinese Mind* (Honolulu: University of Hawaii Press, 1967), pp. 104–131.

23. *Yü-lei*, ch. 116, sec. 21 (p. 4450). The wording is slightly different, but the meaning is the same.

# CHINESE GLOSSARY

*ai chih li* 愛之理
*an* 菴
An-chih 安之
An-ch'ing-fu Shu-yüan 安慶府書院
*an-fu-shih* 按撫使
An Hsi-fan, Wo-su 安希范我素
An-jen 安仁
*an-lo* 安樂
*an-ming* 安命
*an-p'ing shou-tao* 安貧守道
Anu 阿耨
Asakura Gisuke 朝倉儀助

Ch'ai Chung-hsing 柴中行
Chan I-chih, T'i-jen 詹儀之體仁
Chan Jo-shui, Kan-ch'üan 湛若水
　甘泉
*Chan Kan-ch'üan Hsien-sheng wen-chi*
　湛甘泉先生文集
*Chan-t'ang-chuen* 湛堂準
Chan T'i-jen, Yüan-shan 詹體仁
　元善
Chan Wing-tsit 陳榮捷
Ch'an 禪
Chang 章
Chang Chi 張籍
Chang Chieh, Meng-yüan 張杰
　孟遠

Chang Chiu-ch'eng, Tzu-shao,
　Wu-kou 張九成子韶无垢
Chang Cho 張拙
Chang-chou 漳州
*Chang-chou shih-chi* 漳州史蹟
Chang Chün, Wei Kung 張浚魏公
Chang Hsia, Yüan-te 張洽元德
Chang I, Ssu-shu 張繹思叔
Chang Kuei-mu 張貴模
Chang Li-wen 張立文
Chang Liang, Tzu-fang 張良子房
Chang Po-hsing 張伯行
Chang San 張三
Chang Shang-tso, Fu-chih 張商佐
　輔之
Chang Shang-ying, T'ien-chüeh,
　Wu-chin 張商英天覺無盡
Chang Shih, Ch'in-fu, Ching-fu,
　Nan-hsüan 張栻欽夫敬夫南軒
Chang Shu-yeh, Chung-wen Kung
　張叔夜忠文公
Chang Tsai, Heng-ch'ü 張載橫渠
Chang Tsung-yüeh 張宗說
Chang Tun-i 張敦頤
*Chang Tzu Cheng-meng chu* 張子
　正蒙注
*Chang Tzu ch'üan-shu* 張子全書
*Chang Tzu yü-lu* 張子語錄

Chang Ying, Mao-hsien 章穎茂獻
*Ch'ang-hsi so-yü* 長溪瑣語
Ch'ang-lo 長樂
*Ch'ang-p'ing ch'a-yen kung-shih*
    常平茶鹽公事
Ch'ang-ting 長汀
Chao 趙
Chao Ch'i 趙岐
Chao Cho, Ching-chao 趙焯景昭
Chao Ching-ming, Cho-chai
    趙景明拙齋
Chao-chou 趙州
Chao Ch'ung-hsien 趙崇憲
Chao Fan, Ch'ang-fu 趙蕃昌父
Chao Fang 趙汸
Chao Ju-yü 趙汝愚
*Chao-lun* 肇論
Chao Shan-tai 趙善待
Chao Shih-hsia 趙師夏
*Chao-shih k'o-yü* 晁氏客語
Chao Shih-kung 趙師邺
Chao Shih-tuan 趙師端
Chao Shih-yung, Jan-tao 趙師雍
    然道
Chao-wen Shu-yüan 昭文書院
Chao Yen-shu, Tzu-ch'in 趙彥肅
    子欽
Ch'ao-chou 潮州
*ch'ao-feng lang* 朝奉郎
*ch'ao-feng ta-fu* 朝奉大夫
Ch'ao-yang 潮陽
*chen* 震
*Chen-kao* 真誥
Chen Lai 陳來
*Chen-pai wu-shu* 貞白五書
Chen Te-hsiu 真德秀
Chen-tsung 真宗
Ch'en 陳
Ch'en Ch'ang-hou 陳昌侯
Ch'en Chi, Ching-yüan 陳紀景元
Ch'en Chi-ju 陳繼儒
Ch'en Ch'i-chung 陳齊仲
Ch'en Chien 陳建
Ch'en Chih 陳芝

Ch'en Chih, Ch'i-chih 陳埴器之
Ch'en Ching-chih 陳敬之
Ch'en Chiu-ch'uan 陳九川
Ch'en Ch'un, An-ch'ing 陳淳安卿
Ch'en Chün-ch'ing 陳俊卿
Ch'en Fu-liang, Chün-chü 陳傅良
    君舉
Ch'en Hang, Ch'iu-fang, T'ai-ch'u
    陳沆秋舫太初
Ch'en Hou-chih 陳厚之
Ch'en Hsien-chang, Pai-sha 陳獻章
    白沙
Ch'en Hsüan 陳選
Ch'en I, Po-tsao 陳沂伯澡
Ch'en Kang, Cheng-chi 陳剛正己
Ch'en Kuan, Liao-lao, Liao-weng
    陳瓘了老了翁
Ch'en Liang, T'ung-fu 陳亮同甫
*Ch'en Liang chi* 陳亮集
Ch'en Liang-ts'ai 陳良才
Ch'en Lieh 陳烈
Ch'en Lung-cheng, Chi-t'ing
    陳龍正幾亭
Ch'en Mi 陳宓
Ch'en Shih-chih, Yen-chung
    陳士直彥中
Ch'en Shou, Shih-chung 陳守師中
Ch'en Ssu-ch'ien, T'ui-chih 陳思謙
    退之
Ch'en Tan, Ming-chung 陳旦明仲
Ch'en T'uan 陳搏
Ch'en T'ung 陳統
Ch'en Wei-tao 陳衛道
Ch'en Wen-wei, Ts'ai-ch'ing
    陳文蔚才卿
Ch'en Yu 陳樀
Ch'en Yü 陳械
Ch'en Yüan 陳淵
Cheng 鄭
*cheng* 正
Cheng An-tao 鄭安道
Cheng Ch'iao, Yü-chung 鄭樵漁仲
Cheng Chien, Tzu-ming 鄭鑑自明
Cheng-chung 正中

Cheng Chung-li 鄭仲禮

*cheng-chüeh* 正覺

Cheng-ho 政和

Cheng Hsiang, Wei-min Kung
　鄭驤威愍公

*Cheng-hsieh lun* 正邪論

Cheng Hsüan 鄭玄

*Cheng-i* 正異

*Cheng-i hsin-fa* 正易心法

*Cheng-i-t'ang ch'üan-shu* 正誼堂全書

Cheng K'o-hsüeh, Tzu-shang
　鄭可學子上

Cheng Liang-sheng 鄭樑生

*Cheng-meng* 正蒙

*Cheng-meng shih* 正蒙釋

*cheng-ming* 正命

Cheng Po-hsiung, Ching-wang
　鄭伯熊景望

Cheng-shan Shu-yüan 鄭山書院

*cheng-t'ung* 正統

*cheng-tzu* 正字

Ch'eng (king) 成
　　(surname) 程

*ch'eng* (to perfect) 成
　　(sincerity) 誠

Ch'eng Chao-hsiung 程兆熊

Ch'eng Chiung, K'o-chiu 程迥可久

Ch'eng-chung 澄衷

Ch'eng Hao, Ming-tao, Po-ch'un
　程顥明道伯淳

Ch'eng Hsün, Yün-fu 程洵允夫

Ch'eng I, Cheng-shu, I-ch'uan
　程頤正叔伊川

Ch'eng-kuan 澄觀

Ch'eng Kung, Chung-pi, Liu-hu
　程珙仲璧柳湖

Ch'eng Min-cheng 程敏政

Ch'eng Shen-fu 程深父

Ch'eng-shih 程氏

Ch'eng-tsu 成祖

Ch'eng Tuan-li 程端禮

Ch'eng Tuan-meng, Cheng-ssu
　程端蒙正思

Ch'eng T'ung 程曈

Ch'eng Tzu 程子

*Ch'eng Tzu hsiang-pen* 程子詳本

Ch'eng Yung-ch'i 程永奇

Chi 稷

*chi* (contact) 即
　　(incipient) 幾

*Chi-chu* 集註

*Chi-fu ts'ung-shu* 畿輔叢書

*Chi-i* 祭義

*Chi-ku lu* 集古錄

*chi-li* 寂歷

*Chi-t'ing ch'üan-chi* 幾亭全集

Chi-yen 季延

*ch'i* 氣

*Ch'i-meng ch'u-sung* 啟蒙初誦

*ch'i-ping* 氣稟

Ch'i-shui 蘄水

*Ch'i-tung yeh-yü* 齊東野語

Chia 嘉

Chia-ching 嘉靖

*Chia-fan* 家範

Chia-ho 嘉禾

Chia-hui-t'ang 嘉會堂

*chia-jen* 家人

*Chia-t'ai p'u-teng lu* 嘉泰普燈錄

*chia-wu* 甲午

*Chia-yu chi* 嘉祐集

Chiang-chou 江州

*chiang Chung-tzu* 將仲子

Chiang-hsi 江西

Chiang-nan 江南

*Chiang-nan hsi-lu t'i-tien hsing-yü*
　江南西路提點刑獄

Chiang Mo, Te-kung 江默德功

Chiang-shan 江山

Chiang Ssu, Wen-ch'ing 江嗣文卿

Chiang-yu 江右

Chiang Yung, Yüan-shih 江永元適

*ch'iang-tzu* 腔子

Chiao Hsün 焦循

*chiao-shu-lang* 校書郎

Ch'iao-nien 喬年

Chieh 桀

*chieh* 結

Chieh Chih 解智
*chieh-ti* 揭帝
*Chieh-tzu t'ung-lu* 戒子通錄
*chieh-wen* 節文
Chieh-yang 揭陽
*chien* 監
Chien-an 建安
Chien-an Shu-yüan 建安書院
Chien-chou 建州
*Chien-hu chi* 堅瓠集
Chien-ning 建寧
Chien-ou 建甌
Chien-shih Meng-chin 簡氏猛進
Chien-yang 建陽
*Chien-yang hsien-chih* 建陽縣志
Chien-yen 建炎
*Chien-yen i-lai hsi-nien yao-lu* 建炎
    以來繫年要錄
*Chien-yü Hsien-sheng wen-chi*
    健餘先生文集
Ch'ien 錢
*ch'ien* 乾
Ch'ien-chih 謙之
Ch'ien Mu 錢穆
Ch'ien Mu-chih, Tzu-sheng
    錢木之子升
Ch'ien-shan 鉛山
*Ch'ien-shan hsien-chih* 鉛山縣志
Ch'ien-tao 乾道
Ch'ien Te-hung 錢德洪
*chih* (to extend) 致
    (niece) 姪
    (to reach) 至
    (wisdom) 智
*chih-chih* 知止
*chih-li* 支離
Chih-nan Shang-jen 志南上人
Chih-pi-ko 直祕閣
Chih Tun, Tao-lin 支遁道林
*Chih-yen* 知言
*ch'ih-k'ou* 赤口
Ch'ih-ts'ai Shih-mo Chiao 吃菜
    事魔教
Chin (dynasty) 金
    (state) 晉

Chin-ch'eng 金城
Chin Chi-min 金濟民
Chin-hsi 金溪
Chin-hua 金華
*Chin-hua ts'ung-shu* 金華叢書
*Chin-kang ching* 金剛經
Chin-ling 金陵
Chin Lü-hsiang, Jen-shan 金履祥
    仁山
Chin-men 金門
*Chin-men ts'ung-shu* 金門叢書
Chin P'eng-yüeh 金朋說
*chin-shih* 進士
*Chin-shih han-chi ts'ung-k'an* 近世
    漢籍叢刊
*Chin-ssu hsü-lu* 近思續錄
*Chin-ssu lu* 近思錄
*Chin-ssu lu chi-chieh* 近思錄集解
*Chin-ssu lu chi-chu* 近思錄集註
*Chin-ssu lu chi-shuo* 近思錄集說
*Chin-ssu lu pu-chu* 近思錄補註
*Chin-ssu lu t'ai-yao* 近思錄提要
Ch'in 欽
Ch'in Kuei 秦檜
*ching* (quiet, tranquility) 靜
    (reverence, seriousness) 敬
    (well) 井
Ching-an 淨安
Ching-chou 荊州
Ching-hsiang-t'ang 靜香堂
Ching-Hu 荊湖
*Ching-i k'ao* 經義考
Ching-lien 荊聯
Ching-shan 荊山
*ching-she* 精舍
Ching-sheng 淨昇
*Ching-shuo* 經說
*Ching-te ch'uan-teng lu* 景德傳燈錄
*Ching-t'ien lei-shuo* 井田類說
Ching-t'u 淨土
Ch'ing-chiang 清江
Ch'ing-jui-ko 清鎣閣
*ch'ing-hsü-i-ta* 清虛一大
Ch'ing-hu 清湖
Ch'ing-hui 清暉

Ch'ing-li 慶歷

*Ch'ing-tai pi-chi ts'ung-k'an* 清代
筆記叢刊

Ch'ing-tien 青田

Ch'ing-yüan 慶元

Chiu-hua 九華

Chiu-i-shan Shu-yüan 九嶷山書院

*chiu-pen* 舊本

Ch'iu 秋

Ch'iu K'uei 丘葵

*Ch'iu-shih pien* 求是編

Ch'iu Ying, Tzu-fu 丘膺子服

Cho 卓

Cho-chai 拙齊

Chŏng Ch'uman 鄭秋巒

Chou (duke, surname) 周

Chou Chieh, Shu-chin 周介叔瑾

Chou Ch'ing-sou, Lien-fu 周清叟
廉夫

Chou Heng, Tao-t'ung 周衡道通

*Chou-i chu* 周易注

*Chou-i k'ou-i* 周易口義

Chou I-kung 周益公

*Chou-i pen-i* 周易本義

Chou Ju-teng, Hai-men 周汝登
海門

*Chou-kuan* 周官

Chou Kung-shu 周公恕

*Chou-li* 周禮

Chou Mu, Shun-pi 周謨舜弼

Chou Pi-ta 周必大

Chou P'u, Ch'un-jen 周樸純仁

Chou Shen-fu 周深父

*Chou-shu* 周書

Chou Tun-i, Mao-shu, Lien-hsi
周敦頤茂叔濂溪

*Chou Tzu ch'üan-shu* 周子全書

Chou Yeh 周曄

Chou Yü-t'ung 周予同

Chu 祝

Chu-chou 儲州

Chu Ch'üeh 祝確

Chu Fu 朱柈

Chu Heng 朱衡

Chu Hsi, Chung-hui, Hui-an, Tun-
weng, Tzu-yang, Wen Kung,
Yüan-hui 朱熹仲晦晦庵遯翁
紫陽文公元晦

*Chu Hsi chi-ch'ih hsüeh-p'ai Fu-chien
ti-fang-shih tzu-liao* 朱熹及其學派
福建地方史資料

*Chu Hsi hsing-tsung k'ao* 朱熹行踪考

*Chu Hsi ssu-hsiang yen-chiu* 朱熹思想
研究

*Chu Hsi ti ch'ou-o mien-mao* 朱熹的
醜惡面貌

*Chu Hsi yü Chin-men* 朱熹與金門

*Chu-hsüeh lun-chi* 朱學論集

*Chu-hu chi* 燭湖集

Chu-i Shu-yüan 主一書院

Chu I-tsun 朱彝尊

Chu K'e-chia 朱克家

Chu-ko Ch'ien-neng, Ch'eng-chih
諸葛千能誠之

Chu-ko Liang, K'ung-ming, Wu-
hou 諸葛亮孔明武侯

*chu-kuan* 主管

Chu Kuang-t'ing, Kung-yen
朱光庭公掞

*chu-kung* 諸公

Chu Kuo-chen 朱國楨

Chu-lin 竹林

Chu-lin Ching-she 竹林精舍

Chu Lu-shu 朱魯叔

Chu Mu 祝穆

*chu-pu* 主簿

Chu Ron-Guey 朱榮貴

Chu Shu, Shou-chih 朱塾受之

*Chu-Ssu yen-jen* 洙泗言仁

Chu Sung, Wei-chai 朱松韋齋

Chu T'ai-ch'ing 朱泰卿

Chu Tsai, Ching-chih 朱在敬之

*chu-tsai* 主宰

*chu-tso tso-lang* 著作佐郎

Chu Ts'en 朱岑

*Chu Tsu ch'üan-shu* 朱子全書

*Chu Tzu hsin-hsüeh-an* 朱子新學案

*Chu Tzu hsin-t'an-so* 朱子新探索

*Chu Tzu hsing-chuang* 朱子行狀

*Chu Tzu i-shu* 朱子遺書

*Chu Tzu i-tse ssu-i* 朱子易簀私議

*Chu Tzu lun-hsüeh ch'ieh-yao yü* 朱子
論學切要語

*Chu Tzu men-jen* 朱子門人

*Chu Tzu nien-p'u* 朱子年譜

*Chu Tzu nien-p'u k'ao-i* 朱子年譜考異

*Chu Tzu shih-chi* 朱子實紀

*Chu Tzu shih-shih* 朱子事實

*Chu Tzu ssu-shu chi-chu tien-chü k'ao*
朱子四書集註典據考

*Chu Tzu wan-nien ch'üan-lun* 朱子
晚年全論

*Chu Tzu wan-nien ting-lun p'ing-shu*
朱子晚年定論評述

*Chu Tzu wen-chi* 朱子文集

*Chu Tzu wen-chi ta-ch'üan lei-pien*
朱子文集大全類編

*Chu Tzu wen-yü tsuan-pien* 朱子
文語纂編

*Chu Tzu yü-lei* 朱子語類

*Chu Tzu yü-lei p'ing* 朱子語類評

*Chu Tzu yü-lüeh* 朱子語畧

*Chu Wen Kung meng-tien chi* 朱文公
夢奠記

Chu Yeh, Wen-chih 朱埜文之

Chu Yü 朱玉

Ch'u 楚

Ch'u Ch'ai-hsü 儲柴墟

Ch'u-chou 楚州

Ch'u Jen-huo 褚人穫

*Ch'u-shih piao* 出師表

*Ch'u-tz'u* 楚詞

Ch'u Yung, Hsing-chih 儲用行之

*chuan-yün fu-shih* 轉運副使

*ch'uan-ching* 傳經

*Ch'uan-hsi lu* 傳習錄

Ch'uan-i Shu-yüan 傳貽書院

Chuang 莊

Chuang-tsung 莊宗

Chuang Tzu, Chou 莊子周

*Chubaku muchin setsu* 沖漠無朕說

*Chuja haengjang* 朱子行狀

*Chuja haengjang chipchu* 朱子行狀輯注

*Ch'un-ch'iu fan-lu* 春秋繁露

*Ch'un-ch'iu san-chuan hui-t'ung* 春秋
三傳會同

Ch'un-hsi 淳熙

*chung* (central, equilibrium, Mean) 中
(Conscientiousness, loyalty) 忠

Chung Chen 鍾震

*chung-ho* 中和

*Chung-ho chiu-shuo hsü* 中和舊說序

Chung-hua 中華

*Chung-hua ta-tsang-ching* 中華大藏經

Chung-hui (ancient name) 仲虺
(Chu Hsi's name) 仲晦

*Chung-kuo che-hsüeh shih lun-ts'ung*
中國哲學史論叢

*Chung-kuo che-hsüeh ssu-hsiang lun-chi*
中國哲學思想論集

*Chung-kuo che-hsüeh ssu-hsiang lun-chi:
Sung-Ming p'ien* 中國哲學思想
論集：宋明篇

*Chung-kuo che-hsüeh ssu-hsiang-shih*
中國哲學思想史

*Chung-kuo che-hsüeh tz'u-tien ta-ch'üan*
中國哲學辭典大全

*Chung-kuo che-hsüeh yüan-lun: yüan-
hsing p'ien* 中國哲學原論：原性篇

Chung-ni 仲尼

*chung-shu* 忠恕

*Chung-yung* 中庸

*Chung-yung chang-chü* 中庸章句

*Chung-yung chi-lüeh* 中庸輯畧

*Chung-yung chiang-shu* 中庸講疏

*Chung-yung chieh* 中庸解

*Chung-yung huo-wen* 中庸或問

*Chung-yung shuo* 中庸說

*Chung-yung ta-ch'üan* 中庸大全

*Chung-yung tsung-lun* 中庸總論

Ch'ung-an 崇安

*Ch'ung-an hsien-chih* 崇安縣志

*Ch'ung-an-hsien hsin-chih* 崇安縣新志

*Ch'ung-cheng-tien shuo-shu* 崇政殿
說書

Ch'ung-fu 崇福

*Ch'ung-hsü chih-te chen-ching* 沖虛
至德真經

Ch'ung-t'ai 崇泰
Ch'ung-tao-kuan 崇道觀
Ch'ung-yu 冲佑
*Chü-yeh lu* 居業錄
Ch'ü 衢
*ch'ü* 取
Ch'ü-chou 衢州
Ch'ü Yüan 屈原
Ch'üan-chou 泉州
*ch'üan-fu* 泉府
Ch'üan Tsu-wang 全祖望
Chün 鈞
*Ch'ün-chi ch'uan-chieh* 羣己權界
*Ch'ün-fu lu* 羣輔錄

*Daikanwa jiten* 大漢和辭典

En-lao 恩老
*erh* 而
Erh-Ch'eng 二程
*Erh-Ch'eng ch'üan-shu* 二程全書
*Erh-Ch'eng Hsien-sheng yü-lei* 二程
　先生語類

Fa-chou 法舟
*Fa-hua ching* 法華經
Fa-tsang 法藏
Fan Chung-yen 范仲淹
Fan Jan 范染
Fan Ju-kuei 范如奎
Fan Nien-te, Po-ch'ung 范念德伯崇
Fan Tsu-yü 范祖禹
Fan Yüan-yü 范元裕
*fang-chang* 方丈
Fang Hsien-fu, Shu-hsien 方獻夫
　叔賢
Fang I, Pin-wang 方誼賓王
Fang La 方臘
Fang Lei, Keng-tao 方耒耕道
Fang Shih-yao, Po-mu 方士繇伯謨
Fang Tz'u-jung 方次榮
*fei* 費
Fei Hsi 費熙
*Fei Tao-feng i-shu* 費道峯遺書

*Fen-lei Chin-ssu lu chi-chieh* 分類近思
　錄集解
Feng-an 奉安
Feng-ch'eng 豐城
Feng K'o 馮柯
Feng-lien 豐蓮
Feng Yün-hao 馮雲濠
*Fo-fa chin-t'ang-p'ien* 佛法金湯篇
*fo-fa mo-tsung* 佛法魔宗
Fo-ting 佛頂
*Fo-tsu li-tai t'ung-tsai* 佛祖歷代通載
Fu (name) 輔
　(prefect) 傅
*fu* 復
*Fu-chi miao-chi* 孚濟廟記
Fu Ch'eng-tzu 傅誠子
Fu Ch'i, Po-ch'eng 傅耆伯成
Fu-chien 福建
*Fu-chien t'ung-chih* 福建通志
Fu-chou 撫州
Fu-hsi 伏羲
Fu Hsü, Shun-kung 符叙舜功
Fu-k'ou 扶溝
Fu Kuang, Ch'ien-an, Han-ch'ing
　輔廣潛庵漢卿
Fu Meng-ch'üan, Tzu-yüan
　傅夢泉子淵
Fu-ning 福寧
Fu Pi 富弼
Fu Tzu-te 傅自得
Fu Wan 輔萬
*fu-wen* 扶問
Fu-yüeh 傅說
Fujitsuka Chikashi 藤塚鄰

Gao Ling-yin 高令印
*Gimon roku* 疑問錄
*Gōtō kinshi roku* 鼇頭近思錄
Gotō Toshimizu 後藤俊瑞

Han 漢
*Han Ch'ang-li ch'üan-chi* 韓昌黎全集
Han-ch'üan 寒泉
Han-ch'üan Ching-she 寒泉精舍

Han-ch'üan-wu 寒泉塢

Han Fei Tzu 韓非子

Han-hsi Kuan 寒栖館

Han Hsin 韓信

*han-lin* 翰林

Han Mongnin 韓夢麟

Han Shih-ch'i 韓士奇

*Han shu* 漢書

Han T'o-chou 韓侂冑

Han-yang 漢陽

Han Yü 韓愈

*hao* 號

Hao Ching 郝敬

*hao-jan chih ch'i* 浩然之氣

Heng (Mount in Hopei) 恒
    (Mount in Hunan) 衡

Heng-chou 衡州

Heng-shan 恒山

Heng-yang 衡陽

Higashi Masazumi 東正純

Hiroike gakuen 廣池學園

Hiroshima 廣島

Ho 和

*ho* (together, both) 合
    (harmony) 和

Ho Chi, Pei-shan 何基北山

*Ho-ching yü-lu* 和靖語錄

Ho Chü-yüan 何巨元

Ho Hao, Shu-ching 何鎬叔京

Ho-hu 荷湖

*Ho-lin yü-lu* 鶴林玉露

Ho-shan Shu-yüan 鶴山書院

Hou Chung-liang, Shih-sheng
    侯仲良師聖

*Hou-Han shu* 後漢書

Hsi (private name) 熹
    (surname) 奚

Hsi-chin 西津

Hsi-chung 熙中

*hsi-hsin* 洗心

Hsi Kai-ch'ing 襲蓋卿

Hsi-lin 西林

*Hsi-ming* 西銘

Hsi-ning 熙寧

Hsi Shu, Yüan-shan 席書元山

Hsi-t'a 西塔

Hsi-tsu 僖祖

*Hsi-yin-hsüan ts'ung-shu* 惜陰軒叢書

Hsia-men 廈門

Hsiang 湘

Hsiang An-shih, P'ing-fu 項安世
    平父

Hsiang-feng 翔風

Hsiang-shan 象山

*Hsiang-shan ch'üan-chi* 象山全集

*Hsiang-shan ssu-hsiang lin-chung t'ung-
    yü Chu Tzu* 象山思想臨終同於
    朱子

*Hsiang-shan wen-chi* 象山文集

Hsiang-t'an 湘潭

Hsiang Wei-hsin 項維新

*hsiang-yüeh* 鄉約

*hsiao* 孝

*Hsiao ching k'an-wu* 孝經刊誤

Hsiao Ho 蕭何

*Hsiao-hsüeh* 小學

*Hsiao-hsüeh chi-chieh* 小學集解

*Hsiao-hsüeh chi-chu* 小學集註

*Hsiao-hsüeh ch'i-yeh* 小學稽業

*hsiao-kuo* 小過

Hsiao-tsung 孝宗

Hsiao Tzu-liang 蕭子良

*hsiao-wu-niang* 小五娘

*hsiao-ya* 小雅

Hsieh Chiao 謝教

Hsieh Cho-chung 謝綽中

*hsieh-chü* 絜矩

Hsieh Liang-tso, Shang-ts'ai
    謝良佐上蔡

Hsien-an 顯菴

Hsien-ch'ing Ching-she 咸清精舍

Hsien-chou 仙州

Hsien-ch'un 咸淳

*Hsien-p'i lu* 閑闢錄

*hsien-t'ien* 先天

Hsien-t'ung 咸通

*hsin* (faithfulness) 信
    (heart, mind) 心

Hsin-an 新安
*hsin chih te* 心之德
*Hsin ching* 心經
Hsin-chou 信州
*hsin-ch'ou* 辛丑
*hsin-ch'uan* 心傳
*hsin-fa* 心法
Hsin-hsüeh 心學
*hsin i ch'eng-hsing* 心以成性
Hsin-ming 新民
*Hsin-t'i yü hsing-t'i* 心體與性體
*hsin t'ung hsing-ch'ing* 心統性情
*Hsin-ya hsüeh-pao* 新亞學報
*hsing* 性
*Hsing-chih* 性之
*Hsing-chuang* 行狀
*Hsing-li ching-i* 性理精義
*Hsing-li ch'ün-shu chü-chieh* 性理羣書
  句解
*Hsing-li ta-ch'üan* 性理大全
*Hsing-li tzu-hsün* 性理字訓
Hsing Shu, Ho-shu 邢恕和叔
Hsing-tzu 星子
Hsiung Chieh 熊節
Hsiung Chien 熊鑒
Hsiung Kang-ta 熊剛大
Hsiung Meng-chao 熊夢兆
Hsü 許
Hsü Chao-jan 徐昭然
Hsü Ch'eng-chih 徐成之
Hsü Chi, Chieh-hsiao 徐積節孝
Hsü Ch'ien, Pai-yün 許謙白雲
Hsü Chin-chih 許進之
*Hsü Chin-hua ts'ung-shu* 續金華叢書
Hsü Chung-ying 許中應
Hsü Heng, Lu-chai 許衡魯齊
Hsü Hsün-shih, Pi-hsien 胥訓實
  必先
*Hsü ku-tsun-su yü-yao* 續古尊宿語要
Hsü Po 徐焞
Hsü Sheng, Shun-chih 許升順之
*Hsü-shih pi-ching* 徐氏筆精
*Hsü-tsang-ching* 續藏經
Hsü Ts'un, Ch'eng-sou 徐存誠叟

*Hsü tzu-chih t'ung-chien* 續資治通鑑
Hsü Wen-ch'ing, Ssu-yüan 徐文卿
  思遠
Hsü Yen-chang 徐彥章
Hsü Yü, Chü-fu 徐寓居父
Hsü Yüan-p'ing 徐元聘
*hsüan-chiao-lang* 宣教郎
Hsüan-chou 宣州
Hsüan-chüeh 玄覺
Hsüeh Chi-hsüan, Shih-lung
  薛季宣士龍
*Hsüeh-chin t'ao-yüan* 學津討原
Hsüeh Hsüan 薛瑄
Hsüeh-ku, see Liu Hsüeh-ku
*Hsüeh-pu t'ung-pien* 學部通辨
*Hsün-meng hsin-shu* 訓蒙新書
Hsün Tzu, Ch'ing 荀子卿
Hu 胡
*hu* 狐
Hu An-chih, Shu-ch'i 胡安之叔器
Hu An-kuo, Wen-ting 胡安國文定
Hu-chou 湖州
Hu Chü-jen 胡居仁
Hu-Hsiang 湖湘
Hu Hsien, Chi-hsi 胡憲藉溪
Hu Hung (1106–1161) 胡宏
  (1163 *cs*) 胡紘
*hu-jan* 忽然
Hu-kuo 護國
Hu Mei-ch'i 胡美琦
Hu Shih 胡適
Hu Shih, Kuang-chung 胡實廣仲
*Hu Shih Hsien-sheng nien-p'u chien-pien*
  胡適先生年譜簡編
*Hu Shih Hsien-sheng nien-p'u ch'ang-
  p'ien ch'u-kao* 胡適先生年譜長篇
  初稿
*Hu Shih shou-kao* 胡適手稿
*Hu Shih wen-ts'un* 胡適文存
Hu Sung-p'ing 胡頌平
Hu Ta-shih, Chi-sui 胡大時季隨
Hu Ta-yüan, Po-feng 胡大原伯逢
*Hu Tzu chih-yen* 胡子知言
*Hu Tzu chih-yen i-i* 胡子知言疑義

Hu Yen-chung 胡彥仲
Hu Yin, Ming-chung 胡寅明仲
Hu Yung, Po-liang 胡泳伯量
Hu Yüan, An-ting 胡瑗安定
Hua 華
Hua-chou 華州
*hua-t'ou* 話頭
Hua-yen 華嚴
*Hua-yen ching* 華嚴經
*Hua-yen ho-lun* 華嚴合論
*Hua-yen ta-chih* 華嚴大旨
Huai 淮
Huai-an 淮安
Huan-hsi Ching-she 環溪精舍
Huang Chang-chien 黃彰健
Huang Chen 黃震
*Huang-chi ching-shih shu* 皇極經世書
Huang Ch'iao-chung, Tao-fu
　黃樵仲道夫
Huang Chin-shu 黃晉叔
Huang Ch'ing-ch'ing 黃清卿
Huang Hao, Shang-po 黃灝商伯
Huang Hsien-tzu. Ching-chih
　黃顯子敬之
Huang Hsing-tseng, Mien-chih
　黃省曾勉之
Huang Hsün, Tzu-keng 黃笛子耕
Huang I-kang 黃義剛
Huang I-yung 黃義勇
Huang Kan, Chih-ch'ing, Mien-
chai 黃榦直卿勉齋
Huang Lo 黃輅
Huang-lung 黃龍
Huang-mei 黃梅
*huang-men* 黃門
*Huang Mien-chai chi* 黃勉齋集
Huang Po-chia 黃百家
Huang Shih 黃奭
Huang Shih-i 黃士毅
Huang Shu-ching 黃叔璥
Huang Tsung-hsi 黃宗義
*Huang-wang ta-chi* 皇王大紀
Huang Wei-chih, Shu-chang
　黃維之叔張

Huang Yüeh-chou 黃粵洲
Hui-an 晦菴
Hui-an ping-sou 晦菴病叟
Hui-an t'ung-sou 晦菴通叟
Hui-chao 慧照
*Hui-ch'en ch'ien-lu* 揮塵前錄
Hui-chou 徽州
Hui Kuo-kung 徽國公
Hui-weng 晦翁
Hui-yüan 慧遠
*hun* 魂
*hun-lun* 渾淪
*Hu-nan Sung-tai shu-yüan kai-k'uang*
　湖南宋代書院概況
Hung-chien 鴻漸
Hung Ching 洪璟
Hung-ch'ing 鴻慶
*Hung-ch'ing wai-shih* 鴻慶外史
Hung Ch'ü-wu 洪去蕪
*Hung-fan* 洪範
*Hung-lu ssu-ch'ing* 鴻臚寺卿
*huo-jan kuan-t'ung* 豁然貫通
*Huo-wen* 或問
Hyōronsha 評論社


I 益
*i* 義
*I-chieh* 易解
I-chih 一之
*I-chuan* 易傳
*I-ch'uan chi-jang chi* 伊川擊壤集
*I-ch'uan ching-shuo* 伊川經說
*I-ch'uan wen-chi* 伊川文集
*i-erh-erh, erh-erh-i* 一而二二而一
*i-fa* 已發
*I-fa wei-fa chi* 已發未發記
*Igi hwip'yŏn* 理氣彙編
I-hsüan 義玄
*I-hsüeh ch'i-meng* 易學啟蒙
*I-li* 儀禮
I-Lo 伊洛
*I-Lo yüan-yüan lu* 伊洛淵源錄
*I O-hu* 憶鵝湖
*i-pen wan-shu* 一本萬殊

*I-shu* 遺書
*I-shuo* 易說
*i-tan* 一旦
*I-wei t'ung-kua-yen* 易緯通卦驗
I-wu 義烏
I-yin 伊尹
*Ihak t'ongnok* 理學通錄
Iwanami 岩波

Jao-chou 饒州
Jao-kuan 饒關
Jao Lu, Shuang-feng 饒魯雙峯
*jen* (humanity) 仁
    (man) 人
Jen-chih-t'ang-chu 仁智堂主
*jen-hsin* 人心
*jen-shen* 人參
*Jen-shuo* 仁說
*Jen-shuo-t'u* 仁說圖
Jen Yu-wen 簡又文
*jen-yü* 人欲
*Jih-chih lu* 日知錄
*Jin no kenkyū* 仁の研究
Ju 汝
Ju-chou 汝州
*ju-jen* 孺人
*Ju-lin chuan* 儒林傳
*Ju-lin tsung-p'ai* 儒林宗派
Juan Yüan 阮元
Jui-ch'üan 瑞泉
Jui-yen 瑞巖
Jung Chao-tsu 容肇祖
*Jung-ts'un T'ung-shu p'ien* 榕村
    通書篇

Kaibara Ekken 貝原益軒
*Kairoku* 海錄
K'ai-feng 開封
*k'ai-hsi* 開喜
K'ai-shan 開善
K'ai-yüan 開元
Kan 甘
Kan Chieh, Chi-fu 甘節吉父

*Kan-ch'üan Hsien-sheng wen-chi*
    甘泉先生文集
*k'an* 坎
Kaneko Sōsan 金子霜山
Kang Hosuck 姜浩錫
*K'ang-hsi yü-ti chih* 康熙輿地志
K'ang-lu 康廬
Kao 高
Kao P'an-lung, Ching-i 高攀龍
    景逸
Kao-tsu 高祖
Kao-tsung 高宗
Kao Tzu 告子
*Kao Tzu i-shu* 高子遺書
Kao-yao 皐陶
*K'ao-cheng wan-nien ting-lun* 考正
    晚年定論
*k'ao-i* 考異
K'ao-t'ing 考亭
K'ao-t'ing Shu-yüan 考亭書院
*K'ao-t'ing yüan-yüan lu* 考亭淵源錄
*ke* 格
*ke-chih* 格致
*k'e* 克
*K'e-chai chi* 克齋記
*k'e-chi fu-li* 克己復禮
*K'e-chi ming* 克己銘
*k'e-chiang* 客將
*ken* 艮
*keng-hsü* 庚戌
Keng Ping, Chih-chih 耿秉直之
Keng-sang Ch'u 庚桑楚
*keng-wu* 庚午
Ki Taesŭng, Kobong 奇大升高峯
Kim Changsaeng 金長生
Kim Chemin 金濟民
Kimon 崎門
Kin Sai-min 金濟民
*Kinshi roku bikō* 近思錄備攷
*Kinshi roku kōgi: jū-shi moku* 近思錄
    講義：十四目
*Kinshi roku hikki* 近思錄筆記
*Kinshi roku hyōki* 近思錄標記
*Kinshi roku kōsetsu* 近思錄講說

*Kinshi roku rangaisho* 近思錄欄外書

*Kinshi roku sankō* 近思錄參攷

*Kinshi roku setsu* 近思錄說

*Kinshi roku setsuryaku* 近思錄說畧

*Kinshi roku teiyō* 近思錄提要

Kinugawa Tsuyoshi 衣川強

K'o Han, Kuo-ts'ai 柯翰國材

*K'o-i-t'ang wen-chi* 可儀堂文集

*Kobun kyūsho kō* 古文舊書考

Kōdansha 講談社

*ku* 故

Ku-chi 古籍

Ku Ch'i-yüan 顧起元

Ku-chu 孤竹

Ku-lien 谷簾

Ku Lin 顧璘

Ku-shan (monk) 古山

       (mountain) 鼓山

*ku-shih* 故失

*Ku-tsun-su yü-lu* 古尊宿語錄

Ku Yen-wu 顧炎武

*K'u-yai man-lu* 枯崖漫錄

*kua-yü* 寡欲

K'uai-chi 會稽

*kuan* 貫

Kuan Chung 管仲

*Kuan-hsin shuo* 觀心說

*Kuang-ming ching* 光明經

Kuang-tsu 光祖

Kuang-tsung 光宗

Kuang-wu 光武

Kuei-chou 貴州

*Kuei-ch'ü-lai-tz'u* 歸去來辭

*kuei-hai* 癸亥

Kuei-shan 潙山

*Kuei-shan Ling-yu Ch'an-shih yü-lu* 潙山靈祐禪師語錄

*Kuei-shan wen-chi* 龜山文集

*Kuei-shan yü-lu* 龜山語錄

*kuei-shen* 鬼神

*kuei-ssu* 癸巳

*Kuei-ssu Meng Tzu chieh* 癸巳孟子解

Kuei-yang 貴陽

*Kuei-yüan chih-chih* 歸元直指

Kunlun 崑崙

*k'un* 坤

*K'un-chih chi* 困知記

*K'un-hsüeh chi* 困學記

*K'un-yang-fu* 昆陽賦

*kung* 公

*kung-an* 公案

Kung-ch'en 拱辰

Kung Feng, Chung-chih 鞏豐仲至

Kung-fu 公府

Kung Li 龔栗

Kung Mao-liang 龔茂良

Kung-shan 公山

Kung-shu Pan, Ch'iao 公(工)
       輸班巧

Kung-sun Ch'ou 公孫丑

K'ung An-kuo 孔安國

*K'ung-men ch'uan-shou hsin-fa lun* 孔門傳授心法論

K'ung-t'ung tao-shih 空同道士

*K'ung Tzu chia-yü* 孔子家語

K'ung Ying-ta 孔穎達

*Kŭnsarok sŏgŭi* 近思錄釋疑

Kuo Ch'ung-hui 郭沖晦

*kuo-feng* 國風

*Kuo-hsüeh chi-pen ts'ung-shu* 國學
       基本叢書

Kuo Shu-yün, Tzu-ts'ung 郭叔雲
       子從

Kuo Yao-ling 郭堯齡

Kuo Yu-jen, Te-yüan 郭友仁德元

Kusumoto Bun'yū 久須本文雄

Kusumoto Masatsugu 楠本正繼

Kusumoto Sekisui 楠本碩水

Kusumoto Tanzan 楠本端山

Kwŏn Kŭn 權近

Lai-chou 萊州

Lao-Chuang-Lieh 老莊列

*lao-han* 老漢

Lao Tzu 老子

*Lao Tzu chieh* 老子解

Le-t'an 泐潭

Li 李
*li* (Chinese mile) 里
　(principle) 理
　(rites) 禮
　(to separate) 離
Li Ao 李翱
Li Ch'en, Ch'eng-chih 李沉誠之
Li Chi 李杞
*Li chi* 禮記
*Li chi cheng-i* 禮記正義
*Li chi Chung-yung chuan* 禮記中庸傳
Li Ch'ien, Chi-tao 李潛幾道
Li Ching-te 黎靖德
Li Ch'ing-chao, I-an 李清照易安
Li Fan, Ching-tzu 李燔敬子
Li Fang-tzu, Kung-hui, Kuo-chai
　李方子公晦果齋
Li Fu 李紱
Li Hsing-ch'uan 李性傳
Li-hsüeh 理學
*Li-hsüeh tsung-ch'uan* 理學宗傳
*Li-hsüeh tzu-i t'ung-shih* 理學字義
　通釋
Li Hui, Hui-shu 李輝晦叔
Li Hung-tsu, Shou-yüeh 李閎祖
　守約
*li-i fen-shu* 理一分殊
Li Kang, Po-chi 李綱伯紀
Li Kuan, Ch'ou-yüan 李琯稠源
Li Kuang-ti 李光地
Li Kuei-ch'en 李貴臣
Li Kung 李璊
Li Lü 李呂
*li-ming* 立命
Li Mo 李默
Li-niang 麗娘
Li Pi, Chi-chang 李壁季章
*Li-pien* 禮編
Li Po 李白
*Li-sao* 離騷
Li Ssu 李四
Li T'ang-tzu, Yao-ch'ing 李唐咨
　堯卿
Li-tse 麗澤

Li Tseng, Ts'an-chung 李繒參仲
Li Tsu-t'ao 李祖陶
Li Tsung-ssu, Po-chien 李宗思
　伯諫
Li T'ung, Yen-p'ing, Yüan-chung
　李侗延平愿中
*Li Yen-p'ing chi* 李延平集
Li Yüan-han 李元翰
Li Yüan-kang 李元綱
*Li-yün* 禮運
Liang Chang-chü 梁章鉅
*liang-shen* 涼衫
Liang T'ien-hsi 梁天錫
*Liao-chai chi* 了齋集
Liao Te-ming, Tzu-hui 廖德明子晦
*Lieh-kuo lei-pien* 列國類編
Lieh Tzu 列子
Lien-ching 聯經
Lien-hsi 濂溪
Lien Sung-ch'ing 連嵩卿
Lin-an 臨安
Lin Ch'eng-chi, Ching-po 林成季
　井伯
Lin-chi 臨濟
Lin-chi Hui-chao Ch'an-shih yü-lu
　臨濟慧照禪師語錄
Lin-chiang 臨江
Lin Chih, Te-chiu 林至德久
Lin Chih-ch'i 林之奇
Lin-ch'uan 臨川
Lin Hsiang-ju 藺相如
Lin Hsüeh-meng 林學蒙
Lin-ju 臨汝
Lin Kuang 林光
Lin Kuang-ch'ao, Ch'ien-chih
　林光朝謙之
Lin Li 林栗
Lin Piao 林彪
Lin Ta-ch'un, Hsi-chih 林大春熙之
Lin Tzu-yüan 林子淵
Lin Yung-chung, Tse-chih 林用中
　擇之
Ling-fan 靈梵
Ling-ling 零陵

Liu An-shih, Yüan-ch'eng 劉安世
元城
*Liu Chi-san chi* 劉蕺山集
Liu Chih 劉砥
Liu Chin 劉瑾
Liu Ching-chih, Tzu-ho 劉靖之
子和
Liu Ch'ing-chih, Tzu-ch'eng
劉清之子澄
Liu Fu, Chi-chang 劉黼季章
Liu Fu-tseng 劉福增
Liu Hao 劉豪
*Liu Ho-tung ch'üan-chi* 柳河東全集
Liu Hsi 劉熺
Liu Hsüeh-ku 劉學古
Liu Hui 劉煇
Liu Huai, Shu-t'ung 劉淮叔通
Liu, James T. C. 劉子健
Liu Kuang-tsu, Te-hsiu 劉光祖
德修
Liu Kung, Kung-fu 劉珙共甫
Liu Meng-jung, Kung-tu 劉孟容
公度
Liu Mien-chih, Ts'ao-t'ang 劉勉之
草堂
Liu Pao-nan 劉寶楠
Liu Pei, Hsien-chu 劉備先主
Liu Ping, T'ao-chung 劉炳韜仲
Liu P'ing 劉玶
Liu Shang-kung 劉尙恭
*Liu Shen-shu Hsien-sheng i-shu*
劉申叔先生遺書
Liu Shih-p'ei 劉師培
Liu Shu-hsien 劉述先
Liu Ta-chün 劉大鈞
Liu Tsung-chou, Ch'i-shan 劉宗周
蕺山
Liu Tsung-yüan 柳宗元
*Liu Tzu ch'üan-shu i-pien* 劉子全書
遺編
Liu Tzu-hsiang 劉子翔
Liu Tzu-huan, Ch'i-fu 劉子寰圻父
Liu Tzu-hui, Ping-weng, P'ing-
shan, Yen-ch'ung 劉子翬病翁
屏山彥冲

Liu Tzu-yü, Pao-hsüeh 劉子羽寶學
Liu Yao-fu, Ch'un-sou 劉堯夫淳叟
Liu Yüeh 劉爚
*liu-yung* 六用
Liu Yü, Man-weng 劉迂漫翁
Lo (name) 輅
(river) 洛
Lo Ch'in-shun, Cheng-an 羅欽順
整庵
Lo-fou 羅浮
Lo Ju-fang, Chin-hsi 羅汝芳近溪
Lo Po-wen 羅博文
Lo Ta-ching 羅大經
Lo Ts'ung-yen, Yü-chang 羅從彥
豫章
Lo-yang 洛陽
Lokuang 羅光
Lou Liang 婁諒
Lu (mountain) 廬, 蘆
(state) 魯
*Lu-chai hsin-fa* 魯齋心法
Lu Ch'eng, Ch'ing-po, Yüan-ching
陸澄清白原靜
*Lu Chia-shu wen-chi* 陸稼書文集
Lu Ch'ien-heng, Yen-pin 路謙亨
彥彬
Lu Chiu-ling, Tzu-shou 陸九齡子壽
Lu Chiu-shao, Tzu-mei 陸九韶子美
Lu Chung-li, Ch'üeh-chai 逯中立
確齋
Lu Hsiang-shan, Chiu-yüan, Tzu-
ching 陸象山九淵子靜
Lu Lin-chih 陸麟之
Lu-shan (in Fukien) 蘆山
(in Kiangsi) 廬山
Lu Lung-chi 陸隴其
Lu T'an-wei 陸探微
Lu Te-chang 路德章
*Lun-Meng chi-chu* 論孟集註
*Lun-Meng ching-i* 論孟精義
*Lun-yü cheng-i* 論語正義
*Lun-yü chi-chu* 論語集註
*Lun-yü chi-i* 論語集義
*Lun-yü chieh* 論語解
*Lun-yü ching-i* 論語精義

*Lun-yü huo-wen* 論語或問

*Lun-yü shuo* 論語說

*Lun-yü yao-i* 論語要義

Lung-ch'ang 龍場

Lung-ch'ing 隆慶

Lung-hsing 隆興

Lung-hu 龍湖

Lung-she-chou 龍舌洲

Lung-yin 龍隱

Lü Hsi-che, Jing-yang 呂希哲滎陽

Lü Hsien 呂侁

Lü Huan 呂煥

Lü Nan 呂枏

Lü Pen-chung, Chü-jen 呂本中居仁

Lü Shao-hsien 呂紹先

*Lü-shih ch'un-ch'iu* 呂氏春秋

Lü Ta-chün 呂大鈞

Lü Ta-k'uei 呂大奎

Lü Ta-lin, Yü-shu 呂大臨與叔

Lü T'ao 呂燾

Lü Tsu-chien, Tzu-yüeh 呂祖儉 子約

Lü Tsu-ch'ien, Po-kung, Tung-lai 呂祖謙伯恭東萊

Lü Yen 呂炎

*Ma-i i* 麻衣易

Ma-i Tao-che 麻衣道者

*mao* 卯

Mao Hsing-lai 茅星來

Mao Jung 茅容

*Mao-shih cheng-i* 毛詩正義

Mao Tse-tung 毛澤東

Mei-chou 梅州

Mei-hsien 梅縣

Mei-jen 美人

Meitoku shuppansha 明德出版社

Men-yüeh 滿月

*Meng Tzu cheng-i* 孟子正義

*Meng Tzu chi-chu* 孟子集注

*Meng Tzu ching-i* 孟子精義

*Meng Tzu huo-wen* 孟子或問

*Meng Tzu k'ou-i* 孟子口義

*Meng Tzu shuo* 孟子說

*Meng Tzu ta-ch'üan* 孟子大全

*Meng Tzu tzu-i shu-cheng* 孟子字義 疏證

*Meng Tzu yao-chih* 孟子要旨

Mi-an 密菴

Miao-hsi 妙喜

Miao-hsi-an 妙喜菴

*Mien-chai chi* 勉齋集

Min 閩

Min-hsien 閩縣

Minamoto Tadakiyo 源忠精

*ming* 命

Ming-chiao 明教

*Ming-ju hsüeh-an* 明儒學案

*ming-fen* 命分

*Ming shih* 明史

*Ming-tao ch'üan-shu* 明道全書

*Ming-tao Hsien-sheng hsing-chuang* 明道先生行狀

*Ming-tao hsing-chuang* 明道行狀

Ming-tao Shu-yüan 明道書院

*Ming-tao wen-chi* 明道文集

*Ming-yüan lu* 鳴冤錄

Ming-yüeh-t'ang 明月堂

Miura Kunio 三浦國雄

Miyake Shōsai 三宅尚齋

*MO* 摩

*mo* 魔

Mo-chiao 魔教

*mo-fo* 魔佛

MO-ni-chiao 摩尼教

*mo-tsung* 魔宗

Mo Ti, Mo Tzu 墨翟墨子

Morohashi Tetsuji 諸橋轍次

*mou* 畝

Mou Tsung-san 牟宗三

*Mu-chai chi* 牧齋集

*Mu-chung chi* 木鐘集

Mu Hsiu, Po-ch'ang 穆修伯長

Mu-ts'ai 木材

Manhwasa 文化社

Nagasaki 長崎

Nagoya 名古屋

Nakai Chikuzan 中井竹山

Nakamura Shūsai 中村習齋

Nan 南
Nan-ch'ang 南昌
Nan-chien 南劍
*Nan-ch'uan ping-nieh chi* 南川冰蘖集
*Nan-hsüan chi* 南軒集
*Nan-hsüan Hsien-sheng wen-chi*
　南軒先生文集
Nan-hsüan Shu-yüan 南軒書院
*Nan-hua chen-ching* 南華真經
Nan-k'ang 南康
Nan-ming-ching 南溟靖
Nan-p'ing 南平
*Nan-p'ing hsien-chi* 南平縣志
Nan Ta-chi, Yüan-shan 南大吉
　元善
Nan-yüeh 南嶽
*Nan-yüeh ch'ang-ch'ou chi* 南嶽唱酬集
Neng-jen 能仁
Nieh Pao 聶豹
*nien-p'u* 年譜
*Nien-p'u cheng-o* 年譜正譌
Ning-kuo 寧國
Ning-tsung 寧宗
Nisshindō shoten 日進堂書店
*Nü-chieh* 女戒
*Nü Ssu mai-ming* 女巳埋銘

O-hu 鵝湖
O-hu Shu-yüan 鵝湖書院
Okada Takehiko 岡田武彥
O-mei 峨帽
Ōta Kinjō 太田錦城
Ōtsuki Nobuyoshi 大槻信良
O-tzu-feng 鵝子峯
Ogyū Sorai 荻生徂徠
Ou-yang Hsiu 歐陽修
*Ō Yōmei no zenteki shisō kenkyū* 王陽明
　の禪的思想研究

*Pa Hung Ch'ü-wu pen Chu Tzu nien-*
　*p'u* 跋洪去蕪本朱子年譜
*Pai-ch'uan hsüeh-hai* 百川學海
*Pai Hsiang-shan shih-chi* 白香山詩集
*Pai-hu-t'ung* 白虎通

*Pai-lu Shu-yüan chih* 白鹿書院志
Pai-lu-tung-chu 白鹿洞主
*Pai-sha Tzu yen-chiu* 白沙子研究
Pai-shui 白水
Pan Chao 班昭
P'an 潘
P'an Chih 潘植
P'an Ching-hsien, Shu-tu 潘景憲
　叔度
P'an Ching-yü, Shu-ch'ang 潘景愈
　叔昌
P'an Ping, Ch'ien-chih 潘柄謙之
P'an Shih-chü, Tzu-shan 潘時舉
　子善
P'an Yu-kung, Kung-shu 潘友恭
　恭叔
*P'ang Chü-shih yü-lu* 龐居士語錄
P'ang Yün 龐蘊
*pao* (hails) 雹
　　(to wrap) 包
Pao-kao-t'ang 寶誥堂
Pao Ting 包定
*Pao-tsang lun* 寶藏論
Pao-wen-ko 寶文閣
Pao Yang, Hsien-tao 包揚顯道
*Pao-yen-t'ang pi-chi* 寶顏堂祕笈
Pao Yüeh 包約
*Pei-hsi ta-ch'üan chi* 北溪大全集
*Pei-hsi tzu-i* 北溪字義
P'eng Hsing-tsung, Shih-ch'ang
　彭興宗世昌
P'eng Kuei-nien, Tzu-shou 彭龜年
　子壽
P'eng Shih 彭時
P'eng Tan-hsüan 彭澹軒
*pi-shu-lang* 秘書郎
*pi-shu-sheng* 秘書省
*Pi-yen lu* 碧巖錄
*p'i* 否
*pien-hsiu* 編修
*ping-ch'en* 丙辰
*ping-pu lang-kuan* 兵部郎官
Ping-weng 病翁
P'ing-chiang 平江

P'ing-lin 平林
P'ing-ling 平陵
*P'ing-pien ts'e* 平邊策
*po* 剝
Po Chü-i 白居易
Po-i 伯夷
Po-yang 鄱陽
Po-yu 伯有
*p'o* 魄
P'u 溥
*P'u-ch'eng i-shu* 浦城遺書
P'u-t'ien 莆田
P'u-t'ung 普通

*Riku Shōzan, Ō Yōmei* 陸象山王陽明
*Rongochō* 論語徵
*Ryūgan tekagami* 龍龕手鑑

*san* 散
*San-chia li-fan* 三家禮範
San-ch'ü 三衢
San-hsia 三峽
San-kuei 三桂
San-lun 三論
San-min 三民
San-shan 三山
*San-tzu ching* 三字經
*San-yü-t'ang wen-chi* 三魚堂文集
Satō Hitoshi 佐藤仁
Satō Issai 佐藤一齋
Satō Naokata 佐藤直方
*Satō Naokata zensho* 佐藤直方全書
Sawada Bukō 澤田武岡
*Seiza shūsetsu* 靜坐集說
Seng-chao 僧肇
Sha-mao 紗帽
Shan-yang 山陽
Shang-chih 尚智
Shang-jao 上饒
*shang-jen* 上人
Shang-mei 上梅
*Shang-ts'ai yü-lu* 上蔡語錄
Shao 召
Shao-cheng Mao 少正卯

Shao-hsi 紹熙
Shao-hsing 紹興
Shao Shu-i 邵叔義
*Shao Tzu ch'üan-shu* 邵子全書
Shao-wu 邵武
Shao Yung, K'ang-chieh 邵雍康節
Shen 沈
*shen* 神
Shen Chi-tsu 沈繼祖
Shen Hsien 沈僩
*shen-i* 深衣
Shen Kua, Ts'un-chung 沈括存中
Shen Kuei 沈桂
Shen-lang 沈郎
Shen-nung 神農
Shen Pu-hai 申不害
Shen-sheng 申生
Shen-tsung 神宗
*sheng* 生
*Sheng-ch'uan lun* 聖傳論
*Sheng-hsien tao-t'ung ch'uan-shou
tsung-hsü-shuo* 聖賢道統傳授
總叙說
*Sheng-hsüeh hsin-fa* 聖學心法
*sheng-sheng* 生生
*shih* 士
*Shih chi* 史記
*Shih chi-chuan* 詩集傳
*Shih-chieh* 詩解
*shih-chung* 時中
*Shih-hsüeh p'ing-lun* 史學評論
Shih Huang 施璜
Shih Hung-ch'ing 石洪慶
*Shih-huo chih* 食貨志
*shih-jen* 碩人
Shih-jen-ch'iao 碩人橋
*shih-kuan* 史館
Shih-men-wu 石門塢
Shih Pang-yao 施邦曜
*Shih-pien* 詩辨
*Shih-san-ching chu-shu* 十三經注疏
*Shih-shih lun* 釋氏論
*Shih-shih tzu-chien* 釋氏資鑑
*Shih-shuo* 師說

Shih Tun, Tzu-chung 石䃮子重
Shih Yüan-chih 施元之
Shih Yün, Tzu-yün 時澐子雲
Shimada Kan 島田翰
*Shina ni okeru Bukkyō to Jukyō Dokyō*
　　支那ニ於ケル佛教卜儒教道教
Shou-fan shu-t'ang 壽藩書堂
Shu 蜀
Shu, Shou-chih 塾受之
*shu* 恕
*Shu-chi-chuan* 書集傳
Shu-ch'i 叔齊
Shu-chih 叔之
*Shu-i* 書儀
Shu-mi yüan 樞密院
Shu-shan 疎山
*Shu-shuo* 書說
*shu-yüan* 書院
Shui-lien-tung 水簾洞
*Shumon deshi shiji nenkō* 朱門弟子
　　師事年攷
Shun 舜
Shun-ch'ang 順昌
*shun-ming* 順命
Shun-ning 順寧
*shuo* 朔
*Shuo-lüeh* 說畧
*Shuo-yüan* 說苑
Shunjūsha 春秋社
*Shushi* 朱子
*Shushi bunshū koyū meishi sakuin* 朱子
　　文集固有名詞索引
*Shushigaku nyūmon* 朱子學入門
*Shushigaku taikei* 朱子學大系
*Shushi gakuzenkō* 朱子學禪考
*Shushi gorui* 朱子語類
*Shushi gyōjō* 朱子行狀
*Shushi gyōjō Taikei shūchū no igi* 朱子
　　行狀退溪輯注の意義
*Shushi no shisō keisei* 朱子の思想形成
*Shushi shisho shūchū sakuin* 朱子四書
　　集註索引
*Shushi shisho wakumon sakuin* 朱子四
　　書或問索引

Shūeisha 集英社
*Sō-Min jidai jugaku shisō no kenkyū*
　　宋明時代儒學思想の研究
*Sohak chesa* 小學題辭
*Sok kŭnsarok* 續近思錄
*Sŏnghak sipto* 聖學十圖
Ssu (name) 巳
　　　(river) 泗
*ssu* 巳
*Ssu-ch'ao wen-chien lu* 四朝聞見錄
Ssu-hsin Hsin ho-shang 死心新
　　和尚
*Ssu-k'u ch'üan-shu* 四庫全書
*Ssu-k'u ch'üan-shu chen-pen* 四庫全書
　　珍本
*Ssu-k'u ch'üan-shu tsung-mu t'i-yao*
　　四庫全書總目提要
Ssu-ma Fang 司馬邡
Ssu-ma Fu 司馬富
Ssu-ma K'ang 司馬康
Ssu-ma Kuang, Wen-cheng Kung,
　　Wen Kung 司馬光文正公温公
Ssu-ma Liang (bright) 司馬亮
　　　　　　(good) 司馬良
Ssu-ma Mai 司馬邁
Ssu-ma P'o 司馬朴
Ssu-ma Wan 司馬邁
*ssu-ming* 俟命
*Ssu-ming ts'ung-shu* 四明叢書
*Ssu-pu pei-yao* 四部備要
*Ssu-pu ts'ung-k'an* 四部叢刊
*Ssu-shih-erh chang ching* 四十二章經
*Ssu-shih tzu-shu* 四十自述
*Ssu-shu chang-chü chi-chu* 四書章句
　　集註
*Ssu-shu chi-chu* 四書集註
*Ssu-shu huo-wen* 四書或問
*Ssu-shu ta-ch'üan* 四書大全
*ssu-yü* 私欲
Su Ch'e 蘇轍
Su Hsün 蘇洵
Su P'in 蘇玭
Su Ping, Chi-ming 蘇昞季明
Su Shih, Tung-p'o 蘇軾東坡

Sui-te 綏德

*sun* 巽

Sun Ch'eng-tse 孫承澤

Sun Ch'i-feng 孫奇逢

Sun Shu-kung 孫叔拱

Sun Tzu-hsiu, Ching-fu 孫自修敬甫

Sun Yüan-chen 孫原貞

Sun Ying-shih 孫應時

Sung (mountain) 嵩

    (name) 松

Sung-hsi 松溪

Sung Hsiang, Tzu-fei 宋翔子飛

*Sung-jen i-shih lei-pien* 宋人軼事類編

Sung-kao yin-li 嵩高隱吏

*Sung ming-ch'en yen-hsing lu* 宋名臣
    言行錄

*Sung-Ming li-hsüeh kai-lun* 宋明理學
    概論

*Sung-Ming li-hsüeh: Pei-Sung p'ien*
    宋明理學北宋篇

Sung-shan 嵩山

*Sung shih* 宋史

*Sung shih chi-shih pen-mo* 宋史紀事
    本末

*Sung ssu-tzu ch'ao-shih* 宋四子抄釋

*Sung-tai tz'u-lu chih-tu k'ao-shih* 宋代
    祠祿制度考實

*Sung-tai wen-kuan feng-chi chih-tu*
    宋代文官俸給制度

Sung Tuan-i 宋端儀

Sung Yen 松巖

*Sung-Yüan hsüeh-an* 宋元學案

*Sung-Yüan hsüeh-an pu-i* 宋元學案
    補遺


*Ta-hsüeh* 大學

*Ta-hsüeh chang-chü* 大學章句

*Ta-hsüeh Chung-yung chang-chü* 大學
    中庸章句

*Ta-hsüeh huo-wen* 大學或問

Ta-hui, Kao-lao, Miao-shan, P'u-
    chüeh, Tsung-kao 大慧果老妙善
    普覺宗杲

*Ta-hui P'u-chüeh Ch'an-shih yü-lu*
    大慧普覺禪師語錄

*Ta-hui p'u-shuo* 大慧普說

*Ta-hui yü-lu* 大慧語錄

*Ta-kao* 大誥

Ta-kuan-hsüan 達觀軒

Ta-li 大曆

Ta-lin-ku 大林谷

*Ta-pan-jo ching* 大般若經

*Ta-tai li-chi* 大戴禮記

*Ta-tsang-ching* 大藏經

Ta-yin-p'ing 大隱屏

Taedong munhwa yŏn'gu wŏn
    大東文化研究院

Taesan Sŏnsaeng 大山先生

Tai Hsien 戴銑

Tai-tsung Hsin-t'ai 佁宗心泰

Tai Shih-yü 戴師愈

*Tai Tung-yüan ti che-hsüeh* 戴東原
    的哲學

Tai Yung 戴顒

*Taigi roku* 大疑錄

*Taikei shūchū no igi* 退溪輯注の意義

*Taishō daizōkyō* 大正大藏經

*t'ai* 泰

*T'ai-chi* 太極

*T'ai-chi shuo* 太極說

*T'ai-chi-t'u* 太極圖

*T'ai-chi-t'u shuo* 太極圖說

T'ai-chou 台州

*t'ai-hsüeh* 太學

T'ai-ning 泰寧

*T'ai-p'ing ch'ing-hua* 太平清話

T'ai-shan 泰山

T'ai-tsu 太祖

T'ai-tsung 太宗

*tan* 旦

Tan-yang 丹陽

T'an-chou 潭州

T'an-hsi 潭溪

T'an-hsiang 潭湘

Tanaka Kenji 田中謙二

T'ang 湯

*t'ang-chang* 堂長

T'ang-chien 唐鑑
T'ang Ching-ch'uan chi 唐荊川集
T'ang Chün-i 唐君毅
T'ang Chung-yu, Yü-cheng 唐仲友
　與正
T'ang Keng, Tzu-hsi 唐庚子西
T'ang Po-yüan 唐伯元
T'ang-shih 唐石
T'ang Shun-chih 唐順之
T'ang Wen-jo, Li-fu 唐文若立夫
T'ang Yung 湯泳
Tao 道
Tao 道
Tao-ch'ien, Ch'ien-kai-shan,
　Ch'ien-lao 道謙謙開善謙老
Tao-chou 道州
tao-hsin 道心
tao-hsüeh 道學
Tao-hsüeh chuan 道學傳
Tao-i-pien 道一編
tao-jen 道人
Tao-nan yüan-wei 道南源委
Tao-nan Shu-yüan 道南書院
tao-t'ung 道統
Tao-t'ung lu 道統錄
Tao-yüan 道原
T'ao Ch'ien, Yüan-ming 陶潛淵明
Tchou Hi 朱熹
te (to achieve) 得
　(virtue) 德
Te-chih 德之
Te-ch'ing 德清
Teng Chiung, Wei-lao 鄧絅衛老
Teng-feng 登封
Teng Pang-lao 鄧邦老
Teng Yü 鄧禹
T'eng Kung, Te-chang 滕珙德章
T'eng Lin 滕璘
ti (brother) 弟
　(emperor) 帝
ti-kung-lang 廸功郎
Ti-tzu chih 弟子職
t'i 體
t'i-chü 提舉

T'i Hsiao-hsüeh 題小學
t'i-tuan 體段
t'i-yung 體用
t'iao-li 條理
Tieh-ti 鐵笛
T'ien 天
t'ien-chih-hsin 天之心
t'ien-hsin 天心
T'ien-hu 天湖
T'ien-li 天理
T'ien-sheng 天聖
T'ien-t'ai 天台
T'ien-t'ung 天童
T'ien-yen lun 天演論
Ting 丁
Ting Ch'uan-ching 丁傳靖
Ting K'e, Fu-chih 丁克復之
ting-pen 定本
Ting Yao 丁堯
ting-yu 丁酉
t'o-jan 脫然
T'oegye chŏnsŏ 退溪全書
T'oegye hakpo 退溪學報
Tōhō 東豐
Tōhō gakuhō 東方學報
Tokiwa Daijō 常盤大定
Tomoeda Ryūtarō 支枝龍太郎
Tou Ts'ung-chou, Wen-ch'ing
　竇從周文卿
Tsa-i 雜儀
Tsai-ju 宰如
Ts'ai 蔡
ts'ai 才
Ts'ai Ch'en 蔡沈
Ts'ai Hsing-tsung 蔡興宗
Ts'ai Jen-hou 蔡仁厚
Ts'ai Mu 葵謨
Ts'ai Nien-ch'eng, Yüan-ssu 蔡念誠
　元思
Ts'ai-shih chiu-ju shu 蔡氏九儒書
Ts'ai Yüan-ting, Chi-t'ung 蔡元定
　季通
Ts'an-t'ung-ch'i 參同契
ts'ang 倉

Ts'ang-chou Ching-she 滄洲精舍
Ts'ang-chou ping-sou 滄洲病叟
Ts'ang-chou tiao-sou 滄洲釣叟
*Ts'ang-shu* 藏書
Ts'ang-tzu ping-sou 滄子病叟
*Ts'ang-wu so-lu* 滄語瑣錄
Ts'ao Chien, Li-chih 曹建立之
Ts'ao Chin-shu 曹晉叔
*tse* 則
Tseng Chi, Ching-chien 曾極景建
Tseng Kung, Nan-feng 曾鞏南豐
Tseng Pu 曾布
Tseng Shen, Tseng Tzu 曾參曾子
Tseng Ta-ch'ing 曾大卿
Tseng Tsu-tao, Tse-chih 曾祖道
　擇之
Tseng Tzu, see Tseng Shen
Tseng Yüan-po, Nung-ch'ing 曾原
　伯農卿
Tsing Hua 清華
*Tso chuan* 左傳
Tsou Cho-ch'i 鄒琢其
Tsou Hao 鄒浩
Tsou Pin 鄒斌
Tsou Su 鄒訴
*Ts'ui-yen* 萃言
Tsung-hui 宗慧
Tsung-kuei 宗歸
Tsung-mi, Kuei-feng 宗密圭峯
Ts'ung-mu 從穆
Ts'ung-shen, Chao-chou Ho-shang
　從諗趙州和尙
*Ts'ung-shu chi-ch'eng* 叢書集成
Tu Fu, Tzu-mei 杜甫子美
*Tu kao Kuo Yu-jen yü* 讀告郭友仁語
*Tu shih k'ao-i* 杜詩考異
*Tu-shu fen-nien jih-ch'eng* 讀書分年
　日程
*Tu-shu lu* 讀書錄
*Tu-shu shuo* 讀書說
Tu Wei-ming 杜維明
*tuan-chuang* 端莊
Tuan-wa-ch'ih 斷蛙池
Tuan-yu 端友

Tuan Yü-ts'ai 段玉裁
*tui* 兌
*tun* 遯
Tun-weng 遯翁
*t'un* 屯
*Tung-chien lu* 東見錄
Tung Chu, Shu-chung 董銖叔重
Tung Chung-shu 董仲舒
Tung-feng 東峯
Tung I 董琦
*Tung-lai Lü T'ai-shih wen-chi* 東萊呂
　太史文集
Tung-shan 洞山
T'ung-an 同安
*T'ung-chien kang-mu* 通鑑綱目
*t'ung-jen* 同人
T'ung Po-yü, Fei-ch'ing 童伯羽蜚卿
*T'ung-shu* 通書
T'ung-yao 同繇
*tzu* 字
Tzu-ch'an 子產
*Tzu-chih t'ung-chien* 資治通鑑
*Tzu-chih t'ung-chien kang-mu* 資治
　通鑑綱目
Tzu-hsia 子夏
Tzu-hsin 自信
Tzu-i 子儀
*tzu-jan* 自然
*tzu-jan te-chih* 自然得之
Tzu-lai 子來
Tzu-ssu 子思
*tzu-te* 自得
Tzu-yang 紫陽
*Tzu-yang nien-p'u* 紫陽年譜
Tzu-yang Shu-t'ang 紫陽書堂
*Tz'u-hai* 辭海
Tz'u Mu-ma-wang 次牧馬王
*Tz'u-yüan* 辭源

Utsunomiya Ton'an 宇都宮遯庵

*Wai-shu* 外書
Wakabayashi Kansai 若林寬齋
Wakabayashi Kyōsai 若林强齋

Wan Chang 萬章
Wan Hsien-fa 萬先法
*Wan-hsing t'ung-p'u* 萬姓統譜
Wan Jen-chieh, Cheng-ch'un
    萬人傑正淳
Wan-nien Hsiang 萬年鄉
Wan Ssu-t'ung 萬斯同
Wang An-shih, Chieh-fu, Ching
    Kung 王安石介甫荊公
Wang Chi, Lung-hsi 王畿龍溪
*Wang-chih* 王制
Wang Chih-chung 王執中
Wang Chung-lu 汪仲魯
Wang Fu-chih 王夫之
Wang Ken, Hsin-chai 王艮心齋
Wang Kung-ch'en 王拱辰
Wang Kuo 王過
Wang Li-hsing 王力行
Wang Lin-shih, Ch'ien-chung
    王藺時謙中
Wang Mao-hung 王懋竑
*Wang Mei-hsi wen-chi hsü* 王梅溪
    文集序
Wang Ming-ch'ing 王明清
Wang Nien-sun 王念孫
Wang Pi 王弼
*Wang Pi chi chiao-shih* 王弼集校釋
Wang Po, Lu-chai 王柏魯齋
Wang P'o 王朴
Wang Shih-p'eng, Kuei-ling, Mei-
    hsi 王十朋龜齡梅溪
Wang Ts'ao, Tuan-ming 汪藻端明
Wang T'ung, Wen-chung Tzu
    王通文中子
Wang Tzu-ts'ai 王梓材
Wang Yang-ming, Shou-jen
    王陽明守仁
*Wang Yang-ming ch'uan-hsi lu*
    *hsiang-chu chi-p'ing* 王陽明傳習錄
    詳註集評
*Wang Yang-ming yü Ch'an* 王陽明
    與禪
Wang Yen 王衍
Wang Ying-ch'en, Sheng-hsi, Yü-
    shan 汪應辰聖錫玉山

Wang 汪
Wang Ying-lin 王應麟
Wang Yu-kuan 王幼觀
Wang Yü, Tzu-ho 王遇子合
Waseda 早稻田
Watanabe Hiroshi 渡邊浩
Wei 魏
*wei* 尉
Wei-chai 韋齋
Wei Cheng-t'ung 韋政通
Wei Ch'eng-chih 魏誠之
*wei-ch'i* 謂其
Wei Ch'un 魏椿
*wei-fa* 未發
*wei-hsüeh* 偽學
Wei-k'o 惟可
Wei Liao-weng 魏了翁
Wei-lei 畏壘
*Wei-mo ching* 維摩經
Wei-shih 唯識
Wei Shih-meng 魏師孟
Wen 文
*wen* 文
*Wen-chi* 文集
*Wen-chien* 文鑑
Wen-chih 文之
Wen-jui-lou 文瑞樓
Wen Kung 文公
Wen Kung Shu-yüan 文公書院
Wen-hui 文惠
Wen-ling 溫陵
Wen-shan 文山
Wen-tsung Shu-yüan 文宗書院
Wen-yen 文偃
Weng Kuo-liang 翁國樑
Wu (county) 武
    (emperor, king) 武
    (surname) 吳
*wu* (*koan*) 無
    (nonbeing) 無
*wu-ch'en* 戊辰
Wu Ch'eng, Ts'ao-lu 吳澄草廬
Wu Chi, Kung-chi 吳楫公濟
*wu-chi* 無極
*wu-chi erh t'ai-chi* 無極而太極

Wu-chiang Shu-yüan 唔江書院
Wu-chou 婺州
Wu-chün 吳郡
Wu-fu 五夫
Wu Hao 吳浩
*wu-hsin* 無心
*wu-hsing* 五行
Wu Hsiung, Po-ying 吳雄伯英
*wu-hsüeh po-shih* 武學博士
Wu I, Hui-shu 吳翌晦叔
Wu-i 武夷
Wu-i Ching-she 武夷精舍
*Wu-i-shan min-chien ch'uan-shuo*
    武夷山民間傳說
Wu Jen-chieh, Tou-nan 吳仁傑
    斗南
Wu Lieh, Te-fu 吳獵德夫
*Wu-men-kuan* 無門關
Wu Nan, I-chih 吳南宜之
Wu Pi-ta, Po-feng 吳必大伯豐
*wu-shen* 戊申
Wu Shou-ch'ang 吳壽昌
*Wu-teng hui-yüan* 五燈會元
Wu-t'ung 五通
*Wu-tzu chin-ssu lu fa-ming* 五子近思
    錄發明
*wu-wei* 無為
*Wu Wen-ch'eng Kung ch'üan-chi*
    吳文成公全集
Wu Ying, Mou-shih 吳英茂實
*wu-yü* 無欲
Wu Yü-pi 吳與弼
Wu-yüan 婺源


Ya-tung 亞東
Yalu 鴨綠
Yamada Jun 山田準
Yamaguchi Satsujō 山口察常
Yamanoi Yū 山井湧
Yamazaki Ansai 山崎闇齋
Yamazaki Bisei 山崎美成
Yamazaki Michio 山崎道夫
Yanagawa Takayoshi 柳川剛義
*yang* 陽

Yang Chi 楊楫
Yang Chi, Shih-te 楊驥士德
Yang Chien, Ching-chung 楊簡
    敬仲
Yang Chih, Chih-chih 楊至至之
Yang Chu 楊朱
Yang Fang, Tzu-chih 楊方子直
Yang Fu 楊復
*Yang-hao-t'ang chi* 養浩堂記
Yang Hsiung 揚雄
Yang I, Ta-nien 楊億大年
Yang Jin-hsin 楊金鑫
Yang Jo-hai 楊若海
Yang Ju-li 楊汝礪
Yang Lien-sheng 楊聯陞
*Yang-ming ch'uan-hsin lu* 陽明傳信錄
*Yang-ming Hsien-sheng chi-yao*
    陽明先生集要
*Yang-ming yü Chu-Lu i-t'ung ch'ung-
    pien* 陽明與朱陸異同重辨
Yang-p'ing Shu-yüan 陽坪書院
Yang-shan 仰山
Yang Shang-jen 仰上人
Yang Shih, Kuei-shan 楊時龜山
Yang Tao-fu, Chung-ssu 楊道夫
    仲思
Yang Yü-li 楊與立
Yao 堯
Yao-kuan 嶢關
*yao-tz'u* 爻辭
Yasuoka Masahiro 安岡正篤
Yeh (country) 掖
    (name) 埜
*yeh-fu* 野服
Yeh Chu 葉翥
Yeh Kung-hui 葉公回
Yeh Shao-weng 葉紹翁
Yeh Ts'ai 葉采
Yeh Wei-tao, Ho-sun 葉味道賀孫
Yeh Wu-tzu 葉武子
*Yen-ching hsüeh-pao* 燕京學報
*Yen-ching-shih hsü-chi* 研經室續集
Yen-chung 彥忠
Yen Fu 嚴復
Yen-ho 延和

Yen Hui, Yen Tzu, Yen Yüan 顏回顏子顏淵

Yen Hung-k'uei 嚴鴻逵

Yen Jo-ch'ü 閻若璩

Yen Jui 嚴蕊

*Yen-Li i-shu* 顏李遺書

*Yen-Li ts'ung-shu* 顏李叢書

Yen-nan Shu-yüan 燕南書院

Yen-p'ing 延平

*Yen-p'ing fu-chih* 延平府志

Yen-p'ing Shu-yüan 延平書院

*Yen-p'ing ta-wen* 延平答問

Yen Shih-wen, Shih-heng 嚴世文 時亨

Yen Tzu, see Yen Hui

Yen Tzu-chien 顏子堅

Yen Yüan, Hsi-chai 顏元習齋

Yi Hwang, T'oegye 李滉退溪

Yi I, Yulgok 李珥栗谷

*yin* (hidden) 隱 (passive cosmic force) 陰

*Yin-fu ching* 陰符經

Yin Hui-i 尹會一

Yin T'un, Ho-ching, Yen-ming 尹焞和靖彥明

*Ying-lien ts'ung-hua, hsü-hua* 楹聯 叢話續話

Ying Shu, Jen-chung 應恕仁仲

Ying-t'ien 應天

*Young Sun* 人生

Yu 游

*yu* 有

Yu-chou 幽州

Yu-hsi (county) 尤溪 (river) 沈溪

*yu-hsin* 有心

Yu K'ai, Tzu-meng 游開子蒙

Yu Mao, Yen-chih 尤袤延之

Yu Tso 游酢

*yu-tzu* 猶子

Yu Yü 尤焴

*yung* 庸

Yung-an 永安

Yung-chia 永嘉

*Yung-chia cheng-tao ko* 永嘉證道歌

Yung-chou 永州

Yung-ch'üan 湧泉

*Yung-t'ung hsiao-pin* 湧幢小品

Yü (king) 禹 (surname) 喻

*YÜ* 慾

*yü* (desire) 欲 (to give) 與 (preparation) 豫 (rain) 雨

Yü-chen 玉枕

Yü-chang 豫章

Yü Cheng-fu 余正父

Yü Ch'ang-ch'eng 俞長城

Yü Chi 虞集

Yü-chiang 餘江

*Yü chu-sheng* 諭諸生

Yü Liang-neng 喻良能

*Yü-Meng chi-chu* 語孟集註

Yü-shan 玉山

*Yü-shan chiang-i* 玉山講義

*Yü-shuo* 語說

Yü-ssu 玉笥

Yü Sung-chieh, Kuo-hsiu 余宋傑國秀

Yü Ta-ya 余大雅

Yü T'ing-ch'un, Shou-weng 俞廷椿壽翁

*Yü-tsao* 玉藻

Yü Ying-shih 余英時

Yü Yü, Chan-chih 余隅占之

Yü-yüan 玉淵

Yüan 袁

*yüan* (hall) 院 (origination) 元

*Yüan-chüeh ching* 圓覺經

*yüan heng li chen* 元亨利貞

Yüan-hui 元晦

Yüan Shu, Chi-chung 袁樞機仲

*Yüan-tao* 原道

Yüan-tung 遠東

Yüan-wu K'eng-an 圓悟肯菴

Yüan-wu K'e-ch'in 圓悟克勤

*Yüeh chi* 樂記

Yüeh Fei 岳飛
Yüeh-lin Shu-yüan 月林書院
Yüeh-lu 嶽麓
*Yüeh-lu Shu-yüan t'ung-hsün* 嶽麓書院
  通訊
*Yüeh-ming* 說命
*Yüeh-ya-t'ang ts'ung-shu* 粵雅堂叢書
Yün-ho lao-jen 雲壑老人
Yün-ku 雲谷
*Yün-ku-an* 雲谷庵
*Yün-ku chi* 雲谷記
Yün-ku lao-jen 雲谷老人
Yün-men 雲門
*Yün-men Wen-yen Ch'an-shih yü-lu*
  雲門文偃禪師語錄
Yün-t'ai 雲台

Yün-t'ai chen-i 雲台真逸
Yün-t'ai tzu 雲台子
Yün-t'ai wai-shih 雲台外史
Yün-t'ai yin-li 雲台隱吏
*Yün-wo chi-t'an* 雲臥紀談

*Zazen to seiza: Kusumoto Tanzan no
  seiza taininron* 坐禪と靜坐:楠本
  端山 の 靜坐體認論
*Zengaku kenkyū* 禪學研究
*Zhongguo zhexueshi yanjiu* 中國哲學史
  研究
Zia, N. Z. 謝扶雅
*Zoku Yamazaki Ansai zensho* 續山崎
  闇齋全書

# INDEX

Academy. See *Shu-yüan*

An-chih, 472

An-ch'ing-fu Academy, 348

An Hsi-fan, 268

*Analects:* Chu Hsi's emphasis on, 429; commentaries on, 14, 19, 26, 107, 148, 185, 228, 312; comments on, 384; discussion on, 404; interpretations of, 378, 476; on *jen,* 160, 164, 303, 379; language of, 145; Lü Tsu-ch'ien on, 428; on *ming,* 213, 344; order of study of, 5, 331, 364, 387; read by Su Shih, 109–110; on rites, 230; on self-mastery, 175; study of, 99, 338, 376, 425, 503, 566; for women, 541; Yen Tzu as inheritor of, 322; for the young, 388. *See also* Confucius; Four Books

Analogies: in Chuang Tzu, 271; discussed, 271–276; examples of, 273; with grain, 274; with light, 274; with medicine, 274; with a mirror, 273–275, 414; with a pearl, 274; with water, 273, 414; in the *Yü-lei,* 272

Anu Pool, 521

Big dipper, 126–127

Biographical account. See *Hsing-chuang*

Bloom, Irene, 480

Bodhidharma: borrowing from, 526; and Chu Hsi, 330; coming from the West, 532; as model for quiet-sitting, 257–259; pupil of, 532; and teaching meditation, 424

*Book of Changes:* appraised, 491; attributed to Confucius, 101, 191; on Change, 188; Chuang Tzu on, 272; Chu Hsi as an expert on, 559; and Chu I-tsun's theory of transmission, 330–331; com-

mentary on, 108, 112, 134; and divination, 113, 360, 456; hexagrams of, 189, 236, 280, 438, 487; *hsin-fa* in, 305; interpretation of, 406; and Neo-Confucianism, 276; question on, 108; on righteousness and seriousness, 242; on *sheng-sheng,* 497; study of, 364; *T'ai-chi* in, 146–147, 323; Ts'ai Yüan-ting as a specialist on, 96

*Book of History:* analogy of medicine in, 274; appraised, 428, 456; Chu Hsi's commentary on, 28; Chu Hsi's study of, 15, 17; commentaries on, 236, 438; on the Lord-on-High, 187–188, 192; on the moral mind, 471; sixteen-word formula in, 303, 323; study of, 99, 110, 331, 339, 364, 382, 566

*Book of Mencius:* authorship of, 382–383; Chu Hsi's study of, 12–13, 15, 17; commentaries of, 19, 26, 185, 302, 468; explained for Wan Jen-chieh, 115; on Heaven, 192; on *jen,* 159, 164; language of, 145, 384; Lü Tsu-ch'ien and, 428; on the mind, 261; on *ming,* 213, 217; and order in the Four Books, 5; read by Su Shih, 109–110; on strong moving power, 17, 115; on *tzu-te,* 300. *See also* Mencius

*Book of Odes:* and Cheng Ch'iao, 14; Chu Hsi's commentary on, 27, 375, 539, 541; Chu Hsi's explanation of, 26, 566; explained, 109; individual prefaces of, 16, 26; on King Wen, 121; Lü Tsu-ch'ien's explanation of, 428; Mencius on, 382; on the operation of Heaven, 145; on specific principles, 199; teaching of, 99; theory of transmission, 330–331; on *ti,* 187

**Production Notes**

This book was designed by Roger Eggers.
Composition and paging were done on the
Quadex Composing System and typesetting
on the Compugraphic 8400 by the design
and production staff of University of
Hawaii Press.

The text and display typeface is Baskerville.

Offset presswork and binding were done by
Vail-Ballou Press, Inc. Text paper is Glatfelter
Offset Vellum, basis 45.